PEARSON
mybcommlab™

Do your students understand the connection between communication skills and career success? Are you running out of classroom time to practice writing skills and grammar content? Do you want to transform your students into polished communicators? **mybcommlab** can help. **mybcommlab** is the online study tool that helps you transform Business Communication students into polished professionals, ready to take on the challenges of today's business landscape. Go to **www.mybcommlab .com** – *where Practice Makes Polished* – to take advantage of the following interactive tools and browse through the many instructor and student resources.

PRE-TEST, POST-TEST, AND CUSTOMIZED STUDY PLANS

Bring student progress into sharper focus with pre-tests, post-tests, and customized study plans.

When students complete a pre-test, the results generate a customized study plan with remediation activities. Study plans tag incorrect questions from the pre-test to the appropriate textbook learning objective, enabling students to concentrate on only the topics where they need help. Study plans include flash cards, eBook reading assignments, sample documents, and Interactive Lectures. Conclude with the post-test to verify chapter mastery.

GRAMMAR DIAGNOSTIC STUDY PLAN

Assign the Grammar Diagnostic test to see where your students need more support. This customized study plan provides your students with a self-paced learning method designed to improve their grammar skills.

BUSINESS COMMUNICATION MINI-SIMS

The brand new Business Communication Mini-Sims are interactive real-world scenarios that invite students to take on the role of a company decision-maker and apply the concepts they have just learned. Students are scored on the brief simulation and directed to the eBook, quizzes, and other learning aids to reinforce the concepts.

DOCUMENT MAKEOVERS

Help students understand the why and how of polished communication with Document Makeovers. Students can practice identifying communication errors and revising actual documents on Document Makeovers based on chapter objectives.

STUDENT PRESENTATIONS

Show examples of oral presentations from REAL students with the Student Presentations. Your students will learn the ins and outs of delivering an effective presentation by watching these short videos. The Student Presentations incorporate tips on voice, tone, stance, hand gestures, and much more.

Business Communication

Polishing Your Professional Presence

Barbara Shwom
Northwestern University

Lisa Gueldenzoph Snyder
North Carolina A&T State University

Prentice Hall
Boston Columbus Indianapolis New York San Francisco Upper Saddle River
Amsterdam Cape Town Dubai London Madrid Milan Munich Paris Montreal Toronto
Delhi Mexico City São Paulo Sydney Hong Kong Seoul Singapore Taipei Tokyo

Editoral Director: Sally Yagan
Director of Development: Stephen Deitmer
Editor in Chief: Eric Svendsen
Acquisitions Editor: James Heine
Executive Development Editor: Lena Buonanno
Editorial Project Manager: Karin Williams
Editorial Assistant: Jason Calcano
Director of Marketing: Patrice Jones
Marketing Manager: Nikki Jones
Marketing Assistant: Ian Gold
Senior Managing Editor: Judy Leale
Senior Production Project Manager: Karalyn Holland
Senior Operations Supervisor: Arnold Vila
Creative Director: John Christiana
Interior and Cover Designer: John Christiana
Cover Image: Shutterstock
Media Project Manager: Lisa Rinaldi
Acquisitions Editor, Digital Learning & Assessment: Josh Keefe
Multimedia Product Manager: Cathi Profitko
Editorial Media Project Manager: Joan Waxman
Full-Service Project Management: S4Carlisle Publishing Services
Composition: S4Carlisle Publishing Services
Printer/Binder: Courier/Kendallville
Cover Printer: Courier/Kendallville
Text Font: 9.5/11.5 Melior

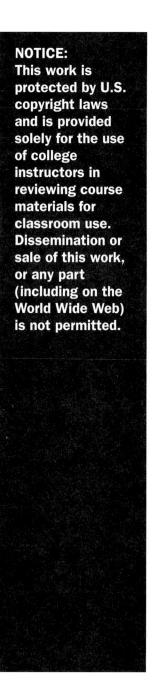
Credits and acknowledgments borrowed from other sources and reproduced, with permission, in this textbook appear on appropriate page within text (or on page CR-1).

Microsoft® and Windows® are registered trademarks of the Microsoft Corporation in the U.S.A. and other countries. Screen shots and icons reprinted with permission from the Microsoft Corporation. This book is not sponsored or endorsed by or affiliated with the Microsoft Corporation.

Library of Congress Cataloging-in-Publication Data

Shwom, Barbara Lynne.
   Business Communication: polishing your professional presence / Barbara Shwom, Lisa Snyder.
      p. cm.
   ISBN-13: 978-0-13-607807-4
   ISBN-10: 0-13-607807-9
   1. Business Communication. 2. Business writing. I. Snyder, Lisa,
1967- II. Title.
   HF5718.S525 2012

                                                            2010043081

Prentice Hall
is an imprint of

www.pearsonhighered.com

10 9 8 7 6 5 4 3 2 1
ISBN 10: 0-13-607807-9
ISBN 13: 978-0-13-607807-4

Dedication

To our husbands for their patience, and to our families for their support.

To our students for helping us be better teachers, and to our colleagues in ABC and business for helping us keep it real.

–Barbara and Lisa

About the Authors

Barbara Shwom

Barbara Shwom, Ph.D., is Professor of Instruction in Writing at Northwestern University, where she teaches in the Weinberg College of Arts and Sciences, Kellogg School of Management, and McCormick School of Engineering and Applied Science. For more than 30 years, she has designed and taught communication courses that have influenced this textbook, including *Writing in Organizations, Communicating Complex Data, Engineering Design and Communication*, and *How to Become an Expert in Roughly 10 Weeks.* Professor Shwom's teaching at Northwestern has been recognized by both an outstanding teacher award and an appointment as a fellow of Northwestern's Searle Center for Teaching Excellence. Professor Shwom has gained industry experience as the managing principal of Communication Partners, a consulting practice that works with clients from a range of industries, including biotechnology, high tech research and development, pharmaceuticals, management consulting, market research, financial services, engineering, and consumer products. Professor Shwom's research interests include evolving genres of business communication, visual communication of data, and methods of persuasion. In addition to many articles, she is also the co-author of a textbook on graphics and visual communication for managers. She currently sits on the editorial review board of *Business Communication Quarterly* and has served as president for both the Association for Business Communication and the Association of Professional Communication Consultants.

Lisa Gueldenzoph Snyder

Lisa Gueldenzoph Snyder, Ph.D., is an Associate Professor and Interim Chairperson of the Department of Business Education in the School of Business and Economics at North Carolina Agricultural and Technical State University in Greensboro. In addition to business communication, she teaches classes in computer applications and e-commerce. She earned a doctorate in Higher Education Administration from Bowling Green State University in Ohio, where she also received a master's degree in Business Education. Her bachelor of science in Business Education is from Northern Michigan University.

Dr. Snyder is widely published in journals such as the *Business Communication Quarterly, Journal of Business Communication, Business Education Digest, The Delta Pi Epsilon Journal,* and *NABTE Review.* She has made over 100 presentations at local, regional, and national professional development events, workshops, and conferences. During her graduate studies, Snyder's doctoral dissertation received the Charles E. Shanklin Award for Research Excellence, and she earned her department's Faculty Award for Academic Excellence. She has received the Innovative Instructional Practices Award from Delta Pi Epsilon, the Distinguished Service Award from the Ohio Business Teachers Association, and the Collegiate Teacher of the Year Award from both the North Carolina Business Education Association and the Southern Business Education Association. Dr. Snyder is also an active member of the Association of Business Communication, Delta Pi Epsilon, and National Business Education Association.

Brief Contents

Features

As students enter the business world, they will need to use technology to communicate with managers, colleagues, and customers. Students will also face new ethical challenges and communicate with a culturally diverse range of colleagues and customers. We integrate technology, ethics, and culture content in each chapter beginning with Chapter 2. Below is a list of the content we provide. In addition, we devote a full chapter to culture, Chapter 2, "Working with Others: Interpersonal, Intercultural, and Team Communication."

ETHICS

CULTURE

TECHNOLOGY

Contents

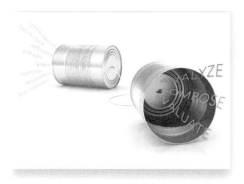

3 Managing the Communication Process: Analyzing, Composing, Evaluating 70

PART 2 Delivering Effective Messages

 Communicating Routine Messages and Building Goodwill 110

 Communicating Persuasive Messages 140

 Communicating Bad-News Messages 182

PART 3 Researching, Proposing, Reporting, and Presenting

7 Finding and Evaluating Business Information 216

8 Preparing Persuasive Business Proposals 252

9 Preparing Business Reports 286

10 Preparing and Delivering Business Presentations 342

PART 4 Persuading an Employer to Hire You

11 Creating Résumés and Cover Letters 390

12 Getting the Job—Interviewing Skills 432

Appendices

Preface

Today's students face communication challenges daily: They write papers, present in class, email instructors, and interview with prospective employers. When students enter the workplace, they face a new set of challenges: communicating with broader audiences, using new technologies, and being more strategic to achieve business goals. Our students' career success—and sometimes even the success of their companies—depends on their ability to be professional, adaptable, and strategic about their communication choices. We wrote this book to help students develop a strong foundation in business communication that leads to smarter choices. We also wrote it to help students develop the kind of communication presence that leads to professional success.

This book will show students how to get the best results from their communication by developing good habits and skills. It will also show students how to adapt to the changing landscape of business communication. The book and online support through **mybcommlab** combine to provide a powerful resource that helps students take charge of their own learning.

Get the Best Results from Your Communication

Getting good results from communication depends on learning a good process and knowing how to apply it in all aspects of communication. This book is designed to help students learn the ACE process, see the process in action, and review the results. The book puts students at the center of the learning process.

Learn the ACE process: Analyze, Compose, Evaluate

At the heart of the book is a flexible communication process called **ACE**—Analyzing, Composing, and Evaluating—that students can apply to any situation, from simple email messages to formal business presentations. We introduce this process in Chapter 3 with a simple graphic and revisit the process throughout the book. As students go through the book, they continue to acquire knowledge about how to apply this framework and why it is important.

Here is what instructors say about the ACE communication model:

"ACE is first introduced in Chapter 3. There is excellent coverage of this process, and I believe this is an excellent instructional technique."

Claudia Orr, *Northern Michigan University*

"I like the proposed text's strategic approach that brings [the ACE Communication Process] in where relevant throughout the text. Relevant repetition of the concept like this helps drive the lesson home."

John Waltman, *Eastern Michigan University*

"I really liked the way the authors introduced the ACE process and explained each segment of that process; appreciated the sample purpose and outcome statements—very valuable to students to understand not just why I'm writing but what I hope to accomplish with this message."

Virginia Hemby, *Middle Tennessee State*

"The ACE communication model is effective and memorable. I like the acronym. It has positive symbolic significance. The three stages (Analyzing, Composing, Evaluating) make sense. The authors' coverage of purpose and desired outcome [in Chapter 3] is excellent. The section on getting the writing process started is excellent."

Jan Costello, *Georgia State University*

FIGURE 3.1 The ACE Communication Process

Here is what students say about the ACE communication model:

"I anticipate using the ACE communication process beyond this course when I write emails, prepare papers, and apply for internships and jobs because the first impression of writing is very important."

Andronico P., *Student at the University of California–Santa Barbara*

"ACE communication process can be helpful for almost any class in college. I plan to use it for my next project for Management class."

Kerim A., *Student at the University of Arizona*

See the Process in Action

Scenarios

Rather than following the pattern of telling students what to do and then illustrating with an example, this book teaches primarily through scenarios. We introduce a communication problem, identify possible solutions, and analyze the results of the writer's choice by applying the principles in the chapter. This approach helps students visualize themselves in the scenario and engage in critical thinking. Here are a few examples of these scenarios:

"This book has a new, refreshing approach to teaching business communication. It is presented in a very personal way with the student being at the center of the learning process instead of seeming like a lecture format."

Joyce Ezrow,
Anne Arundel Community College

- Chapter 3, "Managing the Communication Process: Analyzing, Composing, Evaluating": students assume the role of an employee proposing a summer-hours program to a supervisor.
- Chapter 5, "Communicating Persuasive Messages": students assume the role of a customer service manager who needs to persuade a manager to provide funding for a computer training workshop.
- Chapter 6, "Communicating Bad-News Messages": students assume the role of the owner of a web development business dealing with a new client.
- Chapter 7, "Finding and Evaluating Business Information": students assume they work for a global company seeking an online training system.

Case studies

Each chapter concludes with a case study that places students in a realistic scenario and poses questions related to the content of the chapter. Here are examples of these case studies:

- Chapter 4, "Communicating Routine Messages and Building Goodwill"

  Miguel Ramirez works for his father's insurance company. One day, he is alone in the office and must manage and respond to email, regular mail, and phone communications. How can he use the concepts of the chapter to tackle these tasks?

- Chapter 5, "Communicating Persuasive Messages"

  Kelly Lee and Noah Walker are recent graduates with a great idea for a new business. How can they use the concepts of the chapter to persuade either a bank or family member to loan them funding for the business?

- Chapter 6, "Communicating Bad-News Messages"

  Henry Lai is a student who is receiving bad news from several sources, including his landlord and his car insurance company. How can he use the concepts of the chapter to evaluate and respond to this communication?

Simulations

Role-playing and critical thinking are also reinforced through online simulations at mybcommlab.com. In a series of 12 brief interactive simulations, students get to step into realistic scenarios in which they make—and then see the results of—important,

CASE STUDY Working as a Cross-Cultural Team

This case study will help you review the chapter material by applying it to a specific scenario.

The first three weeks of your internship at Baer, Kramer & Dreslin Market Research in Nashville were great. You enjoyed brainstorming marketing ideas with your manager and designing a survey for an important client. However, the past week has been pure misery. Your supervisor assigned you to join three other interns on a team to create a comprehensive online handbook for interns. Each summer, the company hires seven interns at your location in Nashville and seven more in the company's data processing department in New Delhi, India. You will work on your project with one other intern from the Nashville office and two interns from New Delhi.

Planning the first meeting was difficult. You lost two days of work trying to set a meeting time since there is a 10 1/2 hour time difference between Nashville and New Delhi: at 9 AM Central Daylight Time in Nashville, it is 7:30 PM in New Delhi. You suggested a 7 AM teleconference, but your Nashville teammate, Roberto, said he could not arrive in the office early for a meeting. You suggest an 8:30 AM teleconference, which would be 7 PM in New Delhi, but both your New Delhi teammates, Maansi and Anant, are vague about whether they could stay late. You beg Roberto to arrange to get to work early just one day so that your team can hold a kick-off meeting. Roberto admits that he could easily get to the office early, but prefers to sleep later. "And anyway," he admits, "I didn't sign up for human resources work when I accepted an internship in consumer research. How will this help me get a job?"

Finally, you are able to convince Roberto to accommodate Maansi and Anant. The first meeting is scheduled for 7:30 AM Central Daylight Time. The meeting seems to begin well enough. Everyone arrives on time, the teleconferencing system works, and the meeting starts with friendly introductions. Within five minutes, though, you know you are in trouble. When Anant introduces himself, he speaks so quickly that you miss everything he says. You would be too embarrassed to ask him to repeat it, so

you remain quiet and pretend to understand. After the introductions, things get worse. No one has thought to make an agenda, so no one knows what the team is trying to accomplish. After a few moments of painful silence, you say, "Well maybe we should just start sharing ideas about coming up with a plan for the online handbook."

Anant jumps right in. You don't understand much of what he says, but you do hear the words "user interface," "programming," "database," and "search functions." You and Roberto look at each other in amazement. Why is Anant talking about computer programming? And why is he continuing to talk without stopping for five minutes? Is it rude to interrupt? Finally, Roberto says, "Anant, it sounds like you may have some good ideas, but we don't understand. We thought our job was to plan an online handbook." Anant replied, "That's what I'm talking about." Throughout all of this Maansi remains silent. After the first meeting, you feel that it is going to be a long five weeks until the end of your summer internship.

Review Question 1: *What interpersonal, intercultural, and teamwork communication issues are emerging in this scenario?*

Listening for Understanding

After your first team meeting, Roberto says, "It doesn't sound like Maansi and Anant will be too helpful on this project. Maybe we should do it on our own. We can come up with a plan for a handbook in a week and then coast through the rest of the summer." You think Roberto has a good point. The project would be easier to complete without participating in a cross-cultural team. And you ask yourself "Why *are* Maansi and Anant on this team? Why am *I* on this team? What are we supposed to be doing?"

You decide that this confusion stems from a communication problem—not with Maansi and Anant but with your supervisor. You thought you were listening intently when she asked you to "come up with a plan for an online handbook." But did you really understand what she meant? You were too intimidated to ask any clarifying questions:

everyday business decisions. Each chapter of this text is linked to one simulation that covers several chapter objectives and includes feedback. The simulations span between 5 and 10 minutes and include business-related topics such as how to:

- Write an effective routine message
- Write a persuasive message
- Write a bad-news message
- Develop an effective presentation that meets audience needs and uses visuals as enhancement
- Write an effective cover letter and résumé
- Prepare for a job interview

Review the Results

As part of the scenarios, in each chapter, we provide several targeted examples that highlight core communication skills, such as:

- Analyzing your audience and making choices about the best way to communicate with that audience
- Deciding between a direct or an indirect organization for your message
- Composing a clear message
- Evaluating and improving communication

Students can refer to these examples throughout their college career and into their work career. Here are select examples of the figures students will find in the book:

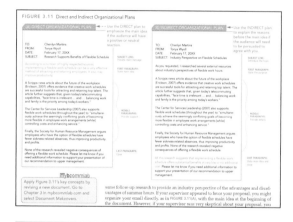

FIGURE 3.11 Direct and Indirect Organizational Plans

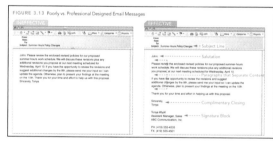

FIGURE 3.13 Poorly vs. Professional Designed Email Messages

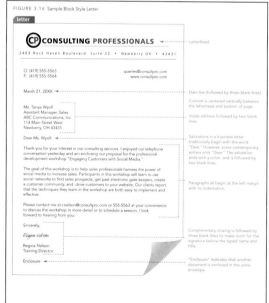

FIGURE 3.16 Sample Block Style Letter

FIGURE 3.17 Formal and Informal Voice Mail Messages

Here is what instructors say about our examples:

"Shwom/Snyder offers believable and engaging examples and scenarios our students can grasp immediately."

Casey Hawley, *Georgia State University*

"I love when the authors show an effective and ineffective example side by side. This provides opportunities for students to analyze and internalize."

Lisa Murray, *University of Tennessee—Knoxville*

"This book covers important information regarding business communication but without a lot of hyperbole and fillers. Important info; no wasted words or space."

Virginia Hemby, *University of Middle Tennessee State*

Here is what students say about our examples:

"I like all the examples of the various communications, such as emails, memos, thank-you notes, etc. I use them as a guide when I am writing."

Kenneth P., *Student at Middle Tennessee State University*

"I liked the letter examples. When I need advice on writing a letter, I have an example to reference very easily."

Paige W., *Student at University of Arizona*

Learn What's Happening Right Now

Business communication is continually evolving. Just 10 years ago, textbooks stressed memos and letters and barely mentioned email. Today, email is the most frequently used medium of communication in business. Meetings used to be held in person; now they are just as likely to be held on the telephone or by video conference. Companies used to reach out to customers by direct mail and brochures. Today, they invite customers to be Facebook fans. Technology is not the only area of change. As students enter the business world, they will face new ethical challenges and communicate with a more culturally diverse range of colleagues and customers.

Every chapter of this book offers insight and advice about how to adapt to the challenges and changes students will face.

New Hires @ Work

The *new hires @ work* feature helps students imagine themselves as part of a larger business communication community. At the beginning of each chapter, a recent graduate describes communication challenges on the job and how communication skills help meet those challenges. Additional *new hires @ work* appear on select pages within each chapter.

Social Media

Businesses are now finding that effective communication through social media—such as blogs, Facebook, and Twitter—can help them stay in touch with customers and employees. Today's students need to know how to responsibly use social media for business purposes, not just personal connections. We integrate coverage of social media in several chapters, including:

Chapter 1, "Becoming a Successful Business Communicator" (page 2)

Chapter 4, "Communicating Routine Messages and Building Goodwill" (page 110)

Chapter 6, "Communicating Bad-News Messages" (page 182)

Chapter 7, "Finding and Evaluating Business Information" (page 216)

new hires @ work

Lydie Modé
Co-founder and Director
Acts of Love Haiti, Inc.
University of South Florida, 2008

ONE CHALLENGE OF BEING PART OF A SMALL ORGANIZATION IS THAT I HAVE TO PLAY MORE THAN ONE ROLE. As co-founder and co-director of Acts of Love, I oversee our written communication with the public. With the rise of social media tools, a nonprofit organization cannot simply rely on a website or monthly newsletter to communicate. We also have to convey a clear and concise message through Facebook, MySpace, Twitter, and blogs. When it comes to writing, I am confident. However, I'm also expected to be present at all public functions and be the spokesperson at many. In my experience, effective written and oral communication skills don't go hand-in-hand. I have had my share of speech anxieties, prompting me to work very hard on improving my oral communication skills.

Ethics, Technology, and Culture

As students move through the book, they will see ethics, technology, and culture integrated into every chapter. In addition, some chapters provide in-depth focus on these topics. For example, Chapter 2, "Working with Others: Interpersonal, Intercultural, and Team Communication," provides frameworks for understanding how cultures differ, and Chapters 9 and 10, "Preparing Business Reports" and "Preparing Business Presentations," help students use writing and presentation technology to get the best results. To build students' skills in ethics, technology, and culture, instructors will find end-of-chapter exercises that challenge students to think critically and apply what they have learned to business situations.

ETHICS Is Blind Carbon Copy (bcc) Like Spying?

In your email program, the bcc—*blind carbon copy*—feature allows you to copy someone on an email without the recipient knowing it. Does sharing an email "secretly" with someone else raise any ethical issues? Consider three different scenarios for sending a bcc.

1. You are sending an email to all employees who are late submitting their travel reimbursement requests, asking them to submit immediately or risk not being reimbursed. The list is long, and if you pasted it into the email cc box, it would fill the screen. By using the bcc feature, you help ensure that your recipients focus on the message content rather than be distracted by an overly long header. In this case, the use of bcc is very functional. You can also argue that it is more ethical than including everyone on the cc line. Recipients don't need to know the names and email addresses of all the others who have missed the deadline. Making this information visible on the email may embarrass some people on the list.

2. You are reporting a problem to the technical support group for one of the software products you use. The head of your IT group has asked that everyone bcc her on all problem reports. She uses these emails as an informal log to track the frequency of problems, but she does not want to be included in follow-up email exchanges. In this case, the use of bcc is also functional and ethical. You are not deceiving the intended recipient or using the information to the disadvantage of the software supplier. The technical support people would act no differently if they knew the head of IT was copied or if the copying was blind.

3. You are writing an email to negotiate the price of a product with a new supplier. Your colleague in another department has asked to be bcc'd on these exchanges. She wants some inside information on the supplier so that she can negotiate a low price on a different product she intends to buy. She would prefer that the supplier not know that she has this extra information. Your colleague argues that her main responsibility is to get the lowest price possible for your company. She has an obligation to use whatever information is available to get that low price. This use of a bcc is much more troubling since your colleague intends to use the information to disadvantage the recipient. This could be considered a form of spying.

As you write emails, how do you decide if you should use a bcc and if it is ethical? Apply these two tests:

1. Are you intending to deceive the "to" recipient about who is receiving the email?

2. Can the recipient be disadvantaged or hurt if the material in the email is shared with the bcc readers and the recipient doesn't know it?

If you can say "yes" to either of these, then do not use the bcc. ■

mybcommlab

For ETHICS exercises, go to Critical Thinking Question 3 on page 134 and Exercise 22a on page 139 or to this chapter's End-of-Chapter Exercises at mybcommlab.com.

TECHNOLOGY Managing Your Social Media Image

Social media can both enhance and detract from your professional image, depending on the content that's "out there" about you and who has access to it.

According to Ponemon Institute, an organization that conducts research on Internet privacy issues, human resource professionals frequently use Internet searches, blog entries, and social networking sites to screen job candidates. A Ponemon survey found that nearly one-third of those web searches led to the candidate being rejected.[18] Similarly, a 2010 survey commissioned by Microsoft found that 79% of U.S. hiring managers and job recruiters research job candidates online, and 70% of managers have rejected candidates based on what they found.[19] Consider, for example, the story of the college student applying for a management consulting internship who lost the job because he described himself on Facebook as being interested in drugs, sex, and violence—using very colorful language. Even though the recruiter knew the young man [...] mpany did not want to risk hiring [...] a job search. One director of a uni- [...] s the story of a company recruiting [...] d difficulty deciding between two [...] earched them both on Google. He [...] ne who had the stronger Google

To manage your online image, follow these guidelines:

Review your current online presence. Google your name to see what results an employer can find. If you believe any of the material may be harmful to you, then work to remove it from the web. Also, modify your Facebook and other social media privacy settings to allow only confirmed friends access to your page. If your friends and acquaintances have posted any negative pictures of you on Facebook, ask to have those pictures removed.

Use a unique and consistent name on all your web profiles. If you have an unusual name, people will easily be able to find you in a web search. However, if you have a common name, consider adding a middle name or middle initial to your web profiles and web entries so that you stand out among all the others who share your name.[23]

Join professional directories. To maximize the positive online information an employer may find about you, add yourself to professional directories such as LinkedIn and Plaxo. Professional networking sites like these enable you to post information about your education, work experience, and professional qualifications. You can also receive recommendations from colleagues and friends to substantiate your qualifications. You may find that you already have a profile on ZoomInfo. ZoomInfo, used heavily by recruiters, continuously updates information about businesses and employees and offers advanced tools to search the information. It combines community-contributed content with content acquired from ZoomInfo's proprietary web crawling to create more than 50 million profiles of business people. ZoomInfo encourages people to update their profiles and there is no cost to do so.

Source: Reprinted with permission from Zoominfo.

Consolidate your web presence by creating a central profile. For example, by creating a Google profile, you can control the information that will appear at the top of a Google search for your name. In this profile, you can create links to other sites on the web that you'd like a potential employer to see.

New Hire at The Baltimore Zoo.
[...]ion from Mimi Bory.

mybcommlab

For a TECHNOLOGY exercise, go to Exercise 12 on page 467 or to this chapter's End-of-Chapter Exercises at mybcommlab.com.

CULTURE Differences in Saying Thank You

A thank-you note or email is more than just a polite gesture. It is a way to show genuine appreciation for the effort someone has made and to make that person feel good about the effort. However, different cultures have different ways of expressing thanks and perhaps different expectations about length and the amount of detail. The following two messages are real thank-you notes business students wrote thanking their supervisors for summer internships. Letter 1 is written by a U.S. student who interned in a U.S. company. Letter 2 is written by a Korean student who interned in a Singapore company. Both letters are very polite and were well received by their audiences. What differences do you notice about the two letters?

Letter 1, the American thank-you letter, follows the advice in this chapter. The letter is:

- personalized and sincerely expresses thanks.
- short and to the point, an appropriate approach in a low-context culture.
- informal, which signals the close working relationship between the student and mentor. This approach is appropriate in cultures with low power distance.

Letter 1: North American Thank You

Dear David:

Thank you for providing me with an internship that exceeded my expectations. I have never had a manager who spent so much time developing my skills. I have learned so much—not only about marketing and strategy but also about how to be a good manager.

I really enjoyed working with you and the rest of the team. I would love to join the group again next summer and would be pleased to hear from you.

Thanks again for everything,

Leslie

Letter 2 is written with the Asian culture in mind. The letter is:

- longer and formal.
- focused at the beginning on the relationship between the writer and audience, which is appropriate in high-context cultures.
- detailed, which signals that the writer has spent much time thinking about what to say to someone he respects. This approach is appropriate in cultures with high power distance.

Letter 2: Asian Thank You

Dear Mr. Jeehun:

Please accept my apology for not writing this letter earlier. After returning to the United States, I was busy with the details of moving.

Now that I reflect on my summer internship at Capital Investors, I see that I was able to complete it successfully primarily thanks to your consideration and support. I especially appreciate that you taught me the values that are necessary to be a successful investment banker.

First, I learned a professional attitude from you. Every kind manner you showed—such as thorough service for clients, a fine sense of being a salesperson, and a charismatic but warm-hearted leadership style—fascinated me.

Second, you showed me devotion to a job. Whenever I watched you absorbed in work, I felt your passion as an investment banker and the dignity of the vocation.

Last but not least, I learned it is possible to be a professional and also enjoy life by seeing you achieve a balance between work and family. It was impressive that you tried hard to invest your time and energy in playing with your children every weekend.

To sum up, having you as a boss during this summer internship was a great professional and personal experience for me. I have decided to look to you as my role model, and I will try to follow you in my career path.

I look forward to seeing you as soon as possible.

Sincerely,

Dong Gyu Lee

---

mybcommlab

For CULTURE exercises, go to Critical Thinking Question 10 on page 134 and Exercise 20 on page 138 or to this chapter's End-of-Chapter Exercises at mybcommlab.com.

Here is what instructors say about our integration of ethics, technology, and culture:

"Integrating ethics, technology, and culture features into chapters throughout the book reinforces students' understanding of the material."

Carolyn Ashe, *University of Houston–Downtown*

"We encounter all three in the modern workplace and to exclude them from our teaching would be negligent. I like the integration into each chapter because it mirrors actual practice where these features are married to our day-to-day business communication functions and part of our response consideration."

Gina L. Genova, *University of California–Santa Barbara*

"I agree wholeheartedly with this approach. The topics of culture and ethics are important considerations in all business communication, particularly communication of which the audience may be unknown or unanticipated. Additionally, knowledge of technology is demanded in modern businesses. Students completing business communication courses should be exposed to the highest variety of channels of communication possible. Included in this demand is the ability to efficiently compose, review, and deliver communications via many channels."

Vanessa Germeroth, *Ozarks Technical Community College*

"The way these three things are incorporated would make me more likely to adopt this book. Business ethics is taught as an elective in our school but many students don't take it. Infusing it into all classes is a much better way to handle it. The same goes for technology issues— explaining them in relation to the course content makes it easier for students to understand the importance of remaining current in technology to make themselves more marketable."

Joyce Ezrow, *Anne Arundel Community College*

Students Can Take Charge of Their Own Learning

In writing this book, we provided instructors with all the support they need to put together a powerful course that helps students polish their professional presence. However, we have also designed this book and the online support, **mybcommlab**, to give students control over their own learning.

A 12-Chapter Book With an Intuitive Format

We have created a focused book that effectively presents and practices the core communication competences in 12 chapters. Part 1, "Understanding the Foundations of Business Communication," addresses the core communication competencies of business communication, ranging from audience analysis and the communication process to document design and collaboration. The remaining parts focus on specific applications of these competencies: delivering effective messages; researching, proposing, reporting, and presenting; and applying and interviewing for a job.

Here is what instructors say about our focused content and number of chapters:

"Shwom/Snyder uses a fresh aproach in economically and efficiently teaching students the essentials to be effective business communicators."

Robert Goldberg, *Prince George's Community College*

"I like the clarity of these chapters and the coverage of the most important topics."

Casey Hawley, *Georgia State University*

"Having only 12 chapters is wonderful! I like how this book is organized."

Joyce Ezrow, *Anne Arundel Community College*

The book's main headings are structured as numbered study questions for you. These questions are answered in subheadings throughout the section. Here is an example of our Chapter 3 content:

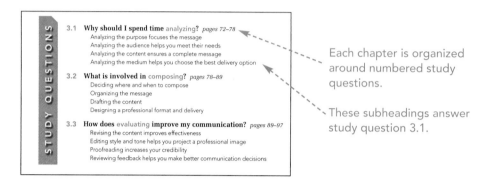

Each chapter is organized around numbered study questions.

These subheadings answer study question 3.1.

Questions and Exercises—Grouped by Study Question

People learn most effectively when they work collaboratively. Business communication is a perfect topic for collaborative learning because communicators need feedback from an audience in order to improve their writing and speaking. Instructors can use many of our exercises for in-class discussions or group exercises to support community-centered learning. By providing opportunities for students to discuss isses, share insights, and build common knowledge, we encourage students to learn together rather than to compete with each other.

The exercises are grouped by Study Questions (1.1, 1.2, 1.3) and then annotated by topic. Instructors can easily identify which skills they wish to reinforce as homework assignments or use for class discussion so they can assess their students' progress. Students can assess their own progress by completing these exercises in mybcommlab and receiving instant feedback.

Here are the categories of questions and exercises that appear at the end of each chapter. Many of the exercises feature either students as the subjects of the scenario or people in business situations.

- **Critical Thinking:** Challenging students' understanding of material in the chapter by encouraging them to reflect on the content and apply it to real-life situations and contexts.

- **Developing Your Communication Skills:** Solving problems to reinforce every main heading in the chapter. These exercises are grouped by Study Questions. The goals of this organization are to make it easier for instructors to assign problems based on study questions, both in the book and in mybcommlab, and to help students efficiently review material that they find difficult by focusing on small segments at a time. If students have difficulty with a particular aspect of a study question, an instructor can easily identify which problems support that study question and assign them as homework or discuss them in class.

- **Writing:** Writing in various media forms for a variety of purposes. Students respond to real-life scenarios and practice the analyzing, composing, and evaluating skills by creating effective messages.

- **Collaborating:** Collaborating on writing activities, research, and team projects. Many of these exercises can be used as in-class activities to reinforce understanding before assigning individual work.

- **Speaking:** Making informal oral presentations and executive briefings. Each chapter includes two sets of speaking exercises: (1) informal oral briefings that require students to "think on their feet" and (2) more formal presentation topics, many of which require students to research and summarize content to share with the class.
- **Grammar:** Helping students improve and reinforce their grammar skills. Solutions to the grammar questions are also located in the back of the book so students can check their progress. For additional help with grammar, students can access Appendix D, "Grammar, Punctuation, Mechanics, and Conventions."

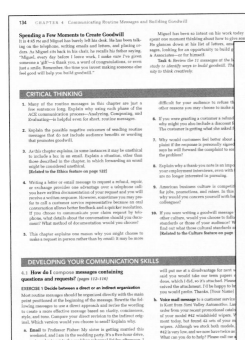

Here is what instructors say about our questions and problems:

"As always, the vignettes are the basis for excellent applications."

Dale Cyphert, *University of Northern Iowa*

In general, these [exercises] are briefer, seem more focused on real work examples, and are organized more logically. I prefer these to my current text."

Fiona Barnes, *Univeristy of Florida*

"I prefer the Shwom/Snyder questions and exercises due to the greater number of choices available."

Tony Corte, *Univeristy of Illinois–Chicago*

"The questions and exercises are certainly more numerous and superior overall to the exercises in most business communication textbooks that I've seen. Most of the textbooks I've viewed focus solely on business situations, which is fine if your class has had a lot of business experience. But students with little experience will relate better to some of your exercises."

Susan Peterson, *Scottsdale Community College*

Facilitate Teaching and Learning Through **mybcommlab**

As teachers, we recognize the importance of online support. Mybcommlab.com is an online course management, testing, and tutorial resource developed by Pearson/Prentice Hall based on input from instructors, students, and book authors.

For instructors . . .

Instructors can integrate mybcommlab.com into their traditional or online courses to whatever degree they'd like: from simply using exercises for homework or tutorials for extra help, to delivering their entire course online. Administrative features bring instructors closer to their students, making managing assignments and evaluating papers more efficient, and save instructors time. For example, instructors can create and deliver assignments online and keep students on track by listing due dates and assignment details in one place. The flexible Gradebook tool captures student grades from self-grading aspects of the site and prebuilt tutorials as well as grades given to writing assignments by the instructor. Instructors can easily assess student and class progress throughout the semester to evaluate effective instruction.

For students . . .

At mybcommlab.com, students complete writing and grammar exercises and receive instant assessment and tutorial help. Resources are available at students' fingertips as they analyze, compose, and evaluate. Students can get the help they need when they need it, without leaving the writing environment.

Students also complete a pre-test, the results of which generate a customized study plan that includes targeted learning activities. Study plans tag incorrect questions from the pre-test to the appropriate textbook study questions, enabling students to concentrate on the topics that they need help with. After students complete the learning activities, they take a post-test to validate that they have mastered the learning objectives.

Mybcommlab.com tools to help students study also include:

Flash Cards: Key terms and definitions are available as flash cards, allowing students to quiz yourself on vocabulary.

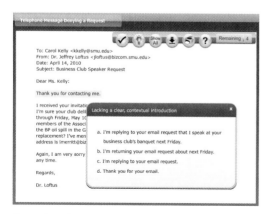

Sample of a Document Makeover

eText reading assignments: A fully searchable eText is available if students wish to read and study in an electronic environment. Students can view all the figures in the book and complete the end-of-chapter questions and exercises.

Grammar and writing tutorials: Students can test and improve their grammar skills and receive instant feedback. Additional tutorials and exercises aid in building the necessary skills to succeed in the course.

Additional mybcommlab.com practice tools help students apply what they learn in class to experiences beyond the book:

Document Makeovers help students build their skills in creating documents that are effective, clear, and audience-centered. Quick multiple-choice questions at the end of each document allow students to assess their progress and continue practicing.

Sample Presentation Videos show college students between the ages of 18 and 22 making presentations. These help students understand how they can make effective public presentations.

Videos tied to each chapter illustrate how textbook concepts are put into practice every day in a variety of real business settings. Accompanying **Video Exercises** help students apply what they saw in the videos to the topics they are studying in class.

Simulations give students the opportunity to role-play in business situations and learn how to think critically and prepare to make tough choices. See page xxii of this preface for more details on the simulations.

Supplements for Instructors: Instructor's Manual, Test Item File, PowerPoint, and Videos on DVD

The following supplements help instructors save time and create productive class experiences. They are all available online through mybcommlab.com and Pearson's Instructor's Resource Center at pearsonhighered.com/educator.

Instructor's Manual

The Instructor's Manual includes Detailed Lecture Outlines and Chapter Summaries prepared by the textbook authors; Social Media examples, In-class Activities, Teaching Tips, and Supplemental Homework Assignments linked to chapter Study Questions; Discussion Starter questions to motivate discussion for each major section of each chapter; and a Video Guide for integration of the *Business Communication* 1st edition Videos on DVD into classroom lectures (description below).

Test Item File and TestGen®

The Test Item File includes 1,200 questions organized by Chapter and Study Question, and annotated with the following information:

Answer feedback: correct answer and brief explanation is given

Difficulty rating: 1 for straight recall, 2 for some analysis, 3 for complex analysis

Question type: multiple choice, true/false, and short-answer/essay

The Association to Advance Collegiate Schools of Business accreditation: AACSB annotation identifies the five categories of AACSB standards (Communication Abilities, Ethical Understanding and Reasoning Abilities, Use of IT, Analytic Skills, Dynamics of the Global Economy, Multicultural and Diversity Understanding, and Reflective Thinking Skills).

Classification: Conceptual, Application, Critical Thinking, or Synthesis

Page reference: where the concept is covered in the main text

The computerized TestGen package allows instructors to customize, save, and generate classroom tests. The test program permits instructors to edit, add, or delete questions from the Test Item Files; analyze test results; and organize a database of tests and student results. This software is flexible and easy to use. It provides many options for organizing and displaying tests, along with search and sort features. The Test Item File is also available in PC, Mac, BlackBoard, WebCT, and Moodle versions.

PowerPoint® Lecture Presentations

A comprehensive set of PowerPoint slides can be used by instructors for class presentations and preparation, or by students for lecture preview or review. The instructor slides include figures from the textbook, key terms, brief chapter summaries, instructor notes, and discussion questions. A more basic version is also available for students to use as a study aid or note-taking guide.

Business Communication 1st edition Videos on DVD

This series of short videos on DVD shows how business communication topics covered in the book apply to real companies. Each video is incorporated into mybcommlab .com and is accompanied by quiz questions for additional chapter-by-chapter remediation. The Video Guide located in the Instructor's Manual includes short synopses of each video, as well as discussion questions and additional multiple choice questions. The DVD is available stand-alone for in-class use. (ISBN 0136078133)

A Word of Thanks

Writing a first edition textbook requires a high performing team to complement what we, as authors, can do. We have been fortunate to work with a such a team of talented and dedicated people at Pearson.

James Heine, Acquisition Editor, provided both leadership and energy, inspiring us to work just a little harder and do just a little more to create the best book possible. Lena Buonanno, Executive Development Editor, worked tirelessly to keep us on track and coordinate all the many elements involved in this complex project. Lena also served as the first and last reader for all of our work, and the book benefited greatly from her objective perspective and keen eye for detail. It also benefited from the sound judgment of Stephen Deitmer, Vice President and Director of Development, who served as arbiter for many of the challenging decisions we needed to make. James, Lena, and Steve spent many, many hours with us over several years—both in person and by teleconference. We are grateful for their guidance and efforts.

We are also grateful to John Christiana, Manager of Design Development, for his vision and playful sense of visual metaphor. The images he chose for the book encourage readers to look at business communication in a new way. Senior Production Project Manager Karalyn Holland, along with Heather Willison from S4Carlisle Publishing Services, did a masterful job of transforming John's graphic vision and our words into a reality: a beautiful and polished book. We offer them our sincere thanks. Project manager Karin Williams was the organizing force behind the supplements and online resources that make this book such a comprehensive package for instructors and students; her energy was matched by that of Kate Moore, Senior Editorial Development Manager, who organized the review panels and focus groups that helped us get vital feedback for the book. But no one's energy could be more contagious than that of Nikki Jones, Marketing Manager; we were inspired by her eagerness to share the book with the business communication community.

Heading the Pearson team were Sally Yagan, Editorial Director, and Eric Svendsen, Editor-in-Chief, who put their faith in this project and could always be counted on to provide perspective and insight. Sally's leadership during the early stages of the book's development provided the solid foundation on which this book was built.

We would also like to acknowledge the contributions of the following people to the instructor supplements: Maureen Steddin; Gina Genova, University of California, Santa Barbara; Randy Gerber, Macomb Community College; Jay Stubblefield, North Carolina Wesleyan College; Melissa Pellarano; and the teams at PreMediaGlobal and ANSRSource.

The feedback and guidance of many business communication instructors and their students helped shape the content and features of this book. We greatly appreciate their assistance and commitment to the craft of preparing students to communicate effectively in business.

Class Testers

We are grateful to both the instructors who class tested manuscript versions of each chapter and to the more than 1,000 students who provided recommendations on how to make the chapters the best they could be.

Carolyn Ashe, *University of Houston–Downtown*
Sherry Baker, *Rich Mountain Community College*
Mary Barton, *University of California–Chico*
Kathleen Blackwell, *University of South Florida*
Deborah Bowen, *University of South Florida*
Cherilyn Boyer, *University of Arizona*
Alma G. Bryant, *University of South Florida*
Kelly Paschal Carr, *Arizona State University*
John Catalini, *University of California–Santa Barbara*
Sandra Chrystal, *University of Southern California*
Janice Cools, *University of South Florida*
Anthony Corte, *University of Illinois–Chicago*
Auli Ek, *University of California–Santa Barbara*
Betty Foust Chapman, *North Carolina A&T State University*
Gina L. Genova, *University of California–Santa Barbara*
K. Virginia Hemby, *Middle Tennessee State University*
Kristie Loescher, *University of Texas–Austin*
Joyce Lopez, *Missouri State University*
Renee McConnell, *University of Arizona, retired*
Elizabeth Metzger, *University of South Florida*
Lisa Murray, *University of Tennessee–Knoxville*
Nancy Nygaard, *University of Wisconsin–Milwaukee*
Claudia Orr, *Northern Michigan University*
Deborah Richey, *Owens Community College*
Sandra S. Rothschild, *University of Arizona, retired*
Stacey Short, *Northern Illinois University*
Jan Starnes, *University of Texas–Austin*
Sally Stanton, *University of Milwaukee*

Acknowledgments

The feedback and guidance of many business communication instructors and their students helped shape the content and features of this book. We greatly appreciate their assistance and commitment to the craft of preparing students to communicate effectively in business.

Consultant Board

Carolyn Ashe,
*University of
Houston–Downtown*

**Lise Diez-
Arguelles,**
*Florida State
University*

Nancy Nygaard,
University of Wisconsin–Milwaukee

Susan A. Peterson,
*Scottsdale Community
College*

Fiona Barnes,
University of Florida

Gina L. Genova,
*University of
California–Santa
Barbara*

**Sandra S.
Rothschild,**
*University of Arizona,
retired*

Anthony Corte,
*University of Illinois–
Chicago*

K. Virginia Hemby,
*Middle Tennessee
State University*

John L. Waltman,
*Eastern Michigan
University*

Jan R. Costello,
*Georgia State
University*

Joyce Lopez,
*Missouri State
University*

Reviewers

Melody Alexander, *Ball State University*
Carolyn Ashe, *University of Houston-Downtown*
Sara Baker, *University of Nebraska–Lincoln*
Sherry Baker, *Rich Mountain Community College*
Fiona Barnes, *University of Florida*
Barclay Barrios, *Florida Atlantic University*
Mary Barton, *University of California–Chico*
Tatiana Batova, *University of Wisconsin–Milwaukee*
Rhonda Baughman, *Brown Mackie College–North Canton*
Reginald Bell, *Prairie View A&M University*
Shavawn Berry, *Arizona State University*
Kara Fahey Blackburn, *Massachusetts Institute of Technology*

Kathleen Blackwell, *University of South Florida*
Cherilyn Boyer, *University of Arizona*
Charlotte Brammer, *Samford University*
Ellen B. Bremen, *Highline Community College*
Alma G. Bryant, *University of South Florida*
Scott Buechler, *Elon University*
Stephen M. Byars, *University of Southern California*
Sharon Cannon, *Washington University in St. Louis*
Brennan Carr, *Long Beach City College*
Kelly Paschal Carr, *Arizona State University*
Rodney Carveth, *Fitchburg State University*
Sandra Chrystal, *University of Southern California*

Jennifer Chunn, *Harrisburg Area Community College*
Paige Clark, *Indiana University*
Dorinda Clippinger, *University of South Carolina*
Anthony Corte, *University of Illinois–Chicago*
Jan R. Costello, *Georgia State University*
Valerie Creelman, *Saint Mary's University*
Mercidee Curry, *Jackson State University*
Dale Cyphert, *University of Northern Iowa*
Babara D'Angelo, *Arizona State University*
Barbara Davis, *University of Memphis*
David Dewberry, *Rider University*
Lise Diez-Arguelles, *Florida State University*
Michael J. Doolin, *Monroe Community College*

Auli Ek, *University of California–Santa Barbara*

Marcella Enos, *Idaho State University*

Donna R. Everett, *Morehead State University*

Joyce Ezrow, *Anne Arundel Community College*

Kathy Fletcher, *Indiana University*

Janis Forman, *University of California*

Jorge Gaytan, *North Carolina A&T State University*

Gina L. Genova, *University of California–Santa Barbara*

Robert J. Goldberg, *Prince George's Community College*

Bob Gregory, *Bellevue University*

Frances K. Griffin, *Oklahoma State University*

Anne Bradstreet Grinols, *Baylor University*

Alice Griswold, *Clarke University*

Susan Hall, *University of West Georgia*

Roxanne Hamilton, *Landmark College*

Lynn Hanson, *Francis Marion University*

William Hargrave, *University of Georgia*

Rachel Harlow, *University of Texas of the Permian Basin*

Patricia L. Harms, *University of North Carolina–Chapel Hill*

Kathleen Haspel, *Fairleigh Dickinson University*

Carolyn Hawley, *Georgia State University*

Susan Heller, *Reading Area Community College*

K. Virginia Hemby, *Middle Tennessee State University*

Ronda Henderson, *Middle Tennessee State University*

Pat Herb, *North Central State College*

Kathy Hill, *Sam Houston State University*

Sheila Hostetler, *Orange Coast College*

Chie Ishihara, *Riverside Community College*

Elizabeth Jackson, *Lone Star College–CyFair*

Kathy Jesiolowski, *Milwaukee Area Technical College*

Carol Johnson-Gerendas, *Texas Wesleyan University*

Marguerite P. Joyce, *Sam Houston State University*

Thomas Kiddie, *West Virginia State University*

Margaret Kilcoyne, *Northwestern State University of Louisiana*

Renee King, *Eastern Illinois University*

Lorraine Krajewski, *Louisiana State University–Shreveport*

Tim Krause, *University of Wisconsin*

Helene Lamarre, *DeVry University*

Christine Laursen, *Red Rocks Community College*

Daisy Lee, *San Jose State University*

Gloria Lessmann, *Bellevue University*

Holly Littlefield, *University of Minnesota*

Joyce Lopez, *Missouri State University*

Jeanette S. Martin, *University of Mississippi*

Gary May, *Clayton State University*

Dorothy McCawley, *University of Florida*

Renee McConnell, *University of Arizona, retired*

Lisa McCormick, *Community College of Allegheny County*

Patricia McLaughlin, *St. Ambrose University*

Jane McPhail, *College of William & Mary*

Lisa Meloncon, *University of Cincinnati*

Elizabeth Metzger, *University of South Florida*

Charles Moses, *Clark Atlanta University*

Lisa Murray, *University of Tennessee–Knoxville*

Dawn New, *Indiana University*

Nancy Nygaard, *University of Wisconsin–Milwaukee*

Claudia Orr, *Northern Michigan University*

Lorelei Ortiz, *St. Edward's University*

Karen Otto, *Florida State University at Jacksonville*

Marvin Parker, *Fort Valley State University*

Lisa Pawlik, *University of Michigan*

Susan A. Peterson, *Scottsdale Community College*

Melinda Phillabaum, *Indiana University*

Deborah Richey, *Owens Community College*

Joy Roach-Duncan, *Murray State University*

Kathleen Robinson, *University of South Florida*

Marcel Marie Robles, *Eastern Kentucky University*

Deborah Britt Roebuck, *Kennesaw State University*

Kimberly Rosenfeld, *Cerritos College*

Chip Rouse, *Stevenson University*

Sandra S. Rothschild, *University of Arizona, retired*

Michael J. Salvo, *Purdue University*

Kathryn Schifferle, *California State University–Chico*

Carolyn Seefer, *Diablo Valley College*

Glenda Seiter, *Northeastern State University*

Teresa Sekine, *Purdue University*

Stacey Short, *Northern Illinois University*

Allen Shubb, *Northeastern Illinois University*

Karen Sneary, *Northwestern Oklahoma State University*

Jason Snyder, *Central Connecticut State University*

Harvey Solganick, *LeTourneau University*

Valarie Spiser-Albert, *University of Texas at San Antonio*

Sally Stanton, *University of Wisconsin–Milwaukee*

Jan Starnes, *University of Texas–Austin*

Kyle Stedman, *University of South Florida*

Natalie Stillman-Webb, *University of Utah*

Robert Stowers, *College of William & Mary*

JoAnn Syverson, *University of Minnesota*

Linda Szul, *Indiana University of Pennsylvania*

Lee Tesdell, *Minnesota State University, Mankato*

Ann Tippett, *Monroe Community College*

Allen Truell, *Ball State University*

Pam Uhlenkamp, *Iowa Central Community College*

Jennifer Veltos, *Minnesota State University, Mankato*

Mary Wallace, *University of Tennessee at Martin*

John L. Waltman, *Eastern Michigan University*

Debra Westerfelt, *Ashland University*

Carol S. White, *Georgia State University*

Julianne White, *Arizona State University*

Beth Williams, *Stark State College*

Lucinda Willis, *Indiana University of Pennsylvania*

Bennie J. Wilson III, *University of Texas–San Antonio*

Maryann Wysor, *Georgia State University*

Robert Yamaguchi, *Fullerton College*

Jensen Zhao, *Ball State University*

Michael Zirulnick, *Fairleigh Dickinson Unviersity*

Gail Zwart, *Norco College–Riverside Community College District*

Accuracy Checkers

Carolyn Ashe, *University of Houston–Downtown*

Cherilyn Boyer, *University of Arizona*

Cole Holmes, *University of Texas–Austin*

Nancy Nygaard, *University of Wisconsin–Milwaukee*

Contributors to the Instructor's Manual

Jan R. Costello, *Georgia State University*

Barbara D'Angelo, *Arizona State University*

Joyce Lopez, *Missouri State University*

Deborah Richey, *Owens Community College*

1 Becoming a Successful Business Communicator

new hires @ work

Lydie Modé
Co-founder and Director
Acts of Love Haiti, Inc.
University of South Florida, 2008

ONE CHALLENGE OF BEING PART OF A SMALL ORGANIZATION IS THAT I HAVE TO PLAY MORE THAN ONE ROLE. As co-founder and co-director of Acts of Love, I oversee our written communication with the public. With the rise of social media tools, a nonprofit organization cannot simply rely on a website or monthly newsletter to communicate. We also have to convey a clear and concise message through Facebook, MySpace, Twitter, and blogs. When it comes to writing, I am confident. However, I'm also expected to be present at all public functions and be the spokesperson at many. In my experience, effective written and oral communication skills don't go hand-in-hand. I have had my share of speech anxieties, prompting me to work very hard on improving my oral communication skills.

Introduction

Do you text, tweet, or use Facebook to keep in touch with friends and family? Do you have conversations with friends and acquaintances at lunch or dinner? Do you email professors with questions, or gesture to friends across the room to wait for you? If so, without even thinking about it, you are engaging in the complex process of **communication**—planning, creating, delivering, and interpreting messages.

The communication skills you have already developed will be valuable to you in the workplace, where communication is considered to be the most important of all abilities you can possess. However, your current skills may not be sufficient to meet many challenges of communicating in the workplace. In your career, you will be required to use many different communication skills to succeed.

For example, you will need to:

- persuade people,
- explain decisions,
- solve problems,
- ensure that everyone is "on the same page," and
- maintain productive working relationships.

This book is designed to help you develop a set of best practices you can use to meet these challenges, no matter what career you pursue.

Think of this first chapter as a preview of the book. Its goal is to help you understand how you will benefit from studying business communication, why being a business communicator is challenging, and what characteristics you should be able demonstrate when you complete this course.

Study Question 1.1

Why should I study business communication?

■ Access this chapter's simulation entitled Successful Business Communication, located at mybcommlab.com.

Studying business communication will offer you many benefits, but two in particular stand out. First, in the job market and at work, being a good communicator will give you a competitive edge over most people who do not possess first-rate communication skills. Second, being a good communicator contributes to your professional and personal success.

Effective business communicators have a competitive edge

The U.S. Department of Labor published a groundbreaking study that identified specific skills that are crucial in the workplace. Many are communication skills:[1]

- Reading
- Writing
- Listening
- Speaking
- Thinking creatively
- Making decisions

- Visualizing concepts
- Solving problems
- Participating as a member of a team
- Exercising leadership
- Negotiating
- Working with diversity

It is not surprising that good communication skills are often listed as a requirement in job advertisements. A study of online job ads found that 63 percent of the ads mentioned communication skills.[2]

Ironically, although these communication skills are important, few people in the workplace have mastered them. In a report produced collaboratively by the Business Roundtable and the Society for Human Resource Management, one-third of the companies surveyed said that most of their employees lack the writing skills needed for the job.[3] Similarly, the New Graduates' Workforce Readiness study found that many employers were dissatisfied with the communication skills of their college graduate employees, specifically citing deficiencies in written communication, leadership, professionalism, and creativity.[4] Even many MBAs are not sufficiently prepared for the communication challenges they face. In fact, in its annual survey of corporate recruiters, the Graduate Management Admissions Council routinely finds that lack of communication ability tops the list of complaints from employers about potential MBA job recruits.[5]

This bad news for the workforce may be good news for you. It means you have an opportunity to stand out in the crowd. If you are able to apply the range of skills you learn in this course, you will be a valuable asset to your business. This will lead to the second benefit: your professional success.

Good communication skills will contribute to your success

Because communication is a valued commodity in the workplace, it can enhance your professional and personal success. Research confirms that communication will help your employer—and you—in a variety of ways:

- **Communication skills will make you a more valuable employee.** Skilled writers have an opportunity to produce documents that save money or generate income. Even a small change in communication can have a large return on investment for an organization. For example, the state of Washington found it was losing tax revenue because businesses did not clearly understand an important letter explaining the requirements about a specific type of tax. The state revised the letter, and after two years, found their improved communication led to an additional $800,000 of tax revenue being collected.[6]

    If you advance to a managerial or executive level, you may have the opportunity to influence how your organization communicates with employees and the general public. That communication can directly impact the organization's success. For example, research by a global consulting firm found that "companies that are highly effective communicators had 47 percent higher total returns to shareholders over the last five years compared with firms that are the least effective communicators."[7]

    Your expertise with **social media**—web-based applications designed to promote social interaction—can benefit your employer also. Companies are now finding that effective communication through social media—such as blogs, Facebook, and Twitter—is improving employee satisfaction and building their brands while expanding their marketing reach.[8] Additionally, if you run your own small business as an entrepreneur, your communication abilities will be especially critical, since most of the communication responsibilities will fall squarely on your shoulders.[9]

- **Communication skills can improve your salary.** Employers value communication-related skills, such as writing, reading, listening, and working well with others.[10] Employers also reward those skills. In fact, your ability to communicate well may even translate into a higher salary. Kip Tindell, the CEO of the Container Store, explains that communication is at the heart of his company's success, and he is willing to pay double the industry average for a great employee who has the right skills. Tindell said "one great person could easily be as productive as three good people," so paying twice as much is a bargain.[11] Tindell's willingness to pay more for good communicators echoes the results of an earlier industry study revealing that people with effective writing skills earn more than three times as much as employees who do not write well.[12] Consider the difference in salary between someone earning $40,000 and an effective communicator earning $120,000 a year!

- **Good communication skills can have a positive impact on your life outside of work.** If you learn good business communication skills—such as speaking and writing clearly, being aware of who will receive your message, listening to others, and persuading others—you can apply those skills in your personal life to improve your relationships with friends and family. In addition, you may be able to use your skills to negotiate a better deal on a car, persuade your cell phone provider to give you a refund, or write an effective application letter for graduate school.

These benefits confirm that studying business communication and practicing your skills will have a positive return on your investment of time and energy.

new hires @ work

Matthew Weiss
Field Representative
U.S. House of Representatives
Hofstra University, 2009

"My college coursework and internships helped me refine my communication skills and become an effective communicator, which is a requirement to succeed in my current job."

Communication The process of planning, creating, delivering, and interpreting messages both verbally (through writing and speaking) and nonverbally (through gestures and symbols).

Social media Web-based applications, such as Facebook and Twitter, designed to promote social interaction.

Why is business communication challenging?

Why is it that many students do not acquire sufficient communication skills as they go through school? Some students do not take business communication courses, while others take the course but do not devote enough time to understand what communication involves because they think it is an "easy" course. However, even for a dedicated student, communicating well in a business context is complex.

Even basic communication is complex

Miscommunication can occur in even the most basic interactions. For example, have you ever done the following:

- Placed an order at a restaurant and received the wrong food?
- Asked someone for directions to a building or a street, received a confusing answer, and had to ask a second person for the same directions?
- Sent an email with an urgent request and waited days for a reply but got none?

A transactional model of communication, illustrated in FIGURE 1.1, helps explain how communication works and why it sometimes doesn't.[13]

The goal of communication is not just for a sender to transmit a message to a receiver, but for a sender and receiver to develop shared meaning by communicating in a dynamic loop, sending and receiving messages back and forth. Achieving that goal requires a number of steps:

1. **Sender encodes a message.** Communication begins when the *sender* has something to "say" to a *receiver*. For example, imagine you need information from a coworker in order to prepare a cost estimate for a proposal you will send to a client tomorrow. To communicate this need to your coworker, you must **encode** the message—put it into words, images, or actions.

FIGURE 1.1
Transactional Model
of Communication

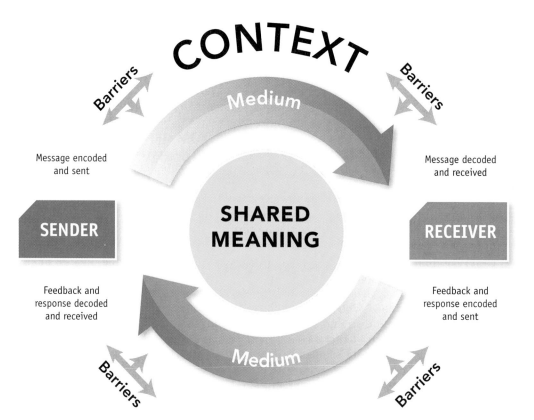

❷ **Sender selects a medium.** The sender transmits a message to the receiver through a **medium**—a channel used to transmit the message, such as a face-to-face conversation, a telephone conversation, a letter, or an email message. While you encode your message to your coworker, you also need to choose your medium. Should you call your coworker, send a quick email, or walk over to her desk to speak to her face-to-face? The medium you choose should depend on which one best supports the purpose of your message (to request information) as well as how best your coworker will process that information. (You will learn more about choosing the best medium for a message in Chapter 3: Managing the Communication Process.)

❸ **Receiver decodes the message.** The receiver **decodes** the message by interpreting the words and actions of a message and attaching meaning to them. This meaning is filtered by the receiver's knowledge, experience, and circumstances. For example, assume you decide to send a simple email message to your coworker requesting information: "How many hours will it take to write the Putney User Manual?" If your coworker does not know you are creating a cost estimate for a proposal, she may decode it incorrectly. She may think you only want a general sense of how long the project will take, and thus she may provide an answer that is not helpful—for example, "It will take about a week if I work on it along with my other projects." This answer will not help you develop a cost estimate. Your ambiguity and your coworker's lack of knowledge are two of the many barriers that can obstruct effective communication. A **barrier** is any obstacle that gets in the way of effective communication.

❹ **Receiver encodes feedback and selects a medium. Feedback** is any form of verbal or nonverbal response to a message. In this case, feedback may simply be a quick email that answers the question: "I estimate the project will take 50 billable hours." Other forms of feedback include requests for clarification or the addition of new ideas to think about: "Did you want to know how many total hours the project will take for billing purposes, or did you want to know when you think we can get it done, so that you can commit to a deadline?"

❺ **Sender and receiver communicate back and forth to create shared meaning.** The original sender decodes (interprets) the recipient's feedback. If the answer responds to the sender's intended meaning, the exchange may be over. However, if the response indicates a difference in understanding, more clarification and more communication may be required. This exchange illustrates how communication is circular. One communication initiates another. The sender becomes the recipient and the recipient becomes the sender, each encoding and decoding messages. By communicating back and forth, the sender and receiver ensure they understand each other, create shared meaning, and experience successful communication.

However, not all communications are successful. As the model suggests, barriers and context add to the complexity.

Barriers and context add to the complexity

Barriers—or obstacles to communication—can occur at any point in the communication process. For example, if you choose to email your coworker but she does not read the email before the proposal is due, your ineffective medium choice is a barrier to communication of the message. If she receives the email, but does not understand what you are asking for, your ineffective wording is a barrier.

Consider how all these possible barriers can interfere with successful communication of even a simple message:

- *Physiological barriers* **arise from a receiver's physical state.** If you are speaking to someone who has a hearing loss or a migraine headache, she may not be able to listen effectively and interpret what you are saying.
- *Psychological barriers* **arise from a receiver's attitudes toward the message or toward the sender.** If you compliment someone who does not trust you, he may interpret that compliment as a subtle criticism. When you are upset, your emotions act as a barrier to effective communication.

Encode To translate the meaning of the message into words, images, and actions.

Medium A channel used to transmit a message. Senders can choose a medium from many options, including face-to-face conversation, videoconference, telephone, letter, memo, email, brochure, website, and group meeting.

Decode To interpret the words and actions of a message and attach meaning to them.

Barrier An obstacle that gets in the way of effective communication.

Feedback Any form of verbal or nonverbal response.

- *Semantic barriers* **arise from language that is ambiguous or difficult to understand.** If a colleague rushes late into a meeting and says to you, "I was held up at the train station," you might ask if the robber had a gun, when your colleague simply meant that the train was delayed.
- *Language barriers* **arise from senders and receivers not using a shared language.** Sometimes the problem is obvious: the sender speaks only Spanish and the receiver speaks only English. Sometimes the problem is less obvious. For example, employees who are new to a company or industry may not yet understand the jargon people use. They may not know that a T&E report is a travel and expense report or that a 483 response is a reply to an informal warning issued by the Federal Drug Administration. Language barriers can also arise from cultural differences. If an American traveling to London is given directions to meet his contact on the first floor of Bain House, the American may decode the message to mean that the meeting will take place on the ground floor of a large home. Instead, the meeting will be one floor above the ground floor (what the United States calls the second floor), in a traditional office building.
- *Mixed messages* **arise from conflicts between verbal and nonverbal communication.** A sender may say one thing but nonverbally communicate something very different. For example, John may tell his boss that he can stay late for a meeting, but his nervous foot tapping and his repeated glances at his watch communicate a different message.

Barriers are not the only challenge to effective communication. Communication is also challenging because it takes place in a specific **context** or set of circumstances. Context influences the purpose of communication, the best medium to use to communicate the message, and how receivers interpret the message.

As an example, assume you work in the software development department of your company and you want to persuade your supervisor to let you work with the marketing team to create a brochure for a new software product, even though you have no experience with marketing or advertising. You may not be successful if you merely state: "I'd like to work with the marketing team to create the brochure." Your supervisor may understand that message, but it will not persuade him. To determine how to achieve your goal, you will need to consider a range of contextual variables: What are the goals of the project? Who else is working on the project and what can you contribute? Does your supervisor like interdisciplinary work teams or does he prefer groups to work separately? How does he prefer to receive messages: in person or by email? Once you have considered these variables, you have a better chance of creating a message that will be both understood and persuasive.

Multiple audiences pose additional challenges

Although the transactional model of communication is comprehensive, it is too limited to capture all the complexities of the communication process in a dynamic business environment. The transactional model depicts communication as happening between two people. However, communication typically occurs among multiple people who encode and decode messages differently and who have different contexts, backgrounds, concerns, and agendas.

Imagine working in an auto parts manufacturing company with team members from different departments: engineering, design, marketing, sales, project management, shipping, and accounting. You are all trying to solve the fortunate problem of having more orders for auto parts than you can fill. With eight people in the meeting, there may be eight different personalities, each with a unique communication style and goal. Some people may be willing to communicate freely, while others may become silent. All the team members presumably want to do what is in the best interest of the company, but each member may have a different point of view about what that is. Sales managers want to meet the needs of current customers and also gain new customers. They may not be thinking about the quality of the auto parts. Project managers, by contrast, may be more interested in maintaining the quality of the auto parts than rushing to meet the needs of current and new customers.

To solve the problem of meeting high demand while maintaining quality, the team will need to listen carefully to each other, negotiate a solution, document agreements, and inform both the CEO and the workers about the company's solution and new priorities. If the team decides the best solution is to slow down new orders, sales managers will need to communicate carefully with disappointed customers to maintain their goodwill. If the team decides to rush and create more auto parts to fill orders, managers need to determine how to ensure product quality.

Becoming an effective communicator in a complex business environment such as this requires that you learn to:

- **communicate with different audiences who have different needs,** including coworkers, managers, customers, and vendors.
- **communicate to achieve different goals,** including gathering information, persuading, negotiating, managing conflict, and making decisions.
- **use written communication methods,** including emails, letters, and reports.
- **use oral communication methods,** including speaking effectively one on one, in small meetings, to large groups, and through distance media such as webcasts, podcasts, and teleconferences.
- **continuously update your communication technology skills to develop competence with new media,** such as wikis, blogs, live chat, and social media outlets.

Mastering these abilities is challenging, which explains why businesses are happy to find employees who have already developed some of the characteristics of successful communicators.

Study Question 1.3

What characteristics do successful business communicators share?

Most people have at least one communication strength. You may be a good writer or a good listener, or you might be very persuasive. However, the best business communicators share the key characteristics illustrated in FIGURE 1.2. These characteristics help business people effectively deal with communication challenges. The remainder of this chapter previews these characteristics, which you will continue to develop throughout the course and throughout your career.

Effective business communicators are . . .

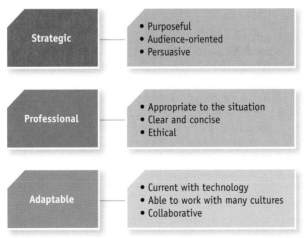

Strategic
- Purposeful
- Audience-oriented
- Persuasive

Professional
- Appropriate to the situation
- Clear and concise
- Ethical

Adaptable
- Current with technology
- Able to work with many cultures
- Collaborative

FIGURE 1.2
Characteristics of Effective Business Communicators

Effective communicators are strategic

The best communicators always have a **communication strategy**—a plan for what and how to communicate to ensure that the message achieves its purpose. Strategic communicators are always making decisions, asking themselves these questions:

Context A set of circumstances that influences the purpose of communication, the best medium to use to communicate the message, and even how receivers interpret a message.

Communication strategy A plan for what and how you are going to communicate to ensure your message achieves your purpose.

- What do you want to accomplish with your message? What is your goal?
- Who is your audience? With whom should you communicate to accomplish your goal?
- What content will your audience need? What content will help you accomplish your goal?
- What medium should you use: a face-to-face meeting, teleconference, email, presentation, report—or a combination of multiple medium options?
- How can you organize the message to state and support your main point?

As these questions suggest, to be a strategic communicator, you must be purposeful, audience-oriented, and—in many cases—persuasive.

Purposeful

When writing or speaking in classes, you probably have a **purpose**—a specific and intended outcome of your communication that defines what you want the recipients of your message to know, do, or feel about the subject of your message. Your purpose might be to merely pass the class, get an A, or impress the instructor. Similarly, successful business communicators plan their writing and speaking to achieve a specific purpose. For example, they might want their recipients to answer a question, accept a proposal, follow directions, or correct an error. The list of potential business purposes is endless.

Business communication is effective when it accomplishes its purpose and achieves its intended outcome. For example, when you write an application letter for a job, the letter is effective if you get an interview. Other features of effective communication—such as grammatical correctness, clarity, and conciseness—will also help you achieve your purpose.

For example, consider the two versions of an email in FIGURE 1.3 by Zack Kramer, a business major and a member of his university's chapter of Students for a Cleaner Environment. The two emails appear to have similar purposes: to get information from a civil engineering professor for one of the club's projects. As you read the two versions, ask yourself which one is more likely to get Zack what he wants.

Audience-oriented

Communication involves more than self-expression. Good business communicators understand that their messages must reach and influence their **audience**, the individual person or people for whom a message is intended. Being able to reach an audience requires first that you be a good reader and listener so that you can understand audience concerns. It then requires that you compose messages that address those concerns and are easy to read.

Reading and listening provide you insights into what is important to the audience. For example, when a good communicator gets an email making a request, she replies only after reading it carefully to identify why the writer is making the request and what kind of answer he needs.

Being a good listener is arguably even more important than being a good reader, since research suggests that people in the workplace spend much more of their communication time listening than they do speaking, reading, or writing.[14] Too often people assume they are good listeners simply because they hear things every day. However, hearing is not the same as listening. **Active listening** is a learned skill that requires you to focus on the speaker, make sense of the information that he or she presented, and when possible, provide feedback about the information to ensure you understand it correctly.

An active listener works to interpret meaning to understand both what a person is saying and why that person is saying it. An active listener will perceive emotional cues and body language—and even think about what is not being said. For example, if a person's voice sounds strained, he may be nervous or concerned about the information he is communicating. Or if a person is using defensive body language, such as crossing her arms, she may feel skeptical or upset, although her words do not convey that same meaning. If you develop good listening skills, your coworkers and customers will communicate with you more frequently and more fully. As a result, you will be able to com-

new hires @ work

Elisa Eminger

Apparel Sales Representative

Outdoor Adventure Sales

Northern Michigan University, 2008

"When you begin your career, there is nothing to prepare you for what you will specifically experience. The biggest part of communicating is listening, and when you listen, you learn."

FIGURE 1.3 Two Versions of an Email Message

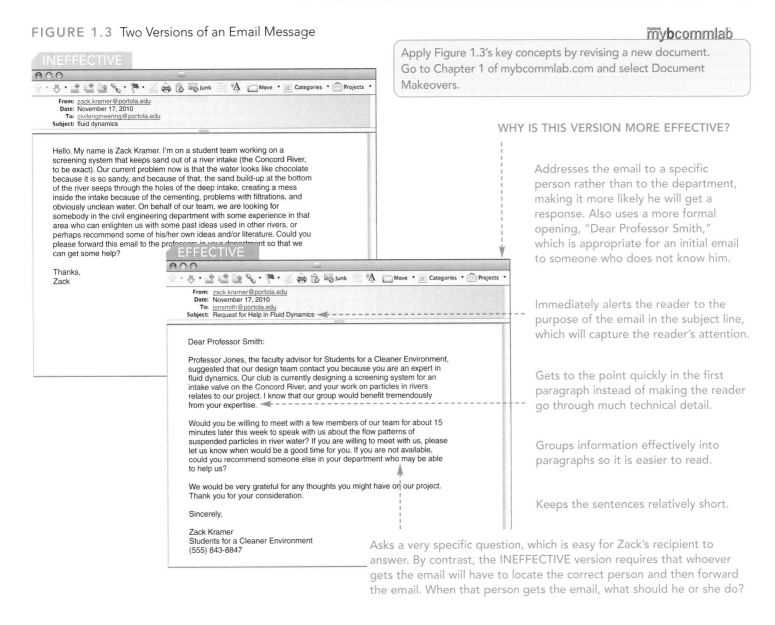

mybcommlab

Apply Figure 1.3's key concepts by revising a new document. Go to Chapter 1 of mybcommlab.com and select Document Makeovers.

WHY IS THIS VERSION MORE EFFECTIVE?

Addresses the email to a specific person rather than to the department, making it more likely he will get a response. Also uses a more formal opening, "Dear Professor Smith," which is appropriate for an initial email to someone who does not know him.

Immediately alerts the reader to the purpose of the email in the subject line, which will capture the reader's attention.

Gets to the point quickly in the first paragraph instead of making the reader go through much technical detail.

Groups information effectively into paragraphs so it is easier to read.

Keeps the sentences relatively short.

Asks a very specific question, which is easy for Zack's recipient to answer. By contrast, the INEFFECTIVE version requires that whoever gets the email will have to locate the correct person and then forward the email. When that person gets the email, what should he or she do?

municate with them more effectively. (You will learn more about active listening in Chapter 2: Working with Others.)

Once you understand your audience, creating an audience-oriented message requires answering two questions:

❶ **What content will your audience need or want?** Your communication should address the questions on the audience's minds and anticipate the possible objections.

❷ **How can you make the message easy for your audience to understand?** You will increase the chances that people will accurately read or listen to the message if you organize it for easy comprehension.

FIGURE 1.4 illustrates two versions of a business memo. To evaluate whether these memos are audience-oriented, try reading them in two steps. First, glance at each memo for about 10 seconds to see what stands out and to determine which version is easier to read. Then, read each memo more carefully to identify which version more clearly provides reasons and explanations that will be compelling to the audience.

Persuasive

When you want to influence people's thoughts or actions, your message needs to be persuasive. **Persuasion** is the process of influencing your audience to agree with your

Purpose The intended outcome of a communication that defines what you want the audience to know, do, or feel about the subject of your message.

Audience Anyone who receives a message and for whom a message is intended; the audience can be one person or many, depending on the number of recipients.

Active listening A learned skill that requires you to focus on the speaker, make sense of the information that is presented, and when possible, provide feedback about the information to ensure understanding.

Persuasion The process of influencing your audience to agree with your point of view, recommendation, or request.

FIGURE 1.4 Two Versions of a Business Recommendation

TO: Matt Leonard
FROM: Alan Dubay
DATE: February 12, 20XX
SUBJECT: Santé Système Blood Pressure Monitor

Santé Système has expressed interest in participating in the manufacture of our new home blood pressure monitor in France. On my recent trip to Europe, I had the opportunity of discussing this with George Bonet of our French subsidiary. The situation in France is that registration will take upwards of 12–18 months unless some local assembly/manufacturing can occur within France. If some assembly process could occur at Santé, George projects that registration could be accomplished within six months. Currently, two competitors, Acme and Globics, are pressing for large-scale automated programs of similar technology. Our French subsidiary has a number of Santé units out on trial now, which have been well received but further activity will be extremely difficult pending registration. Could I ask you and your people to investigate the possibility of providing Santé with parts, which they can assemble and incorporate into locally produced final packaging? George will be forwarding to Santé about 25 sets of parts that Santé can use to develop an assembly procedure. Once they have assembled a complete monitor, we can test it and make a decision. George projects first-year sales of such a blood pressure monitor in France to be between 8,000–10,000 units.

I am enclosing for your examination a mock-up monitor produced by Santé. Please keep me informed of progress as the evaluation continues.

AUDIENCE-ORIENTED
FEATURES

TO: Matt Leonard
FROM: Alan Dubay
DATE: February 12, 20XX
SUBJECT: Recommendation to Evaluate Partnership with Santé Système ◄------------- Subject line identifies the purpose of the message.

Recommendation ◄-- Recommendation is easy to find.
On my recent trip to Europe, I met with George Bonet of our French subsidiary to discuss a partnership with Santé Système for manufacturing our new home blood pressure monitors in France. Based on this conversation, I recommend that we evaluate the possibility of Santé's participation by allowing them to assemble several test units for us.

Rationale for Working with Santé ◄-- Headings outline the organization.
- **Working with Santé will substantially speed the process of getting the product on the market in France.** Registration in France will take 12 to 18 months if assembly occurs in the United States. If assembly takes place in France, registration will take only six months. Our French subsidiary has a number of monitors out on trial now. The units have been well received, but we will have difficulty growing sales until the product is registered.
- **Working with Santé, we may be able to beat our competitors to market.** Our ◄------- Bullets list reasons and next steps.
  competitors, Acme and Globics, are pressing for large-scale production programs of similar technology.
- **Getting to market quickly will allow us to capture a share of a substantial market.**
  George projects first-year sales of such a monitor in France to be between 8,000 and ◄----- Content provides information audience needs.
  10,000 units.

Next Steps
Will you please:
- Investigate the possibility of providing Santé with components that they can assemble and incorporate into locally produced final packages. George will be forwarding to Santé about 25 sets of parts to use to develop an assembly procedure. We can then (1) test a prototype on an in-house machine to understand its performance and (2) make a decision.
- Examine the enclosed mock-up kit produced by Santé, which demonstrates their proposed look of the product and confirm that it is acceptable.

Pleast let me know by February 25 if you anticipate any problems with the procedure.

point of view, recommendation, or request. In your daily life, you often need to communicate persuasively. You may be persuading people to accept a proposal or recommendation, give you a refund, agree with your argument, donate money to a charity, become a customer, or remain a customer—the list goes on and on. The more persuasive you are, the more effective your communication will be.

Being persuasive requires thinking about the topic from your audience's point of view. What benefits do you offer? What audience objections do you need to address? What reasons and factual evidence support your claim? In FIGURE 1.5, Fran Patera of MaxiWeb Web Hosting wants to persuade a potential customer to switch to MaxiWeb as its Internet provider. As you read Fran's message, notice how she uses all these persuasive techniques. (You will learn more about persuasion in Chapter 5: Communicating Persuasive Messages.)

Effective communicators are professional

Professionalism refers to the qualities that make you appear businesslike in the workplace. Professionalism is expressed by your actions, your attire, the wording of an email, your body language during a meeting, your tone of voice on the telephone—not to mention your attention to correct grammar and proofreading. However, professionalism goes beyond projecting a professional image. It also involves living up to the standards of your profession, including ethical standards.

An effective professional communicator demonstrates three very different aspects of professionalism. These include being:

- appropriate to the situation
- clear and concise
- ethical

Appropriate to the situation

Different situations require different behavior. For example, if you have lunch with friends, you may not think to stand up when a new person joins you at the table or to formally introduce that person to the others. In addition, you may assume it is okay to tell your friends funny stories about another student. However, during a business lunch, professionalism requires that you observe etiquette and actively participate in conversations without disrespecting others. Etiquette errors become barriers that interfere with how the recipients of your message perceive you.

Professionalism is just as important in writing as it is in speaking. For example, assume you just found out you have to cancel your evening plans because your marketing team needs to finish a new client proposal before an 8 AM meeting. You may want to send a message to your team like this: *"hey guys, i hope you didn't get too wasted last night, cuz we gotta pull an all-nighter tonite to get that crappy project done by 8 AM or you-know-who will kick our butts! i'll order pizza–any requests?"*

The informal tone, style, and wording may reflect how you feel. However, informality can be a problem since someone can forward that email to others at the company. The challenge is to be professional in your work email without being overly formal. In this case, the more professional email uses standard English and eliminates references to personal life as well as negative references to the project and supervisor: *"Hi John, Deepa, and Elaine: It looks as if we will have to work late tonight to meet the 8 AM deadline. I'll order a pizza for us—any requests?"*

Consider the two emails in FIGURE 1.6 on page 15. In the INEFFECTIVE version, the rambling style—including typographical errors—not only gives the impression that the writer is immature and unprofessional, it also leads to wordiness and an unorganized narrative that is difficult to follow. In the EFFECTIVE email, the writer conveys a more professional image. In addition, the sentences are shorter and the ideas are better organized for easy reading.

Professionalism The qualities that make you appear businesslike in the workplace.

FIGURE 1.5 Persuasive Letter

`letter`

2929 Avenue of the West, Houston, TX 77002

June 25, 20XX

Mr. Will Johnson
SaveOnCrafts
1349 Lothrop Street
Topeka, KS 66605

Dear Mr. Johnson:

Thank you for meeting with me last week to discuss changing your web hosting company from your current provider, to MaxiWeb. We believe that MaxiWeb will offer you two important benefits:

The first benefit is reliability. With our integrated backup systems, we average only five minutes of outage time per month. According to an independent survey published in *E-Commerce Today*, your current provider loses connectivity at least once per day. I have enclosed an article from *E-Commerce Today* that provides a method for estimating what this amount of down time may be costing your company in lost sales.

> Benefit 1: Reliability will result in fewer lost sales.

The second benefit is responsiveness and customer service. MaxiWeb has the highest customer service rating in the industry. Unlike many other providers, we offer 24-hour telephone support from our home office in Houston. Our average time for resolving problems is less than 30 minutes.

> Benefit 2: Excellent customer service will solve problems quickly.

At the meeting, you expressed concern that MaxiWeb may cost more per month than your current service. As an attachment to this letter, I've included a detailed comparison between MaxiWeb's flat fee, which includes all services, and Interflex's fee structure, which requires you to pay for each service separately. By the time you add up all the extra services you need, I think you will find that Interflex's yearly cost is 10 percent more than our flat fee.

> Response to a known objection: MaxiWeb will not cost more than the competition.

Only a few days are necessary to set up and test your site. We will be glad to coordinate that work with your IT department. In more than 95 percent of cases, the actual transfer is so quick and seamless that you will not lose even one sale from your site.

> Response to an anticipated objection: Transition to a new provider will be easy.

I will call you next week to see if you have any additional questions. We are ready to begin the transfer process as soon as you authorize it.

> Closing emphasizes next steps and makes it easy for Mr. Johnson to implement a change.

Sincerely,

Fran Patera

Fran Patera
Director of Sales

Enclosures

FIGURE 1.6 Two Emails Illustrating Different Levels of Professionalism

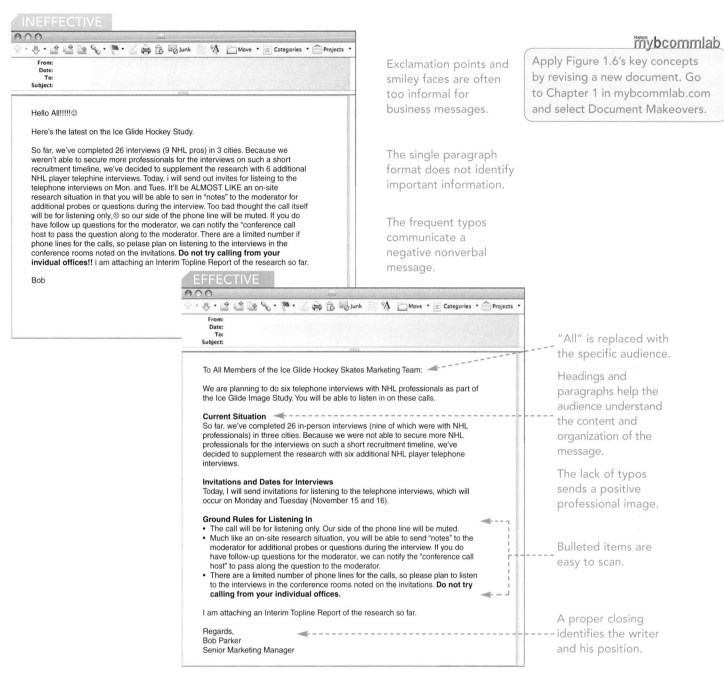

Exclamation points and smiley faces are often too informal for business messages.

Apply Figure 1.6's key concepts by revising a new document. Go to Chapter 1 in mybcommlab.com and select Document Makeovers.

The single paragraph format does not identify important information.

The frequent typos communicate a negative nonverbal message.

"All" is replaced with the specific audience.

Headings and paragraphs help the audience understand the content and organization of the message.

The lack of typos sends a positive professional image.

Bulleted items are easy to scan.

A proper closing identifies the writer and his position.

Clear and concise

In school, you may have developed a wordy writing style to fulfill word count requirements in assignments like a 500-word essay. You may also have developed the habit of writing complicated sentences in order to sound sophisticated and well educated. If you have developed these habits, you will need to change them to sound professional in the workplace. In business, people value clarity and conciseness. **Clarity** is the quality of being unambiguous and easy to understand. Clear communication. It has only one possible meaning. In addition, it uses simple words in well-constructed sentences and well-organized paragraphs. **Conciseness** means that a message uses no more words than necessary to accomplish its purpose. Clarity and conciseness are valued in business because time is a scarce resource. Your audience will understand clear and concise language faster than wordy and complicated language.

Consider the two versions of a voice mail message in **FIGURE 1.7**. The ineffective message is long and rambling. The effective message is short and to the point.

Clarity The quality of being unambiguous and easy to understand. Clear communication uses relatively simple words in well-constructed sentences and well-organized paragraphs.

Conciseness Using no more words than necessary for a message to accomplish its purpose.

INEFFECTIVE	EFFECTIVE
Hi, Ahmad. This is Don. The meeting yesterday went on for two hours after you left, and there was a lot of discussion about the new pricing system and how it will affect our sales and marketing campaign. No one could really agree about what the impact will be, which isn't surprising since we didn't have your charts to review, and we never agree about anything right away, so we decided to hold another meeting on Friday, which you are welcome to come to but you don't really have to. But what we do need from you are the sales projections for the four regions, which you never got a chance to present yesterday. Can you get those to Mary by Friday morning? Also, if you don't plan to come and there's anything else you want us to discuss, let me know.	Hi, Ahmad. This is Don. I'm sorry we didn't have a chance to discuss your sales projections at the meeting yesterday. We've scheduled a new meeting to discuss them at 2 PM on Friday. Could you let me know if you are available to attend? If not, please get the sales projections to Mary by noon on Friday so she can distribute them at the meeting. Thanks.

To leave a clear and concise voice message—or any spoken message—it is crucial to plan in advance. If you were writing the message in an email, you would be able to produce a quick draft and then go back to revise for clarity and conciseness. With voice mail, revising would require rerecording the entire message, which is not always possible.

Ethical

As a professional, you are likely to face a number of ethical dilemmas that are difficult to resolve. **Ethics** refers to the principles you use to guide decision making, leading you to do the right thing. However, the right thing is not always immediately obvious, and making the wrong decision may put your career, your colleagues, your customers, or your company at risk.

For example, assume your supervisor asks your team to prepare a persuasive presentation to support her recommendation that your company move some of its manufacturing facilities to Mexico. Most of your research supports the move because it will save the company money without decreasing product quality. However, you are not certain you have done enough research into the labor situation in Mexico. You have heard rumors that the move may expose the company to risks resulting from excessive employee absenteeism and turnover. You don't have time to do more research because your supervisor is presenting the information tomorrow. Here is your ethical dilemma: Should you mention the potential risk, which will weaken your argument? Or should you ignore this potential risk and present the strongest case you can to support the move to Mexico? After all, your supervisor has asked you to put together a strong argument, since management really wants to move several facilities to Mexico. In addition, you have no actual evidence that there will be a labor problem.

This scenario highlights two kinds of ethical challenges. The first is your responsibility to tell the truth. If your presentation gives the impression that no problems exist in moving facilities to Mexico, you would not be living up to that responsibility. The second ethical challenge is your responsibility to your supervisor and your organization. If your supervisor wants a change that you believe may be risky to the organization, you are in a bind. You might think, *"I'll just give my supervisor the strong argument she asked for, and she can do with it what she likes."* However, if you feel tempted to do this, you might want to impose the headline test on your actions. How would you feel if the company had problems in Mexico, and you opened the newspaper to read this headline: *"Business analyst neglected to inform company of potential labor risks"*? If the headline makes you feel uncomfortable or guilty about your actions, then you have probably acted against your own ethical principles. In general, it is better to tell the entire truth to your supervisor: there are unconfirmed rumors of labor unrest in Mexico that should be investigated before reaching a final decision. This allows everyone to make the best and most informed decision.

As a business communicator, you may not always easily identify the best and most ethical course of action to take. However, a good communicator recognizes the responsibility to try. Jeff Bezos, the CEO of Amazon.com, illustrated this characteristic in handling an ethical and public relations crisis. Amazon realized it was inadvertently acting unethically by selling electronic access to books that it did not own the digital copyrights to sell, including George Orwell's novel *1984*. To correct that ethical mistake, Amazon deleted the books from customers' online libraries and returned the purchase price to the customers.

Amazon thought this was the ethical thing to do, but customers who had purchased the books were angry. What right did Amazon have to delete the books from their library, without any warning or communication? Imagine how you would feel if you needed a book from your electronic library to study for an exam the next day and the book had simply disappeared. While Bezos could easily have defended his actions, instead he posted on the Amazon discussion forum the message in FIGURE 1.8, taking responsibility for his actions and acknowledging the ethical responsibility to treat people fairly.[15]

discussion forum posting

This is an apology for the way we previously handled illegally sold copies of *1984* and other novels on Kindle. Our "solution" to the problem was stupid, thoughtless, and painfully out of line with our principles. It is wholly self-inflicted, and we deserve the criticism we've received. We will use the scar tissue from this painful mistake to help make better decisions going forward, ones that match our mission.

With deep apology to our customers,

Jeff Bezos, Founder & CEO
Amazon.com

FIGURE 1.8
Discussion Forum Posting

Customer response in the discussion forum was overwhelmingly positive, and the media picked up the story, praising Bezos for taking responsibility for the company's actions.

Effective communicators are adaptable

The business world evolves continually, requiring you to adapt both as an employee and a communicator. For example, a person who began to work for IBM in the mid 1980s joined a company whose key business was building and selling stand-alone mainframe computers for large corporate clients. IBM basically had one product to make and one product to sell to one kind of customer. Communication with those clients—and with colleagues—took place by phone calls, letters, memos, and face-to-face meetings.

However, in a few short years, the world changed dramatically. IBM employees saw the company's one product being overshadowed by the personal computer and networks. The Internet was rapidly growing as both a means of communication and a business platform. Clients were now looking for software solutions, not hardware products. So IBM changed its focus from being a product provider to a service provider.

During this change, an employee who wanted to remain at IBM had to learn to adapt—no longer focusing on communicating the benefits of one product, but listening to client needs and providing a solution to those needs. Employees also had to adapt to other cultures, since IBM's customer base outside the United States was growing. In addition, employees needed to become more collaborative, as IBM created more global teams to serve its global customers. And new communication media—email, video conferencing, online meetings—were replacing the old ones.[16]

It is impossible to predict how business will change in the future and how communication will change as a result. In this decade, dramatic transformations are already occurring with the proliferation of global outsourcing and social media—Twitter, Facebook, blogs, and viral videos. Only one thing is certain: more change will come, and as a business communicator, you must learn to adapt—to new technologies, new cultures, and new ways of working with others.

Ethics A set of principles that guide decision making and lead someone to do the right thing.

LinkedIn, a social networking site for professionals, grew from a half million members in 2004 to 75 million members in 2010.

Current with technology

Technology reduces the distance between communicators, allowing an immediate exchange of information across miles and time zones. It enables people to meet online and share documents instantaneously, even though they are in different countries. Effective business communicators stay current with technological advances to communicate effectively in today's Digital Age. That means taking advantage of equipment such as smart phones and applications like Web 2.0 (and 3.0) technology as well as using social media such as Facebook and Twitter. Currently, companies use social media outlets not only to market and promote their products and services but also to improve two-way communication with employees.

Technology changes so quickly that the hardware and software applications you use in school can be outdated by the time you reach the workplace. Each year, business communicators have more technology options and more technology challenges. As a result, communicators continually need to address three questions: What is the best technology for the task? How can I use technology to enable more effective communication? And how can I avoid the technology traps that get in my way?

For example, imagine you are working for a company in Palo Alto, California. You are collaborating on a project with a team in your company's Tokyo office, where the time zone is 16 hours ahead. At the end of your workday at 5 PM, it is 9 AM the next day in Tokyo. You need to update your Tokyo colleagues about your accomplishments on the project for the day so they can continue the work. What technologies can you use to do this? If you conduct a pro-con analysis, you'll see that no one technology is perfect. You will need to make thoughtful decisions.

- **Should you call your colleagues to let them know the status of the project?** The advantage of a phone call is that your colleagues can ask questions. The disadvantage is that there is no written documentation of your update. If someone in Tokyo misses your phone call, he won't have access to the information.

- **Should you email your colleague?** Email is very efficient, and it allows you to communicate with many people at once. However, email is not always reliable because there may be network delays or someone's spam filter may block your message.

- **Should you upload your documents to the company intranet?** This offers the advantage of having all the documents in a central location that employees with the password can access. The disadvantage, though, is that your colleagues in Tokyo will need to remember to go to the site to download documents. The documents aren't delivered to their mailboxes.

- **Should you use a team wiki**—a collaborative web application accessible by multiple users—that allows everyone to constantly update material to a shared space? This offers the same advantages and disadvantages as the company intranet. In addition, wikis allow people to better track the history of changes.

Technological competence goes beyond selecting a communication technology. It also requires knowing how to avoid traps. Have you experienced any of these situations?

- You've created a PowerPoint presentation that includes some specialized fonts. When you present it using someone else's computer, your specialized fonts don't work. All you see is gibberish. (To solve this problem, communicators need to learn how to "embed" fonts within a PowerPoint or Word document.)

- Your classmate sends you a web document filled with pictures. When you open the document, you see no pictures. Instead, you see boxes with red Xs in them. (This problem is solved by "inserting" graphics rather than pasting them.)

- You've created a graph in Excel that you need to import into PowerPoint. When you import it, all the colors in the graph change. (To avoid this problem, experiment with all the different paste options in PowerPoint.)

- You've produced an email that is well designed using color and professional formatting. When your audience receives the message, all the formatting is gone and the text has run together. (This problem is difficult to solve, since different email programs show formatting in different ways. A smart communicator will ensure that email will be readable in its plainest form.)

As a good communicator, you don't need to know all technologies, but you do need to think about the implications of technology choices and use your options wisely.

You also need to be adaptable to new technologies as they arise. Currently, both for-profit and not-for-profit organizations are exploring ways to enhance communication through social media—blogs, wikis, virtual worlds, and social networking websites such as Facebook, LinkedIn, and Twitter. Social media also includes multimedia outlets like YouTube, Skype, and Slideshare. The list of applications and outlets grows as technology advances. Dose of Digital, an e-marketing company specializing in the pharmaceutical and healthcare industry, has identified *Seven Uses of Social Media in Business—the 7 Cs:*[17] communicating, cause support/sponsorship, contests, consumer research, connecting others, customer service, and community building. Here are some examples of how businesses are taking advantage of social media:

- **Communicating.** Twitter is an effective method of sharing short bursts of information with a mass audience. Gartner, Inc.—a leading IT research company—reported that many companies use Twitter externally for direct marketing communication and internally to report informal project updates.[18] Companies also use social media for two-way communication with audiences. For example, when Eastman Kodak asked its social media followers for input on a name for a new product, the company received over 20,000 submissions in four days. In response to growing social media coverage, Kodak created a chief listening officer position to serve as an "air traffic controller" of the company's incoming and outgoing social media communications.[19]

- **Cause Support/Sponsorship.** Many companies, such as Bank of America and RE/MAX, support the Susan B. Komen breast cancer organization by displaying the pink ribbon on their products, websites, and Facebook pages. Facebook fans often can donate directly through the company's site, with the company sometimes offering incentives such as discounts or matching donations.

- **Contests.** Novartis—a pharmaceutical company and early adopter of social media—used YouTube in 2007 to solicit video submissions to raise awareness of the importance of flu vaccinations.[20] Online contests can provide good public relations and promote brand awareness.

- **Consumer Research.** Social media has expanded the ways that a company can distribute surveys to gather data about consumer preferences and behavior. Links to surveys can be emailed to customers and also posted on corporate websites, promoted on blogs, and integrated into Facebook pages, as illustrated in FIGURE 1.9.

By being adaptable to changes in technology, businesses are creating communication opportunities and strengthening their connections with employees, customers, and the general public.

Able to work with other cultures

As workplaces become more diverse and companies become more global, the chances increase that you will be communicating with people of many countries and backgrounds. Some people may not be native English speakers. In those cases, keep your writing and speaking easy to understand by using short sentences and avoiding idiomatic language—such as "we are on the same page"—that may cause confusion.

However, even people who are very adept at English may come from cultures that approach business and communication differently than you do. **Culture** refers to the learned and shared patterns in a society. People demonstrate their culture through values, ideas, attitudes—and their approach to communication. While it would be nearly impossible to memorize a list of cultural differences among countries, effective communicators approach their tasks with an open mind and are ready to adapt to different cultural needs. Some cultures, like the Chinese, are more formal than others. Chinese businesspeople follow a prescribed set of rules about how to show respect to managers and other senior colleagues. People from other cultures, like Germans, are more concerned with punctuality, and may be offended if someone arrives at a meeting 10 minutes late. By increasing your awareness of cultural differences and keeping an open dialogue with your colleagues, you can adapt your behavior as needed.

Culture The learned and shared patterns in a society. People demonstrate their culture through values, ideas, and attitudes.

FIGURE 1.9 Consumer Survey on a Facebook Page

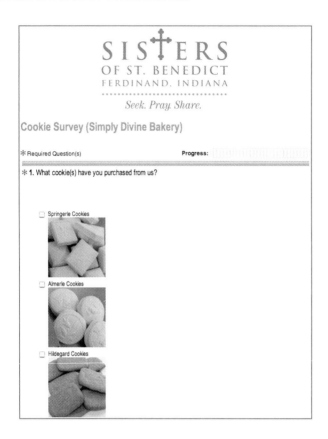

The following scenarios focus on two communication challenges between a British and Chinese company doing business together.[21] The challenges arise from one key difference between Chinese and British business cultures: Chinese businesses are very hierarchical, while British businesses are more egalitarian or democratic. That means in China, senior members of the company are accorded special respect and treated differently than their employees. By contrast, in Britain everyone is accorded equal respect.

- A company from Great Britain hired a Chinese firm to act as the sales representative for its products in China. The British regional manager in charge of Asia Pacific sales created an email distribution list to communicate efficiently with the entire group in China. The head of sales in China was insulted at being included in the list with junior colleagues. This method of communication does not show the head of sales enough respect.

- Later in this partnership, the British head of the Chinese office invited a delegation of Chinese sales representatives to Great Britain for a technical meeting about the products they would sell. The meeting was held in the factory where the products would be produced. The British director of sales and marketing presided over the meeting and sat at the head of the table. The Chinese representatives sat around the table. Since the room and table were small, the British representatives sat in chairs against the walls of the room rather than crowding in around the table. The British director made a brief welcoming speech and then asked his staff members to introduce themselves. He then asked the Chinese staff members to introduce themselves. The head of the Chinese delegation looked confused and later admitted that he felt the British were condescending and disrespectful. The seating arrangements suggested that this was not a meeting of equals, and the speaking roles made him feel he was not given adequate respect as an equal.

As you can see from these two scenarios, basic communication decisions that seem normal in your own cultural context may offend colleagues from another culture. The British manager could have avoided miscommunication by learning more about the

Chinese corporate culture. In the first scenario, the manager could have sent the communication only to the Chinese director who then could decide how to communicate the information to his employees. In the second scenario, the British manager could have shared an agenda in advance with the Chinese director, found a bigger room, requested that the Chinese director sit next to him at the head of the table, and introduced the Chinese director immediately, giving him an opportunity to speak and express appreciation.

Cultural sensitivity does not refer only to international communication. People who differ in age and in gender may also be separated by cultural differences. Even within the same country, younger people are likely to be less hierarchical and formal than their older counterparts. While the older head of the Chinese delegation may have been insulted that the British introduced themselves first, the younger members of the delegation may have responded differently. They may have identified more with their younger British counterparts and felt that respect must be earned rather than accorded by hierarchy.[22]

Although you will not be able to predict every intercultural problem even if you conduct comprehensive research on the culture with which you are working, your attempt to accommodate the cultural differences will communicate professionalism and respect.

Collaborative

In school, you complete much of your work on your own. Even when you work on a group project or study with other students, the grade you earn at the end of the class is usually an individual one. In business, while you will routinely have to communicate as an individual, many of your projects will be team-based because they are too big to be completed by just one person. As a result, **collaboration**—working together to achieve a common goal—is crucial in the workplace.

Being collaborative requires that you adapt to the working style of many different people. In addition, it requires that you coordinate, compromise, negotiate, and manage conflict. Consider the following scenario. You work for an airline and have been assigned to a cross-disciplinary team that is researching various ways to decrease costs. Your team has 30 days to complete its research and present findings and recommendations to management. Think about all the decisions you need to make to coordinate your work:

- How to identify talents of team members and divide the research
- How and when to share information with each other
- What criteria to use to evaluate the options
- Which options to present to management
- How to organize your presentation
- How to divide the task of writing the presentation
- How to organize and deliver your recommendations to management

In the process of working together and making these decisions, you and your teammates are likely to experience disagreements and conflicts. Perhaps one teammate firmly believes, based on his research, that the best option for decreasing costs is to eliminate the lowest volume routes that the airline flies, while another teammate argues that this option has hidden public relations costs. As this scenario suggests, effective communicators need to know more than just how to research, write, and present. They also need to know how to coordinate work, manage conflicts, and negotiate agreements.

IN SUMMARY, this chapter provides a broad overview of business communication and the many skills you need to be effective in the workplace. Practicing to be a strategic, professional, and adaptable communicator will give you a competitive edge that will make you a valuable employee, potentially increase your salary outlook, and enhance communication in all facets of your life. Each chapter in this textbook focuses on a different aspect of business communication—from working with others and communicating specific kinds of messages to preparing proposals and reports and interviewing for a job. The goal of this book is to provide you with the skills and insight you need to make good decisions for every communication challenge you face.

Collaboration The process of working together to achieve a common goal.

CHAPTER 1 Summary

1.1 Why should I study business communication? *(pages 4–5)*

- **Effective business communicators have a competitive edge.** Communication—planning, producing, delivering, and interpreting messages—is regarded as one of the most important business abilities. Yet employers find too few people who communicate well.
- **Good communication skills will contribute to your success.** Communication will not only help you find a job but will also make you a more valuable employee, and perhaps even increase your salary. Good communication skills can help you in your personal life as well.

1.2 Why is business communication challenging? *(pages 6–9)*

- **Even basic communication is complex.** As the transactional model of communication demonstrates, communication involves many steps: encoding a message, selecting an appropriate medium, decoding the message, and providing effective feedback.
- **Barriers and context add to the complexity.** Effective communication requires overcoming physiological, psychological, semantic, and linguistic barriers. It also requires adapting to the context of a situation. You will need to think about how best to accomplish your purpose, considering the audience and the business situation.
- **Multiple audiences pose additional challenges.** Often you will communicate with more than one person, requiring you to think about all their contexts, backgrounds, concerns, and agendas.

1.3 What characteristics do successful business communicators share? *(pages 9–21)*

- **Effective communicators are strategic.** Effective communicators are purposeful and design their communication to achieve a specific outcome. They are also audience-oriented, considering what content the audience requires and also what organization, format, and language will make the content easy to understand. Finally, when their purpose requires it, they know how to be persuasive and influence the audience's thoughts and actions. Three useful techniques for persuasion are identifying benefits, providing reasons and evidence to support the main ideas, and anticipating audience objections.
- **Effective communicators are professional.** Professionalism refers to the qualities that make you appear businesslike. Business communicators appear professional when they act in a manner appropriate to the situation, are clear and concise, and live up to the ethical standards of their profession.
- **Effective communicators are adaptable.** Being adaptable means being willing and able to change to meet new business needs. In business, communicators must adapt to remain current with technology, which changes very quickly. In addition, since business is increasingly global and values diversity, communicators must adapt to working with other cultures. Finally, since many business projects require teamwork and coordination with others, communicators must adapt their work styles to collaborate well with others.

PEARSON mybcommlab *Are you an active learner? Go to mybcommlab.com to master Chapter 1 content. Chapter 1 interactive activities include:*

- Customizable Study Plan and Chapter 1 practice quizzes
- Chapter 1 Simulation, Successful Business Communication, that helps you think critically and prepare to make choices in the business world
- Flash Cards for mastering the definition of chapter terms

- Chapter 1 Video Exercise, Effective vs. Ineffective Communication, which shows you how textbook concepts are put into practice every day
- Interactive Lessons that visually review key chapter concepts
- Document Makeovers for hands-on, scored practice in revising documents

STRATEGIC

Purposeful

Stephanie Crim

Marketing Analyst, BP
University of Southern California, 2007

"In my business communication course in school, I learned to focus on the purpose and put the key message up front. At work, this is helpful when explaining complex issues as the audience understands the key message before we get into the detailed analysis."

Audience-Oriented

Rasheite Radcliff

Freelance Writer and Teacher
Bradley University, 2009

"I think what I apply most from my courses is identifying and understanding my audience. I always evaluate the intended readers of anything I compose, and I try to make sure that things will make sense from their perspective. You really have to put yourself in their shoes."

Persuasive

Ellen Hildebrand

Associate Media Manager
Miller-Coors
Northwestern University, 2004

"A lot of my job requires persuasion—of the agency, internal clients, and external audiences. I have learned that knowing your audience is critical to effective persuasion. As a result, I ask questions to learn about my audience and tailor my communication style to influence their thinking."

PROFESSIONAL

Appropriate to the Situation

Jose Campoy

Management Analyst, U.S. Department of Defense
University of Arizona, 2009

"I work with many different people at all levels across the federal government. Sometimes it's challenging. I apply what I learned in my bcom class to consider the context of a situation and modify my behavior and professionalism to match. Some situations require more formality than others."

Clear and Concise

Kalani Miller

Co-owner, MIKOH Swimwear
University of California – Santa Barbara, 2009

"The communication courses I took helped prepare me to run my own business efficiently. Most professionals do not have time to read "fluff" or "beat around the bush." They want to know what you need and when you need it, so it is important to be clear and concise in every message."

Ethical

Travis English

Sales Operator, Best Buy
North Carolina A&T State University, 2008

"One thing I learned was to be ethical in my communication with customers. In the technology business, it's important not to talk over people's heads. I never promise too much, and if I don't know the answer, I find someone who does."

ADAPTABLE

Current with Technology

Miachelle DePiano

Technical Writer, Intel
Arizona State University, 2008

"Intel is a global company, which means that most of our communications and meetings are via email or chat. With communication that is global and asynchronous, you have to deal with language barriers, cultural differences, electronic translators, and time zones. Add to this dynamic the "faceless" nature of the communication, and it can make communicating effectively a real challenge."

Able to Work with Other Cultures

Ingrid Holguin

Writer/Teacher, Avalon School in Seoul, Korea
University of South Florida, 2009

"My business communication class helped to prepare me for intercultural communication. Miscommunication with other cultures can be frustrating. If you lose your temper, the other party shuts down and a brick wall builds up. You must be patient when you're asked many questions to ensure they understand. Similarly, you have to ask many questions yourself, to ensure you understand."

Collaborative

Amado Villarreal

Project Engineer, CH2M Hill Constructors, Northwestern University, 2009

"I am glad I was able to practice collaborative work in school. It is challenging to establish yourself when meeting new people. When you enter the workplace, no one knows who you are or what you can do. You must be willing to start conversations with people so you can begin to create relationships and learn how the company operates and what role your job takes in the overall success of the company."

KEY TERMS QUICK ACCESS REVIEW

Active listening p. 10	**Conciseness** p. 15	**Feedback** p. 7
Audience p. 10	**Context** p. 8	**Medium** p. 7
Barrier p. 7	**Culture** p. 19	**Persuasion** p. 11
Clarity p. 15	**Decode** p. 7	**Professionalism** p. 13
Collaboration p. 21	**Encode** p. 6	**Purpose** p. 10
Communication p. 4	**Ethics** p. 16	**Social media** p. 5
Communication strategy p. 9		

CRITICAL THINKING

1. The chapter recommends that communicators address potential audience objections. Describe a situation—either from your personal experience or a theoretical business scenario—where it would be wiser to ignore potential audience objections.

2. In audience-oriented writing, you can make key ideas easy to find by using headings. How can you make important ideas stand out in a voice mail message?

3. Imagine that you are trying to persuade a teammate to agree with an idea for a presentation and the teammate accuses you of being manipulative—trying to influence someone for your personal benefit. What is the difference between being persuasive and being manipulative?

4. Assume that your supervisor asked you to lie to a customer in an email about why a shipment is delayed. Would it be unethical for you to write the email if you believe it is wrong to lie? Conversely, would it be unethical for you to refuse to write the email if you believe you have a responsibility to your employer? How would you resolve this issue?

5. Imagine you have been asked to collaborate on a project with a colleague whose work style is very different from yours. For example, you like to plan carefully and follow a schedule, while your colleague is spontaneous. You like to write thorough drafts that require only minimal revision, while your colleague likes to write incomplete drafts and revise heavily later. Based on these differences, you think it would be more efficient and cost effective for the company to have you work on this project by yourself. Should you make that argument to your supervisor? What might be the benefits of collaborating? What are the drawbacks?

6. Although it is important to consider your audience's potential questions and objections when you communicate, you may not always know a lot about the people in your audience in advance. Imagine, for example, that you are sending a business proposal to a new client you have never met before. How can you learn more about your audience before writing the proposal?

7. Cross-cultural communication requires you to use clear language. What are some of the other challenges of communicating across cultures?

8. Students who are not used to writing professional emails sometimes make the mistake of composing them as if they were text messages. What are some key elements of text messages that you should avoid in professional emails?

9. Based on your experience, what are some of the benefits of new communication technologies, such as Web 2.0 and social media? What are some of the challenges they pose?

10. Readers often judge a person's professionalism based on whether a document is spell-checked and free of grammatical errors. Do you believe this is a fair basis for making a judgment?

DEVELOPING YOUR COMMUNICATION SKILLS

1.1 Why should I study business communication?
(pages 4–5)

EXERCISE 1 Effective business communicators have a competitive edge

Review the communication skills outlined in this chapter. How many of them do you possess? Which ones do you need to improve upon? How do you think you can improve these skills? Outline your answers in a paragraph or two.

EXERCISE 2 Good communication skills will contribute to your success

Use an online job bank such as Monster, to search for job advertisements related to your career goals. How many of them include communication skills in their descriptions or requirements? Summarize your findings in a paragraph that outlines your career goals, two or three jobs you found, and the communication skills they require.

1.2 Why is business communication challenging?
(pages 6–9)

EXERCISE 3 Even basic communication is complex

Think of a personal or business experience when someone "decoded" your message incorrectly and misinterpreted your meaning. Write a brief paragraph explaining the situation and the result.

EXERCISE 4 Barriers and context add to the complexity

Think of a personal or business experience when you did not achieve a communication goal. Use the transactional model of communication presented in this chapter to describe why your communication was unsuccessful. Outline what you could have done to improve the experience. Summarize your explanation in a paragraph or two.

EXERCISE 5 Multiple audiences pose additional challenges

Think of a personal or business experience when you were communicating with multiple people who had different needs or different levels of knowledge. In a paragraph or two, describe the situation, how you handled it, and whether you believe that communication was successful.

1.3 What characteristics do successful business communicators share? *(pages 9–21)*

EXERCISE 6 Effective communicators are strategic – being purposeful

Read the following memo and identify its main purpose. Rewrite the subject line and the first sentence of the memo to make them clearer.

TO:	Gloria Paradi
FROM:	Josh Benson
DATE:	March 23, 20XX
SUBJECT:	Staffing

This office has not had the benefit of full staffing at any time in the past year. There is no relief from continual pressure due to a limitation of staff. An analysis of overtime during the November/December time period provides a clear indication of the inability of the office to enjoy full coverage of all the required work within regular work hours. Additional help can be usefully provided in purchasing, design, fabrication, assembly, and shipping since we are understaffed in all areas. As we can set aside no time for training right now, it is required that all new employees be experienced.

Accompanies Exercise 6

EXERCISE 7 Effective communicators are strategic – being audience-oriented

In the early 1990s, the United States government's General Services Administration (GSA) posted the following bulletin on the walls of buildings around Washington, D.C., to warn workers about the dangers of working around pigeon droppings. After you read this message, recommend three changes to make it easier for the audience to find the most important ideas.

Bulletin: Potential Biological Hazard

Background: During evaluations in a historic building that GSA proposes to restore, a large accumulation of pigeon droppings was discovered, which had collected through long habitation of the birds. Samples of the droppings were collected and analyzed by the Centers for Disease Control in Atlanta, Georgia.

Discussion: The CDC identified the droppings as containing a fungus capable of causing very serious infection in humans. This fungus is called "Cryptococcus Neoformans." It attacks the lungs, central nervous system, skin, eyes, liver, and joints and has a marked target of the brain and meninges. It is contained in the accumulation of excretion of birds and pigeons in old nesting areas and in soil contaminated with bird and pigeon droppings.

Workers who work around or demolish bird and especially pigeon habitations should use extreme caution due to the potential risk of illness involved when disturbing accumulation prior to decontamination. Infection is primarily due to inhalation. Prevention is possible by wearing appropriate facemasks and personal protective clothing.

Recommendation: If such an area is identified, do not disturb it. Leave the area and report the finding immediately to your supervisor. Supervisors will coordinate with Regional Accident and Fire Prevention Branches for evaluation, preventive measures, and decontamination action.

Further information: Avoid a suspected area until it has been determined not hazardous.

Accompanies Exercise 7

EXERCISE 8 Effective communicators are strategic – being persuasive

You are the manager of a large supermarket that borders a residential neighborhood. A customer who lives nearby comes into the store and says, "I am completely out of patience with the trucks that make deliveries to your store. Deliveries start at 7 AM and end at 9 PM. Early in the morning and into the evening, trucks are banging their trailers into the loading docks. And the engines! The drivers keep the trucks running while they're making deliveries. I can't talk with friends in my yard because of all the noise of the trucks. And it's not just the noise. The trucks also block the alley so I sometimes cannot get out of my garage to get to work in the morning."

To respond, you could just choose to explain the situation. Clear reasons exist for each of the behaviors that the neighbor is complaining about:

- Local laws have set truck delivery hours from 7 AM to 9 PM. To accommodate all the deliveries, management needs to spread them throughout the day.
- The engines are on in refrigerator trucks because they run the generators that keep food from spoiling.
- The trucks block the alley for only a short time while they are waiting for other trucks to leave. Drivers politely move if they are asked.

However, suppose your main goal is to retain this "neighbor" as a customer and increase goodwill. In that case, you may choose to respond in a way that is more persuasive. Brainstorm content to include in your response. As you brainstorm, consider these persuasive techniques:

- Show that you understand your audience's concern.
- Address the objections.
- Show the benefits to the audience.

As part of your brainstorm, think of possible solutions to the problem. If you mention possible solutions, your response may be even more persuasive.

EXERCISE 9 Effective communicators are professional – being appropriate

You work for HungerFighters United, a not-for-profit organization dedicated to eradicating hunger in the United States. One of your colleagues, Sheryl Greene, drafts a letter to a potential donor who has also expressed an interest in volunteering for your organization. Sheryl gives you a copy of the letter to review before sending it. You think the tone is friendly, but you wonder if Sheryl is projecting a sufficiently professional image of herself and HungerFighters. Identify at least five changes you would suggest that Sheryl make.

December 14, 20XX

Ms. Anita Lawrence
4949 Daily Drive
Cleveland, OH 44101

Dear Anita:
As mentioned in my voice mail to you today, I am enclosing my card and other information that you might be interested in.

I have been with HungerFighters United in the Detroit Office since 1997 and have just moved to Development Director of the Midwest region . . . long title but the work is pretty much the same except I've expanded from Detroit to 11 states and am encouraged by the wonderful reception I've received and especially, by the powerful resources Midwesterners are sharing with the families we serve.

Steve Cannon mentioned that you might consider reaching out to others in your circle of friends. If you would like to host a gathering in or around your area, that would be an idea. We have wonderful stories to tell, literature to share, and handouts people can take home. Or, a small group in a restaurant or your home is also effective. At any rate, this serves as an introduction to our efforts and ideas on expanding the help we need to end hunger.

I wish you and yours a wonderful holiday season and look forward to talking to you in the New Year.

Gratefully,

Sheryl Greene
Director of Development

Accompanies Exercise 9

EXERCISE 10 Effective communicators are professional – being clear and concise

Select a message you received, such as a letter from a company or an email from a colleague. Identify specific content that can be revised to be clearer and more concise. Offer specific revisions based on the content presented in the chapter. Prepare to present your suggestions in class.

EXERCISE 11 Effective communicators are professional – being ethical

Your supervisor is preparing a speech for the company's chief executive officer to distribute to shareholders. He asks you to read the speech and provide feedback on how effective you think it will be. As you read the speech, you think you recognize some of the points—and the wording—from a speech by a financial analyst you heard a few weeks ago on C-SPAN television. You fear your supervisor's speech is plagiarized. You wonder if you should tell him that you recognize some of that speech from another source, but you decide not to for two reasons. First, if you tell your supervisor the speech sounds familiar, he may get angry or insulted. Second, the speech was televised very late at night, so it's unlikely that many people watched it. Evaluate the pros and cons of that choice. Is your choice ethical?

EXERCISE 12 Effective communicators are adaptable – current with technology

You are planning to hold a conference call with three other people, and you are looking for a technology that balances expense and convenience. Three kinds of conference call services are available to you:

- **Option 1:** Everyone calls in to a toll-free number. Your credit card will be charged 4 cents per minute for each person on the call. If people need to join the call late, they can do so without inconveniencing the rest of the participants.
- **Option 2:** Everyone calls in to a long-distance number. Each person pays whatever he or she would normally pay for a long distance call. For two people, it will be free because their telephone service offers free long-distance. The remaining two people will each pay 7 cents per minute. They will each need to be reimbursed. This option offers the same call-in convenience as Option 1.
- **Option 3:** You initiate a web-based conference call, using Skype. This call will be free for everyone. However, all participants need to be available at the moment you call them. Otherwise, you will need to repeatedly redial their number until they are available. If, for some reason, their call is dropped, they will have no easy way to rejoin the conference call.

The technology choice must balance costs versus convenience. Which option would you choose—and why?

EXERCISE 13 Effective communicators are adaptable – collaborative

You are working with a team of five colleagues to research and write a report recommending a new sales strategy for your client. Because you are a very good writer, you are designated the lead writer on the project. Everyone else is writing drafts—except for one colleague, Emma Yamaguchi. Emma has recently transferred to the United States from the Tokyo office, and her English writing is weak. Your team thinks Emma is contributing quite a lot to the project with her statistical analysis, which is strong. Everyone is happy with the distribution of labor—except Emma. She transferred to the United States to improve her written English, and now she finds she isn't being given the opportunity. Fortunately, she confides in you and tells you that she'd like to help with writing the report. How can Emma contribute in ways that will help improve her English writing but will not compromise the quality of the final product? Think of two or three ideas that you can suggest to the team and Emma.

EXERCISE 14 Effective communicators are adaptable – able to work with other cultures

Re-read Exercise 13. Assume that you suggested to Emma that she write one short section of the report, which another teammate can then edit. Emma writes her part, and you volunteer to edit that section. Emma gasps when she sees all your edits. She looks down and tells you she is ashamed to have submitted such poor quality work.

You are shocked by her response because you were helping her learn to write better English. As you read more about Japanese culture, you think that your response has made Emma "lose face," that is, feel embarrassed. How could you handle the situation differently in the future? What approach can you take that will make Emma feel comfortable rather than ashamed?

WRITING

EXERCISE 15 Analyzing communication effectiveness

In January 1996, Philadelphia experienced one of the most paralyzing snowstorms in its history. In one day, two and a half feet of snow fell, making travel treacherous. Some employers closed their doors completely. Others encouraged their workers to stay at home. Still others expected everyone to fight through the storm to get to work.

J. Richard Carnall, chair of PNC Bank's mutual fund operation, was one of the employers who expected workers to be at work during the storm. On the day following the snowstorm, Carnall was furious that only 30 percent of the staff reported to work. He wrote a memo to employees stating that he "was disappointed to not see more employees at work." He said, "While I don't confuse our goal with emergency personnel working in hospitals, we have, nonetheless, chosen a profession that demands our uninterrupted servicing ability." Mr. Carnall praised those who made it in to work, but pointed out that more workers should have taken advantage of local hotels the night before, adding that employees "who typically experience unplowed streets near your homes should use common sense" next time. To ensure that employees are more prepared to do battle with future winter storms, Mr. Carnall promised that specific "crisis services" individuals will be "stationed" at area hotels the day before a storm to emphasize the "criticality" of getting to work.

Employees who received this memo were very upset. In fact, one worker leaked the story to *The Wall Street Journal,* which published it, causing significant embarrassment to the writer.[23]

Is Mr. Carnall being strategic and professional in writing this memo?

Write an email to your instructor, analyzing the effectiveness of Mr. Carnall's communication according to the following criteria:

1. Strategic—purposeful, audience-oriented, persuasive
2. Professional—appropriate to the situation, clear and concise, ethical

Explain why you think the communication does or does not meet each of those criteria.

EXERCISE 16 Analyzing communication effectiveness

In July 2007, Apple released the iPhone at a price of $599. Only two months later, the company dropped the price by 33 percent to $399. The early iPhone customers were angry about the sudden drop in price and felt they had overpaid for the product. See the letter on page 28 that Steve Jobs wrote to these customers. Not surprisingly, members of the news media received the message and shared it with the general public.[24] Write a one- or two-paragraph email to your instructor, providing your assessment of whether or not you think this is an effective business communication. Provide support for your answer.

COLLABORATING

EXERCISE 17 Planning a virtual team meeting

Imagine that you are working on a team with members in the United States, Singapore, and the Netherlands. You need to check in with each other at least once a week to address issues and plan for the upcoming week. This requires that you decide on a technology for your weekly discussions. You are considering the following options:

- Email
- Wiki
- Internet chat
- Teleconferences
- Videoconferences

Use your favorite search engine to learn more about these technologies. If you have five members in your team, assign one technology to each team member. Then collaborate to create a chart that analyzes the pros and cons of each option. As a team, determine which technology (or technologies) you would choose and explain why.

EXERCISE 18 Increasing cultural sensitivity

Divide into teams of three to five students—or work as a whole class. Select at least three cultures not represented by anyone on your team. When you identify cultures, do not limit yourself to thinking about different countries of origin. Also consider the following:

- Region of the country (for example, the south or the northeast in the United States)

- Ethnicity
- Age (for example, people in their teens, twenties, thirties, forties, and so on)
- Gender
- Disability

For each of the cultures you have identified, list two or three "communication characteristics"—things to keep in mind when communicating to people of that culture. Illustrate each with a concrete example.

Prepare a class presentation of your findings. If the findings of different teams conflict, have a class discussion about why two teams draw two different conclusions about a particular culture.

To All iPhone Customers:

I have received hundreds of emails from iPhone customers who are upset about Apple dropping the price of the iPhone by $200 two months after it went on sale. After reading every one of these emails, I have some observations and conclusions.

First, I am sure that we are making the correct decision to lower the price of the 8GB iPhone from $599 to $399, and that now is the right time to do it. iPhone is a breakthrough product, and we have the chance to 'go for it' this holiday season. iPhone is so far ahead of the competition, and now it will be affordable by even more customers. It benefits both Apple and every iPhone user to get as many new customers as possible in the iPhone 'tent.' We strongly believe the $399 price will help us do just that this holiday season.

Second, being in technology for 30+ years I can attest to the fact that the technology road is bumpy. There is always change and improvement, and there is always someone who bought a product before a particular cutoff date and misses the new price or the new operating system or the new whatever. This is life in the technology lane. If you always wait for the next price cut or to buy the new improved model, you'll never buy any technology product because there is always something better and less expensive on the horizon. The good news is that if you buy products from companies that support them well, like Apple tries to do, you will receive years of useful and satisfying service from them even as newer models are introduced.

Third, even though we are making the right decision to lower the price of iPhone, and even though the technology road is bumpy, we need to do a better job taking care of our early iPhone customers as we aggressively go after new ones with a lower price. Our early customers trusted us, and we must live up to that trust with our actions in moments like these.

Therefore, we have decided to offer every iPhone customer who purchased an iPhone from either Apple or AT&T, and who is not receiving a rebate or any other consideration, a $100 store credit towards the purchase of any product at an Apple Retail Store or the Apple Online Store. Details are still being worked out and will be posted on Apple's website next week. Stay tuned. We want to do the right thing for our valued iPhone customers.

We apologize for disappointing some of you, and we are doing our best to live up to your high expectations of Apple.

Steve Jobs
Apple CEO

Accompanies Exercise 16

SPEAKING

EXERCISE 19 Informal impromptu presentations

a. Describe a time when you were very successful at achieving a specific communication goal, such as persuading someone to do something. Identify at least one reason for your success.

b. Describe a time when you wanted to achieve a specific goal with communication but were unsuccessful. Identify at least one reason that you weren't successful.

c. Based on your experience, give your classmates one or two tips about collaborating successfully with a teammate.

d. Do you think you are better at writing or at speaking? Provide examples to support your answer.

e. When you have communicated with people from a different culture, what was your biggest challenge?

EXERCISE 20 Executive briefings

a. **Are they thinking like a business communicator?** Find an "official email" that you have received from an organization you do business with: for example, your school, employer, bank, insurance company, or retail store. Analyze the message to determine if the writers were thinking like business communicators as described in this chapter. Identify two features of the email that you can discuss: both can be effective, both can be ineffective, or you can discuss one of each.

b. **Analyzing cultures:** Select a country that you have visited or would like to visit some day, and conduct a web search or library search about communication in that country. (Be sure your sources are authoritative. Do not use Wikipedia.) Make two or three recommendations about communication for colleagues who will be traveling to that country.

c. **Analyzing professionalism:** Imagine you are a small business owner and need to purchase a product or service (for example, executive coaching). Find two competitive websites that offer what you've chosen. Imagine you were going to choose a vendor based on the professionalism of the website. Prepare a brief presentation about which site inspires more confidence—and explain why.

GRAMMAR

Nouns and pronouns (See Appendix D—Section 1.1.1)

Rekey (or download from mybcommlab.com) the following two paragraphs, correcting the errors in use or formation of nouns and pronouns. Underline all your corrections.

Whomever answers the phone may be the only contact a caller has with a business. Everyone has their own personal preferences. However, find out how your employer wants the telephone answered, what your expected to say. When you pick up the phone, its important to speak politely and provide identifying information. Clearly state the company's name and you're name. Should you identify the Department, too?

These are the kinds of questions to settle before the phone rings. If the caller asks for you by name, say, "This is me." Don't leave the caller wondering who he or she has reached. Remember that when on the telephone at work, you are the Company.

2 Working with Others
Interpersonal, Intercultural, and Team Communication

new hires @ work

Jessica Lavery
Account Services Executive
ESPN
Northwestern University, 2009

" COMMUNICATING EFFECTIVELY IS ESSENTIAL IN MY ROLE AT ESPN. I depend on numerous sales and marketing counterparts across different advertising mediums and in different states across the country. For a given project, it is not uncommon to have 25 people, who are never in the same room together, contributing to the final result. Effective communication is essential to keep the project on track and on time. "

Introduction

Whether you work for a large company or a small one, you will interact with many people on the job: coworkers and teammates, supervisors and managers, vendors and service providers, and customers and clients. Your ability to work well with these people depends on your interpersonal communication skill. This chapter will help you increase those skills so you can create positive and productive working relationships.

First, the chapter addresses how to be an effective listener and speaker. Then it helps you apply your listening and speaking skills in three challenging contexts that arise when you work with others:

- Managing conflict
- Communicating with people from diverse cultures
- Communicating in teams

What listening skills will help me communicate better with others?

■ Access this chapter's simulation entitled Interpersonal Communication and Teamwork, located at mybcommlab.com.

Every day, without thinking about it, you engage in an important communication skill—listening. In fact, research shows that college students spend more than half their communication time listening.[1] For new employees in the workplace, listening is the most frequently used communication skill.[2]

Most people assume they are good listeners because they have so much listening experience. Yet decades of research show that people typically listen at only 25 percent efficiency.[3,4] As a result, they often mishear, misinterpret, misunderstand, and misremember. In business, this **passive listening**—hearing what someone says without actively paying attention to ensure understanding—leads to costly mistakes, unhappy employees, and customer complaints. Here are examples:

- An employee does not pay attention to a customer reciting a mailing address and then sends a shipment of 1,000 computers to Springfield, Massachusetts, rather than Springfield, Illinois. The shipping and return charges are extremely high, and the customer is angry because the computers haven't arrived.
- A customer service representative fails to listen carefully to a customer reporting a software problem and routes the call to a hardware engineer. The result is wasted time for employees and perhaps a lost customer.
- A manager does not listen carefully—or ask good follow-up questions—when an employee says she is sick and needs to go home. The manager requires that the employee stay, which exposes the entire office to a contagious flu.

People rarely become better listeners on their own. However, with study and training, you can become an active listener and significantly improve your communication skills. **Active listening** is a process of focusing attentively on what a speaker says, actively working to understand and interpret the content, and then responding to acknowledge understanding. This section will help you develop four categories of active listening skills:

- Hearing
- Comprehending and interpreting
- Evaluating
- Responding

Most of these same skills—especially interpreting and evaluating—are equally useful when you "listen" to what people say in their writing. Understanding the meaning of an email message can be as difficult as understanding the meaning of a conversation.

Hearing accurately

Listening typically starts with hearing: perceiving sounds and focusing on them. Since sounds are all around us, listening requires that you first distinguish the sounds you need and want to listen to, and then concentrate on fully hearing those sounds.

Some barriers to hearing are physiological. For example, you might have a temporary hearing problem, such as blocked ears due to a head cold. One significant physiological barrier to hearing is the speed at which your brain can process what you hear. Most people can process information twice as fast as the average person speaks. While you are waiting to process more information, your brain is not fully engaged and may begin to wander rather than actively listen and focus on the words you hear. Similarly, if you choose to multitask while listening, your brain becomes engaged in a different task, and you won't accurately hear what the speaker says.

The environment around you may also distract you from hearing well. Think about the last time you tried to have a conversation in a noisy restaurant or talk on your cell phone while standing at a busy intersection. You probably found it difficult to concentrate on what the other person was saying. At work, you may be distracted by ringing telephones, people passing by your desk, or noise from the next office.

The key to hearing accurately is focus. Look at the speaker and concentrate on what he or she says. Make a comment or ask a question to keep yourself engaged. A benefit of this approach is that you earn the respect of the speaker by being so attentive.

Comprehending and interpreting

You might very clearly hear someone speaking in Portuguese, Dutch, or Arabic, but you probably can't comprehend all those languages. Listening **comprehension** refers to how well you understand what you hear. In culturally diverse workplaces, language differences—including accents—can become significant barriers, but they are not the only obstacles to comprehension. You may have difficulty comprehending vocabulary or jargon that is unfamiliar to you. For example, imagine that you accompany a sick friend to a medical appointment. You hear the physician tell an assistant: "The patient presented with febrile illness." Unless you have medical training, you probably won't comprehend that this means your friend suddenly got a high fever. You may also have difficulty comprehending something that is explained badly, is confusing, or is contradictory.

Interpretation is different from comprehension. **Interpretation** involves analyzing the meaning of what you hear, read, or see to determine its intention. You might misunderstand a comment because you interpret it from a different frame of reference. For example, imagine you work in your company's Los Angeles office and your colleague is meeting with clients in Boston. Late in the evening, you receive an email from your colleague saying he needs information for a client meeting, and he'd like you to email it to him first thing in the morning. You could interpret that statement in two different ways. Does he want the information by 9 AM in Boston (Eastern time) or by 9 AM in Los Angeles (Pacific time)? If you interpret the statement from your frame of reference—Pacific time—you may be sending the summary too late (noon Eastern time).

Understanding what someone really means also requires being empathetic and paying attention to feelings. Research suggests that some people may be more naturally empathetic listeners than others.[5,6] Some people tend to pay attention to the literal content of communication, while others are skilled at focusing on the emotional content. Consider this scenario: Ron rushes late into a meeting with Dan and Erica. Dan asks him if everything is okay. Ron looks distracted and tense but says, "I'm okay." After Ron leaves the meeting room, Erica comments that Ron seemed very upset when he arrived. Dan responds, "There's no problem. He said he's okay." Dan focused on the content of the words, while Erica focused on the emotional meaning behind them.

Even if you are not naturally empathetic, you can train yourself to comprehend and interpret more effectively by "listening" to nonverbal communication and by verifying your understanding through questions and paraphrase.

"Listen" to nonverbal communication

Nonverbal communication refers to messages that are conveyed through something other than words—through tone of voice, facial expressions, gestures, body language, or other behavior. Consider how all these forms of nonverbal communication can help you better understand and interpret someone's meaning:

- **Emphasis and tone of voice.** Words carry different meanings depending on how they are said. Imagine someone speaking the simple phrase "I called him." Say that

Passive listening Hearing what someone says without actively paying attention to ensure understanding.

Active listening A process of focusing attentively on what a speaker says, actively working to understand and interpret the content and then responding to acknowledge understanding.

Comprehension How well you understand what you hear or read.

Interpretation Analyzing the meaning of what you hear, read, or see to determine its intention.

Nonverbal communication Messages conveyed through means other than words, for example tone of voice, facial expressions, gestures, and body language.

phrase three times, each time emphasizing a different word: "*I* called him"—"I *called* him"—"I called *him*." What three different meanings do those three statements convey? Now imagine saying those three words in an angry tone of voice and a happy tone of voice. Each time, you will be conveying a different meaning. As a good listener, you will benefit from paying close attention to tone of voice and letting it influence your interpretation of what you hear.

- **Facial expressions.** If someone says "hello" with a smile, you will interpret a very different meaning than if someone says "hello" with lowered eyebrows and a clenched jaw. While experts may disagree about whether facial expression is an unconscious reflection of emotion or a conscious technique that people use to convey meaning, most people agree that facial expression is an important element of communication.[7] Beware, though, of assuming that all people interpret facial expressions in the same way. As you will read in the Culture feature (page 35), biologists have determined that facial expressions are not universal among all cultures.

- **Body language, posture, and gestures.** You can uncover clues about a person's attitude toward what he or she is saying by observing body language. Is that person ashamed, proud, or uncertain? The speaker's posture—and even eye contact or lack of it—can help you interpret that attitude. In fact, you can often interpret attitude from body language without listening to any words.

Remember, though, that body language and gestures may be ambiguous. As FIGURE 2.1 illustrates, gestures need to be interpreted in the context of facial expressions. Both pictures illustrate people leaning forward in a conversation. In the picture on the left, leaning forward with a smiling face communicates openness. On the right, leaning forward with a clenched jaw communicates hostility.

FIGURE 2.1 Nonverbal Signals Have Multiple Meanings

GESTURE	DOES IT MEAN THIS?	OR THIS?
Leaning forward	Openness	Hostility
Eye contact	Friendliness	Anger
Lack of eye contact	Shyness, Respect	Guilt, Disrespect
Wrinkled forehead	Concentration	Anger, Frustration
Straight posture	Self-confidence	Rigidity

CULTURE   Facial Expressions Are Not Universal

Not all cultures around the world interpret facial expressions the same way. In fact, research suggests that people from East Asia (for example, China, Japan, and Korea) focus mainly on the eyes when they are reading facial expressions. By contrast, people from the West (for example, the United States, Germany, and Mexico) focus on the entire face, including both the eyes and the mouth.[8]

Surprise   Shock

As a result of this difference in perception, people from East Asia sometimes confuse surprise, shock, fear, and anger since these emotions are difficult to extract from the eyes alone. As the figure to the left illustrates, key differences in these emotions are reflected by the mouth.

The East Asian focus on the eyes is also reflected in their *emoticons*—the series of characters used to represent facial expressions in emails. As the following table illustrates, in American emoticons, the face is represented on its side, and differences of emotion are represented by the mouth. In East Asian emoticons, the face is right side up, and differences in emotion are expressed by the eyes.

How Emoticons Differ between Eastern and Western Cultures

EMOTION	WEST	EAST
Surprise	:-0	o.o
Sad	:-(	(;_;)

PEARSON
mybcommlab

For a CULTURE exercise, go to Exercise 28 on page 68 or to this chapter's End-of-Chapter Exercises at mybcommlab.com.

In addition, gestures must be interpreted within the context of culture. In Japan it is a sign of respect to avoid eye contact and look down when an older or more powerful person is talking to you. In the United States, looking away when someone is talking is often interepretd as a sign of disrespect or guilt. Before reaching a conclusion about what nonverbal communication means, consider alternative meanings.

- **Behavior.** Observing behavior can also help you interpret meaning, especially if the behavior is inconsistent with a spoken statement. For example, imagine that a customer is complaining that the zipper on a jacket is broken and asks you to find a duplicate with a functioning zipper. As you observe the customer struggle with the zipper, you realize that this particular zipper is not broken but instead requires more fine motor control than the customer has. Rather than searching for a duplicate item, you might respond, "Some people have a hard time with this zipper because it is so small and hard to grip. Can I help you find a jacket with a better zipper?" In this case, observing behavior provides more information than listening to language.

Ask questions and paraphrase to ensure understanding

In addition to "listening" to nonverbal behavior, you can improve comprehension and understanding by asking questions and by paraphrasing. Questions are very straightforward. You can ask someone to repeat what he or she is saying, or you can offer two alternative meanings and ask which is correct. For example, you could ask your colleague, "By 'first thing in the morning,' do you mean 9 AM Boston time or when I get in to work in the morning in Los Angeles?"

Paraphrasing is a little more complicated. Paraphrase involves restating what you hear in different words to ensure that you completely understand. Because meaning has multiple dimensions, you might paraphrase in multiple ways to capture those dimensions. As FIGURE 2.2 illustrates, you can paraphrase to ensure you understand

Paraphrase Restating someone's point in different words.

literal content, the ultimate intention, and the emotional content—or feeling—behind the speaker's statement.

FIGURE 2.2
Paraphrasing for Content,
Intent, and Feeling

Comment from the supervisor:
"I'd like all employees to take at least half of their vacation days by November 1."

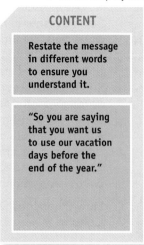

CONTENT

Restate the message in different words to ensure you understand it.

"So you are saying that you want us to use our vacation days before the end of the year."

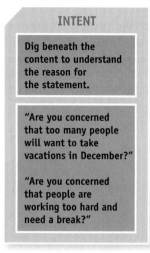

INTENT

Dig beneath the content to understand the reason for the statement.

"Are you concerned that too many people will want to take vacations in December?"

"Are you concerned that people are working too hard and need a break?"

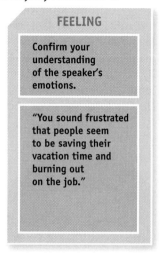

FEELING

Confirm your understanding of the speaker's emotions.

"You sound frustrated that people seem to be saving their vacation time and burning out on the job."

Evaluating

Once you fully understand what someone says, you can **evaluate**. Evaluating is the practice of critically reviewing and judging what you hear. Is it accurate, well-supported, and convincing? As a listener, you may find it difficult to reach a fair evaluation of what you hear. Think of all the things that can block a fair evaluation. First, you may prejudge a speaker, especially if you find that speaker to be annoying or distracting. Second, you may prejudge an idea, especially if it is an idea you have already considered and dismissed. If you don't listen carefully to the speaker's rationale or explanation, you lose the opportunity to reconsider your previous evaluation. Third, you may jump to conclusions based on the beginning of a message and interrupt the speaker or tune out while you wait your turn to speak.

Making good business decisions depends on your ability to evaluate what you hear. For example, imagine that you own a children's clothing store. In a meeting with your employees, the assistant manager suggests that you open another store in an up-and-coming neighborhood on the west side of the city. For support, she points to the growing population in the neighborhood and the fact that the three new stores that opened in that neighborhood are doing very well.

Evaluating that proposal fairly requires that you remain open-minded. Even if you live far away from the west side of the city and would prefer a closer location, you need to consider the business arguments. Evaluating that proposal fairly also requires that you critically analyze what you hear. Does the success of other new stores necessarily mean that a children's clothing store will succeed? To evaluate that opinion, you would need to know how many children live in the area and what competition exists.

Finally, evaluating fairly requires that you separate emotions from logic. Your assistant manager may try to convince you that a store in that neighborhood will be a path to wealth and prestige, since the neighborhood is so desirable. These emotional appeals may be strong enough to make you want a store in that neighborhood, even if the rent is extremely expensive and the children's clothing market in the neighborhood is not big enough to ensure a profit.

Responding

Responding has two roles in the listening process: It lets the speaker know that you understand the point, and it initiates the next step in the conversation. Some responses will quickly stop any further exchange, while others will move the discussion forward. For example, a response such as "That's a ridiculous idea" may discourage someone's further input, whereas you could encourage a speaker with a more tactful response: "That's interesting. How would that work?"

Responses can be verbal and nonverbal. On some occasions, the nonverbal messages communicate more fully than the verbal ones. Imagine a coworker says, "I need some advice about how to describe our new product." You verbally respond, "Okay." But what is your nonverbal message? Did you make eye contact with your colleague and smile as you said okay? Did you gesture for her to take a seat? Or did you keep your eyes on your computer, sigh deeply, and tense your body? Whichever approach you take, your colleague will interpret your response based on your nonverbal message. In other words, how you say something is often taken more seriously than what you say.

To become a more effective responder, pay attention to the type of response you offer. As FIGURE 2.3 illustrates, you can respond to a speaker in many different ways. For example, you can ask a question, give your opinion or advice, disagree, or express empathy.

SPEAKER: "The auditors are coming tomorrow to look at our books. We're not ready. I don't know what to do."

FIGURE 2.3
Five Ways to Respond

YOUR RESPONSE OPTIONS	
Ask a Question	What do we need to do to get ready? How long do you think it will take?
Give an Opinion	I think if you have most of the documents they will need tomorrow, they can get a good start.
Give Advice	Let's try to reschedule the audit until next week.
Argue/Disagree	Actually, I think we are ready. We have completed everything on the checklist.
Express Empathy	It's nerve-wracking to get everything ready for a major audit. You're doing fine, and I'll be glad to help.

This set of active listening skills—hearing, comprehending and interpreting, evaluating, and responding—will help you better understand what people say and use that information effectively. In addition, being a good listener offers another important business benefit. It can persuade others to listen more carefully to you, too, and to accept your point of view. As one organizational leader explains, "if people feel they were listened to, that their views were taken into account, that they had a chance to show you the world from their point of view, they're going to be much more likely to go along with a decision."[9]

Study Question 2.2

What speaking strategies will encourage others to listen to me and understand what I am saying?

Listeners and speakers are partners in the communication process. Just as listeners need to work hard to understand meaning, speakers need to work hard to engage listeners and make meaning clear. This section provides seven general speaking strategies that you can use to communicate productively:

- Focus on your audience
- Share the conversation
- Use clear, concrete, unambiguous language
- Support your message with good nonverbal communication
- Avoid language that triggers a negative response
- Frame negative comments positively
- Be aware of gender-specific communication styles

Evaluating The practice of critically reviewing and judging communication.

Focus on your audience

Many speakers fail to connect with the audience's interests or knowledge about a topic. Before speaking, take time to analyze your audience by considering the following questions:

- Why will they be interested in what you are saying?
- What barriers will prevent them from listening carefully?
- What questions or objections may they have?
- What is the best way to connect with them?

Imagine, for example, that you want to ask a coworker to help you with a project, and you approach this person while he is concentrating on his own work. At the beginning of this conversation, he knows nothing about your project. He is focusing on something else, not on you, which may prevent him from listening carefully. He also may object to helping because he is too busy. To communicate effectively with this audience, don't begin the conversation by describing the project in detail and then finally ask for help. Your coworker is probably not interested in the details and will tune you out by the time you make your request. Instead, you might begin by saying "I could really use your help on my current project. It requires some database programming that I've never done before. I know you have lots of database experience." This opening effectively helps your audience understand why you are communicating. To prevent your audience from objecting that he is too busy, you may also add "I don't think it will take much time, but if it does, I'll be glad to help you on your project, too." At that point, your coworker will probably say, "Tell me more about your project and what you need." Your audience will be ready to listen.

Share the conversation

Have you ever noticed how some speakers, once they have "the floor," continue talking for a long time and resist all attempts of other people to share the conversation? They may even say, "Please let me finish" or "Don't interrupt me." In a conversation, each participant deserves a turn. A good interpersonal communicator will avoid monologues and instead share the conversation with others. When you have finished making your point clearly and concisely, invite your audience to respond or add to the conversation. You can do this by asking a question designed to move the conversation forward. It can be as simple as "What do you think?" Or it can be more situation-specific, for example: "Has anyone else tried this approach in the past?"

Use clear, concrete, unambiguous language

Unambiguous language is phrasing that has only one meaning. By contrast, *ambiguous language* may mean different things to different people. For example, imagine someone tells you, "Deliver the package next door." If you have offices on either side of you, it's ambiguous which one should get the package—and you have a 50-50 chance of making a mistake. Similarly, if your supervisor says, "This project is your responsibility," you may assume "your responsibility" means that you have to do the project by yourself. However, your supervisor may mean that you are in charge of the project and need to assemble a team to get the work done.

Pronouns, if not used precisely, can be ambiguous. Consider the word "they" in this statement: "I called the purchasing managers about the new vendors we want to use. *They* are too busy to meet with us for a few weeks." Who is too busy? The purchasing managers or the vendors? Although it is more effective to avoid ambiguous language in the first place, active listeners know to ask questions to clarify the meaning when they are unsure what the speaker meant.

Support your message with good nonverbal communication

Many studies on the role of nonverbal communication have found that a speaker's body language, facial expressions, gestures, and tone of voice carry more weight than the speaker's words.[10] As a speaker, you can use nonverbal communication in three ways to enhance your communication:

- **Use body language and eye contact to engage your audience.** This means facing your audience and maintaining eye contact with your audience as you speak, keeping your facial expressions positive, and keeping your posture relaxed rather than stiff or clenched. You may also find it effective to mirror the body language of your audience. Recent research has shown that job candidates who demonstrate confidence and mirror the interviewer's gestures are more likely to get a positive response.[11]

- **Use a strong and positive tone of voice.** If you want your audience to be receptive to your ideas, speak in an enthusiastic or energetic tone of voice.[12] Do not undermine your persuasiveness by sounding hesitant or doubtful.

- **Use gestures and facial expressions that complement your message.** In a conversation, your nonverbal communication can either conflict with a message or complement it. For example, if you say you are confident, but you fidget or frown while you speak, your audience will not have confidence in your words. By contrast, if you smile and use effective gestures, your audience will better sense your confidence. In addition, listeners remember what you say better when nonverbal signals reinforce your words.[13]

Avoid language that triggers a negative response

Just as your choice of language can encourage listeners to pay careful attention, it can also evoke negative emotional responses. If you make your audience defensive or angry, they may refuse to pay attention to your ideas. The following four specific types of language—biased language, provocative questions, accusatory language, and trigger words—can cause communication problems and negative feelings.

Biased language

Biased language suggests prejudice, prejudgment, or disrespect. When you use this kind of language, two things can happen. First, it can shut down the conversation. If you turn to a coworker at a meeting and say, "Kevin, as our resident geek, tell us your opinion on whether we should upgrade our computer operating system," Kevin may not be open and honest about his ideas since you've labeled him as a "geek." Unbiased language would be: "Kevin, you're familiar with the pros and cons of the new operating system upgrade. Do you think we should implement it now or wait?"

Biased language can also encourage others to prejudge ideas without even hearing them through. Imagine introducing an addition to a meeting agenda in this way: "Clive wants a few minutes in the meeting to regale us with his latest and greatest idea." This language diminishes Clive's idea, and it prejudices others against taking the idea seriously. Unbiased language is more respectful: "Clive has an item he'd like to address."

Provocative questions

Typically, questions are a positive part of the communication process: they help you share information, uncover opinions, and confirm understanding. These genuine requests for information and opinion are *authentic questions*. In contrast to authentic questions, *provocative questions* are designed to annoy and inflame. For example, assume that after three days of work, your IT support professional says to you, "We've finally solved the problem with the online database." An authentic question would be "What was the problem?" or "How did you figure it out?" By contrast, a provocative question might be "We have three days of bad data now. Why didn't you find the solution earlier?" This question will lead the IT professional to be defensive and negative. As a result, you will not learn anything that will help you avoid the problem the next time.

Accusatory language

The provocative question "Why didn't you find the solution earlier?" is also an example of *accusatory language.* It focuses negative attention on the person ("you") rather than on the issue. FIGURE 2.4 provides additional examples of accusatory language along with alternative phrasings. Notice that some of the alternative phrasings use what interpersonal communication experts call *"I" language.* "I" language focuses on how you respond to or feel about the other person's behavior and focuses on your perception rather than assigning blame. This encourages dialogue with the other person. However, it does not imply that the word "I" is always good and "you" is always accusatory. If every sentence begins with "I," your audience will think you are egotistical. Conversely, many sentences that include "you" can be very positive especially when you focus on audience benefits or offer a compliment (for example, "You did a great job on that project").[14] This positive language, as contrasted with accusatory language, encourages people to listen to your point of view and respond.

FIGURE 2.4
Accusatory Language and
Alternative Phrasings

INEFFECTIVE: ACCUSATORY LANGUAGE	EFFECTIVE: ALTERNATIVE PHRASING
We now have three days of bad data. Why didn't you solve the problem earlier?	I'm concerned that we won't have time to eliminate the bad data from our results.
Your instructions are confusing.	I got lost on step three of the instructions. Could you please explain further?
Your interpretation of this rule is wrong.	I understood the rule differently.
This is the third time this month you've been late.	I'm uncomfortable making excuses when people call for you. That's why I hope you can arrive on time.

Trigger words

Biased language, provocative questions, and accusatory language may trigger emotional responses. Everyone is sensitive about some topic or issue. Emotional responses may also be triggered by certain words or phrases that people dislike. For example, some people get upset when they hear *absolutes,* words like *always* and *never,* that are likely to be exaggerations: "You never get to work on time." "You always forget your keys." "No one ever answers the phone in this office." These absolute words, often combined with an accusatory "you," can create obstacles to effective communication. People may also get upset when they hear a phrase like "It's none of your business" or "That doesn't concern you." They feel dismissed. While you cannot anticipate all the trigger words that might upset people, always pay attention to emotional responses and avoid triggers when you recognize them.

Frame negative comments positively

You may find that you need to offer constructive criticism to a coworker or an employee. If you phrase that criticism simply as a negative statement, your listener may become defensive or tune out. David C. Novak, Chairman, CEO, and president of Yum Brands—whose chains include KFC, Pizza Hut, Taco Bell, and Long John Silver's—offers two pieces of advice for giving feedback: start out positively and avoid the word "but." In an interview with the *New York Times,* he said:

> The best way to give feedback is to start out with, "This is what I appreciate about you." They might have great strategy, good vision, they're good at execution, or whatever you think they're really doing well. When you start out by talking to people about what they're doing well, that makes them very receptive for feedback because at least you're giving them credit for what they've done. Then I say, "And you can be even more effective if you do this." I think that really works. "But" can be a killer word. "And" really recognizes the appreciation part. If you say "but," it throws all the appreciation out the window.[15]

Be aware of gender-specific communication styles

Men and women are often socialized to behave differently from each other and thus may develop different gender-related styles of communication. Neither style is better than the other. However, communication can break down if people are intolerant of other speaking styles or draw incorrect judgments about a speaker based on his or her style.

As sociolinguist Deborah Tannen points out, men are often socialized to value autonomy and independence and therefore learn to communicate in ways that assert independence, power, and their place in the social hierarchy.[16] For example, in conversations, men tend to interrupt more than women do.[17] In contrast to men, women are often socialized to value connections with other people and to communicate in ways that preserve equity and relationship. Thus, women tend to wait their turn to speak as an act of respect to the speaker. In addition, women tend to minimize the assertiveness of what they say by using what linguists call *hedges*, *hesitations*, and *tag questions*:[18]

Hedge: I don't know if this is a good idea, but we could get an editor for our presentation slides.
Hesitation: Um, well, we could, uh, we could get an editor for our presentation slides.
Tag Question: We can get an editor, can't we?

Gender-specific characteristics may have negative results in conversation. Interruptions can easily lead to a communication breakdown, especially when men interrupt women. While males are often very comfortable with interruptions and interrupt right back, women are more likely to get angry or feel silenced. Tag questions, hesitations, and hedges also cause problems. They lead some listeners to conclude that the speaker lacks confidence and thus does not deserve to be taken seriously.[19,20] However, by recognizing gendered characteristics of your own and others' language, you can avoid drawing incorrect conclusions about others and instead pay more attention to their ideas.

Study Question 2.3

How can I manage interpersonal conflict?

Even if you follow all of this chapter's advice about listening and speaking, conflict will inevitably arise when you work with others. Conflict can include differences in opinion, disagreements about how to handle issues, complaints about performance or fairness, criticism about the behavior of others, and personality conflicts between people who just do not get along.

Conflict is one of the most significant and costly problems in a workplace. In Great Britain alone, researchers found that business conflict costs more than £33 billion (almost $50 billion) per year.[21] These costs result from wasted time, loss of productivity, poor decision making, absenteeism, legal fees, and employee turnover. In fact, a study of exit interviews from people who voluntarily left jobs found that more than 50 percent of all departures resulted from unresolved interpersonal conflict.[22] For every employee who leaves, a business needs to hire and train a new employee, which costs 1.5 times that employee's salary.[23]

Not all workplace conflict is bad. Conflict can be divided into two broad categories: **cognitive conflicts**, which result from differences in understanding content or tasks, and **affective conflicts**, which result from differences in personalities and relationships. All high-performing work teams experience cognitive conflict—or disagreements—about a project.[24] Working through these conflicts can have positive results on the quality of team decisions and the final work product. For example, two people working on a marketing plan may disagree about the best way to reach the company's target market. If they

Cognitive conflict A conflict that results from differences in understanding content or tasks. Working through a cognitive conflict often leads to better decisions and work products.

Affective conflict A conflict that results from differences in personalities and relationships. If affective conflicts remain unstated and unaddressed, they can lead to tension, stress, and dysfunctional work processes.

work through this cognitive conflict and achieve consensus, the result may be better than if they pursued only one idea.

However, problems arise if teams allow these cognitive conflicts to become affective conflicts. If the two people working on the marketing plan cannot agree and leave the meeting in anger, this emotional conflict may damage the working relationship. Problems also arise if conflicts remain unstated and unaddressed, leading to tension, stress, and dysfunctional work processes.

Although people often use the term *conflict resolution* to discuss handling conflict, *conflict management* is a more helpful term. While conflict resolution implies that the conflict will go away, conflict management recognizes that some conflicts cannot be resolved. The next section of the chapter offers you a two-step process for managing conflict: first identify the cause of the conflict and then decide how to respond.

Identify the cause of the conflict

As FIGURE 2.5 illustrates, cognitive and affective conflicts generally occur for a few well-defined reasons. Note in FIGURE 2.5 that the line between cognitive and affective conflicts can be unclear. In fact, it is sometimes difficult to know whether a conflict is cognitive or affective—for example, whether you truly object to that person's idea (cognitive) or you simply do not like that person (affective). However, analyzing the cause of a conflict is useful because different causes call for conflict management strategies.

FIGURE 2.5
Causes of Conflict

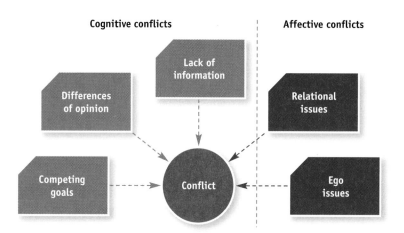

Competing goals

People who collaborate may not always be motivated to achieve the same goals. In fact, for a business to succeed, it must work toward a number of goals that are sometimes in competition with each other. A business strives to make a profit while planning for future growth, keeping employees and customers satisfied, and meeting governmental requirements for employee and consumer safety. Employees have their own goals, such as increasing their income, enhancing their reputation, gaining new customers, getting a promotion, or spending more quality time with family and friends.

Conflicts routinely arise because people work with different goals in mind. Consider this scenario:

> Marcus and Allison of Green Earth Landscapes are barely speaking to each other. This morning, Marcus promised one of the company's best customers, a large museum, that Green Earth could complete a major landscape installation by the end of October. Marcus's supervisor had told him that keeping this customer happy was a high priority since the museum was responsible for 30 percent of Green Earth's income last year. When Marcus approached Allison, who does the scheduling, Allison exploded: "We are 100 percent

booked through the end of the year. We cannot take on any new projects, no matter who the client is. I received explicit instructions from the head of project management that we need to keep costs down. I'm not going to schedule any overtime. We'd lose money rather than make it. Why didn't you talk to me before you made a promise?"

Marcus's goal is to keep the customer happy, while Allison's goal is to keep costs in line by eliminating all overtime. This example illustrates how easily competing goals—a cognitive conflict—can disintegrate into an affective conflict. Allison thinks Marcus does what he wants without concern for the consequences. Marcus thinks Allison always argues with him and that she doesn't understand the big picture of how the company works. By recognizing that they each are trying to achieve different goals, they can discuss the issue with their supervisors to determine which goal has priority. At that point, they can agree to satisfy the most important goal or collaborate to find a solution that addresses both goals.

Differences of opinion

Even if people agree on a goal, they may have differences of opinion about how to achieve it. Consider this scenario:

> Rotel Plumbing Supplies wants to become the premier plumbing distributor in the Southwest. What is the best way to accomplish this goal? Valerie argues that investing in marketing and customer relations is the key since Rotel needs more and bigger customers. Corinne argues that investing in distribution is the key. To be the premier distributor, Rotel needs to guarantee next-day delivery, which will require creating more distribution centers.

Differences of opinion also can easily lead to affective conflicts, especially if the differences result in a contest of wills. Differences of opinion are best resolved by a rational decision-making process, which may involve some compromise.

Lack of information

People often draw conclusions or make decisions based on faulty assumptions. They do not have all the information they need, and they may not even know they are missing information. This lack of information leads to significant workplace conflict. Consider this scenario:

> Janelle gave her sales team a schedule of dates to submit quarterly sales data. She told them she expected them to meet these dates. On the due date for the fourth quarter data, Shawn realized that he could include a very large sale worth hundreds of thousands of dollars if he waited just a few days to submit his figures. He knew that Janelle, his supervisor, was interested in increased sales figures, so he decided to wait and surprise her with unexpectedly positive results. The next morning, Shawn arrived to work at 9 AM to find an angry email from Janelle: "Where are your sales figures? I was up all night preparing a presentation for management at 8 AM and didn't realize until 4 AM that you hadn't submitted your numbers. You knew they were due yesterday. I looked like a fool at the meeting."

Shawn was working on the assumption that Janelle cared more about an increase in reported sales than about his punctuality. He never verified that assumption with Janelle. He wanted to surprise her with the big sale. For her part, Janelle failed to tell Shawn and the others how important it was that she received their reports on time this quarter. Janelle did not consider that her staff might need to know she had scheduled an 8 AM presentation that required up-to-date data. From her perspective, she had already told them she expected them to deliver the figures on time. No further information was necessary.

This conflict could have been avoided if Janelle and Shawn had shared more information with each other. When Janelle sent the schedule of dates to her sales team, she could have explained *why* she needed the sales figures on specific dates. More importantly, Shawn should have asked Janelle for an extension on the fourth quarter deadline so he could include the increased sales numbers.

Relational issues

Sometimes people just don't get along well, and they don't work to overcome their differences.

You may have heard the old adage, *"We like those most who are most like us."* In a workplace context, this means that most of us prefer to work with people whose styles resemble our own. For example, if you are detail-oriented, you most likely feel comfortable working with other detail-oriented people. If you like to make quick decisions, you enjoy working with other decisive people. Styles that differ from our own often create tension—they violate our comfort zones—and we may place a negative label on that behavior. We may also begin to treat the other person badly, which leads to conflict. A more productive perspective is to realize that different styles may complement each other and help a team achieve balance.

The following example illustrates how relational conflicts can stand in the way of productive discussions about content and substance:

> At first, Derek was excited to work on a new project with his consulting company's biggest client because it would give him a chance to learn new skills and gain valuable exposure. However, from the first day of the project, he has been in conflict with his new teammate Ed. Ed interrupts him, argues against his ideas, and then tries to take credit for his ideas when they work. Sometimes Ed has a good idea of his own, but Derek has difficulty acknowledging it because he is so angry at Ed most of the time. Derek thinks that Ed is egotistical and stubborn. He often finds himself arguing against an idea just because Ed brought it up.

Personality conflicts like this are costly to a business. A survey conducted by researchers at the University of North Carolina found that:

- 53 percent of workers said they lost time at work because they worried about confrontations with coworkers
- 37 percent said that arguments with colleagues caused them to reduce their commitment to the job
- 22 percent said that they put less effort into their work because of conflicts with colleagues[25]

Relational conflicts do not simply go away if you ignore them. When you have a personality clash with someone, explore ways to resolve it. Pick your battles, and argue only about things that make a real difference. Ask if you can meet to discuss the cause of the conflict, being sure to listen actively by focusing on the content rather than personalities. Use neutral rather than accusatory language. Ask for help from managers, if you need it. Mediation from supervisors may sometimes be necessary.

Ego issues

Ego conflicts threaten someone's sense of professional identity or self-image. In professional contexts, people typically see themselves as honest, reasonable, intelligent, and committed to the well-being of the organization. When someone accuses you of something negative or challenges your sense of identity, you may find it difficult to work productively with that person. Consider the following scenario:

> Nadia is the youngest customer relationship manager in the company, and she is proud of her quick rise through the ranks. In three years, she has progressed faster than any other employee and is responsible for 35 percent of the company's sales. Yet whenever she meets with Brian, the head of engineering, to discuss her customers' needs, she feels personally insulted. If Brian does not like what she proposes for a project, he often says, "We can't do that. You're not an engineer. You don't know what you're talking about." Or he might say, "How old are you? You've only been here for three years. I've been doing this kind of work for 20 years, and I know the best way to get it done." Things are so strained between Brian and Nadia that they avoid face-to-face encounters, resorting to email to discuss projects.

When a conflict becomes personal, as this one has, one wise approach is to shift the focus back to business. Nadia might say, "I know you have 20 years of experience. That's why I'm sure you can help me meet this customer's needs." This approach not only shifts the focus of the conversation, but it also offers Brian a subtle compliment and may make him more willing to take Nadia seriously.

Select an appropriate management technique

As the scenarios in the previous section suggest, not all conflicts are best managed the same way. If you are involved in affective conflict—one that focuses on relationships or ego—you will need to address the emotional issues before you can productively discuss the content of your work. If you are involved in a cognitive conflict, however, you can consider five different strategies to move toward an acceptable outcome—avoid confrontation, accommodate or give in, compete to win, compromise, or collaborate.[26] Each strategy has pros and cons.

Avoid confrontation

Instead of addressing a conflict, you may choose to avoid a conflict: deny the problem exists, change the topic, screen your telephone calls, or even avoid the person completely, as Nadia and Brian did in the previous example. Avoidance is occasionally a good choice, especially when you believe you have no chance of resolving the conflict to your satisfaction and it does not interfere with productivity.

More often, however, everyone loses when you avoid a conflict. If problems are not addressed, they tend to get worse. If Brian and Nadia continue to avoid each other and communicate only by email, they will have no opportunity to develop a sense of shared goals that will allow them to work in the best interest of the business. Ultimately, the customers will suffer. Instead of avoidance, Nadia and Brian need to adopt a different strategy.

Accommodate or give in

Accommodating essentially means that you give in and you allow the other person to have his or her own way. Graciously accommodating is a wise choice if you decide that your position was wrong and you change your mind. Accommodating is also an excellent choice when the conflict is trivial or you don't care deeply about the result. That is why accommodation is often part of a good negotiation strategy: you give in about something less important to you so that you can get your way on something more important. Finally, accommodating can be a good choice if maintaining a harmonious relationship with the other person is more important than the outcome of the issue.

Accommodating does pose a danger if you give in to the point of sacrificing your principles and beliefs. Such accommodation can lead to loss of self-esteem or ineffective results. For example, assume you are assigned to a marketing team consisting of people with diverse backgrounds. Your team's goal is to generate cutting-edge marketing ideas for the company's new product. During the group's first brainstorming session, many ideas are suggested. However, as soon as the marketing manager expresses an opinion about one, everyone immediately agrees with him. You think a different idea might work better, but don't want to be the only dissenting voice. To show that you "fit with the company," you "go along to get along." This is an example of **groupthink**, a process by which people strive for group unanimity and consensus by eliminating all critical thinking that threatens consensus. A groupthink approach to eliminating conflict can lead a group to ignore differing opinions that may be valuable, settle on a solution that may be wrong, and sacrifice creativity and innovation.[27]

Compete to win

Sometimes a conflict becomes a contest, with participants competing to win, even at another person's expense. Like accommodating, competing results in an "I win, you lose" outcome. Competitive tactics can include finding fault or blaming others, rejecting the other party's point of view, and minimizing one's own responsibility for a mistake. Some

Groupthink A process by which a group reaches a decision by eliminating all critical thinking that threatens consensus.

competitive conflicts are decided by third parties, such as boards of directors, voters, supervisors, or CEOs.

Competitive approaches to resolving conflicts may result in quick solutions, but they often lead to relational conflicts. For example, Marcus and Allison of Green Earth (first introduced on page 42) could bring their conflict to the president of the company to decide which goal to prioritize: keeping customers happy or keeping costs down. If the president decided to accommodate old customers, Marcus and Allison would have a clear direction, but they would still need to work out the personal anger that had developed between them.

Compromise

Compromising is a more cooperative approach than competing. In a compromise, all the parties involved get something they want or can accept, but everyone also needs to sacrifice something.

Compromising is often a good way to achieve workable solutions under time pressure. Imagine that Valerie and Corinne of Rotel Plumbing (see page 43) need to present a budget to the board of directors the next day, even though they continue to have differences of opinion about how best to achieve the goal of being the premier plumbing supplier in the Southwest: should they invest in marketing or distribution? They could reach a compromise and create budgets for two smaller projects—one on marketing and another on distribution. Neither will get everything she wants, but this solution offers several benefits: each will get part of what she wants, they will be able to project a united front at the board of directors meeting, and they will gather data from the two projects that may help them resolve their difference of opinion.

Compromise is also a good approach when people have competing goals. Marcus and Allison of the Green Earth scenario have different goals based on their roles in the company. To solve the immediate conflict of how to accommodate the important museum project without scheduling overtime, Marcus and Allison could reach a compromise solution: Allison will schedule workers for the museum project, and Marcus will talk with other clients to see if some existing projects can move to the first of the year. By compromising, each person's goal is partially achieved.

Collaborate to find the best solution

Although collaboration is a time-consuming approach, it is often the best approach for managing complex conflicts. In collaboration, all the parties work together to determine the best possible solution. For example, Marcus and Allison could have realized they would not be able to easily resolve their conflict because their supervisors gave them conflicting requirements. While they could individually talk to their supervisors, another approach would be to work together to find a solution in the best interest of the company. Perhaps the company could charge more for rush jobs, give clients the option of paying a retainer to leave space on the Green Earth schedule, or develop a new procedure for calculating revenues versus overtime costs. Marcus and Allison could then present these collaborative solutions in a meeting with their two supervisors. Collaboration like this has the benefit not only of providing a solution but also ensuring buy-in from all parties and strengthening the relationships between people.

Study Question 2.4

How can I improve my communication with people from different cultures?

You may have heard the saying, "We cannot escape our culture." **Culture** describes the attitudes and behaviors that characterize a group of people. Differences in culture exist among countries, such as the United States and France, as well as subsets of a population, such as urban and rural. People are shaped by the cultures they come from, and they develop a set of assumptions about how to act based on these cultures. For example, for most Americans, the following statements are noncontroversial truths:

- If you have a 10 AM appointment, you should arrive a little before 10 AM to be on time.
- If someone makes a mistake, it's best to be honest (though polite) and point it out so that he or she has an opportunity to correct the mistake.
- To be efficient, it is important to get right to business quickly at a meeting.
- If you are a man, as a sign of politeness, you should allow a woman to enter a doorway before you or exit an elevator before you.

Not every culture subscribes to these codes of behavior, however. For example, in a Latin American culture—that is, in the cultures of North or South American countries where Spanish or Portuguese are spoken—you would be rude to jump immediately to business at the beginning of a meeting, especially a first meeting. Latin American cultures value getting to know the other person and building a relationship of trust. In Korea, a young woman would be rude to exit an elevator before an elderly man because respecting elders is highly valued in the Korean culture. Although it would be unrealistic to try to learn about every culture all at once, you can prepare yourself to communicate with people from other cultures by taking two important steps. First, understand some of the key ways that cultures differ, and second, develop communication strategies that help you communicate with diverse groups.

Understand how cultures differ

Because workplaces are increasingly multicultural and businesses are increasingly global, learning about other cultures is required, not optional. Cultural understanding will help you avoid misinterpreting verbal and nonverbal communication of colleagues and customers who do not share your culture. It will also help you to avoid displaying **ethnocentrism**—an inappropriate belief that your own culture is superior to all others. People who are ethnocentric are often trapped by cultural **stereotypes**—oversimplified images or generalizations of a group. While stereotypes may describe a generally observed cultural norm, if you assume everyone from that culture follows that norm, you ignore the fact that individuals are, in fact, individual and influenced by many different things in their lives: education, travel, family values, friendships, and job requirements. Just as it is wrong to assume that all Americans are loud (a common stereotype), it would be equally wrong to assume that all the French are rude.

Although it is important to avoid cultural stereotypes, it is equally important to recognize that cultures do differ. Over the years, anthropologists, sociologists, and intercultural experts have identified many dimensions of those differences. This section covers five of those dimensions, all of which have implications for business communication.

High context versus low context

Anthropologist Edward T. Hall first used the term **context** to describe how people deliver, receive, and interpret messages.[28] Countries exist on a continuum from high context to low context, as illustrated in FIGURE 2.6. In a *high-context* culture, such as China or Japan, communicators convey meaning not just by words but also by all the context surrounding the words: how something is said, the nonverbal behavior of the communicator and audience, the history of the relationship between the two communicators, and even the silences in the conversation. In a *low-context* culture, such as the United States or Canada, communicators rely less on context and more on explicit language to communicate a message as clearly and unambiguously as possible.

Reflecting this difference, people in the United States typically value direct conversations that immediately get to the point, while people from Japan rely on more subtle cues. If a Japanese business person wants to say "no," she may not actually use that word but instead may respond with silence or with a reserved reply such as "That is very interesting." She will rely on you to interpret the message correctly, based on the context of the communication.

Culture The attitudes and behaviors that characterize a group of people.

Ethnocentrism An inappropriate belief that your own culture is superior to all others.

Stereotypes Oversimplified images or generalizations of a group.

Context A term that describes how people in a culture deliver, receive, and interpret messages. Low-context cultures rely on explicit language to communicate. High-context cultures derive meaning not just from words but from everything surrounding the words.

FIGURE 2.6 Continuum of Low- to High-context Cultures

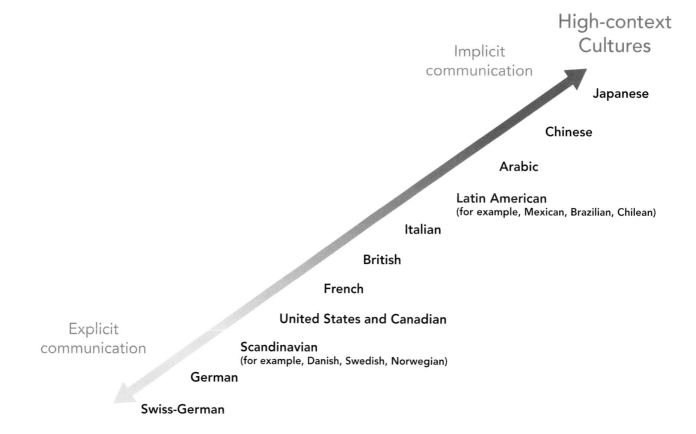

Individualism versus collectivism

Individualism versus collectivism is one of the key dimensions of culture identified by Dutch intercultural expert Geert Hofstede.[29] In an **individualistic culture**, people value an individual's achievements, satisfaction, and independent thinking. By contrast, in **collectivist cultures**, people put the good of the group or organization before their own individual interests. Obligation and loyalty to the group are more important than one's own achievement. Harmony is extremely important.

Individualist and collectivist values influence communication and business in a number of ways. In the individualistic United States, many companies reward individual leaders—for example, CEOs and other executives—with multi-million dollar bonuses for the companies' successes. By contrast, in more collectivist China, PepsiCo learned that rewarding an individual leader was not an effective incentive. When one highly regarded manager chose to divide his bonus equally among his employees, PepsiCo changed its practice to reward an entire group when goals are met.[30] Similarly, in collectivist cultures, employees may be embarrassed—or even ashamed—if they are singled out and praised for accomplishments, while in individualist cultures, employees expect to be acknowledged for individual achievements. Although people in the United States tend to think of individualism as the norm, there are significantly more collectivist cultures in the world than individualist cultures.[31]

Power distance

Power distance is the term Hofstede developed to describe how cultures perceive inequality and authority. In cultures with high power distance, organizations are very formal and hierarchical with a clear separation between superiors and subordinates.

People are granted respect based on their position alone. In high power-distance cultures, people typically expect to conduct business with others of equal rank. To send a junior executive to meet with a CEO would be considered an insult to the CEO.

By contrast, cultures with low power distance believe in social equality and therefore have a more relaxed attitude about title and status. Seniority and age alone do not earn someone respect. Younger workers expect to be taken seriously and respected for the quality of their work despite their lower status. In low power-distance cultures, people progress to a first-name basis much more quickly than in high power-distance cultures.

While there is often a correlation between power distance and context, this is not always the case. For example, French culture is relatively low context and direct. However, the French have more respect for formality and authority than other people from low-context cultures, such as Canada.

Uncertainty avoidance

Uncertainty avoidance relates to how comfortable a culture is with ambiguity, risk, and change. Cultures that are uncomfortable with them tend to rely on rituals, rules, and codes of conduct that help make the future more predictable. For example, employees in these cultures tend to like clear guidelines that lead to a predictable result. These employees value learning by observation so that results are repeatable. By contrast, cultures that are more comfortable with uncertainty and ambiguity tend to like more flexible work environments that allow risk-taking and entrepreneurial behavior. These employees value learning by doing, even though the result may be less predictable.

Attitudes toward uncertainty and ambiguity affect communication on many levels. Cultures that avoid uncertainty are often collectivist and tend to be cautious about integrating new people into a group. They also value harmony and consensus. Cultures that tolerate uncertainty are open to new people, new ideas, and risks.

Time orientation

In addition to cultural context, anthropologist Edward T. Hall introduced the terms *monochronic* and *polychronic* to describe two very different cultural orientations toward time. **Monochronic cultures**, like the United States and Northern European countries, value punctuality and efficiency. Meetings begin on time and are expected to follow a set agenda. Deadlines are usually strict. While most monochronic cultures are also individualistic, some collectivist cultures, like Japan, also value punctuality and efficiency. In their view, keeping to an agreed schedule shows respect for the entire group. **Polychronic cultures** are more relaxed about time and punctuality. Polychronic cultures typically put people and relationships before schedules. In a meeting, participants may easily change the order of items on the agenda. While it is important for work to be completed, people may choose to spend time building a relationship over completing a task. In polychronic cultures, deadlines can often be adjusted.

Understanding the various approaches to time is crucial to maintaining smooth relationships. An American who lived for many years in both Denmark and Latin America said, "When you are invited to dinner at 7 PM in Denmark, this means you'll be sitting at the table at 7 PM. When you are invited to dinner at 7 PM in Argentina, this means you'll be expected to arrive at around 8 PM. The only thing they have in common is this: for both cultures, to arrive at 7 PM would be rude."

Develop strategies that help you communicate with diverse groups

You may not know the cultural backgrounds of the people you work with. Here are strategies to help you communicate and work well with people regardless of their backgrounds:

- **When in doubt, exhibit formality and respect.** Americans are often less formal than people from European and Eastern cultures. In situations where you might think people appear impersonal and distant, they believe they are behaving with propriety

Individualistic culture A culture that values an individual's achievements, satisfaction, and independent thinking.

Collectivist culture A culture that puts the good of the group or organization before people's individual interests.

Power distance A characteristic of cultures that describes how the culture perceives inequality and authority.

Uncertainty avoidance A measure of how comfortable a culture is with ambiguity, risk, and change.

Monochronic culture A culture that values punctuality and efficiency.

Polychronic culture A culture that has a relaxed attitude toward time and punctuality.

and decorum. To maintain formality and respect, address people by their last names ("Hello, Ms. Tsai") until they ask you to call them by their first names ("Hi, Fu-Nien"). Be polite and courteous. Try to learn about the culture of the people you'll be working with. When appropriate, learn how to greet people in their native language. During conversations, listen carefully, respect other people's perspectives, defer judgment, and ask for feedback to ensure effective communication. Be respectful, and avoid attempts at humor because someone from another culture may not understand the humor.

- **Pay attention to the other person's nonverbal communication and, when appropriate, mirror it.** If you are doing business with someone from another culture, pay attention to how that person acts. Does she maintain eye contact? Does he shake hands vigorously? Also, pay attention to how closely people stand together to talk. In the United States, a comfortable conversational distance ranges from four feet to seven feet. In Northern Europe, the distance is half that much, close enough for a handshake. In Latin America and Southern Europe, the distance is less, and in the Middle East, the distance may be as close as one foot.[32] By observing and learning, you can avoid cultural mistakes.

- **Be clear and concise.** Be very specific with your choice of words when communicating with people from different cultures. Avoid **idioms**, that is expressions that mean something other than the literal meaning of their words, Idioms like "drive me up the wall" and "pass with flying colors" are culture-specific and as a result may confuse people from other cultures. Similarly avoid **jargon**, the specialized language of a specific field. Even business jargon like "in the red" or "headcount" may be unfamiliar to people from other cultures.

- **Talk slowly.** People can hear and understand you better if you talk relatively slowly and pronounce words clearly.

- **Request feedback to ensure understanding.** When speaking with people from different cultures, do not assume that their smiles and head nodding means they understand what you are saying. These nonverbal responses mean different things in

 ETHICS Nike Faces Ethical Challenges Abroad

Even when you embrace diversity, overcome stereotypes, and research the differences of other cultures, you may face ethical issues or conflicts in values that stand in the way of successful business relationships. Problems may arise when people from different cultures assume that their way of doing business is the best or only way. Even more serious problems may arise if a company based in the United States works with a foreign partner who is involved in practices considered unethical in U.S. culture. Examples of such practices include the following:

- Bribery
- Use of child or slave labor
- Poor working conditions
- No limit on working hours, no minimum for wages
- Unequal treatment of women
- Disregard for the environment
- Nepotism (for example, hiring or promoting only relatives of managers or company owners)

Nike faced an ethical dilemma with one overseas partner. Like many other organizations, Nike contracted with manufacturing facilities in countries, including Indonesia, where laborers are paid less than in the United States. This wage difference is not unethical. However, the factories also employed child labor, since children as young as 14 can legally work in factories in Indonesia.[33] In addition, reports emerged that the working conditions in these factories were

unsafe, in part because Indonesia does not have the same safety regulations as the United States. *The Washington Post* reported that workers at nine Indonesian factories under contract by Nike said they had suffered or witnessed sexual and verbal abuse.[34]

Was Nike responsible for the working conditions and abuse at these overseas facilities? Were the company's local contractors responsible? Nike called the findings disturbing and promised to fix the problems by investigating the abuse allegations and establishing a "new system that would allow workers to file grievances." The company also said it would take "severe measures against managers who engage in these practices."

However, Nike's response was too late to repair damage to its reputation. Critics accused Nike of taking advantage of different ethical practices to increase profits. Since then, Nike has successfully worked to institute safety standards, increase the minimum age of workers and minimum wages, and sever relations with manufacturers guilty of abuse.[35] To ensure that these ethical violations do not arise again, human rights organizations continue to monitor Nike and other sports brands that manufacture products in Asia.[36] ■

PEARSON
mybcommlab

For an ETHICS exercise, go to Exercise 16 on page 66 or to this chapter's End-of-Chapter Exercises at mybcommlab.com.

different countries. Instead, ask friendly questions that encourage people to give you verbal feedback so you can ensure mutual understanding.

- **Smile.** While it may sound like a cliché, smiling is a universal language. It expresses openness, friendliness, and willingness to communicate. In addition, it puts others at ease.

Study Question 2.5

How can I work effectively as part of a team?

This chapter so far has focused on developing communication skills to help you work effectively with others. In workplace environments, your work with others will often be accomplished in teams. A team is more than a group of people working together. An effective **team** involves two or more people who recognize and share a commitment to a specific, common goal and who collaborate in their efforts to achieve that goal.[37]

Teams are integral to an organization's success largely because one individual does not have all the skills needed to compete in today's business world. In addition, if a company needs to bring a product to market before a competitor does, it cannot wait for one or two people to do all the work involved. Instead, the company must rely on a well-coordinated team, each person doing his or her part to achieve the common goal. Individuals benefit from teamwork, too. By working on a team, you will use your best individual strengths while learning new skills from others, improve your interpersonal skills, and expand your personal network. This section suggests six ways you and your teammates can improve team performance and make teamwork an enjoyable experience.

Assemble an effective team

If you have the opportunity to assemble a team for a project, choose carefully. Friends are not always the best choices for teammates. The most effective team will be one with the right skills and attitudes to get the job done well. To select strong team members, ask yourself the following questions:

- **What are the skills needed to complete this team project effectively?** If your project involves market research, identify who has experience conducting surveys.
- **What skills am I lacking that I can identify in prospective team members?** If your project involves working with colleagues in a country you know nothing about, identify someone who has experience with that culture.
- **Who has the time and resources to contribute effectively to the team project?** You may have someone in mind, but that person may be working on several other projects and not have time to do a good job on your team. Ask that person to recommend someone else.
- **Who may be most interested in this topic (and therefore motivated to participate)?** You may know someone who has worked on the topic before, or you might consider a new employee who you know is eager to learn about the topic.
- **Who is easy to work with?** To do their project well, team members need more than just skills and knowledge. They also need to know how to work with others and be able to identify, confront, and resolve issues as they arise.

How big should your team be? Although team sizes vary greatly based on the goal of the team, smaller team sizes of three to five people are typically more productive than larger ones. You may have heard the phrase "too many cooks spoil the broth." If you have more team members than duties to share, people may "get in the way" by trying to help without having a specific purpose to fulfill. Teams of three or five people also eliminate the possibility of a 50/50 split if the team votes on a decision. If you need a larger team for larger projects, consider breaking it into subteams.

Idiom An expression that means something other than the literal meaning of its words.

Jargon The specialized language of a specific field.

Team Two or more people who recognize and share a commitment to a specific, common goal and who collaborate in their efforts to achieve that goal.

Agree on team goals and standards

For a team to be successful, all team members need to agree on key elements at the beginning of the project:[38]

- **Goals.** Good teams are goal-oriented. All members understand their purpose as a team, share a concrete goal and vision for success, and believe that what they are doing is worthwhile. They know their work will make a significant contribution to their organization, their client, the community, or something they care about. In addition, each individual member must be willing to do whatever it takes to make the team successful, including helping each other if the need arises. To promote commitment, teams should make sure that all members get a chance to participate in decisions and feel they are being heard.
- **Expected results.** Good teams are also results-oriented. In other words, the team's success is measured by results, not effort, and the team is organized to achieve those results. Specifically:
  - All team members have a clear role and are held accountable for their contributions.
  - Workload is divided equitably. Some tasks may require more effort than others, so it is important to discuss the work to ensure that the team is aware of each member's responsibilities and no one is overburdened with too much work.
  - The team has an effective communication system to keep all team members informed in a timely way.
  - Team members give each other prompt and helpful feedback on their performance so each can do his or her best work.
- **Team standards.** Finally, good teams have standards and hold each team member accountable for them. You may develop standards about any or all of the following topics: conducting meetings, communicating between meetings, keeping records, making decisions, and managing conflict. Working together to create team standards helps a team get off to a strong start. If conflict begins to arise during a project, the team standards can help a team resolve the conflict.

Give the team time to develop

While some teams get off to a fast start, most teams need time to develop their collaborative working relationship. FIGURE 2.7 illustrates a model for understanding team development first proposed by Bruce W. Tuckman. He identified four stages of development in teams that had no formal team training: forming, storming, norming, and performing.[39] One reason to study teamwork in a business communication course is so that you can move more quickly to the performing stage.

What happens in each stage?

- **Forming**. When a team first begins to form, everyone is usually polite and considerate. You exchange information about your schedules, when and where you can

FIGURE 2.7
Stages of Team Development:
What Team Members Do
at Each Stage

FORMING	STORMING	NORMING	PERFORMING
Exchange vital information	Experience conflict and tension	Discuss and resolve problems	Work collaboratively
Learn about each other	Feel disillusioned and discouraged	Create standards for communicating	Use individual differences as a source of strength
Have high expectations for success	Identify reasons for conflict	Plan regular meetings	Put project above individual goals
Act politely and considerately		Hold members accountable	Achieve high level of productivity

meet, and how you can contact each other. Usually, expectations for the team and its success are high, and conflicts are not evident.

- **Storming**. The team eventually begins to encounter problems that don't solve themselves. Members begin to feel tense and anxious about the success of the project. Some team members may begin to feel disillusioned and discouraged. As you experience conflict, try to identify the reasons for the conflict to help the group move to the next stage of development.

- **Norming**. Norming begins when team members start to manage conflict and establish a consensus about how to work together efficiently. This is the stage at which many teams decide to create standards about communication and accountability.

- **Performing**. At the performing stage of team development, team members have learned how to work collaboratively and are able to use their differences as a source of strength, not weakness. While problems will continue to arise, a performing team feels comfortable confronting and resolving the problems that might jeopardize the success of the project. Members begin to enjoy working together and are glad they don't have to complete the project alone. They often get so involved and excited about what they are doing that they lose track of time, and the success of the project becomes more important than individual goals.

A performing team may also evolve into a *high-performing team*: a team whose members are deeply committed to each other's growth and success.[40] Achieving this level of performance requires time commitment and hard work. However, when you get there you will find the team experience to be exhilarating and rewarding.

Develop good leadership

Every team needs good *leadership* to provide direction and manage the team's activities. A team leader may not be the team member who has the most creative ideas. An effective leader is the person who has the skills to motivate people, manage work processes, and help the team succeed.

A team can establish leadership in a number of ways. One person can serve as leader, leadership can rotate during phases of the project, or different leaders can take responsibility for different aspects of the project. It is not crucial for the team to have one single leader. However, it is crucial for the team to have capable leadership that keeps the good of the team in mind. Remember that if you volunteer to be a team leader, that role does not put you in charge of the team. Instead, it puts you in service of the team.

Here is a partial list of ways that a leader can serve the team and help it succeed:

- **Establish and maintain a vision of the future.** One of the most valuable roles for any leader is to keep the team focused on their ultimate goal and remind the team why that goal is valuable. Teams can easily get bogged down in the details of the work and forget why the project is worthwhile. A good leader will reenergize team members, refocus them on the goal, and make the team believe in itself.

- **Create a supportive climate.** Teams work best when team members feel that they can take risks and that they will be listened to and respected. A team leader can set the tone for the team by encouraging creativity and being respectful to everyone.

- **Delegate responsiblity and assign tasks equitably.** Delegating responsibility and assigning tasks is a balancing act. On the one hand, the team needs to take full advantage of its human resources and assign people tasks that call on their strengths. On the other hand, teams need to provide members with opportunities to learn, stretch, and develop new skills. A good leader can help maintain this balance by considering each individual's talents and goals. In addition, a good team leader can help ensure that workloads are shared equitably. As a project progresses, work assignments may need to shift: some tasks may prove to be bigger than anticipated, some may be smaller, and new tasks may arise.

- **Establish a timeline.** Once the team collaboratively determines a plan for their project, a team leader can oversee the creation of a timeline to plan the team's progress and ensure deadlines will be met. Then, throughout the process, a leader can help the team reevaluate and reassess the plan.

Forming A stage of team development in which members get to know each other.

Storming A stage of team development in which teams experience conflict and begin to confront differences.

Norming A stage of team development in which team members learn how to manage conflict and work with each other effectively.

Performing A stage of team development in which team members work collaboratively and achieve a high level of productivity.

- **Keep the project on track.** Although individual members of the team may work on separate tasks, a good leader will bring the team together throughout the project to discuss progress, encourage group feedback, and share ideas. Scheduling regular meetings keeps the project on track to meet established deadlines while also allowing for changes in the plan based on continual input and feedback.
- **Manage meetings effectively and encourage positive collaboration.** A good leader will use effective listening, questioning, and restating techniques to ensure that all members of the team participate in meetings and provide input. Leaders also encourage positive collaboration among team members and referee any unconstructive feedback or personality conflicts.
- **Ensure effective decision making.** While teams can take many approaches to decision-making, important decisions should never be made by giving in to the team member who is the loudest and most assertive. A team leader can ensure that the team makes fact-based judgments and is able to support all its decisions with sound evidence and reasoning. Although a good leader will help a team work toward consensus, the leader must also protect the team against reaching consensus quickly by groupthink.
- **Resolve differences.** When team members have differences of opinion and need an impartial point of view, a team leader can take responsibility for listening carefully and offering a resolution.

Plan for effective meetings

Team meetings are crucial for determining tasks, sharing ideas, and making decisions. To avoid falling into the trap of holding too many meetings where not enough gets done, plan your meetings in advance following these guidelines:

- **Create an agenda.** Base the agenda—a detailed plan for the meeting—on input from each team member. At the top of the agenda, include the day, time, and place of the meeting. Also state the purpose of the meeting. This will help keep the discussion on track. List all the topics to be discussed—or all the decisions to be made—and estimate the amount of time each item will require. Although you may need to be flexible with time during the meeting, the time estimates will help the team get through all the topics efficiently. Assign each topic to a team member and ensure that all team members have some responsibility during the meeting. If team members are not responsible for anything on the agenda, reconsider whether they need to attend the meeting.

  FIGURE 2.8 shows an agenda for a team that is working to develop an online handbook for summer interns. Notice that the agenda provides the list of topics to be discussed, the names of the individuals responsible for each item, and the amount of time to spend discussing each item.
- **Distribute the agenda sufficiently in advance.** Distributing the agenda before the meeting ensures that all the team members know what will be expected, who is responsible, and what their roles will be during the meeting.
- **Assign someone to serve as a timekeeper during the meeting.** The timekeeper can keep track of how well the meeting follows the agenda. If the meeting becomes sidetracked on unrelated matters or if participants get stuck on unproductive tangents, the timekeeper can bring the conversation back to the necessary topic.
- **Assign someone to serve as a note taker during the meeting.** The note taker will produce **meeting minutes**, a written description of what was discussed, what was decided, and what actions will follow.

  FIGURE 2.8 also shows the minutes of the online handbook team's meeting. Notice that the minutes focus on what the team decided and do not repeat everything that was said. The minutes also include assignments (who agreed to do what) and deadlines (when they agreed to do it).
- **Plan for followup.** Include a wrap-up as the last item on your agenda. This reminds you to end the meeting by reviewing the actions and deadlines that everyone agreed upon and scheduling the next meeting's time and place.

FIGURE 2.8 Agenda and Minutes

agenda

AGENDA

Online Internship Handbook Team

Human Resources Conference Room
Tuesday, July 31, 20XX
4:00 – 5:00 PM

MEETING PURPOSE:
To kick off the internship handbook project and develop a six-week plan.

I. Introductions   5–10 min.

    a. Jay Macintosh, Intern to Director for Human Resources, Team Leader
    b. Rachel Ferrera, Intern to Assistant to CEO
    c. Arnie Glover, Intern to Temp Pool Supervisor
    d. Roberto Washington, Intern, Web Development Department

II. Project Overview   - Jay Macintosh   10–15 min.

    a. Brainstorm Initial Ideas for Topic Content
    b. Assign Responsibilities

III. Web Development Support   - Roberto Washington   10–15 min.

    a. Discuss Format / Layout Options
    b. Determine Resource Needs (Materials)

IV. Six-Week Timeline   - Jay Macintosh   10–15 min.
    a. Meeting Times
    b. Progress Reports and Submission Schedule
    c. Interns Who Will Provide Feedback:
        1. Sarah Fernandez, Marketing Department
        2. Paul Mason, Research & Development
        3. Soren Afzabi, Research & Development
        4. Melanie Godfarb, Accounting

V. Other?   5–10 min.

VI. Due Next Week: Content Reports

minutes

MINUTES

Online Internship Handbook Team

Human Resources Conference Room
July 31, 20XX

Present: Jay Macintosh, Intern to Director for Human Resources, Team Leader
         Rachel Ferrera, Intern to Assistant to CEO
         Arnie Glover, Intern for Temp Pool Supervisor
         Roberto Washington, Intern, Web Development Department

I. **Introductions:** Jay Macintosh called the meeting to order, introduced himself, and asked the others to state their department, experience, and skills.

II. **Project Overview:** Jay Macintosh explained the project goals. The team brainstormed ideas for topics and assigned content as follows:

    a. Welcome to the Company   - Rachel Ferrera
        1. History of the Organization
        2. Mission / Vision Statements
        3. Organizational Chart
        4. Your Role as an Intern

    b. Policies and Procedures   - Arnie Glover
        1. Maintaining Work Hours and Reporting Absences
        2. Sending and Responding to Email
        3. Logging Telephone Calls
        4. Using the Internet
        5. Using Social Media
        6. Submitting Reimbursement Requests

    c. Human Resources   - Jay Macintosh
        1. Salary and Payroll Procedures
        2. Health Benefits
        3. Educational Resources
        4. Applying for Permanent Employment

III. **Web Development Support:** Roberto Washington explained company policies about website format, layout, and design options. The team discussed where on the current company website the internship handbook should be located. **Decision:** Roberto will check with his supervisor about content and resource needs and report to the team by email before the end of the week.

IV. **Six-Week Timeline: Decisions:**
    1. We will meet on Tuesdays from 3–5 PM. Between meetings we will update each other by email.
    2. Jay will send our weekly meeting minutes to his supervisor as our progress reports.
    3. We will send the completed version of our first draft to the other interns who volunteered for this project to get their feedback by Week 3.
    4. We will submit a draft to the Director of Human Resources by Week 4.
    5. Roberto will begin putting the material on the web in Week 5.

V. **Next meeting:** The team will meet on August 7 to discuss the content reports.

Be a good team member

Although a team works together to achieve a common goal, it is still made up of individuals. Each individual needs to take responsibility for his or her own tasks and also contribute to a productive working relationship with others. To be a good team member, follow these guidelines:

- **Make a commitment to the team and its goals.** At times, it may be tempting to do minimal work for the team and assume that others will take up the slack. But a team will succeed only if everyone shares a similar level of commitment. Every member must be reliable and pull his or her own weight. In addition, every team member must be willing to do whatever it takes to make the team successful, including helping each other if the need arises.

- **Create a collaborative working climate.** To work well together, team members need to trust each other and believe that everyone is working in the team's best interests. That means, as a good team member, you need to be worthy of that trust. Listen to your teammates without criticism or judgment and give everyone a chance to participate in decision-making. Respond constructively to feedback

mybcommlab

Apply Figure 2.8's key concepts by revising a new document. Go to Chapter 2 in mybcommlab.com and select Document Makeovers.

Agenda A detailed plan or outline of the items to be discussed at a meeting.

Meeting minutes Notes that describe what was discussed at a meeting, what was decided, and what actions will follow.

TECHNOLOGY   Conferencing, Collaborating, and Managing

Advances in technology have made it easier for teams to work collaboratively, whether in the same office or across the globe. Three types of technology have become standard for workplace teams.

Conferencing Tools

One challenge of teamwork is finding the best—and most cost effective—ways to meet. In a global workplace, team members are often in different locations. In that case, you can choose three levels of technology for meeting.

- **Teleconferences** allow people to meet by telephone. If participants need to see the same materials, documents can be distributed in advance by email.

- **Web conferences** are like teleconferences except participants are also able to share computer screens and see the same presentation file, spreadsheet, or website. The meeting leader controls what everyone sees.

- **Video conferences** typically require special equipment that allows you to share video images of your conference room with people in another location. Video conferences are especially good if you are meeting distant teammates for the first time and want to put a face with the name and voice. Video conferences are also good if people need to hold a lively discussion where many people will be talking and you want to be able to identify who is speaking.

Collaborating Tools

When teammates need to work on the same document or spreadsheet, file sharing tools like Google Docs ensure that everyone can access the most up-to-date version available. Google, Yahoo, and other technology providers also offer calendar sharing. If all team members keep their calendars up to date, you can easily find when others have free time. You can also post important team milestones to everyone's individual calendars.

Project Management Tools

Technology has also eased the burden of creating project management tools like Gantt charts. A *Gantt chart* (named after its inventor, Henry Gantt) is a project scheduling tool that helps you plan and track specific tasks over time. As the illustration below shows, one advantage of a Gantt chart is that it helps you manage time by identifying tasks that can take place simultaneously versus those that need to be completed sequentially.

If you create your chart as a word processing or spreadsheet file, you will be able to share it electronically with your team members to ensure that everyone knows how to keep the project on track.

PEARSON mybcommlab

> For TECHNOLOGY exercises, go to Exercises 24 and 25 on page 67 or to this chapter's End-of-Chapter Exercises at mybcommlab.com.

Gantt Chart

Assignment Key

Team	Alma	Fiona	John	Michael

Project: Client Web Site Development

Current Week → (4/20 to 4/27)

Tasks	3/2 to 3/9	3/9 to 3/16	3/16 to 3/30	3/30 to 4/6	4/6 to 4/13	4/13 to 4/20	4/20 to 4/27	4/27 to 5/4	5/4 to 5/11	5/11 to 5/19	5/19 to 5/25	5/25 to 6/1
Document Client Requirements	*	*										
Acquire Client Approval - Requirements		■										
Create Code			■	■								
Create Artwork Alternatives			■									
Present Artwork Alternative					■							
Acquire Client Approval - Artwork					■							
Integrate Artwork and Code						■	■					
User Testing									**	**		
Fix Bugs and User Interface Issues									■	■		
Present Final Site to Client											■	
Acquire Client Approval - Final Site											■	
Launch Site												■

* Michael is lead   ** Alma manages multiple testers from outside of team

from others, and address conflicts when they arise rather than letting them grow silently and weaken team cohesion.

- **Support and encourage your teammates.** Individuals appreciate recognition, even when they are working as a team. A good team member will show gratitude for the efforts of others and identify how individual contributions support the larger team effort.

- **Support team decisions.** Even if the team has made a decision that differs from what you wanted, once the decision is made, support that decision and work toward implementing it. If you have concern about the decision or believe it may cause problems, voice your concerns to the team. Do not try to undermine the decision.

- **Focus on continuous quality improvement.** No matter how well your team is performing, individual team members may see ways that the team can do better. By making productive suggestions, you can help improve the team and its results.

IN SUMMARY, the interpersonal skills you learned in this chapter are wide-ranging—spanning from basic listening and speaking skills to the more complex skills of managing conflict, working with people from other cultures, and working well in teams. As you move forward through the course, you will find many opportunities to apply these skills both in the classroom and within team projects.

2.1 **What listening skills will help me communicate better with others?** *(pages 32–37)*

Use active listening techniques to ensure understanding. These include:

- **Hearing accurately** by eliminating distractions to focus on the speaker.
- **Comprehending and interpreting** what is being said by observing people's behavior, listening to their nonverbal communication, being aware of tone of voice and emphasis, and paraphrasing.
- **Evaluating** to judge objectively what you hear. Remain open-minded, separate ideas from the speaker, and use sound reasoning.
- **Responding** to let the speaker know you understand and to initiate the next step in the conversation.

2.2 **What speaking strategies will encourage others to listen to me and understand what I am saying?** *(pages 37–41)*

- **Focus on your audience** to analyze the audience's interests.
- **Share the conversation** by inviting others to speak.
- **Use clear, concrete, and unambiguous language** to avoid misinterpretation.
- **Support your message with good nonverbal communication** that reinforces your spoken message.
- **Avoid language that triggers a negative response.**
- **Frame negative comments positively.**
- **Be aware of gender-specific communication styles.**

2.3 **How can I manage interpersonal conflict?** *(pages 41–46)*

While cognitive conflict can be productive in improving team outcomes, affective conflict focusing on personalities does not enhance team performance. To manage conflict:

- **Identify the cause of the conflict,** which can include competing goals, differences of opinion, lack of information, relational issues, and ego issues.
- **Select an appropriate management technique.** You might avoid confrontation, accommodate or give in, compete to win, compromise, or collaborate to find the best solution.

2.4 **How can I improve my communication with people from different cultures?** *(pages 46–51)*

- **Understand how cultures differ.** Low-context cultures value explicit communication, while high-context cultures rely more on subtle cues. Individualist cultures value an individual's achievements, while collectivist cultures put the good of the group first. Cultures with high power distance are very hierarchical. Low power-distance cultures are less formal. Cultures also differ in their tolerance for uncertainty (including ambiguity, risk, and change) and their orientation toward time.
- **Develop strategies that help you communicate with diverse groups.** Be relatively formal, mirror the other person's behavior, be clear and concise, talk slowly, request feedback to ensure understanding, and smile to express friendliness and willingness to communicate.

2.5 **How can I work effectively as part of a team?** *(pages 51–57)*

- **Assemble an effective team** of people with the skills, resources, and attitude to succeed.
- **Agree on team goals and standards.** Do not expect the team to perform at a high level immediately.
- **Give the team time to develop** through the stages of forming, storming, norming, and performing.
- **Develop good leadership** practices.
- **Plan for effective meetings.**
- **Be a good team member** by doing your job and supporting team members.

PEARSON
mybcommlab™ *Are you an active learner? Go to mybcommlab.com to master Chapter 2 content. Chapter 2 interactive activities include:*

- Customizable Study Plan and Chapter 2 practice quizzes
- Chapter 2 Simulation, Interpersonal Communication and Teamwork, that helps you think critically and prepare to make choices in the business world
- Flash Cards for mastering the definition of chapter terms

- Chapter 2 Video Exercise, Mastering Interpersonal Communication, which shows you how textbook concepts are put into practice every day
- Interactive Lessons that visually review key chapter concepts
- Document Makeovers for hands-on, scored practice in revising documents

LISTENING

- Hear accurately to comprehend and interpret meaning.
- "Listen" to nonverbal communication.
- Ask questions and paraphrase to ensure understanding.
- Evaluate information: is it accurate, well-supported, and convincing?
- Respond to provide feedback.

SPEAKING

- Focus on your audience.
- Share the conversation.
- Use clear, concrete, unambiguous language.
- Support your message with good eye contact, strong and positive tone, and complementary gestures and facial expressions.
- Avoid biased, provocative, or accusatory language.
- Be aware of gender-specific styles.

MANAGING CONFLICT

- Identify conflict as affective or cognitive.
- Identify the reason for the conflict.
- Shift focus away from ego and back to business.
- Decide how to manage conflict: avoid confrontation, accommodate, give in, compete to win, compromise, or collaborate to find the best solution.

COMMUNICATING ACROSS CULTURES

- Understand how cultures differ.
- Identify dimensions of the specific culture: high or low context? individualistic or collectivistic? high or low power distance? comfortable or uncomfortable with uncertainty? monochronic or polychronic?
- Develop strategies to communicate with diverse groups: use formality and respect, pay attention to nonverbal cues, be clear and concise, talk slowly, and request feedback to ensure understanding.

WORKING IN TEAMS

- Assemble effective teams by identifying skills, resources, and interests.
- Determine goals and standards.
- Plan time to form, storm, norm, and perform.
- Develop good leadership by focusing on the purpose, encouraging participation, creating timelines, assigning tasks, keeping the project on track, and resolving differences.
- Plan effective meetings supported by agendas and minutes.
- Be a good team member through commitment, collaboration, and continuous quality improvement.

KEY TERMS QUICK ACCESS REVIEW

Active listening *p. 32*	Forming *p. 52*	Paraphrase *p. 35*
Affective conflict *p. 41*	Groupthink *p. 45*	Passive listening *p. 32*
Agenda *p. 54*	Idiom *p. 50*	Performing *p. 53*
Cognitive conflict *p. 41*	Individualistic culture *p. 48*	Polychronic culture *p. 49*
Collectivist culture *p. 48*	Interpretation *p. 33*	Power distance *p. 48*
Comprehension *p. 33*	Jargon *p. 50*	Stereotypes *p. 47*
Context *p. 47*	Meeting minutes *p. 54*	Storming *p. 53*
Culture *p. 46*	Monochronic culture *p. 49*	Team *p. 51*
Ethnocentrism *p. 47*	Nonverbal communication *p. 33*	Uncertainty avoidance *p. 49*
Evaluating *p. 36*	Norming *p. 53*	

CASE STUDY Working as a Cross-Cultural Team

This case study will help you review the chapter material by applying it to a specific scenario.

The first three weeks of your internship at Baer, Kramer & Dreslin Market Research in Nashville were great. You enjoyed brainstorming marketing ideas with your manager and designing a survey for an important client. However, the past week has been pure misery. Your supervisor assigned you to join three other interns on a team to create a comprehensive online handbook for interns. Each summer, the company hires seven interns at your location in Nashville and seven more in the company's data processing department in New Delhi, India. You will work on your project with one other intern from the Nashville office and two interns from New Delhi.

Planning the first meeting was difficult. You lost two days of work trying to set a meeting time since there is a 10 1/2 hour time difference between Nashville and New Delhi: at 9 AM Central Daylight Time in Nashville, it is 7:30 PM in New Delhi. You suggested a 7 AM teleconference, but your Nashville teammate, Roberto, said he could not arrive in the office early for a meeting. You suggest an 8:30 AM teleconference, which would be 7 PM in New Delhi, but both your New Delhi teammates, Maansi and Anant, are vague about whether they could stay late. You beg Roberto to arrange to get to work early just one day so that your team can hold a kick-off meeting. Roberto admits that he could easily get to the office early, but prefers to sleep later. "And anyway," he admits, "I didn't sign up for human resources work when I accepted an internship in consumer research. How will this help me get a job?"

Finally, you are able to convince Roberto to accommodate Maansi and Anant. The first meeting is scheduled for 7:30 AM Central Daylight Time. The meeting seems to begin well enough. Everyone arrives on time, the teleconferencing system works, and the meeting starts with friendly introductions. Within five minutes, though, you know you are in trouble. When Anant introduces himself, he speaks so quickly that you miss everything he says. You would be too embarrassed to ask him to repeat it, so you remain quiet and pretend to understand. After the introductions, things get worse. No one has thought to make an agenda, so no one knows what the team is trying to accomplish. After a few moments of painful silence, you say, "Well maybe we should just start sharing ideas about coming up with a plan for the online handbook."

Anant jumps right in. You don't understand much of what he says, but you do hear the words "user interface," "programming," "database," and "search functions." You and Roberto look at each other in amazement. Why is Anant talking about computer programming? And why is he continuing to talk without stopping for five minutes? Is it rude to interrupt? Finally, Roberto says, "Anant, it sounds like you may have some good ideas, but we don't understand. We thought our job was to plan an online handbook." Anant replied, "That's what I'm talking about." Throughout all of this Maansi remains silent. After the first meeting, you feel that it is going to be a long five weeks until the end of your summer internship.

Review Question 1: *What interpersonal, intercultural, and teamwork communication issues are emerging in this scenario?*

Listening for Understanding

After your first team meeting, Roberto says, "It doesn't sound like Maansi and Anant will be too helpful on this project. Maybe we should do it on our own. We can come up with a plan for a handbook in a week and then coast through the rest of the summer." You think Roberto has a good point. The project would be easier to complete without participating in a cross-cultural team. And you ask yourself "Why *are* Maansi and Anant on this team? Why am *I* on this team? What are we supposed to be doing?"

You decide that this confusion stems from a communication problem—not with Maansi and Anant but with your supervisor. You thought you were listening intently when she asked you to "come up with a plan for an online handbook." But did you really understand what she meant? You were too intimidated to ask any clarifying questions:

- What does "plan" mean? What is the goal of the team?
- Is there some reason you and Roberto were put on the team? Is there some specific reason Maansi and Anant are on the team?
- What should be the final deliverable this summer?

With these questions in mind, you propose this plan to Roberto: "Let's try to arrange a meeting with our supervisor this afternoon. Rather than just sitting there and listening, let's ask lots of questions to be sure we understand. At the end of the meeting, we can summarize what we learned and email it to Maansi and Anant. We need to be sure we all have the same idea of what we are supposed to do."

Review Question 2: *Listening involves a number of specific skills: hearing, comprehending and interpreting, evaluating and responding. Which of these areas contributed to the communication problem in this scenario? Identify specific examples.*

Framing Negative Criticism Positively

Fortunately, the meeting with your supervisor is very helpful. Through much questioning and paraphrasing, you and Roberto identify four tasks for the summer: evaluate the material in the current paper handbook, gather information from current interns in both locations, put together a content outline for the website, and develop an easy-to-use structure for the website.

Although the meeting is successful, you are angry at Roberto because he simply cannot hide his contempt for this project. Before the meeting, he whispers to you, "Let's just get this meeting over with. No one needs a handbook. This project is just more busywork for interns." You find it difficult to begin focusing on content in the meeting because you are fuming about Roberto's attitude. Originally, you were looking forward to working with Roberto because he is very smart and creative, but now you are afraid that his attitude may stand in the way of completing the project.

You prepare two different ways to talk with Roberto about this:

- **Option 1.** "Roberto, you are so negative all the time. I know you really don't want to do this project, but that's our job. We both need good evaluations from this internship. If you don't change your mind-set, you'll cause us both to fail."

- **Option 2.** "Roberto, I'm really looking forward to working with you. You always have such great ideas. But, I'm worried that you don't think this project is important and won't give it your best effort. I want to get a strong evaluation from this internship. I know if we work together we can plan a great handbook—and I think we can have a good time working together."

Review Question 3: *How would you describe the difference between the two approaches? Which approach would help Roberto accept the criticism?*

Understanding Conflict

By the second week of the project, the team is working efficiently, with all team members doing their tasks. Yet there is tension at every team meeting. Roberto appears to be looking for the fastest way through the project, and he gets frustrated with your attention to detail. You also are losing patience with Roberto. He is capable of great work, but it is never quite finished. Meanwhile, Maansi and Anant continue to focus just on the programming aspects of the online handbook and aren't interested in talking about content. When you ask Maansi to help you gather information about content needs from New Delhi interns, she says, "I won't have time to do that. We can take content from the current handbook. To have an excellent handbook, what's really important is developing an interactive website." You find this insulting, since you have been working hard to develop content.

Before bad feelings take over, you decide to schedule a meeting with your supervisor to talk about these conflicts and see if she has any ideas about how to handle them. She asks, "What kind of conflicts are these? Are these personality conflicts? Or do the conflicts stem from differences of opinion about how to get the best handbook? Or do team members have competing goals?" As you think about the problems, you realize these conflicts go beyond simple personality clashes.

The conflict with Roberto seems to be one of competing goals. Your goal is to create a great handbook. Roberto's goal from the start has been to work on a project that will look good on his résumé. Perhaps you and Roberto can talk and find common ground between these two goals.

The conflict with Maansi and Anant is different. They seem to want an excellent handbook. However, they have a very different opinion about what is required to achieve that goal. They believe that programming is the key. Existing content can simply be imported into the new site. As a result, they are not interested in interviewing their fellow interns to gather information. The New Delhi interns may need different information from the handbook, but you have no way to find out. Perhaps the best way to address this conflict is simply to accommodate Maansi and Anant and let them focus solely on programming. You and Roberto can determine a different way to gather information from New Delhi interns.

Review Question 4: *Besides accommodating, what specific actions could you take to manage the conflict with Maansi and Anant if you decided to avoid, compete, compromise, or collaborate? Which approach do you believe would lead to the best outcome?*

Managing Cultural Diversity

To streamline communication while working with Anant and Maansi, you set weekly meeting times on Tuesdays and Thursdays at 8 AM Central Daylight Time, which fortunately works well for both the U.S. and India team members. Every meeting has an agenda, and teams exchange important information in writing before and after the meeting, which eases the problem of understanding foreign accents. (You were surprised that Anant had as much difficulty understanding your southern American accent as you had understanding his Indian accent. But he had learned British English.)

Nonetheless, your team has had some real difficulties working together. Anant and Maansi always seem busy with several projects, not just the internship project, and do not treat this one with any urgency. They are very indirect in presenting what they have accomplished, and you are never confident about how far along they are. At one meeting, when you ask Maansi to see their prototype website so that you can figure out how to structure your content, she becomes silent. You hadn't meant the question as a criticism, but perhaps she understood it that way. Anant, by contrast, is never silent and is always trying to engage in an intellectual debate about various programming techniques. Trying to figure out how to communicate with people from other cultures without knowing them or their culture has proved very challenging.

Review Question 5: *What factors may explain the cultural differences between the U.S. and Indian team members?*

Reaping the Benefits of Teamwork
At the end of the summer internship, despite the conflicts and your communication challenges, you are surprised at all your team accomplished. Working as a team, you:

- Interviewed all the current interns and compiled the results into a report identifying the most important content for the handbook
- Developed a site map for the handbook
- Wrote content for two sections of the handbook
- Gathered inspirational quotations from senior management

- Programmed a prototype site
- Conducted a round of user testing
- Developed a list of necessary revisions

You think about two of Roberto's comments from earlier in the summer. At one point he complained, "You know, it doesn't sound like Maansi and Anant will be too helpful on this project. Maybe we should do it on our own." It would have been easier to create the content with just you and Roberto, but consider how much less work would have been done: no site mapping, no programming, and no user testing. You needed people with programming expertise on your team to get that done. At another point, Roberto asked, "How will this help me get a job?" The answer to that question is now obvious: You learned to work collaboratively with others, manage conflict, and complete a complicated project. Compared to other interns who learned only technical skills in market research, you have developed a transferrable set of skills that will be crucial on the job no matter what field you enter.

Review Question 6: *Section 2.5 describes some of the characteristics that successful teams share. This team ultimately was successful. How did it demonstrate these characteristics?*

CRITICAL THINKING

1. Explain a situation—either at home, school, or work—in which you passively listened and neglected to hear important information. Describe the negative result and identify how you could have used the active listening strategies to improve your communication process.

2. Designers of consumer products argue that to understand what customers really need, you have to do more than listen to what they say. You have to observe what they do. Why do you think there is often a gap between what people say and what they do?

3. Review the speaking strategies listed at the beginning of Study Question 2.2 on page 37. Divide them into two lists: strategies that you currently try to use when you speak and strategies that you typically do not think about. Of the strategies that you typically do not think about, identify one that you'd like to begin using immediately and explain why.

4. What words or phrases trigger a negative emotional response from you? If someone repeatedly uses one of your "trigger words," what are your options for responding? Which option would you choose?

5. Some organizations provide the services of mediators to help resolve workplace conflicts. What are the advantages of having a disinterested party resolve a conflict? What are the advantages of having people involved in the conflict work it out on their own?

6. As described in this chapter, people from the United States are typically both very individualistic and monochronic. How do these characteristics complement each other? How might they contradict each other? Explain your reasoning.

7. Imagine you have been hired by a global company that is holding a two-week orientation for all new employees at the head office in San Francisco. You will be staying in a hotel for two weeks, and you have been assigned to share a room with a new employee from Zurich, Switzerland. What can you do to find out in advance a little bit about the culture in Zurich? Once you have identified some characteristics of that culture, what can you do to ensure that you do not stereotype your roommate?

8. Explain a team situation in which you experienced conflict. What was the purpose of the team? Why did the affective and/or cognitive conflict occur? How did the team resolve the conflict? What was the impact on the final product?

9. Imagine you have a teammate who wants to do all the project work himself because he does not trust anyone else on the team to produce high-quality results. How would you respond to that teammate?

10. Groupthink occurs when people convince each other to agree. What are the problems with groupthink, and what can you do to avoid the groupthink syndrome?

DEVELOPING YOUR COMMUNICATION SKILLS

2.1 What listening skills will help me communicate better with others? *(pages 32–37)*

EXERCISE 1 Hearing accurately

In each of the following situations, identify what you can do to improve the ability of listeners to hear.

a. One member of your team has a hearing impairment and often misses key things that are said at meetings. Suggest at least four things that you and the rest of the team can do to make it easier for your teammate to hear well. Suggest at least four things your hearing-impaired teammate can do to hear you better.

b. At departmental meetings, your mind wanders when your boss is speaking because he has a monotonous tone of voice and rarely gets to the point. As a result, during the last two meetings you have missed important information. What can you do to improve your ability to hear what your boss says?

EXERCISE 2 Comprehending and interpreting

a. **Listening to tone of voice.** A speaker's tone of voice and emphasis provide clues about his or her attitudes and feelings. Imagine at least two different ways that you can say each of the following four statements. What are the different meanings conveyed by the different sets of nonverbal cues?
   1. I didn't do anything wrong.
   2. We need to talk now.
   3. I'll give you my phone number after the meeting.
   4. When did you come up with that idea?

b. **Paraphrasing to ensure understanding.** Learning how to paraphrase in multiple ways is challenging. Note the two conversational exchanges in the next column, with paraphrases in **boldface**. Identify which **boldface** statements are paraphrases of content, intent, and feeling. Remember, when you paraphrase for content, you state your understanding of the explicit message. When you paraphrase for intent, you try to uncover why someone made that statement. When you paraphrase for feelings, you try to uncover the emotions in the statement.

EXERCISE 3 Evaluating

Your coworker Bob is always complaining about something and offers nothing but negative comments at meetings. He came into your office this morning to share a proposal he plans to make in a manager's meeting tomorrow. He proposes that the department change the hiring requirements so that all new hires have three years of experience in addition to a bachelor's degree. He claims that "A college education is not sufficient for the job." He supports his claim with this evidence: "The two newest employees, fresh out of college, have been making mistakes and cannot seem to learn the details of the job. We have no time to train them. We need to hire people who are already trained." He asks if you will support his idea at the meeting.

Your immediate reaction is "I don't know." You have made friends with one of the new hires, and you know from your own

1. **Accounts payable:** We keep getting invoices for partial shipments, and I can't figure out when a purchase order is completely filled. I can't pay an invoice for a partial shipment. The purchase order has to be closed out before we pay the invoice. **Purchasing: So, you are saying that our computer system will not allow you to pay a partial invoice?**
   Accounts payable: I don't know. The computer system might allow it.
   Purchasing: So, it's company policy not to pay partial invoices?
   Accounts payable: Well, it's not really a company policy. It's just so confusing to match these partial invoices with purchase orders. I'm never sure I get it right, so I don't think it's a good idea for us to do this.
   Purchasing: You sound like you might want some help with the invoices since you're spending so much time matching the invoices with the purchase order. Would you like me to match them for you? Because I wrote the purchase orders, I can do it more easily.
   Accounts payable: That sounds like a good idea.

2. **Interviewer:** What gets you excited about public relations?
   Interviewee: I've been thinking about public relations for a long time.
   Interviewer: Your goal has always been to go into public relations?
   Interviewee: Well, no. My original goal was to be a lawyer, and I worked as a paralegal for a few years, but there was really no career path, so I decided to do something else.
   Interviewer: So, you were frustrated and that led to a career change?
   Interviewee: Yes, exactly. I want to do something that allows me to be more creative and contribute more to an organization.
   Interviewer: You believe that public relations will make better use of your talents.

Accompanies Exercise 2

experience it takes time to learn a job. You were hired right out of college too. You will need to evaluate this proposal critically before you take a stance. What steps would you take to evaluate what you heard?

EXERCISE 4 Responding

Assume you are working on a project with three other people. One of your teammates provides great ideas during team meetings, but consistently misses deadlines and provides only partial work. Her lack of follow-through has significantly slowed the project, and you are now concerned that your team will not complete the project on time. Your teammate says she will meet the next deadline. How could you effectively respond to her statement? Practice six different kinds of responses:

a. Ask a question.

b. Make a judgment.

c. Contribute an opinion.

d. Give advice.

e. Argue or disagree.

f. Express empathy.

Identify the one response you think is best and be prepared to discuss your answer in class.

2.2 What speaking strategies will encourage others to listen to me and understand what I am saying?

(pages 37–41)

EXERCISE 5 Focus on your audience

Imagine you receive a phone call from an actual friend or relative who asks you "How is school going?" or "How is your job?" Write a two-paragraph email to your instructor:

- In the first paragraph, identify the friend or relative you have in mind and explain what you think that person really wants to know in asking that question.
- In the second paragraph, explain how you will respond. What will you tell your friend or relative and why? What won't you tell him or her and why?

EXERCISE 6 Share the conversation

Observe a conversation at a meeting or between two or three people at lunch or dinner. Does any one person monopolize the conversation? If so, does that have any negative results? If the conversation is shared fairly, how long is each person's typical turn? How do people signal that they want to speak?

EXERCISE 7 Use clear, concrete, unambiguous language

Each of the sentences below contains at least one ambiguous phrase. Identify the possible ambiguity and rephrase the statement so that it has one clear, concrete meaning. Feel free to make up details if necessary.

a. You did a great job on that report.

b. Mary's job performance hasn't been satisfactory this year.

c. Our presentation needs to be perfect.

d. There are just a few small problems to clear up before signing the contract.

e. Clean up the conference room before the end of the day.

f. Let's talk after the project is finished.

EXERCISE 8 Support your message with good nonverbal communication

Ask someone you do not know for directions to a nearby location, and pay attention to that person's verbal and nonverbal communication.

- What is that person's verbal message; in other words, does the person provide directions or decline to help, or say something else?
- What nonverbal elements support that message?
- Are there any nonverbal elements that conflict with that message?

EXERCISE 9 Avoid language that triggers a negative response

Read the following scenario and identify alternatives for the biased language.

Your first job after graduating is as an internal consultant with a small, local company. On your first day of work, the vice president who hired you asked you to come to a meeting where he will introduce you to the head of every department in the company. As you stand up at the front of the conference room, the vice president says, "I'd like to introduce the _____ who has been hired to help us." Imagine that the blank was filled in with each of the following terms (consider only the gender terms appropriate for you):

- Young lady/Young man
- Woman/Man
- Gal/Guy
- Expert
- Consultant
- Genius
- College girl/College boy

Which term(s) would you prefer the vice president use to introduce you? What are the problems with each of the remaining terms? What kinds of bias, if any, do they represent?

EXERCISE 10 Frame negative comments positively

Although most people do not enjoy providing negative feedback, it is necessary in most work environments. People respond better to negative feedback if it is framed in a positive way and if the criticism is not preceded by "but." For each of the following scenarios, provide criticism, starting out with a positive comment and avoiding "but."

a. You asked your assistant, Paulo, to make 50 photocopies of 15 individual handout sheets that you will use during the training session you are conducting tomorrow. Paulo decided that it would be easier for you to distribute the handouts as one set, so he collated and stapled the photocopies. However, your plan was to distribute each handout separately at specific points throughout the training session. How do you respond to Paulo?

b. Your supervisor, Jean, asks you to suggest how the department can improve employee morale, which has been low since she took over six months ago. The former supervisor often told people they were doing a good job, but Jean has not mentioned anything to anyone—positive or negative. You are sure that employee morale would improve dramatically if she would share encouraging feedback once in awhile. How do you tell her this?

c. You and Sheena met during your company orientation two years ago and were placed in similar positions in two different departments. Since then, you have met for lunch once a week. Sheena is known for gossiping about coworkers, and even though you know it's not appropriate, you often look forward to her tantalizing tales. You don't share the gossip with others, but you know Sheena does, and you believe this may be why you have been promoted twice while she has remained in the same position. After the standard gossip-fest at lunch today, Sheena mentions that she was passed over yet again for a promotion. She asks you why you think she can't seem to get ahead in the company. You do not want to hurt her feelings, but you do want to see her succeed. How do you respond?

EXERCISE 11 Be aware of gender-specific communication styles

Although there is no absolute "female" communication style or "male" communication style, researchers in sociolinguistics have identified a number of widespread differences between the way men and women typically communicate. In business, people need to accommodate different styles in order to work well together. In small groups (or as a whole class), discuss the following three scenarios. In your past experience, have you noticed these types of differences? What would you recommend the participants do to bridge the differences?

a. Ella and Michael are assigned to work on a project together. Ella goes to her supervisor to ask for clarification of details and to ensure she understands what the project requires. By contrast, Michael jumps right in and begins to work. He says he'll figure it out along the way. Michael tells Ella she's wasting time. Ella believes Michael hates to ask for help or directions.

b. In meetings, Richard illustrates his points with metaphors about war and sports: "I think we'll score a touchdown with this new product. But if we don't get it to market soon, the competition will outflank us." By contrast, Alice uses anecdotes and metaphors about relationships and home: "Our products are always the bridesmaids. This one will be the bride." Richard and Alice understand the other person's metaphors, but they are not comfortable with them.

c. At the monthly department meeting, Denise and James's manager asked for suggestions about how to research a client problem. Denise spoke immediately and began to make a suggestion. Before she had time to finish, James interrupted and said, "That gives me another idea," and he began presenting his thoughts. The conversation in the meeting then focused on James's idea. Denise waited for a break in the conversation, to return to her point. She quietly tried to interrupt, but could not break the momentum of the conversation. She left the meeting feeling angry with James.

2.3 How can I manage interpersonal conflict?

(pages 41–46)

EXERCISE 12 Identify the cause of the conflict

Identifying the cause of conflict is not always easy. Review the five different causes of conflict you learned in this chapter: competing goals, differences of opinion, lack of information, relational issues, and ego issues. For each of the following scenarios, identify the cause—or causes—of the conflict and explain your reasoning.

a. Your company is planning to install a new air conditioning system for the administrative offices. The Vice President of Operations has asked you and a coworker to research air conditioning systems and to recommend one. You and your coworker have narrowed your search to two systems, but you've

reached an impasse. Your coworker argues that you should propose the AirCo system because it is the most cost-efficient to install. You, by contrast, want to propose CoolRite because it has the best long-term reliability record.

b. You and two classmates have decided to start a small business to help fund your college education. As part of your planning, you have asked an art student friend to design a logo for you. You have all decided that, above all else, the logo must look professional. Your friend gives you four options to choose from, but you and your business partners cannot agree on an option.

c. It's 9 AM on Tuesday morning, and it doesn't look as if your team paper will be finished and edited to hand in by the 10 AM deadline. When you received the parts from everyone on Monday at 8 PM, you saw many grammatical and formatting errors that you needed to fix. You've been working on the paper all night. Your teammates say, "Just print it out and hand it in. It's good enough—and it's important that the paper be in on time." You say, "We'll get points off for grammar errors—and the paper will only be an hour or so late." Your teammates are getting very angry and feel as though you are holding them hostage, since the edited version of the paper is on your computer. One of your teammates says, "You are such a nit-picky perfectionist. That's what we get for having an English major on our team!"

EXERCISE 13 Select an appropriate management technique

You and a teammate are working on a presentation that will be given at a budget meeting on Monday. On Thursday night, you think the project is far from complete. You'd like the presentation to be as polished as possible, so you suggest to your teammate that you get together over the weekend to finish it. He says that he wants to finish the presentation by Friday because he wants to relax over the weekend. You begin to argue. You know you won't be able to complete the presentation in one day. What is the cause of this conflict and how would you respond?

In a memo to your instructor, explain how you could use each of the following conflict management techniques:

- **Avoid:** How could you avoid dealing with the conflict?
- **Accommodate:** What would you do to accommodate your teammate?
- **Compete:** What would a competitive approach look like?
- **Compromise:** What would a compromise look like?
- **Collaborate:** What would you do to try to collaborate?

Then identify the approach you would recommend and explain your selection.

2.4 How can I improve my communication with people from different cultures? *(pages 46–51)*

EXERCISE 14 Understand how cultures differ

Nonverbal communication differs among cultures. For example, eye contact is important to establish credibility in the United States. However, people in Japan and other Asian cultures often show respect by avoiding direct eye contact. Using an Internet search engine or sources recommended by your instructor, research nonverbal communication in a country or culture other than the United States. (Tip: use the search terms *nonverbal communication* and the name of the country of your choice.) Be prepared to share your findings with the class.

EXERCISE 15 Develop strategies that help you communicate with diverse groups

Imagine you are talking to a group of international business people and in conversation you use one of the following idiomatic phrases (or another one of your choice):

- Drive me up the wall
- Out of sync
- Out of the box
- Threw me for a loop
- That's cool

Your international visitors ask you to explain. How would you explain that phrase? What could you have said instead of that phrase in the first place to be more easily understood?

EXERCISE 16 Intercultural issues
[Related to the Ethics feature on page 50]

As you learned in this chapter, different cultures often have different perceptions about ethical issues, which affect international business interactions. Using your library's online index of business-related publications, find at least two recent articles about instances of bribery between the United States and foreign countries. What companies were involved? How large were the bribes? What was offered in exchange for the bribes? Were either of the companies charged under the Foreign Corrupt Practices Act? Summarize your findings in a paragraph or two. Then use your favorite web searching tool—such as Google or Bing—to find one of the online "Bribe Payers' Indexes." How do the countries in your articles rank on the list? Add this documentation to your summary and be prepared to share your findings in class.

2.5 How can I work effectively as part of a team?
(pages 51–57)

EXERCISE 17 Assemble an effective team

Assume you are the president of your school's student investment club. The provost emailed you to let you know that your group is eligible to apply for a $5,000 grant to support students' travel expenses to attend professional development opportunities, such as conferences and symposiums. You need to submit a three- to five-page proposal that justifies your group's financial need, outlines the potential use of the funds, and demonstrates how your group will benefit. The grant is competitive, and proposals are due in two weeks. You have eight people on your executive board but know that's too many people to collaborate on this project. Select three or four of the following people to help you write the proposal. Justify your selections both in terms of how they would benefit the project as well as how the remaining people would not.

- **Jill Hawthorne, Vice President** – Jill is a junior and has been a member of the group since her freshman year. She will run for president next year. She admits her writing skills are not good, but she is very creative and never misses a meeting.
- **Amber Robinson, Treasurer** – Amber is a senior accounting major. She has been the treasurer for the last two years. She will graduate this semester and has missed the last several meetings because she has been out of town on job interviews.

- **Pilar Seehorn, Secretary** – Pilar is a sophomore. She never says anything during meetings but takes excellent minutes. She writes well and regularly sends emails to the executive board and membership about upcoming events and activities.
- **Michael Anderson, Professional Development** – Michael is a senior, but needs another year to graduate. He arranges all the group's educational activities. He's a self-proclaimed people person and is very outgoing, but he struggles with written assignments.
- **David Miller, Membership** – David is a junior marketing major. He is very creative and outgoing. He managed to increase your group's membership by 50 percent in the last two semesters. He writes well and helped write a similar proposal for a different group last year.
- **Manuel Hernandez, Publicity** – Manuel is a sophomore accounting major. He is new on the executive board, but he attends every meeting, writes well, and is very eager to help the group. He is interested in taking over as treasurer next semester after Amber graduates.
- **Jon Sawyer, Fundraising** – Jon is a junior finance major. With Michael's help, he raised over $1,000 last semester for the group's professional development fund. Jon is very task-oriented, works hard, and writes well. He has already asked if he could help you with the proposal.
- **Sabrina Trotter, Service Learning** – Sabrina is a junior management major. She organizes the club's volunteer activities. With David's help, she has managed to double the level of charitable involvement. She has also asked if she could help you with the proposal.

EXERCISE 18 Agree on team goals and standards

Search the web for "team contract," and find three examples that outline goals and standards for productive working teams. What content do the examples share? What differences exist? Consider a recent team experience that could have benefited from a team contract. What elements from the sample contracts would you recommend? Create an outline of the topics you would include in a team contract for a similar group experience.

EXERCISE 19 Give the team time to develop

Some teams do not advance through all stages of the forming, storming, norming, and performing process. Some teams get stuck in the storming stage and never reach norming, which is the stage where team members work effectively with each other. Other teams work through their conflicts but run out of time before they can effectively perform. Summarize one of your recent team experiences using some (but not all) of the following questions to help you describe the development of your team:

- What was the goal or purpose of the team?
- How was the team formed (for example, assigned or selected)?
- What happened during the forming stage?
- Did the team experience any storming? If so, describe what happened.
- Did your team develop an approach to working together well? If so, what was it? If not, why not?

- Did the team end up accomplishing its goal?
- Would you want to work with that team again?

EXERCISE 20 Develop good leadership

Some people are born leaders. Other people have to work hard to develop good leadership skills. Researchers have investigated leadership styles for decades. As early as 1939, Kurt Lewin identified three major leadership styles—authoritarian (autocratic), participative (democratic), and delegative (laissez-faire).[41] Search the web to learn more about leadership styles and identify one that best represents a leadership style with which you would be comfortable. Document your source, describe the leadership style, and explain how it best fits your personality. Summarize your findings in a few paragraphs.

EXERCISE 21 Plan for effective meetings

Meetings are common—often daily—events for most business people. You may be asked to take minutes at a meeting, either as one of your team assignments or for someone who is not able to attend the meeting. To practice your note-taking skills, watch a half-hour news broadcast, either by a local news station or a national network. Or attend a seminar or workshop offered by your school. Record the important information you hear, and organize content for easy reference. Since you won't have an agenda, you will need to listen (and watch) carefully for major ideas. Create a professional-looking document similar to the sample provided in the chapter. Proofread carefully before submitting your minutes to your instructor.

EXERCISE 22 Be a good team member

For each of the following scenarios, identify the conflict and describe how you would respond. Explain your reasoning.

a. You and four other students have just been assigned to work together on a presentation that will be delivered in three weeks. You are appointed as the team leader. After class, you meet briefly with your team to determine when you can schedule time in the next few days to meet in the library to plan your project. However, a single day and time does not seem to work well for the entire group. Joe, who is already late for his next class, gets impatient and says to go ahead and meet without him. He'll go along with whatever the group decides and walks away. When asked for his contact information, he says, "Don't bother. I'll catch up with you next class."

b. Your group meets later that evening without Joe and assigns tasks to all team members. At the next class session, you tell Joe that the rest of the team members will research the content and that he has been assigned to put the content together in a PowerPoint file and present the summary slide. Joe says, "That's nuts! I'd have to wait to work on the file until the rest of you guys have finished your work, which will probably be the night before the presentation. No way! That's not fair!" You disagree.

c. You agreed to swap assignments with Joe, but he did not send his part of the content to you by the deadline. You call him to ask if you can help, and he says, "Don't worry. I'm working on it now, and I'll bring it to the presentation tomorrow." You tell him that you can't create a summary slide if you don't have his information. He says, "You can work it in tomorrow before class and fake your way through a summary. No problem." You disagree.

d. During your presentation, Joe's part took less than one minute, which meant you had to fill the extra time during the summary to ensure your team met the 10-minute requirement. Although you managed to fake your way through the presentation, you did not feel that you did as well as you could have if Joe had provided his information on time. Back at your seats, Joe says to you, "Great job! We pulled it together. I think we had the best presentation in the class." You disagree.

e. At the next class session, your instructor asks your team to write a one-paragraph assessment of its effectiveness, both in terms of the team's collaborative process and the quality of the presentation. Each team member must sign the assessment. Joe thinks everything was great. You disagree.

WRITING

EXERCISE 23 Analyzing team effectiveness

Select a recent team experience in which you participated, whether for a sport, organization, or class project. In a few paragraphs, describe the team and identify the goal for the activity. Then outline the pros and cons of the experience. Was the team successful? Which benefits of effective teamwork did your group experience? Did conflict occur? What changes may have improved the team's effectiveness?

EXERCISE 24 Selecting web conferencing tools
[Related to the Technology feature on page 56]

Assume your company is looking to invest in a permanent web conferencing system to support communication with your global subsidiaries. Currently, you use basic conference call technology to communicate. Your supervisor, Maury Phillips, specifically thinks a web conferencing tool that allows shared desktop technology among all users would be most effective. Research a company that develops these tools and outline the tools' features in a one-page summary.

EXERCISE 25 Using Google docs for collaboration
[Related to the Technology feature on page 56]

Go to Google docs at www.docs.google.com and create a Google account if you do not already have one. If you are not familiar with the applications, learn about them by watching the video or doing the "try it now" demonstration. Once you are familiar with the applications, create a few sample files—a document, spreadsheet, and presentation—to become familiar with the file creation process. Practice sharing files with others and saving them as web pages. Email your sample documents to your instructor to document your Google docs experience.

COLLABORATING

EXERCISE 26 Improving active listening skills

In groups of four, assign one of these roles to each group member: Speaker, Listener 1, Listener 2, and Observer. Complete the following exercise:

- **Speaker:** Talk for two to three minutes about a problem you faced in a past job search or a concern you have about a future job search.
- **Listeners:** Use clarifying questions and paraphrases to understand the speaker's content, intent, and feelings. Consider nonverbal messages as you paraphrase.
- **Speaker:** After the conversation ends, describe the degree to which you feel satisfied that the paraphrasing represented meaning accurately.
- **Observer:** Point out specific examples of effective and ineffective techniques the listeners used.
- **Listeners:** Discuss how the paraphrasing and questioning felt. Was it difficult? Awkward? Useful in uncovering additional meaning? How did you pick up on nonverbal cues?
- **Each Individual:** Based on what you learned from this exercise, write an email to your instructor explaining the challenges and benefits of active listening. Use examples from the exercise to support your analysis.

Accompanies Exercise 26

EXERCISE 27 Analyzing trigger words

Work with a group of three or four classmates to analyze trigger words. Each person should identify at least two words or phrases that he or she reacts to negatively. Tell your team how you react when you hear the words you suggest. Also try to identify the source of this reaction. Does it result from your upbringing, your past experiences, or an association with a particular person? Summarize your team's discussion and prepare to report to the rest of the class the most interesting insights.

EXERCISE 28 Comparing cultural differences – [Related to the Culture feature on page 35]

Have each person in your team select a different country. Be sure the countries represent a range of geographical regions. Research your selected country to determine the cultural differences, such as customs and body language, that could affect your ability to communicate effectively with people from this country. (Tip: begin your search on the web, using the search terms "doing business in *Country*," or "business etiquette in *Country*," inserting the name of the country you are researching.) Then compare your findings with your teammates. If you were hosting a business meeting with representatives from each country, what factors would you have to consider? As a team, write a memo to your instructor that summarizes your findings.

SPEAKING

EXERCISE 29 Making informal impromptu presentations

For each of the following topics, prepare a five-minute presentation:

a. Identify your collaborative strengths and weaknesses and describe one way you could improve your communication skills to become a better team member.

b. Describe a recent team experience in which your group suffered from an affective conflict. How was the conflict resolved? If it wasn't, how could it have been resolved?

c. Describe a team situation in which your group experienced groupthink. How could it have been avoided?

d. Have you used an electronic collaboration tool that you have found effective? Describe the tool, how you have used it, and why you like it.

EXERCISE 30 Presenting executive briefings

As a team, prepare a five-minute presentation on one of the following topics. Include at least one visual aid.

a. You work for a company in Detroit, Michigan, and the vice president of purchasing is planning a series of teleconferences with business suppliers in various parts of the world: China, Saudi Arabia, Israel, India, and Costa Rica. Each country is in a different time zone. The vice president has asked you to help schedule these meetings. He would like each meeting to take place during the standard workweek for the country and he wants to avoid offending any participants by suggesting a meeting time that conflicts with any weekly or daily religious observations for the dominant religions in these countries: Buddhism, Islam, Judaism, Hinduism, and Christianity. Research the time zones, standard workweek, and days of religious observation in the various countries. Prepare a five-minute briefing for the vice president, proposing a series of meeting times and supporting your proposal with your research. Include at least one visual aid.

b. Your company is considering installing videoconferencing equipment to support meetings between employees in distant locations. However, your manager is concerned that the challenges of videoconferencing will outweigh the benefits. Your manager has asked you to prepare a five-minute presentation outlining some challenges and benefits of videoconferencing, which you will present at the beginning of an executive committee meeting. Prepare that presentation, including at least one visual aid. You can find information about videoconferencing by conducting a web search using combinations of the terms *videoconferencing benefits challenges*. Also try *virtual collaboration*.

c. Your company is considering offering a seminar or workshop in conflict management. You have been asked to research possible courses. Conduct a web search to identify three training seminars in conflict management. Prepare a five-minute executive briefing providing details about the three courses, comparing them in terms of length, content, and cost, and recommending one of them. Include at least one visual aid.

GRAMMAR

Verbs (See Appendix D—Section 1.1.2)

Rekey (or download from mybcommlab.com) the following paragraph, correcting the errors in use or formation of verbs. Underline all your corrections.

If my first boss had ran his businesses the way he answered the phone, he would have went broke long ago. Usually he grabbed the receiver and growls, "Barker." The person at the other end probably thought, "That don't sound like a human, more like a rottweiler." If George Barker was a dog, he would probably be more courteous on the phone. No doubt there was lots of offended customers. The other day he asked my coworker, Jess, and me to stop by his office. He still answered the phone the same way. George's phone offenses amounts to quite a long list. Instead of "barking," there is several other things he could say. "Hello, Barker Contracting" or "This is George Barker" make a better impression.

3 Managing the Communication Process

Analyzing, Composing, Evaluating

online reports
face-to-face
websites
emails
letters
meetings
newsletters
text messages

ANALYZE
COMPOSE
EVALUATE

new hires @ work

Hilary Corna
Senior Executive Officer
Toyota Motor Asia Pacific
Elon University, 2007

"**EVEN IN THE SIMPLE PROCESS OF TYPING AN EMAIL, I FOLLOW A COMMUNICATION PROCESS.** I first identify the purpose of the communication and then consider the audience and the details they need. As I compose the message, I always review and confirm that the key point of the email is clear and I have stated any specific requests I have for the audience. In meetings, I follow a process also. Before speaking, I usually compose a visual in my notes to develop a clear and concise message to avoid any misunderstanding. As I speak, I observe many things to evaluate the merit of my comments. I observe people, their responses, facial expressions, body language, and more. As I've practiced this skill, I almost do it subconsciously now."

Introduction

In the workplace, you will face communication tasks that range from preparing a simple email to planning a complex, hour-long presentation. In this chapter, you will learn a flexible communication process called **ACE**—**A**nalyzing, **C**omposing, and **E**valuating—that you can apply in any situation, no matter how simple or how complex. As FIGURE 3.1 shows, each ACE step plays a unique role in successfully communicating a message.

Analyzing "sets the stage" for your business message and helps you make good decisions. Before you begin to compose, analyze four important elements. First, determine your **purpose**—the reason why you are communicating and the outcome you want to achieve. Second, analyze your **audience**—the recipients of your communication. Who are they and what are their concerns and interests? Third, determine the **content** they need—the specific information to include—which is the substance of your message. Do you have all the content you need? If not, where will you find it? Fourth, determine the best **medium**—how you will deliver your message—by analyzing your options. Should you communicate by telephone, face-to-face meeting, email, letter, text message, website, or some other option? Taking the time to analyze these four elements will help you complete the second ACE step: composing.

Composing involves more than putting words on the page or speaking them aloud. It is a multi-step process. The first step is to use what you learned while analyzing to plan your message. Determine what content you will include and how you will organize it to ensure that the message flows logically and makes sense from your audience's perspective. Once you have this plan in place, you are better able to draft your message and format it with appropriate paragraphs and headings so that your audience finds important ideas.

Evaluating is the process of reviewing your message on multiple levels. First, determine if you have included the content necessary to achieve your goal and have organized it well. Next, evaluate whether the word usage and style are professional and effective. Finally, consider whether the format makes the document easy to read and communicates a professional image. As part of the evaluating process, share your draft with others to get feedback. Reviewing your message and considering feedback may lead you to return to the first step of the process—analyzing—to reconsider the decisions you made about purpose, audience, content, and medium. This circular approach helps ensure effective communication.

At first, you may be concerned that following these steps will be time consuming and unnecessary. However, as with any other skill, once you learn the steps and they become familiar, you will get more consistent results with less effort. In the sections that follow, we take a closer look at each step in the ACE process.

FIGURE 3.1 The ACE Communication Process

Why should I spend time analyzing?

Many people fail to communicate effectively because they do not think about what they want their message to accomplish and how they want their audience to respond. Instead, they jump ahead to composing the message. This section describes four important elements you should analyze before you start to compose: *purpose*, *audience*, *content requirements*, and *medium*. Analyzing each element serves a distinct purpose.

Analyzing the purpose focuses the message

Before thinking about *what* you are communicating, analyze *why* you are communicating. Think about "why" from two points of view: (1) what is your purpose for communicating, and (2) what is the outcome you would like to achieve?

What is my purpose?

Every business message has a purpose:

- *inform* employees of a workshop
- *persuade* a customer to purchase a product
- *report* financial information
- *analyze* which proposal to accept
- *propose* a solution to the problem of increased shipping

All of these messages must also create or maintain **goodwill**, a positive relationship between you (or your company) and the audience.

What outcome would I like to achieve?

Purpose statements alone are too general to help you think strategically about the best content to use. As part of your analysis, also identify your desired **outcome**, what you want your audience to know or do as a result of the communication. FIGURE 3.2 compares three purpose statements and related outcome statements.

PURPOSE	DESIRED OUTCOME
To inform my client that I cannot take on a new project right now.	My client will postpone the project rather than hire someone else to do it.
To persuade my supervisor to support a plan to implement flexible summer hours.	My supervisor will present the plan to upper management.
To ask my supervisor for an extension on an assignment deadline.	My supervisor will let me submit the assignment on Monday so I can finish it over the weekend.

Keeping your purpose and desired outcome in mind as you write your message helps you evaluate whether your content supports your goal. For example, consider how you would address the first item in Figure 3.2. If you think about only your general purpose, you might draft a message that thanks the client for his interest, explains that you cannot take on the project right now because you are fully booked, and concludes with a goodwill statement about looking forward to future opportunities. However, if you think about your desired outcome, you may decide that you do not want to lose the project or the client. How can you persuade the client to postpone the project? What will you say to the client if he cannot postpone the project? How will you persuade the client to return to your company for future projects? Thinking about outcome often helps you refine your purpose and your content. Consider the revision in FIGURE 3.3, which achieves the purpose and the desired outcome.

DRAFT	REVISION
PURPOSE: *To inform my client that I cannot take on a new project right now.*	**DESIRED OUTCOME:** *My client will postpone the project rather than hire someone else to do it.*
Thank you for contacting us. We are fully booked right now and cannot meet your schedule. We are grateful that you thought of us and look forward to working with you in the future.	Thank you for contacting us about your new project. We would like to help you with this project, and are confident we can do a fast and outstanding job since we have worked with you so closely in the past. However, we are fully booked until June.
	If you are able to postpone your project for six weeks, we can provide you with our top marketing team and will be glad to extend a 10% discount over our regular fees.

new hires @ work

Dylan Alperin

Global Supply Chain Rotational Associate

Colgate-Palmolive Company

University of Tennessee, 2009

"When I choose a method to communicate, I think about how disruptive my communication will be: is it best to physically go to my audience's office, telephone, email, or IM?"

FIGURE 3.2

Examples of Purpose and Outcome Statements

Analyzing The process of looking critically at four elements of your message: purpose, audience, content, and medium.

Purpose The reason why you are communicating and the outcome you want to achieve.

Audience The recipients of your communication.

Content The substance of your message.

Medium The method you use to deliver your message (for example, telephone, face-to-face meeting, email, letter, text message, or website).

Composing The multi-step process of producing content, organizing it so that it is understandable from the audience's perspective, putting it into coherent sentences and logical paragraphs, and then designing a format or delivery approach that is professional and makes the communication easy to follow.

Evaluating The process of reviewing your communication to ensure it is complete, clear, concise, easy to understand, and error-free.

Goodwill The positive relationship between you (or your company) and your audience.

Outcome What you want your audience to know or do as a result of the communication.

FIGURE 3.3

Achieving a Desired Outcome

FIGURE 3.4 Informational Message—No Persuasion Needed

Will the outcome require persuasion?

At this early stage of analysis, you will find it useful to consider whether achieving your outcome will require simply providing information or if it will also require some persuasion. **Persuasion** is the ability to influence an audience to agree with your point of view, accept your recommendation, or grant your request.

If your communication is purely informative, no persuasion is necessary. For example, an email to all department employees about a room change for a meeting simply needs to provide clear and complete information as shown in FIGURE 3.4 (left). Other examples of informational messages include meeting minutes, instructions, and progress reports.

However, many business messages require a persuasive approach. They need to influence a recipient either to agree with an idea or to take action. For example, assume you want to convince your supervisor, Cherilyn Martins, to implement a summer-hours work schedule for your department. Your standard workday hours begin at 9 AM and end at 5 PM. A flexible summer-hours schedule would allow employees to begin and end an hour earlier so that they can take advantage of the increased daylight and warmer weather during the summer. You propose that your department's workday hours begin at 8 AM between June 1 and August 31. Because you want to motivate action, this message clearly needs to be persuasive. FIGURE 3.5 shows your purpose statement and desired outcome statement. With this desired outcome in mind, you can analyze the audience to get a clearer idea of how you can influence them and achieve this outcome.

FIGURE 3.5 Sample Purpose and Outcome Statements

PURPOSE	DESIRED OUTCOME
To persuade my supervisor to approve a summer-hours work schedule.	My supervisor will support the proposal and believe it is in the best interest of the department to adopt the plan. She will forward the proposal to upper management and request a meeting to discuss it, with the goal of having the proposal accepted in time to implement for the summer.

Analyzing the audience helps you meet their needs

Analyzing your audience helps you determine specific content to include. Messages often have both primary and secondary audiences. Your **primary audience** is the direct recipient of your message, in other words, the person or people to whom your message is addressed. Your **secondary audience** is anyone else who may receive a copy of your message (or hear about it), either from you or from the primary audience. For example, if you email your supervisor about incorporating a flexible summer-hours schedule and she likes the idea, she may forward your message to the vice president of operations. Although you planned your message for your supervisor—the primary audience—the vice president becomes a secondary audience.

Once you have identified your audience, consider the questions listed in FIGURE 3.6 to determine what content to include as well as how and when to deliver the message. The answers in the figure relate to the summer-hours work schedule scenario.

To be persuasive, it is important to analyze **audience benefits**—advantages the recipient gains from agreeing with or acting on your message. People are more likely to go along with what you propose if they understand the advantages they—or the business—will gain from granting your request.

Unfortunately, people who are trying to persuade others often make the mistake of emphasizing their own benefits. Focusing on the benefits to you is easy. For example, by implementing a summer-hours schedule, you get to leave work an hour

---

1. **What does the primary and secondary audience already know?**

   My primary audience already knows about the structure of our current workday, so I do not need to explain that.

2. **What information does the audience need to know—and why?**

   My supervisor and upper management need to know what I mean by "summer hours," how summer hours will work in our department, and how the change will affect the productivity of the department during the summer months.

3. **When does the audience need this information?**

   My supervisor needs the information soon so we can gain support from upper management in time to implement the change for the coming summer.

4. **How will the audience react to this information?**

   I don't know how my supervisor or upper management will react, so I will try to anticipate potential problems and provide solutions.

If the purpose is primarily persuasive, also consider these questions:

5. **What questions or objections will my audience have?**

   My audience may ask these questions:

   - How will we ensure that someone is available to answer phone calls after 4 PM if all employees ask to start and end their day earlier?

   - When workdays begin and end earlier, will we have to rearrange lunch hours and breaks? How will we handle that?

   - Will there be additional costs?

   - Has this plan worked well in other departments or companies?

   - Will anyone think this schedule is unfair?

   - Is there any evidence to support the benefits?

6. **How will my audience benefit from my idea or proposal?**

   - Providing flexible summer hours may improve employee morale, which may lead to other benefits, such as reduced employee turnover rates, increased employee productivity, and increased quarterly sales figures.

   - Providing flexible summer hours may improve employees' perceptions of the supervisor.

FIGURE 3.6
Audience Analysis Questions

---

earlier each day. You have more time to enjoy outdoor activities, family, and friends. Further, if you have the option to choose summer hours or regular hours each day, you can take advantage of the flexibility to schedule your work hours to meet your own needs. These outcomes are good for you, but they do not suggest any benefits for your supervisor or company. Therefore, they are not likely to persuade your audience.

The challenge is to determine audience-focused benefits, like those listed in Figure 3.6, item 6, and then select the ones that will be most effective. You would certainly want to stress that a flexible summer schedule will improve morale, reduce turnover rates, and increase productivity. However, you may choose to leave out the other potential benefits. It will be hard to prove that quarterly sales figures will increase, and it would be unwise to suggest that summer hours will improve employees' perceptions of your supervisor. Although your supervisor may find this a valid reason to change the work schedule, your secondary audience—the vice president—may not.

Persuasion The ability to influence your audience to agree with your point of view, accept your recommendation, or grant your request.

Primary audience The person or people to whom your message is addressed.

Secondary audience People other than the primary audience who may receive a copy or hear about your message.

Audience benefits Advantages the recipient gains from agreeing with or acting on your message.

Analyzing the content ensures a complete message

In addition to analyzing your purpose and audience, you also need to analyze your content requirements. Do you know enough about the topic or situation to compose your message? Do you have enough data to support your main ideas? Or do you need to do additional research?

For example, assume you have identified the list of potential benefits for a summer hours plan illustrated in **Figure 3.6**, as well as the list of questions your supervisor may ask. Before composing, you will need to gather the required information. You may be able to get it from *internal sources* such as company reports, databases, and experts. Or you may have to consult *external sources* such as industry journals, web-based search tools, or experts outside your company. The following research would provide you with strong content.

- To learn whether other departments in the company have implemented summer hours, you will need to consult internal sources. You may call or email other managers, contact your human resources office, or research the company's employee handbook.
- To learn whether employees will support the summer schedule or think it is unfair, you may need to survey employees.
- To learn whether other companies have found a summer-hours schedule to provide tangible benefits, such as increased productivity, you would need to search external sources. You could conduct **primary research**, which involves collecting your own original data. For example, you may call the human resources departments of other local companies. A more efficient method might be to look in libraries or online sources for **secondary research**, which is information other people have collected. An article by the Society for Human Resource Management titled "Workplace Flexibility has Bottom-Line Implications" may be helpful because it suggests a benefit of flextime: employees who have the option of flexible schedules have fewer sickness-related absences.[1]

You may decide to postpone some of this time-consuming research until you learn whether your supervisor is receptive to the idea of summer work hours. However, your initial communication with your supervisor will be stronger if you can communicate that you have done at least a little research and have objective support for your proposal. More detailed information about finding and evaluating sources is available in Chapter 7.

Analyzing the medium helps you choose the best delivery option

You can use several methods to communicate a message. For example, you could send an email, write a text message, have a face-to-face conversation, or publish your message through a social media site. FIGURE 3.7 lists many common methods of communication and identifies the advantages and disadvantages of each.

Making a good choice about the best medium to use is challenging. For example, if you need to send detailed financial data to your supervisor, you might choose to present that information in a spreadsheet and attach it to an email that summarizes the data. However, if the spreadsheet requires a more detailed explanation, a face-to-face meeting might be more effective. As new mediums develop, the choices become even more challenging, and people find uses for new communication technology. For example, a *blog* can be used to begin a discussion within the department about summer hours. If management is concerned that employees will think summer hours are unfair, a blog discussion can provide insight into employees' real feelings and give people a chance to express their points of view.

Primary research Collecting your own original data.

Secondary research Searching published reports, articles, and books for information other people have collected.

FIGURE 3.7 Selecting the Best Medium to Communicate Your Message

MEDIUM	ADVANTAGES	DISADVANTAGES
Face-to-Face *(one-to-one conversation)*	• Allows personal explanation targeted to an individual • Provides for immediate feedback	• Is not efficient for disseminating information to many people • Is not usually permanently documented (recorded)
Meeting *(several people)*	• Disseminates information to many people • Provides for immediate feedback • Is documented by minutes	• Can be difficult to schedule • Is time consuming—takes employees away from assigned duties
Telephone	• Allows personal explanation targeted to an individual • Allows short messages to be delivered via voice mail if individuals are not at their desks • Can provide for immediate feedback if the person answers the phone	• Is time consuming if individual calls need to be made to several people • Is not usually permanently documented (recorded)
Text Message, Instant Message	• Allows quick communication • Creates a permanent record (if saved)	• Is not efficient if message is long, complex, or sensitive • Does not ensure immediate feedback
Email	• Allows quick communication • Disseminates information to one or many people • Creates a permanent record if saved or printed	• May not be a private and secure medium for sending sensitive content • Does not ensure immediate feedback because not everyone checks email regularly
Memo *(printed hardcopy to audiences within the organization)*	• Can accompany original documents or forms that need signatures • Can be used for employees who have no access to email • Creates a permanent record	• Incurs costs to copy to many people • Is delivered more slowly than email • Does not provide for immediate feedback
Letter *(printed on letterhead and sent to audiences outside the organization)*	• Projects a more "official" or formal image than email • Can accompany original documents, such as forms with signatures • Creates a permanent record	• Incurs cost of letterhead and postage • Takes at least a day to deliver • Does not provide for immediate feedback
Newsletter *(printed hardcopy, html-designed email, or attachment)*	• Disseminates a lot of information to many people simultaneously • Creates a permanent record	• Incurs cost to copy and distribute by mail • Does not provide for immediate feedback
Website	• Makes information available to anyone with access • Can be password protected to limit access • Enables combinations of text, video, and audio through podcasts, MP3 files, webcasts, webinars, and web-conferencing tools • Is easy to keep up to date • May provide for feedback (wikis)	• Is not effective with audiences who have limited Internet access • Requires the audience to access the site • May not reach the audience • Does not provide for immediate feedback • May not provide a permanent record, unless web files are archived
Social Media: Networking Websites *(for example, Facebook, LinkedIn)*	• Allows you to communicate to a community of people who have linked with you and expressed an interest • Allows interactive communication • Is easy to keep up to date	• Requires the audience to access the site • May not reach the audience • May reach unintended audiences
Social Media: Wikis, Blogs, and Microblogs *(like Twitter)*	• Broadcasts short messaging bursts through micro-blogging tools such as Twitter and other SMS applications • Encourages discussion • Is easy to keep up to date • Allows interactive communication • Provides a complete record	• Is not effective with audiences who have limited Internet access • Requires the audience to access the site or actively request messages be sent to them • May not reach the audience

ETHICS How to Handle Information That Conflicts with Your Position

Inexperienced communicators often make the mistake of looking for content that supports their own point of view, rather than looking for content that provides a complete picture. As an ethical business communicator, you have the responsibility to provide information that allows your audience to make good business decisions—even if that information conflicts with your own ideas.

Suppose that you used an online database to find sources of information about flexible work hours. Your search results include positive information from a nonprofit workforce newsletter and two independent news agencies. You select information from each source to prepare a short email report intended to persuade your supervisor to adopt flexible summer hours. However, suppose you also find a source that suggests that implementing a summer-hours work schedule allows some employees to take advantage of the flexibility in inappropriate ways, such as both arriving to work late and leaving early. Should you include this information or ignore it because it will weaken your point?

If you fail to address relevant information that contradicts your point of view, you are committing an ethical error of omission. Instead of ignoring that information, analyze it. Is it strong enough to make you modify your point of view? Is it weak enough that you can argue against it? Does it bring up a problem that you can solve? The most ethical approach is to report the information, cite the source, and then provide a solution to the problem the source raises. For example, you could suggest that the company implement a reporting process that documents employees' actual work hours. By addressing potentially negative information, you demonstrate your integrity as a business communicator, as well as your ability to think critically and solve problems. ■

mybcommlab

For an ETHICS exercise, go to Critical Thinking on page 101 or to this chapter's End-of-Chapter Exercises at mybcommlab.com.

Study Question 3.2

What is involved in composing?

■ Access this chapter's simulation entitled The Communication Process, located at mybcommlab.com.

Composing involves more than just putting words on a page or speaking spontaneously during business meetings or presentations. Composing includes organizing the content so that it is understandable from the audience's perspective, putting that content into coherent sentences and logical paragraphs, and then designing a format or medium that is professional and makes the communication easy to follow.

Composing is certainly easier if you have effectively analyzed your communication situation before sitting down to write. However, even a simple and well-planned message benefits from at least two drafts. The first draft allows you to get your thoughts on paper. The second draft allows you to refine your thoughts and pay more attention to evaluating the language and grammar. More complex messages may require more drafts to make the message complete, clear, and persuasive. This section helps you think through some key elements of the composing process: deciding where and when to compose, organizing the message, drafting the message, and designing a professional format and delivery.

Deciding where and when to compose

When you write a short email or plan a brief telephone call, you may not need to pay much attention to your environment. However, when you are preparing a complex report or presentation, you'll benefit from making good decisions about where and when to compose.

First, identify what kind of composing environment is comfortable for you. Avoid areas where you find it difficult to focus. Some writers like a quiet location with few distractions. Others prefer to work with background noise, such as soft music or the sounds of a crowded coffee shop. At work you may not have the option to write anywhere except in your office, so create an environment that helps you focus on your writing.

Next, plan how you will handle interruptions and distractions. If your telephone rings, will you answer it instead of focusing on your task? If someone stops by your office or desk, will you stop to chat? If you get bored, will you be tempted to check email or work on something else? You can be more successful at composing if you take control of your environment and plan how to get the work done.

Finally, estimate how much time you will need to compose and decide how to manage that time. For example, if you will be making a brief presentation to a new client, you might decide to allocate four hours to prepare for the meeting. While you may be tempted to leave the task to the morning of the meeting, you could also divide the four hours differently. You could spend two hours preparing your presentation on one day and then rehearse the presentation in front of a friend or colleague the next day. Based on the feedback you receive, you can then spend the final hour developing your ideas and refining your approach.

Planning your composing time is even more important when you prepare a long document or presentation. These messages take more time to analyze, compose, and evaluate. Although estimating how much time you need may be difficult at first, you may find it useful to estimate at least an hour per page and work backwards from your document's due date. For example, assume you have collected and organized the data needed to write a five-page report due in 10 days. To compose a quality product, spend one or two hours a day writing, and take a day off from writing now and then. This expanded process takes no more time than cramming five hours into the day before the deadline. However, it ensures you have a fresh perspective every day and helps you use your time in a more constructive way. Just as exercising for long periods is more taxing than exercising in short bursts, working your brain for an extended period is also more stressful. A more effective composing process will result in a more effective communication.

Organizing the message

Composing is much faster and more effective if you begin with an organizational plan that addresses at least two issues: What is the overall organization of the communication? Where will you state your main point?

What is the overall organization of the communication?

Every email, letter, report, or presentation you prepare needs an organization that is logical and easy for your audience to follow. *Outlining* is an all-purpose organizing tool that can help you plan this organization. An outline allows you to break a topic into major ideas and supporting details and then list that content in the order you will present it. For example, assume you researched information about summer-hours schedules and need to put together a report for your supervisor. FIGURE 3.8 illustrates a traditional outline format for a long document, such as a report or proposal that may require several heading levels with multiple points under each topic.

Not every outline needs to be elaborate. You do not need a detailed traditional outline format for brief messages, such as emails or short presentations at meetings. As FIGURE 3.9(A) illustrates, outlining a short informative email message may require only a few bullet points. Each bullet point will become a short paragraph in the email. Outlining the content for a short discussion during a meeting may require just a list of questions you will answer, like that illustrated in FIGURE 3.9(B).

FIGURE 3.8 Traditional Outline

`outline`

Outline: Proposal for Summer-Hours Work Schedule

PURPOSE: To propose that ABC Communications' Sales Department adopt a summer-hours work schedule between June 1 and August 31.

Introduction
- Statement of problem
- Proposed solution

Detailed Description of Proposed Summer-Hours Work Schedule
- Flextime options emphasizing core workday hours
- Suggested policies to ensure balanced staffing

Benefits (documented by primary and secondary research)
- Increased employee morale
- Reduced employee turnover rates
- Increased employee productivity

Implementation Plan
- Survey employees to assess flextime preferences
- Develop policies and procedures
- Create an assessment plan

FIGURE 3.9
Short Outlines

(A) NOTES FOR PLANNING AN EMAIL	(B) OUTLINE FOR DISCUSSION AT A MEETING
Notes for Email to Cherilyn SUBJECT: Update on Summer-Hours Schedule Proposal - Ask for feedback on attached rough draft - Briefly explain research gathered to date - Outline information to be included - Thank her for taking time to provide input	Overview of Summer-Hours Schedule Proposal 1. What is a flexible summer-hours schedule? 2. How will the company benefit from the schedule? 3. How will we avoid/overcome potential problems? 4. When/how will we implement the schedule? 5. How will we assess the schedule's effectiveness?

Finally, if you are a visual thinker, you might organize your communication using a *tree chart*, like that in FIGURE 3.10, which lets you see the hierarchical structure and connections between your ideas.

FIGURE 3.10 Tree Chart Outline

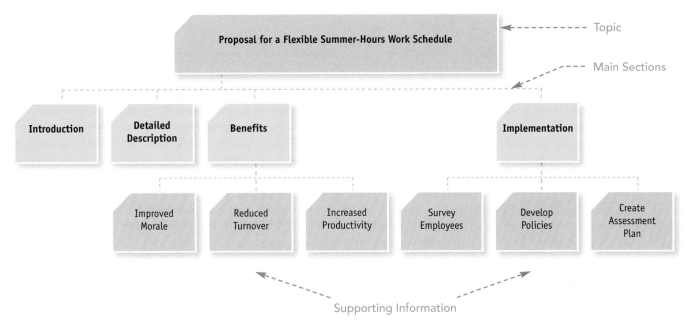

Where should I state the main point—at the beginning or the end?

After you plan the overall organization of your communication, consider where you want to place the main idea. Do you want to state it directly at the beginning of the communication, or do you want to be indirect by building up to the point and placing it near the end of the message?

In most situations, audiences will become impatient if they don't know why you are communicating with them and how the details support your message. To avoid this problem, skilled business communicators use a **direct organizational plan** by stating the purpose and main idea of their message before the supporting details. The direct plan eases the job of the audience. Once readers and listeners understand the main idea of your message, they can more easily follow your line of reasoning. The direct organizational plan follows this sequence:

❶ Present the main idea of the message in the first paragraph, or in the beginning of a long document.
❷ Provide supporting information and related details in the middle paragraph(s).
❸ Conclude the message with a call to action, any applicable deadlines, and contact information.

However, in certain circumstances, you may want to use an **indirect organizational plan**— stating the main idea after supporting information and related details. The indirect approach may be effective when you are communicating negative news to people who will not expect it, when you anticipate that your audience will be resistant, or when you need to provide explanation before your main point makes sense. The indirect organizational plan follows this sequence:

❶ Open with a general statement about the topic that usually indicates the purpose.
❷ Provide supporting information and related details in the middle paragraph(s).
❸ Present the main idea of the message after the supporting details.
❹ Conclude the message with a call to action, any applicable deadlines, and contact information.

FIGURE 3.11 demonstrates the differences between the direct and indirect approaches to communicate research on flexible summer hours. Imagine that you presented the summer-hours proposal to your supervisor in a meeting and she requested that you email her

Direct organizational plan Stating the purpose and main idea of the message before the supporting details.

Indirect organizational plan Stating the purpose and main idea of the message after the supporting details.

FIGURE 3.11 Direct and Indirect Organizational Plans

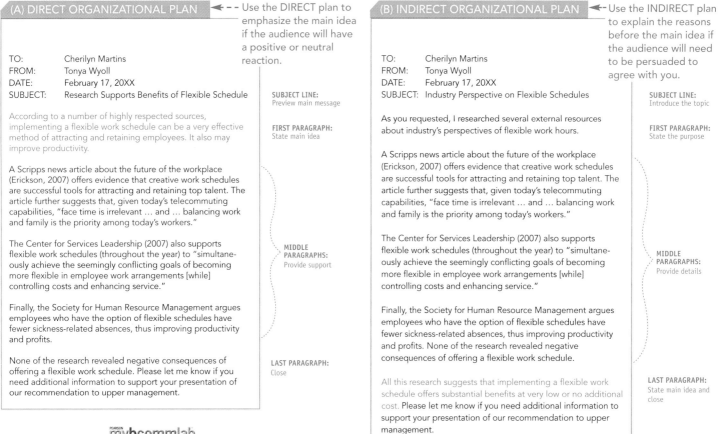

some follow-up research to provide an industry perspective of the advantages and disadvantages of summer hours. If your supervisor appeared to favor your proposal, you might organize your email directly, as in FIGURE 3.11(A), with the main idea at the beginning of the document. However, if your supervisor was very skeptical about your proposal, you might organize your email indirectly, as in FIGURE 3.11(B), with the main idea appearing after the supporting details. Also note the difference in the **subject line**—the line at the top of the email that communicates what the message is about and influences whether the audience will open the message. In the direct approach, the subject line previews the main message of the email. In the indirect approach, the subject line is more neutral and just indicates the purpose and topic. Because the audience is expecting the email, the subject line does not need to be more explicit about how it relates to the audience.

Drafting the content

Once you have an organizational plan, the next composing step is to draft your message. **Drafting** is a creative process. If you are writing, drafting involves getting the information on paper (or the computer screen). If you are speaking, it means saying your message aloud or in your head so that you can hear it and evaluate it. Using your outline as a guide, you can begin to draft with a degree of freedom knowing that your first draft will not be your final product.

Untrained writers often create barriers to their creativity and slow the drafting process by stopping frequently to evaluate what they have written before finishing their thoughts. If you feel a sentence has to be perfect before you begin the next sentence, you suffer from the *perfectionist syndrome*. The best method for dealing with this problem is to ignore the editor in your brain while you write and focus on getting words on the page without evaluating them. Assuming you have given yourself sufficient time to write, you will be able to revise your message after you compose. Switching between drafting and revising is inefficient because the two activities require very different mental processes. In contrast to the creative process of drafting, **revising** is a logical process that involves evaluating the effectiveness of your message in relation to your audience and purpose, and then making changes in content, organization, or wording, as necessary. You can be more creative in your drafting and more logical in your revising if you separate the activities.

A second barrier that many writers face at the drafting stage is **writer's block**: an inability to begin or continue writing. Symptoms include staring at a blank page or a blank computer monitor without a clue of how to begin. This inability to write is often a result of procrastination or impatience. If you wait until the last minute to work on an assignment, the stress of the coming deadline can block your creative writing skills. Although using the ACE process will help reduce the problem, you may still experience moments when you cannot think of what to say. When this happens, you can try several techniques to unblock your thoughts.

One technique to overcome writer's block is *free writing:* writing down anything that comes to mind regardless of whether it is appropriate or even meaningful. The result is that you will create some content that is usable for your message, even if you won't use all of it. See FIGURE 3.12 for an example of free writing.

FIGURE 3.12
Example of Free Writing

> Okay … I need to start the introduction of this report with a statement of the problem and the purpose of the report. There really wasn't a serious problem, but the summer-hours plan sounded like a good idea to me. A friend told me about it at his company, I mentioned it to some colleagues here, and they thought I should recommend it. So what's the problem? Well, low morale could be contributing to our typical third-quarter sales slump. The summer numbers are always the lowest each year. I can document this with the data I collected from the last 10 years. But since I found that data *after* I started the research, it shouldn't really be the problem we're trying to solve, just a possible benefit of the schedule. So the summer flex hours could be a solution that boosts morale and productivity thereby potentially increasing third-quarter sales. If I start with that in the introduction and document support with findings from sources in the middle, I could close with assessment recommendations that evaluate both morale and sales.

Review your free writing results to determine which points you want to include, and then highlight or copy those points into a second document. Don't be too quick to delete all your text from your free-writing experience because you may change your mind and need to refer to your thought process again.

A second technique to avoid writer's block is *thinking aloud*, which is similar to free writing except that you speak rather than write. If you don't write or type quickly, thinking aloud helps get your ideas "out in the air." Some writers find it useful to record their thoughts, play back the recording, and then type the most important points they hear. In fact, writers who struggle with awkward wording when they write often find recording their thoughts to be an effective way to ensure that their business writing has a conversational tone.

Finally, one of the fastest ways to overcome writer's block is to write the easiest parts first. Using a word processing program to compose allows you to begin your draft at any point in the document. You can easily cut and paste or insert text throughout the writing and evaluating process. Most writers find that once they have some words on the page, the rest of the content more easily falls into place.

Designing a professional format and delivery

After you have composed your message, arrange it into a professional format that is easy to read and understand. A document's format plays a role similar to your dress and behavior in face-to-face communication. If the style looks professional, then it communicates to an audience that you are professional. If the format is difficult to read or confusing, then it undermines your credibility.

Although the specific techniques you use for designing your communication will depend on the medium you choose for the message, some consistent design principles apply to all media. For example, good business communicators:

- start with a purpose-driven introduction
- break their message into short chunks (paragraphs)

Subject line The line at the top of an email that communicates what the message is about and influences whether the audience will open the message.

Drafting A creative process that involves getting information on the paper or computer screen before revising and editing it.

Revising A logical process that involves evaluating the effectiveness of your message in relation to your audience and purpose and then making changes in content, organization, or wording, as necessary.

Writer's block An inability to begin or continue writing.

- begin each paragraph with a strong **topic sentence** that identifies the main point or overall idea of the paragraph
- signal shifts in content by using headings or words such as "first" and "second"
- use parallel bullet lists for easy comprehension and skimming
- end with a specific conclusion or recommendation

The following sections give examples of professional formats for email messages, memos, letters, and voice mail messages. Other chapters will discuss methods of creating professional formats for longer, more complex documents, such as reports and presentations. A comprehensive formatting guide is available in Appendix B: Business Document Formatting Guide and online at mybcommlab.com.

Email messages

Business email messages should focus on only one topic, which should be clearly identified in the subject line. However, one topic does not mean the message should contain only one paragraph. Consider the two versions of the email message in FIGURE 3.13. Both versions contain the same information—the subject line and sentences are identical. However, the design is very different. Examine the layout. Which one looks more readable? Which one looks better organized? Which one looks more professional?

FIGURE 3.13 Poorly vs. Professionally Designed Email Messages

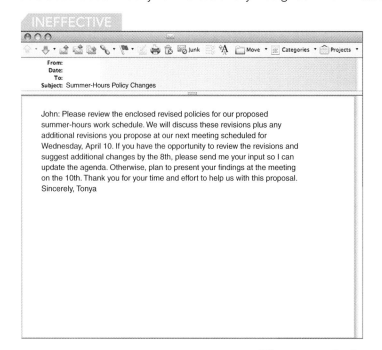
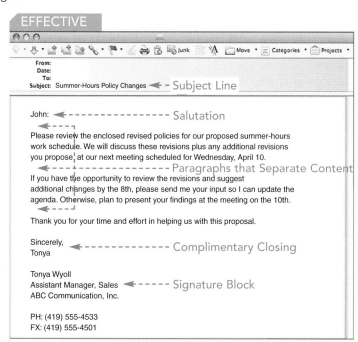

When you write longer emails, you can enhance the organization and design even further by using three important techniques:

- Begin with a focused first paragraph that identifies your purpose and previews your content. Strong first paragraphs are increasingly important as more people read emails on mobile devices with small screens. Those readers appreciate getting the core of the message without having to scroll repeatedly.
- Use **topic-specific headings**, section or paragraph titles that are short but include a key idea. For example, instead of using a generic heading like "Benefits," compose a topic-specific heading such as "Benefits of a Flexible Summer Schedule" that helps the audience understand the content of the paragraph.
- Format important lists vertically, as **bullet point lists**, with each item preceded by a dot or other simple shape. The content you are reading now is part of a bullet point list. Notice that the listed items are grammatically parallel. In other words, they each have the same grammatical structure. In this list, each item begins with a verb.

The email in FIGURE 3.14 illustrates all three techniques.

FIGURE 3.14 Email with Focused Opening, Topic-Specific Headings, and Bullet Points

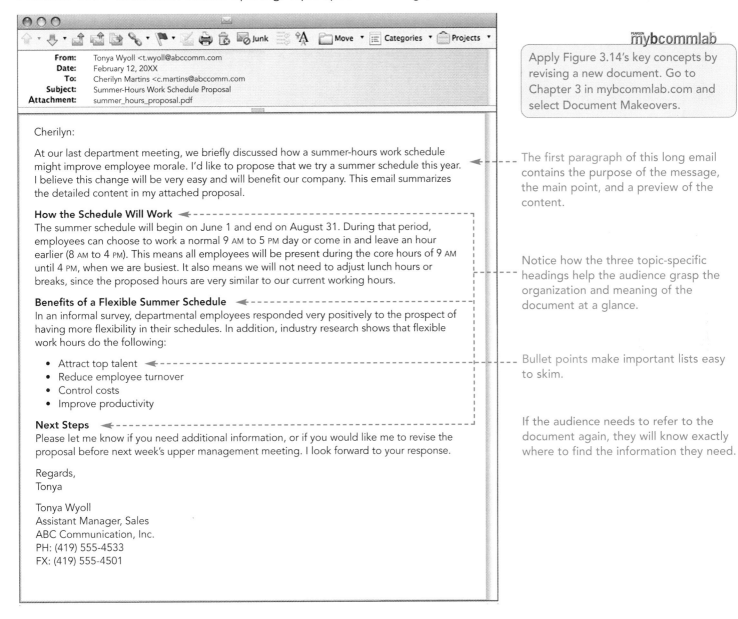

The first paragraph of this long email contains the purpose of the message, the main point, and a preview of the content.

Notice how the three topic-specific headings help the audience grasp the organization and meaning of the document at a glance.

Bullet points make important lists easy to skim.

If the audience needs to refer to the document again, they will know exactly where to find the information they need.

Memos

Memos are hardcopy documents typically sent to **internal audiences**, people within your organization. Before email existed, organizations frequently relied on memos for internal communication. Today, you are likely to see memos only in specialized situations—for example, accompanying documents that cannot be sent electronically, such as booklets, pamphlets, or contracts and legal documents that require signatures. You may also see people producing memo reports if they have important information that is too long for a typical email message but too short for a formal report with a title page and table of contents.

FIGURE 3.15 provides a memo version of the email message in FIGURE 3.14. As this figure illustrates, memos have a lot in common with emails. The standard headings in memos—to, from, date, and subject—are similar to those displayed in email messages that you receive. However, the order and alignment are standardized and may differ from the order used in your email application. In addition, like emails, memos should use an effective subject line, be restricted to one topic, use short paragraphs, and use headings to make the document easier to skim.

Memos differ structurally from emails in three key ways. First, memos do not include a salutation, like "Hello, John" or "Dear Cleo." Second, memos do not include

Topic sentence Sentence that identifies the main point or overall idea of the paragraph. Most frequently, it is the first sentence in a paragraph.

Topic-specific headings Section or paragraph titles that are short but include key ideas. They are often in the form of a short sentence and include a verb.

Bullet point list A vertically formatted list, with each item preceded by a dot or other simple shape.

Memos Hardcopy documents, following a set format, typically sent to internal audiences.

Internal audiences People with whom you communicate inside your organization.

FIGURE 3.15 Memo Format

Memo headings follow a standard order. The words following the colons are aligned.

Memos include no salutation ┄┄┄┄┄┄┄┄┄┄►

Paragraph structure for memos is identical to that for emails.

Memos do not include a complimentary closing or signature block. The attachment notation draws the audience's attention to the supporting document.

memo

TO: Ms. Cherilyn Martins, Vice President, Sales
FROM: Ms. Tonya Wyoll, Assistant Manager, Sales
DATE: February 12, 20XX
SUBJECT: Summer-Hours Work Schedule Proposal

At our last department meeting, we briefly discussed how a summer-hours work schedule might improve employee morale. I'd like to propose that we try a summer schedule this year. I believe this change will be very easy and will benefit our company. This memo summarizes the content in my detailed proposal, which is attached.

How the Schedule Will Work
The summer schedule will begin on June 1 and end on August 31. During that period, employees can choose to work a normal 9 AM to 5 PM day or come in and leave an hour earlier (8 AM to 4 PM). This means all employees will be present during the core hours of 9 AM until 4 PM, when we are busiest. It also means we will not need to adjust lunch hours or breaks, since the proposed hours are very similar to our current working hours.

Benefits of a Flexible Summer Schedule
In an informal survey, departmental employees responded very positively to the prospect of having more flexibility in their schedules. In addition, industry research shows that flexible work hours do the following:
- Attract top talent
- Reduce employee turnover
- Control costs
- Improve productivity

Next Steps
Please let me know if you need additional information, or if you would like me to revise the proposal before next week's upper management meeting. I look forward to your response.

Attachment

complimentary closings and signatures at the end, like "Sincerely, Jeff" or "Best regards, Sanjay." The "To" and "From" lines at the top of the memo are the only parts that identify the recipient and sender. Finally, memos are often longer than the recommended length for emails. Memos can be several pages long when they are used to communicate detailed information such as new procedures or changes in policy. That is why you will sometimes see people write a long document in memo form and attach it to an email as an alternative to writing a long email.

In longer memos, as with longer emails, topic-specific headings help organize the reading experience. In some memos or memo reports, you may decide to use headings composed as questions. If you created a question outline (like FIGURE 3.9(B) on page 80), you can simply transfer those questions from your outline to your memo report. For more detailed advice on formatting memos, see Appendix B or visit mybcommlab.com.

Letters

In contrast to memos, which are intended for internal audiences, **letters** are generally intended for **external audiences**: people outside your organization, such as customers or clients. A letter is considered a more formal method of communication than an email message or memo. As a result, letters are sometimes used for internal communication when the situation calls for formality. For example, you might receive a letter offering you a promotion, or you might write a formal letter of resignation if you were leaving a job.

When letters are sent as hard copy, they are printed on company letterhead. Letters can also be sent electronically as email attachments. In fact, many companies use electronic letterhead templates so that letters attached to emails will look the same as

CULTURE Composing for an International Audience

As a business communicator, you will certainly be working with people who are different from you. You may even find yourself working in another country, communicating primarily with people from a different culture. Therefore, it is important to think about cultural differences as part of the ACE process. As you analyze your audience, consider how familiar they are with American English, whether their culture values formality or informality in communication, and even whether their culture considers it more respectful to start doing business quickly or to take a few minutes to establish a personal relationship. The communication you compose should reflect what you learn. Failure to analyze international audiences can lead to miscommunication and surprises. Consider these two anecdotes from business professionals who communicate cross culturally.

Matt Woolsey, a learning and development professional who has worked for several consulting companies, tells the story of a company email that failed to communicate across cultures:

> In 2000 and 2003, our company conducted an employee engagement survey, which we called a "health check." It was so successful and we learned so much about employees' needs that we decided to repeat the survey in 2010. However, between 2003 and 2010, the company had grown substantially. It now had 1,400 employees in 17 offices around the world—including offices in India, China, and Japan. When we conducted the survey this time, we got almost no responses from the employees in Asia. In fact, most Asian employees had not even opened up the email.
>
> We couldn't figure out why the response rate was so low until we talked to some employees in India and learned that they assumed from the subject line the email—"It's time to do a health check."—was a reminder to go visit a doctor. The metaphor "health check" did not communicate effectively across cultures.

Laurent Caron, who works for Google Spain, has an international background. He grew up in France, attended college in the United States, and studied abroad in Argentina. He is fluent in French, English, and Spanish. Laurent made the following observation:

> When I first moved to Spain, I was surprised that Spaniards had different expectations than the French about levels of formality. For example, both French and Spanish languages have two distinctive forms of the pronoun 'you.' The informal 'you' (*tu* in French, *tú* in Spanish) is used with friends and family while the formal one (*vous* and *usted* respectively) is to be used with strangers, elder people, and professional acquaintances.
>
> The two forms of 'you' are so similar in French and Spanish that it took me some time to realize that the two cultures apply different rules for using them. The French vigorously maintain the distinction between *tu* and *vous*. The difference is so engrained in the French mind that if you call someone *tu* when the situation dictates the use of *vous*, you will catch that person off guard. Spaniards, however, are much more relaxed and mostly use the informal form. Even in a business environment, it is very common to be treated as *tú* seconds after meeting a person for the first time. Now when I travel to France, I often make the mistake of being too informal. I always need to think about my audience and where I am before I speak.

mybcommlab

For a CULTURE exercise, go to Exercise 19 on page 107 or to this chapter's End-of-Chapter Exercises at mybcommlab.com.

---

printed letters. An attached letter maintains the formality of the message, while the email transmission takes advantage of the quick delivery and electronic documentation.

You may have learned in a keyboarding class that several letter formats exist, such as block style, modified block, and simplified. However, block style, as shown in FIGURE 3.16 and throughout this text, is the most efficient letter style and the one most commonly used in business. Block style letters use no indentions or centering. Instead, all elements begin at the left margin. Paragraphs are separated with a double space. Guidelines for formatting letters and examples of modified block style can be found in Appendix B and on mybcommlab.com.

Voice mail messages

You may think it is odd to consider the design of oral communication since people consider design a visual concept. However, you should apply to voice mail the same principles used in designing emails: focus on one topic, keep the message short, make the main

Letters Formal correspondence, generally intended for external audiences.

External audiences People with whom you communicate outside your organization.

FIGURE 3.16 Sample Block Style Letter

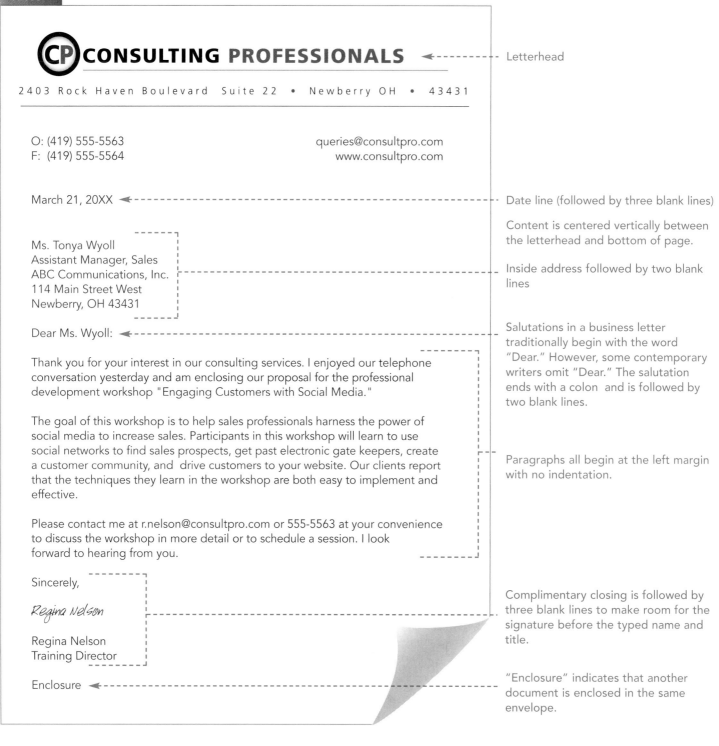

letter

CP CONSULTING PROFESSIONALS ◄------ Letterhead

2403 Rock Haven Boulevard   Suite 22 • Newberry OH • 43431

O: (419) 555-5563   queries@consultpro.com
F: (419) 555-5564   www.consultpro.com

March 21, 20XX ◄--- Date line (followed by three blank lines)

                                                            Content is centered vertically between
                                                            the letterhead and bottom of page.

Ms. Tonya Wyoll   Inside address followed by two blank
Assistant Manager, Sales   lines
ABC Communications, Inc.
114 Main Street West
Newberry, OH 43431

Dear Ms. Wyoll: ◄--- Salutations in a business letter
                                                            traditionally begin with the word
Thank you for your interest in our consulting services. I enjoyed our telephone   "Dear." However, some contemporary
conversation yesterday and am enclosing our proposal for the professional   writers omit "Dear." The salutation
development workshop "Engaging Customers with Social Media."   ends with a colon and is followed by
                                                            two blank lines.
The goal of this workshop is to help sales professionals harness the power of
social media to increase sales. Participants in this workshop will learn to use
social networks to find sales prospects, get past electronic gate keepers, create
a customer community, and drive customers to your website. Our clients report   Paragraphs all begin at the left margin
that the techniques they learn in the workshop are both easy to implement and   with no indentation.
effective.

Please contact me at r.nelson@consultpro.com or 555-5563 at your convenience
to discuss the workshop in more detail or to schedule a session. I look
forward to hearing from you.

Sincerely,

Regina Nelson   Complimentary closing is followed by
                                                            three blank lines to make room for the
Regina Nelson   signature before the typed name and
Training Director   title.

Enclosure ◄-- "Enclosure" indicates that another
                                                            document is enclosed in the same
                                                            envelope.

point easy to find, and provide contact information. Take a few minutes to plan your message before speaking. Below is one good approach for organizing a voice mail message.

- **Greet the recipient** by name to personalize the message.
- **Identify yourself** and include your affiliation or position if the audience is not familiar with you. Leave a callback number if you want a return call.
- **State your purpose and main point.** Let your audience know why you are calling.
- **Follow up with details.** Use signal words to help your audience keep track of ideas. If you say at the beginning of the message that you want to talk about two topics, mention each of those topics by signaling them with words like "first" and "second."
- **Identify actions.** Do you want your audience to return your call, send you something, or do something else? If you are requesting an action, be both polite and specific.
- **Provide contact information.** Even if you state your contact information at the beginning, repeat it, and speak slowly when leaving your telephone number. Your audience should not have to listen to your message again to know the number to call.
- **Sign off.** Say goodbye.

FIGURE 3.17 illustrates two voice mail messages. Although FIGURE 3.17(A) is more formal than FIGURE 3.17(B), both include all the elements described above.

FIGURE 3.17 Formal and Informal Voice Mail Messages

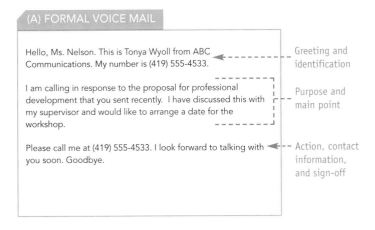
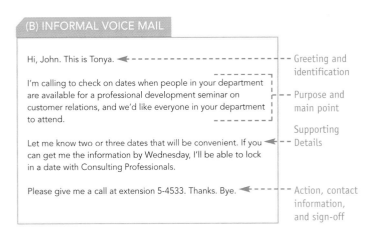

How does evaluating improve my communication?

The final step in the ACE process is **evaluating** your communication to ensure it is complete, clear, concise, easy to understand, and error-free.

Evaluation may occur at different points for written and oral communication. For example, written communication allows you to evaluate *before* delivering your message. You can take the time to reread, revise, and edit—and then send. Inexperienced business writers often skip the evaluating stage of writing because they believe it's more efficient to treat their first draft as a final draft. However, most experienced business writers know that a first draft is rarely good enough. If you write your first draft quickly to get your ideas on the page, you may include incomplete thoughts, awkward sentences, and grammatical errors that you will need to correct. Computer editing tools such as spelling and grammar checkers will catch some of these problems but not all of them. For example, these checkers don't catch incomplete thoughts, and they don't catch misused homonyms, such as *capital* and *capitol*. In addition, by the time you get to the end of your first draft, you may have discovered new ideas about what to say and how to say it. The evaluating phase gives you the opportunity to make those changes before you send the message.

By contrast, oral communication allows you to evaluate *while* you are delivering the message based on immediate feedback you receive. For example, imagine that you are making a point in a meeting. As you look around the room, you can gauge your audience's reaction and begin to adjust or revise your explanation on the spot. Written communication does not provide this type of immediate feedback or the opportunity to revise your message as you are communicating it.

This section describes four ways to evaluate your communication: revising the content, editing the style and tone, proofreading for errors, and using feedback to improve your future communication.

Revising the content improves effectiveness

Even if you are a good writer, you need to review and revise the content of a first draft. First drafts are opportunities for you to examine and think through your ideas. As you review the draft, you may see that you have left out an idea, changed your logic, or written a long-winded explanation because you did not understand your material well enough yet to be concise. As you evaluate your content, ask yourself these questions: Is it complete and well organized? Is it clear? Is it concise?

Completeness

As a first step in the revising process, re-read the entire document from the audience's perspective. Think about the analysis stage of the ACE process and the purpose and outcome you identified for the communication. Ask yourself if the document has the right information and the right approach to achieve your goal:

- **Are your purpose and your main point clear?** Underline your purpose and main point. If you cannot find explicit statements to underline, then revise to add those sentences.
- **Have you provided all the information you need to support your purpose?** Consider all the things you believe your audience will need to know. Then review your draft document, putting a mark next to each of these items. If any information is missing, revise. If you cannot imagine what your audience will need to know, ask friends or colleagues to provide feedback. Do they have any unanswered questions after reading your draft? If so, revise.
- **Will the organization of that information make sense to the audience?** Read the topic sentences of each paragraph. Does each topic sentence identify the main idea of the paragraph? If not, then add new topic sentences. Do the details of the paragraph relate to the topic sentence? If not, revise the details. Does the progression from one topic sentence to the next seem logical? If not, then identify what is missing.
- **Is the message persuasive enough to be successful?** If your message is intended to be persuasive, identify key objections your audience may have. If you have not addressed these objections, consider revising. Also identify audience benefits. If you have not stressed these, consider revising. Additional persuasive techniques are addressed in Chapter 5.

You will find it easier to revise if you have some distance from your draft. Put it away overnight—or for a few hours—and then read it with fresh eyes.

Clarity

Clarity refers to using clear wording that an audience can easily understand. One of the first mistakes many new employees make is to try to impress colleagues, managers, and customers by using big words in long sentences. However, people are rarely impressed by writing that is long and difficult to understand. The purpose of business writing is to express meaning as quickly and simply as possible rather than to impress people with vocabulary. Remember to keep it simple.

For example, the author of the poorly worded sentences in FIGURE 3.18 incorrectly uses formal (often stilted) wording. The clearly worded sentences intend the same meaning, but use short, simple wording so the audience can clearly understand the message.

Good business communicators also avoid **abstract wording**—language that refers to broad concepts that an audience can interpret in multiple ways. Consider the sentence "We need to solve the transportation problem ASAP." In this sentence, the terms "transporta-

POORLY WORDED	CLEARLY WORDED
• Please affix the appropriate amount of postage to the mailing package. • I sincerely appreciate your exertion on this critically important endeavor.	• Please put a first-class stamp on the envelope. • Thank you for your work on this important project.

FIGURE 3.18
Using Clear Wording

tion" "problem" and ASAP are abstract. What do they mean? A dictionary defines transportation as conveyance (carrying, moving, shipping, or hauling), but does everyone think of the same kind of transportation when they visualize the word? Probably not. Similarly, what does "problem" mean in this context? Does it mean that the transportation is delayed or too expensive? Does ASAP mean by today, or by the end of the week, or whenever you have the time to do it? Using abstract and ambiguous wording results in miscommunication if your audience infers a different meaning than you intended. **Concrete wording** is specific. The more concrete the language is, the more likely it is that you and your audience will interpret the same message in the same way: "By tomorrow morning, we need to determine why trucking shipments are leaving the warehouse one to two days late."

Conciseness

In business communication, shorter is usually better. **Concise** communication is short and to the point, expressing its idea clearly in the fewest possible words. Whether your message is oral or written, a well-constructed, concise message saves the audience time. As entrepreneur Guy Kawasaki, managing director of Garage Technology Ventures, explains, schools "should teach students how to communicate in five-sentence emails and with 10-slide PowerPoint presentations. If they just taught every student that, American business would be much better off. . . . No one wants to read 'War and Peace' emails. Who has the time? Ditto with 60 PowerPoint slides for a one-hour meeting."[2]

FIGURE 3.19 provides examples of how you can edit wordy phrases to be more clear and concise.

WORDY	CONCISE
• This email is in reference to our approval of your prior request . . . • Enclosed in this mailing you will find three photocopies . . . • If you have any questions, please do not hesitate to contact me at . . .	• We approve your request . . . • Enclosed are three copies . . . • Please contact me if you have any questions . . .

FIGURE 3.19
Using Concise Wording

You can also make writing more concise by eliminating obvious fillers and any information that is not necessary or helpful to achieve your purpose. When you include extra words and unnecessary information, you waste your time as you compose the message as well as the audience's time as they read or listen to it. Consider the examples in FIGURE 3.20.

Clarity Using clear wording that an audience can easily understand.

Abstract wording Language that refers to broad concepts that an audience can interpret in multiple ways.

Concrete wording Language that is specific, making it likely that everyone will interpret it the same way.

Conciseness Expressing an idea clearly in the fewest possible words.

WORDY	CONCISE
• As you know, we met yesterday to discuss next year's budget. Based on the auditor's review, I recommend that we . . . • As your assistant manager, I am suggesting that we review our departmental procedures. • There are three people who will attend the meeting.	• Based on the auditor's review of our budget, I recommend that we . . . • I suggest we review our departmental procedures. • Three people will attend the meeting.

FIGURE 3.20
Eliminating Unnecessary Words

Concise wording also eliminates **redundancies**, the unnecessary repetition of an idea. Consider the examples in FIGURE 3.21 (redundant phrases appear in red in the left column).

FIGURE 3.21
Avoiding Redundancies

REDUNDANT	CONCISE
• Please refer back to the minutes from our last department meeting.	• Please refer to the minutes from our last department meeting.
• Advance planning on our project will allow our departments to combine together our resources and divide up the work to be done.	• Good project planning will allow our departments to combine resources and divide the work.
• The first issue we need to address is travel reimbursement. Travel reimbursement is an important issue to address because nearly 70% of our employees have expense accounts.	• First, we need to address travel reimbursement because nearly 70% of our employees have expense accounts.

The White House published this photo of President Barack Obama editing a speech on health care in the Oval Office, September 9, 2009.
(Official White House Photo by Pete Souza)

Editing style and tone helps you project a professional image

All good communicators, including business communicators, also evaluate and edit their documents to ensure a professional style and tone. **Style** refers to how you express yourself rather than what you say. Do you use positive or negative language, big words or small words, long sentences or short sentences, strong active verbs or weak passive voice?

Your style choices will affect the tone of your communication. **Tone** is the image your language projects about you based on how the language sounds to the audience. Tone in writing is similar to your tone of voice when you speak. Your tone can be friendly or angry, positive or negative, formal or casual, professional or unprofessional, courteous or rude. In a business message, you should not take advantage of all these options. Your tone should be professional and courteous at all times, even when you are frustrated and angry. For example, when replying to an angry customer about a problem with his recent purchase, you need to ensure that the tone of your message is polite and reassuring, even if this particular customer often complains or does not understand how to use the product correctly. To ensure a professional style and tone, use positive wording, a conversational style, and active voice. Avoid slang and clichés.

Use positive wording

Whenever possible, effective business writers choose positive wording to communicate their messages, even in negative situations. *Positive wording* creates an optimistic, encouraging, and often more informative message. For example, consider the sentences in FIGURE 3.22. The sentences on the left focus on the negative meaning of the messages. Note how in each example subtle changes in wording on the right focus on the positive meaning.

FIGURE 3.22
Using Positive Wording

NEGATIVE	POSITIVE
• We will not be able to approve a new budget until the analysis is complete.	• We will be able to approve a new budget when the analysis is complete.
• The board has not yet voted on the salary increases.	• The board will vote on the salary increases at the next board meeting.
• If you do not sign the form before 5 PM, we will not be able to fund your travel request.	• If you sign the form before 5 PM, we will be able to the fund your travel request.

Use a conversational style

Business writing also should be *conversational* rather than academic. Academic writing often sounds too formal for everyday communication. Conversational writing style uses relatively short sentences and familiar words. When read aloud, the text should sound like the writer is talking with the audience. See the examples in FIGURE 3.23. Read the sentences on the left aloud. Would you speak this way to someone? Probably not. The sentences on the right convey the same meaning but with a better conversational style.

TOO FORMAL	CONVERSATIONAL
• Henceforth all documentation is to be completed within two business days.	• Please complete all forms within two business days.
• As per your instructions, I have initiated discussions with the previously identified employees.	• I began talking with the employees you mentioned last week.
• This new policy will facilitate the implementation of more beneficial scheduling decisions.	• This new policy will let us schedule shipments more efficiently.

FIGURE 3.23
Using Conversational Style

Use an active voice

Voice refers to the relationship between the subject and verb in a sentence. In **active voice** sentences, the subject performs the action of the verb.

          subject   **verb**
ACTIVE VOICE: The employees completed the project early.

In **passive voice** sentences, the subject does not perform the action of the verb. Instead, the subject receives the action expressed by the verb.

          subject   **verb phrase**
PASSIVE VOICE: The project was completed early.

In business writing, active voice should dominate because it leads to a clear and lively style of writing, while passive voice leads to a wordier and often weaker style. However, passive voice may be a good choice in a number of special circumstances, for example, when you do not want to assign blame. You may also choose passive voice when you want to emphasize a certain word by placing it in the subject of the sentence. See FIGURE 3.24 for examples.

FIGURE 3.24
Choosing between Active and Passive Voice

WHICH IS BETTER?

PASSIVE VOICE: Because the project was completed early, a bonus was given to the employees.

ACTIVE VOICE: Because they completed the project early, the employees received a bonus.

The active sentence makes it clear that the employees were responsible for completing the project ahead of time.

PASSIVE VOICE: The meeting was scheduled for Friday afternoon.

ACTIVE VOICE: Camilla scheduled the meeting for Friday afternoon.

In this case, passive voice may be more effective because it allows you to put the important word "meeting" at the beginning of the sentence. However, if your audience needs to know who scheduled the meeting, then active voice may be effective.

Redundancy Unnecessary repetition of an idea.

Style How you express yourself.

Tone The image of yourself that your language projects based on how the message sounds to the recipient.

Active voice A sentence structure in which the subject performs the action of the verb.

Passive voice A sentence structure in which the subject is passive and receives the action expressed by the verb.

Eliminate slang and clichés

To communicate effectively in business, you need to use words that your audience will understand. **Slang** is nonstandard, informal language that may work well within a certain group but often excludes people from different countries, cultures, and social groups. Examples of slang include *cool, my bad, off the chain, plugged in,* and *go missing.* As you edit, eliminate all nonstandard usage.

Clichés are commonplace and often overused phrases that have lost their force and meaning. Like slang, clichés are also specific to cultures and languages, and they may exclude international audiences. Would a businessperson who learned English in India or China understand what the following clichés mean?

- His proposal **is all over the map.**

  Means . . . His proposal is **disorganized.**

- Hiring him was **a bad call.**

  Means . . . Hiring him was **a bad decision.**

- **The bottom fell out** of that investment.

  Means . . . The investment **lost money.**

Proofreading increases your credibility

In written communication, **proofreading** is an important step of the evaluation process. You can spend hours writing a report, but if that writing is full of errors, your audience may focus more on your mistakes than on your message. In addition, your audience may assume that you lack attention to detail. Therefore, a quick scan of a document is not a sufficient proofreading technique. In the sections that follow, you will learn the steps you can use to check your documents carefully and systematically for all types of errors.

Familiarize yourself with five types of errors

Most writing errors fall into one of five categories: content errors, typographical and spelling errors, usage errors, grammatical errors, or format errors.

Content errors are mistakes in the substance of a message. Examples of content errors include incorrect information or missing information. To check for content errors, review dates and days of the week, confirm locations and times of meetings, and verify lists and spelling of names. You may be too close to or familiar with the material to determine if there is missing content, so ask a colleague to help you proofread, and ask for specific feedback about information you should include.

Spelling errors result from your lack of knowledge about how to spell a word. *Typographical errors* are mistakes made in typing. Typing too quickly often results in misspellings, transposed letters, and duplications. Automated spelling checkers may help you proofread for spelling and typographical errors, but do not depend on the computer to find all your mistakes. For example, if you type the word "saw" instead of "was," the spell checker will not identify the word as incorrectly spelled. To catch these errors, look up the spelling of all words that you are not confident you have spelling correctly. In addition, look for typos as you read and also check all numbers, including those in addresses and phone numbers. Neither the spelling nor grammar tools will know if numbers are correct.

Usage errors are errors in the way language is used. For example, if you use the word "imply" when you mean "infer" or use the word "economical" when you mean "economic," you have committed a usage error. It is difficult to catch these when you proofread on your own, since you originally chose the wrong words. However, other readers can often catch them for you.

Grammatical errors are violations of grammar rules. These errors include sentence fragments, run-on sentences, shifts in tense, incorrect pronouns, and incorrect subject-verb agreement (just to name a few). Although grammar checkers can help you identify these problems, they may also suggest inappropriate changes. You need to identify and correct grammatical errors on your own and validate the suggestions offered by the automated tools. Refresh your memory of grammar rules by reviewing

Appendix D on page A-37 and completing the grammar exercises at the end of each chapter of this text. You can also go to mybcommlab.com for additional assistance.

Format errors are inconsistencies in design techniques within a document, such as including both indented and block-style paragraphs, bullets that do not align correctly, and differences in font sizes or styles. These errors often occur when you cut and paste text from other documents. Other formatting problems occur when spaces are used to align text rather than tabs, which can be set as left, centered, or right aligned. Correctly using word processing formatting techniques ensures the professional design of your documents.

Check systematically for errors

To check systematically for all these types of errors, follow these guidelines:

- **Read your work multiple times.** The errors listed in the previous section are very different from each other and very difficult to catch in one reading. If you proofread just once for all errors, you most likely will not find them all. However, if you narrow each proofreading to scan for a particular problem, you will be more successful finding your mistakes.

- **Look for your own common errors.** Most writers repeat the same kinds of errors based on their individual writing style. Identify your common errors by reviewing your graded writing assignments or asking your instructor for assistance. Make a list of these errors and look for them in your drafts. For example, if you often misuse commas, proofread your draft once just for commas. If you also notice that you often use the word "there" instead of "their," proofread a second time just for those words and stop each time you find either word to determine if you have used it correctly.

- **Read your work later.** If possible, put some time between your composing and evaluating stages. Too often, writers quickly compose a first draft and immediately try to proofread their work. Taking even a five-minute break can clear your thoughts and let you proofread with a more objective and fresh perspective. Read each word and proofread slowly through the message. Some writers find it helpful to read from the bottom up. They start with the last sentence and read up the page sentence by sentence. This backward approach slows your reading pace and lets you examine the information out of context to help you find typos and missing words.

- **Read your draft aloud.** Generally, people speak more slowly than they read. Therefore, reading your draft aloud slows your reading pace and helps you focus on the text and find more errors. Also, when you hear what you have written, you are more likely to identify a missing word or notice awkward phrasing.

- **Swap with a colleague.** For a more objective perspective, ask a colleague to proofread your draft. Even good writers miss some of their own writing errors. Because you wrote the content and you know exactly what you meant when you composed the draft, your brain can fill in missing words or information. An objective reader can sometime find errors that you may have overlooked. If you routinely proofread others' work, you may want to familiarize yourself with the standard symbols that professional proofreaders use to mark errors (see Appendix F to learn proofreading marks).

Take advantage of technology tools

In addition to the spelling and grammar tools already discussed, many word processors contain other tools that help you evaluate, revise, and edit. For example, Microsoft Word's spelling and grammar tool includes a reading level analysis, which assesses the readability of your writing based on sentence length and the number of long, multisyllabic words it contains. The test then assigns your writing a grade level. Don't assume that your documents should match the grade level of your audience. Because business writing should be short and simple, most messages should be written at eighth-grade level or less. See FIGURE 3.25 for examples.

Slang Nonstandard, informal language that may communicate well within a certain group but often excludes people from different countries, cultures, and social groups.

Clichés Commonplace and often overused phrases that have lost their force and meaning.

Proofreading A systematic process of reviewing writing for errors.

FIGURE 3.25
Examples of Reading Levels

INAPPROPRIATE	APPROPRIATE
Grade Level 12.3: Henceforth, all documentation is to be completed within two business days.	**Grade Level 5.2:** Please complete all forms within two business days.
Grade Level 14.8: As per your instructions, I have initiated discussions with the previously identified employees.	**Grade Level 6.0:** I began talking with the employees you mentioned last week.
Grade Level 16.6: This new policy will facilitate the implementation of more beneficial scheduling decisions.	**Grade Level 8.3:** This new policy will let us schedule shipments more efficiently.

The thesaurus is another tool that can help you during the composing and evaluating processes. A *thesaurus* is a reference that provides synonyms and antonyms. *Synonyms* are words that have the same or similar meaning, such as "quickly" and "rapidly." *Antonyms* are words that have opposite meanings, such as "clear" and "confusing." When you have trouble looking for the right word to express the meaning of your message, use your word processing software's thesaurus to identify options. However, choose carefully among the words that you see in the thesaurus and look up unfamiliar words in the dictionary before using them. Even when a thesaurus lists two words as synonyms, they may not have the exact meaning. For example, a thesaurus usually lists the word "privileges" as a synonym for "benefits."[3] However, if you were writing a memo about "employee benefits," you could not simply swap the word "privileges" for "benefits." "Employee benefits" has a different meaning than "employee privileges."

Reviewing feedback helps you make better communication decisions

As you learned in Chapter 1, business communication is a two-way transaction. In its simplest form, you send a message and, whether you ask for it or not, you get feedback that indicates how effectively you have communicated. This feedback can come in many forms: a complaint, a compliment, compliance with a request, phone calls asking for clarification, nods and smiles, or puzzled looks. When you get feedback, take a moment to consider it and to learn from it. For example, if you receive no response to an email message, does that mean the audience did not believe a response was important? Or perhaps the subject line failed to capture the audience's attention? If you write a set of directions and your audience gets lost, does that mean they are poor readers, or that you included ambiguous information, or that you missed a step? What you learn will help you make better decisions the next time you communicate.

If you have used the ACE process to get feedback on the first draft of a message, then you can use that feedback to make changes immediately, before you complete a document. For example, when you share your summer-hours proposal with your supervisor, she may suggest that you reorganize your content, include additional possible disadvantages, or develop an assessment plan as part of the proposal. This feedback will require you to spend more time analyzing, composing, and evaluating, which may be disappointing if you thought you were done with the writing process. However, it will lead to a more successful proposal.

TECHNOLOGY Using "Track Changes" to Get Feedback on a Draft

When you ask others to review your writing, the *track changes* feature in many word processing programs is a useful tool. Rather than printing a hard copy of a draft and marking the changes by hand, your coworkers can make their changes electronically.

As you can see in the following example, *track changes* allows you to make corrections, suggest content to add and delete, and insert comments. The comment boxes include the reviewers' initials so you know who is making the comment. Additionally, the word processing program automatically assigns different colors to each reviewer so you can easily see who made what comment or change. You can then review the sug-

gested changes one by one and accept or reject them. You can also review each comment, make appropriate changes, and then delete the comment from the document.

When completing the final draft of a collaboratively edited document, accept all the tracked changes and delete all the comments before saving to avoid sending a message that allows the audience to see your edits.

mybcommlab

For a TECHNOLOGY exercise, go to Exercise 18 on pages 106–107 or to this chapter's End-of-Chapter Exercises at mybcommlab.com.

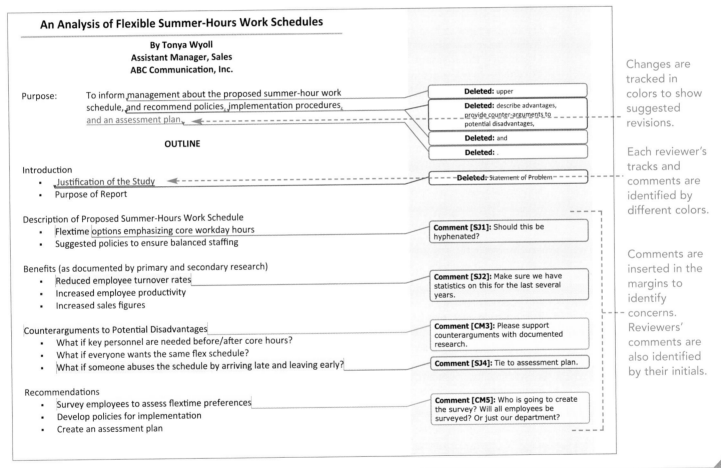

IN SUMMARY, the ACE process will help you communicate more effectively by ensuring that you analyze, compose, and evaluate in a systematic way. In the following chapters, you will have an opportunity to apply this process to a range of business communications from short, routine communications through complex reports and presentations. Short email messages may take only a few minutes to analyze, compose, and evaluate, while the more complex communications will require more time. However, as you become a more experienced communicator, you will increasingly be able to go through each step of the process more quickly and effectively regardless of the length or purpose of your communication. If you follow the process well, your communications will more likely achieve your purpose and project a professional image.

CHAPTER **3** **Summary**

The ACE process—Analyzing, Composing, Evaluating—provides a structured way to communicate successfully. This approach helps you make good choices about what content to include, how to organize the content, how to draft efficiently, and how to evaluate your communication objectively.

3.1 Why should I spend time analyzing? *(pages 72–78)*

- **Analyzing the purpose focuses the message.** Develop an outcome-oriented purpose statement, consider how you will maintain goodwill, and determine whether your message will need to be persuasive.
- **Analyzing the audience helps you meet their needs.** Think about what the audience needs to know, how they will benefit from your message, and their possible objections. Consider both the primary audience and possible secondary audiences.
- **Analyzing the content ensures a complete message** so you know whether you have enough information or need to conduct additional primary or secondary research.
- **Analyzing the medium helps you choose the best delivery option**—such as an email, memo, letter, or social media—to ensure that your message reaches your audience effectively.

3.2 What is involved in composing? *(pages 78–89)*

- **Deciding where and when to compose** begins by considering your environment, avoiding distractions, and planning your time.
- **Organizing the message** requires that you determine the overall structure of the communication. Long documents may benefit from using a multilevel outline. To organize short documents, you can use a more informal outline. When organizing, also decide where to state the main point. Messages can be organized using either the direct organizational plan (main idea first) or the indirect organizational plan (supporting details before main idea).
- **Drafting the content** is a creative process. Save revising (a logical process) until later. Use strategies like free writing to avoid writer's block.
- **Designing a professional format and delivery** requires that you consider specific formatting techniques for emails, memos (for internal audiences), letters (for external audiences), and voice mail messages. When appropriate, use topic-specific headings to signal the structure and meaning of the document.

3.3 How does evaluating improve my communication? *(pages 89–97)*

When you evaluate, you assess whether your communication will be effective and then make changes to prove it. You can evaluate in four ways:

- **Revising the content improves effectiveness** by ensuring your communication has the right information and approach to meet its goals. As you revise, look to see that your document is complete, clear, and concise.
- **Editing style and tone helps you project a professional image.** Use positive wording, a conversational style, and active voice. Eliminate slang, clichés, and unnecessary passive voice.
- **Proofreading increases your credibility.** To improve your proofreading skills, familiarize yourself with the different kinds of errors: content, spelling and typographical, usage, grammatical, and format. Systematically check for these errors, and take advantage of technology tools.
- **Reviewing feedback helps you make better communication decisions.**

PEARSON
mybcommlab *Are you an active learner? Go to mybcommlab.com to master Chapter 3 content. Chapter 3 interactive activities include:*

- Customizable Study Plan and Chapter 3 practice quizzes
- Chapter 3 Simulation, The Communication Process, that helps you think critically and prepare to make choices in the business world
- Flash Cards for mastering the definition of chapter terms

- Chapter 3 Video Exercise, Planning Business Messages, which shows you how textbook concepts are put into practice every day
- Interactive Lessons that visually review key chapter concepts
- Document Makeovers for hands-on, scored practice in revising documents

Use This ACE Checklist to Guide You through the Communication Process...

ANALYZING	COMPOSING	EVALUATING
• What is the purpose of the message and what do I want the outcome of this communication to be? • Who is my audience and what do they need to know? • What do I need to say or write in order to meet audience needs and achieve the desired outcome? • Where can I get additional information if I need it? • What is the best medium for this message based on the audience and content?	• How can I organize the message logically? • Where should I state the main point: at the beginning (direct organizational plan) or at the end (indirect organizational plan)? • How can I make the organization clear using topic-specific headings and good paragraphing? • How should I format this message to support my purpose and be professional?	• Is the information complete, concise, clear, and correct? • Have I anticipated and addressed my audience's questions and concerns? • Is the tone appropriate? • Is the message well organized and designed so that the audience can skim the text and follow the flow of my logic? • Is the message professionally formatted and effectively proofread?

FIRST DRAFT

To ALL: We need to reschedule our meeting for next week. Sorry for the inconvenience.

thnx, dale

First draft is quickly written with only the writer in mind.

Revised draft considers audience needs and uses the ACE process to achieve a more effective message.

REVISED DRAFT

To All Budget Committee Members:

We need to reschedule our budget meeting. Are you available on Thursday, September 13, at 2 PM?

The accounting department is backlogged and won't have the projections we need to make informed decisions about the budget until Wednesday.

Please reply to all before you leave the office so I can finalize our meeting arrangements. I will reply tomorrow morning to confirm the day/time and location.

Thank you,
Dale

Dale Levitz, Office Manager
ABC Communications
dlevitz@abccomm.com
(419) 555-4525

Message uses a professional format that is easy to skim.

The purpose of the message is clearly stated in the first paragraph.

The middle paragraph provides details.

The closing requests a response.

Complimentary closing is professional.

Signature block includes contact information.

KEY TERMS QUICK ACCESS REVIEW

Abstract wording *p. 90*

Active voice *p. 93*

Analyzing *p. 72*

Audience *p. 72*

Audience benefits *p. 74*

Bullet point list *p. 84*

Clarity *p. 90*

Clichés *p. 94*

Composing *p. 72*

Conciseness *p. 91*

Concrete wording *p. 91*

Content *p. 72*

Direct organizational plan *p. 81*

Drafting *p. 82*

Evaluating *p. 72*

External audiences *p. 86*

Goodwill *p. 73*

Indirect organizational plan *p. 81*

Internal audiences *p. 85*

Letters *p. 86*

Medium *p. 72*

Memos *p. 85*

Outcome *p. 73*

Passive voice *p. 93*

Persuasion *p. 74*

Primary audience *p. 74*

Primary research *p. 76*

Proofreading *p. 94*

Purpose *p. 72*

Redundancy *p. 92*

Revising *p. 83*

Secondary audience *p. 74*

Secondary research *p. 76*

Slang *p. 94*

Style *p. 92*

Subject line *p. 82*

Tone *p. 92*

Topic sentence *p. 84*

Topic-specific headings *p. 84*

Writer's block *p. 83*

CASE STUDY Using ACE to Improve Communication Results

This case study will help you review the chapter material by applying it to a specific business situation.

Suppose your employer asks you to inform everyone in the Customer Relations department about an upcoming workshop on communication skills. You quickly create a flyer with the following information and post copies on the break room bulletin board and in the cafeteria.

> Communication Skills
> Workshop
> Wednesday, November 1 @ 2:30 PM
> Training Room A

Although your department includes 60 people, when you arrive for the workshop, only four people are there. What went wrong? How could using ACE help improve the communication results?

What Is the Desired Outcome?

Your supervisor may have simply instructed you to tell the employees about the workshop, but what is the desired outcome? Your supervisor wants most of the department's 60 employees to attend. Simply telling employees that the workshop exists will not make them attend. They need to be persuaded.

What Content Does the Audience Need?

What will the audience need to hear to make them want to attend? To answer this question, you need to analyze the audience and anticipate their questions and objections.

The 60 employees in the Customer Relations Department are busy. They also believe they are already good communicators—after all, they are in Customer Relations. They will attend a workshop only if they are required, if they believe they will benefit, or if they believe it will be fun. Here are some questions that will be on their minds when they hear about the workshop and some possible objections they may have to attending.

Possible Questions:

- Is this workshop required?
- Is the presenter good?
- How long will the workshop last?
- Will it be worthwhile?
- How will I benefit from attending?
- Will my manager be upset if I don't attend?

Possible Objections:

- I have too much work to do.
- I studied communication in school.
- Somebody needs to answer the phones.
- I'm not interested.
- A workshop won't help me get promoted.

Review Question 1: *What other questions and objections can you anticipate? If you were going to revise the communication, which questions and objections would you want to answer directly? Are there any you would choose not to address? If so, why?*

Which Medium Is Best?

You realize now that a flyer was not the most effective way to communicate about the workshop because some people simply walk past flyers without reading them. What other options would be better?

Review Question 2: *What are the advantages and disadvantages of the following other options: making an announcement on the company's internal website, sending a memo to each employee, sending an email to each employee, calling each employee?*

How Can I Structure My Content?

Assume that you decide to send an email and now have the challenge of structuring the content. The next page shows a draft.

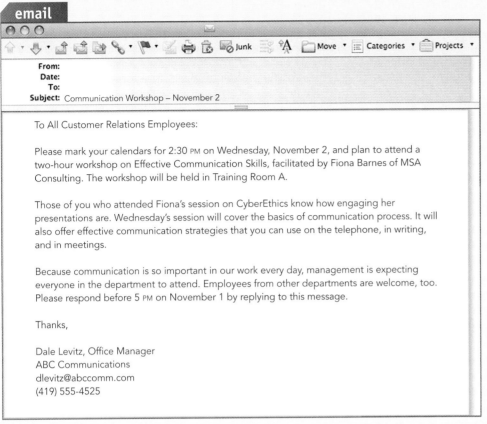

email

From:
Date:
To:
Subject: Communication Workshop – November 2

To All Customer Relations Employees:

Please mark your calendars for 2:30 PM on Wednesday, November 2, and plan to attend a two-hour workshop on Effective Communication Skills, facilitated by Fiona Barnes of MSA Consulting. The workshop will be held in Training Room A.

Those of you who attended Fiona's session on CyberEthics know how engaging her presentations are. Wednesday's session will cover the basics of communication process. It will also offer effective communication strategies that you can use on the telephone, in writing, and in meetings.

Because communication is so important in our work every day, management is expecting everyone in the department to attend. Employees from other departments are welcome, too. Please respond before 5 PM on November 1 by replying to this message.

Thanks,

Dale Levitz, Office Manager
ABC Communications
dlevitz@abccomm.com
(419) 555-4525

Accompanies Review Question 3

Review Question 3: *Review how the ACE process led to this improved message above:*

Analyzing:

1. What information in the revised version addresses the need for persuasion?

2. How does the email message emphasize reader benefits?

3. What content appears in the email that was not included in the original flyer? Why is that content useful?

Composing:

4. Is the information in the email organized effectively? Explain.

5. What determines which information goes in which paragraph?

6. How would you decide whether to organize the content directly or indirectly?

Evaluating:

7. In evaluating content, are there additional persuasive points you could add?

8. Does this email message use clear and concise wording as well as professional tone and style?

9. Which elements promote a conversational style?

10. When proofing this email, which content elements would you proofread for accuracy?

11. Is the message designed well? Explain.

12. Would you keep the current subject line or would you revise it? Explain.

CRITICAL THINKING

1. Think about the last paper, report, letter, or business email you wrote. What percent of your writing time did you spend on each element of the ACE process (**A**nalyzing, **C**omposing, and **E**valuating)? Will you change your approach in the future? Explain why or why not.

2. Analyzing your audience helps you compose effective messages. However, sometimes you may need to communicate with people you do not know. What methods can you suggest to learn about and analyze an unfamiliar audience?

3. Assume that you work for a company that designs and manufactures uniforms and protective equipment. Your company would like to expand its offerings and is considering manufacturing firefighter uniforms. As part of the research necessary to make this decision, your supervisor has asked you to gather information about the market for these uniforms. How big is it? Is it growing or shrinking? In your research, you found this statement on the Education-Portal.com website: "According to the Bureau of Labor Statistics, www.bls.gov, the occupation of firefighter is projected to grow faster than the average for all oc-

cupations through the year 2014." However, you also found several newspaper sources on the web that cite shrinking budgets and personnel cutbacks in fire departments. How would you present this conflicting information in your report? Would you need to do any additional research on the topic before composing? If so, what questions would you research? **[Related to the Ethics feature on page 78]**

4. Assume that you work at a bookstore near campus and would like to propose to your supervisor that the bookstore stay open two hours later each evening during the week. You need to choose whether to write your proposal in an email or to request a face-to-face meeting. Your supervisor has no preference about how you communicate. Which medium would you choose and why?

5. Referring back to question 4, assume that when you either write or speak to your supervisor proposing expanded evening hours, you decide to organize your message indirectly, building up to the main point. Since you are using an indirect organization, what content can you include in the

introduction of the email or opening of the conversation that will help your audience follow your logic and understand where you are going? Provide an example.

6. Assume you work for a supervisor who generally prefers to receive email messages rather than have face-to-face meetings. Identify at least two circumstances in which you believe it would be better to request a meeting to discuss an issue rather than send an email. Explain your rationale.

7. Explain a situation in which you have experienced writer's block. What were you writing about? How much time did you have to complete the project? Which of the suggestions to overcome writer's block from the chapter might have helped you? Which ones will you use in the future?

8. Retrieve a recent email message that you wrote to someone other than your family and friends. Do you believe that the email portrays a professional image? If so, what elements of

the email create that image? If not, what elements undermine that image?

9. Retrieve and read three email messages (or a class paper) you recently wrote, and begin to create your personal list of common errors. To help you identify them, ask a colleague to help you assess your messages, or seek assistance from your school's writing center. What kinds of errors do you frequently make? How can you ensure you do not continue to make these errors in the future?

10. Much of the advice about evaluating in this chapter refers to written communication. What are some ways that you can evaluate your oral communication, for example when you speak at a meeting or interview, leave a voice message, or give an oral presentation? Consider things that you can do in advance of delivering the oral message, things that you can do while you are delivering the message, and things you can do afterwards that will help you improve your communication in the future.

DEVELOPING YOUR COMMUNICATION SKILLS

3.1 Why should I spend time analyzing? *(pages 72–78)*

EXERCISE 1 Analyzing the purpose focuses the message

For each of the following business communication situations, (1) identify a desired outcome, (2) identify whether achieving that outcome will require persuasion, and (3) explain your reasoning. For those situations that require persuasion, list at least two audience benefits that would make your message more persuasive.

a. Informing department employees of a new form to use when requesting expense reimbursement.

b. Convincing your supervisor to create a new staff position in your department.

c. Informing a subordinate of his frequent tardiness and poor performance, and encouraging improvement.

d. Documenting a subordinate's tardiness and poor performance and recommending the employee's termination in a memo report to your supervisor.

e. Informing department employees of a mandatory change in vacation policy: If vacation days are not used by the end of the year, they will be lost.

EXERCISE 2 Analyzing the audience helps you meet their needs

Currently your company does not provide company cell phones for members of the sales force who travel as part of their regular job responsibilities. Instead, salespeople are required to submit monthly reimbursement requests for business-related calls made on personal cell phones. This process is time consuming for salespeople. You would like to propose that the sales department purchase cell phones for all salespeople to use for business calls only and then simply pay the monthly bill. What questions and objections do you think the sales force will have with this proposal? How will you address them?

EXERCISE 3 Analyzing the content ensures a complete message

Your supervisor asks you to give a brief presentation at your company's annual sales meeting that analyzes sales trends for each of the company's three regions over four years. You collect the data about gross sales and then create the following exhibit.

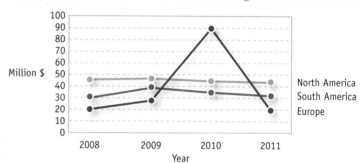

Accompanies Exercise 3

As you look at the graph, you realize it will raise questions during the presentation and that you should prepare answers. What questions and observations about sales do you think your graph will raise? What additional research would you do to answer those questions?

EXERCISE 4 Analyzing the medium helps you choose the best delivery option

For each of the following scenarios, identify which medium would be the best choice to communicate your message. Select your choice from the list of medium options in **Figure 3.7** on page 77 or other options you may deem appropriate. Explain your reasoning.

a. Your employer leaves a message on your voice mail asking you to work overtime this weekend, but you plan to attend your cousin's out-of-town wedding. What medium would you use to explain why you can't work overtime?

b. You are developing a new procedure manual for the sales associates in your department and need input on several issues from your department manager and training staff. What medium would you use to gather the input you need?

c. Your supervisor approves your request to schedule a one-hour yoga class each Wednesday after work. This class is ongoing. How do you (1) inform all the employees of this new program and (2) keep the program publicized through the course of the year?

d. You ordered 14 boxes of 8 1/2" × 11" copy paper from a local office supply store, but you received 11 boxes of 8 1/2" × 14" legal paper. After you talk with Paul, an associate manager of the store, he personally delivers the 14 boxes of standard copy paper to your office, carries the boxes into your supply room, and retrieves the boxes of legal paper—all within an hour of your initial contact. You are so impressed with Paul's personal attention and quick service that you want to inform his supervisor. How do you contact Paul's supervisor to recognize his efforts?

e. The weekly Wednesday yoga classes have been so popular that your supervisor suggests expanding the program to include weekly healthy living tips, fitness information, and healthy recipe ideas. How do you deliver this information to your employees each week? Explain how your choice of medium changes based on each of the following number of employees: 50 employees, 500 employees, and 5,000 employees.

3.2 What is involved
in composing? *(pages 78–89)*

EXERCISE 5 Deciding where and when to compose

Assume you are interning part-time for a marketing company this semester while taking classes. Your supervisor's project team is working on an ad campaign for a new client that produces big and tall men's apparel. In preparation for the team's initial brainstorming session next week, you've been asked to gather preliminary information about the client's leading competitors. You've researched the three companies that currently dominate the market and have gathered sample TV ads, website screen shots, and print media sources. You need to create a five-page report that summarizes your research. The report is due in seven days. How much time do you estimate you will need to compose and evaluate this report? How would you spread that work over the seven days?

EXERCISE 6 Organizing the message

Compare the following email messages. Email A uses a direct organizational plan. Email B uses an indirect organizational plan. Note that the only difference between these two messages is the placement of the main idea: "My analysis determined that Adaptive Solutions' website is more effective based on its ease of use, comprehensive content, and general appearance."

a. Under what circumstances would Nichole choose to write this message to Susan with the direct organizational plan? Explain at least two circumstances.

b. Under what circumstances would Nichole write this same message with the indirect organizational plan? Explain at least two circumstances.

c. Which organizational plan would you use and why?

d. How would you revise this message (regardless of the organizational plan) to emphasize audience benefits?

EMAIL A	EMAIL B
Susan: As you requested, I compared the websites of our two main competitors: Creative Communications (CC) and Adaptive Solutions (AS). My analysis determined that Adaptive Solutions' website is more effective based on its ease of use, comprehensive content, and general appearance. The AS website uses a consistent navigation format throughout. By contrast, the CC menus differ on several pages, which make finding specific information very difficult. Additionally, the AS website describes workshop topics, provides sample PowerPoint demonstrations, and links their handout examples. The CC site lists their workshop topics with a brief description of each, but does not provide additional materials. Finally, the overall appearance of the AS website is more professional. The content is well organized and the text is easy to read. I found it difficult to find information at the CC site and had a hard time reading the 10-point text. Let me know if you need a more detailed analysis of these two sites. I look forward to working on our own company's web design team. Best, Nichole Nichole Perkins Communications Consultant PH: 510.555.4512 FX: 510.555.4513	Susan: As you requested, I compared the websites of our two main competitors: Creative Communications (CC) and Adaptive Solutions (AS). The AS website uses a consistent navigation format throughout. By contrast, the CC menus differ on several pages, which make finding specific information very difficult. Additionally, the AS website describes workshop topics, provides sample PowerPoint demonstrations, and links their handout examples. The CC site lists their workshop topics with a brief description of each, but does not provide additional materials. Finally, the overall appearance of the AS website is more professional. The content is well organized and the text is easy to read. I found it difficult to find information at the CC site and had a hard time reading the 10-point text. My analysis determined that Adaptive Solutions' website is more effective based on its ease of use, comprehensive content, and general appearance. Let me know if you need a more detailed analysis of these two sites. I look forward to working on our own company's web design team. Best, Nichole Nichole Perkins Communications Consultant PH: 510.555.4512 FX: 510.555.4513

Accompanies Exercise 6

EXERCISE 7 Drafting the content

Select a topic you're researching for a class or group project—or a topic assigned by your instructor. Use free writing to fill at least a half page (typed and single spaced). Print the page and review your freewriting. Then, in a separate paragraph, identify how you might use this freewritten material in your project.

EXERCISE 8 Designing a professional format and delivery

Use the formatting techniques outlined in the chapter to improve the draft letter from Kirchen Art Musuem. Determine the best place for paragraph breaks. Add headings if you believe they are useful. Break up paragraphs into bullet points if you find lists.

3.3 How does evaluating improve my communication?

(pages 89–97)

EXERCISE 9 Revising the content improves effectiveness: Clarity and conciseness

Edit the following sentences to improve their clarity and conciseness:

a. The emergence of the Information Age and its corresponding technology has forever modified our societal norms and the methodologies of conducting business in today's world of Corporate America.

b. Computer technology and its associated software applications in conjunction with the widespread usage of the World Wide Web have had the most profound and visible effects of any invention in modern history.

c. Technologies have dramatically impacted and modified our complex communication systems, exchanges of information, and our commercial endeavors.

d. As technology permeates nearly every facet of business entities, the question is whether today's college students receive adequate information and assistance as they prepare for the high-tech world of business.

e. A multitude of employers are now testing prospective employees prior to employment to determine if their information technology knowledge and skill levels will meet or exceed their technology expectations in terms of meeting their workplace needs.

f. For people in the workforce who lack the absolutely essential knowledge and skills to succeed in today's highly competitive world of work, many institutions of higher learning are now beginning to offer distance-learning courses at an astronomical rate.

KIRCHEN ART MUSEUM
2815 CLAIRMONT AVE.
BIRMINGHAM, ALABAMA 35222

Dear Past Member:

Think spring. Think Impressionists. Our blockbuster exhibition—*The Influence of Impressionism*—promises to be the finest exhibition on Impressionism ever assembled by any museum in the past 40 years. So why not get ahead of the crowds? We want to make sure you have exclusive access to this extraordinary show opening in March. In fact, for immediate access to *The Influence of Impressionism* bring the enclosed reply to the museum on March 18 or 19 to join and attend the Member Previews before the exhibition opens to the public. As a member, you'll also receive a members-only behind-the-scenes experience by attending one of our exhibition lectures given by the curator and private viewings of the exhibition the first hour of every day—and every Thursday evening for members only. *The Influence of Impressionism* will surely be the highlight of our year—and yours. This landmark exhibition will showcase nearly 250 pivotal paintings, sculptures, drawings, and prints. The exhibit will include some of the most famous works of artists like Matisse, Monet, and Degas. Remember, membership benefits extend beyond special exhibitions. There are more than 260,000 works of art in our collection for you to enjoy. Be part of it all and experience the benefits of membership. These include free admission every day to the entire museum, dining in our world class rooftop restaurant, member discounts at all of our fabulous museum stores, and access to our Members Lounge. Renew your membership today, and mark your calendar for your exclusive member-only hours to visit *The Influence of Impressionism.*

Sincerely,

Kara Waltman

Kara Waltman
Director of Annual Giving

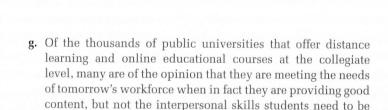

Accompanies Exercise 8

g. Of the thousands of public universities that offer distance learning and online educational courses at the collegiate level, many are of the opinion that they are meeting the needs of tomorrow's workforce when in fact they are providing good content, but not the interpersonal skills students need to be successful in workplace situations.

h. At the same time that the greater society in general and the world of academia in particular race to stay abreast of the wealth of new technologies and the newest software and hardware available, they appear to be unable to stem the tide of the growing and dangerously pervasive problem of unethical computer use that permeates society.

i. It is incredible to believe that for some people the ethical problems of piracy, identity theft, and computer fraud were unexpected surprises.

j. Our morals and values can become subjective considering that what one believes is morally incorrect may not be conceived as such by someone else.

EXERCISE 10 Revising the content improves effectiveness: Unnecessary wording and redundancies

Edit the following sentences to eliminate unnecessary wording and redundancies.

a. You asked me to provide you with my recommendation for the new sales position, and I believe that Sarah Miller is the best candidate.

b. Next month's board meeting will be held on the second Tuesday of the month, September 8.

c. Please take into consideration the fact that I will not be available in the afternoon on the 8th.

d. I need advance notice to prepare a speaking presentation on the basic fundamentals of this project.

e. We combined together the proposals, and after close scrutiny of the results have come to the consensus of opinion that this project will be our first priority.

f. Foreign imports are an essential necessity in our business.

g. We extend our grateful thanks that your future plans have secured our company's good success.

h. I sincerely believe we can solve the problem by hiring two knowledge experts to work for a limited period of time.

i. He will refer back to the survey responses and separate out the negative comments so we do not repeat the same problems again.

j. Whether or not they agree with the temporary reprieve, this issue still remains a problem.

EXERCISE 11 Editing style and tone helps you project a professional image: Positive wording

Edit the following negatively worded sentences to sound more positive:

a. He will not do well on the employment exam if he does not review the company's procedures.

b. The committee will not make their decision until next week.

c. The workers will receive no bonus if they do not submit their performance evaluations on time.

d. If you do not present your corporate ID card at the new cafeteria, you will not receive the 10 percent discount.

e. The project is not yet complete.

f. The reception will not be scheduled if the clients do not sign the contract.

g. I cannot attend the meeting if this report is not finished on time.

h. Because the construction plans were not delivered, we could not determine a timeline for completion.

i. Please do not schedule meetings on Fridays because the sales associates can't attend.

j. You do not have access to those documents because you neglected to complete the registration form.

EXERCISE 12 Editing style and tone helps you project a professional image: Conversational style

Edit the following sentences to improve their conversational style:

a. We do not concur that an equally advantageous investment opportunity will manifest itself again in the future.

b. Scheduling of the meeting is contingent upon affirmative responses from all constituents.

c. Kindly refrain from all interruptions for the duration of the presentation.

d. Our clients' allegiance rests upon our satisfactory achievement of performance criteria.

e. Utilize the most recently approved form to make your request to receive reimbursement for your travel expenses.

f. Apprise the departmental workers under your supervision that their efforts have been recognized and duly noted with appreciation.

g. We are satisfied with our pre-identified levels for end-of-year sales requirements.

h. I am curious as to your thought processes concerning the amendments to the proposal.

i. My opinion is that his work is not of the caliber to warrant promotion to division manager.

j. I would appreciate your perspectives on this issue in support of my decision-making process.

EXERCISE 13 Editing style and tone helps you project a professional image: Active voice

Edit the following sentences to change passive voice to active voice. (Note: You will need to supply a subject for the active verbs in some sentences.)

a. The proposal was written by the marketing team based on in-depth research.

b. The decision was made to extend overtime allowances by 10 percent.

c. Because two proposals were submitted, a meeting was scheduled to discuss the differences.

d. The survey instrument was created to gather information about the employees' perspectives.

e. The report will be delivered tomorrow so a decision can be made before the end of the week.

f. The problem can be solved only after the data have been analyzed.

g. His marketing plan was presented with very convincing supporting documentation.

h. Positive feedback about the presentation was received from the clients.

i. The salary increase will be seen in your next pay check.

j. The retirement party for Ira will be held at the College Club next week.

EXERCISE 14 Editing style and tone helps you project a professional image: Eliminating slang and clichés

Edit the following sentences by removing the slang and clichés (in italics) to clarify the meaning. If you are unfamiliar with the cliché, look it up online before editing.

a. Everyone in the department knows that the *buck stops here.*

b. His manager thinks she needs to *dangle a carrot* in front of him to get anything done.

c. Personally, I think this proposal will go *gang-busters* with upper management.

d. She has really been *a good soldier* about the change in leadership.

e. The union representative said we need to *sweeten the pot* if we want to end the labor strike.

f. He will be *swimming with the sharks* if he tries to present that proposal to the management team.

g. If this stock offer is not accepted, we may *take a bath.*

h. To be successful in business, you really need to *think outside the box.*

EXERCISE 15 Proofreading increases your credibility

Proofread the IT department meeting minutes (on this page), looking for the following types of errors: content, spelling and typographical, usage, grammatical, and format. If you would like to practice using the standard proofreading marks, you will find them in Appendix F.

EXERCISE 16 Proofreading increases your credibility: Checking systematically for errors

Type the following paragraph in a word processing software application of your choice, or download a copy from **mybcommlab.** Enter the words and punctuation exactly as shown. Highlight any errors that you see. Then run the application's spelling and grammar tools. Make a list of any (a) spelling errors that the spell-checker did *not* find and (b) changes the grammar checker suggested that would create an error. Do the results of this exercise change the methods you will use for proofreading in the future? Summarize your findings in an email message or memo to your instructor.

Do to recent security events, are technology upgrades our scheduled to be implemented at the beginning of next months. This change requires you to ask yourself what applications you current use and predicted those you may knee during the next fiscal year. How will you now what you might need in the future? That is a difficult question to answers. However, you're in put is necessary to assure that hour resources our used correct. Thank in advance for you're effort too improve this process.

Accompanies Exercise 16

IT Department Meeting Minutes
November 31, 20XX

Pat Wall, IT Division Manger, called the meeting to order at 2:05 PM. All IT Department employees was in attendance.

1. New Position – Rick Smeldon from Human Resources reported that the new IT position was posted November 1. Applications will be received through the first of the year. The recruitment committee will revue applications in early January and plans to conduct on-sight interviews during mid- to late Jnauary. HR plans to have the position filled by February 1.

2. IT Procedures Manual – The corporate office has asked the Department to update the IT Procedures Manual given change in policies and technology upgrades during the last two years. Bonita Ramirez and Sammie Taylor will co-chair the commitee to revise the current manual. Employees were asked to review and provide suggestion by the end of the month. A draft willbe provided at the December Department meeting.

3. Holiday Party – Sheldon Miller volunteered to organize the Department's Holiday Party. The date is yet to be determined but in holding with past tradition an after-hours pot-luck event will be scheduled in the employee lounge. Everyone is asked to bring a rapped gift ($10 limit) to exchange. Details will outlined by email in a few week. Flyers will be posted as reminder.

4. Help Desk Requests. Pat Wall stated that although our help desk requests have increased by 12% since last quarter. Unfortunately, we have not kept up with the program. Our response rates declined by 8%. New initiatives were discussed, and will be reiterated at our next department meeting.

Pat Wall adjourned the meeting at 1:55 PM

Respectully submitted by,

Jan Davis
Administrative Assistant
IT Department

Accompanies Exercise 15

EXERCISE 17 Editing style and tone helps you project a professional image: Improving reading level

Identify a paragraph that you find complicated and difficult to read from any of these sources: a paper you have written for class, a document you have written for work, a letter or email you recently received, a textbook, flyer, magazine, or brochure. If you do not already have an electronic copy of the paragraph, key it into your word processing software. Using the application's technology tools (or an online tool you find through a web search), determine the grade level of the paragraph.

Then make a copy of the paragraph and rewrite it in a conversational style using simple words in short sentences. Determine the revised version's grade level and print. In a three- to five-minute presentation to the class, display both the original and revised versions and describe how you revised the paragraph to be more readable. Identify which version you believe is most effective and explain why.

EXERCISE 18 Using "track changes" to get feedback on a draft [Related to the Technology feature on page 97]

Download the text from Exercise 16 from **mybcommlab** or type the text exactly as shown. Use that text as the body of a memo to

All Employees from you. Date it with today's date and create an appropriate subject line. Then edit the text, using your word processing application's track changes tools to show the corrections. Insert comments to indicate any suggestions or questions for the author.

EXERCISE 19 Adapting your communication approach to other cultures [Related to the Culture feature on page 87]

Assume you are a manager at a bank in Chicago and want to market new savings products to a growing Hispanic population. You are looking forward to Carlos Sanchez joining your marketing team, since he has experience working with this population. At the first team meeting, you make several enthusiastic suggestions about ways to market these products and you expect Carlos and other teammates to debate with you, point out weaknesses in your ideas, and make alternative suggestions. However, Carlos remains quiet. He simply nods and says, "That sounds like a good idea." You can't understand why he has so little to offer. After the meeting, you mention your concern to another colleague who suggests that Carlos is reluctant to disagree with you. Since Carlos grew up in a Latin American culture, he may see himself as below you in the hierarchy of the team and feel that contradicting you may seem disrespectful.

For the second team meeting, you want to communicate differently with Carlos, so that he feels more comfortable contributing. Use your favorite web search engine to research sources that provide information about working effectively with people from Latin American cultures. Identify some different ways you might begin the meeting so that Carlos can offer his perspective and suggestions without worrying about disrespecting you.

WRITING

EXERCISE 20 Analyzing, composing, evaluating

a. Assume you are a member of a student organization that wants to organize a business-dress fashion show for students on your campus. Select a clothing store in your area that sells reasonably priced business attire, such as suits, shoes, and accessories. You want to showcase the store's products in your fashion show by borrowing a dozen outfits and accessories (six for men, six for women) that will be modeled during the show. Further, you would like a representative from the store to participate in the fashion show by explaining the appropriate fit of clothing, such as the right length of a tie and the position of a cuff for men, and the height of a heel, length of a skirt, and appropriate jewelry for women.

Use the list of ACE questions in the visual summary on page 99 to work through the ACE communication process and determine how you would communicate this message to the store manager. Then prepare the communication. If you choose a written medium, write the document. If you choose an oral medium, write a script.

After completely evaluating your final draft, print your message and submit it to your instructor. Also submit, on a separate sheet, a paragraph explaining how you implemented the ACE process and how it helped you prepare this communication.

b. Assume your student group has successfully organized a business-dress fashion show (see question 20a), which will be presented on February 3 at 7 PM. You now need to compose an email that will invite business majors to attend the show, free of charge. Use the list of ACE questions in the visual summary on page 99 to work through the ACE communication process and determine the information you will include in the email to interest your audience and persuade them to attend. Compose a draft of the email and ask at least two students who are not in your class to read the draft and provide feedback. Do they find it clear and persuasive? Revise

your draft based on their feedback, evaluate it thoroughly, and submit both your first draft and your revised draft to your instructor. On a separate sheet, submit a paragraph explaining how you changed your draft based on feedback.

EXERCISE 21 Revising and designing

a. Craig and Darryl work for a product design firm in New York. This morning, Craig received a call from a client in Chicago, asking if he and Darryl could fly to Chicago to consult on a new project. Craig and Darryl agreed, checked their calendars, and chose a 2 PM flight from JFK Airport the next day. However, when Craig called American Airlines to book two seats for the flight, he learned that no seats were available. He did a little research and decided that, of the options available, he would prefer to take a later flight leaving from Newark airport. See the draft of Craig's email to Darryl below. Revise this email to (1) use a direct organization and (2) arrange the material into effective paragraphs.

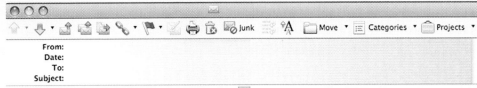

Darryl,

I just got off the phone with American Airlines. There are no seats available on the 2 PM flight from JFK that we planned to take tomorrow. If we have to take a later flight, I'd like to attend my staff meeting at 3 PM. I checked on the late flights out of JFK. They are at 7 PM and 9:30 PM, but are very expensive. Also, I remember that the last time we flew out of JFK in the late afternoon, the traffic was awful. I also checked flights from Newark so we can take the train from Penn Station. Starting at 6 PM there are hourly flights, and the fares are significantly cheaper. Let me know what you think.

Accompanies Exercise 21a

b. Alex and Marika are planning to attend an 8 AM meeting with their boss to discuss a report they completed the night before. On the way to work, Alex gets into a car accident. The following paragraph (right) is the voice message Alex leaves Marika to tell her that he will not be able to get to work in time for the meeting. He also needs to tell Marika where to find the photocopies of the report he made last night. Before Alex gets to the end of his message, the electronic "operator" interrupts and says: "If you are satisfied with this message, press 1. If you would like to record the message again, press 2." Alex realizes he should revise the message, and he presses 2. Revise this message for Alex.

> Marika, this is Alex. You won't believe what happened on the way to work today. I was driving down Sherman Avenue when a car ran a red light and hit me. I'm okay, but I'm at least 30 minutes from work and my car is undrivable. I can't leave anyway because the police officer is writing up the report really slowly, and I need to wait to get my license back and to make sure the tow truck comes for my car. Then I'll need to get a taxi. I'm really glad I have my cell phone with me. Otherwise, I'd be in big trouble. I don't know when I'll get to work, so can you present our report at the meeting this morning? The photocopies are on Lucy's desk because . . ."

Accompanies Exercise 21b

COLLABORATING

EXERCISE 22 Writing collaboratively

Everyone enjoys getting compliments. Working with a team of students, identify one administrative office at your school that you think is very helpful or is in some other way doing a good job. Examples of administrative offices include admissions, financial aid, student housing, technology support, and athletics, among others. Alternatively, you can select a student club, a local store, or a local restaurant. As a team, brainstorm a list of reasons why you believe they are doing a good job and some evidence to support those reasons. From your brainstormed list, identify the best ideas to include in a letter designed to express appreciation and provide positive feedback. Use ACE to analyze your purpose and audience, compose a draft, and evaluate it. Submit your finished version to your instructor (and mail it to the intended audience).

EXERCISE 23 Providing and receiving feedback

Feedback is a valuable element of the evaluation process, but many writers find it challenging both to provide effective feedback and to use the feedback they receive. This collaborative activity is designed to give you practice in giving and receiving feedback.

Identify an administrative office at your school that you believe could be more helpful or could make a change that will benefit students. Examples of administrative offices include admissions, financial aid, student housing, technology support, and athletics, among others. Alternatively, you can select a student club, a local store, or a local restaurant. Before coming to class, write a letter to the person in charge of that organization, offering your proposed change and providing reasons. Be sure to analyze purpose, audience, and content before you write. In class, in groups of three or four, read each others' draft letters and, through discussion, provide feedback to the writer. First discuss the elements of the letter you believe are effective, and then discuss recommended changes. In your evaluation, use the questions in the evaluation checklist on page 99.

Based on the feedback you receive, revise your letter and then evaluate it. Submit to your instructor your first draft and revision.

EXERCISE 24 Exploring slang and clichés

Working with a team of students, make a list of 10 slang terms or cliché phrases that you use or hear on a regular basis. For each item on your list, type a complete sentence that uses the slang term or cliché. Under each sample sentence, create an edited version that communicates the same meaning without the slang or cliché.

Example: Slang: Let's make sure we are on the same page.
            Revision: Let's make sure we understand the
                       situation the same way.

SPEAKING

EXERCISE 25 Impromptu presentations

Select one of the following topics and plan a brief one- to two-minute presentation that you organize using a direct organizational plan. Begin with the main idea, followed by supporting information, and concluding with a short summary or wrap-up. Then select a second topic and plan a brief presentation that you organize with an indirect plan. For this presentation, begin with supporting information, followed by the main point with a brief summary or wrap-up at the end.

a. Describe your last vacation.

b. Explain why you chose your major.

c. Describe your dream job.

d. Explain why you selected this university/college.

e. Where do you see yourself in five years?

EXERCISE 26 Executive briefings

Prepare presentations for the following exercises:

a. **Analyzing websites:** Visit the website of a successful, well-known company, and print the first page. Based on your analysis, what is the purpose of the page? Who is the primary audience? Who might be the secondary audience? Is the page persuasive? Identify the content of the page and explain how it supports the purpose of the page.

Prepare a three- to five-minute presentation that conveys this information to the class. Display the website if possible.

b. **The art of persuasion:** Most business communication uses some level of persuasion. Presenting audience benefits is just one of many strategies writers use to persuade their audience. Search the web for other methods of persuasion that are applicable to business communication and prepare a three- to five-minute presentation that outlines this information for the class.

c. **A method to the medium:** Selecting the best medium for your business communication is often difficult. Assume you need to communicate with your professor. Create a realistic scenario or perhaps share a personal experience. In a three- to five-minute presentation to the class, describe the situation you need to communicate and outline the pros and cons of using a face-to-face conversation, telephone call, email message, or memorandum.

d. **Designing effective documents:** Select a business letter that one member of your group has received, for example a sales letter, a letter from a bank or insurance company, a promotional letter from a credit card company, or a letter soliciting donations for a charity. As a group, identify features of this letter that you believe are effective, making the letter professional-looking and easy to read. Also identify features that you find ineffective. In a three- to five-minute presentation, present your analysis. Either display or distribute a copy of the letter.

GRAMMAR

Adjectives and adverbs (See Appendix D—Section 1.1.3)

Retype (or download from mybcommlab.com) the following paragraph, correcting the errors in use or formation of adjectives and adverbs. Underline all your corrections.

Does your telephone etiquette speak good of you? Because most people answer their own phones at work, poor phone manners make both you and your company look badly. Which greeting will make the best impression: "How may I help you?" or "What do you want?" It is important to sound cheerfully on the phone.

Even if you don't feel well, try to respond positively. A more simple way to sound positive is to smile when speaking. Smiling actually does make a person seem more friendlier over the phone. Some people like to have the most unique telephone greeting in the office: "Yo, super service representative Skip speaking!" A greeting like that just makes "Skip" seem real unprofessional. Instead of being named "Best Employee of the Month," he is likely to be awarded "Worse Phone Manners of the Year."

4 Communicating Routine Messages and Building Goodwill

new hires @ work

Kalani Miller
Co-owner
MIKOH Swimwear
University of California—Santa Barbara, 2009

"ROUTINE MESSAGES ARE SIGNIFICANT because they form the basis of professional relationships. To ensure a positive image, I always evaluate my messages for a professional style and tone. For example, since I travel so much and my phone does not work in foreign countries, it is easiest for me to respond by email so I make sure my cell phone's voice mail greeting encourages callers to email me for the most efficient response. This attention to detail—even for routine messages—ensures effective communication and builds goodwill."

Introduction

Businesses produce millions of messages every day as a routine part of getting work done. These **routine business messages** take the form of emails, memos, letters, text messages, telephone calls, face-to-face conversations—even tweets. Examples of routine business messages include:

- requesting a correction to a shipment that included the wrong merchandise
- responding to a request to present quarterly sales data at a meeting
- explaining a travel expense to the accounting department
- sending a coworker updated charts that she requested

Routine messages such as these are short, straightforward, and not sensitive. They do not require you to persuade your audience to accept your point. Nor do they require thinking about how to prevent your audience from being upset. They simply require that you be clear, complete, and respectful. However, meeting just these requirements can be challenging. You need to decide how to phrase your main point, how to organize the message, what information to include, and how to evaluate the message to ensure that it is concise and easy to understand.

Chapter 3 showed you how to use the ACE process (Analyze, Compose, Evaluate) to make these kinds of decisions for all messages, including routine messages. Chapter 4 offers guidelines for composing specific types of routine messages, including questions and requests, informational messages, and **goodwill messages**—messages that give you the opportunity to establish and sustain a positive relationship with your audience. Throughout the chapter, you will see the ACE logo at points where the discussion offers new insight on how to use ACE to prepare these communications.

Study Question 4.1

How do I compose messages containing questions and requests?

People ask questions and make requests daily, but not all requests are equal. In some instances, you will be asking people to do things that clearly are part of their job responsibilities. In other cases, you will be asking people to do you a favor, something that they have no obligation to do. This second kind of request often requires more explanation and persuasion. However, in both cases, you want to ensure that your audience responds well. You can do this by following the guidelines in this section.

Decide between a direct or an indirect organization

When you compose a request message, like any other message, you need to decide between direct and indirect organization of the content. In other words, where in the message will you state your main idea, in this case your question? In a message with a direct organization, your question appears toward the beginning, often as early as the first sentence. Explanatory details follow. In a message with an indirect organization, your question appears later in the communication after a brief explanation. For most requests, a direct organization is the better choice. FIGURE 4.1 illustrates the difference between the two.

At first glance, it may seem that the indirect version is more polite because it is less assertive than the direct version. However, the direct version phrases the request equally politely. In addition, the direct version is easier to understand because it gets to the point quickly and lets the audience know why they are reading the message. By contrast, the indirect version requires the audience to read through all the details before learning why the details are important. As a result, the audience may need to reread the message. Put yourself in the audience's position: with dozens of messages to navigate throughout the day, your audience will appreciate messages that are organized directly.

■ Access this chapter's simulation entitled Routine Messages, located at mybcommlab.com.

FIGURE 4.1 A Direct Organization Is Best for Most Requests

indirect organization

The latest version I have of the third-quarter sales figures is dated three weeks ago. I know your report is not yet complete, but we will be discussing the data in tomorrow's budget meeting at 4 PM. Can you please send me the latest draft? Thanks!

Details lead up to the request.

direct organization

Please send me the latest draft of the third-quarter sales figures. I know your report is not yet complete, but we will be discussing the data in tomorrow's budget meeting at 4 PM, and the latest draft I have was dated three weeks ago. Thanks!

Request comes first, followed by details.

However, in some circumstances, you may find it's better to use an indirect organization for requests. If the audience will be confused by your question or request, a brief introduction can provide helpful context. For example, imagine that you are working for a construction firm in Murfreesboro, Tennessee, and a company hires you to build an office building in Indianapolis, Indiana. Your business banker in Tennessee, Jerry, used to work in Indianapolis and may have some useful information for you. To ask Jerry for this information by email, an indirect organization is appropriate because Jerry could be confused by your question without some introductory context. FIGURE 4.2 illustrates the difference between a direct and indirect organization for this message.

Note that choosing direct or indirect organization will affect how you phrase the subject line. When you choose direct organization, you can state your request explicitly in the subject line. The indirect organization requires that the subject line be more neutral and only indicate the general purpose of the email.

FIGURE 4.2 An Indirect Organization Is Useful for Confusing Questions

direct organization

SUBJECT: Request for names of contractors in Indianapolis

Hello, Jerry:

Would you please look over the attached list of contractors in Indianapolis and suggest a few others that I can ask to submit a bid for work on a new office building?

My company has won a contract for a large office building in Indianapolis, and we're now contacting subcontractors to request bids on the job. I'm having difficulty identifying qualified heating and cooling contractors.

I need six and have only three. I know that you worked in Indianapolis for many years, arranging construction loans, so I am sure you are familiar with heating and cooling contractors there. I'd really appreciate your help and will be glad to return the favor whenever possible.

Thanks,

Bob

Robert Golterman
Golterman Construction
9898 Weldon Highway
Murfreesboro, TN 37129
Telephone: 615-555-8388

WHY IS THIS VERSION INEFFECTIVE?

If you haven't talked to Jerry recently, he will probably be confused by this unusual and unexpected request.

After reading or hearing the details, Jerry will need to review the request again.

indirect organization

SUBJECT: Request for a small favor

Hello, Jerry:

I have a favor to ask. I know that you worked in Indianapolis for many years arranging construction loans, so I am sure you are familiar with heating and cooling contractors there. My company has won a contract for a large office building in Indianapolis, and we're now contacting subcontractors to request bids on the job. I'm having difficulty identifying qualified heating and cooling contractors. I need six and have only three.

Could you please look over my attached list of contractors and suggest a few more I can add? I'd really appreciate your help and will be glad to return the favor whenever possible.

Thanks,

Bob

Robert Golterman
Golterman Construction
9898 Weldon Highway
Murfreesboro, TN 37129
Telephone: 615-555-8388

WHY IS THIS VERSION MORE EFFECTIVE?

First sentence signals to Jerry that a request is coming.

Details prepare him for the request.

Following the details, the request will make sense to Jerry.

Wherever you place your request, phrase it so that your audience knows exactly what you are asking and will be able to answer easily. If you have a series of questions, list or number them so that the audience can respond to each question individually. In all cases, avoid simply implying your request, which requires your audience to figure out exactly what you want. Imagine, for example, the following version of the message communicated in Figure 4.1:

> The latest version I have of the third quarter sales figures is dated three weeks ago. I know your report is not yet complete, but we will be discussing the data in tomorrow's budget meeting at 4 PM. *I will not be able to prepare for the meeting if I don't have the latest draft.*

The audience needs to read through the entire message and then decide whether you are saying that you have decided not to prepare for the meeting or if you would like an updated draft so that you can prepare. To eliminate that ambiguity, state your request explicitly.

ACE

Provide reasons for the request

As you analyze the content to include in the message, consider how much detail the audience needs to know. As the example in Figure 4.2 illustrates, unless the reason for your request is obvious, you will need to explain it. The message in Figure 4.2 requires a substantial explanation. Other messages will require much less. For example, most customer requests for refunds or merchandise exchanges—sometimes called *claim requests*—require little explanation.

Routine business message A nonsensitive, straightforward communication that asks questions, answers questions, provides information, or confirms agreements.

Goodwill message Any message that gives you the opportunity to establish and maintain a positive relationship with your audience.

FIGURE 4.3 provides an example of a request a customer submitted to a company that shipped the wrong order. Many companies provide online customer service support, and this message was entered on the company's website. Notice that it begins with the direct request for a return authorization number, which is the first step in initiating a product return. Although it may seem abrupt to begin the message by stating what you want, your audience will appreciate the direct approach. Companies deal with many claim messages each day, and readers need to find the main point quickly. If a claim request requires more explanation or evidence, you would write a persuasive claim, which is described in Chapter 5.

FIGURE 4.3
Request Requiring Brief Explanation

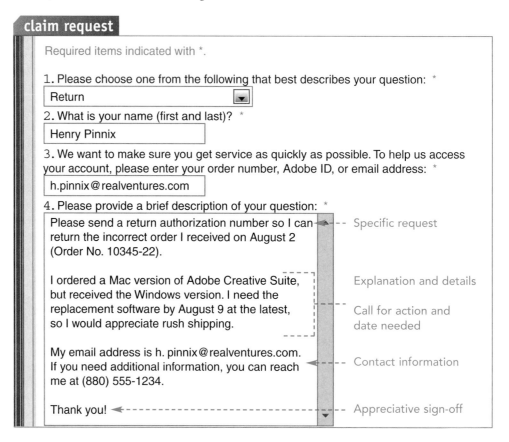

claim request

Required items indicated with *.

1. Please choose one from the following that best describes your question: *

Return

2. What is your name (first and last)? *

Henry Pinnix

3. We want to make sure you get service as quickly as possible. To help us access your account, please enter your order number, Adobe ID, or email address: *

h.pinnix@realventures.com

4. Please provide a brief description of your question: *

Please send a return authorization number so I can return the incorrect order I received on August 2 (Order No. 10345-22).   ◄--- Specific request

I ordered a Mac version of Adobe Creative Suite, but received the Windows version. I need the replacement software by August 9 at the latest, so I would appreciate rush shipping.   Explanation and details

Call for action and date needed

My email address is h. pinnix@realventures.com. If you need additional information, you can reach me at (880) 555-1234.   ◄--- Contact information

Thank you! ◄------------------------------- Appreciative sign-off

Adopt a "you" perspective and include audience benefits

Like other communications, routine requests will get the best reception from your audience if you compose the message from the audience's perspective, not just your own. A **"you" perspective** involves more than just using the word "you" in the message, although that is one technique that helps. It also involves focusing on what the audience needs and how the audience benefits from your message. To determine **audience benefits**, analyze the positive outcomes your audience will experience by responding favorably to your request. Audience benefits are not as important in routine requests as they are in persuasive requests, when the audience may be resistant to your proposal. However, benefits can promote goodwill in *all* your messages. Consider the example in FIGURE 4.4.

The "you" perspective message has a different focus than the "I" perspective version. Instead of addressing why "I" need to get the sales figures, it focuses on how "you" (the audience) will benefit from sending the figures. This helps the audience feel more positive about taking the time to perform the task.

Creating a "you" perspective can be challenging because it requires you to consider other people's viewpoints. Although you can never be certain what someone else will perceive as a benefit, brainstorming ideas can help. As you brainstorm, analyze two different categories of benefits. **Internal benefits** are advantages that your audience directly receives from complying with your request, for example, reduced workload, increased

"I" PERSPECTIVE	"YOU" PERSPECTIVE
Please send me the latest draft of the third-quarter sales figures. I will be presenting the data in tomorrow's budget meeting, and the latest draft I have was dated three weeks ago. Thanks!	Will you please send me your updated third-quarter sales figures today? If the budget committee has the figures to discuss at tomorrow's meeting, they can get you a preliminary budget by Thursday, and you'll be able to start planning next year's sales forecasts.

FIGURE 4.4
"I" versus "You" Perspective

professional recognition, or financial gains. Figure 4.4 illustrates an internal benefit: by sending the sales figures, the audience will receive the budget information she needs to begin planning sales forecasts. **External benefits** are advantages that someone else—a third party—gains. For example, your communication may have positive effects on people or things your audience cares about. Consider these examples:

Internal benefit: By volunteering for this project, you will be eligible for a bonus of 5 percent of your salary.

External benefit: By volunteering your time during Help Our Community Day, you will not only help our department achieve its community service goals, but you'll also be helping our local schools.

Notice that in all examples, the word "you" is associated with polite requests and audience benefits. This is a positive use of "you." To be effective, avoid using "you" in negative ways—for example issuing orders and accusations. In those cases, use impersonal expressions rather than "you."

Accusatory statement: You made errors on the forms. You must correct and resubmit them.

Impersonal statement: Please correct the highlighted errors and resubmit the forms.

Conclude with gratitude and a call for action

Two elements are typical at the end of requests: (1) an expression of gratitude or thanks and (2) a specific call for action that makes clear what you need and when you need it. In short requests, such as the previous examples, a simple "Thanks" may be all that's needed to show your gratitude for the audience's predicted response. However, when you are requesting a favor or something that will be an inconvenience, your audience will appreciate a fuller expression of gratitude.

FIGURE 4.5 illustrates a short request that is spoken but could also be emailed. In this case, Stan's manager is asking Stan to give a presentation at a meeting, on short notice. The manager chose a face-to-face conversation because doing so might encourage Stan to respond more positively. Stan would most likely find it more difficult to decline the request in a face-to-face conversation, or over the phone, than if he had received the same message by email.

"You" perspective An approach to communication that presents the information from the audience's point of view. The "you" perspective focuses on what the audience needs and how the audience benefits from your message.

Audience benefits The positive outcomes your audience will experience by responding favorably to your request.

Internal benefits Advantages that the audience will directly receive from complying with your request. These may include a reduced workload, increased professional recognition, or financial gains.

External benefits Advantages that someone else—a third party—gains when your audience complies with a request.

FIGURE 4.5 Spoken or Emailed Request for a Favor

Begins by stating the request. No introduction is needed.

Provides concise explanation and rationale for request

Expresses gratitude and offers possible audience benefit

Concludes with call for action

request

Hi, Stan. Can you cover for me at the 2 PM division meeting today? I have a client lunch I'm sure will run long, and you know all the data we need to report—you researched everything and put it together. I'd appreciate your help, and this might be a great opportunity for you to impress the VP. Sound okay?

FIGURE 4.6 illustrates a more complex request that requires a detailed call for action as well as expressions of gratitude.

FIGURE 4.6 Written Request for Information

letter

Tabor College
Reed Hall, Box 1054
Lineville, VA 28615
January 14, 20XX

Ms. Paulina Rashid, Advisor
Students in Free Enterprise
Atlantic University
410 Bedden Hall
Patterson, VA 28664

Dear Ms. Rashid:

My cousin, Marlina Robertson, is a member of the Students in Free Enterprise (SiFE) chapter you advise at Atlantic University. She gave me your name and address. We are hoping to start our own SiFE club here at Tabor College and would greatly appreciate your answers to a few questions that I did not find answered on the SiFE website (www.sife.org).

1. How many student members are required for a club to be recognized by the governing international organization?

2. Does the governing organization provide any financial assistance for newly developed clubs to support on-campus promotions for membership drives, such as t-shirts and brochures?

3. Do you develop relationships with other SiFE clubs to collaborate on projects? Or are the projects competitive?

Since our first membership drive is scheduled in March, could you get back to us before January 31? If you prefer to discuss my questions by phone, please call me at your convenience at (409) 555-1234.

If SiFE projects can be collaborative, rather than competitive, we would enjoy developing a collaborative relationship with your SiFE club to design a joint project that would benefit both our campuses and communities. I look forward to talking with you about that once our club is under way.

Thank you for sharing your knowledge with us.

Sincerely,

Dominique Robertson

Dominique Robertson
Tabor College

Annotations (left margin):

The letter begins with an introduction, and the first paragraph ends with the request, phrased politely.

Mentioning the website shows the reader that you have done research before writing and are not wasting her time.

Numbered questions help the audience respond to each item in the reply.

The letter indicates when a response is needed.

An alternate reply method (phone call) gives the reader flexibility.

The potential "collaborative relationship" may be perceived as a benefit.

A "thank you" at the end expresses gratitude.

How do I compose informational messages?

Not all routine messages involve requests or questions. You will sometimes be writing to convey information. For example, you may be replying to requests, responding to claims, confirming information, making announcements, or providing instructions. You can consider these messages routine if the information will not surprise, disappoint, or anger the audience. The following sections explain how to address each kind of informational message.

TECHNOLOGY Taking Advantage of Instant Messaging in Business

Businesses are increasingly using instant messaging (IM) for informal and formal communication. In some businesses, people use free public IM programs (such as Google Talk and Yahoo Messenger) to communicate with coworkers just as they do with family and friends. In other businesses, IM has become an official communication channel with specialized corporate IM platforms installed and regulated by the IT department and available only to employees of that company. The financial services industry uses IM heavily because it allows people to communicate very quickly to take advantage of changes in financial markets. The Union Bank of Switzerland estimated that in one month their company generates 65 million IM messages.[1] Technology experts predict that business use of IM will continue to grow and that by 2013, 95 percent of employees in major global companies will use IM as a primary communication tool, generating 46 billion IMs per year.[2]

At ZS Associates, a global management consulting firm with more than 1300 employees and 19 offices worldwide, Google Talk is used extensively in the company's Software Development Group, which has around 100 people. Jes Sherborne, Managing Principal for Software Development, requires that all of his employees use Google Talk. Sherborne said IM "fills a really interesting niche. People use Google Talk here to show that they are available to be interrupted with a quick question or to provide a piece of information to help a colleague get over a hurdle. If you're busy and don't want to be disturbed, you can designate you're 'busy' and you won't receive IMs. It's much less intrusive than someone knocking on your door or calling you up."

In addition to improving productivity by managing interruptions,[3] IM provides businesses other benefits, including the ability to communicate real-time information, improved efficiency for geographically dispersed workgroups, and multitasking with multiple communication channels. Employees can simultaneously speak to a customer on the tele-phone, receive IM updates from a colleague, and research solutions on the Internet.

Despite these benefits, if a business has no IM standards, IM use can lead to problems with maintaining security, archiving messages, and preventing employee misuse. If your company does not have standards, the following guidelines are a good starting place for business communication:[4]

1. **Focus on business.** Even if your coworker's IM status says he is not busy, do not interrupt with personal messages. Limit your workplace IMs to workplace topics.

2. **Keep messages simple.** IM users expect text will be brief and to the point. Use IM to ask short questions, make quick announcements, or list brief answers that you need to communicate immediately.

3. **Use a professional-sounding IM username.** An IM username should be easily identified and attached to a business email address. Do not use anonymous usernames, such as "HomeAlone," "Wasco21," or "Liv2Ski." Instead, use a combination of your first and last name, such as "PatriciaH," "PHarmon" or patricia.harmon.

4. **Be professional and confidential.** Assume that other people will read your IM messages. Use language that you would feel comfortable having anyone read, and never convey company-sensitive information, such as stock information, company merger news, or plans for layoffs.

5. **Save important messages.** If your organization has a centralized IM system, then your messages will automatically be archived. If not, keep your own records so that you can refer to messages in the future.

PEARSON **mybcommlab**

For TECHNOLOGY exercises, go to Exercise 18 on pages 137–138 and Exercise 22b on page 139 or to this chapter's End-of-Chapter Exercises at mybcommlab.com.

Reply to questions with a direct answer

Most answers to questions benefit from a direct organization:

- Begin with the direct response and then provide explanatory details.
- For a message with multiple questions, follow the organization of the original message, answering each question in sequence.
- End with a friendly closing.

See FIGURE 4.7 for an example of a written reply to a request for information. It is a response to the letter in FIGURE 4.6 on page 116, which a student wrote to an advisor at another college requesting information about a student club. As the advisor prepares to respond to the student's request for information, she uses ACE to analyze the purpose, audience, content, and medium. Her purpose is not just to provide the requested information, but also to encourage the students to pursue their plans. Since her audience will probably respond favorably to the message, the writer can begin with a positive response and number her answers to mirror the student's original letter. The advisor decides that a letter is the best medium because she can mail sample brochures and flyers with the letter.

FIGURE 4.7 Written Reply to a Request for Information

letter

ATLANTIC UNIVERSITY
Patterson, VA 28664

January 18, 20XX

Ms. Dominique Robertson
Tabor College
Reed Hall, Box 1054
Lineville, VA 28615

Dear Ms. Robertson:

The opening builds goodwill by including a congratulatory statement. It quickly gets to the point by indicating that the requested items are included.

Congratulations on your goal to begin a SiFE club at Tabor College. Below are the answers to your questions.

The responses to the questions are numbered.

Each numbered item begins with a direct answer to the corresponding question.

The paragraphs provide additional related information, including suggestions, references to sample documents, and additional contact information.

1. Your campus club can be as small or large as you like. SiFE does not require a specific number of student members to recognize a campus club. However, based on our experience, you should have at least 15 active members (including your executive officers) to ensure your club's success. Of course, the more members you have the better.

2. Although SiFE does not provide financial assistance to help you promote your club, I am enclosing several sample documents that we have successfully used here. Your cousin, Marlina, has helped us design many of these materials. Her desktop publishing skills are exceptional. Perhaps she can share these files with you.

3. We look forward to developing a collaborative relationship with your SiFE club. Our current president is Colin Withers. His email address is cwithers@atlantic.edu. Please contact him to discuss this possibility.

The closing includes contact information and a friendly offer for additional assistance.

If you have any other questions, please feel free to call me at (409) 123-9874. I would be happy to serve as a mentor until you establish your own faculty advisor.

Best regards,

Paulina Rashid

Paulina Rashid, M.Ed.
SiFE Faculty Advisor

Enclosures

When someone asks you a question in a face-to-face or telephone conversation, you can organize your message exactly as you would when writing a response. If your response is not controversial or likely to disappoint, begin with a direct answer and then follow up with details. If you do not have the answer immediately available, then say that right away.

For example, imagine that Stan is responding to the question his manager asked him in Figure 4.5 on page 115. Stan's manager cannot attend a meeting and asks Stan to attend and present his department's report. Even if Stan decides he cannot provide a definitive answer at that moment, he can still provide a short and direct answer: "I would like to review the research for about 15 minutes to see if I can effectively present the information. Can I call you back?" After determining that he feels comfortable with the task, Stan can either email his response to his supervisor or he can call.

Respond to customer requests by creating goodwill

When a customer requests a refund, exchange, or repair, the business has an opportunity to create goodwill. Assuming that the business decides to satisfy the claim, a well-written response can strengthen its relationship with the customer. According to research reported by marketing expert Phillip Kotler, 34 percent of consumers who file complaints will do business with a company again if their complaint is resolved. As many as 95 percent will do business again if the complaint is handled quickly.[5]

When composing positive responses to customer requests, use the same general format as other routine replies:

- **Begin with the positive response** (in this case, that you can grant the claim). Your subject line may be neutral ("Response to Your Request for Platinum Status") or positive ("Congratulations on Your New Elite Status"). The first paragraph should always be positive. Avoid sounding as if you are doing the customer a favor. For example, do not say, "Although you have not reached the required number of frequent flyer miles to achieve platinum status, we will make an exception in your case because you are a valuable customer." Instead, say, "Because we value your loyalty, we are pleased to offer you platinum status."

- **Follow up with any necessary information.** If a customer has reported a problem, explain the reason behind it and your plans to prevent it from reoccurring. A good explanation can win consumer confidence,[6] while an explanation that sounds like an excuse will result in a negative reaction.[7] Although it is not necessary to apologize, it is also important not to blame the customer. You can win customer confidence and strengthen customer loyalty simply by expressing genuine concern.[8]

- **End with a friendly closing.** For example, express appreciation.

> "You are correct. Your cell phone account was incorrectly billed last month. We have credited your account for $32.60. If you have further questions, please call us at 1-800-555-1234. Thank you for choosing CoastTel."

FIGURE 4.8 illustrates a positive response to the claim in Figure 4.3 on page 114. Notice that the sales representative does not apologize but does include a goodwill strategy at the end.

FIGURE 4.8 Positive Response to a Claim Request

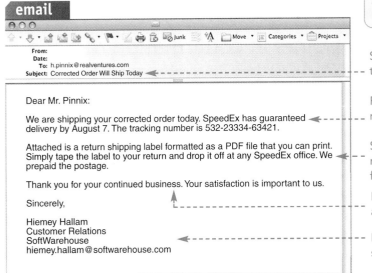

PEARSON mybcommlab

> Apply Figure 4.8's key concepts by revising a new document. Go to Chapter 4 in mybcommlab.com and select Document Makeovers.

email

From:
Date:
To: h.pinnix@realventures.com
Subject: Corrected Order Will Ship Today

Dear Mr. Pinnix:

We are shipping your corrected order today. SpeedEx has guaranteed delivery by August 7. The tracking number is 532-23334-63421.

Attached is a return shipping label formatted as a PDF file that you can print. Simply tape the label to your return and drop it off at any SpeedEx office. We prepaid the postage.

Thank you for your continued business. Your satisfaction is important to us.

Sincerely,

Hiemey Hallam
Customer Relations
SoftWarehouse
hiemey.hallam@softwarehouse.com

Subject line communicates the positive response.

First sentence restates the positive response. No introduction is needed.

Second paragraph explains how to return and offers an audience benefit: free shipping on the return.

Last paragraph expresses appreciation and desire for continued business.

Email ends with complimentary closing, signature, and contact information.

Social media networks such as Twitter offer businesses expanded opportunities to receive customer suggestions and complaints—and respond to them quickly to satisfy customers and maintain goodwill. Whole Foods Market, the world's leading natural and organic grocer, is a cutting-edge user of Twitter. The company's Integrated Media team monitors all tweets that mention Whole Foods Market and addresses complaints immediately. FIGURE 4.9 illustrates one such exchange. (In the figure, each tweet is numbered in the order it was sent.) A customer in London complained that the apples he purchased at his last trip to Whole Foods Market were not good and that his local store was "understaffed at the till" (the British word for cash register). The Integrated Media team at Whole Foods Market responded within a few hours and defused the situation—in fact, making the initially irate customer feel much better about his Whole Foods Market experience. Each tweet from Whole Foods (#2 and #4) was clear and respectful, expressing a "you" perspective in fewer than 140 characters.

FIGURE 4.9 Twitter Exchange Responding to Customer Complaint

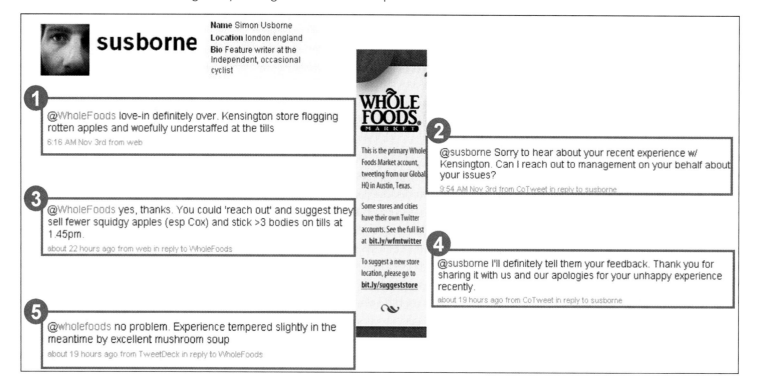

Highlight key points in confirmation messages

A **confirmation** is a message acknowledging that you have received information or checking that you have understood information correctly. When you make oral agreements with someone, it's a good practice to confirm those agreements in writing. For example, assume that while you are eating lunch in the break room, you discuss with a colleague the need to change the scheduled day and time of a meeting. You might make mental notes of the possible scheduling options and write them on a napkin during the conversation. However, when you return to your office, you discover that you accidentally threw away the napkin. Now you're relying only on your memory. You decide to confirm the information with your colleague and email him so you have his response in writing. Compare the two versions of the confirmation email drafts in FIGURE 4.10. The effective version is not only clearer, it is also more professional.

FIGURE 4.10 Two Versions of an Email Confirming Information

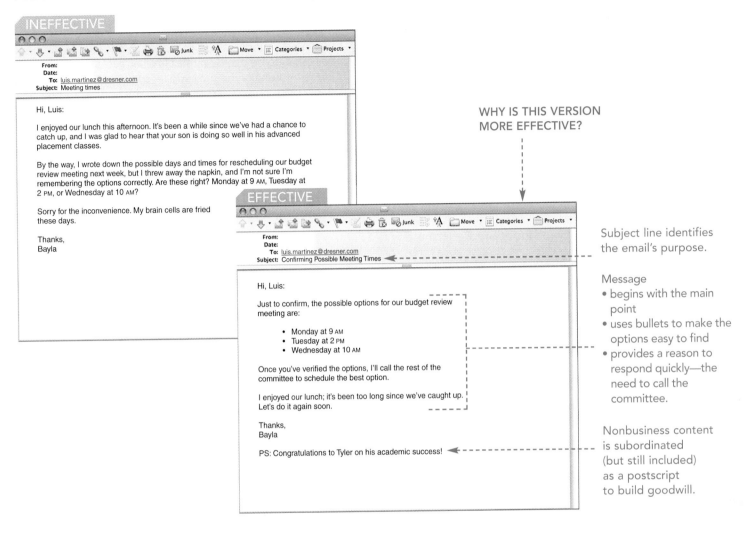

WHY IS THIS VERSION MORE EFFECTIVE?

Subject line identifies the email's purpose.

Message
- begins with the main point
- uses bullets to make the options easy to find
- provides a reason to respond quickly—the need to call the committee.

Nonbusiness content is subordinated (but still included) as a postscript to build goodwill.

Organize routine announcements so they are easy to skim

Announcements are messages that publicly notify an audience of information they need or want to know. For example, you might notify:

- customers about a sale or a change in policy
- employees about a new CEO or promotions within the organization
- the public about job opportunities in your company

You can announce information through any medium. You can publish announcements to the general public through newspapers, television, radio, and company websites. For announcements to employees at your company, you can use the company website, memos or email, or a flyer. Announcements to customers are typically sent by letter or email, but you may also post them on social networking sites like Facebook.

How does an announcement email differ from other emails you may write? One difference is that an announcement will go to a broad audience, not just one or two people. Another difference is that an announcement rarely requires a response. It is usually a one-way, informational communication. However, like any other routine communication, a good announcement will clearly state its purpose and be organized so that the audience can find important information.

Confirmation An acknowledgment that you have received information or understood a message correctly.

Announcement A communication that publicly notifies an audience of information they need or want to know.

ETHICS Is Blind Carbon Copy (bcc) Like Spying?

In your email program, the bcc—*blind carbon copy*—feature allows you to copy someone on an email without the recipient knowing it. Does sharing an email "secretly" with someone else raise any ethical issues? Consider three different scenarios for sending a *bcc*.

1. You are sending an email to all employees who are late submitting their travel reimbursement requests, asking them to submit immediately or risk not being reimbursed. The list is long, and if you pasted it into the email cc box, it would fill the screen. By using the bcc feature, you help ensure that your recipients focus on the message content rather than be distracted by an overly long header. In this case, the use of bcc is very functional. You can also argue that it is more ethical than including everyone on the cc line. Recipients don't need to know the names and email addresses of all the others who have missed the deadline. Making this information visible on the email may embarrass some people on the list.

2. You are reporting a problem to the technical support group for one of the software products you use. The head of your IT group has asked that everyone bcc her on all problem reports. She uses these emails as an informal log to track the frequency of problems, but she does not want to be included in follow-up email exchanges. In this case, the use of bcc is also functional and ethical. You are not deceiving the intended recipient or using the information to the disadvantage of the software supplier. The technical support people would act no differently if they knew the head of IT was copied or if the copying was blind.

3. You are writing an email to negotiate the price of a product with a new supplier. Your colleague in another department has asked to be bcc'd on these exchanges. She wants some inside information on the supplier so that she can negotiate a low price on a different product she intends to buy. She would prefer that the supplier not know that she has this extra information. Your colleague argues that her main responsibility is to get the lowest price possible for your company. She has an obligation to use whatever information is available to get that low price. This use of a bcc is much more troubling since your colleague intends to use the information to disadvantage the recipient. This could be considered a form of spying.

As you write emails, how do you decide if you should use a bcc and if it is ethical? Apply these two tests:

1. Are you intending to deceive the "to" recipient about who is receiving the email?

2. Can the recipient be disadvantaged or hurt if the material in the email is shared with the bcc readers and the recipient doesn't know it?

If you can say "yes" to either of these, then do not use the bcc. ■

mybcommlab

For ETHICS exercises, go to Critical Thinking Question 3 on page 134 and Exercise 22a on page 139 or to this chapter's End-of-Chapter Exercises at mybcommlab.com.

FIGURE 4.11 illustrates a routine announcement to bank customers. The bank is changing some of its policies and is required by law to notify customers. This announcement avoids legal language. Instead, it uses informal language ("we're"), active voice, and bullet points to entice the audience to read it.

Format instructions so readers can easily follow the steps

In addition to requests and replies, routine business messages may include procedure information or brief instructions about how to do things. Examples include:

- directions to complete a new travel authorization form
- instructions to process budget requests
- procedures for submitting reimbursement documentation

Good instructions allow the audience to understand the task and complete it accurately. To make it easy for the audience to follow the instructions, use these guidelines:

- **Begin with a brief overview** that helps your audience understand when and why they need to use the instructions.

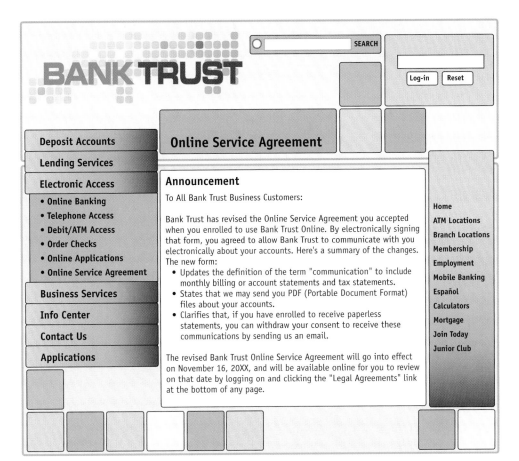

FIGURE 4.11
Routine Informational Announcement

- **Divide the instructions into numbered or bulleted steps**, including only one action per step. Numbers are more effective than bullets when you want to be able to refer to other steps in the procedure. For example, you might want to direct your audience to return to a specific step or to skip a step under specific conditions. However, if the sequence or order is not important, bullets are acceptable.
- **Begin each step with an action verb**, using **parallel phrasing**—the same grammatical form for each item. There is one exception to this rule. If an instruction is conditional, in other words it needs to be performed only under certain conditions, begin the step by identifying the condition (see item #6 in Figure 4.12 as an example).
- If a step requires explanation, **place the explanation after the action** rather than before it (see item #5 in Figure 4.12).

FIGURE 4.12 illustrates these guidelines.

Study Question 4.3

What kinds of messages build goodwill in my business relationships?

Business depends on good relationships. As Linda Hudson, President of BAE Systems, the largest military vehicle business in the world, explains, "It's incredibly important to realize that relationships define everything that we do, and it's all about the quality of those relationships that makes an organization work."[9] *Goodwill* is a term used to describe the attitude of friendliness and caring that is central to creating, solidifying, and maintaining relationships.

Parallel phrasing Using the same grammatical form for each item in a list.

FIGURE 4.12 Memo Providing Instructions

memo

TO: All Employees

FROM: Luka Mirkovic, VP Accounting Division

DATE: July 15, 20XX

SUBJECT: New Procedures for Travel Authorization

Acme has a new travel authorization form. Below are instructions for completing it correctly. If you submit the form before you travel, your absence from the office will be recorded as a travel day and will not count against your sick days or vacation days.

1. Enter your name in **box A**.

2. Enter your employee ID number in **box B**.

3. Enter the travel destination in **box C**.

4. Enter the purpose of the travel in **box D**.

5. Enter the dates you will be away from the office in **box E**. Date formats must be entered as MM/DD/YYYY, for example 06/04/20XX to 06/07/20XX.

6. If you will be away from the office for two or more days, identify in **box F** the name of the individual who will be responsible for your office duties while you are traveling. If you are away for fewer than two days, skip **box F**.

7. Ask your supervisor to sign and date in **box G**, indicating his/her approval of your travel authorization.

If you have questions, contact Ryan Devlin at Ext. 6632.

First paragraph begins with an overview of the procedure, outlining its purpose and benefits to motivate the reader.

Actions are divided into numbered steps.

Steps 1–5 and Step 7 begin with an action verb, using parallel phrasing.

In Step 5, explanations come after the action.

Step 6 begins with a conditional phrase because the step needs to be completed only under certain conditions.

new hires @ work

Nicole Thomas

Associate Consultant, Kroll

University of Florida, 2008

"I spend at least an hour each day writing emails to coworkers, managers, and clients. Some tricks I use include numbering questions, writing short and specific subject lines, and dividing an email into short paragraphs."

Throughout this chapter, you have seen examples of goodwill techniques: expressing appreciation, offering help, using a "you" perspective, and highlighting audience benefits. While some of these techniques might appear to be embellishments to make the message more polite, these audience-oriented expressions in fact serve two important communication goals. They make your audience more receptive to your message, and they make your audience feel good about their business relationship with you. With a good business relationship established, you will be able to work more easily and effectively with people whether they are coworkers, managers, vendors, customers, or clients.

Because relationships are so important, you will want to take advantage of opportunities to express appreciation and thoughtfulness, both in your routine communication and also in special messages designed primarily to communicate goodwill and keep the channels of communication open. These include thank-you messages, congratulations, expressions of sympathy, and for-your-information messages.

Thank-you messages

Thank-you messages offer you the opportunity to express appreciation and make your audience feel good about something they have done for you. You might write a thank-you message to a client who hosts you during a recent business dinner, to someone who writes a recommendation or reference letter for you, or to colleagues who send you congratulatory gifts when you are promoted. Thank-you messages also offer you the opportunity to express and display your professionalism. A well-written thank-you letter following a job interview communicates to an employer that you are motivated, thoughtful, and articulate.

The form your message takes will depend on the situation. Thank-you messages range from formal letters to informal emails, handwritten notes, or telephone calls. Following a job interview, you would choose to write a formal letter and, if time allows, send it by mail. The letter may be typed—or handwritten if your handwriting is legible.

Thank-you message An expression of appreciation when someone has done something for you.

C U L T U R E Differences in Saying Thank You

A thank-you note or email is more than just a polite gesture. It is a way to show genuine appreciation for the effort someone has made and to make that person feel good about the effort. However, different cultures have different ways of expressing thanks and perhaps different expectations about length and the amount of detail. The following two messages are real thank-you notes business students wrote thanking their supervisors for summer internships. Letter 1 is written by a U.S. student who interned in a U.S. company. Letter 2 is written by a Korean student who interned in a Singapore company. Both letters are very polite and were well received by their audiences. What differences do you notice about the two letters?

Letter 1, the American thank-you letter, follows the advice in this chapter. The letter is:

- personalized and sincerely expresses thanks.
- short and to the point, an appropriate approach in a low-context culture.
- informal, which signals the close working relationship between the student and mentor. This approach is appropriate in cultures with low power distance.

Letter 2 is written with the Asian culture in mind. The letter is:

- longer and formal.
- focused at the beginning on the relationship between the writer and audience, which is appropriate in high-context cultures.
- detailed, which signals that the writer has spent much time thinking about what to say to someone he respects. This approach is appropriate in cultures with high power distance.

Letter 1: North American Thank You

Dear David:

Thank you for providing me with an internship that exceeded my expectations. I have never had a manager who spent so much time developing my skills. I have learned so much—not only about marketing and strategy but also about how to be a good manager.

I really enjoyed working with you and the rest of the team. I would love to join the group again next summer and would be pleased to hear from you.

Thanks again for everything,

Leslie

Letter 2: Asian Thank You

Dear Mr. Jeehun:

Please accept my apology for not writing this letter earlier. After returning to the United States, I was busy with the details of moving.

Now that I reflect on my summer internship at Capital Investors, I see that I was able to complete it successfully primarily thanks to your consideration and support. I especially appreciate that you taught me the values that are necessary to be a successful investment banker.

First, I learned a professional attitude from you. Every kind manner you showed—such as thorough service for clients, a fine sense of being a salesperson, and a charismatic but warm-hearted leadership style—fascinated me.

Second, you showed me devotion to a job. Whenever I watched you absorbed in work, I felt your passion as an investment banker and the dignity of the vocation.

Last but not least, I learned it is possible to be a professional and also enjoy life by seeing you achieve a balance between work and family. It was impressive that you tried hard to invest your time and energy in playing with your children every weekend.

To sum up, having you as a boss during this summer internship was a great professional and personal experience for me. I have decided to look to you as my role model, and I will try to follow you in my career path.

I look forward to seeing you as soon as possible.

Sincerely,

Dong Gyu Lee

PEARSON mybcommlab

For CULTURE exercises, go to Critical Thinking Question 10 on page 134 and Exercise 20 on page 138 or to this chapter's End-of-Chapter Exercises at mybcommlab.com.

In informal situations, an email is appropriate. However, your audience may perceive a handwritten note to be an even more meaningful expression of gratitude since handwritten notes are so rare in today's digital age. FIGURE 4.13 illustrates a handwritten thank-you note.

FIGURE 4.13
Handwritten Thank-You Note

Hi, Tom:

Thank you for inviting me to your club while I was in Santa Barbara last week. I really enjoyed the spa, and the workout equipment was spectacular. If I had access to that kind of facility around here, I would be in great shape.

I look forward to seeing you again next month for our regional conference in Phoenix.

Regards,
Holt

Message begins with the thank you, followed by supporting comments.

Message concludes with a forward-looking statement.

The main challenge in writing a good thank-you note is to include specific content that relates to the act for which you are thanking someone. In Figure 4.13, Holt was easily able to write a customized note since he was thanking Tom for a specific act of hospitality. The problem arises when you need to write many similar notes—for example, in the scenario illustrated in FIGURE 4.14: writing a thank-you note to guest speakers. In

FIGURE 4.14   Generic versus Personalized Thank-You Note

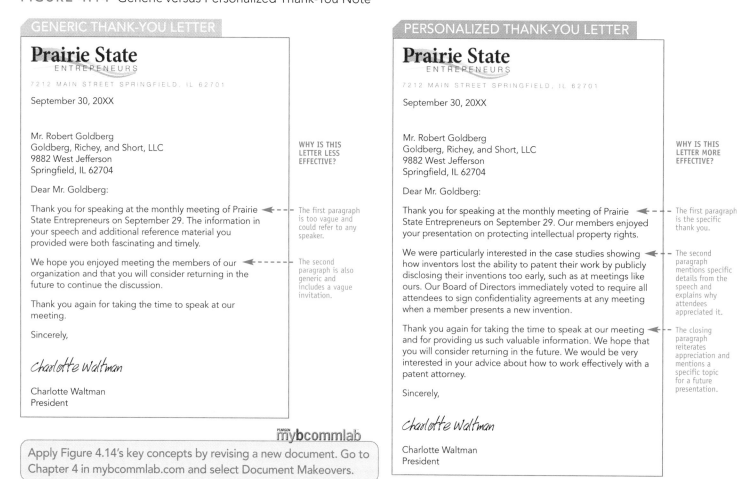

GENERIC THANK-YOU LETTER

Prairie State
ENTREPRENEURS
7212 MAIN STREET SPRINGFIELD, IL 62701

September 30, 20XX

Mr. Robert Goldberg
Goldberg, Richey, and Short, LLC
9882 West Jefferson
Springfield, IL 62704

Dear Mr. Goldberg:

Thank you for speaking at the monthly meeting of Prairie State Entrepreneurs on September 29. The information in your speech and additional reference material you provided were both fascinating and timely.

We hope you enjoyed meeting the members of our organization and that you will consider returning in the future to continue the discussion.

Thank you again for taking the time to speak at our meeting.

Sincerely,

Charlotte Waltman

Charlotte Waltman
President

WHY IS THIS LETTER LESS EFFECTIVE?

The first paragraph is too vague and could refer to any speaker.

The second paragraph is also generic and includes a vague invitation.

PERSONALIZED THANK-YOU LETTER

Prairie State
ENTREPRENEURS
7212 MAIN STREET SPRINGFIELD, IL 62701

September 30, 20XX

Mr. Robert Goldberg
Goldberg, Richey, and Short, LLC
9882 West Jefferson
Springfield, IL 62704

Dear Mr. Goldberg:

Thank you for speaking at the monthly meeting of Prairie State Entrepreneurs on September 29. Our members enjoyed your presentation on protecting intellectual property rights.

We were particularly interested in the case studies showing how inventors lost the ability to patent their work by publicly disclosing their inventions too early, such as at meetings like ours. Our Board of Directors immediately voted to require all attendees to sign confidentiality agreements at any meeting when a member presents a new invention.

Thank you again for taking the time to speak at our meeting and for providing us such valuable information. We hope that you will consider returning in the future. We would be very interested in your advice about how to work effectively with a patent attorney.

Sincerely,

Charlotte Waltman

Charlotte Waltman
President

WHY IS THIS LETTER MORE EFFECTIVE?

The first paragraph is the specific thank you.

The second paragraph mentions specific details from the speech and explains why attendees appreciated it.

The closing paragraph reiterates appreciation and mentions a specific topic for a future presentation.

PEARSON mybcommlab

Apply Figure 4.14's key concepts by revising a new document. Go to Chapter 4 in mybcommlab.com and select Document Makeovers.

those cases, it may be tempting to write one message and send it to everyone. However, as the first example in Figure 4.14 illustrates, a generic note like that loses much of its effectiveness because it could be used for any speaker by just changing the names and the topic description. The second example in Figure 4.14 is more effective. By including details relating to the speech, the personalized version sounds more sincere and will make the audience feel genuinely appreciated.

Congratulatory messages

Congratulatory messages build goodwill by recognizing someone's achievements or important events. These events could be professional or personal. For example, you can write a congratulatory message when your supervisor is promoted, your colleague has a baby, or your customer wins her city's entrepreneur-of-the-year award.

As with all routine messages, organize congratulatory notes directly by identifying the purpose for writing in the first sentence. Then provide any supporting details, followed by a friendly closing. Note the differences between the two email messages in FIGURE 4.15.

Congratulatory message Communication sent to recognize someone's achievements or important events.

FIGURE 4.15 Congratulatory Email Message

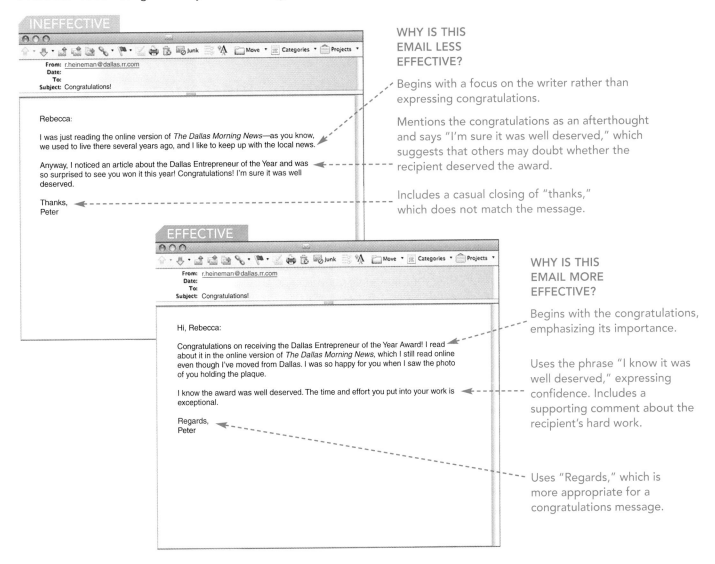

WHY IS THIS EMAIL LESS EFFECTIVE?

Begins with a focus on the writer rather than expressing congratulations.

Mentions the congratulations as an afterthought and says "I'm sure it was well deserved," which suggests that others may doubt whether the recipient deserved the award.

Includes a casual closing of "thanks," which does not match the message.

WHY IS THIS EMAIL MORE EFFECTIVE?

Begins with the congratulations, emphasizing its importance.

Uses the phrase "I know it was well deserved," expressing confidence. Includes a supporting comment about the recipient's hard work.

Uses "Regards," which is more appropriate for a congratulations message.

Sympathy messages

Even when you do not have a close personal relationship with coworkers or business acquaintances, they will appreciate your expressions of sympathy when they have experienced a loss. Many people do not know what to say when a colleague becomes seriously ill or has experienced a death in the family. Although you can take advantage of get-well cards and sympathy notes to deliver your messages, also include a few lines that show your compassion and understanding. Just like thank-you notes, **sympathy messages** (also called **condolences**) are more meaningful when handwritten and sent shortly after you hear about the situation. Read the example in FIGURE 4.16.

FIGURE 4.16
Sympathy Message

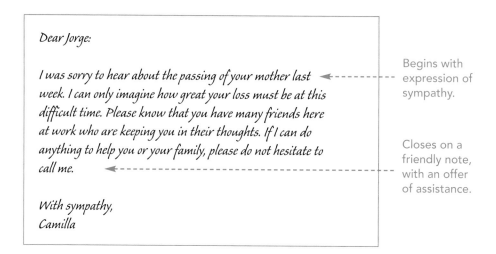

Dear Jorge:

I was sorry to hear about the passing of your mother last week. I can only imagine how great your loss must be at this difficult time. Please know that you have many friends here at work who are keeping you in their thoughts. If I can do anything to help you or your family, please do not hesitate to call me.

With sympathy,
Camilla

Begins with expression of sympathy.

Closes on a friendly note, with an offer of assistance.

"For-your-information" messages

This final category of goodwill messages, illustrated in FIGURE 4.17, has no formal name, but you can think of them as **for-your-information messages**: messages sent to pass along information or communicate something you believe your audience will appreciate. For example, when reading an article on the web about a new restaurant in New Orleans, you may remember that a customer is planning a vacation in New Orleans the next month. Or while talking to your tax accountant, you may learn about a new tax rule that you think a colleague may appreciate knowing. It would be easy simply to ignore those thoughts and go about your business.

However, taking the opportunity to pass along this information leads to several benefits. First, you keep channels of communication open, which is an important part of networking. Every business relationship benefits from periodic communication to ensure that your audience continues to think about you. These messages serve that goal. Second, friendly messages such as these solidify relationships because they make both parties feel good. You will get personal satisfaction from writing these messages, and your audience will be pleased to hear from you. Finally, these messages may start a dialogue that can lead to possible business benefits.

FIGURE 4.17
For-Your-Information Message

Dear Renee:

I heard something about you at dinner last night that I thought you'd enjoy hearing, too. Maggie and Lou Embry, two business acquaintances, mentioned that their daughter, Venita, interned at Regal Enterprises this summer and that she worked for you. When I told them that you and I were long-time friends, they could not stop talking about how wonderful you were to Venita and how much she learned from the internship. I thought you'd appreciate knowing how much your intern valued you as a mentor.

Let's get together soon.

Rick

The message begins by explaining its purpose. The main point of the message comes later.

For the main point to make sense, Renee will need some context. The middle of the message provides this context.

The main point at the end is indirect and follows from the context.

The message closes on a friendly note.

IN SUMMARY, routine and goodwill messages like those explained in this chapter are fundamental elements of business communication. They are the day-to-day messages you produce to get work done and to build and maintain healthy working relationships. To accomplish your goals with these messages, use the ACE process that you learned in Chapter 3: analyze, compose, and evaluate. The ACE process will help ensure that you target the message to your purpose and audience, make it easy to understand, and avoid errors that will undermine your professionalism.

Sympathy message (also called **condolences**) A message that expresses compassion and understanding when someone experiences a loss.

For-your-information message A message written as an act of kindness to pass along information you think someone may appreciate knowing.

CHAPTER 4 Summary

4.1 How do I compose messages containing questions and requests?

(pages 112–116)

Most workplace communications are routine business messages that are short and to the point. Use the ACE process to make good decisions when analyzing, composing, and evaluating your messages.

- **Decide between a direct or an indirect organization** when composing routine messages that ask questions or make requests. In most cases, state your request directly. However, if the audience needs information to understand or be convinced about your request, use an indirect organization.
- **Provide reasons for the request** when necessary.
- **Adopt a "you" perspective and include audience benefits** in all messages that ask questions or make requests. Internal benefits are advantages that your audience directly receives, and external benefits are advantages that someone else gains.
- **Conclude with gratitude and a call for action.**

4.2 How do I compose informational messages? *(pages 116–123)*

- **Reply to questions with a direct answer.** Begin with a positive response, follow the organization of the original message—using corresponding numbers when appropriate—and end with a friendly closing.
- **Respond to customer requests by creating goodwill.** This is especially important when customers are requesting refunds, exchanges, or repairs.
- **Highlight key points in confirmation messages.** A confirmation is a message acknowledging that you have received information or checking that you have understood information correctly.
- **Organize routine announcements so they are easy to skim.** Announcements are messages that publicly notify an audience of information they need or want to know.
- **Format instructions so readers can easily follow the steps.** Begin with an overview, divide instructions into numbered or bulleted lists, and begin each step with an action verb or a conditional phrase, if the step is necessary only under certain conditions. Use parallel phrasing to ensure the same grammatical form for each item. Position any needed explanation after the action rather than before it.

4.3 What kinds of messages build goodwill in my business relationships? *(pages 123–129)*

Goodwill is a term used to describe the attitude of friendliness and caring that is central to creating, solidifying, and maintaining relationships.

- **Thank-you messages** offer you the opportunity to express appreciation and make your audience feel good about something they have done for you. They also offer you the opportunity to express and display your professionalism. Thank-you messages range from formal letters to informal emails, handwritten notes, or telephone calls. The main challenge in writing a good thank-you note is to include specific content that relates to the act for which you are thanking someone. A generic note loses much of its effectiveness.
- **Congratulatory messages** build goodwill by recognizing someone else's achievements or important events. These events could be professional or personal.
- **Sympathy messages** are written to colleagues and business acquaintances to show your compassion and understanding. Although you can take advantage of get-well cards and sympathy notes to deliver your messages, also include a few hand-written lines to personalize the message and promote goodwill.
- **"For-your-information" messages** are sent to pass along information or communicate something you believe your audience will appreciate. These friendly messages keep channels of communication open, solidify relationships, and initiate dialogues that may lead to business benefits.

PEARSON
mybcommlab™
Are you an active learner? Go to mybcommlab.com to master Chapter 4 content. Chapter 4 interactive activities include:

- Customizable Study Plan and Chapter 4 practice quizzes
- Chapter 4 Simulation, Routine Messages, that helps you think critically and prepare to make choices in the business world
- Flash Cards for mastering the definition of chapter terms

- Chapter 4 Video Exercise, Writing Routine & Positive Messages, which shows you how textbook concepts are put into practice every day
- Interactive Lessons that visually review key chapter concepts
- Document Makeovers for hands-on, scored practice in revising documents

Will you please send me your updated third-quarter sales figures today? If the budget committee has the figures to discuss at tomorrow's meeting, they can get you a preliminary budget by Thursday, and you'll be able to start planning next year's sales forecasts. Thanks.

Dear Jerry: I have a favor to ask. I know that you worked in Indianapolis for many years arranging construction loans, so I am sure you are familiar with heating and cooling contractors there. My company has won a contract for a large office building in Indianapolis, and we're now contacting subcontractors to request bids on the job. I'm having difficulty identifying qualified heating and cooling contractors. I need six and have only three.

Could you please look over my attached list of contractors and suggest a few more I can add? I'd really appreciate your help and will be glad to return the favor whenever possible.

Dear Mr. Pinnix:

We are shipping your corrected order today. SpeedEx has guaranteed delivery by August 7. The tracking number is 532-23334-63421.

Attached is a return shipping label formatted as a PDF file that you can print. Simply tape the label to your return and drop it off at any SpeedEx office. We prepaid the postage.

Thank you for your continued business. Your satisfaction is important to us.

Sincerely,

Dear Renee:

I heard something about you at dinner last night that I thought you'd enjoy hearing, too. Maggie and Lou Embry, two business acquaintances, mentioned that their daughter, Venita, interned at Regal Enterprises this summer and that she worked for you. When I told them that you and I were long-time friends, they could not stop talking about how wonderful you were to Venita and how much she learned from the internship. I thought you'd appreciate knowing how much your intern valued you as a mentor.

Let's get together soon.

Rick

4.1 How do I compose messages containing questions and requests?

Be DIRECT when your audience will easily understand your question and why you are asking it.

Be INDIRECT when the audience needs to understand the context of the situation to make sense of your question or request.

In every routine message, adopt a "you" perspective and include audience benefits.

4.2 How do I compose informational messages?

Begin with the main idea.

Highlight benefits, if there are any.

Follow up with the details. Number or bullet them if they are a list.

End with a friendly closing or contact information as appropriate.

4.3 What kinds of messages build goodwill in my business relationships?

Compose thank-you messages, congratulatory messages, sympathy messages, and FYI messages to create, solidify, and maintain relationships.

Depending on the context:
- Express professionalism.
- Include specific content.
- Recognize achievements.
- Show compassion and understanding.
- Personalize the messages.

131

KEY TERMS QUICK ACCESS REVIEW

Announcement   *p. 121*

Audience benefits   *p. 114*

Confirmation   *p. 120*

Congratulatory message   *p. 127*

External benefits   *p. 115*

For-your-information message   *p. 128*

Goodwill message   *p. 112*

Internal benefits   *p. 114*

Parallel phrasing   *p. 123*

Routine business message   *p. 112*

Sympathy message (also called **condolences**)   *p. 128*

Thank-you message   *p. 124*

"You" perspective   *p. 114*

CASE STUDY A Day's Worth of Routine Messages

This case study will help you review the chapter material by applying it to a specific scenario.

For the past year, Miguel Ramirez has worked for his father's insurance agency, Ramirez & Associates Insurance. The small company has only five employees: Miguel and his father, Carlos; Melinda and Reggie, both senior associates; and Theresa, the office manager.

On a Friday morning, Miguel opens the office and checks the company's voice mail. The first message is from his father saying he won't be in today because he decided to leave for vacation one day early. The second message is from Reggie reminding everyone that he will be out calling on clients. The third message from Melinda says that the insurance supplier she planned to visit next week requested that she come today instead, so she will be out of the office all day. The last message is from Theresa, the office manager, who says she has the flu and will not be in today. This leaves Miguel in charge.

Miguel sits down at Theresa's computer and opens the central email for the office. He also glances at the stack of regular mail on Theresa's desk. Here is a summary of the 11 messages he found.

In the Email:

1. A notice from one of the insurance companies whose products Ramirez & Associates sells. The company has adjusted auto insurance rates and coverage for all customers in the state based on claims and costs from the previous year. These changes will affect almost all customers.

2. A notice from another company that they will not renew the insurance for a customer who filed three claims during the past year.

3. Two requests for insurance quotes from new customers.

4. A request from a summer intern for a job recommendation.

5. A request from a corporate client asking that Ramirez & Associates confirm the details of an insurance policy covering their fleet of 1,000 cars.

6. A notice that a customer's claim for wind damage to her garage will be completely covered by the insuring company, minus the $250 deductible.

7. An email from Melinda asking someone in the office to place an order of office supplies with Office-To-Go. She left the list of supplies on her desk, and she needs the items by Monday.

In the Regular Mail:

8. Three insurance policies that need to be mailed to customers. These policies are complex, and the customers will not understand the details without a clear summary.

9. An invitation addressed to Miguel's father, Carlos, asking him to speak at a college career night next month. The school requests a reply within 10 days, and Miguel's father is not going to be back to the office for two weeks.

10. A letter from the National Association of Insurance and Financial Advisors indicating that Carlos Ramirez has been nominated for the prestigious John Newton Russell Memorial Award, the industry's highest honor.

11. A news release from Office-To-Go, one of the major office equipment suppliers in the area. The company has been purchased by a larger corporation, which may affect pricing and delivery policies. The news release offers no details, but raises many questions about whether Office-To-Go will remain competitive with other suppliers.

Analyzing Tasks and Choosing the Best Medium

Since Miguel is alone, he decides to spend the day following up on business leads, answering the phone, and responding to email and letters. As a first step, Miguel uses the first phase of the ACE process to analyze his communication tasks using three criteria: Do others need the information quickly? Will the task be easy for me to do, or should someone else handle it later? Is it in the business's best interest for me to answer quickly?

Task 1: *Review the 11 messages and prioritize each item by putting a **1** next to those that must be handled today, a **2** next to items that should be handled today if there is time, and a **3** next to items that can wait. Then, for each item, do a quick analysis. Identify the purpose of Miguel's communication, the audience, and the best medium option: letter, memo, email, IM, telephone, meeting, etc. Be prepared to explain your choices.*

Composing Good News in Response to a Claim

Miguel has good news to deliver to his client, Kristina Ivanska. He received an email from her insurer saying that the company will pay 100 percent of the replacement/repair cost for her roof, which was severely damaged in a wind storm, minus the $250 deductible.

Ms. Ivanska will get her payment in two installments. She will immediately receive a check for $7242, which is the value of her seven-year-old roof. Then when she has the roof repaired, the company will pay the difference between what they have already paid and the actual repair cost minus the $250 insurance deductible. She doesn't need to rush to have the roof repaired since she has up to 180 days to submit the bill for the repairs.

Miguel is eager to communicate this news to Ms. Ivanska, so he decides to call her. He begins the conversation with good news: "Ms. Ivanska, I wanted to let you know that Bill Baker, the insurance adjuster, will be stopping by your house next week with a check for $7,242 to cover your roof damage." Much to Miguel's surprise, Ms. Ivanska was very upset. She said: "But I just got an estimate from the roofing company for $9,850 to replace the roof. I thought my insurance covered 'replacement value.' There's a $2,500 difference! How can I pay for that?"

Miguel immediately realizes that he had organized his message the wrong way. He tries to calm Ms. Ivanska: "Don't worry. The insurance will cover the full cost except for your $250 deductible. I'm just explaining it wrong. Let me write you a letter, and I'll drop it by your house on my way home. It will make everything clear."

Task 2: *Write the good news letter for Miguel. Be sure that it:*

- *delivers the good news in a way that Ms. Ivanska will understand and calms her concerns*
- *explains what the insurance company will do and what she needs to do*

- *reestablishes her confidence in Ramirez & Associates as an insurance broker*

Evaluating a Routine Letter

After he handles the priority messages, Miguel turns his attention to the Office-To-Go announcement. Although it looks like a routine message, it is bad news to Miguel because he spent the past two months researching new office furniture and computer equipment from Office-To-Go. He made his choices and was about to prepare a proposal for his father. Now it is unclear whether the new vendor will carry the same brands, charge the same prices, or have the same service agreements.

Miguel decides to write a letter to Office-To-Go requesting information that will help him decide whether to find a new vendor. Miguel composed the following letter quickly and hopes to revise it by the end of the day.

Task 3: *Evaluate this letter and suggest revisions and corrections Miguel should make before sending it.*

---

letter

Ramirez & Associates Insurance

8713 Hillview | Quincy, MA 02170 | 800-551-9000 | fax: 617-555-0000

November 18, 20XX

Sales Manager
Office-To-Go
7633 Raintree Drive
Weymouth, MA 02188

Subject: Your Recent Announcement

I have been planning a large order of furniture and computer equipment with Office-To-Go and was very upset to receive the announcement that your company has merged with another and may not be carrying the same items. Ramirez & Associates has been a loyal customer of Office-To-Go for the past five years, and this change will greatly inconvenience us.

I need to determine whether to continue my plans to order from your company or to switch to another office equipment supplier in the South Shore area. To make a decision, I need to know whether you will be honoring the prices in your current furniture and equipment catalog and what discounts you will offer for bulk purchases. That assumes, of course, that you will be carrying the same items as in your current catalog. Will you?

I also need to know what freight company you will be using and how insurance will be handled. Will OTG technicians set up the furniture and equipment delivered? What's the turnaround time from order to delivery? Since I'm also deciding on whether to use OTG for other things, I'd also like to know whether OTG will be able to personalize stationery on site, or will it have to be outsourced?

Please respond by November 30 so that I may place an order by the end of the year. You can contact me at the phone number provided above or by email (mramirez@ramirezinsurance.com).

Sincerely,

Miguel Ramirez

Spending a Few Moments to Create Goodwill

It is 4:45 PM and Miguel has barely left his desk. He has been talking on the telephone, writing emails and letters, and placing orders. As Miguel sits back in his chair, he recalls his father saying, "Miguel, every day before I leave work, I make sure I've given someone a 'gift'—a thank you, a word of congratulations, or even just a smile. Remember, the time you invest making someone else feel good will help you build goodwill."

Miguel has been so intent on his work today that he hasn't spent one moment thinking about how to give someone a "gift." He glances down at his list of letters, emails, and voice messages, looking for an opportunity to build goodwill for Ramirez & Associates—or for himself.

Task 4: *Review the 11 messages at the beginning of this case study to identify ways to build goodwill. This is a good opportunity to think creatively.*

CRITICAL THINKING

1. Many of the routine messages in this chapter are just a few sentences long. Explain why using each phase of the ACE communication process—Analyzing, Composing, and Evaluating—is helpful even for short, routine messages.

2. Explain the possible negative outcomes of sending routine messages that do not include audience benefits or wording that promotes goodwill.

3. As this chapter explains, in some instances it may be unethical to include a bcc in an email. Explain a situation, other than those described in the chapter, in which forwarding an email might be considered unethical.
   [Related to the Ethics feature on page 122]

4. Writing a letter or email message to request a refund, repair, or exchange provides one advantage over a telephone call: you have written documentation of your request and you will receive a written response. However, sometimes you may prefer to call a customer service representative because an oral conversation allows better feedback and a quicker resolution. If you choose to communicate your claim request by telephone, what details about the conversation should you document? What method of documentation would you choose?

5. This chapter explains one reason why you might choose to make a request in person rather than by email: it may be more

difficult for your audience to refuse the request. What are other reasons you may choose to make a request in person?

6. If you were granting a customer a refund for a faulty product, why might you also include a discount for a future purchase? The customer is getting what she asked for, so why do more?

7. Why would customers feel better about a response to a complaint if the response is personally signed and if the responder says he will forward the complaint to someone who can solve the problem?

8. Explain why a thank-you note is an important follow-up to all your employment interviews, even with those companies you are no longer interested in pursuing.

9. American business culture is competitive. People compete for jobs, promotions, and raises. In this competitive culture, why would you concern yourself with building goodwill with colleagues?

10. If you were writing a goodwill message to someone from another culture, would you choose to follow your own cultural standards or those of your audience? Why? How could you find out what those cultural standards are?
    [Related to the Culture feature on page 125]

DEVELOPING YOUR COMMUNICATION SKILLS

4.1 **How do I compose messages containing questions and requests?** *(pages 112–116)*

EXERCISE 1 Decide between a direct or an indirect organization

Most routine messages should be organized directly with the main point positioned at the beginning of the message. Rewrite the following messages to use a direct approach and revise the wording to create a more effective message based on clarity, conciseness, style, and tone. Compare your direct revision to the indirect original. Which version would you choose to send? Explain why.

a. **Email** to Professor Fisher: My sister is getting married this weekend, and I am in the wedding party. It's a five-hour drive, so in order to get to the wedding rehearsal Friday afternoon, I have to leave before noon on Friday, which means I won't be able to attend our 2 PM class. I know that missing your lecture

will put me at a disadvantage for next week's exam, but you said you would take our term papers early if we got them done, which I did, so it's attached. Please confirm that you received the attachment. I'd be happy to bring by a hard copy if you would prefer. Thanks, [Your Name]

b. **Voice mail message** to a customer service department: Hi. This is Kent from Simi Valley Automotive. Last week, we placed an order from your recent promotional catalog. We ordered 24 sets of your model #42 windshield wipers. We received the shipment today, but found 42 sets of your model #24 windshield wipers. Although we stock both models, our supply of model #42 is very low, and we now have twice as many model #24 sets. What can you do to help? Please call me at 555-1234. Thanks!

c. **Letter** to a prospective tenant: Dear Mr. Abrams: Thank you for your recent request for additional information about our summer rental facilities. I agree that we have several interesting options to choose from, and without specific pricing details, it is difficult to make an informed decision. If you reserve your rental from the attached pricing list before April 1, I can offer you a 10 percent discount. Enclosed is the price list you requested. Thanks, [Your Name]

d. Memo to department managers: As you know, recycling is a very important goal for our company. Our efforts to make the planet clean and green extend beyond our corporate walls. We encourage every employee to recycle at home as well as work. The original blue recycling containers that were placed in each break room and reception area several years ago will be replaced with larger green containers that have separate receptacles for paper, plastic, glass, and metals. Please remind the employees in your department to recycle as much as possible. Thanks, [Your Name]

e. Face-to-face conversation: Hi, Hiro: You know that memo about the new travel forms we're supposed to use? Well, I'm going to a conference next week in Las Vegas—nice, huh?—although I've already asked Thad to cover for me while I'm gone, after reading the memo, I wasn't sure if we had to ask someone who is actually in our department to cover for us. I was hired to replace Thad when he moved up to management, so he knows my job better than anyone else—not that I think there will be much for him to do while I'm gone—but I didn't want my travel request to get hung up in the process if I had to ask someone else. Do you know?

EXERCISE 2 Provide reasons for the request

Your first job after college required you to move to a new city, Louisville, Kentucky, where you don't know anyone. You want to get involved with activities outside of work where you can meet people, so you attend a meeting of the Young Professionals Association of Louisville. Because you enjoyed the meeting, you sign up to join and provide your credit card number for the membership fee. Two weeks later as you review your online credit card statement information, you notice that your annual dues were charged at $100 premium member fee rather than the $50 new-member fee that was advertised during the meeting. To get your $50 back, you email the organization. You do not know the name of the president or the treasurer. However, you do have a general email address: YPAL@louisville.net. Draft your email requesting a refund.

EXERCISE 3 Adopt a "you" perspective and include audience benefits

For each claim response below, revise the message to use the "you" perspective and include audience benefits.

a. Thank you for contacting us about the Internet outage in your area. We restored the connection.

b. We are sorry that one of the pizzas delivered to your office last week was cold. Enclosed is a refund.

c. We regret that one of the eight office chairs you ordered was damaged during delivery. We are shipping a replacement today.

d. You're right. You were charged incorrectly. We will credit your account today.

e. The headset you returned could not be repaired. We're enclosing a new one for your convenience.

EXERCISE 4 Conclude with gratitude and a call for action

The following email exchange consists of five separate short messages. Revise the messages to conclude with an appropriate call for action. Where appropriate, include other techniques such as an expression of gratitude, a "you" perspective, and audience benefits.

a. Hi, Peter: Will you be able to take on the new Meggison marketing project? I'm simply overwhelmed with the Pagel campaign and don't know how I would handle both projects simultaneously. Thanks, Larry

b. Hi, Larry: Sure, I can work on the Meggison project.—Peter

c. Peter: I am so glad you accepted my offer to lead the new Meggison marketing project. I have so much on my plate right now, you just can't imagine! I expect you will call me with any questions you have. I need your proposal as soon as possible.—Larry

d. Larry: Attached is my rough draft for the Meggison proposal.—Peter

e. Peter: Attached are my suggested revisions for the Meggison proposal.—Larry

4.2 How do I compose informational messages?
(pages 116–123)

EXERCISE 5 Reply to questions with a direct answer

As the director of human resources at UrbanLife, you receive several requests each week from students for information about internship opportunities at your company. Although you respond to each request individually, you often reply with the same information. Rather than typing the same information each time, you decide to create a template of responses that you can cut, paste, and modify as necessary to personalize each message. The questions often include the following:

- Do you provide internships? *Answer:* Yes.
- If so, in what areas? *Answer:* All departments.
- What is the timeline for submitting applications? *Answer:* Usually a four- to six-week response.
- When during the academic year do you hire interns? *Answer:* Accepted throughout the year.

Draft a sample email response that you could use to respond to any request for internship information. Include the suggested elements: begin with the positive response, include all requested information, and end with a friendly closing. Remember the importance of creating goodwill with your response by striking an appropriate tone.

EXERCISE 6 Respond to customer requests by creating goodwill

Callan Reis wrote to her company's employee benefits director to appeal the director's decision not to reimburse certain health care expenses. The benefits director drafted the following message, responding positively to Callan's appeal. However, in evaluating this message before sending, the writer determined the message did not do a good job of promoting goodwill. What changes would you recommend to the writer?

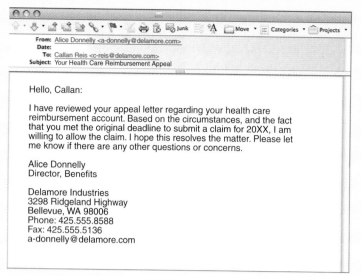

Accompanies Exercise 6

EXERCISE 7 Highlight key points in confirmation messages

As a new intern at a large marketing company, you provide assistance to a wide variety of project managers and their staff. The diverse experience is a great learning experience but requires significant attention to detail to ensure you remember what you're supposed to do for whom and by when. You have been keeping detailed notes, but sometimes in the course of running an errand, someone will ask you to do something when you don't have your notes with you. This happened today. As you were copying documents and collating materials into presentation packets for a client meeting, Lydia Homer, the team leader for the project presentation, looked in the copy room and said, "Don't forget to include the original RFP in the packets. When you're done with all that, take the packets to Brian for labeling. Use the 5164 size. Sally has the list of names. Thanks." Before you could respond, Lydia hurried down the hall to another meeting. You realize you don't know what an RFP is, you don't know Brian or Sally, and now you can't remember whether she said 5164 or 5614. Since your copy machine has another 500 pages to print, you decide to email Lydia confirming the information and asking for clarification. Draft the message.

EXERCISE 8 Organize routine announcements so they are easy to skim

You manage *City Kids,* a large daycare facility in the downtown area. You want to announce your expanded hours to your current clientele as well as employees of local businesses (potential customers) near your facility. Your old hours were 7:30 AM to 6:30 PM. Beginning the first of next month, you will be open from 7:00 AM until 7:00 PM. The daycare facility has a comprehensive website and an active listserv that includes every parent's email address. Create additional information to draft an announcement and identify the media options you could use to distribute this message. How would the draft change based on the medium?

EXERCISE 9 Format instructions so readers can easily follow the steps

Your company is planning to recruit new employees at several college-sponsored job fairs and has decided to staff the booths with current employees from throughout the company. You have a full schedule of volunteers for the fairs. You wrote the short set of instructions in the following paragraph, which you plan to distribute at an orientation session for volunteers. Before the session, though, you decide to revise the instructions to make them easier to follow. Reformat (and if necessary, revise) the following text to create a one-page instruction sheet for volunteers. As you revise, consider which steps are separate and which can be grouped together.

> ### Protocol for Job Fair Booth Volunteers
> Greet the student (that is, prospective employee). Shake hands and introduce yourself. Ask the student's name. Give the student the company brochure. Outline the nature of the jobs you are recruiting for, without going into too much detail. Focus on the benefits of working for our company. Ask if the student has any questions. Answer any questions you can and take notes about any question that you cannot answer. Thank the student for his or her interest in our company and wish the student good luck in his or her job search.

Accompanies Exercise 9

4.3 What kinds of messages build goodwill in my business relationships? *(pages 123–129)*

EXERCISE 10 Thank-you messages

You work for a large tax accounting firm, and one of your satisfied customers, Andrea Stockton, wrote a very complimentary email about you to the senior vice president. The customer also referred a colleague (Evan Russert) to your company based on your work. The senior vice president forwarded you a copy of this email. Send your customer a thank-you message.

EXERCISE 11 Congratulatory messages

This is your fifth year as the head of new client development for a small consulting company. Your assistant, Madeline, has been extremely helpful since your first day. After 30 years of service to the company, Madeline is retiring. You have organized her retirement party and selected a beautifully inscribed silver plaque. However, you're not sure what to write in her farewell card. Although you will miss her knowledge and talents, you know she is looking forward to retirement and plans to begin with a two-week Caribbean cruise. Draft a congratulatory message to Madeline.

EXERCISE 12 Sympathy messages

You are a sales consultant for a regional distribution company. Your biggest client, Jana, has also become a good friend. Last year, Jana's son, Brian, was diagnosed with leukemia. Your client meetings have been less frequent lately since Jana has been working from home, but you've managed to stay in contact by email. This morning, the first email you open is from Jana. It's a message sent to dozens of people informing them that Brian died peacefully in his sleep a week ago. Jana's message thanks the group for their continued support during the past year, and indicates that donations can be made in Brian's name to the Children's Leukemia Center. Although your instinct is to reply by email, you know a hand-written sympathy note is more appropriate. Draft your message.

EXERCISE 13 "For-your-information" messages

Jim O'Callahan is your company's vice president of marketing. Last week you sat next to Jim at a business dinner. In conversation, Jim mentioned how much he admired Abraham Lincoln as a leader. The next day as you were browsing through your local bookstore, you saw a book by Eric Foner, *The Fiery Trial: Abraham Lincoln and American Slavery.* This made you think of Jim's comments, and you bought the book. You're only three chapters through it but you are really enjoying it. You wonder if Jim has read it. Write a message to Jim that lets him know about this new book.

WRITING

EXERCISE 14 Writing routine messages

Each of the following messages has a problem. It may be too short, too wordy, or have the wrong tone. For each of the scenarios represented by the message, compose a new message that you believe is well-organized, includes enough information to be effective, and builds goodwill. Create any additional information that you need.

a. **Email:** Hi, Jane: Attached are the files you requested. Regards, Jill.

b. **Voice mail message:** This is Maria Martinez from Accounting. I need more information than you provided on your recent travel expense report. Please call me at Ext. 1440 as soon as possible. Thanks.

c. **Memo:** To All Employees: Please stop throwing away your plastic water bottles. We have recycling bins in several convenient locations. Thanks!

d. **Flyer posted in break room:** Volunteers Needed for Blood Drive—Call Ext. 550 for Info!

e. **Comment made during a meeting:** As the chair of the social committee, I think it's important that we do a better job of recognizing birthdays in our department. I'll take the responsibility of buying and routing cards for signatures prior to each person's birthday, but you all need to chip in. Five dollars per person will cover the cost of the card and muffin from the coffee shop. Sound okay?

EXERCISE 15 Requesting a favor

You own a consulting business that provides communication training. This morning, Tim Merrick of LabCorp left a voice mail message on your office phone requesting that you present a one-hour email etiquette workshop for his staff of 25 people next week during their professional development retreat. You have presented several workshops for Tim's company in the past and look forward to continuing your business relationship with him, but you will be out of town next week on another consulting job and won't be available. Rather than reply to Tim with bad news, you would prefer to find a replacement and decide to ask one of your associates, Kathryn, to conduct the email etiquette workshop. Although Kathryn has not presented this topic before, she is an excellent presenter. You have an email etiquette PowerPoint presentation, handout materials, and group activities you have used successfully in the past. Kathryn just needs to get familiar with the content to prepare for the workshop. Since you need a response quickly, you decide to send an email to Kathryn. Use the ACE process to analyze the situation, compose the email, and evaulate it. Submit your final draft email to your instructor.

EXERCISE 16 Requesting information

In your role as a human resources specialist, you help new employees determine which retirement benefit packages best fit their personal needs. After spending the entire morning meeting separately with three people about the same issues, you realize that you typically ask each person the same questions. Rather than continuing to take the time to collect this information in person, you decide it would be more efficient to have employees prepare this information ahead of time. Your questions involve their current age and planned retirement age, minimum level of annual income needed in retirement for recurring expenses, anticipated special circumstances in retirement (such as children's college tuition or weddings), desired lifestyle during retirement, and current rate of savings. You also need to know whether they prefer low-risk investments that are more stable but may provide less return on investment or high-risk investments that are less stable but may provide a high return on investment. Compose a memo to new employees that will be included with their orientation materials. Your memo should indicate that as a human resources specialist, you are available to schedule individual appointments to discuss retirement benefit packages. You would like the new employees to bring typed responses to these questions to their scheduled appointments.

EXERCISE 17 Respond to claim requests by creating goodwill

Assume you are a private attorney running your practice out of your home. A friend suggests that creating a website for your business might enhance your client base and recommends a college student, Kent Miller. You contact Kent, discuss content and images, and agree to his hourly fees. A week later, Kent sends you a draft of your website and an invoice for $300. The site looks great, so you send him a check and thank him for his work. A few days later, Kent emails you indicating that although he looks forward to continuing to work on your website project, he is concerned that the check you sent was for $200, which was $100 less than the invoiced amount. You refer to your checking account register and realize you made a mistake. Respond to Kent's email.

EXERCISE 18 Writing an informational memo about instant messaging [Related to the Technology feature on page 117]

You work in the IT department of Pullman Daniels Brokerage (PDB). PDB would like to implement a standardized Instant Messaging system that will allow brokers and financial managers to communicate with each other and clients. With this form of instant communication, PDB professionals and clients can take better advantage of changes in the financial markets and specific securities.

The vice president of PDB has asked you to do some research and answer these questions:

- What are the key issues or challenges in implementing a companywide IM solution?
- What are the benefits of such a system?

- What are some of the features that such a system must include in the financial services industry?

You use the Internet to see what other financial services organizations are doing and to learn about requirements. Among other sources, you find the home page for the Financial Services Instant Messaging Association. Based on your research, write a one- to two-page informational memo to the head of the firm, answering his questions. Use ACE to analyze the audience and content needs, compose the draft, and evaluate it.

COLLABORATING

EXERCISE 19 Identifying audience benefits

As a team, assume that you are the human resources staff for a small regional hospital with a workforce of approximately 500 (physicians, nurses, administrators, support staff, and volunteers). Your department routinely sends messages to all employees. For each of the "To All" scenarios below, brainstorm audience benefits that you can incorporate into the message. Revise each message to include at least one audience benefit and build goodwill.

a. To All: The employee parking area will be repaved next week. The crew will pave the north half of the lot on Monday and the south half on Tuesday. Although half of the employee lot will be available at all times, arrangements have been made with the volunteer transportation services unit to run shuttles every 10 minutes from the overflow parking area to the main hospital entrance. Thank you for your cooperation.—HR Dept.

b. To All: Next Friday between 10 AM and 2 PM, the Volunteers' Association will be hosting a bake sale in the lobby area outside the cafeteria. All proceeds from the sale will support the new free clinic. Donations are also accepted. Thank you for supporting this worthy cause!—HR Dept.

c. To All: Our new insurance forms are now available. Please stop by the HR Dept. to register for the new coverage options. If you don't update your records by the end of the month, you will not be able to select plan options until the next quarter.—HR Dept.

d. To All: The gift shop in the lobby will be renovated next month. To help reduce the inventory before the renovations

begin, all items have been reduced 25 percent. As usual, your hospital ID badge gives you an extra 10 percent discount. Thanks for helping us clear the shelves before we tear them down!—HR Dept.

e. To All: Although our hospital campus has been tobacco-free for several years, we've recently received several complaints from the custodian services supervisor that cigarette butts have been found in the garbage cans of several employee bathrooms throughout the building. Please refrain from using any tobacco products in the hospital or on the grounds. Thank you for your cooperation.—HR Dept.

EXERCISE 20 Exploring cultural expectations
[Related to the Culture feature on page 125]

As a team, select a country and research its customs and expectations for showing gratitude, saying thank you, and building goodwill. For example, what are the customs and expectations about gift giving: is it expected, discouraged, or optional? Is a thank you in writing more appropriate than orally? Or is an oral thank you more expected? Each team member should look at different sources and discuss similarities and differences among their findings. Potential resources include the eDiplomat and the CyborLink websites. Use your favorite search engines to find others. Prepare a two-minute presentation for your class about saying thank you and building goodwill in that country. Be sure to include a list of your sources and be prepared to identify which one was most helpful and why.

SPEAKING

EXERCISE 21 Making informal/impromptu presentations

a. Identify a routine message you recently wrote and explain the purpose, audience, content, and medium of the message. Was the message successful in achieving its purpose? How do you know? Share your information with your class in a short, informal oral presentation.

b. Identify one situation in which a business sent you a goodwill message or added goodwill content to a routine message. In a short, informal presentation, explain what the business communicated to you and whether the goodwill message made you feel positively about the business. Explain why or why not.

c. Explain how you have built and maintained goodwill with your friends. Provide at least three examples.

EXERCISE 22 Presenting executive briefings

a. Imagine that your business wants to create a policy about when and how to use the blind carbon copy feature in emails. Your team has been assigned to draft that policy. As a team, brainstorm situations when using blind carbon copy is effective and acceptable as well as some situations when it is not. Develop a short set of guidelines and share them in class using a three- to five-minute presentation that includes one or two slides. **[Related to the Ethics feature on page 122]**

b. Imagine that your business wants to create a policy for using Instant Messaging at work. Your team has been assigned to draft that policy. As a team, brainstorm ways of using instant messages that would be productive at work as well as ways that would be disruptive. Develop a short set of guidelines for using IM at work and present these to the class in a three- to five-minute slide presentation.
[Related to the Technology feature on page 117]

GRAMMAR

Prepositions and conjunctions (See Appendix D—Section 1.1.4)

In the following paragraph, identify the prepositions (P), coordinating conjunctions (CC), correlative conjunctions (CorC), subordinating conjunctions (SC), and conjunctive adverbs (CA). There are a total of 10 prepositions and conjunctions. Count correlative conjunction pairs as one.

> The way you begin a business call is very important; however, the conclusion is equally important. Have you ever been caught in an awkward spot, wondering who should end the call? If you initiated the call, the convention is for you to conclude it. After you have obtained the information you need, thank the person you called and then say good-bye. The person at the other end either can just say good-bye or can end with a pleasantry: for example, "I'm glad I could help."

5 Communicating Persuasive Messages

new hires @ work

Aznir Haron
Assistant Director
Gifted and Talented Youth Program
Montclair State University, 2005

TO GENERATE REVENUE SUCCESSFULLY, we must persuade parents to enroll their gifted and talented children in our program by convincing them that we are the best in the region and that we provide a challenging educational program not being offered in the regular school setting. We focus on the excellence of our program's trained faculty and unique curriculum that is tailored to meet each gifted child's unique needs. This is our best approach to market the program and sustain our clientele.

Introduction

In Chapters 3 and 4, you learned how to use the ACE process to prepare well-constructed routine messages that target your audience. However, what should you do if you anticipate your audience may not accept your message or agree with your request? In this chapter, you'll learn to make your messages persuasive. **Persuasion** is the process of influencing your audience to agree with your point of view, recommendation, or request.

In your daily life, you often need to communicate persuasively. You may want to persuade friends to go to a movie. As a student, you may need to persuade your advisor or dean to grant you credit for a course taken at another school. As a consumer, you may need to persuade a manufacturer to give you a refund for a faulty product. In the workplace, you may need to:

- influence customers to shop at your store rather than your competitors'
- sell a new service to a potential client who has not heard of your company
- recommend a policy change to a supervisor

Being persuasive requires that you analyze your audience to understand why they may resist your ideas. It also requires understanding persuasive techniques that will help you overcome resistance. The ACE process will help you achieve that understanding and choose effective persuasive strategies when communicating in typical business situations.

How can the ACE process help me persuade my audience?

To be persuasive, a message must do more than just state your point of view. It must motivate your audience to agree with it. Using the ACE process will help you develop a message that accomplishes this goal.

For example, assume that you are Pedro Baca, a customer service manager for an e-commerce and mail order company that has an annual goal to increase profits by improving customer service and cutting costs. To improve customer service, the company installed new computer software that tracks customer orders and allows customer service representatives to provide customers with immediate, accurate information. To cut costs, the company eliminated the training budget. Now you have a dilemma. Your employees received only a brief orientation and don't know how to use all the features of the new software. Customer complaints have increased, and you fear the company may alienate customers because of poor service. To solve this problem, you want to persuade your supervisor, Maria, to authorize money for training.

Your first thought is to write a quick email to Maria to request the funds. You sit down at the computer and write the message in FIGURE 5.1. This message simply asks for what you want.

As you review this message, you wonder how Maria will react. Instead of sending the message, you rethink it using the ACE process.

FIGURE 5.1
An Unpersuasive Request

> **email**
>
> To: Maria Cardoni <mcardoni@pilotproducts.com>
> From: Pedro Baca <pbaca@pilotproducts.com>
> Subject: Request for Funding
>
> Maria:
>
> I am requesting funding to support a computer training workshop to ensure my department's employees will be more productive and customer complaints will decrease. I will call your assistant to schedule an appointment to discuss this soon.
>
> Thanks,
> Pedro

Analyzing helps you plan your message

In persuasive situations, you will increase your chances of getting a positive response by spending extra time on the analyzing phase of the ACE communication process. Recall that analyzing involves thinking strategically about your:

- purpose, desired outcome, and business results
- audiences' and stakeholders' needs
- content needs
- medium choices

Analyze your purpose, desired outcome, and business result

Before focusing on what you will say in your message, think about why you are communicating. What is the purpose of the message (why you are communicating) and what outcome would you like to achieve (how would you like your audience to respond)? If your audience agrees to your request or recommendation, what will the business result be? Understanding how your request will affect others and your business helps you anticipate audience response.

Your message to persuade Maria has the following purpose, outcome, and result:

- The *purpose* is to request funding to support a training workshop.
- The *outcome* is that your audience (your supervisor) will provide the requested funds.
- The *result* is that the employees will be more productive and provide improved customer service.

Analyze your audiences' and stakeholders' needs

Once you have determined your purpose, desired outcome, and business result, consider how to persuade your audience. Because persuasion involves influencing your audience's thinking and behavior, the more you know about your audience, the more persuasive you can be. Audience analysis involves imagining yourself in your audience's position and interpreting your message from your audience's perspective.

Consider both the **primary audience**, the direct recipient of the message, as well as the **secondary audience**, other people who may read or hear your message. The secondary audience may receive a copy of your message either from you or from your primary audience. You may even want to consider stakeholders who may be affected by the message. In the computer training workshop example, your supervisor (Maria) is your primary audience. The secondary audience may include the vice president of finance if Maria forwards your request to approve additional funds. Additional stakeholders include employees in the department and customers. Although employees and customers will not see your message, they will certainly be affected by the outcome that results.

To create a persuasive message for your audience, focus on information needs, motivation and benefits, and potential resistance.

- **Information: What does your audience know about the situation? What do you need to tell your audience?** Maria knows that budget cuts have eliminated all professional development activities throughout the organization. She also knows that the company is committed to improving customer service. However, she does not yet know that productivity and customer service have suffered in your department because employees have not been trained to use the new computer systems.
- **Motivation and benefits: What will motivate your audience to accept your idea or comply with your request? How will your audience benefit from your proposed idea?** Maria probably will be motivated to solve the problem once she is aware that it exists. She and the company will benefit from improved productivity and customer satisfaction, as long as it does not cost too much. The vice president of finance may be motivated to solve the problem if he understands that his investment in the new computer system is not yielding the expected benefit.

■ Access this chapter's simulation entitled Persuasive Messages, located at mybcommlab.com.

Persuasion The process of influencing your audience to agree with your point of view, accept your recommendation, or grant your request.

Primary audience The direct recipients of your message.

Secondary audience People other than the primary audience who may read or hear your message. These include people to whom you have sent a copy of your message as well as people to whom your audience has forwarded a copy.

- **Potential resistance: What concerns and objections will the audience have?** Maria may have two concerns. She may argue that training is the wrong solution since employees received some training when the system was installed. She may also argue that the department simply cannot afford the training. She may be hesitant to bring a request for funds to the vice president of finance since the company is committed to cutting costs. The vice president of finance will be opposed to spending more money unless he can see a clear financial benefit.

Analyze content needs

Based on your audience analysis, you can determine what content you will need to provide.

- **Information:** You will need to inform Maria that a costly problem exists and that the problem is related to insufficient training. You may have to research the actual costs associated with this problem.
- **Motivation and benefits:** For Maria, the main benefits to stress are cost savings, improved productivity, and customer retention. For the vice president of finance, you can stress an additional benefit: the training will increase the value of the investment he has already made in purchasing customer service software. The company will not see benefits from the software until the representatives are adequately trained.
- **Response to potential resistance:** Once you anticipate potential objections, you may respond to them in two different ways: **refutation** and **concession**. You can refute the points by trying to prove that they are wrong. Alternatively, you can concede the points by admitting that the opposing point of view has merit but does not invalidate your argument. Think of refutation as saying *"No, that is wrong, and here's why,"* while concession is saying, *"Yes, but . . . ."* Whichever approach you use, be sure to state the opposing argument fairly and thoroughly and to let the audience know that you understand their concerns.

  Since you anticipate Maria may object to your request for training funds, develop responses to her objections as part of your planning process. For example:

  Objection: Employees already received sufficient training.

  Refutation: The training taught the employees only the minimum features necessary to operate the system. They do not know how to use several of the software functions necessary to deal effectively with customers' needs.

  Objection: Training is costly, and one of our corporate goals is to cut costs.

  Concession: Yes, training is costly. But customer service problems caused by insufficient training will cost even more.

Analyze medium choices

Selecting the best medium for your persuasive message depends on many variables:

- The number of people in your audience and your ability to reach them all in a timely way
- The complexity of your content
- The amount of resistance you expect
- Your audience's communication preferences

If you need to persuade only one person, consider that person's communication preferences. For example, if you know your audience will be more open to discussing an issue in person, plan a face-to-face meeting or a phone call. However, if you think your audience would prefer to spend time considering a response to your message without being put "on the spot" in a face-to-face conversation, then communicate by email or voice mail message instead. If you need to persuade many people, you may want to plan a meeting where you can make a persuasive presentation. Alternatively, you may want to email all the people involved. An email will also allow you to send a copy to a broader secondary audience of people who will be affected by your proposal or idea.

FIGURE 5.2 summarizes reasons why you might choose various medium options when you need to persuade an audience.

FIGURE 5.2 Selecting the Best Medium for Persuasive Messages

Choose one of the selected medium options when you want to do the following:	One-to-One	Group Meeting	Telephone	Text/IM	Email	Memo	Letter	Newsletter	Website	Social Networking	Wikis, Blogs
Audience-Related Criteria											
Target a personal appeal to an individual	■		■	■	■		■				
Communicate with large audiences		■		■	■	■		■	■	■	■
Communicate with people already interested in your topic	■	■	■	■	■	■	■	■	■	■	■
Communicate with potential audiences you can't yet identify									■	■	■
Content- and Response-Related Criteria											
Communicate a complex message	■	■	■		■	■	■	■	■		
Include additional documents or support material (images, charts, video, etc.) that may help persuade your audience	■	■			■	■	■	■	■	■	■
Receive immediate feedback, so you can alter your appeal "on the fly," if necessary	■	■	■								■
Take time to think about any objections in the audience's reply, collect evidence if necessary, and compose a response				■	■	■	■				
Give the audience time to consider your appeal carefully before responding				■	■	■	■	■	■	■	■
Make it more uncomfortable for the audience to respond negatively (given the interpersonal interaction)	■	■	■								

Because persuasion is a process, it often requires multiple communications, with each message contributing to your persuasive goal. For example, if you know that Maria does not like surprise requests, you might consider sending an email message to mention your training idea and schedule an appointment to discuss the issue in more detail. The email must be persuasive to ensure that Maria will meet with you and be interested in what you have to say.

Refutation A response intended to prove an objection is wrong.

Concession An admission that the opposing point of view has merit but does not invalidate your argument.

Composing implements the persuasive plan

While the analyzing stage helps you make a persuasive plan, the composing stage helps you put the plan into action and draft the message. As **FIGURE 5.3** illustrates, a planned message will be much more persuasive than a message composed without planning.

FIGURE 5.3 Composing an Effective Persuasive Message

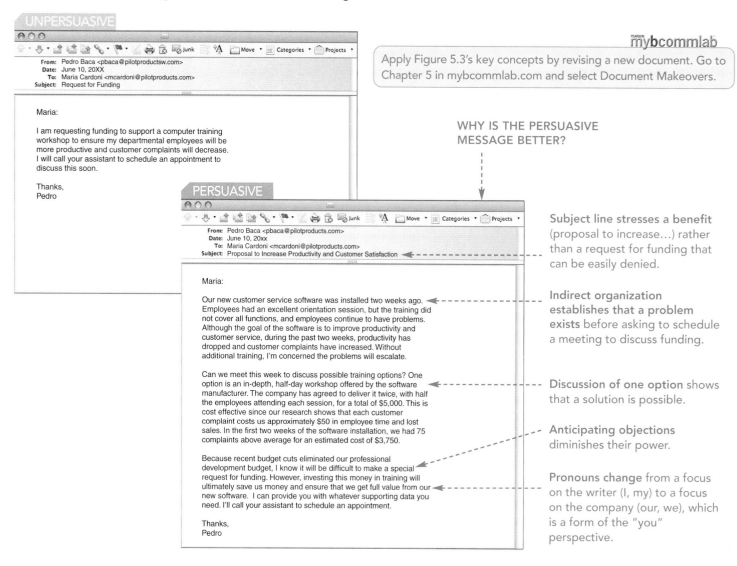

WHY IS THE PERSUASIVE MESSAGE BETTER?

Subject line stresses a benefit (proposal to increase...) rather than a request for funding that can be easily denied.

Indirect organization establishes that a problem exists before asking to schedule a meeting to discuss funding.

Discussion of one option shows that a solution is possible.

Anticipating objections diminishes their power.

Pronouns change from a focus on the writer (I, my) to a focus on the company (our, we), which is a form of the "you" perspective.

Apply Figure 5.3's key concepts by revising a new document. Go to Chapter 5 in mybcommlab.com and select Document Makeovers.

Evaluating helps you review the draft for effectiveness

Even when you have planned your message well and composed it carefully, take additional time to evaluate your decisions before communicating. Ask yourself several questions to ensure you have implemented a good persuasive strategy. Here is how you, as Pedro, might evaluate the persuasive message in Figure 5.3:

- **Have I convincingly shown that a problem or opportunity exists?** The email shows that productivity is dropping and customer complaints are rising. The email also shows that customer complaints are costly.
- **Is the proposed solution or plan a good one?** The email presents the training option as a realistic solution that is also cost effective.
- **Is the evidence and reasoning sound?** You provide documented evidence that each complaint costs $50. You provide sound reasoning that the cost of training is less than the cost of the problem.
- **Have I addressed any objections that I can anticipate?** The email addresses Maria's potential objections: initial training should have been sufficient, the company has no money, and it's difficult to secure special funding.
- **Have I stressed benefits?** Most of the benefits are implied. If we solve the problems then, by implication, we will increase productivity, reduce complaints, and retain

more customers. The last paragraph addresses one additional benefit: getting full value from the customer service software.

- **Is the message easy to read?** The structure of the email is logical (problem, request for meeting to discuss possible solutions, next steps), and the email uses effective paragraphing techniques.
- **Is the information complete, concise, clear, and correct?** It includes all the necessary information and nothing else. The wording is clear, and the language and content are correct.
- **Do I need to change anything to get the result I want from my audience?** Evaluate the message from Maria's perspective. Will she believe a problem exists and your solution is reasonable? Will she believe she will benefit from meeting with you? If so, then the message is ready to send. If not, then revise the message to accomplish your purpose.

Although Pedro's final email to Maria is much longer than his original draft, the revised message takes advantage of the ACE process and has a greater chance of helping Pedro gain funding because its content and structure are persuasive.

Study Question 5.2

What are the basic elements of persuasion?

To develop the most persuasive content for your communication, you will need to understand the basics of persuasion. What kind of content will motivate your audience to trust you, believe your points, agree with your position, and do what you request?

You learned about three elements of persuasion in Section 5.1 when Pedro prepared his email to Maria. His persuasive strategy included the following:

- Establishing a problem or need
- Focusing on benefits
- Anticipating objections

This section addresses three additional persuasive elements that have been recognized as important since the time of Aristotle:[1]

- Building credibility
- Constructing a logical argument
- Appealing to emotion

Most persuasive business arguments combine all these elements, but may emphasize one more than another.[2]

Building credibility

When trying to persuade an audience, you will be more effective if you have **credibility**—that is, if your audience believes you have expertise and are trustworthy based on your knowledge, character, reputation, and behavior.[3] You may already have credibility with your audience if they know and respect you or if you are an acknowledged expert.[4] In these cases, you will not need to focus on building credibility in your message. Frequently, however, you will need to establish credibility with your audience to be persuasive. In these cases, use the following techniques:

- **Spend time getting to know your audience.** Have you ever noticed how skilled salespeople often spend a few minutes chatting with potential customers before trying to make a sale?[5] Talking with your audience before trying to persuade them helps you understand their concerns and allows you to build rapport and trust. It is easier to persuade an audience who likes you than one who does not know you.
- **Introduce yourself effectively.** You can build credibility with your audience by mentioning key credentials including education, experience, and expertise. You can also mention your relationship with someone the audience knows, respects,

new hires @ work

Matthew Weiss

Field Representative
United States House of Representatives

Hofstra University, 2009

"Although some messages are more persuasive than others, I find that most communication requires some level of persuasion. I have learned to think on my feet to use different techniques of persuasion."

Credibility An audience's belief that you have expertise and are trustworthy based on your character, reputation, and behavior.

and believes to be credible. This *affinity* with a credible source will help convince the audience that you are trustworthy.

- **Present your ideas effectively.** The quality of your communication also builds credibility. Audiences are more likely to believe you if you present an unbiased point of view, organize your ideas logically, and support those ideas with good research and sound reasoning. Even if you are not an expert yourself, you can add weight to your ideas by citing authorities and experts.

Because credibility is so critical for capturing an audience's attention and persuading them to listen, small companies often devote substantial space on their websites to building credibility. FIGURE 5.4 illustrates how one small company presents itself to instill confidence in readers.

FIGURE 5.4 A Small Business Website That Builds Credibility

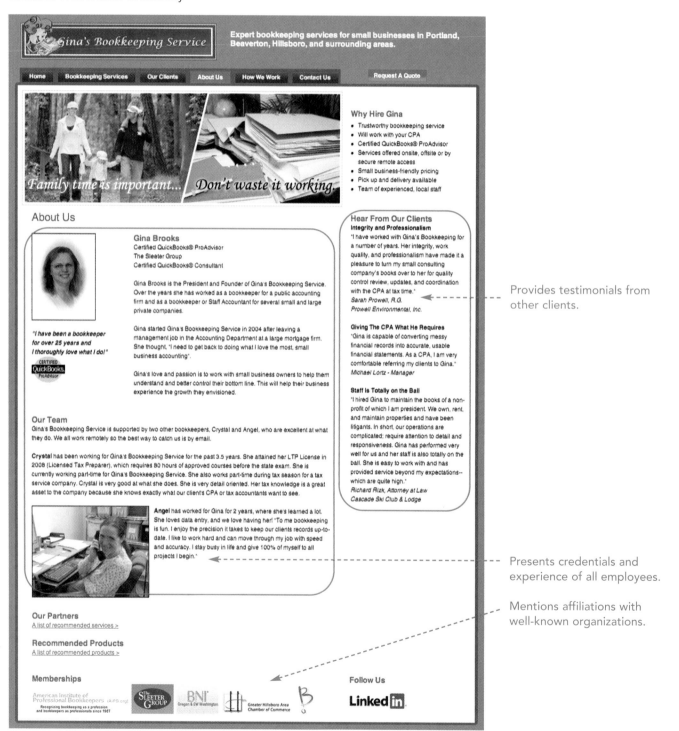

Provides testimonials from other clients.

Presents credentials and experience of all employees.

Mentions affiliations with well-known organizations.

While credibility is important, it has two important limitations as a persuasive technique:

- **Credibility is hard to earn and easy to lose.** A person with a reputation for honesty can quickly lose credibility by making statements that prove to be untrue or making promises that are not fulfilled. For example, in 2009, after Toyota recalled 3.8 million vehicles for "unintended acceleration," Toyota Group Vice President Bob Carter stated Toyotas had no additional problems and accused critics of engaging in "unwarranted speculation." Soon after, however, additional problems, including braking problems, came to light. Carter admitted he "shot some of [his] personal credibility" with his earlier comments.[6]
- **Credibility alone often is not strong enough** to change the mind of someone who is deeply interested in an issue, including people committed to an opposing point of view.[7] For example, Steve Jobs, the CEO of Apple, has a great deal of credibility as a technology innovator and a producer of award-winning products. However, that credibility—even coupled with the quality and credibility of Apple products—has persuaded fewer than 10 percent of computer buyers to purchase Macs.[8] Credibility cannot overcome the resistance caused by higher costs and entrenched corporate commitment to Microsoft operating systems.

Credibility may convince your audience to trust you, but successfully persuading an audience will require additional persuasive techniques, including a logical argument.

Constructing a logical argument

Logical arguments provide the foundation for most persuasive business messages. **Argumentation** means taking a position, supporting the position with reasons, and then documenting those reasons with evidence.

In Section 5.1, you considered how Pedro could persuade his supervisor, Maria, to support his request for funds to provide computer training to the customer service department. Pedro emailed Maria a short version of his argument (see Figure 5.3 on page 146) to persuade her to meet with him. Assume that Maria responded to Pedro with an email that said the following: "Pedro, your recommendation makes sense, and your timing is good. I am scheduled to meet with the vice president of finance tomorrow morning and would like to present your recommendation so that we can schedule the training as soon as possible. Please write a one-page document outlining the reasons and evidence that I can bring to the meeting. Thanks, Maria."

FIGURE 5.5 offers one way to structure that argument logically by defining the position, identifying reasons, and outlining evidence.

Argumentation A persuasive appeal that supports a position with reasons and evidence.

FIGURE 5.5 Structure of a Logical Argument

In a logical argument like the one represented in Figure 5.5, the quality of your evidence is important. You can collect evidence from original research that you conduct (primary research) or by reading research that others have conducted (secondary research). Your evidence may take different forms, depending on the reason you are trying to support and the needs of your audience. Consider the types of evidence that Pedro can use to support his argument:

- **Numerical data.** Many business arguments are based on numbers. Some arguments require data about costs, time, or revenue. Other arguments require data about customer preferences or business trends. You may find some of the numbers you need in published sources. Others will come from company records or from surveys and questionnaires. You can present this data in tables, graphs, or paragraphs. Pedro's current argument requesting funds to support a computer training workshop relies primarily on numerical data about the number of customer complaints, number of customers served, and cost of customer complaints.

- **Facts.** A fact is documented information that someone can verify. If the fact is not already well known to the audience, it will be important to cite the source, for example:

    According to Bain & Co. consultants, retaining and deepening an existing customer relationship can be 5 to 10 times more profitable than acquiring a new one.[9]

- **Expert authority.** For additional support, you may cite the opinions of people with acknowledged expertise. For example:

    According to sales expert Jonathan Farrington, "the cost of an unhappy customer is much greater than the cost of any individual lost sale." It also includes the loss of that person's future business and the potential lost sales from people who have talked to the unhappy customer.[10]

- **Personal experience.** Your experiences and observations may provide compelling support for a claim, although they are rarely conclusive on their own. For example:

    This software is too difficult to learn without training. I've spent 10 hours trying to learn all its functions, and I still can't figure out how to issue a refund.

- **Examples.** Although examples are not conclusive evidence, they can clarify your point and help your audience understand. For example:

    Customer complaints have increased 50 percent. We have received complaints about dropped calls, orders being lost, and refunds not being credited.

Pedro uses most of this evidence in his one-page memo for Maria and the vice president of finance. The memo, illustrated in FIGURE 5.6, follows the logical structure outlined in Figure 5.5. It also anticipates objections and stresses benefits. Pedro's logical writing style and thorough analysis will give him a good deal of credibility with his audience.

Appealing to your audience's emotions

Although logic is critical for business decisions, logic alone may not always be enough to persuade an audience. You may also need to appeal to their emotions.[11] Psychologists and other researchers have identified several techniques for engaging your audience on an emotional level.

Appeal to your audience's emotional and psychological needs

You may wonder how you can address your audience's psychological needs, especially when communicating with an audience you do not know. However, psychologist Abraham Maslow argued that all people—even people of different cultures and different generations—share a common set of needs.[12] At the basic level are physiological needs of food, clothing, and shelter. Once those needs are met, people will seek to meet

FIGURE 5.6 Logical Argument for Computer Training

memo

TO: Maria Cardoni
FROM: Pedro Baca
DATE: June 11, 20XX
SUBJECT: Proposed Solution for Costly Customer Service Problems

Subject line focuses on solving a cost problem, which will interest the VP.

Problem

Two weeks ago, the customer service department installed new software designed to improve productivity and customer service. Employees received the standard three-hour orientation that comes with the software package. However, the training did not cover the customized functions necessary to process returns, exchanges, and refunds.

In the two weeks that employees have been using the software, we have logged 75 complaints more than average. Customers have complained about dropped calls, exchanged orders being lost, and refunds not being credited. In addition, because representatives are addressing so many time-consuming complaints, they are handling fewer calls, and their productivity has decreased by 15 percent. Although we cannot prove that lack of training on the new software caused the customer service problems, the coincidence is too great to be ignored.

The first two paragraphs document the problem and anticipate the objection that employees have received sufficient training.

These problems are costly to our company. Last year, we researched the cost of customer complaints and determined that each complaint costs us approximately $50 in employee time and lost sales. This means that in the past two weeks, handling the 75 additional complaints has cost us $3750. If these problems continue, costs will conservatively exceed $10,000 in two months.

We also need to consider the long-term costs of unhappy customers. According to sales expert Jonathan Farrington, "the cost of an unhappy customer is much greater than the cost of any individual lost sale."* It includes the loss of that person's future business and the potential lost sales from people who have talked to the unhappy customer.

The next two paragraphs document the immediate and long-term costs of the problem. Pedro cites both research conducted by the department and a sales authority.

Proposed Solution

I have discussed this problem with the software developer, Mark Richey from Viking Systems, and he has agreed to provide an additional three-hour training session for all employees addressing the important customized functions in our system. To ensure that all employees are trained, he has also agreed to deliver the session twice, with half of the representatives attending each session.

The first paragraph of this section provides the details of the solution.

The cost for this customized training will be $5000, the exact amount it would have cost us to add the training to our original purchase. Although the amount may seem expensive, it is actually cost effective, considering the losses we project if the customer service problems persist. I do not believe employees will be able to master the system without training. I've spent 10 hours trying to learn all the functions of the new system on my own, and I still cannot figure out how to issue a refund.

The second paragraph presents the cost and anticipates several objections: Viking Systems is charging too much, the training will not be cost effective, and employees can learn on their own.

Mark is prepared to deliver the session next week if we can approve the funding. The more quickly we provide the training, the more quickly we can realize the customer service benefits from the company's investment in the new system.

The final paragraph reminds the audience of the main benefit of funding training—it is the only way the department will receive the intended results from the new system.

* Farrington, J. (2008). Customer complaints: The income multiplier effect. *CRM-Daily.com*. Retrieved from *http://www.crm-daily.com*

increasingly higher levels of need. Advertisers routinely appeal to these needs as part of their persuasive strategy:

- **Safety.** Advertisements for home security systems appeal to the audience's desire for safety. Banks and investment companies appeal to the audience's desire for financial security.
- **Love and belonging.** Commercials for hair products and cosmetics appeal to the audience's desire to be attractive and admired. Commercials for convenience foods

ETHICS Avoiding Logical Fallacies

When constructing an argument, you may be tempted to strengthen a weak position by overstating your case, diverting attention from problems with your position, or even attacking an opponent. These violations of logical reasoning that lead to a flawed argument are called **fallacies**, and intentionally using them is both dishonest and misleading.

Pedro might have used some of the following fallacies in his argument to Maria and the vice president of finance. Fortunately he did not. As you read each, identify what is misleading about the statement.

It is important to avoid fallacies in your own communication and also to recognize fallacies when others use them so that you are not persuaded by unsound ideas. ■

PEARSON
mybcommlab

For an ETHICS exercise, go to Exercise 6 on page 177 or to this chapter's End-of-Chapter Exercises at mybcommlab.com.

Type of Fallacy	Description	Example Fallacy from Pedro to Maria
Appeal to popular opinion	Offering as evidence statements such as "everybody knows"	*Everybody knows that without training, new computer systems lead to productivity losses. It's obvious.*
Hasty generalization	Drawing a conclusion from a sample that is either too small or does not represent the larger population	*Two of our most experienced sales reps say that they are having difficulty with the computer system. If they are having trouble, it's likely everyone is.*
Ignoring the burden of proof	Stating a claim but providing no evidence to support it	*Providing computer training will immediately reverse our losses.*
False cause	Assuming there is a cause and effect between two things without proving the relationship	*As soon as we got new computers, customer complaints increased. Obviously, the new system is the cause.*
False analogy	Supporting an idea by comparing it to something that is not comparable	*We require everyone to receive sufficient instruction before operating a car. Similarly, we should require all customer service reps to get sufficient training before operating the new computer system.*
False dilemma	Asserting that only two choices exist, while ignoring other options	*Either we provide more training or we will continue to see losses in productivity.*
Red herring	Focusing on an irrelevant issue to draw attention away from a central issue	*If management wants to cut budgets, then it would be much better to eliminate executive bonuses. The company spends millions on bonuses, and what benefit do we see from that?*
Ad hominem attack	Attacking a person who disagrees with you rather than addressing the issues	*The managers who instituted the budget cuts are just a bunch of pencil pushers who don't have any idea what employees really need to do their jobs well.*

appeal to the audience's desire for dinners that bring the family closer, even if they have no time to cook.

- **Self-esteem.** Advertisements for charities often appeal to the increase in audience self-esteem that will result from the good works enabled by the donation: *Your donation of a dollar a day will prevent a child from starving.* Advertisements for educational institutions focus on the respect you earn—and the self-respect you feel—from completing your education.
- **Self-actualization.** The U.S. Army's long-lived advertising slogan "Be all that you can be" appealed to people's desire to make the most of their abilities. Advertisements for luxury travel experiences often appeal to travelers who want to "find themselves" in exotic places.

You can make use of these appeals in your business communication. For example, assume you want to persuade someone to donate to a charity. You can appeal to your audience's self-esteem by praising them for past actions, focusing on how they will make a difference in the world, showing them that their actions are greatly needed, or

Fallacy A violation of logical reasoning that leads to a flawed argument.

even complimenting them for their character. FIGURE 5.7 illustrates a fundraising message that uses all these emotional appeals to persuade a donor who has supported a charitable organization in the past.

mybcommlab

Apply Figure 5.7's key concepts by revising a new document. Go to Chapter 5 in mybcommlab.com and select Document Makeovers.

FIGURE 5.7 Persuasive Fundraising Message Using Emotional Appeals

letter

The Greenwald Center

2025 Chatham Drive   •   Burlingame, CA 94010   •   P: 808.555.1477   •   F: 808.555.1478

November 18, 20XX

Ms. Julie Benjamin
106 W. Third Avenue
San Mateo, CA 94401

Dear Ms. Benjamin:

Thank you for your past support of The Greenwald Center. Your generosity has helped create opportunities and successes for people in our community who live with disabilities. As you make your year-ending giving decisions, please consider renewing your support with a gift of $100.

Each year at The Greenwald Center, 5,000 people with disabilities strive to increase their independence one step at a time—finding accessible housing or steady employment, learning to read or cook, or managing household finances. The Greenwald Center supports these efforts one person at a time, helping people achieve their individual goals. As our four-star rating from Charity Navigator indicates, every dollar that you contribute goes directly toward helping people.

Here are some of the successes your contribution supported this past year:

- 350 people found jobs ranging from car porter to sales representative
- 93 people learned to read bus signs, make medical appointments, and conduct personal banking on their own
- 100 percent of families surveyed have learned ways to assist their children's development at home

In an era of shrinking government support, we increasingly rely on sustainable funding from friends like you, extraordinary people who see ability in everyone. Your gift can help train a literacy volunteer, facilitate a "mock" interview session, hire a guest cooking instructor or, in other ways, support the success of people living with disabilities.

Please use the enclosed self-addressed stamped envelope to return your pledge today or contribute on our website at www.greenwaldcenter.org.

Thank you for generously continuing to support The Greenwald Center.

Sincerely,

Allan I. Bergman

Allan I. Bergman
President/CEO

P.S. As a token of our appreciation, we have enclosed a DVD, *Introduction to The Greenwald Center,* so that you can see the good work you are supporting. We also have a limited number of tickets available for a December 15 holiday concert at City Orchestra. The tickets sell for $75 each, but we will give them free of charge to donors who request them, on first-come first-served basis.

Annotations:

HOW DOES THIS LETTER APPEAL TO SELF-ESTEEM?

Praises past action.

Provides quantitative data to illustrate that donors' support makes a difference.

Shows that the support is greatly needed.

Compliments donors as exceptional people.

Concludes by assuming that this good person will, of course, continue to exhibit the same generosity.

In addition to appealing to self-esteem, the letter in Figure 5.7 uses additional persuasive techniques based on psychological principles that have been proven effective in engaging people's emotions.[13] These principles are summarized in FIGURE 5.8.

FIGURE 5.8 Techniques for Appealing to Emotion

Principle	How It Is Used in Figure 5.7
Consistency People like to act consistently and to make decisions similar to the ones they made in the past. Remind your audience they have made similar decisions in the past.	*Thank you for your past support of The Greenwald Center. Your generosity has helped create opportunities and successes for people in our community who live with disabilities.*
Social Proof People follow the lead of others they respect. Include names and testimonials.	*As our four-star rating from Charity Navigator indicates, every dollar that you contribute goes directly toward helping people.*
Liking People respond more positively to those whom they like and who like them. Show that you appreciate your audience.	*In an era of shrinking government support, we increasingly rely on sustainable funding from friends like you, extraordinary people who see ability in everyone.*
Reciprocity People want to reciprocate if they receive a gift. The gift can be as small as a compliment or a recommendation of a book to read.	*P.S. As a token of our appreciation, we have enclosed a mini-DVD Introduction to The Greenwald Center so that you can see the good work you are supporting.*
Scarcity People want things more if those things are scarce. Highlight the exclusivity of your offer.	*We also have a limited number of tickets available for a December 15 holiday concert at City Orchestra. The tickets sell for $75 each, but we will give them free of charge to donors who request them, on first-come first-served basis.*

Adapted from Cialdini, R. (2001, October). "Harnessing the Science of Persuasion." *Harvard Business Review.*

Show your own emotional commitment

If you want your audience to commit to an idea, they need to know that you are committed to it also. In other words, you will be more persuasive if you speak—or write—from the heart.[14] One reason that Rio de Janeiro won the bid for the 2016 Olympics may have been that Brazilian President Luiz Inacio Lula da Silva demonstrated extraordinary emotional commitment to hosting the Olympics. Not only did he spend two years personally lobbying the Olympic committee and other heads of state, he also spent the week before the final vote in Copenhagen visiting with members of the International Olympic Committee to make his case. The day before the vote, he gave a heartfelt speech explaining what it would mean to South America to host the Olympic Games for the first time in the competition's history. He described how athletes throughout South America would be affected by being part of this experience—and how the world would take notice if the International Olympic Committee awarded this honor to a continent that it had previously ignored. After the speech, Lula said, "It was extraordinary the emotion we put into our presentation . . . I almost cried two times during my speech."[15] One delegate of the International Olympic Committee commented, "I told the president (Lula), whom I know very well for a long time, that his speech went under my skin."[16]

Use compelling evidence and powerful language

Evidence is typically the "logic" part of an argument. However, compelling evidence is presented in clear and vivid language that can also touch an audience emotionally and motivate them to act.[17] For example, the late Diana, Princess of Wales, once spoke at a seminar sponsored by the Landmines Survivors Network and the Mines Advisory Board in London. Her goals were to persuade the English government and people to support an international ban on landmines and to increase foreign aid to remove landmines from poor countries in Africa, where mines continue to harm people long after a war has ended. In this speech, Princess Diana explicitly chose not to describe the injuries of children who are victims of these mines. Instead, she focused on alarming facts, such as these:

For the mine is a stealthy killer. Long after conflict is ended, its innocent victims die or are wounded singly, in countries of which we hear little. Their lonely fate is never reported. The world, with its many other preoccupations, remains largely unmoved by a death roll of something like 800 people every month—many of them women and children. Those who are not killed outright—and they number another 1,200 a month—suffer terrible injuries and are handicapped for life. I was in Angola in January with the British Red Cross—a country where there are 15 million landmines in a population, Ladies and Gentlemen, of 10 million—with the desire of drawing world attention to this vital, but hitherto largely neglected issue.[18]

Powerful facts can be powerful persuaders. A week after Diana gave this speech, then British Prime Minister Tony Blair led the British government to reverse its former position against banning landmines. Six months later, 125 countries signed an international agreement to ban landmines. Although Diana's speech was not the sole cause of these changes, it played a role in changing hearts and minds.

Study Question 5.3

What types of business messages typically require persuasion?

In business, the following types of communication typically require persuasion to influence and motivate the audience:

- Recommendations for action
- Requests for favors
- Persuasive customer claims
- Sales messages

This section provides examples for each message type. Chapter 11 covers another example—job application letters.

Recommendations for action

When you make a **recommendation**, you establish that a problem or a need exists, and then you show how your solution is effective. The content of your recommendation can include a range of persuasive elements: focusing on benefits, anticipating objections, building credibility, constructing a logical argument, and appealing to the audience's emotion.

One challenge is to determine the order for this content. Should your recommendation be direct, starting with the main point? Or should it be indirect, building up to the main point? FIGURE 5.9 shows an outline for both direct and indirect recommendations. The left column provides specific criteria to help you determine which organization you should choose. For example, if the audience requests your recommendation, be direct. However, if your recommendation will come as a surprise, you may want to organize it indirectly.

As an example, assume you manage a 20-person technology support department in a company of 500 employees. Your staff supports every department in the company, from the proprietary accounting software for payroll to the janitorial staff's application for online supply requisition. Currently, you assign technicians as problems arise. The next technician in the rotation handles the next problem, no matter which department requests support. However, staff members have developed specialized skills by working repeatedly with specific software applications. Therefore, you believe the company would benefit from decentralizing technical support and assigning technicians to specific units. This would shift the supervisory lines from your technical support department to the various departments throughout the company. You mention the plan to your staff. They like it because it would provide them with more specialized experience and streamline their duties.

Recommendation A business message that suggests a solution to a business problem.

FIGURE 5.9 Two Ways to Organize Recommendation Messages

Use **DIRECT ORGANIZATION** if...	**DIRECT ORGANIZATION** follows this pattern...
your audience • requests the recommendation, prefers directness, or is likely to react positively, **and the recommendation will not** • negatively affect stakeholders or require additional effort from stakeholders.	**BEGIN WITH MAIN POINT** Propose a specific recommendation. **PROVIDE CONTEXT** • Identify the issue, problem, or opportunity. • Provide evidence that the problem or opportunity is significant. **SUPPORT YOUR PROPOSAL** For example: • Justify recommendations with persuasive rationale. • Describe alternative solutions and negative implications. • Address potential objections • Stress benefits. **MOTIVATE ACTION** Conclude with call to action.

Use **INDIRECT ORGANIZATION** if ...	**INDIRECT ORGANIZATION** follows this pattern ...
your audience • is not expecting the recommendation, • prefers indirectness, or • is likely to react negatively, **and the recommendation will** • negatively affect stakeholders, or • require additional effort from stakeholders.	**BEGIN WITH CONTEXT** • Identify the issue, problem, or opportunity. • Provide evidence that the problem or opportunity is significant. **OPTIONAL: ELIMINATE OTHER ALTERNATIVES** • Describe alternative solutions and negative implications. **STATE MAIN POINT** • Propose a specific recommendation. **SUPPORT YOUR PROPOSAL** For example: • Justify recommendations with persuasive rationale. • Address potential objections. • Stress benefits. **MOTIVATE ACTION** Conclude with call to action.

You decide to prepare a persuasive recommendation for the vice president (VP) of operations. Although the primary audience is the VP, you decide to copy your message to all the department heads (the secondary audience) since your proposed change would affect them.

In this situation, which organizational plan would be better? Consider two scenarios:

• Assume that your audience did not request the information. However, you predict they will not be surprised by your recommendation. You think the primary audience, the VP of operations, prefers direct messages. You also think he will react positively to your recommendation since he personally requests the same tech support person when he needs assistance. Since other department heads have complained about slow response times when requesting technical support, you think the secondary audience won't need significant persuading either. You believe all stakeholders will benefit from the change even though it will require significant effort to reorganize. Therefore, you draft the direct message in **FIGURE 5.10**.

- Now assume a different scenario. The VP of operations is newly appointed to the position. Given that he's been on the job only a few weeks, he may be very surprised at a recommendation to reorganize your department. Since he is new, you can't be sure whether he prefers directness or if he will react positively. Although the recommendation will not negatively affect stakeholders, the change will require significant effort to reassign supervisory roles. In fact, you predict several of the department heads may not appreciate having to manage and house your technical staff in their departments. Under these circumstances, you would draft a message like the indirect recommendation in FIGURE 5.10. The last two paragraphs of the messages are identical. Notice three main differences in the indirect version: the wording of the subject line, the position of the recommendation, and the extra background information.

FIGURE 5.10 Persuasive Recommendation (Email Message)

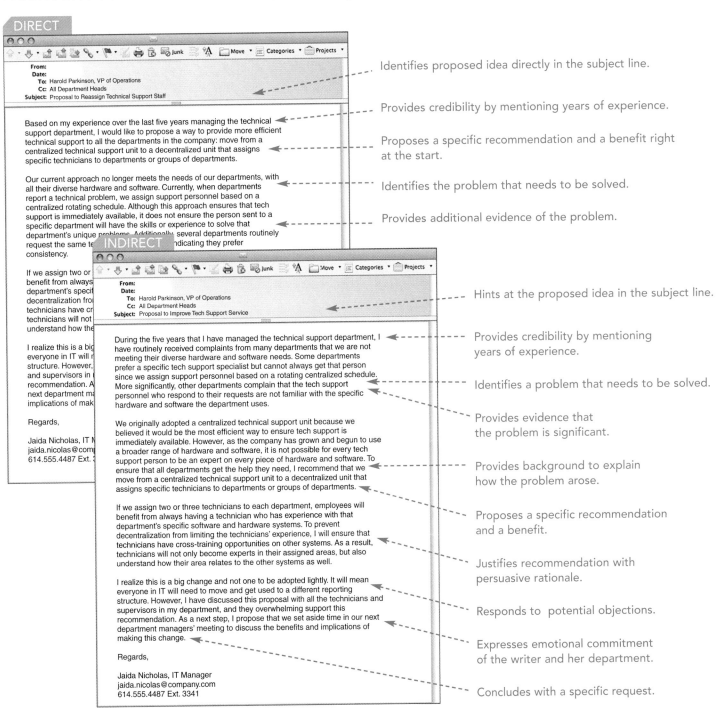

TECHNOLOGY   Writing Recommendations with Presentation Software

Many businesses routinely write recommendations using presentation software like PowerPoint. These documents provide all their evidence and reasoning clearly on the slides, since the audience will refer to the slides later when making decisions. Four key principles will help you assemble a logical and persuasive recommendation presentation:

1. Organize your presentation into well-defined sections that signal your logic.
2. Design every slide to support one main idea.
3. Write *message headlines*: short sentences or meaningful phrases at the top of the slide, representing your main ideas.
4. Present material in the body of the slide that supports the main idea in your headline.

To see these four principles in action, review the following recommendation presentation. The presentation, written by a not-for-profit organization, is designed to persuade state legislators to require calorie labeling in Illinois restaurants. The presentation is divided into three sections: Problem, Causes, and Proposed Solution.

As you read the presentation, notice how it follows the four principles. The persuasive argument flows from slide to slide. You can follow the argument just by reading the slide headlines.

PEARSON
mybcommlab

For a TECHNOLOGY exercise, go to Exercise 12 on page 178 or to this chapter's End-of-Chapter Exercises at mybcommlab.com.

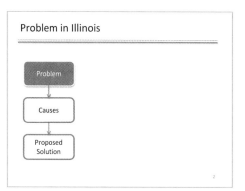

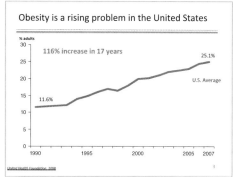

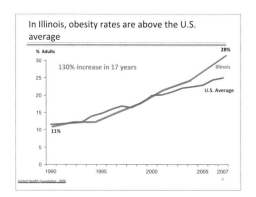

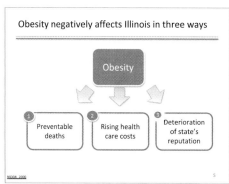

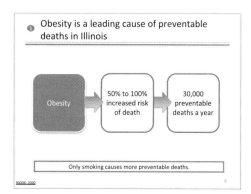

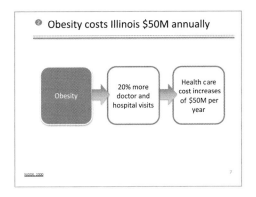

❷ Obesity costs Illinois $50M annually

Obesity → 20% more doctor and hospital visits → Health care cost increases of $50M per year

NIDDK, 2000   7

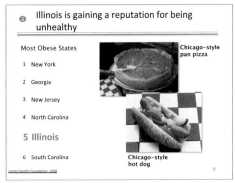

❸ Illinois is gaining a reputation for being unhealthy

Most Obese States

1 New York
2 Georgia
3 New Jersey
4 North Carolina
5 **Illinois**
6 South Carolina

Chicago-style pan pizza

Chicago-style hot dog

United Health Foundation, 2008   8

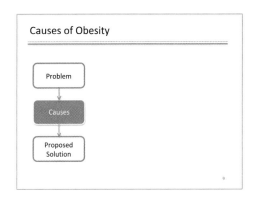

Causes of Obesity

Problem → Causes → Proposed Solution

9

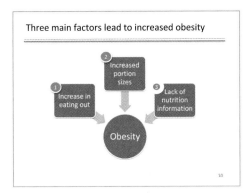

Three main factors lead to increased obesity

① Increase in eating out
② Increased portion sizes
③ Lack of nutrition information
→ Obesity

10

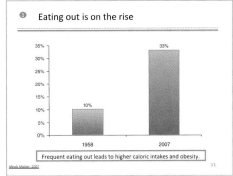

❶ Eating out is on the rise

- 1958: 10%
- 2007: 33%

Frequent eating out leads to higher caloric intakes and obesity.

Meals Matter, 2007   11

❷ Portion sizes have increased since the 1950s

Average Portion Sizes

	Then	Now	% Increase
French fries	2.4 oz	7.1 oz	300%
Muffin	3.0 oz	6.5 oz	216%
Fountain soda	7.0 oz	12.0 to 64.0 oz	170% - 815%
Pasta serving	1.5 cups	3 cups	200%
Chocolate bar	1.0 oz	2.6 to 8.0 oz	260% - 800%

Meals Matter, 2007   12

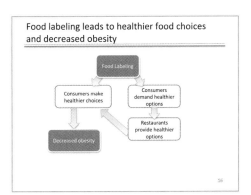

❸ Healthy decisions are hard to make without nutrition information

- Wendy's: Chicken BLT Salad — 780
- Dunkin Donuts: Cake donut — 280
- McDonald's: Big Mac — 540
- Starbucks: Strawberry Frappuccino — 570

Calorie counts are surprising

13

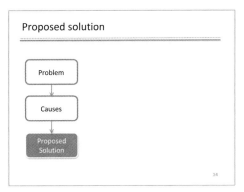

Proposed solution

Problem → Causes → Proposed Solution

14

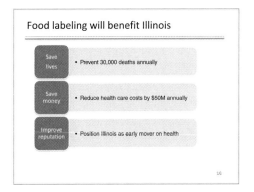

A food labeling plan is straightforward and easy to implement

Who	What	When
• Chain restaurants • 15 or more locations in the United States	• Required to list calories on menus • Enforced by city governments	• Implementation within a year

New York City implemented a similar plan without problems.

15

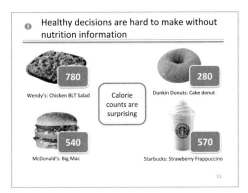

Food labeling leads to healthier food choices and decreased obesity

Food Labeling → Consumers make healthier choices → Consumers demand healthier options → Restaurants provide healthier options → Decreased obesity

16

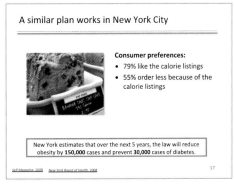

A similar plan works in New York City

Consumer preferences:
- 79% like the calorie listings
- 55% order less because of the calorie listings

New York estimates that over the next 5 years, the law will reduce obesity by **150,000** cases and prevent **30,000** cases of diabetes.

Self Magazine, 2008   New York Board of Health, 2008   17

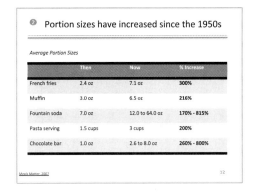

Food labeling will benefit Illinois

- Save lives — • Prevent 30,000 deaths annually
- Save money — • Reduce health care costs by $50M annually
- Improve reputation — • Position Illinois as early mover on health

16

Requests for favors

When you ask people to do something that is easy for them to accomplish or that they will be happy to do, little persuasion is required. By contrast, more persuasion is required if you ask people to do something that involves effort, requires them to choose between alternatives, or differs from their plans. In those cases, you will need to make a **persuasive request** that helps the audience feel good about doing the favor. If possible, the request will also show how the audience will benefit from helping you.

For example, assume that as a member of your state's bar association, you volunteered to help organize a local awards luncheon for the 450 association members in your area. This morning—less than a week before the event—you receive a phone call from the keynote speaker, the mayor, indicating that she is no longer able to speak at the luncheon due to a death in the family. You have just a few days to find a replacement. Fortunately, you know the perfect person to contact. Dr. Gunther Maher was your business law professor in college. He retired last year and has many anecdotes he can share during a keynote presentation. Your concern is whether he is available and, more importantly, whether he would be willing to make the presentation with less than a week to prepare. To plan your persuasive request, you use the ACE process.

Analyzing

As you analyze, answer the following questions:

- **Purpose: What is my purpose, desired outcome, and business result?** You want Dr. Maher to agree to deliver the bar association keynote presentation next week. If he agrees, the result will be that the attendees will not mind that the original presenter cancelled.

- **Information needs: What does Dr. Maher need to know (what does he already know)?** Dr. Maher may not remember who you are, so you will need to reintroduce yourself. He then needs to know the date and time of the bar association awards luncheon, the length of his presentation, why you are asking him to speak at the last minute, and what you would like him to speak about.

- **Motivation and benefits: What will motivate Dr. Maher to comply with my request? How will he benefit?** You can appeal to Dr. Maher's self-esteem. Dr. Maher may be persuaded if he believes that he can influence the careers of hundreds of lawyers. He might have chosen to become a professor to help mold the minds of future professionals. This keynote gives him the opportunity to further influence many of today's lawyers. This is a benefit to him since it helps him achieve his personal goals.

- **Potential resistance: What concerns and objections will he have?** He may be concerned that he has to prepare carefully for the presentation and he does not have time.

- **Medium: What is the best medium for this message based on the purpose, audience, and content?** You need to know quickly if Dr. Maher can fulfill your request, so a telephone conversation is the best medium. In a telephone call, you can also answer any questions he has.

Composing

As you compose (in this case, as you prepare what you plan to say on the telephone), answer the following questions:

- **Should the message be direct—with the main point at the beginning—or indirect?** You decide that you need to begin the conversation by reintroducing yourself and building your credibility as a business professional and active member of the bar association. Your request will be indirect, coming after you have reestablished this relationship.

- **How can I best organize the message?** You decide to make an outline to ensure that you effectively present your argument and justify your request.
  - Introduce yourself as a former student.
  - Mention how much you liked his course.

- Preface the request by indicating you're calling to ask an important favor.
- Explain the request, specifically indicating the date of the keynote address.
- Use the persuasive strategy outlined in the analysis: mention his years of experience, wealth of knowledge, and ability to make a significant difference in the professional careers of hundreds of lawyers.
- Repeat the request by specifically asking for his agreement.
- If he agrees, thank him for agreeing and provide additional details.
- If he declines, thank him for considering the request.

- **How should I format this message to be professional and support my purpose?** Since the message will take the form of a telephone conversation, you don't have to worry about the format, but you do need to make sure you sound professional.

You dial Dr. Maher's telephone number, but he doesn't answer. You get his voice mail. FIGURE 5.11 illustrates a voice mail message that makes the persuasive request.

FIGURE 5.11 A Persuasive Request (Voice Mail Message)

voice mail message

Hello, Dr. Maher. This is Alexa Hampton. I was in your business law class several years ago and found it very useful. I now work as an associate lawyer at Betts, Miller, and Russo here in town, and I'm calling to ask you a favor.

Begins with an introduction, establishes credibility, and indicates general reason for calling.

I'm on the planning committee for the local bar association, and our awards luncheon is next Monday. The mayor was our original keynote speaker, but a sudden death in the family prevents her from attending. I immediately thought of you as a replacement. Would you be able to deliver a one-hour speech based on anecdotes and lessons you learned during your career?

Provides context.

Makes a direct request.

Addresses potential objection: he will not have time to research material for a speech.

Your years of experience and wealth of knowledge could make a significant difference in the professional lives of the 450 lawyers who will attend the luncheon. In a one-hour speech, you will address more people than you were able to teach in an entire academic year as a business law professor. I know you are the perfect keynote replacement for the mayor.

Motivates with self-esteem by praising Dr. Maher's experience and knowledge.

Includes audience benefits: he will continue to make a difference in the lives of others.

Please call me at 555-1887 as soon as you get this message so we can discuss the details. I look forward to talking with you soon. Again, Alexa Hampton, 555-1887. Thank you.

Concludes with a call for action: requests reply and provides phone number.

Evaluating

Consider the voice mail message from Dr. Maher's perspective. How would you react if you received this message? Was the message persuasive enough to justify a positive response? The better you know the audience—in this case, Dr. Maher—the more likely you are to create a persuasive message.

Persuasive customer claims

You have probably read store policies with the phrases "no returns," "all sales are final," or "limited warranty." If you want to request a refund or adjustment to a sales transaction, you need to create a **customer claim** message that persuades the seller that a policy should not apply in your situation or that it is in the seller's best interest to fulfill your request.

Persuasive request A request that persuades the audience to do you a favor by making the audience feel good about doing the favor and, if possible, stressing audience benefits.

Customer claim A request that a store or a vendor accept a return, refund money, exchange an item, or perform a repair.

For example, assume you are starting a home-based business and need a scanner. You purchase a refurbished scanner from a discount electronics store, E-Tronics, which clearly posts its no-return policy in the store and on every receipt. Although the sales associate who helped you with the purchase assured you that the scanner would work with your specific laptop model, you cannot get the scanner to work. You decide to bring both your laptop and the scanner to E-Tronics so the "Tech Team" can fix your problem. However, after seeing your laptop, they explain that the scanner model was discontinued before your laptop model was created. Therefore, the driver that you need to enable the laptop to communicate with the scanner does not exist. They would be happy to sell you a scanner that would work with your laptop, but they cannot exchange it for your current scanner or refund your money. After explaining to the store's manager that a sales associate assured you the scanner and laptop were compatible, the manager provides you with the E-Tronics customer service address where you can request a refund or exchange. You return home to draft your persuasive claim letter. Where do you begin?

Analyzing

As you analyze, answer the following questions:

- **Purpose, desired outcome, and business result: What do I want the audience to do after receiving this message?** You want the store to exchange the scanner for the one that works with your laptop.
- **Information needs: What does the audience need to know?** The audience needs to know what happened and why you are requesting an exchange. The audience also needs to know why you believe their policy should not apply in this instance.
- **Motivation and benefits: What will motivate the audience to accept your idea? How will the audience benefit?** The audience will be motivated by appeals to fairness and integrity: you purchased the scanner because the sales associate assured you the original scanner would actually work with your specific laptop model. The benefit is that you will continue to be a customer.
- **Potential resistance: What concerns and objections will the audience have?** The audience may resist because the store's stated policy allows no exceptions. Therefore, it is important to stress that you are requesting an exchange because of a mistake the store made, not a mistake that you made. You can also overcome resistance by showing you are willing to purchase a more expensive item if necessary.
- **Medium: What is the best medium for this message based on the purpose, audience, and content?** By following the store's policies, you start with a letter to begin the claim process and receive a claim number. Then you plan to follow-up with a telephone call to speak directly with someone.

Composing

As you compose, answer the following questions:

- **Should the message be direct—with the main point at the beginning—or indirect?** Since you're writing to a customer service department that knows most messages are based on problems, they will not be surprised to receive your message. You decide to state the main point directly.
- **How can I best organize the message?** Divide the message into clear paragraphs: (1) state the request, (2) explain the problem, (3) demonstrate goodwill and understanding, and explain why the policy should not apply, and (4) conclude by providing contact information and expressing continued confidence in the store.
- **How should I format this message to be professional and support my purpose?** Use a standard business letter format, keep it neat and professional, and avoid emotions.

Based on these decisions, you draft the letter illustrated in FIGURE 5.12.

FIGURE 5.12 Persuasive Claim (Letter)

letter

ELAINE MACKIEWETZ
4218 Paragon Trail, Apt. 32
Eagle Heights, OH 43434
(419) 555-8623

October 13, 20XX

E-Tronics, Inc.
Customer Service Department
5522 Industrial Parkway West
Chicago, IL 60660

Ladies and Gentlemen:

Directly states the reason for the letter.

My local E-Tronics store in Eagle Heights, Ohio, sold me a refurbished scanner that does not work with my computer's operating system. I would like to exchange it for one that does work with my computer.

Clearly explains the evolution of the problem and the technical details.

On October 10, 20XX (see attached receipt), I purchased a refurbished HP scanner, Model #5770, because a sales associate at the store mistakenly assured me that this HP scanner would work with my Toshiba Protégé Z500-S9050 laptop, which is running Windows 7. It was only when I got home that I discovered that a driver does not exist for Windows 7, only for Vista and Windows XP.

Demonstrates understanding and goodwill.

Explains why the policy should be waived in this case.

Appeals to fairness.

Any sales associate can make an honest mistake, and I am very willing to return this scanner and purchase one, even a more expensive one, that works with my computer. However, my local store will not exchange the scanner because of your no returns / no exchange policy. Although I understand that such a policy may be necessary to keep prices low, in this instance, I believe that my request to exchange this scanner for one that will work with my laptop is reasonable given that I received incorrect sales advice.

Closes positively with a forward-looking statement emphasizing continued business relationship (audience benefit).

Please call me at (419) 555-8623 to discuss how we can resolve this matter. I look forward to hearing from you and enjoying future purchases from your stores.

Sincerely,

Elaine Mackiewetz

Elaine Mackiewetz

Evaluating

After drafting the letter but before sending it, evaluate it from the audience's point of view. Consider how it meets the following evaluation criteria:

- **Have I convincingly shown that a problem exists?** The problem is directly stated in the first paragraph.
- **Is the proposed solution or plan a good one?** It seems fair to both sides: you get equipment that works and the store loses no revenue from the exchange.
- **Is the evidence and reasoning sound?** The second paragraph clearly explains the evolution of the problem, providing enough technical details that the audience can verify the problem.
- **Have I addressed any objections that I can anticipate?** The third paragraph explains why the policy should be waived in this case, and it appeals to the audience's sense of fairness.

- **Have I stressed benefits?** The ending refers to "enjoying future purchases," which could be perceived as a benefit from granting the request.
- **Is the message easy to read?** It uses the correct format for a letter, and the paragraphs are well organized.
- **Is the information complete, concise, clear, and correct?** It effectively gets to the point, explains the problem, demonstrates understanding, offers a solution, builds goodwill by emphasizing a positive business relationship, and closes on a forward-looking note.
- **Do I need to change anything to get the result I want from my audience?** The letter is effective, but you may want to follow up with a telephone call to get the desired result.

Sales messages

Persuasion is also an important element in most sales messages, where your goal is to motivate someone to buy a product or service. Sales and marketing people often use the acronym **AIDA**—**A**ttention, **I**nterest, **D**esire, and **A**ction—to create effective messages in sales letters, brochures, advertisements, and websites. FIGURE 5.13 summarizes the four AIDA components.

FIGURE 5.13
AIDA Approach for Organizing
Sales Messages

Attention: Grab your audience's attention so they want to know more

Interest: Build their interest by meeting their needs and emphasizing benefits

Desire: Create desire through authority, social proof, or perceived scarcity

Action: Make it easy for the audience to act and respond

AIDA relies on the basic components of persuasion that you learned in Section 5.2: build credibility, construct logical arguments, and appeal to emotion.

- **Attention.** The first part of a sales message should grab the audience's attention. Your wording should make the audience want to read or hear more about your product or service by focusing their awareness. Extreme examples include the phrases "You've Won a Million Dollars!" or "Watch as many movies as you want for only $8.99 a month!" If you read the fine print, you know that neither claim is completely true, but they do grab the reader's initial attention. In business communication, you can grab the audience's attention in a professional way by sharing a startling fact, thought-provoking story, or motivating question. Consider these examples:

Startling Fact:	Did you know that 50 percent of all small businesses fail within the first five years?
Thought-Provoking Story:	Imagine yourself running your own business with no one to answer to except yourself! You're the boss. Your ideas are taken seriously, and everyone looks to you for guidance. Sound too good to be true? For most people it is, but entrepreneurs who use our CustomerBase software suite have a good chance of achieving this dream.
Motivating Question:	Would you like to achieve your full financial potential rather than limiting your income to a monthly salary? Of course! Make your dream job come true with the CustomerBase software suite designed to build your business and increase your financial success.

- **Interest.** After gaining the audience's attention, you need to build their interest in the product or service by describing how you can meet their needs. The ACE process can help you do this. One of the first steps of the ACE process is to analyze your audience. The better you know your audience, the more likely you are to understand—and potentially meet—their needs. You can build interest by emphasizing how your product or service meets those needs—and provides additional benefits. Consider these examples:

Meeting Needs:	In addition to organizing and maintaining your customer information, CustomerBase also tracks your employees' sales by region, department, and individual person. This new feature makes identifying individual sales quotas a breeze. You'll never have to analyze convoluted spreadsheets again. Let CustomerBase do the work for you.
Audience Benefits:	The CustomerBase software suite eliminates the stress of managing your customer relationships. With one user-friendly interface, you can easily keep track of information about your customers and their needs, generate custom-designed reports, and effortlessly maintain contact with your customers.

- **Desire.** Creating a sense of desire involves reducing the audience's resistance to the sales message, which is especially important when you create **unsolicited sales communication,** or cold-call sales messages—messages you send to audiences who did not request the information. However, reducing resistance is also important in **solicited sales communication**—messages you send to audiences who did request the information. Although customers who request information want the product or service, you may have to reduce their resistance if the price is more than they predicted or if the item does not fulfill all their needs. To create a sense of desire, consider using one of the principles of persuasion introduced in Figure 5.8 on page 154. Social proof and scarcity can be particularly useful approaches:

Social Proof:	A survey of 2,500 CustomerBase users from across the country indicates that the use of the software contributes to increased sales and long-term business success. Over 85 percent of these businesses say they reached their target market sales goals within the first two years. Compare that to the national failure rate and it's easy to see how your investment in CustomerBase is a sound investment in your future success.
Scarcity:	For a limited time, we can offer you substantial savings on your CustomerBase contract. By placing your order today, you will receive free technical support for the first six months of your service contract. This offer is available only to first-time customers.

- **Action.** The final step of the AIDA persuasive strategy is to motivate your customer to act and purchase the product or service. If you want to motivate the customer to download your software package, the message should take the form of an email that includes a link to easily download the product. If your sales message is a phone call, you should be able to process the customer's order over the telephone. If you are mailing a letter or sales brochure, enclose a postage-paid return envelope in which the customer can easily place an order. Motivating action requires a professional approach. You do not want to assume the customer will purchase the product, but you don't want to use weak wording either. Motivate action by making the response easy and using strong, yet professional wording.

Easy Response:	Click here to download a free two-week trial copy of CustomerBase. After two weeks, you will be prompted to download the full version, which can be easily charged to your credit card account.
Strong, Professional Wording:	In the meantime, please call me at 800-555-1234 to discuss how CustomerBase can enhance your business success.

AIDA An acronym used in marketing to suggest the organization of sales communication: Attention, Interest, Desire, Action.

Unsolicited sales communication Sales messages you send to audiences who did not request the information, also called "cold-call sales messages."

Solicited sales communication A response to a request for sales information.

FIGURE 5.14 provides an example of a sales message that uses the AIDA strategy.

Although AIDA is usually associated with sales messages to a general audience, you can use the AIDA approach even more effectively in situations when you know the audience. For those messages, you can apply your knowledge of audience needs to determine what specific information will effectively grab their attention, build interest, create desire, and motivate action.

FIGURE 5.14 Unsolicited Sales Message

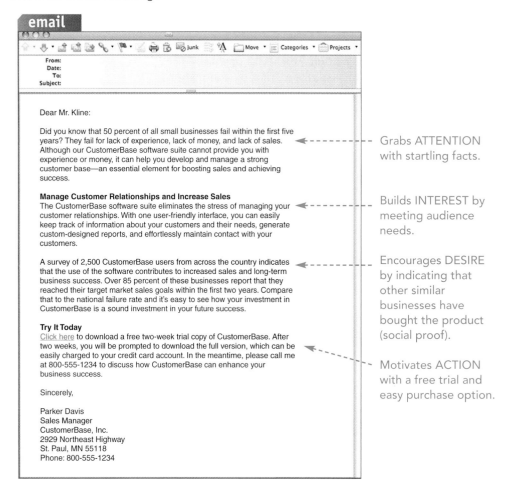

Study Question 5.4

How can I use persuasion to improve teamwork and collaboration?

This section shows you two very different ways that persuasive skills can help you be a better team leader and team member.

Persuasion helps you motivate others

Have you ever been part of a work team with members who had other priorities or did minimal work? Even if you are not designated as a team leader, you can adopt a leadership role and use your persuasive skills to help the team—and individual team members—get back on track. In this context, persuasion means influencing your team members' attitudes to bring about a change in behavior.

Effective team leaders use the following techniques to influence attitudes and motivate people to make a commitment to a team:

- **Remind the team why the work is important.** As you learned in Chapter 2, the best teams share a concrete goal and vision for success.[19] Depending on the project, success may mean that the company will launch a new product or save time and money. Success may mean that the organization will better understand the competition or that each team member will receive a bonus. If team members lose sight of the goal, remind them of their vision for success and why it is important.
- **Help others feel pride in their work.** People lose motivation when they feel unappreciated and when they do not feel good about their work. By showing appreciation and acknowledging team members' contributions, you can persuade team members to continue working at a high level.
- **Understand and acknowledge the emotions of team members.** Emotions can stand in the way of a team's success. If a team member is angry or frustrated or feels excluded from decision making, productivity will decline. Rather than try to convince someone to feel differently, actively listen to him or her, try to understand the feelings, and acknowledge the validity of those feelings. With that kind of support, many team members persuade themselves to make some changes and work harder.[20]
- **Make it possible for a team member to succeed.** Sometimes, external factors stand in the way of team success. For example, team members may have competing responsibilities at home and may not be able to commit to the team as fully as necessary. If you help people resolve these conflicts you may be able to persuade them to work harder on your project. Can you reschedule a meeting? Allow them to work from home? Redistribute tasks? Help them with another project that is taking too much of their time? Helping others makes it more possible for them to participate in the team and may also lead them to reciprocate and do more for your project.[21]

Persuasion helps a team make better decisions

In the context of decision making, you might think that persuasion means influencing your audience to agree with you and make the decision you prefer. However, when you work in a team, persuading others to agree with you can be counterproductive, leading to the type of *groupthink* described in Chapter 2. The goal of team decision making is to generate the best possible solution based on everyone's input. Ideally, the team's decision will be better than any decision an individual team member could make alone.

Consider this example: Nicole, Phil, and Ben are on a three-person team charged with researching and recommending a new approach for training their company's employees. Thus far, the team has investigated three options. Each team member believes a different option is best.

① Nicole supports contracting with Tech Solutions, Inc., a locally owned, private training company that provides tailored educational experiences either on site or at Tech Solutions' training facility a few miles away. The cost is calculated per each training session offered, rather than per student. This pricing will lower overall costs.

② Phil believes sending employees to City Community College is the best choice. A satellite campus a few blocks from the company's office offers courses toward certificate and associate degree programs. Costs are based on regular community college tuition for the courses. He proposes that the company reimburse employees for each course they pass at a grade of C or above.

③ Ben recommends working with State University, which offers tailored professional development courses for corporate customers; certificate training; and bachelor's and graduate degree programs. Their campus is several miles away, but they provide free childcare services for students enrolled in evening classes. State University offers a special tuition discount to corporate partners.

How can the team decide which idea best serves the company's and employees' needs? One approach is to ask the team members to make a case for their selection and allow other team members to challenge the selection. The dialog in FIGURE 5.15 is an example of a conversation designed to facilitate effective decision making. Notice how each team member plans his or her contributions to include persuasive arguments.

FIGURE 5.15
Persuasive
Conversation/
Collaboration

Ben

We have three proposals and three different opinions about which is best for our company training program. Nicole recommends Tech Solutions. Phil suggests the community college, and I prefer the university. Let's discuss our options and come up with the best solution. Nicole, what do you like about Tech Solutions?

Meeting opens with a summary of the situation and requests information about each preference.

Nicole

I've taken several classes with them. They're very professional, have great instructors, and usually provide the training materials as part of the course cost. I'm sure we'd have to buy books at either the community college or university.

Nicole identifies the key benefits of the Tech Solutions option.

Ben

Can classes at Tech Solutions count toward degrees or certificate training?

Ben challenges the position to bring out more details.

Nicole

I don't think so, but they can provide courses that prepare for the certificate exams. They don't proctor the actual exams, though. We'd have to outsource that.

As a result of this challenge, more details about the Tech Solutions option emerge.

Phil

For those of us who work in IT, certificates and licensing are the biggest issues. The community college offers both the preparation classes and the exams. You can find most of the technical stuff online, so I'm not concerned about book costs.

Phil identifies a limitation in Tech Solutions and explains how the community college option overcomes that limitation.

Ben

Phil, if the university offers the same classes and exams, why do you prefer the community college?

Ben probes to uncover more details about the community college option.

Phil

I like that they are so close. I could take a class during my lunch hour. I got my associate's degree there and know a lot of the IT faculty. They're really great.

Phil identifies the key benefits of the community college option.

Ben

We have inside information on all three options: Nicole took classes at Tech Solutions, Phil graduated from City Community College, and I went to State University. Let's create a chart to compare the three options.

Ben suggests focusing the conversation on objective (logical) reasoning to make a decision.

External Training Options

	TECH SOLUTIONS	CITY COMMUNITY COLLEGE	STATE UNIVERSITY
Tailored Courses	Yes	No	Yes
Certificate Courses	Yes	Yes	Yes
Licensing Exams	No	Yes	Yes
Associate Degrees	No	Yes	No
Bachelor Degrees	No	No	Yes
Graduate Degrees	No	No	Yes
Locations	Onsite/Few miles	Few blocks	Several miles
Conveniences	Books included	Online resources	Free child care
Costs for tailored courses	$3000/day	N/A	$3000/day
Costs for standard courses	N/A	$90/credit hour	$150/credit hour discounted to $120 for corporate partners

FIGURE 5.15
Continued

Ben

The chart shows that the university provides more options in terms of courses, exams, and degrees. I can personally attest to the professionalism and quality of the faculty. And the free child care may outweigh the distance to drive from our office. But, the university costs the most per course.

Ben focuses on comparable information and pros/cons. Mentions professionalism and quality of faculty, which Nicole had earlier noted as a benefit of Tech Solutions.

Nicole

Those are good points in favor of the university. Now that I look at the chart, I do not see many benefits for Tech Solutions—except that they offer customized training onsite. Do you think we could persuade the university to offer customized training onsite for us? Some schools do that.

As Nicole listens to Ben's argument, she reevaluates her position on Tech Solutions. Since Tech Solutions offers only one real benefit over the university—onsite training—Nicole suggests a way to get that benefit from the university.

Ben

Let's call their professional development division to find out. If we offer them enough business for specialized training, they will probably send instructors to our company. Phil, would the university work for you and the rest of the IT staff? You can complete certificate and licensing requirements, and there's an online degree program.

Ben aims to persuade Phil that the university may meet his needs also.

Phil

Well, yes ... it would work. But, the company will be paying $150/credit hour, when we can get the same required courses from the community college for $90/hour.

In responding to Ben's attempt at persuasion, Phil raises the question about whether the extra cost of the university is worthwhile—especially for the certificate courses that are also offered by the city college.

Ben

Good point. What we really need is a combined solution. As Nicole said, there's no real benefit to Tech Solutions, so let's focus on the benefits of State University and City College.

How about this? Let's propose that our company work with the professional development office of State University to design and deliver onsite training for our specialized courses because that will be both high quality and cost effective. However, for certificate, licensing, and degree courses, let's propose that the company reimburse at City College's $90/credit hour rate. Then employees can decide whether they would rather opt for the lower cost and convenience of City College or pay $60/credit hour of their own money for the greater flexibility of the university.

Ben proposes a collaborative solution that meets the range of needs identified in the conversation. It allows employees flexibility and also saves the company money.

Nicole

That would be great. I could enroll in an online master's degree program at the university, and it would cost me only $60/credit hour.

Phil

And I could take certificate courses at lunchtime at the City College at no cost to me.

Nicole and Phil confirm the benefits of that solution for meeting their individual needs.

Ben

This is a really creative solution that meets the company's and employees' needs—at the best cost for the company. Let's write our recommendation memo.

This collaborative conversation has not only helped the team arrive at a good solution, it has also helped them develop the arguments they need to persuade others.

As Figure 5.15 illustrates, persuasion is key to reaching a collaborative solution. While all team members make a strong case for their preferred alternative, they also listen carefully and are willing to change their minds. People who are not willing to give up their position do not work well in collaborative environments and are not effective team members.

CULTURE   Adapting Persuasive Appeals

While many people believe that the key to persuasion is providing a strong, logical argument, you've learned in this chapter that persuasion depends on many additional factors: strengthening your credibility, engaging your audience's emotions, and adapting to their preferences.

Adapting is particularly important when you want to persuade people from different cultures. You may need to adapt in these ways:

- Using a different medium for persuasion
- Emphasizing different persuasive content
- Accommodating a different decision-making process

Below are two scenarios involving cross-cultural persuasion. If you were involved in these scenarios, what would you do? After deciding, compare your answers with those below (upside down).

1. You are working on a project with a team of people from Mexico and the United States, communicating primarily by email. One of your Mexican teammates often takes three to four days to respond to messages that you have marked urgent. So far, this has not been a problem. However, now you need a quick response from him. Your team is running late on a project deadline, and your ability to meet this deadline will have a great impact on your performance review. How would you persuade your Mexican teammate to respond to you quickly and to help meet the deadline?
    a. Write an email message politely explaining exactly what you need and by when. Apologize for the short notice and explain that you will both share the success for meeting the deadline or the blame for missing it.
    b. Write an email message explaining the urgency of the situation, providing detailed instructions, and show-

ing appreciation for his extraordinary efforts to help you. Follow the email with a telephone call to ensure he understands.
    c. Call on the telephone to explain the situation and ask for help. Ask about his workload to see if your request is realistic. Invite him to call you to ask for help in meeting the deadline, and end the conversation by saying you hope to meet in the future.

2. You are part of a team that is presenting a proposal to a client in the Netherlands. Your client has sent you a list of people who will be attending the meeting, along with background information on each. You notice that they represent a wide range of functions in the company. You also notice that no senior decision maker will be attending the meeting. Typically when your company presents a persuasive proposal, you target the senior decision maker and aim primarily to persuade that person. This approach has been successful and led to quick sales. In this case, what should your team do?
    a. Call your main contact and persuade him or her to include a senior decision maker in the meeting, rearranging the time of the meeting if necessary.
    b. Structure your presentation to provide specific information on the benefits of your product for each of the functional areas attending the meeting.
    c. Structure your presentation in the same way you would if a senior decision maker attended, leave a handout, and encourage your main contact to pass this information along to the senior decision maker.

PEARSON
mybcommlab
For a CULTURE exercise, go to Exercise 15 on page 178 or to this chapter's End-of-Chapter Exercises at mybcommlab.com.

Answers

1. C is the best choice. In Mexico, it is important to develop working relationships. A phone call signals that you are making an effort to build a relationship. In addition, by asking about your colleague's workload, you are showing that you recognize the value of his work and that you are not egotistical. This will provide you with credibility. By building a relationship and your credibility, you increase the chances that your colleague will make an extra effort to help you.[22]

2. B is the best choice. Although the Netherlands is a highly individualistic culture, important business decisions are made by consensus.[23] This means that you will achieve more success if you persuade each person in the meeting that his or her specific functional area will benefit from your product.

IN SUMMARY, being a persuasive business communicator requires that you adopt a "you" perspective and understand what will motivate your audience as well as what will prevent them from agreeing with you. The techniques you learned in this chapter are tools that you can use to address your audience's needs and concerns—and help your audience agree with and accept your ideas. If your content is sufficiently targeted to your audience, you may find that they will persuade themselves to agree with you.

CHAPTER 5 Summary

5.1 How can the ACE process help me persuade my audience? *(pages 142–147)*

- **Analyzing helps you plan your message** by focusing on your purpose, desired outcome, and business result. Analyzing your primary and secondary audiences' (and stakeholders') needs help you determine the content of the message. If you anticipate specific objections, you can use refutation or concession to address them. Analyzing also helps you select the best medium based on audience-, content-, and response-related criteria.
- **Composing implements the persuasive plan** by putting words into action.
- **Evaluating helps you review the draft for effectiveness** by considering whether the message is convincing, proposes a good solution, includes sound reasoning, anticipates possible objections, and stresses audience benefits. Evaluating also ensures a complete, concise, clear, and correct message.

5.2 What are the basic elements of persuasion? *(pages 147–155)*

- **Building credibility** enhances the audience's perception that you have expertise and are trustworthy. You can build credibility by getting to know the audience, introducing yourself effectively, and presenting your ideas persuasively.
- **Constructing a logical argument** involves making a claim that is supported by reasons and evidence, which can be in the form of numerical data, facts, expert opinion, personal experience, or examples. When constructing arguments, avoid fallacies, which are violations of logic. They are dishonest and misleading.
- **Appealing to your audience's emotions** helps you sell your persuasive idea. You can do this by appealing to your audience's emotional or psychological needs, such as safety, love and belonging, self-esteem, and self-actualization. Other psychological principles include consistency, social proof, liking, reciprocity, and scarcity. You can show your own emotional commitment by using compelling evidence and powerful language.

5.3 What types of business messages typically require persuasion? *(pages 155–166)*

- **Recommendations for action** require that you convince someone that a problem or opportunity exists and that your idea is a good way to address it.
- **Requests for favors** involve asking people to do something that takes effort, requires them to make choices, or differs from what they had planned to do. For persuasive requests, you can motivate your audience to comply by making them feel good about their actions or showing them how they will benefit.
- **Persuasive customer claims** are used when a seller is not obligated to approve a refund, exchange, or repair. Therefore, you need to persuade the seller that its policy should not apply in your situation or that it is in the seller's best interest to grant your request.
- **Sales messages** often incorporate the components of AIDA—an acronym used in marketing to suggest the organization of sales communication: Attention, Interest, Desire, and Action. These components are useful in both solicited and unsolicited sales communication.

5.4 How can I use persuasion to improve teamwork and collaboration? *(pages 166–170)*

- **Persuasion helps you motivate others** on your team. Even if you are not the designated team leader, you can use persuasive techniques, such as reminding the team why the work is important, helping others feel pride in their work, acknowledging team members' emotions, and making it possible for each team member to succeed.
- **Persuasion helps a team make better decisions.** When team members have different ideas, the goal should not be for one team member to persuade another to agree with his or her position. Instead, team members should present the best cases for their ideas so that the team can critically evaluate options and develop a collaborative solution.

PEARSON
mybcommlab
Are you an active learner? Go to mybcommlab.com to master Chapter 5 content. Chapter 5 interactive activities include:

- Customizable Study Plan and Chapter 5 practice quizzes
- Chapter 5 Simulation, Persuasive Messages, that helps you think critically and prepare to make choices in the business world
- Flash Cards for mastering the definition of chapter terms
- Chapter 5 Video Exercise, Writing Persuasive Messages, which shows you how textbook concepts are put into practice every day
- Interactive Lessons that visually review key chapter concepts
- Document Makeovers for hands-on, scored practice in revising documents

5.1 What ACE questions will help me prepare a persuasive message?

ANALYZING

Analyzing Helps You Plan Your Message

- Purpose, outcome, business result: What do I want to happen?
- Information needs: What does my audience need to know?
- Motivation and Benefits:
  - What will motivate the audience to accept my idea?
  - How will the audience benefit?
- Potential resistance: What concerns and objections will the audience have?
- Medium choices: What is the best medium to achieve my purpose and outcome?

Evaluating Helps You Review the Draft for Effectiveness

Composing Implements the Persuasive Plan

EVALUATING

- Have I convincingly shown that a problem or opportunity exists?
- Is the proposed solution or plan a good one?
- Is the evidence and reasoning sound?
- Have I addressed potential objections?
- Have I stressed benefits?
- Is the message easy to read?
- Is this information complete, concise, clear, and correct?
- Do I need to change anything to get the result I want?

5.2 How does this message combine the basic elements of persuasion?

Builds credibility

Establishes a problem
States the request
Anticipates objections

Presents a logical argument

Focuses on benefits to audience and appeals to emotion

Makes it easy to respond

Hello, Dr. Maher. This is Alexa Hampton. I was in your business law class several years ago and now work as an associate lawyer at Betts, Miller, and Russo here in town. I'm calling to ask you a favor.

I'm on the planning committee for the local bar association, and our awards luncheon is next Monday. The mayor was our original keynote speaker, but a sudden death in the family prevents her from attending. I immediately thought of you as a replacement. Would you be able to deliver a one-hour speech based on anecdotes and lessons you learned during your career?

Your years of experience and wealth of knowledge could make a significant difference in the professional lives of the 450 lawyers who will attend the luncheon. In a one-hour speech, you will address more people than you were able to teach in an entire academic year as a business law professor. I know you are the perfect keynote replacement for the mayor.

Please call me at 555-1887 as soon as you get this message so we can discuss the details. I look forward to talking with you soon. Again, Alexa Hampton, 555-1887. Thank you.

5.3 How can persuasion help teams reach better solutions?

| **Phil: City College**
Benefit: low cost, good location | **Nicole: Tech Solutions**
Benefit: customized onsite training, good instructors | **Ben: State University**
Benefit: more degree options, good instructors |

The team collaborates to:
- identify the strengths and benefits of each team member's proposal
- challenge each of the proposed ideas by asking questions and focusing on logical reasoning
- develop a chart to compare the options
- reevaluate original positions and create a collaborative solution

Collaborative Solution

1. City College for certificate, licensing, and degree courses (fully reimbursed by company at $90/credit hour)
2. State University as an option for degree courses (reimbursed at City College rate of $90/credit hour)
3. State University for company-wide onsite customized training (high quality/cost effective)

CASE STUDY Starting a New Business

This case study will help you review the chapter material by applying it to a specific scenario.

Kelly Lee and Noah Walker meet in a marketing class and recognize they have two things in common. First, they enjoy working with animals. Kelly's family breeds Irish Setters, and Noah works part time in a veterinary office. Second, they both want to be entrepreneurs. After some initial market analysis, they decide to collaborate on creating a pet daycare center, Pet Haven, which will offer daily workouts for the animals, hourly playtime and petting with individual handlers, and clean and roomy cages or containment areas.

To get Pet Haven up and running, Kelly and Noah realize they must persuade either a bank or other investors to give them a small business loan. Then they must persuade potential customers to use their service.

Persuading Lenders to Fund a Loan

When Kelly and Noah go to the bank to discuss a loan for Pet Haven, the banker is interested in the idea but tells them their interest rate will be very high because they have an insufficient credit history and no collateral for the loan. To secure a more reasonable rate, he suggests they ask relatives to co-sign the loan application. In other words, their parents would have to agree to repay the loan if Kelly and Noah could not.

Kelly and Noah decide they need to convince their parents that Pet Haven is a sound financial idea. To prepare for these meetings, they brainstorm a list of questions their parents could ask:

- Are you ready to run a business?
- What services will you provide? How do you know these are the right services? What will you need in order to deliver these services?
- Who is your customer base? Are there enough customers to support your business?
- What is the competition in our city? What will you offer to make you stand out?
- Have these kinds of pet daycare businesses been successful in other towns?

- How will you market your services to your customers? How will you communicate and what will you communicate?
- What kind of licensing and credentials do you need?
- Do you have a location yet? What kind of space do you need? What kinds of equipment do you need?
- What will the start-up costs be for leases, employees, licenses, advertising, and equipment?
- What size loan do you need? How will you repay this loan from cash flow?
- Why don't you get a job first and get some experience? You can open a business later.

Review Question 1: *How can Kelly and Noah prepare for a successfully persuasive conversation with their parents?*

   a. *What questions require a logical argument, using claims, reasons, and evidence?*

   b. *How should Kelly and Noah gather information to support these arguments?*

   c. *How can Kelly and Noah establish credibility about their ability to run a business and repay a loan?*

   d. *What kinds of emotional appeals might be effective as part of their argument to their parents, to motivate action?*

Identifying Benefits and Objections

Based on Kelly's and Noah's persuasive business plans, their parents agree to co-sign the loan. However, they insist that Kelly and Noah begin to market their business before graduation. As a next step, Kelly and Noah decide to learn more about their potential customers:

- What do they know about pet daycare services?
- What benefits will they perceive from the service?
- What objections and concerns may prevent them from using the service?

Review Question 2: *How can Noah and Kelly learn this information? What would you do?*

   a. *Alone, or with a small group, search the Internet for animal or pet daycare centers. Select at least two companies and read their websites thoroughly. List the customer benefits that each company stresses. Which benefits seem most compelling? What benefits would you recommend Noah and Kelly stress? Can you think of other potential benefits that you did not read in competitors' websites?*

b. *In small groups or as a class, brainstorm objections that pet owners may raise about the pet daycare concept. What may prevent pet owners from using Pet Haven's services? What will convince them to send their pets? Prepare for this brainstorm by talking to friends and relatives outside of class and getting their opinions. For each objection or question, give Kelly and Noah ideas about how to anticipate those issues in their marketing materials. What objections should they refute and how? What objections might they concede and how?*

Writing a Persuasive Sales Letter

As a next step, Kelly and Noah compose two sales letters for Pet Haven. One is targeted to pet owners in the area. The other is more personalized, targeted to pet owners Kelly and Noah know.

Review Question 3: *Noah and Kelly have brainstormed some claims that they would like to include in the sales letters. Evaluate each claim to determine if it can be supported or if it represents a logical fallacy. If it can be supported, what kinds of evidence would be effective for each claim? Where can Kelly and Noah find this evidence?*

- If you have a pet and work all day, you can either allow your pet to remain lonely or take advantage of high-quality daycare services.
- Pets that are stimulated during the day are happier and healthier than pets left alone.
- If you are willing to bring a child to day care, then you should certainly be willing to do the same for your pet.
- Day care is as good as medicine for a pet's health. For example, Mrs. Jones's dog was sickly before becoming a daycare client. Now the dog is healthy and energetic.
- Daycare clients receive a discount on routine grooming.

Review Question 4: *Noah and Kelly have decided to use the AIDA form for both letters. Alone or working with a small group of classmates, draft either of the sales letters. Use your imagination to develop specific details for the pet owners Kelly and Noah know. End each letter by asking the audience to go to the Pet Haven website for more information.*

In class, compare and evaluate the various letters to see different implementations of AIDA.

CRITICAL THINKING

1. This chapter defines persuasion as the "process of influencing your audience to agree with your point of view, recommendation, or request." In what way is persuasion a process?

2. When you identify potential audience objections to your ideas—as part of planning a letter, email, or report—should you address those objections directly as part of your persuasive strategy? Or should you ignore them? Describe a situation where it might be better to address possible objections. Then identify another situation where it might be better to ignore potential objections until your audience actually objects.

3. If you are persuading someone to make a business decision, why is it important to include a strong logical argument rather than just appeal to that person's emotions?

4. Motivating your audience is particularly important when you are asking them to do something that is difficult or that they are resistant to doing. Imagine you are writing a persuasive email, requesting a colleague to organize your company's annual summer picnic this year. Assume the recipient would be initially resistant because of the responsibility and effort required. What content could you include to motivate that person to agree to the job?

5. Suppose you are making a presentation to your boss that recommends a change that will eliminate budget overruns. Is it important to present details about the budget overruns, or is it better just to focus on your solution to this problem? How would you decide the best approach?

6. A study conducted on a college campus found that students soliciting donations from other students were twice as effective when they began their request by saying "I am a student here, too."[24] How would you explain this success? Why did this statement make the students more persuasive to their audience?

7. In what key ways is a persuasive customer claim different from other kinds of requests, such as requests for information, a favor, or a donation? Why are different persuasive techniques necessary?

8. AIDA—attention, interest, desire, and action—is a long-established and widely used pattern for persuasive sales messages. Why do you think the approach works so well?

9. If the goal of persuasion is to influence people to agree with your point of view, why is listening an important skill in persuasion?

10. In this chapter, you learned about how fallacious reasoning can be unethical if you intentionally use it to mislead your audience. What else could you do in an attempt to persuade that could be considered unethical?

DEVELOPING YOUR COMMUNICATION SKILLS

5.1 How can the ACE process help me persuade my audience? *(pages 142–147)*

EXERCISE 1 Analyzing helps you plan your message

Assume that you have the opportunity to travel to China during the summer as part of a Global Business Initiatives project at your school. The goal of the trip is to visit businesses in that country, learn more about the differences between American and Chinese businesses, and to make some international contacts. The school will provide the funding for your trip. Each student, however, is asked to request donations from local companies to support the project. You decide to approach Keith Dinsmore, the president of a shoe manufacturing company in your community, to request a donation. You selected this person because he graduated from your university and because many of his company's products are manufactured in China. Analyze the communication situation to plan your communication:

a. What should be the specific purpose of your communication? What specific outcome do you want? Will you ask for a specific amount of money or will you have some other message?

b. What information will Mr. Dinsmore need?

c. What reasons or benefits can you offer Mr. Dinsmore to support why he should donate?

d. What objections do you anticipate? Prepare possible responses for each objection.

e. What medium should you use to communicate with Mr. Dinsmore? Should you make your request by letter, email, or should you ask to meet in person? What are the advantages and disadvantages of each option?

EXERCISE 2 Composing implements the persuasive plan

Refer to Exercise 1. Assume that you chose to write a persuasive letter or email to Mr. Dinsmore. Based on your analysis from that exercise, compose a first draft of the letter.

EXERCISE 3 Evaluating helps you review the draft for effectiveness

Refer to Exercises 1 and 2. Evaluate your first draft and explain how it meets the following criteria. If it doesn't, identify how you could modify the message.

a. Have I convincingly shown that a problem or opportunity exists?

b. Is the proposed solution or plan a good one?

c. Is the evidence and reasoning sound?

d. Have I addressed any objections that I can anticipate and have I stressed benefits?

e. Is the message easy to read?

f. Is the information complete, concise, clear, and correct?

g. Do I need to change anything to get the result I want from my audience?

5.2 What are the basic elements of persuasion? *(pages 147–155)*

EXERCISE 4 Building credibility

a. In your entrepreneurship class, you and three classmates developed an idea that you would like to turn into a business: a tutoring service for high school and middle school students in your community. Tutors would be students at your college or university who are majoring in the subject that they are tutoring and who have prior experience tutoring in the subject. The tutoring services would be advertised online. Prices would be $40/hour if the clients come to campus and $50/hour if tutors go to the clients' homes or other locations. For the business to succeed, you know that you will need to build credibility with the local school administration and with local families. Review the approaches to building credibility on pages 147–149. How would you build credibility for yourself and your new company?

b. You are a sales associate in the fine china and glassware department of an exclusive department store. Every few months, your department runs a big sale, and your manager requires all associates to call customers to persuade them to come to the store and shop during the sale. You feel that you have very little credibility in these phone calls. The customers believe you are just interested in increasing your sales commission. Brainstorm ways that you can build your credibility in these calls so that more people will be persuaded to shop during the sale.

EXERCISE 5 Constructing a logical argument

You work for a development and construction company that specializes in commercial real estate. You need to make a persuasive presentation to your town council, requesting that the town rezone a parcel of land—Parcel 5812—from residential to commercial in a fast-growing area so you can build a retail shopping area anchored by a grocery store. Based on your research, you are going to provide three reasons why the town should rezone the land for a new shopping area:

1. The residential population in the area is growing while nearby shopping options are not.
2. The nearest grocery store, which is four miles away in a different town, is accessible only by a two-lane highway, suggesting that without a nearby store traffic congestion may increase.
3. The retail space will stimulate growth and help increase the town tax base.

What kind of evidence would you include to support each of these three reasons? For example, what kind of evidence would help you prove the residential population is growing?

EXERCISE 6 Avoiding logical fallacies
[Related to the Ethics feature on page 152]

The following list includes examples of weak and illogical arguments. Explain the problem with each. Why should you disagree with each statement?

a. Of the three ad campaigns presented by the marketing department, I think we should go with the second one because it's the best.

b. The media is biased against our products. For the past two days, the *City Journal* has featured stories about our competitors but hasn't mentioned us.

c. Our current travel authorization forms are not efficient. We should either not require authorization or decline all travel requests.

d. I'm not surprised sales have dropped. The sales reps are completely incompetent.

e. If democracy is the best way to run a government, then it must be the best way to run a company also.

f. Sales in our international branches nearly doubled after the CEO hired a new assistant. We should promote the assistant to vice president of sales.

EXERCISE 7 Appealing to your audience's emotions

You are a real estate agent who has just shown a home to Tom and Serena Phillips, a young professional couple who seemed very interested in the property. They are looking to start a family in the next few years and like the large backyard. They also like the neighborhood and reputation of the local schools. Most importantly, the house is in their price range. They are hesitant to make an offer on the house, however, because it's a large investment and because the house needs new carpeting.

You know this house will not stay on the market long. In fact, you have two other buyers who have shown an interest. However, you think this is a perfect house for Tom and Serena, and you'd like to persuade them to make an offer. They have the facts, so you decide to compose a message that emphasizes emotional appeals. Review all the techniques for motivating an audience on pages 150–155. Using at least three of the techniques, develop content that you could use in your message.

5.3 What types of business messages typically require persuasion? *(pages 155–166)*

EXERCISE 8 Recommendations for action

You are the director of volunteer services for a regional hospital. Most of your volunteers are retirees who work four-hour shifts one or two days a week providing various services, such as transporting patients to X-ray, delivering lab results to doctors' offices, and greeting visitors in reception areas. During the summers, many of your volunteers go on vacation, which leaves you with a lot of empty shifts to fill. During a directors' meeting, you suggest that

the hospital create a summer student volunteer program to recruit high school and college students. The job would provide valuable experience to students interested in pursuing a medical career. However, several of the department heads expressed concern about whether the student volunteers would be mature enough or responsible enough to commit to unpaid summer work. You believe that requiring high GPAs, letters of recommendations, and interviews will help the hospital select mature and responsible students. The committee asks you to write a recommendation report outlining the idea in more detail. Write a persuasive recommendation using the following outline:

- Propose a specific recommendation.
- Identify the problem that needs solving.
- Provide evidence that the problem is important.
- Describe alternate solutions and implications.
- Support your chosen recommendation with persuasive reasoning, stressing benefits.
- Address potential objections.
- Conclude by requesting action.

EXERCISE 9 Requests for favors

Assume you are a sales representative for Acme Widget Company. Acme has just developed a new and improved widget, which you are planning to present to your biggest account, Southline Manufacturing, in two days. You are proofreading your sales presentation when your mother calls to share the sad news that your favorite uncle passed away this morning and your aunt has asked you to deliver the eulogy. Your uncle had been ill for some time, so the news was not a shock. However, the fact that the funeral conflicts with your presentation Monday morning does cause concern. You know you have to attend the funeral. Your choice is to ask the client to reschedule the meeting or ask a colleague to make your presentation for you. Since Southline wants to make an immediate purchasing decision, you decide to ask another sales representative, Jamal Harrison, to fill in for you. Jamal does not know anything about the customer, but he is familiar with the new widget and he has exceptional presentation skills. Consider audience benefits and persuasive techniques to convince Jamal to fill in for you. Draft the message, using whichever medium you think is most appropriate.

EXERCISE 10 Persuasive customer claims

Assume you are the purchasing agent for Henderson Market Research. You process orders for office supplies, equipment, and furniture. The chairs in the executive conference room are 20 years old and show signs of wear and tear. The CFO approved the funds to purchase new chairs, and the CEO's administrative assistant, Ronda, selected the style and color to coordinate with the room. You process the order with the same local office furniture company you've always used and were pleased to receive a substantial discount because the chairs Ronda selected are being discontinued and the store is selling its remaining stock. All sales of discontinued merchandise are final. Three weeks later when the chairs arrive, Ronda calls you complaining that the chairs are the wrong color. She wanted black chairs, but received brown. Ronda complains that the brown chairs simply will not work with the color scheme in the conference room. You quickly retrieve your order and realize that you entered the wrong SKU number. You tell Ronda you will try to take care of it as quickly as possible. Compose a message to the office furniture company—Winchester Furniture—explaining the problem, requesting they replace the chairs. Your contact person at the furniture company is Danielle Connors.

Use the ACE process. Identify the purpose and outcome of your message. Analyze your audience to determine questions and objections on their minds. Identify how you will build credibility, construct a logical argument, and motivate action.

EXERCISE 11 Sales messages: AIDA

You are the assistant sales director for a company that is a market leader in the hand sanitizer industry. You have a new product—the SaniPlus—that you plan to target to existing business customers through unsolicited sales messages. The product is a portable, touch-free dispenser of hand sanitizer. The dispenser stands on the floor, can be positioned in strategic locations, and can be moved to other locations. The director of sales asks you to draft a letter that incorporates the AIDA elements to persuade existing customers to purchase your new product. Create information about the product to support your persuasive message.

EXERCISE 12 Writing logical arguments with presentation software [Related to the Technology feature on page 158]

As a team, find a website that effectively uses the techniques and principles described in this chapter to persuade its audience. Develop a short slide presentation that identifies three ways in which the website is persuasive. Organize your slides this way:

Slide 1. Your title slide. Include the name of the website, a screen shot of the home page, and information that identifies your team and assignment.
Slide 2. Identify the purpose and audience of the website.
Slide 3. Identify and illustrate the first way in which the site is persuasive.
Slide 4. Identify and illustrate the second way in which the site is persuasive.
Slide 5. Identify and illustrate the third way in which the site is persuasive.

For slides 2–5, use a message headline that briefly states the main point of the slide. Then, on the body of the slide, present evidence to support the headline. Evidence can include screen shots, excerpts of text, pictures, etc. Use the presentation on pages 158–159 as an example of how to write message headlines and support them on the slide.

5.4 How can I use persuasion to improve teamwork and collaboration? *(pages 166–170)*

EXERCISE 13 Persuasion helps you motivate others

In small groups, describe recent situations when you had to use persuasion to motivate others on a team. If you were successful, explain the strategies or techniques from this chapter that you used to persuade your audience. If you were not successful, identify a strategy or technique that you could have used. Record comments from each person in the group and analyze your findings. What commonalities exist? Prepare a short report that summarizes your findings.

EXERCISE 14 Persuasion helps a team make better decisions

Assume that you and two or three other students in your class have been appointed as a committee to propose a guest speaker to talk to your business communication class. The speaker can be from the business community, the not-for-profit world, your school, or some other context. The only requirements are that the speaker lives or works within 100 miles of your location and that the speaker can address a topic that is, in some way, relevant to the material of the course. As a team, propose one speaker by following this process:

- Identify several possible candidates.
- Develop criteria for making a decision.
- Discuss and evaluate all the candidates, following the example of the collaborative conversation in Figure 5.15.
- Collaboratively select one candidate.
- Write a persuasive memo to your instructor proposing that speaker and providing reasons to support your recommendation.

EXERCISE 15 Values and persuasion [Related to the Culture feature on page 170]

If you attend a school with people from other cultures, interview two or three people of these cultures to gather information about how they would approach the same persuasive task in their home cultures—for example, asking a professor to speak at an event, asking a supervisor to be assigned to a specific project, asking an acquaintance for a ride to the airport. Compare results relating to different cultures and write a brief memo to your instructor describing your findings. Be sure to support each finding with evidence.

WRITING

EXERCISE 16 Writing a request—intern needed

You are the head of the accounting department for a large company that hires student interns each summer. You have always requested two or three interns depending on the needs of your staff. In years past, the human resources (HR) department not only fulfilled your intern requests, but they were also able to send you students who were accounting majors. This year, however, HR announced that due to budget cuts, the internship pool would be reduced by half. You can request an intern—only one—but HR will assign interns only to selected departments, and they cannot guarantee your intern, if assigned, will actually be an accounting major. HR will determine the intern assignments based on justified requests from each department head. During a department meeting with your staff, you explain the situation and ask for their input. The group offers the following justification:

- The accounting department employs 15 full-time staff members. Your department is one of the smallest in the company, yet is responsible for critical operational and budgetary responsibilities upon which all other departments depend.
- The company's fiscal year ends June 30, which means significant work is required in the summer months to generate year-end reports in addition to regular accounting operations.
- Coincidentally, two employees in the accounting department will be out on maternity leave, one during May and June, and the other during June and July. These absences will further limit the department's ability to fulfill their end-of-year responsibilities.

Use the ACE process to write a memo to the HR department requesting an intern (accounting major, if possible) for your department. Do not simply repeat the points outlined above. Develop credibility, put the arguments in an effective order, supply evidence to support your arguments, and use techniques to motivate action.

EXERCISE 17 Writing a persuasive recommendation – University laptops

A friend attends Northern Michigan University (NMU), where all students receive a laptop as part of their tuition. Many of the classes at NMU use e-books, which significantly reduce textbook costs. You believe the students at your campus would benefit from the savings as well as the technology. You want to persuade your school's administration to become a "laptop campus." However, you predict many objections. The costs to purchase and maintain the laptops are an obvious concern. Other potential problems include theft and misuse. Additionally, some faculty may not want students to be distracted by web browsing and social networking during class. To prepare a persuasive communication, first identify possible concessions or refutations for these and other objections. Then focus on audience benefits and other persuasive strategies you learned in this chapter. Compose a letter requesting a meeting to discuss the program in more detail, and then draft a presentation to use during the meeting.

EXERCISE 18 Writing a persuasive recommendation – afterschool program

You are an employee of a mid-sized company. You estimate 40 percent of the employees have school-aged children. You want to persuade the company to create an afterschool program in the empty warehouse space adjacent to the office building. Obvious objections include the expenses for personnel, decorating and furnishing the space, toys, and additional liability insurance. Brainstorm other possible obstacles, determine audience benefits (for all stakeholders), and use effective persuasive techniques to sell your idea. Write a short recommendation to the company president.

COLLABORATING

EXERCISE 19 Reaching a team decision

As a team, identify an issue in your school or community that you believe should be addressed. Pick an issue that is important to everyone in your team. For example, you may believe the school should offer more career assistance, better dining options, or better on-campus transportation. Then, as a team, follow this process:

1. Identify several possible solutions.
2. Use the example of the collaborative conversation in Figure 5.15 on pages 168–169 to develop and challenge strong arguments for each solution.
3. Collaboratively determine a team recommendation.
4. Write a memo to your instructor identifying the issue, your team's proposed solution, and the reasons to support it.

EXERCISE 20 Gathering information and evidence

Referring to Exercise 19, gather additional information and evidence to support your team's position. Each person in your team should ask 10 other students whether they support your proposal and why. Your goal is to collect persuasive evidence from students to justify and document your recommendation. Spend a day or two gathering the feedback and then compare your findings with your team. Identify commonalities among the responses and make a list of persuasive reasons to support your recommendation. Based on your findings, draft a persuasive letter to the person or committee in a position to implement your recommendation.

SPEAKING

EXERCISE 21 Impromptu presentations

Make a one- to two-minute presentation designed to persuade your classmates to do one of the following:

a. Change their major to yours.
b. Join a new student organization that has an expensive membership fee.
c. Attend graduate school full time immediately after graduation and defer full time work, OR
   Attend graduate school part time while working full time, OR
   Defer graduate school for a few years to work full time.
d. Spend a year doing public service before entering the workforce.

e. Begin contributing to individual retirement accounts as soon as they can.

In your presentation, include at least one statement designed to establish credibility, one logical argument with reasons and evidence, and one benefit designed to motivate.

EXERCISE 22 Impromptu speaking—business role plays

In a one- to two-minute presentation, explain how you would persuade your audience in each of the following business situations:

a. Assume you are the new director of fundraising for a nonprofit organization. In the past, your organization has created targeted fundraising events, such as galas and pledge drives, to increase donations and contributions. You think a monthly e-newsletter to regular donors could keep them informed of how their money is put to use and promote the events now promoted only through fundraising letters and web advertising. Although collecting email addresses and developing an email database would be time consuming, you believe the benefits would certainly outweigh the effort.

The board of directors supports your idea, but the membership director—who would be responsible for collecting the email addresses and distributing the monthly e-newsletter—is resistant because she is very busy and does not have the time. You see her at lunch and decide to discuss the matter with her individually. In one to two minutes, persuade her to agree to this idea.

b. You are on a sales team that is planning an important presentation for a prospective client. During the meeting, the team leader discusses the content to present and the kind of visual aids and handouts to create. During the discussion, you are surprised that no one mentions an audience analysis. You believe that an audience analysis is necessary to create a presentation that meets the client's need. In one to two minutes, persuade your team to analyze the audience.

c. You coordinate the purchase of office supplies and equipment for your company. Since the company began 22 years ago, it has used Office Rx as its supply and equipment vendor. You call or email them with your order, and they personally deliver it to your office within a few business days. As a small local company, they do not support online ordering. However, they do not charge delivery fees. Although the ordering process is tedious, you prefer this company over the larger online vendors because of their low prices and friendly customer service. In fact, you usually always speak with the same person, Annette. During a telephone conversation with Annette to place a new order, you decide to ask her about the possibility of online ordering. She indicates that they had never considered online ordering because of their small size and local clientele. In one to two minutes, persuade Annette to develop an online ordering system. Address possible objections and include benefits for both Annette's company and yours.

EXERCISE 23 Presenting executive briefings—research

Conduct research to prepare for a three- to five-minute presentation on one of the following topics. Prepare a visual aid to support your presentation.

a. Select two universities that offer competing business graduate programs. Research basic information about both programs (such as location, enrollment size, tuition, and faculty) and then persuade your audience why one university is a better option than the other.

b. Select two companies that offer comparable entry-level jobs for your major. Research basic information about both options and then persuade your audience why they should apply to work at one company rather than the other.

c. Select two comparable wireless communication companies that provide service in your area. Research basic information about both service providers and then persuade your audience why one option is better than the other.

d. Assume your audience is in the market for a new car. Research the pros and cons of leasing versus purchasing. Choose the option you prefer and convince your audience to agree.

e. Your company has five mini-vans in the motor pool that it purchased 10 years ago and need to be replaced. The most important criteria are that the mini-vans have at least a six-person capacity and are fuel efficient. Research current purchasing options and create a visual comparing your three top choices and providing a well-supported recommendation for one of the options.

f. Your company is planning a summer picnic in the green space behind your office building for your employees and their families. Roughly 200 people plan to attend. Research two local catering companies and make a persuasive recommendation based on your findings. Create a visual to support your presentation.

g. Your employer would like to contract with a university to offer an online MBA program to support employees' continuing education. Research the current opportunities available online and create a visual recommending one.

h. You can use technology to enhance communication and persuasion. For example, in addition to processing your purchases, Amazon.com suggests other products you might be interested in based on your prior selections. In effect, Amazon is persuading you to view other items you might not have considered. This is an example of persuasive technology. Research the concept of persuasive technology and report your findings in a brief presentation. Write a one-page summary (executive briefing) that defines persuasive technology, describes two examples (other than Amazon), and explains your perception of how the technology affects the audience. Prepare to present your summary to the class.

GRAMMAR

EXERCISE 24 Phrases and clauses
(See Appendix D—Section 1.2.2)

It is easier to write grammatical sentences when you understand the difference between phrases and clauses. In the following paragraph, circle or highlight each phrase. Underline each dependent clause once and each independent clause twice. There are a total of 10 dependent and independent clauses and a total of 15 phrases.

In the list of tech-etiquette offenders, the "misguided multitasker" may be the worst, although the "broadcaster" is a close second. Holding their BlackBerries under the table, multitaskers send email or text messages during meetings. The nonverbal message that they are sending to everyone else is that the meeting is not important to them. Broadcasters use their cell phones anytime, anywhere, and they apparently don't mind being overheard by others. On a crowded elevator, they will discuss the intimate details of a medical procedure or they will talk loudly about confidential business matters.

6 Communicating Bad-News Messages

new hires @ work

Bryon Creech
Logistics Manager of Well Services
Schlumberger
University of Tennessee, Knoxville, 2009

"WHEN I CREATE A NEW LOGISTICAL PROGRAM, I also have to implement it, which means getting everyone on board with the new processes. Change is often perceived as very negative, even when the results will eventually be positive. When I communicate changes in processes, I relate why the change is necessary and how it will be more efficient. I have to think about how my audience will perceive my message, decide whether I'll start with the main idea or work my way up to it, and then arrange my ideas so that I can positively present information that would otherwise have been seen as bad news."

183

Introduction

During your working career, you will have to deliver messages that disappoint, inconvenience, or even anger your audience. For example, you might need to:

- tell a coworker you cannot help with a project
- explain an unexpected problem
- deny a customer's request for a refund
- reject an employee's request for a promotion, raise, or time off
- turn down someone who applied for a job

If you communicate this bad news ineffectively, you risk not only angering people, but also hurting your own business by potentially losing customers, clients, or employees. Will customers no longer do business with you if you deny their refund? Will employees' productivity decline if you reject their request for a raise? In complex situations, legal liabilities may also be an issue. For example, if you cannot fulfill a contract you previously agreed to, you have to communicate the bad news as well as deal with the consequences of breaking (or modifying) the contract.

This chapter outlines several techniques that you can use to communicate bad news while maintaining the audience's goodwill. The chapter also shows you can adapt the ACE process to achieve these goals.

Study Question 6.1

How will the ACE process help me deliver bad news effectively?

Access this chapter's simulation entitled Negative Messages, located at mybcommlab.com.

Bad-news messages are challenging to compose because they require you to achieve a number of goals that are incompatible at first glance. The ACE process can help you make good decisions that will achieve these goals.

Delivering bad news requires balancing four goals

To communicate bad-news messages well, you must balance four goals:

❶ **Conveying the news clearly, yet sensitively to protect the audience's self-esteem.** The audience should understand the message without feeling personally offended. The message should allow the audience to maintain their self-esteem and a positive self-image.

❷ **Convincing the audience to accept the bad news.** If the audience does not accept the news and comply with it, you may have to spend additional time and energy re-explaining the message or dealing with the audience's noncompliance.

❸ **Projecting a positive image of yourself and your organization.** If a bad-news message is both sensitive and reasonable, it will project a positive image of you and your organization. It will also allow your audience to maintain a positive self-image. Both of these are necessary to maintain **goodwill**, the positive relationship between you and your audience.

❹ **Avoiding legal complications and liabilities.** People may turn to the courts if they feel they have been treated unfairly. When communicating bad news, avoid potential legal action by stating clear facts and using logical arguments.

FIGURE 6.1 is an example of a job rejection letter that aims to achieve all four goals.

FIGURE 6.1 Example of a Bad-News Message

letter

▮|**Paradigm** DESIGN GROUP

9453 Ventura Way
St. Louis, MO 63044

www.Paradigm.Design.com
800.555.6674 | Fax: 314.555.6675

March 15, 20XX

HOW DOES THE LETTER ACHIEVE THE GOALS?

Mr. Harsha Patel
925 Rosedale Street
St. Paul, MN 55118

Dear Harsha:

Thank you for taking the time to meet with our hiring committee and sharing information about your background and qualifications. We enjoyed meeting you and discussing your career goals.

Projects a positive image of the organization by thanking the candidate, showing appreciation for his effort, and expressing interest in his background.

Following the interviews, the hiring committee further reviewed the needs of our marketing department. After much consideration, we have offered the position to another candidate.

Conveys the bad news clearly but sensitively by using positive phrasing.

We wish you every personal and professional success with your job search and future career. Thank you for your interest in our organization.

Sincerely,

Meredith Baldwin

Meredith Baldwin
Human Resources Manager
Paradigm Design Group

Convinces the audience to accept the bad news by making clear that the decision is final: another candidate has been offered the job.

Avoids legal complications by saying nothing that can be interpreted as age, gender, or racial discrimination.

The ACE process helps you balance the goals

You can succeed in balancing the four goals of bad-news messages by practicing and applying the ACE process. FIGURE 6.2 demonstrates a helpful set of questions for adapting ACE to bad-news messages. As you work through a specific communication challenge, you may identify additional helpful questions.

The next three sections of this chapter address each stage of the ACE process separately and cover each question posed in Figure 6.2. How can you analyze and plan a bad-news message? What strategies are useful for composing the message? What special challenges occur when evaluating bad-news messages?

Goodwill The positive relationship between you and your audience.

FIGURE 6.2 Using ACE for Bad-News Messages

- What is the bad news?
- What business result do I want to achieve?
- How will the audience react to this news?
- What justification and explanation should I include? Is there anything I can say to soften the bad news?
- Should I include an apology?
- Can I do anything else to project a positive image and maintain goodwill?
- What is the best medium for this message?

- Is the bad news stated clearly yet sensitively?
- Will the message convince the audience to accept the bad news?
- Does the message project a good image of me and maintain goodwill with the audience?
- Will the message achieve a good business result?
- Have I avoided legal complications?

- Should I begin with the bad news or build up to it?
- How can I clearly phrase the bad news?
- What content and techniques should I use to soften the impact of the message?
- How can I close the message appropriately?

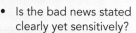
Study Question 6.2

How should I analyze and plan a bad-news message?

 Before composing a bad-news message, analyze the situation by asking yourself several questions that help you develop content and choose the best medium.

Ask questions that help you develop content

Assume you run a one-person web development business. Yesterday, you made a proposal to a new client, Great Expectations Books, a small local business, to add an ecommerce function to its website. After meeting with the manager, you proposed installing an inventory database and online ordering function within a month.

However, today you receive a request from a long-time client, South Shore Community Television (SSCT), who needs your immediate help with a critical repair to its website. This client is one week away from a major fundraising pledge drive and needs the online pledge function repaired.

You feel obligated to help SSCT for two reasons: you originally programmed the SSCT website and may be the only person who can fix it quickly, and SSCT is a long-time client who gives you a lot of business each year. Although you made a commitment to Great Expectations and do not want to disappoint this new client, you decide to inform the manager at Great Expectations that you cannot meet the original deadline and need a two-week extension.

How will you deliver this bad news? Analyzing is crucial to developing a message that supports your business goals and positively affects audience reaction. Consider the analyzing questions outlined in Figure 6.2.

- **What is the bad news?** The bad news is that you cannot meet the original deadline, but you can get the job done with an additional two weeks.

- **What business result would you like to achieve in communicating the bad news?** You would like Great Expectations to grant you an extension rather than withdraw its agreement and hire a new web developer.

- **How will the audience react to this news?** Although you cannot exactly predict the audience's reaction, you can think about the situation from Great Expectations' perspective. They currently do not use an ecommerce function and have an informational website that works. You also know they plan to launch an "order online" advertising campaign at the end of the month. You think Great Expectations will be disappointed with the extended deadline, but they won't be upset enough to find a different website developer. You would like them to accept your request and postpone their ad campaign for two weeks.

- **What justification and explanation should I include?** To be effective, a bad-news message should explain the reasons behind the bad news. Of all the features in your message, this explanation has the most power to influence the audience to accept your bad news.[1] Consider the questions the audience may have: "Why can't you deliver your services in the agreed-on time? Why do you need an additional two weeks?" If you want a continued relationship with Great Expectations, you will need to provide a reason for the delay. You can explain, for example, that another client has had an emergency that only you can handle. You do not need to give the name of the client or explain the nature of the emergency.

- **Is there anything I can say to soften the bad news? For example, is there any good news to include? Will the audience benefit in any way? Does this cloud have a silver lining?** To soften the bad news, you can communicate to Great Expectations that you value their business. You can also let them know why the other client's request took priority without making Great Expectations feel less important. If you are not able to think of any direct audience benefits in this situation, you can subtly suggest that this situation demonstrates that your commitment to customers extends beyond the website development process. You are available for updates and revisions, especially in critical circumstances when time is an issue. Finally, you might find a *silver lining*, or a hidden benefit, in this delay. For example, with more time before programming the ecommerce site, Great Expectations can survey customers to learn more about how they would like the site organized.

- **Should I include an apology?** Because you were responsible for not meeting the agreed on deadline—and perhaps delaying Great Expectations' advertising campaign—you decide that you owe this new client a sincere apology that acknowledges that you understand the implications of this delay.

- **Can I do anything else to project a positive image and maintain goodwill and the relationship?** Your professionalism and apology will project a positive image. In addition, you can offer your client an alternative, rather than simply agreeing to your request. For example, Great Expectations might allow you to complete the most critical parts of the project by the original deadline, with the rest coming later. By giving them options, you can manage the relationship.

Select the best medium to achieve your goal

The final analyzing question in Figure 6.2 focuses on choosing a medium. When you communicate bad news, select a medium that best fits the purpose of the message, the audience, and the situation. FIGURE 6.3 outlines the advantages and disadvantages of various medium options for communicating bad-news messages.

What medium should you use to communicate the bad news to your client, Great Expectations Books? Only three options in Figure 6.3 are good choices: a face-to-face meeting, telephone conversation, or email message. Letters take too long to arrive, memos are for internal communication, text messages are too informal, and the other choices—newsletters, websites, social networking, wikis, and blogs—are clearly not good choices for individual communication.

Of the three acceptable choices, which is best? A face-to-face meeting would be appropriate, but may take some time to arrange. Both email and telephone have advantages and disadvantages. A telephone call allows you to make a personal contact and to hear your audience's tone of voice. You will be able to gauge whether they are upset or

new hires @ work

Bridget Forney
Account Executive, PROFILES, Inc.
Stevenson University, 2008

"It is challenging to find the best way to communicate bad news to clients. I have to carefully consider not only how to word the message, but whether I should send an email, make a phone call, or arrange to meet in person."

not, and you can adjust your message accordingly. However, the Great Expectations manager may not answer the phone immediately, and you will not want to leave the bad news in a voice mail. If you ask for a return call, you may play telephone tag all day. If your audience does answer the telephone, your call may be putting him on the spot, suggesting that he needs to answer you immediately. An email may make your audience feel less pressured, allowing more time to review the original contract and to think about whether this delay will have serious impacts.

In this case, no one best medium choice exists. You will need to weigh the pros and cons, thinking about how your audience will react to a surprising telephone call versus an email. You will need to adjust the wording of your message based on your medium.

FIGURE 6.3 Selecting the Best Medium for Bad-News Messages

	One-to-One	Group Meeting	Telephone	Text/IM	Email	Memo	Letter	Newsletter	Website	Social Networking	Wikis, Blogs
Audience-Related Criteria											
Share bad news with a single person	■		■	■	■		■				
Communicate to many employees and shareholders simultaneously		■		■	■	■		■	■	■	
Provide instantaneous news to people at geographically diverse locations				■	■				■	■	■
Share bad news with the public									■	■	■
Content- and Response-Related Criteria											
Share insignificant bad news quickly, such as letting your lunch appointment know you're running a few minutes late			■	■	■						
Share important bad news in a way that does not seem impersonal or evasive	■	■	■		■	■	■				
Hear your audience's tone of voice and silences, which convey meaning and feedback	■	■	■								
See facial expressions and body language, and hear tone of voice, which convey meaning and feedback	■	■									
Encourage immediate discussion of the news	■	■	■	■						■	■
Prevent immediate discussion or give the audience (and you) time to carefully consider a response					■	■	■	■	■	■	■
Ensure that you have written documentation of the communication					■	■	■	■	■	■	■

TECHNOLOGY Can I Use Email or Text Messages for Bad News?

Communicators often wonder whether they should avoid email or text messages for delivering bad news and instead talk to their audience in person or on the telephone. Stacy Brice, CEO of AssistU—a consulting company that trains, coaches, and provides referrals for virtual assistants—argues in favor of the face-to-face approach: "If you've ever opened an email containing bad news, you know it feels like you're being slammed face first into a wall going 60 miles per hour."[2]

Nonetheless, some companies unwisely choose to use email to deliver bad news about firings and layoffs. In one highly publicized incident, Radio Shack sent emails to 400 workers at its headquarters, notifying them that they were being let go. Infuriated workers who felt the company was treating them disrespectfully immediately leaked this action to the press. Human resources professionals commenting on this case unanimously agreed that firing by email is a bad practice because it is impersonal and rude.[3]

Even worse is the practice of firing someone by text message, which some companies have justified because their workforce is young and comfortable with that medium. Katy Tanner, a clerk at a body piercing studio, received the following text message when she was home sick with a migraine:

> "Hi Katy its alex from the shop. Sorry 2 do this by text but ive been trying to call u + ur phones been switched off. Ive had a meeting with jon + ian and weve reviewed your sales figures and they're not really up to the level we need. As a result we will not require your services any more. You will receive your last pay packet on Friday 28th july. Thank you for your time with us."[4]

Is email ever a good choice for communicating bad news? It may be in these circumstances.

- **If you want to give your audience time to think carefully before having to reply.** In the Great Expectations scenario, you may choose to communicate the bad news by email to give your audience time to think about the implications of the news and to consider the way best to respond to your request.

- **If it is crucial that you avoid miscommunication and misinformation.** Researchers have found that people who are uncomfortable communicating bad news face-to-face are more likely to sugarcoat the bad news when talking in person to reduce their own and their audience's discomfort. This distortion can lead to misunderstandings. By contrast, communicators are more likely to be accurate, complete, and honest in email because they do not worry about being confronted by an angry audience.[5]

- **If you need to communicate bad news to many people in different locations at exactly the same time.** In January 2009, Steve Ballmer, CEO of Microsoft, sent a message to all Microsoft employees explaining how Microsoft would be responding to deteriorating economic conditions.[6] In that email, he announced that the company would be eliminating 5,000 positions over 18 months. This included laying off 1,400 people that day. Fortunately, Ballmer followed much of the advice that this chapter offers. He signaled at the beginning of the email that he would be communicating difficult news. He provided detailed justification for the company's decision and showed respect for the hard work of all employees. Even more fortunately, the company made the wise decision to communicate individually and in person to the 1,400 people who were laid off.

PEARSON mybcommlab

For a TECHNOLOGY exercise, go to Exercise 5 on page 210 or to this chapter's End-of-Chapter Exercises at mybcommlab.com.

For a TECHNOLOGY exercise, go to Exercise 5 on page 210 or to this chapter's End-of-Chapter Exercises at mybcommlab.com.

Study Question 6.3

What are effective strategies for composing bad-news messages?

The analyzing questions on page 186 help you develop *what to say* in a bad-news message. The composing questions in this section focus on *how to say it*.

ACE

- Should I begin with the bad news or build up to it?
- How should I phrase the bad news?
- What is the best way to soften the impact of the message?
- How can I close the message appropriately?

Decide where to state the bad news

As you learned in Chapters 3 and 4, most routine business communication benefits from a *direct organization*, stating the purpose and main idea of the message before the supporting details. Audiences who are inundated with too much information and have too little time may not have the patience to search through a message—or sit through several minutes of an introductory explanation—to learn the main idea.

Even in bad-news situations, the direct approach may be a good idea, especially if your audience is expecting to hear from you and the news will not come as a big surprise. In other bad-news situations, you can help your audience better understand and accept the news by using an *indirect organization*, by placing the main idea after the supporting details. Conveying bad news too abruptly might confuse, upset, or anger your audience. An indirect organization allows you to prepare the audience and explain your position before delivering the bad news.

FIGURE 6.4 outlines the differences between the direct and indirect approaches for communicating bad news and identifies the situations when you would choose each. Note that the content communicated in each version is nearly the same. The difference between the two methods is the placement of the bad news and the use of a **buffer**—an introductory sentence or paragraph that leads up to and softens the bad-news message.

FIGURE 6.4
Two Ways to Organize
Bad-News Messages

Use **DIRECT ORGANIZATION** if...	**DIRECT ORGANIZATION** follows pattern:
your audience • is unlikely to be upset or angry, or • expects the news and will not be surprised, **and the recommendation** • is easy to explain and understand, • is important for the audience to see immediately, or • is relevant to health and safety.	**STATE THE BAD NEWS DIRECTLY.** (main idea) **Provide supporting explanation.** **Conclude with goodwill.**

Use **INDIRECT ORGANIZATION** if...	**INDIRECT ORGANIZATION** follows this pattern:
your audience • is likely to be upset or angry, or • does not expect the news and will be surprised, **and the recommendation** • is difficult to understand without introductory explanation.	**Begin with a buffer.** **Provide supporting explanation.** **SUBORDINATE THE BAD NEWS.** (main idea) **Conclude with goodwill.**

FIGURE 6.5, an announcement warning customers about a health and safety problem, illustrates a message that needs to be communicated directly. If the main message is buried, as it is in the indirect version in Figure 6.5, the audience may mistake the letter for a routine communication and decide not to read it. The direct version solves that problem by stating the message in the first sentence.

FIGURE 6.6 on page 192, by contrast, illustrates a bad news message that needs to be organized indirectly. Assume you work for RemCo, a company that developed Vi-Spy, a virus protection and spyware removal program. The program continually protects against the latest viruses as long as the users routinely download new virus definitions. One of your corporate clients calls you in a panic. They relied on your product to protect their computers, but many of the computers in the system are now infected with a virus that they cannot remove. The only way to eliminate the virus from the infected computers is to reformat their hard drives, deleting all of the data and programs. Your client is claiming that your company's Vi-Spy software doesn't work. They not only want a refund, they want you to pay the costs of reclaiming the disks and data.

FIGURE 6.5 Example of Bad News Requiring a Direct Organization

INEFFECTIVE (INDIRECT)

Dear Richards Electronics Customer:

Thank you for your recent purchase of our LS520 microwave oven.

Although all of our products are rigorously tested before they are put on the market, we have found some minor abnormalities with the model LS520 under certain conditions. Recent customer experience revealed risk of overheating and fire when the microwave operates at the highest level for more than one hour. Therefore, we are recalling the LS520 and will either refund your full purchase price or exchange your microwave for another product.

Please contact the retail store where you purchased your LS520 microwave to arrange to return it, or call our toll-free number to request free express shipping pickup. We regret the inconvenience this recall will cause you but assure you that your health and safety are our primary concern.

Regards,

WHAT'S WRONG WITH THE INEFFECTIVE VERSION?

The ineffective version is indirect. It begins by thanking customers for their purchase. Although this is a neutral buffer, it could be potentially misleading. The audience may assume this message is a routine thank-you letter and not read the rest of the message, putting them at risk for a kitchen fire.

No important ideas stand out. Someone reading quickly may miss the main point.

EFFECTIVE (DIRECT)

IMPORTANT PRODUCT SAFETY RECALL NOTICE
RICHARDS LS520 MICROWAVE OVEN FIRE HAZARD

Dear Richards Electronics Customer:

Richards Electronics is voluntarily recalling the LS520 microwave oven because we have received 11 reports worldwide of overheating and fires when the oven operates for longer than one hour at full power.

Our records indicate you have purchased this model. To protect your health and safety, Richards advises you to take the following steps:

- Stop using the microwave oven immediately.
- Return the product to the retail store where you purchased it, or call us toll free at 888-123-4567 to request free express shipping pickup. You can either receive a full refund or exchange your microwave for another model.

We apologize for the inconvenience this recall will cause you. We are modifying our research protocols to ensure future products exceed all industry specifications. Your safety and satisfaction with our products are our primary goals.

Regards,

WHY IS THE EFFECTIVE VERSION BETTER?

The effective version gets to the point directly by announcing the product recall in a headline and then repeating the main idea—the bad news—in the first sentence. Although the audience will be surprised and potentially upset with this information, their health is too important not to grab their attention.

It highlights the necessary actions so they stand out.

It concludes with goodwill by assuring readers that the company is taking action to prevent similar problems in the future.

After investigating the cause of the problem, you need to explain that the client was in fact responsible for the problem based on a complex set of circumstances. This message is not only likely to upset the audience, it also will be difficult to understand without introductory explanation. As a result, the indirect version of the email illustrated in **FIGURE 6.6** will be more effective than the direct version.

Buffer An introductory sentence or paragraph that leads up to and softens the bad news.

FIGURE 6.6 Example of Bad News Requiring an Indirect Organization

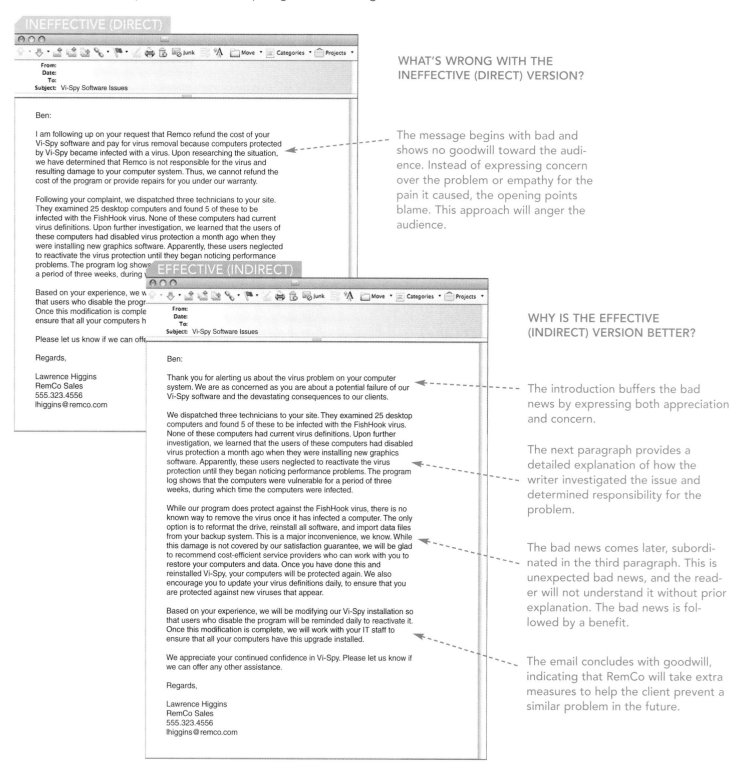

WHAT'S WRONG WITH THE INEFFECTIVE (DIRECT) VERSION?

The message begins with bad and shows no goodwill toward the audience. Instead of expressing concern over the problem or empathy for the pain it caused, the opening points blame. This approach will anger the audience.

WHY IS THE EFFECTIVE (INDIRECT) VERSION BETTER?

The introduction buffers the bad news by expressing both appreciation and concern.

The next paragraph provides a detailed explanation of how the writer investigated the issue and determined responsibility for the problem.

The bad news comes later, subordinated in the third paragraph. This is unexpected bad news, and the reader will not understand it without prior explanation. The bad news is followed by a benefit.

The email concludes with goodwill, indicating that RemCo will take extra measures to help the client prevent a similar problem in the future.

Phrase the bad news clearly

The best way to ensure the audience understands the bad news is to state it clearly. If you convey bad news in vague terms or only imply the answer, the audience may misunderstand. For example, assume you work for a company that sells MP3 players. You receive an emailed request from a customer to replace the broken screen of his recently purchased player since it is still under warranty. Consider the two versions of your email reply in FIGURE 6.7.

FIGURE 6.7 Phrase the Bad News Clearly

INEFFECTIVE

We received your request to replace the broken screen on your MP3 player. We are enclosing a list of authorized third-party dealers who can replace the screen within two days for a very reasonable charge.

EFFECTIVE

We received your request to replace the broken screen on your MP3 player. Although our warranty covers defects in the equipment, it does not cover broken screens, since that kind of damage typically results from accidents rather than defects. However, we are enclosing a list of authorized third-party dealers who will replace the screen within two business days for a very reasonable charge. They also offer a discount on cases that include screen protectors.

WHAT'S WRONG WITH THE INEFFECTIVE VERSION?

The customer may assume that he can send you the bill for the "very reasonable charge" since you did not state that the damage to the MP3 is not covered under the product's warranty.

WHY IS THE EFFECTIVE VERSION BETTER?

The effective version clearly states that the warranty does not cover broken screens.

It also offers advice about how to prevent broken screens in the future.

Soften the bad news

Regardless of whether you present the bad news directly or indirectly, you want to "soften the blow" of the bad news, even if it is expected. You can do this in several ways:

- Develop an effective buffer
- Position good news ahead of bad news
- Subordinate the bad news
- Use positive or neutral language

Develop an effective buffer

Buffers are introductory statements that lead up to bad news and soften its impact. Buffers may provide a context for the message or provide positive information that builds goodwill. They can also "hook" the audience and get them interested in your message. For example, imagine that you have scheduled a meeting with 30 employees to discuss the problem of having to either reduce everyone's hours by 10 percent or lay off three people. FIGURE 6.8 suggests several buffer statements you could use at the beginning of the meeting to encourage your audience to listen to the rest of your message with a positive attitude.

Notice that all the buffer statements in Figure 6.8 signal that bad news may be coming later in the message. A buffer statement that does not provide this signal may mislead—and ultimately anger—the audience.

Position good news ahead of bad news

One of the best ways to buffer bad news is to begin with good news and audience benefits, if there are any. United Airlines used this technique when it communicated bad news to its frequent flyers. The airline would be increasing by 25 percent the number of award points a flyer had to spend to receive a free flight. In addition, the airline would be charging fees for free flights booked within 14 days of travel. Instead of beginning the message on its website with this negative information, United first emphasized some additional changes in the frequent flyer program that would benefit

new hires @ work

Jason Calcaño

Editorial Assistant, Pearson Education

Rutgers University, 2010

"I report to three editors and sometimes have too much work to meet a deadline. If I communicate this bad news by clearly and respectfully explaining what I need and why, the editor usually agrees."

FIGURE 6.8 Types of Buffer Statements

BUFFER	EXAMPLE
Background Information	Over the past six months, the economy has slowed, and our sales have dropped significantly.
Facts That Signal a Problem	In order to stay in business, our store needs to meet its payroll obligations.
Good News	Despite the soft economy and slowing sales, we have identified a way to keep the store open and meet our payroll obligations.
Thanks or Compliments	Thank you for your efforts this past year to improve sales at our store. Your knowledge of the merchandise and concern for customers have resulted in our highest-ever customer satisfaction rating, even in these difficult economic times.
Generally Accepted Truths	In these lean times, we need to watch our budget and eliminate all unnecessary spending. This will require sacrifices from us all.
Empathy with Audience	I know how hard you have worked to keep costs down, so I understand how you might think we're unfair coming back to you this year with yet another request.

customers. These changes included an increase in the number of seats available for free travel and a reduced number of award points required for certain free flights. By positioning the good news ahead of the bad news, United was able to soften the bad news by putting it in a larger context.[7]

Subordinate the bad news

Although you need to state bad news clearly, you can ease its impact by using subtle subordinating techniques, such as *passive voice* or a *subordinate clause*.

Recall from Chapter 3 that *voice* refers to the relationship between the subject and verb in a sentence. In *active voice* sentences, the subject performs the action of the verb. In *passive voice* sentences, the subject does not perform the action of the verb. In the following examples, the passive version avoids placing blame on the audience.

      Subject Verb   Verb

ACTIVE: You damaged your MP3 player and invalidated the warranty.

            Subject   Verb

PASSIVE: Your MP3 player was damaged by an accident or misuse, invalidating the warranty.

Putting the bad news in a subordinate clause means preceding the bad news with a word like "although," which will de-emphasize the bad news. The following examples show a comparison of bad news in the main clause and in a subordinate clause. The bad news is italicized.

> **Main clause:** *The repairs on your MP3 player are not covered by the warranty.* However, we have enclosed a list of third-party vendors who can replace the screen within two days for a very reasonable charge.
>
> **Subordinate clause:** *Although the repairs on your MP3 player are not covered by warranty*, we have enclosed a list of third-party vendors who can replace the screen within two days for a very reasonable charge.

Notice that when you place the bad news in a subordinate clause ("Although the repairs on your MP3 player are not covered by the warranty"), you can emphasize the good news ("we have enclosed a list of third-party vendors") in the main clause.

Another way to de-emphasize the bad news while remaining clear is to put the bad news in a main clause surrounded by two subordinate clauses.

> **Main clauses surrounded by subordinate clauses:** Although our warranty covers defects in the equipment, *it does not cover broken screens*, since that kind of damage typically results from accidents rather than defects.

CULTURE Did You Hear the Bad News?

In the United States and many other Western business cultures, people tend to communicate bad news explicitly. They may soften the bad news by using a buffer or subordinating it, but at some point in the message, they will state the bad news. For example, if you ask an American whether he has finished analyzing data for a meeting, a bad-news answer might sound like this:

- *Although the analysis is not complete, we have enough for the meeting.*
- *The analysis was more difficult than I anticipated, so I am not quite ready.*

Sometimes an American will imply the bad news, but even then the message is obvious.

- *If we can move the meeting to Friday, I will be able to complete the analysis.*

By contrast, in many Eastern cultures, including India, people say "no" in a very different way. They may ignore the question, change the subject, respond with another question, or make a statement from which you will infer the negative news. In *Speaking of India*, intercultural expert Craig Storti illustrates a range of possible ways someone from India might say no without actually saying it:[8]

- *Who exactly is going to be at the meeting?*
- *Do you mean all the data?*

- *Is tomorrow good for you?*
- *Let me ask my team.*
- *We'll try our best.*
- *We have been working late every night.*

Within the Indian culture, these answers would not be considered evasive. The audience would understand that all these answers equally mean that the analysis is not ready and the speaker is uncomfortable saying "no."

When you communicate with people from different cultures, listen very carefully to be sure you hear the bad news and do not assume a positive answer. Similarly, you may need to change the way you deliver bad news—and even good news. For example, if an American answers "*the analysis will probably be ready*," someone from India may assume that you are saying "no." Any kind of qualification or hesitation will be perceived as a negative reply. The best way to say yes in India is to say "yes" and to repeat the detail:

- *Yes, we will be ready tomorrow.*

For CULTURE exercises, go to Critical Thinking Question 4 on page 208 and Exercises 23 and 26 on page 214 or to this chapter's End-of-Chapter Exercises at mybcommlab.com.

Use positive or neutral language

The language you use in bad-news messages influences the audience's response as much as the organization of the message itself. The tone and style of the message should help the audience feel good about you, the situation, and themselves. The following guidelines will help you evaluate your messages for effective language.

- **Avoid blaming your audience.** Your audience will be more open to accepting the bad news if you treat them politely and respectfully. Show that you understand their needs and concerns. Avoid using language that is accusatory or blaming. For example, if you use the word "you" too much in a bad-news message, the audience might feel blamed rather than respected.

  Accusatory: Your warranty does not cover breakages that you caused.

  More neutral: The warranty does not cover accidental breakage.

  Accusatory: Because you did not purchase an extended warranty, you forfeited your right to free repairs.

  More neutral: The repair would have been covered free of charge under our extended warranty.

- **Eliminate excessive negatives.** First drafts of bad-news messages often use words like "unfortunately" to convey the bad news. As much as possible, review your wording and remove negative words and phrases like these: *unfortunately, we cannot, your fault, unable, unwilling, misunderstand, regret, violate, refuse, reject, deny.*

Negative: Unfortunately, we cannot repair your MP3 player free of charge.

More positive: Your warranty includes repair only for manufacturer's defects, not for accidental breakage.

Remember, though, that you must remain clear, which will often require using some negative words.

Close the message positively

Several strategies help create a sense of goodwill when communicating bad-news messages, including using a positive opening, explaining audience benefits, and subordinating the bad news. The conclusion provides an additional opportunity to stress the positive, instill confidence, and promote goodwill. A positive closing does not mention the negative news or apologize for it. The closing should be forward-looking and optimistic. Depending on the situation, any of the following approaches may be appropriate:

- **Propose a solution.** If your bad news focuses on a problem, you may want to conclude by proposing a solution: "To increase your investment return next year, I suggest we rebalance your portfolio to include less risky investments."
- **Propose an alternative.** If you are refusing a request, consider whether you can grant a portion of the request or offer an alternative: "We encourage you to contact our affiliates to see if they have any internship openings for the coming summer. Enclosed is a brochure listing all our affiliates and their locations."
- **Create options for future business.** If you are turning down a vendor's proposal because of technical requirements, you could close your response by inviting the vendor to submit a proposal for a different project. "Our next round of requests for proposals will begin in six months. We hope you will consider submitting a proposal that meets the enclosed technical requirements."
- **Focus on a benefit.** When communicating negative situations, try to focus on the "silver lining," if one exists. For example, assume you learn that a new product designed by your company has flaws. When communicating this bad news to management, conclude by stressing good news: "Fortunately, the flaw appeared before the design went into production."

Study Question 6.4

How should I evaluate bad-news messages?

For any communication, evaluation is important to ensure that your message is effective. For sensitive communication like bad-news messages, evaluation is particularly important because communication can have significant negative business results.

As you evaluate your message, look at it objectively and consider whether it is clear, easy to understand, and honest. Also consider whether you are communicating a sense of goodwill toward your audience. Then, step back and put yourself in your audience's position to evaluate how they are likely to respond and whether the message will achieve the business result that you intend.

Evaluate the message's clarity, honesty, and sense of goodwill

Consider the scenario on page 186 of this chapter. You want to give your new client, Great Expectations Books, the bad news that you cannot complete their project as quickly as you initially promised. You had determined that both telephone and email were appropriate medium choices. In this situation, however, you decide to convey the bad news in a telephone call rather than by email for a more personal touch.

You plan the message before calling. Here is your first version, which takes a direct approach:

> Hello, Bill. I have some bad news. Due to circumstances beyond my control, I cannot begin working on your website for two weeks. As a result, it will take me an additional two weeks to complete the project. I hope that you will understand and be willing to reschedule your promotional campaign accordingly.

Before you make the phone call, evaluate this message. It is certainly concise, clear, and easy to understand. However, is it honest? You say circumstances are beyond your control, but that is not true. You can choose to work with Great Expectations rather than your other client.

Also consider how effective this message will be for maintaining the client relationship. It does not communicate a sense of goodwill or make the client feel valued. It does not express appreciation or apologize. It offers no good news or any alternatives. It does not give the client any reason to work with you rather than hire someone else to do the job. This message clearly needs revising.

For your second draft, you make a few changes. You use an indirect organization to build up to the bad news, eliminate dishonesty, provide some reasons for the news, and express appreciation:

> Hello, Bill. I'd like to talk with you about the completion date I promised for your project. One of my other clients has a time-sensitive web emergency that has to be addressed by next week. Since their website is uniquely programmed, I am the only person who can solve this problem. As a result, I will not be able to begin your project for two weeks. I appreciate your understanding and your willingness to reschedule your promotional campaign.

Is the second draft better? It softens the unexpected bad news by moving it later in the message. In addition, this version provides an honest explanation without giving too much information about the other client, and it does express some appreciation. However, it still doesn't apologize, offer alternatives, communicate goodwill, or indicate that Great Expectations is a valuable customer. It is even a little presumptuous, assuming that Bill will accept the bad news graciously and reschedule his promotional campaign.

Evaluate the business result

Review the message from your audience's point of view and think carefully about the business result. Your goal is to get your client to extend the deadline. However, the first two drafts of the message gave your client no reason to comply with your request. If you want this new client to accept your news, you may need to take a different approach. So you try a third version: one that offers alternatives and provides a better possible business result. You also rethink the purpose of this message. Do you want to impose bad news on your new client? Or would it be better to make a request and allow your client to determine if he can afford to wait for you?

> Hello, Bill. I have a favor to ask. Would it be possible to extend the due date for your project for two weeks? As I mentioned yesterday, I'm committed to doing the best possible job for all my clients, and I plan to do an outstanding job for you. However, one of my other clients—a not-for-profit agency—has an emergency and requires a last-minute reprogramming of their website so that it will work with a new server. The work must be done before the launch of their annual pledge drive next week. Because I did the original programming, I'm the only person who can reprogram the system quickly. I realize that I made a commitment to you, and I apologize for any inconvenience a delay will cause. I would very much appreciate your extending the deadline. If that is not possible, could we identify the most crucial elements of the project that need to be done by the original deadline, with the remainder coming later?

The evaluation process led to a very different message than the first draft. The most important change is that you are giving your client the opportunity to do you a favor or to say "no, you may not extend the deadline" and to negotiate a mutually acceptable solution. This message is much more likely to achieve a good business result than the two previous versions.

What types of bad-news messages are common in business?

Most people deliver bad-news messages only on rare occasions. However, certain situations do require communicating bad news: denying a request or turning down an invitation, denying a consumer claim, rejecting a recommendation or proposal, identifying issues or problems, and communicating negative change. This section provides examples of each, with annotations explaining what makes them effective.

Denying requests or turning down invitations

When you cannot—or are not willing to—grant a request or accept an invitation, you need to find a tactful, professional way to say "no" and, at the same time, not make your audience feel guilty for asking.

The strategies outlined in this chapter can help you tactfully justify your negative response. For example, recall the voice mail message from Alexa Hampton in Chapter 5 on page 161 that asked Dr. Maher—a retired business law professor—to fill in for the mayor as a keynote speaker at the local bar association's awards luncheon. Assume that Dr. Maher is leaving the day before the luncheon for a two-week cruise. He needs to deny Alexa's request and leaves the voice message in FIGURE 6.9. He decides on a direct approach. Although Alexa may be disappointed, Dr. Maher knows she will not be offended or hurt by the direct approach.

mybcommlab

Apply Figure 6.9's key concepts by revising a new document. Go to Chapter 6 in mybcommlab.com and select Document Makeovers.

FIGURE 6.9 Telephone Message Denying a Request

voice mail message

Hello, Ms. Hampton. This is Dr. Maher returning your call. We seem to be playing telephone tag.

I am sorry I will not be able to accept your invitation to speak at the luncheon next week. I am honored that you thought of me to replace the mayor as the keynote speaker. If I wasn't leaving Sunday for a two-week cruise, I would have enjoyed the opportunity.

I hope you're able to find a replacement in time for the event. Please keep me in mind for future occasions. I'd be happy to help you out when I can.

Goodbye.

Refers to Alexa's message to put the call in context.

- States the bad news directly.
- Notes appreciation for the request to ensure goodwill.
- Provides only a brief explanation since Alexa will not be surprised or upset by this news.

Closes with a positive and future-oriented statement.

Denying customer claims

When denying a customer claim request, maintaining goodwill is important because you want to retain your customers' future business as well as win the business of their colleagues and acquaintances. Bad news about customer service travels fast and far. Research shows that customers tell nearly twice as many people about their bad experiences than they tell about their good experiences.[9]

What communication techniques help customers feel good about continuing their relationship with a company? When you have to communicate bad news, customers need to know that you value them and have acceptable reasons for denying their request. Most importantly, customers need to know the company has corrected all errors and is willing to apologize if the company is at fault. If customers are happy with the resolution, they are likely to remain customers.[10]

FIGURE 6.10 offers an example of a denial message that follows these guidelines. John Stevens, an unhappy customer, emailed Tuttle Office Supply, asking them to replace 10 printers visibly damaged during shipping. He also requested on-site service to ensure the remaining 15 printers sent in the shipment are undamaged. Maggie Scher, the customer care representative at Tuttle Office Supply, is able to replace the broken printers. However, she also has to communicate the bad news that the company cannot provide on-site service.

Note how the email reply in Figure 6.10 softens the bad news in four ways:

- positioning the good news before the bad news as a buffer
- subordinating the bad news in an "although" clause
- offering an alternative solution to the request for on-site service
- expressing empathy

Notice that the tone of the email is both factual and polite. It is designed to convince the customer that Tuttle Office Supplies values this customer.

FIGURE 6.10 Email Denying Part of a Claim Request

email

Mr. Stevens:

Thank you for contacting Tuttle Office Supply about the 10 printers that were damaged in shipment due to packaging problems. We are sorry you have experienced this inconvenience. To return the printers, please contact United Packers and Shippers (800-555-1297) who will supply you with new boxes and packing and pick-up instructions. Please charge the shipping to this account number: 86-2457-31. As soon as we receive the printers, we will ship you replacements by express delivery.   ← Positions good news first, as a buffer.

If you are concerned that the remaining 15 printers also may have suffered some damage, please run the included diagnostic program, which should catch any problems. Although onsite maintenance is not part of your contract, if any printer fails the test or malfunctions within the extended warranty period, please call us immediately at (800-555-6123), and we will arrange a return and replacement.   ← Subordinates the bad news in an "although" clause ("Although on-site maintenance is not part of your contract . . .") and offers an alternative solution.

We appreciate your continued loyalty and look forward to fulfilling all your office supply needs.   ← Closes with a forward-looking statement.

Maggie Scher
Customer Care Representative
818-423-2251 Ext. 4053

If you have no good news to offer in response to a customer claim, you still need to be polite, demonstrate understanding, and offer clear reasons and alternatives. For example, imagine you work in the reservations office for Greenways Hotel. You receive a telephone call from a guest who is cancelling a prepaid reservation for a one-night stay and requesting a refund. The guest had reserved the room at a deeply discounted nonrefundable rate, and company policy prevents you from refunding reservations made at this discounted rate.

How will you deny that request and still maintain positive customer relations and goodwill? While it is tempting simply to say "Company policy does not allow refunds for nonrefundable rates," this approach will not win customer loyalty. Instead of referring to the policy, explain the reasoning behind the policy and the refusal. FIGURE 6.11 illustrates one way to deliver the bad news.

Rejecting recommendations or proposals

In today's team-based businesses, collaboration increases the number of ideas that are generated. It also creates situations where you often have to decline more ideas than you accept to complete a project. How do you tactfully turn down someone's recommendation while maintaining goodwill and ensuring that the person will continue to contribute ideas for future projects? The key is to express appreciation and provide a convincing explanation. For example, assume Sam emailed his supervisor, Tena, a detailed description of a recommendation for a client project. Unfortunately, Tena decides not to implement it and needs to explain why. She writes the email in FIGURE 6.12. Although the message delivers bad news, it maintains goodwill. It is polite and respectful, uses neutral language, and has a conversational tone.

FIGURE 6.11 Denying a Claim Request

telephone conversation

Mr. Franks, thank you for letting us know in advance about the cancellation. We are sorry you won't be able to stay with us. ◄------------------- First paragraph offers a buffer: thanking the audience and expressing appreciation.

I see you booked the room at our nonrefundable weekend getaway rate. We offer this rate at a 50 percent discount as a benefit to people who are able to plan their travel early. Our ability to offer these discounts depends on being able to count on the income from these rooms. Although your deposit cannot be refunded with this discounted rate, we would like you to stay here the next time you are in Memphis, so we'll be glad to offer you an upgrade voucher for your next stay. ◄------------- Second paragraph provides a full explanation of the rationale for a policy and subordinates the bad news.

◄------------- Conversation ends with goodwill: offering a discount for future use.

FIGURE 6.12 Rejecting a Recommendation

email

SUBJECT: Recommendation for Additional Focus Groups

Hi, Sam:

Thank you for your input on the Patterson project. I appreciate the time and effort you ◄---- put into your recommendation. ----- The message is indirect. It begins by expressing thanks and appreciation for Sam's effort.

I agree that we could offer Patterson more comprehensive market research if we scheduled five additional focus groups. In fact, I shared your proposal with the Patterson marketing team. Although Patterson does not want to spend the extra time ◄---- or money for additional focus groups, they were impressed with your analysis and would like you to take the lead in analyzing the current focus group findings. ----- The bad news is in the middle of the message. The explanation is detailed enough to answer Sam's questions.

Will you be able to present your results at this Friday's meeting? I look forward to ◄---- hearing your analysis. ----- The forward-looking statement ends the message positively. It also politely closes the door on Sam's original suggestion, implying that Tena's answer is final.

Regards,
Tena

PEARSON mybcommlab

Apply Figure 6.12's key concepts by revising a new document. Go to Chapter 6 in mybcommlab.com and select Document Makeovers.

Identifying issues or problems

In your business dealings with other companies, you may need to identify an issue or problem. For example, you may need to tell a client that project results are disappointing, or tell vendors their service is poor. Although you might think that being sensitive to a vendor about bad news is not as important as being sensitive to a client, in most cases, you want to fix the problem and continue a positive business relationship. In addition, a disgruntled vendor can easily damage your reputation by complaining to your customers and competitors.

Consider the example of Esther Davies, the vice president of corporate communications at Central Auto Fabricators. Esther has to communicate bad news to a vendor, Morrell Public Relations. Morrell has failed to deliver two agreed-upon services: a publication of a feature story in a prominent auto industry trade magazine and an invitation from one of the leading trade organizations to speak at their next convention.

Esther needs to communicate to Cara Denholm, her contact at Morrell, that if Morrell cannot deliver on its agreements, then Esther will need to cancel the PR agreement. The best medium will be a face-to-face meeting or a telephone conversation, since this allows for discussion. However, since Esther has not been able to contact Cara by telephone, she decides to write the letter in FIGURE 6.13. One advantage of a letter is that it documents the communication in writing. Like other bad-news communications, this letter needs to balance a clear statement of the bad news with positive statements of goodwill.

FIGURE 6.13 Identifying an Issue or Problem

letter

CENTRAL
AUTO FABRICATORS, Inc.

22 Denwood Avenue,   Chicago, IL 60601 | 312.555.8447

April 2, 20XX

Ms. Cara Denholm
Morrell Public Relations
7943 Callaway Drive
Barrington, IL 60010

Dear Cara:

I am concerned that Morrell is not delivering the publicity our company needs. Since I have not been able to reach you by telephone, I am writing this letter to be sure that we have a mutual understanding.

When we hired your firm six months ago, our goal was to increase our company's exposure among automobile manufacturers and others in the auto industry. To help us achieve this goal, Morrell agreed to two major accomplishments:

- A feature story about our business in a top auto industry publication.
- An invitation for our CEO to give a speech at one of three trade organizations.

So far, no one in the company has been interviewed for a feature story, and our CEO has received no invitations for speaking engagements.

We cannot afford to wait much longer. If your agency is not able to deliver on these promises within 90 days, we will be forced to cancel our agreement according to the provisions of the contract we signed.

We've admired the work Morrell has done for other companies like ours and hope you can deliver the same level of results for us. I'd like to schedule a phone conversation next week to discuss how we can work together to achieve these goals.

Sincerely,

Esther Davies

Esther Davies, Vice President
Corporate Communications

The opening paragraph directly states the problem in very general terms.

The next two paragraphs remind the audience of their commitments.

Using "we," "our," and "us" rather than "you" softens the impact of the bad news.

Using bullets to itemize what the writer wants highlights the information.

The bad news is clearly presented, and the ultimatum is specifically outlined.

The closing paragraph builds goodwill by being positive and forward-looking.

ETHICS Apologizing for Mistakes

Imagine that you or your company makes a mistake that harms people—or potentially could harm people. You may have manufactured a faulty product, failed to deliver on a service that you promised, or inconvenienced a customer thereby costing her additional money and time. What is the most ethical way to communicate to your stakeholders about this problem?

Some people believe it is dangerous to apologize because it puts a business in a defensive position that could imply legal liability. However, in a research study titled, "Companies Can Apologize: Corporate Apologies and Legal Liability," the authors argue that apologies can have a positive effect.[11] A well-timed, strategically worded apology can improve a company's public image, facilitate forgiveness, and even decrease damages if a case goes to court. Taking a "you perspective" in the face of a mistake is not only ethical, but also a good business decision.

Companies that successfully communicate about mistakes often include these four elements in their apology:

- Acknowledging the mistake
- Expressing sympathy and concern
- Explaining how the mistake occurred
- Showing how they will prevent the problem from reoccurring

You can see these elements at work in an apology written by the CEO of JetBlue Airlines. In 2007, a winter storm caused JetBlue to experience flight delays, cancellations, and baggage loss that inconvenienced hundreds of customers around the country. The news media immediately picked up the story, painting a negative picture of JetBlue. Rather than respond defensively, JetBlue's CEO David Neelman apologized in personal letters to passengers, on the company website, on YouTube, and on television talk shows. Here is the text of the written apology, which received an overwhelmingly positive response from both customers and the public:[12]

mybcommlab

For an ETHICS exercise, go to Exercise 17 on page 212 or to this chapter's End-of-Chapter Exercises at mybcomlab.com.

Dear JetBlue Customers:

We are sorry and embarrassed. But most of all, we are deeply sorry.

Last week was the worst operational week in JetBlue's seven-year history. Following the severe winter ice storm in the Northeast, we subjected our customers to unacceptable delays, flight cancellations, lost baggage, and other major inconveniences. The storm disrupted the movement of aircraft, and, more importantly, disrupted the movement of JetBlue's pilot and in-flight crewmembers who were depending on those planes to get them to the airports where they were scheduled to serve you. With the busy President's Day weekend upon us, rebooking opportunities were scarce and hold times at 1-800-JETBLUE were unacceptably long or not even available, further hindering our recovery efforts.

Words cannot express how truly sorry we are for the anxiety, frustration, and inconvenience that we caused. This is especially saddening because JetBlue was founded on the promise of bringing humanity back to air travel and making the experience of flying happier and easier for everyone who chooses to fly with us. We know we failed to deliver on this promise last week.

We are committed to you, our valued customers, and are taking immediate corrective steps to regain your confidence in us. We have begun putting a comprehensive plan in place to provide better and more timely information to you, more tools and resources for our crewmembers, and improved procedures for handling operational difficulties in the future. We are confident, as a result of these actions, that JetBlue will emerge as a more reliable and even more customer-responsive airline than ever before.

Most importantly, we have published the JetBlue Airways Customer Bill of Rights—our official commitment to you of how we will handle operational interruptions going forward—including details of compensation. I have a video message to share with you about this industry leading action.

You deserved better—a lot better—from us last week. Nothing is more important than regaining your trust and all of us here hope you will give us the opportunity to welcome you onboard again soon and provide you the positive JetBlue Experience you have come to expect from us.

Sincerely,

David

Communicating negative change

There's a saying that "nothing is constant in business except change." To remain competitive, businesses need to change their procedures and policies in response to the state of the economy, customer needs, and new opportunities that arise. Change is so pervasive in business and industry that "change management" has emerged as a discipline to help organizations and individuals implement and adapt to change. Communication is typically an element in change management plans, especially when change negatively affects an audience, as is the case with layoffs and reductions in benefits.

For example, assume Jason Easterling, CEO of Reliant Textiles, needs to communicate to all employees in the Fayetteville, North Carolina, plant that the plant will be closing and all operations will be moving to the Columbia, South Carolina, facility. Only half the employees will be offered transfers. While this is a final decision, he needs to help employees accept the decision and secure their assistance with the plant closing.

Because he wants all plant employees to learn this news at the same time, he holds a meeting. However, since some employees work a night shift and cannot attend the meeting, he sends the email in FIGURE 6.14 immediately after the meeting so that he can communicate simultaneously with everyone in the facility.

FIGURE 6.14 Communicating Change

> **email**
>
> From: jason.easterling@relianttextile.com
> To: Employees@relianttextile.com
> Date: February 8, 20XX
> Subject: Fayetteville Plant Transition
>
> Colleagues:
>
> With deep regret, I must inform you that as of April 1, 20XX, the Fayetteville, NC, manufacturing facility will be discontinuing operations and closing permanently.
>
> This decision has been difficult for the company's management and board of directors since the plant has been in operation for more than 25 years and many of you have been working in the plant since it first opened. But increasing competition from lower-cost apparel manufacturers overseas along with the plant's older and less efficient equipment have made it too costly to keep the plant open. We will be consolidating all of our manufacturing in the Columbia, South Carolina, plant with its newer, more efficient equipment.
>
> We know this transition will be difficult for you and your family. To help you, the company will be providing severance payments based on your years of service, employment counseling, and advice about how to apply for unemployment and insurance benefits.
>
> You will receive a complete packet of information next Monday, February 14, including details about your severance payment and final date of employment. Some of you will be asked to stay on until closing to help with the final shutdown of plant operations. Others will be leaving before April 1. Your final date of employment will be included in your packet.
>
> We sincerely appreciate all you have contributed over the years. We thank you for your service to the company and offer you best wishes for the future.
>
> Jason E. Easterling
> President and Chief Executive Officer
> Reliant Textiles

Email is a good medium choice because this message needs to reach a large audience simultaneously. Not everyone is available to come to the meeting.

States the bad news directly. The writer knows the audience will be looking for the bad news, so he makes it easy to find.

Explains the reasons for plant closing.

Expresses empathy and focuses on what this closing means to the audience. Also explains how the company will help.

Offers specific details and suggests that the decision is final.

Ends with a sincere expression of appreciation.

IN SUMMARY, presenting bad news requires that you balance many goals that are not always easy to combine. This chapter provides techniques that will help you state bad news clearly and also soften its negative effect. Your overall business goal should be to maintain positive relations. While you may disappoint your audience, you still want them to understand your rationale, to believe you are reasonable, and to feel good about you and about themselves.

CHAPTER 6 Summary

6.1 How will the ACE process help me deliver bad news effectively?

(pages 184–186)

- **Delivering bad news requires balancing four goals:** conveying the news clearly yet sensitively to protect the audience's self-esteem, convincing the audience to accept the bad news as both reasonable and final, projecting a positive image of you and your organization, and avoiding legal complications and liabilities.
- **The ACE process helps you balance the goals** and communicate clearly while you maintain goodwill.

6.2 How should I analyze and plan a bad-news message? *(page 186–189)*

- **Ask questions that help you develop content.** Bad-news messages require planning to achieve a good business goal without alienating your audience. To begin planning, ask questions such as these:
  - What is the bad news? What business result would I like to achieve in communicating the news?
  - How will the audience react to this news?
  - What justification and explanation should I include?
  - Is there anything I can say to soften the bad news? For example, is there any good news to include? Will the audience benefit in any way? Does this cloud have a silver lining?
  - Should I include an apology?
  - Can I do anything else to project a positive image and maintain goodwill?
- **Select the best medium to achieve your goal.** Consider audience-related criteria, such as whether you need to share the bad news with one or many people. Also consider content- and response-related criteria, such as whether you want to see or hear the audience's reaction, receive their immediate feedback, or give the audience time to consider a response carefully.

6.3 What are effective strategies for composing bad-news messages?

(pages 189–196)

- **Decide where to state the bad news.** State it at the beginning (direct organization) when the bad news is expected, easy to understand, unlikely to upset the audience, or relevant to health and safety. In other situations, use an indirect organization, stating the bad news after an explanation.
- **Phrase the bad news clearly.**
- **Soften the bad news** with a buffer, subordination, and positive or neutral language. You may also use passive voice, rather than active voice, to subordinate the bad news. Position good news ahead of bad news, when possible.
- **Close the message positively** to promote goodwill.

6.4 How should I evaluate bad-news messages? *(pages 196–197)*

- **Evaluate the message's clarity, honesty, and sense of goodwill.** Look at your message objectively and consider whether it is clear, easy to understand, and honest. Also consider whether the message will maintain a positive relationship with your audience.
- **Evaluate the business result.** Review the message from your audience's point of view and consider how the audience is likely to respond. Will the message achieve your intended outcome? Will it hurt or help your business?

6.5 What types of bad-news messages are common in business? *(pages 198–203)*

In business, you may face certain recurring situations that require you to deliver bad news:

- **Denying requests or turning down invitations**
- **Denying customer claims**
- **Rejecting recommendations or proposals**
- **Identifying issues or problems**
- **Communicating negative change**

In each situation, follow the basic guidelines for bad-news messages, and adapt the message to your specific content.

PEARSON mybcommlab *Are you an active learner? Go to mybcommlab.com to master Chapter 6 content. Chapter 6 interactive activities include:*

- Customizable Study Plan and Chapter 6 practice quizzes
- Chapter 6 Simulation, Negative Messages, that helps you think critically and prepare to make choices in the business world
- Flash Cards for mastering the definition of chapter terms

- Chapter 6 Video Exercise, Writing Negative Messages, which shows you how textbook concepts are put into practice every day
- Interactive Lessons that visually review key chapter concepts
- Document Makeovers for hands-on, scored practice in revising documents

- What is the bad news?
- What business result do I want to achieve?
- How will the audience react to this news?
- What justification and explanation should I include? Is there anything I can say to soften the bad news?
- Should I include an apology?
- Can I do anything else to project a positive image and maintain goodwill?
- What is the best medium for this message?

- Is the bad news stated clearly yet sensitively?
- Will the message convince the audience to accept the bad news?
- Does the message project a good image of me and maintain goodwill with the audience?
- Will the message achieve a good business result?
- Have I avoided legal complications?

- Should I begin with the bad news or build up to it?
- How can I clearly phrase the bad news?
- What content and techniques should I use to soften the impact of the message?
- How can I close the message appropriately?

Mr. Stevens:

Thank you for contacting Tuttle Office Supply about the 10 printers that were damaged in shipment due to packaging problems. We are sorry you have experienced this inconvenience. To return the printers, please contact United Packers and Shippers (800-555-1297) who will supply you with new boxes and packing and pick-up instructions. Please charge the shipping to this account number: 86-2457-31. As soon as we receive the printers, we will ship you replacements by express delivery.

If you are concerned that the remaining 15 printers also may have suffered some damage, please run the included diagnostic program, which should catch any problems. Although onsite maintenance is not part of your contract, if any printer fails the test or malfunctions within the extended warranty period, please call us immediately at (800-555-6123), and we will arrange a return and replacement.

We appreciate your continued loyalty and look forward to fulfilling all your office supply needs.

Maggie Scher
Customer Care Representative
818-423-2251 Ext. 4053

HOW CAN I SOFTEN THE BAD NEWS?

Develop an effective buffer.

Position good news ahead of bad news.

Subordinate the bad news.

Use positive or neutral language.

Close the message positively.

Buffer *p. 190*   **Goodwill** *p. 184*

CASE STUDY Making the Best of Bad News

This case study will help you review the chapter material by applying it to a specific scenario.

Henry Lai is having a bad week. On Monday, Henry got into a minor car accident on his way to his business communication class. It was his third accident of the year, and he was late for class. Today, he is almost late again. As Henry left his apartment, his neighbor stopped him in the hallway to ask if he read the landlord's email announcing an increase in rent. Henry does not know how he'll handle these extra expenses. On top of a rent increase, he may need to pay for a repair to his broken computer printer, which may not be covered by a manufacturer warranty. And he also needs to help pay for the anniversary party he and his brothers are throwing for their parents in May.

Henry slips into class just in time to get Professor Anderson's assignment sheet. As Henry reads it, he begins to smile. This is an assignment he can definitely handle. Professor Anderson is requiring students to pick one or two types of writing—routine, persuasive, good news, or bad news—and over the next five weeks collect samples to analyze. The goal is to evaluate these pieces according to the guidelines in the textbook and suggest revisions. A lot is going on in Henry's life, and many people are communicating with him. In fact, he could begin the assignment right after class by reading his landlord's email about the rent increase.

Henry has to read the letter twice to understand what it means, and when he finally understands, he is shocked. This isn't what he expected at all! His family has had City Mutual Insurance since before he was born. How could they drop him?

Review Question 2: *A reader should be able to understand a bad-news letter quickly—and not feel insulted or abandoned. How would you advise City Mutual to revise its letter?*

Bad News from the Professor

After arriving late to his business communication class a third time, Henry is not surprised to see an email from Professor Anderson in his inbox. Professor Anderson has a strict attendance policy for her course, which Henry is finding difficult to follow. If this is a bad-news email, Henry hopes it is well written. He does not want to be in the position of critiquing his teacher in his final project.

Henry reads the email, reproduced on the next page, and wonders: "If I can't pass the course, maybe I should drop it. Is that really the goal of this email?"

Review Question 3: *Is this an effective bad-news email? Would you recommend that Professor Anderson make any revisions?*

As a Customer, How Do I Feel?

As Henry prepares to write his final business communication report by analyzing messages he has received during the term, he thinks about how important it is for a business to communicate

Softening the Impact of Bad News

After class, Henry rushed to the computer lab on campus to check his email. Would his landlord raise the rent to more than he could afford? He is not looking forward to reading the bad news. See the landlord's email message to the right.

As Henry finishes reading, he thinks, "I'd like to stay. This must be a pretty good email." Would you agree?

Review Question 1: *Evaluate this email. Would you recommend any revisions?*

Bad News in the Mail

When Henry returns home from class, he finds a letter in his mailbox from his auto insurance company. He opens it, glances at it quickly, and then puts it aside. At first glance, the letter appears to be announcing a raise in premiums. He doesn't have time to read it carefully. Later that evening, though, he decides to pick it up again to read more carefully. See the letter on the next page.

email

Dear Tenants:

When you get your lease in the next few months, you will see a 15 percent raise in rent. I want to explain to you why rent is increasing. I value each of you as tenants and neighbors, and I hope you will understand and choose to stay at 727 Seward Street.

As you probably know, both property taxes and the cost of heating fuel have increased this past year. This winter, it cost me 20 percent more to heat your apartments—and mine—than the year before. My total costs as landlord have gone up 30 percent.

The rent increase barely covers these increased costs. In addition, during this upcoming year, I will be painting the halls and buying new equipment for the laundry room. I want this building to remain a good place for us to live, and like every year in the past, this year I will make more improvements.

I know more rent is a hardship since many of you are in school as well as working. But the rent here is still the most reasonable in the neighborhood.

Please let me know if you don't plan to stay, but I hope you do.

Sincerely,
Edward Nikaza

Accompanies Question 1

letter

City Mutual Insurance

8851 Lincoln Way, St. Louis, MO 63114

March 15, 20XX

Mr. Henry Lai
727 Seward Street
Chesterfield, MO 63005

Dear Mr. Lai:

At City Mutual Insurance, our ability to provide cost-effective insurance to all our customers depends on our periodically assessing and reevaluating risk. Our internal guidelines and policies are carefully constructed to ensure that we remain a financially secure company. It is in this way that we can provide financial security to our customers in their times of need. Our guidelines take into account a number of risk factors, including a customer's driving record.

When a customer account falls out of the accepted parameters, we have the legal option to cancel or refuse to renew automobile insurance at the next renewal date. Based on your recent record of chargeable automobile accidents, our guidelines require that your automobile insurance be cancelled 30 days from the date of this letter. You will receive a pro-rated reimbursement check within 60 days, as required by law.

We encourage you to act quickly to secure new insurance since all registered automobiles in your state must have insurance.

Adjustment Department
City Mutual Insurance

Accompanies Question 2

email

Dear Henry:

This week you arrived late to class for the third time. As you know, you can have no more than two unexcused absences or four late arrivals and still pass the class. I cannot stress enough how serious this is. Business Communication 371 is a requirement for graduation in your major. You must receive at least a C in this course. With one more absence or late arrival, you will need to repeat the course in order to graduate.

Professor Anderson

Accompanies Question 3

From: Tanya Corros <Tanya@gremlincorp.com>
Date: April 1, 20XX
To: Henry Lai <Henry.Lai@popmail.com>
Subject: Repair Options for Gremlin 2740n Printer

Dear Mr. Lai:

As a follow-up to our telephone conversation today, I have reviewed your warranty as well as the notes from the authorized technician who examined your nonfunctioning Gremlin 2740n wireless laser printer. The warranty protects your printer against manufacturer defects and mechanical failure for one year from the date of purchase. However, it specifically excludes damage from accidents and misuse.

According to our technician, a bent fuser usually results from dropping the printer or dropping something on the printer. Therefore, that damage is not covered by our warranty, even though you purchased the printer less than three months ago.

We can offer two suggestions for cost-effectively repairing or replacing your printer. First, if you used a credit card to purchase the printer, consider contacting the company to see if it offers buyer protection plans that insure your purchases against accidental loss or damage. If you must pay for your own repairs, you may find it more cost effective to purchase a factory-authorized refurbished printer directly from Gremlin. We will be pleased to offer you a $50 discount on this purchase.

Thank you for being a Gremlin customer. We look forward to being your printer of choice long into the future.

Sincerely,
Tanya Corros

effectively with its customers. Henry asks himself, "As a customer, how do I feel about the people who have been communicating with me? How do I feel about my landlord, City Mutual Insurance, and Professor Anderson? Would I choose to have a continuing relationship with them or do business with them again? Will I spread a good word about them?" These questions remain on Henry's mind as he analyzes his last set of business messages: a letter from the manufacturer of his broken computer printer (to the left) and a voice mail from the River Inn where he planned his parents' anniversary party (below). Would he choose to do business with these organizations again?

Review Question 4: *Based on these bad-news communications, would you like to do business with these organizations?*

voice mail

Mr. Lai. This is Darryl at the River Inn. We need to make some changes in the arrangements for your party in May. The room you reserved is undergoing extensive repairs for water damage caused by the storm and will not be ready by the 15th of next month. All of our other rooms are taken for that evening. Is it possible for you to change the date of your event to Sunday the 29th? If not, we will be glad to completely refund your deposit. Please return my call at your earliest convenience. I'm at 678-957-1344.

CRITICAL THINKING

1. Identify a situation that required you to share bad news in the past. Were you successful in achieving a balance between clarity and maintaining goodwill? If so, how did you accomplish that? If not, how could you have achieved a balance, based on reading this chapter?

2. Analyzing how the negative information will affect your audience is an important first step to create an effective bad-news message. Assume you are replying to a customer who submitted a claim for a defective product. The customer sent this email: *"Dear Sir or Madam: I bought a GreenLife outdoor bird fountain during your summer clearance sale last month. I assembled it myself, and it worked perfectly for several weeks until yesterday. For some reason, the fountain will no longer work. I've already thrown out the box the fountain came in (and my receipt), but I know you'll want to keep me as a customer by replacing the fountain or refunding my money. I look forward to your reply."* Unfortunately, in addition to not refunding sales without receipts, you are not able to exchange clearance items due to your store's "all sales are final" policy. You do not know this customer. How do you think the bad news will affect the customer? How can you frame the bad news to maintain that customer's business in the future?

3. Sincere apologies can be effective tools for communicating bad news. By contrast, insincere apologies can alienate your audience. Think of a situation in which you might want to offer someone an apology. Phrase that apology in an insincere way, as if you don't really mean to apologize. Then change it to sound sincere. Describe some of the features that distinguish the two kinds of apologies.

4. Before communicating bad news in cross-cultural situations, you should research the cultures' expectations about the organization of bad-news messages. Some cultures prefer directness, and others value indirectness. Assume you are presenting bad news in a face-to-face meeting with stakeholders who represent several different cultures, including high-context cultures (Arabic and Latin American) as well as low-context cultures (German and Scandinavian). How do you balance their differing perspectives about how bad news should be presented?
[Related to the Culture feature on page 195]

5. When possible, face-to-face meetings are usually the best medium for sharing bad news, even if they need to be supplemented with an email or memo for documentation. If you are apprehensive about communicating bad news in person, what can you do to prepare yourself for a face-to-face meeting?

6. Assume you are on the executive board of an organization, and one of your friends is chair of the organization's fundraising committee. Your friend has been doing a bad job, and the board has asked you to replace him. How would you communicate this bad news?

7. "Do you want the good news first or the bad news?" This question is a common method of beginning a face-to-face conversation when you have both good and bad news to share with an audience. The response usually is based on the situation. As suggested in this chapter, you should often position the good news ahead of bad news in business communication. However, describe a specific situation in which you

might decide to share the bad news before the good news. Create a scenario that is not already presented in the chapter.

8. The chapter suggests that you do not justify refusing a customer claim by saying "it's company policy." Instead, explain the rationale for the policy, without mentioning policy. What if you do not understand the rationale behind a policy? What can you do?

9. Some people might consider positive language as sugarcoating bad news and being insincere. What are the benefits of using positive language when communicating bad-news messages?

10. One goal of communicating bad news is to convince your audience that the bad news is final and they should accept it. Can you think of any situations in which you might not want to convince the audience the news is final?

DEVELOPING YOUR COMMUNICATION SKILLS

6.1 How will the ACE process help me deliver bad news effectively? *(pages 184–186)*

EXERCISE 1 Delivering bad news requires balancing four goals

Describe a situation in which you have given someone bad news. Answer each of the following questions by describing how you met the goal. Or, if you did not meet the goal, identify how you could have.

a. Did you convey the news clearly, yet sensitively to protect the audience's self-esteem? If so, how?

b. Were you able to convince the audience to accept the bad news as both reasonable and final? What techniques did you use?

c. Did you project a positive image of yourself (or your organization)? If so, how?

d. If applicable, were you able to avoid legal complications or liabilities?

EXERCISE 2 The ACE process helps you balance the goals

You are a customer service agent for a company that sells gifts, cards, and seasonal items such as holiday ornaments through catalog and online sales. Through your website, a customer orders personalized holiday cards, approves the personalization information when finalizing the order, and receives a confirmation email with a sample of the personalized card. Two weeks later when the customer receives the order, she calls you to complain about a misspelling on the cards. Because she approved the personalization when ordering the cards and did not reply to the email confirming the order, you cannot refund her purchase (obviously, the cards cannot be resold). How would you balance the four goals in your response? Consider both the wording of the response and how you organize the message.

a. How would you phrase the bad news so that it is clear but also protects the audience's self-esteem and maintains goodwill?

b. How would you convince the audience to accept the bad news as both reasonable and final?

c. How would you project a positive image of yourself and your organization?

d. Can you imagine any legal complications that might arise from this scenario? How could you avoid them?

6.2 How should I analyze and plan a bad-news message? *(pages 186–189)*

EXERCISE 3 Ask questions that help you develop content

Assume you manage a video processing lab where customers bring in old home movies and have them transferred to DVDs. Yesterday, a long-time client brought in a video of her daughter's wedding and plans to pick up the DVD in two weeks after she returns from vacation. Today, one of your employees accidentally damaged the video tape and all your efforts to retrieve the data have failed. Answer these questions:

a. What is the bad news?

b. What business result do I want to achieve in communicating it?

c. How will the audience react to this information?

d. How do I want the audience to respond?

e. What justification and explanation should I include?

f. Is there anything I can say to soften the bad news? For example, is there any good news to include (audience benefits)?

g. Should I include an apology?

Be sure to explain and justify your answers.

EXERCISE 4 Should I include an apology?

Consider each of the following bad-news scenarios and determine whether you would apologize in your response to each. Justify your decision by explaining how the apology would affect the audience and your organization.

a. Advising a supervisor about a mistake in the sales figures from last quarter's income summary report.

b. Telling a vendor that you are selecting a competitor's proposal for a project.

c. Denying a customer's request for a refund because the receipt was not provided.

d. Rejecting an employee's request for a transfer to a different department due to budget issues.

e. Refusing a colleague's request to change vacation dates with you because you have already booked your flight.

EXERCISE 5 Select the best medium to achieve your goal
[Related to the Technology feature on page 189]

Assume you manage a local clothing store. One of your part-time employees who frequently misses work or arrives late emails to ask you to recommend her for a supervisory position. How will you communicate the bad news that you do not feel comfortable recommending her for a promotion? What is the best medium for communication: would you write an email or choose face-to-face communication? Would you state the bad news directly or indirectly? Explain your reasoning.

6.3 What are effective strategies for composing bad-news messages? *(pages 189–196)*

EXERCISE 6 Decide where to state the bad news

For each of the following scenarios, explain whether you would use the direct or indirect organizational plan for communicating the bad news, and justify your decision:

a. You are a marketing representative for a textbook publishing company. You told a customer that a new edition of a book would be available by July 1, in plenty of time to prepare for use in the fall semester. Today you learn that the book's publication has been delayed and that it won't be available until August 15, just days before the semester begins. How would you organize the message communicating this information to the customer?

b. Part of your job as the assistant manager of a large department store is to evaluate trainees as they transition from probationary status to regular full-time employees. Most of the time, you are able to begin your face-to-face conversations with positive feedback before subordinating any constructive criticism. However, today you have to tell Phillip that if he wants to continue to work for the store, he will remain on probationary status for two more weeks. He has not yet demonstrated that he can process returns on his own, and he struggles with the computer when processing any transaction. In fact, none of his supervisors could provide any positive feedback. How would you begin your face-to-face conversation with Phillip?

c. You are the chief financial officer for a large consulting company. Due to the recent economic downturn in your industry, the board of directors asks you to reduce the budget by 20 percent and strongly recommends cutting staff, which is the largest individual line item in your budget. Rather than lay off 20 percent of your employees, you suggest the company incorporate a furlough program that reduces the workweek from five to four days. Departments will rotate off days among their staff to ensure adequate coverage Mondays through Fridays. The board approves your plan and asks you to create a preliminary outline of a memo that the CEO will send to employees, explaining the furlough program. Explain whether you would organize the message directly or indirectly, and compose a rough outline of the content.

EXERCISE 7 Phrase the bad news clearly

The following badly written messages are partial responses to the scenarios outlined in Exercise 6 ("Decide where to state the bad news"). Revise the wording to state the bad news more clearly. For each response, identify (1) what phrase is ambiguous, (2) how the audience might misinterpret it, and (3) what you could say instead.

a. (See Exercise 6a): Thank you for ordering the new marketing textbook, *Marketing Concepts, Third Edition,* by Allen and Tate. We are sure you and your students will be pleased with this new edition. The revised shipping date is August 10 and should be in your mailbox no later than August 15.

b. (See Exercise 6b): Your probationary period has been extended for two weeks.

c. (See Exercise 6c): To help the company stay in business during these tough economic times, changes will be made to our staffing procedures to reduce the budget by 20 percent. Check with your department supervisors to determine how this change will affect you.

EXERCISE 8 Soften the bad news

Rewrite each of the following badly written messages to soften the impact of the bad news:

a. Thank you for your recent order. I'm sorry you think your shipment was not complete. According to our records, all the items you ordered were delivered. Please refer to the attached copies of your order form and packing slip to confirm your complete shipment.

b. Although I hate to do it, we cannot offer bonuses this year due to declining sales. I'm sorry to disappoint you, especially during the holiday season. Better luck next year!

c. As we indicated last month, travel budgets have been frozen until next quarter. Why did you submit a request when you knew I'd have to deny it?

d. Thank you for your email indicating concern about the monthly premiums for family health insurance coverage. I agree that the difference between employee-only coverage ($10) and family coverage ($345) is unreasonable. Your proposal to split the difference makes sense. I wish I could support it, but the premiums are set by the insurance company.

e. Sorry to hear your iPod broke after only a week. We sell them, but we don't fix them. You'll have to contact the manufacturer, who offered the warranty.

EXERCISE 9 Close the message positively

For each of the badly written messages outlined in Exercise 8 "Soften the bad news", create a concluding statement or paragraph that closes the message positively. Use one or more of the following techniques: propose a solution, propose an alternative, create options for future business, and focus on a benefit.

6.4 How should I evaluate bad-news messages?
(pages 196–197)

EXERCISE 10 Evaluate the message's clarity, honesty, and sense of goodwill

Two months ago, Marla requested a week of vacation in early June to participate in her children's end-of-year school activities. However, yesterday she found out her husband's family reunion would be held over the July 4 holiday. She decides to email her supervisor, Paul, to see if she can request a change in her vacation schedule. Unfortunately, Paul is not able to grant her request. Evaluate Paul's email message on page 211. Is it clear and easy to understand? Is it honest? Does it project a sense of goodwill with the audience? What changes would you recommend?

email

Marla:

I received your recent request to change your vacation week from the first week of June to the first week of July. Unfortunately, that's just not possible this year because of the end-of-year reports due by July 3. Also, as I am sure you are aware, company policy clearly states that vacations cannot be taken adjacent to scheduled holidays. Let me know if you'd like to select a different vacation week or keep your current first week of June.

Regards,
Paul

Accompanies Exercise 10

EXERCISE 11 Evaluate the business result

You are an event planning consultant at Renew Retreat Center. Several months ago, Rena Murphy at Smith-Harrison and Associates (SMA) called you to coordinate their annual volunteer training seminar to be held at the retreat center May 1–2. Rena booked the center from 1 PM on Friday, May 1, through 6 PM on Saturday, May 2. Today is April 1, and Rena emails you to begin working on the logistics of the seminar. As you retrieve the reservation from the system, you realize you accidentally mixed up the reservation. You have SMA coming in at 6 PM on Friday and leaving by 1 PM on Saturday. Other events have already been booked before and after these times, and it would be difficult to make changes. Saturday afternoon's event is a wedding, and you're quite sure the invitations have already been sent. How do you communicate this bad news to Rena without losing the event? Evaluate the email message to Rena, located to the right. Assume you would like to retain this customer's business. Do you think that message will help you achieve the result? If so, why? If not, how would you recommend changing it?

6.5 What types of bad-news messages are common in business? *(pages 198–203)*

EXERCISE 12 Denying requests or turning down invitations

Assume you are a business professional who hires management majors for internship positions from the regional university located in your city. Paolo Miguel, one of your current interns, emailed you to request that you serve as the advisor next year for the university's chapter of Future Business Leaders of America. In his request, Paolo emphasized how much the students can learn from you and how your management skills can help ensure the organization's future success. Given your workload and other community service commitments, you don't think you'll have enough time to devote to this student organization. How will you effectively decline Paolo's request? Compose an email response.

EXERCISE 13 Denying customer claims

You are the shipping manager for a toy company that does most of its sales through catalog and online ordering. However, you also sell

email

Dear Rena:

I am so sorry, but I did not record your May 1–2 reservation correctly. I mixed up the times and have your group scheduled to arrive at 6 PM on Friday, May 1, and leaving by 1 PM on Saturday. Unfortunately, we have already booked other events for Friday and Saturday afternoons. I'm sorry that we have to cut your seminar so short and hope that you won't cancel your event. To make up for the inconvenience, I can provide a 20 percent discount on your room rates. Please let me know when a good time to call might be so we can better discuss your options.

Sincerely,
[Your Name]

Accompanies Exercise 11

products to select local retailers across the country, including Toys R Us. Martha Hagler of Delaware, Ohio, ordered a train set for her grandson's fifth birthday. The large set came in a unique tin container, which was damaged during shipping. Martha emailed your company to complain about the damage and request that a replacement be shipped to her overnight. Her grandson's birthday is in three days, and she wants another train set before the party. However, because the tin containers are made by another manufacturer and you are currently out of stock, you cannot replace her order before the party. Reply to Ms. Hagler with the bad news and an alternative solution.

EXERCISE 14 Rejecting recommendations or proposals

You are the assistant principal at a large metropolitan high school. The head of the business education department, Jacqueline DeMarta, has complained for years that the computer labs need to be updated. This morning, she emailed a proposal to purchase 30 new laptop computers that could be used in several classrooms to support teaching and learning. The laptops she wants are $1,000 each. You do not have the funds in the budget to cover her request, and you are concerned that the laptops would be easier to steal than standard desktop computers. Your school has experienced several break-ins in the last year, and you do not want to provide additional targets for future robberies. Rather than completely deny her request, email Ms. DeMarta with an alternative solution. Research desktop computers priced at $750 or less that would be applicable for a high school computer lab. Using what you have learned, compose a response to Ms. DeMarta.

EXERCISE 15 Identifying issues or problems

You run an online business selling unique gifts from a wide variety of manufacturers. A new customer placed an order for a product that was back-ordered by the manufacturer. Two weeks later, when you checked on the status of the shipment, you discovered that the manufacturer discontinued the product. You spent several hours researching similar products from other manufacturers but have not yet found a viable replacement. You know you need to contact your customer to indicate that the product is no longer available. Decide on at least one strategy to buffer the bad news (see Figure 6.8 on page 194). Determine the best medium, and draft an effective message.

EXERCISE 16 Communicating negative change

You work for Plimpton Financial Services, a company that offers an extremely generous tuition plan for employees. The company pays 100 percent of college tuition for the children of all employees who have worked at the company for more than five years. This benefit can be worth hundreds of thousands of dollars for employees with multiple children. The CEO of Plimpton explains why the company has been so generous: "If we can take away the worry of paying for college, employees will concentrate more and be more productive. We value our employees, and this is a great way to keep them."

Because of difficulties in the financial market, Plimpton has decided to phase out this benefit over a period of five years. This news will disappoint and anger many people who have been staying at the company in order to receive the benefit.

Your job is to plan the announcement. Use the ACE process to analyze the audience and compose a message. Since you do not have an actual audience available, imagine yourself as an employee of Plimpton, who has three children to put through college.

EXERCISE 17 Apologizing for a mistake
[Related to the Ethics feature on page 202]

Kosta Browne Winery is a small business in Sebastopol, California, that is in an enviable position. The vineyard has more demand for its wines than they can produce. Kosta Browne distributes its products through a private customer list and offers customers a specific allocation—the maximum number of bottles they are able to purchase. Potential customers interested in the wine can request to be on a waiting list for future allocations.

One season, the customers on the waiting list received a happy surprise: an email explaining that the winery would soon send them an order form for purchasing wine. These customers weren't expecting an offer this year, and were pleased to receive it. Unfortunately, that email was a mistake. It should have been sent only to current customers—not to those on the waiting list. The mistake was compounded by the fact that, a few minutes later, waiting list customers received a second email, saying they would receive no wine. How should Kosta Browne address this problem?

The company decided to deliver the bad news quickly, directly, and personally. According to co-owner Mike Browne, "We were sick to our stomachs when the wrong communication

Accompanies Exercise 17

Mike Browne, Dan Kosta, and Chris Costello – the founders of Kosta Browne Winery in Sebastopol, California

---

letter

January 23, 20XX

Mr. Ben Forman
1234 Damian Lane
Bolingbroke, IL

Dear Ben:

Thank you for recently joining the Kosta Browne mailing list. Regrettably, one of the first correspondences we have had with you may not have been an enjoyable experience! On the evening of Monday, January 19, we sent you two errant emails regarding your account and allocations for our upcoming release of Appellation Pinot Noirs. We sincerely apologize for the confusion that was caused by this mistake.

We appreciate that you have taken the time and interest to join our waiting list, and we look forward to offering you wine in the future. Since we have a limited amount of wine that is already allocated to mailing list members, we regrettably cannot offer you wine as a consolation at this time. However, we have marked your account to reflect that you received these misdirected emails so that when we are able to offer you an allocation, you will receive a discount on our first shipment as a token of our appreciation for your patience and continued support.

If you have any further questions or comments, please contact our offices directly 707-555-7430. We would be happy to talk with you.

Sincerely yours,

Dan Kosta and Mike Browne

Accompanies Exercise 17

went out. Writing a personal letter was important to us since our customers and our future customers are extremely important to us." Page 212 shows the letter mailed to each customer on the waiting list who received the incorrect email. Review this letter and evaluate whether (and how) it follows the advice in this chapter.

WRITING

EXERCISE 18 Cancelling a keynote speaker

Your company has invited one of its biggest clients, Vince Embry, to be a keynote speaker at a company retreat. Vince has cancelled other engagements and arranged his calendar to accommodate your schedule. Vince also purchased an airline ticket at his own expense and has begun writing his speech. However, you've just learned that the company must cancel the retreat due to budget cuts. Create a message to Vince communicating the bad news that the retreat is cancelled so he will not have the opportunity to speak. Consider what you can offer that will make up for his inconvenience and expense.

EXERCISE 19 Responding to a customer's complaint

You are a manager at Home Goods, which sells a wide variety of bath, kitchen, and other household items. Several months ago, you offered a special sale on a specific FreshAir humidifier, Model 2850. A customer who purchased one of these humidifiers returned to your store last week to purchase more filters for the humidifier. However, your store no longer carries the FreshAir brand. Although the store offers several replacement filters for other brands, you do not carry the specific model the customer requires. He wrote a letter to "The Manager" complaining about the problem and indicating that he plans to tell everyone he knows not to bother buying products from your store since you don't stock the items needed to maintain them. Although you don't have the filters in your store, you can special order them. How do you respond to the letter? What medium would you use? Draft a message.

EXERCISE 20 Responding to a customer request

Assume you manage a catering business. Two weeks ago, you met with Ellyn Jones to discuss the details of catering a reception for her parents' 50th wedding anniversary. The party is in another week. She indicated that her maximum catering budget for the party is $2,500, and she signed a contract that outlined a price of $25 per person for up to 100 guests. The contract provided for several "finger-food" stations, including a sushi bar, crudités, hot hors d'oeuvres, and a large cake in addition to punch, tea, and coffee. You special order the sushi from an out-of-town supplier to be shipped fresh just in time for the event. The rest of the items are available locally and can be prepared a day in advance. Today, Ellyn emails you with some bad news. Her mother decided most of the relatives won't like sushi and would like to replace that station with a chocolate fountain. Additionally, she would like to increase the head count to 120. Your heart sinks when you read the message. With these changes you will no longer be able to keep the price within Ellyn's budget. Not only will you have to pay a $200 cancellation fee if you cancel the sushi order, but renting the chocolate fountain and buying the chocolate, dipping foods, and skewers will cost $300 more than the sushi it is replacing. In addition, accommodating 20 additional guests will cost $500. These changes bring the cost of catering to $1,000 over Ellyn's budget. How do you respond? Decide what your message will be, medium you will use, and how you will organize the message. Compose a draft.

EXERCISE 21 Giving bad news to your manager

You are a part-time accountant for a small, local retail company. You provide Patricia Zho, the owner of the company, with quarterly reports summarizing her income and expenses. Together you determine a budget and compare it to actual data to help make important decisions such as ordering merchandise and providing raises.

After two years of continual losses in sales, you believe Patricia must reduce her payroll. She has consistently refused to consider this suggestion in the past, stating that her employees are like family, and she cannot reduce their wages or fire anyone. She'd rather go out of business. At this point, the data are telling you that she will have to close her doors if she does not reduce payroll. Five people are on the payroll, averaging $35,000 a year each. Sales continue to decline, as described in the following table. Inventory costs her 40 percent of the sales price. To help her understand the situation, write a memo giving her the bad news. If possible, support it with a graph that visually represents the data.

Quarter	Sales
20XX–Q1	$510,000
20XX–Q2	$480,000
20XX–Q3	$452,000
20XX–Q4	$412,000
20XY–Q1	$389,000
20XY–Q2	$381,000
20XY–Q3	$325,000
20XY–Q4	$315,000

Accompanies Exercise 21

EXERCISE 22 Rejecting a job applicant

You are the hiring manager for a mid-sized company. You have narrowed the applicants for a managerial position to two: (1) a 22-year-old college graduate who interned at a different division of your company two summers ago but has no additional industry experience and (2) a 48-year-old MBA with over 20 years of experience related to your industry. Although the older candidate is better qualified, your budget restrictions will not allow you to meet the older candidate's salary requirements. Who do you hire? Indicate the medium you would choose and draft a bad-news message to the applicant you do not hire.

COLLABORATING

EXERCISE 23 Preparing to communicate bad news in other countries [Related to the Culture feature on page 195]

Your team is organizing a training seminar for new managers who will be working closely with clients in the four largest markets in your industry: Brazil, Russia, India, and China. You know that businesspeople in these countries have differing expectations about how bad news should be communicated. Use the resources available on mybcommlab.com to research the differences. Assign one country to each of the four members in your team. Each team member should write a paragraph summarizing best practices for communicating bad news. Then collaborate on a one-page memo that provides information new managers would find useful when communicating bad news to clients from each of these countries. Be sure your memo includes an introduction and conclusion.

EXERCISE 24 Preparing to communicate change

Assume the dean of academic affairs at your school is considering adding a one-credit senior seminar as a requirement for graduation. Although the seminar will provide soon-to-be graduates with beneficial information, such as interviewing skills and résumé writing, most students perceive the additional requirement as bad news. To help the dean "sell" the bad news to the student body, your group has been asked to collect student responses that the administration can address. Each member of your group is assigned to collect input from 10 students across campus (be sure to tell them this is a hypothetical scenario). Do they think the senior seminar requirement is a good idea? If not, why not? Meet as a group to combine all members' data and summarize your findings to provide the dean with an audience analysis. Provide suggestions about how the dean can best create a message that addresses the concerns of those students who will consider the change to be bad news.

SPEAKING

EXERCISE 25 Making informal/impromptu presentations

Plan a brief (less than one minute) response for the following scenarios:

a. Your brother gave you two tickets to the final game of the basketball championship series, since he would be out of town and could not use his tickets. You plan to go to the game, and you offered the extra ticket to a friend—a real basketball fan who has done you a number of favors. The day before the game, your brother calls, says his travel plans have changed, and he wants to go to the game with you. How would you tell your friend you can no longer take him to the game?

b. You have promised to send 10 bound copies of a document to your client by overnight express delivery. He needs to distribute these documents to his board of directors at a meeting the next afternoon. You packaged the reports, brought them to the express delivery company, filled out the address form, and paid for early morning delivery. Later that night, however, you realized that you made a mistake when filling out the address form. You included the wrong zip code, so the package is on its way to Iowa instead of Michigan. How will you tell your client that the package will not be delivered on time?

EXERCISE 26 Executive briefing [Related to the Culture feature on page 195]

You are working with an international team of research and design specialists that includes engineers from subsidiary offices in several countries. Last week, you tried to tell Bhavna Asnani from the Mumbai office that there was a serious problem with her report. Although Bhavna speaks fluent English, you had difficulty ensuring that she understood the problem. She kept changing the subject. Then she merely agreed with your comments rather than questioning the process or determining a solution to the problem. This morning you shared the scenario with your supervisor, who explained how Indian cultures react to and communicate bad news. Now the conversation makes more sense to you, and you wish you had not been so direct with the bad news. To ensure you don't make the same mistake, you decide to begin to research how to communicate effectively with international audiences. Use sources such as CyborLink.com and MannersInternational.com and summarize your findings in a five-minute presentation including at least one visual aid.

GRAMMAR

EXERCISE 27 Common sentence errors: Run-ons and comma splices (See Appendix D—Section 1.3)

Rekey (or download from mybcommlab.com) the following paragraph, correcting the 10 run-on or fused sentences and comma splices (see Sections 1.3.1 and 1.3.2). Underline all your corrections.

One business etiquette consultant believes that good telephone manners begin in childhood, children should be taught how to answer the phone courteously and take messages. Diane Eaves says, "I work with a lot of people who are technically ready for work however, they apparently missed a lot of the teaching of manners." For instance, asking who is calling can be taught in childhood then it will be a habit. Parents know how annoying it is to have a child report that "somebody called and wants you to call back" Sonny doesn't remember who it was and didn't write down the number. Thank goodness for caller ID it can be a big help, nevertheless, children should be taught to ask for and write down names and numbers. It's surprising how many people don't identify themselves when they make business calls, they expect listeners to recognize their voice. That may be OK if you speak frequently with the caller on the other hand it's mystifying when a voice you don't recognize launches right into a subject. It is the caller's responsibility to identify himself or herself, if he or she doesn't you can politely say, "Excuse me, I didn't catch your name."

7 Finding and Evaluating Business Information

new hires @ work

Amado Villarreal
Project Engineer
CH2M Hill Constructors, Inc.
Northwestern University, 2009

"**MY BOSS OFTEN ASKS ME TO FIND INFORMATION** about permit and certification requirements. To gather that information, I first get a clear understanding of what I need to find and then develop key words to search for it. Most of the material is on our internal website, which contains guidelines, protocols, and information from past projects. For information not on that site, I search externally. I also reach out to others in the company since the people at CH2M Hill are very open to questions. When the research is complete, I organize it in a binder to present for review."

Introduction

In the workplace, you may be assigned jobs or projects that require you to conduct research and share the results. For example, you may be asked to:

- investigate why product sales declined
- determine which product features are most important to your customers
- compare benefits packages offered by your company and its competitors
- analyze how new state tax laws will affect your company
- decide where to open a new store

Employers won't expect you to have all the information you need at your fingertips, but they will expect you to conduct research to get the information.

You probably have developed some research skills in other classes that assigned research papers. These skills will be useful to you since academic research and workplace research both require you to identify research questions, find appropriate sources, extract the right information, combine it with information from other sources, and present it in a useful format.

However, workplace research and academic research differ in two key ways: their starting points and their goals. Academic research typically starts with a topic. You need to focus on that topic, identify a research question, and then structure the research. The goal of most academic research is for you—the researcher—to learn. Workplace research, by contrast, typically starts with a specific question or problem. The aim of the research is to find, analyze, and organize information that will help answer the question or solve the problem.

Chapters 7, 8, 9, and 10 address issues of conducting and reporting business research. Chapter 7 focuses on the research process itself. Chapters 8, 9, and 10 focus on using and presenting research (as well as other kinds of information) in proposals, reports, and presentations. All four chapters rely on the ACE process. This chapter pays particular attention to the analyzing phase, which is when research begins, as well as to evaluating—especially evaluating the credibility of sources and the usefulness of the research results.

Study Question 7.1

How do I determine what information I need?

■ Access this chapter's simulation entitled How to Find, Interpret, and Use Business Data Effectively, located at mybcommlab.com.

Because most business research starts with a specific question or problem, you will have a distinct advantage over someone writing an academic paper who starts with only a general research topic and needs to develop a research question. However, you will still benefit from following a structured process that helps you understand exactly what you are looking for and where to look for it.

As you read this chapter, keep the following research scenario in mind: Assume that you are Alan Cotton, Learning and Development Manager for Ipswich Brands, a large consumer product company with offices around the globe. You report to Mitchell Harris, Chief Learning Officer. Your department is responsible for orienting new employees and providing training and professional development opportunities for employees in all the company's offices. Specific tasks include designing instructional materials, organizing training sessions, training new trainers, maintaining employee training records, and providing data for supervisors to use during performance reviews.

Currently, the company's system for managing these tasks is expensive and inefficient. All training is conducted face-to-face, with trainers traveling to the specific offices or employees traveling to a central location. In addition, all training schedules and records exist only on one central computer at the company's headquarters. To reduce costs and improve efficiency, you suggest that the company invest in a learning management system (LMS) that will allow the company to provide some training online as well as manage all the content and record keeping for the system. Mitchell thinks it's a great idea and asks you to research and recommend a learning management system. He gives you four weeks to complete this project.

You have a lot of research ahead of you before you can determine which system to recommend. Here are some of the specific questions you will need to answer:

- What are the major differences between the types of learning management systems: products primarily used in academia (such as Blackboard or Desire2Learn), products specifically designed for business use (such as eLeaP and Plateau), and open source products that can be customized (such as Moodle and ATutor)?

- What criteria should you use to evaluate LMS packages?
- What are the experiences of other companies with specific LMS packages?
- What are the costs of different options?

As you research, you will think of other questions. Where do you find the data you need to answer all these questions? And once you find the data, how do you evaluate whether the information is useful?

Analyze the research question and topic

Be sure you have a good understanding of your major research question or problem as well as the assumptions it is based upon. You may need to broaden the question to find the information you need. For example, in the Ipswich Brands scenario, Mitchell Harris asked you to research which learning management system is best for the company. This question assumes that a learning management system in general is the best solution to the problem of excess training expense and inefficient content management and record keeping. Perhaps a different kind of solution may be better. Based on this analysis, you might broaden your research questions to include those illustrated in FIGURE 7.1. Notice that each research question also includes subquestions that you will need to explore to answer your main question.

Research Question 1:	**Would a learning management system (LMS) be an effective tool for our company?**
	• What specific training and content management needs does our company have?
	• What current problems are we facing?
	• What are options for solving these problems?
	• Is an LMS the best option?
Research Question 2:	**If an LMS would be effective, which one is the best option to meet our specific training needs?**
	• What are the various options for LMS programs?
	• What criteria will we use to judge the options?
	• Which option best meets the criteria?
Research Question 3:	**What will be the cost of the recommended option?**
	• What is the initial purchase and installation cost?
	• What are the ongoing costs, such as customer support?

FIGURE 7.1
Questions to Guide LMS Research

Before doing in-depth research to explore these specific questions, it is also important to understand your general topic. You can do this through background research that helps you understand your topic's history, context and structure, and categories.[1] FIGURE 7.2 illustrates a set of background questions and then adapts those questions to apply to each learning management system. For your specific topic, you will need to decide which questions listed in the figure are most important.

You may not directly include the results of this background research in your final presentation or report. However, gaining a broader background understanding of your topic can help you structure your research. For example, doing background research on the various types of learning management systems may help you narrow your detailed research to focus on one particular type. Similarly, doing background research on the parts and functions of a learning management system may help you identify which functions—for example, online training or record keeping—are most important to your company.

Identify audience concerns and needs

What questions will your audience expect you to answer when you present the research? What sources will your audience expect you to consult? Taking the time to analyze the audience and other stakeholders enables you to consider the problem from their point of view and identify concerns that you will need to address. For example, in the LMS research, your primary audience is your supervisor, Mitchell Harris, who

FIGURE 7.2　Background Research Questions

History	When and why did X first develop?	When and why did learning management systems first develop?
	How has X developed over time?	How have learning management systems changed and why? What have been the biggest influences on these systems?
Context and Structure	How does X function as part of a larger context or system?	How does a learning management system fit into a larger system of workplace training and development? What role does it play in relationship to the other elements in the system?
	What else exists that serves similar purposes?	Instead of a learning management system, what else could help solve our problem?
	What are the parts of X and how do the parts fit and work together?	What are the various elements of a learning management system? How do all the parts work together?
Categories	What types or categories of X exist?	What kinds of learning management systems are there? How are they grouped, and why are they grouped that way?
	How do different types of X compare and contrast with each other?	How do typical academic learning management systems, like Blackboard and Desire2Learn, compare and contrast with those primarily used in the workplace, like ePlateau and NetLeap?

asked you to research LMS training options. You also have a secondary audience: the company's senior-level decision makers who will finance a learning management system. Additional stakeholders include the employees who will be affected by the integration of a learning management system (or other changes to the current training practices). To analyze the audience and stakeholders, ask yourself these questions:

- Who is the primary audience?
- Who is the secondary audience?
- Who else may be affected by this problem or decision?
- What does the audience already know? What do they need to know?
- What questions will your audience expect you to answer when you present the research?
- What sources will your audience expect you to consult?

That final question—what sources will your audience expect you to consult—is important for your credibility. If you perform a quick Google search or rely on a general and nonvalidated source like Wikipedia, even for background information, your audience may not respect your findings. A professional audience is more likely to value your information if you use professional and highly credible sources. These sources include journals and websites published by professional associations in the industry, research published in academic journals, books by reputable authors and publishers, and newspapers. For example, in researching options for learning management systems, your audience may expect you to consult:

- *T&D*, a journal published by the American Society for Training and Development (ASTD)
- *Training*, another journal in the training industry
- *Learning Circuits*, ASTD's website devoted to e-learning
- Books like *The E-Learning Handbook: A Comprehensive Guide to Online Learning* by Carliner and Shank
- The websites and marketing departments of each learning management system you are considering

Your audience may even expect you to conduct your own original research, such as interviewing people who have experience with your topic or surveying potential stakeholders.

Establish the scope of the research

The **scope** of a research study refers to the range of your research: how broad or narrow will it be? Establishing the scope is like looking through binoculars. You can choose to view the landscape of a large area (broad scope) or to focus on the details of a small object (narrow scope). In your LMS research, you may look broadly at the information about many LMS packages to determine if online content management and training would be an effective format for your company. However, to determine which system is the best option, you might have to narrow your focus to collect a lot of information about two or three packages.

Establishing the scope of your research also allows you to define the limitations of your research. **Limitations** are the characteristics of the research that prevent you from generalizing your findings more broadly. For example, if you choose to narrow the scope of your research to established LMS packages that have been widely used and reviewed rather than investigating new options, then you cannot generalize and say you have selected the best of all possible learning management systems—just the best widely reviewed system.

How do you decide on the scope of the research? The answer depends on the needs of the project, the amount of time available, and what you learn in your initial research. For example, if you have only a week to research learning management systems, you may limit your research to include only material that is available from companies and product reviews in professional journals. With more time available, you may choose to interview users of the programs. If you learn in your initial background research that only two programs seem appropriate for your company, then you may decide to narrow your research to focus deeply on those two programs.

Define research activities

Research activities are the steps you will take to answer the research questions. For example, how will you research the currently available learning management systems? How will you determine the most relevant criteria for judging the options? For each question, list possible steps you might take to find the necessary information. As you can tell from FIGURE 7.3, a list of research activities helps you identify sources for the information. Typically, sources fall into one of three categories: primary, secondary, and tertiary sources.

Primary sources provide raw data. You can collect primary data by surveying, interviewing, or observing people. If you survey users of different learning management systems, you are conducting primary research. Another form of primary research involves reading primary texts—such as texts written by the subjects you are researching—for example the websites and marketing materials of various LMS providers. Primary research may be quantitative or qualitative. **Quantitative research** gathers numerical data, such as structured survey responses to which you can assign numbers. Quantitative research allows you to classify, count, and compare, and thus identify patterns. By contrast, **qualitative research** gathers data in the form of open-ended responses and observations that provide insights into the attitudes, values, and concerns of the research subjects.

Secondary sources are the results of other people's research. You may find this research in articles, books, or research reports, usually written by the researchers themselves. If you find a journal article comparing three learning management systems, that is a secondary source.

Tertiary sources are books and articles that synthesize material from secondary sources, framing them for general readers. Tertiary sources include encyclopedias, textbooks, online tools like Wikipedia, and the results of most standard web searches. Sources like these are often very good for background research. However, they may oversimplify the research they present. You will have more credibility if you try to find the original material that these sources summarize.

For the lpswich Brands LMS project, you will need to do a good deal of primary research. For example, you could read websites and marketing materials of several learning management systems, speak to salespeople, interview users of these systems, and interview people within your organization to identify criteria for judging the options. Good secondary sources will also make your job easier. If you can find reviews of different systems or case studies describing how people have used learning management systems, you

Scope The range of your research: a broad scope includes a wide range of content, while a narrow scope focuses on specific aspects of the topic.

Limitations The characteristics of the research that prevent you from generalizing your findings more broadly.

Primary sources Sources from which you collect your own raw data.

Quantitative research Research that relies on numerical data, such as that gathered from structured survey responses to which you can assign numbers.

Qualitative research Research that provides insight into the attitudes, values, and concerns of research subjects through interviews and observation.

Secondary sources The results of other people's research that you consult as part of your research.

Tertiary sources Books and articles that synthesize material from secondary sources.

FIGURE 7.3 Examples of Research Activities to Answer Research Questions

Research Question 1:   Would an LMS be an effective training tool for the company?

SPECIFIC QUESTION	RESEARCH ACTIVITY
What specific training and content management needs does our company have?	Interview department heads in the company.
What current problems are we facing?	Interview the chief learning officer and department heads.
What are alternatives/options for solving these problems?	Survey other companies and research training and education journals, books, and websites.
Is an LMS the best option?	Compare options against the company's training needs.

Research Question 2:   If an LMS would be effective, which one is the best option to meet the company's specific training needs?

SPECIFIC QUESTION	RESEARCH ACTIVITY
What are the various options for LMS programs?	Review training and education journals, books, and websites. Do a web search for LMS programs. Speak to other companies in the industry.
What criteria will we use to judge the options?	Interview chief learning officer and department heads.
Which option best meets the criteria?	Conduct a comparative analysis to compare alternatives against selected criteria.

Research Question 3:   What will be the cost of the selected option?

SPECIFIC QUESTION	RESEARCH ACTIVITY
What is the initial purchase and installation cost?	Speak to the sales department of the selected company.
What are the ongoing costs, such as customer support?	Speak to sales department of the selected company. Interview other companies using the system.

will be able to save time. Although you should not rely on the material from a tertiary source—like a Wikipedia article on learning management systems—quickly reading that article or a summary article on the ASTD website may be a good place to get background information or a list of other resources to consult.

Develop a work plan

The last step before beginning your research is to develop a work plan like that illustrated in FIGURE 7.4 to help you track your progress over time and ensure you meet deadlines. Although you may need to modify your work plan as you discover new information and find alternative solutions to your problem, an initial plan helps you focus on the project. The work plan in Figure 7.4 spreads the research over three weeks, leaving you one week to prepare your presentation. The plan begins with the research questions, which form the basis for the research activities. From there, you can chart your goals for determining key findings, implications, conclusions, and recommendations.

Figure 7.4 provides a closeup view of the first three columns of the work plan. You will notice that it lists the tasks by question, not by sequential due date because you may conduct several research tasks concurrently, during the same week. In addition, if you are already interviewing people in other companies to find out how they handle training and record keeping (Research Question 1), you may also want to find out what specific learning management system they use (Research Question 2) and what the costs are (Research Question 3).

The work plan also creates space for recording results. This will help you organize your final report or presentation. By taking the time to organize your data as you analyze it, you will be better prepared to translate it into meaningful information that effectively answers your research questions. You may need to create a modified version of the table to fit your notes. The next sections describe where you can find sources of information to fill in the work plan.

FIGURE 7.4 Developing a Work Plan

RESEARCH QUESTIONS	RESEARCH ACTIVITIES	TARGET DATE	KEY FINDINGS	IMPLICATIONS/ CONCLUSIONS	RECOMMENDA-TIONS

RESEARCH QUESTIONS	RESEARCH ACTIVITIES	TARGET DATE
Background Research • What are the various types of learning management and course management systems? • How do the types compare? • What are the various elements of a system and how do they work?	Research training and education journals, books, and websites.	Weeks 1–2
	Find and interview LMS expert.	Week 1
1. Would an LMS be an effective training tool for our company? • What specific training and content management needs does our company have? • What current problems are we facing? • What are alternatives/options for solving these problems? • Is an LMS the best option?	Interview the company's chief learning officer and department heads.	Week 2
	Survey or interview other companies.	Week 2
	Research training and education journals, books, and websites.	Weeks 1–2
	Compare options against company's training needs.	Week 2
2. If an LMS would be effective, which one is the best option to meet our specific training needs? • What are the various options for LMS programs? • What criteria will we use to judge the options? • Which option best meets the criteria?	Review training and education journals, books, and websites.	Week 1
	Do a web search for LMS programs.	Week 1
	Speak to other companies in the industry.	Week 2
	Interview chief learning officer and department heads.	Week 1
	Conduct a detailed comparative analysis.	Week 3
	Compare alternatives against selection criteria.	Week 3
3. What is the cost of the selected option? • What are the initial purchase and installation costs? • What are the ongoing costs, such as customer support?	Speak to the sales department of selected company.	Week 3
	Interview other companies using the system.	Week 3

PEARSON
mybcommlab

Apply Figure 7.4's key concepts by revising a new document. Go to Chapter 7 in mybcommlab.com and select Document Makeovers.

Study Question 7.2

How do I conduct and evaluate research in print and online sources?

Many students use only Google when conducting research. This is a shortsighted approach since you will not be able to find all the information you need through a web search, and many sources you do find will not be relevant or useful. Finding the best information requires you to use a variety of research tools and methods.

To be an efficient researcher, you need to learn how to:

• search the web strategically
• use an online index or database to find articles from print publications

- use a library or bookseller to find relevant books
- follow leads in good sources
- evaluate your sources for credibility

This section presents many different types of search tools. FIGURE 7.5 summarizes these different tools and identifies what you can find with each.

FIGURE 7.5 Tools for Finding Research Sources

TOOL . . .	SUCH AS . . .	SEARCHES . . .	TO FIND . . .
General Search Engine	Google, Yahoo, Bing	Web	Publicly available content
Deep Web Search Engine	Science.gov, Biznar.com	Web	Specialized content on the web, often not accessible through a general search engine
Online Publication Index	New York Times Index	One publication, such as the *New York Times*	Articles in that publication
Online Article Database	Ebsco Business Source Premier Lexis/Nexis Sociological Abstracts	Abstracts and full texts of thousands of publications, gathered together in the database	Articles originally published in print journals, magazines, and newspapers
Online Business Research Tools	Thomson One Banker IBIS World Hoover's Standard and Poor's Yahoo Finance	Corporate and industry research reports from various sources	Company, industry, and market data
Library Online Catalog	Northwestern University NUCat University of Michigan Mirlyn University of Wisconsin MadCat	The library's paper and electronic holdings	Books and other publications available through that library
Online Bookstore	Amazon.com, Borders.com	Books available through that online bookstore and other used booksellers	Books available for sale

Search the web strategically

A basic search engine, like Google, Bing, Yahoo, or AltaVista, indexes sites throughout the web. When you type search terms into the engine, it links you to sites that use those terms. The sites that appear at the top or on the side of the results page are usually those whose organizations have paid a fee to be featured in the search results. The main body of the results page begins with sites that are frequently accessed or that most closely match your search terms. As you go further into the list, the results are likely to be less relevant.

Although searching the web seems easy, finding useful information is challenging. A Google search for the words *"learning management systems"* returns more than 56 million results. Which ones will be relevant to you? The following search tips will help narrow your search.

- **Use quotation marks around your phrase.** If you need an exact match, use quotation marks around your key word or phrase. For example, keying *"learning management systems"* will result in a list of resources that include the exact phrase rather than sites that include those three words anywhere on the page. This reduces the results from 56 million to 790,000.
- **Add more words to the search.** Think of words that you believe must be included on a website that is relevant to your research, and add that word to your search

terms. Keying *"learning management system"* and *corporate* will give you only sites that include both phrases. This will get you closer to your goal. If you would like only corporate systems that offer "assessment" features, add that term to your search. If you want to find articles that compare *"learning management systems"* and *"course management systems,"* perform a search using both phrases, each in its own set of quotation marks. If you would like to see if specific companies use a learning management system, then search for that company's name along with "learning management system."

- **Exclude words from the search.** Using the minus symbol (–) before a search term tells a search engine to exclude pages that mention that term. If you want to find information about learning management systems that do not use open source software, try this search string: *"learning management system" –"open source."*

- **Use wildcards.** When you play a card game, a designated wildcard can represent any other card in the deck. When you conduct a search in most web search engines, you can use an asterisk (*) as a wildcard symbol within a phrase to represent an unknown word. For example, if you would like to find websites about companies that have selected the specific learning management system Plateau, try constructing a search using a short sentence like this: *"* selects Plateau."* This search will yield websites that include this short sentence, no matter what the first word is—for example "Internal Revenue Service selects Plateau" or "General Electric selects Plateau." Vary the wording and word order of that sentence to provide even more results. Using the search string *"* chooses Plateau"* yields different results, for example, "Singapore Airlines chooses Plateau."

- **Use Boolean operators.** In many search engines, you can use the words AND, OR, and NOT (spelled in ALL CAPS and called Boolean operators after mathematician George Boole) along with key words to expand or reduce your search results. For example, results from a search on *"learning management" AND "system"* would include only pages that contained both "learning management" and "system." However, searching for *"learning management" AND (system OR software)* would result in pages that contained the phrase "learning management" with either the word "system" or the word "software," which would provide a much longer list of results.

- **Use synonyms or alternative wording.** As you search the web, pay attention to terms that are frequently used to discuss your subject, and conduct a web search for those terms. For example, discussions of "learning management systems" often use the term "e-learning." You can conduct a search using that term itself.

- **Search for specific file types.** In addition to websites, you can also search for documents that are on the web, such as PDF (Portable Document Format) files, using the advanced search functions of most search engines. On Google, for example, you can search *"learning management system" filetype:pdf.* Similarly, to find Word documents, search *"learning management system" filetype:doc.* Using specific file types in your search may help you find additional articles, documents, or case studies published by reputable organizations.

- **Search for expert blogs.** Many experts write and publish blogs on their topics of expertise. Reading those blogs is similar to interviewing experts. To find those blogs, you can type into the search engine the name of your subject plus the word "blog." Be sure to read the author's biographical profile to ensure that he or she has professional credentials and is an expert.

Use an online index or database to find articles and business data

Almost every academic and public library purchases subscriptions to specific publications like the *Wall Street Journal* and the *Journal of International Business Studies.* They also purchase subscriptions to online databases, such as Lexis-Nexis, that collect articles from thousands of publications, including newspapers like the *New York*

TECHNOLOGY   Going beneath the Surface of the Web

An enormous amount of information is available to researchers through the web, but not all of that information is easy to find. Most people rely on search engines like Google and Yahoo! to find web-based information. However, those search engines gather information from the surface of the web, which is just a small percentage of what is available. As a researcher, you will want to go more deeply into the web, finding not just free information aimed at the public and consumers, but also information aimed at professionals and information in publications that require a subscription. To find that information, familiarize yourself with *deep web* portals.[2]

Deep web portals perform *federated searches*. These search engines select several very useful databases available on the web and conduct your search on those databases. By doing this, they provide high-quality research knowledge designed for professionals.

For business research, you will find three deep web portals particularly useful:

- **Biznar.** This site is designed for professional business researchers and searches highly credible sources.

- **Science.gov.** This database provides access to federally sponsored research on almost any topic.

- **ipl2.** This merger of two portals—the Librarian's Internet Index and the Internet Public Library—provides access to

trustworthy websites on a number of topics, including business.

For example, imagine you work for a real estate development company interested in incorporating solar power in the new houses it builds. You have been asked to research cost-effective options for solar power. If you conduct a Google search for "cost-effective solar power," you will find websites that offer devices for sale, blog entries about solar power, articles about installing solar power published on "how to" websites, and many other links that may not be useful. By contrast, if you search the same topic on science.gov, you will find material from the U.S. Department of Energy and the journal *Electric Light and Power*. This material is typically well-researched and designed for professional audiences.

Even when using material found through the reliable deep web portals, you need to verify the credibility and objectivity of the source. For example, you can go to the website of *Electric Light and Power* so that you are knowledgeable about the magazine and the types of articles it publishes.

mybcommlab

For TECHNOLOGY exercises, go to Exercise 6 on page 246 and Exercise 29c on page 250 or to this chapter's End-of-Chapter Exercises at mybcommlab.com.

Times, magazines like *Business Week*, professional publications (also called trade journals) like *Financial News*, and academic journals like *Alt-J: Research in Learning Technology*. Articles from these publications are not available through a Google search because they require a paid subscription.

These articles are regarded as more reliable than websites because editors carefully review them. Articles in academic journals offer another advantage: they are both written and peer reviewed by professionals in the field. The *peer review* process is designed to ensure that articles are accurate and honest.

You can check with your university or public library to learn what online databases are available. Searching for articles in these databases resembles searching the web. You must use good search terms to get relevant results. In addition, database searches allow you to limit results even further by identifying important characteristics of the articles. For example, you can specify that you want only articles that are peer reviewed, published within a certain date range, and available in full text online. FIGURE 7.6 illustrates search results from one widely available database, *Business Source Premier*.

You can also use online databases and other research tools to find business data and analyses. For example, research organizations, such as Standard & Poor's, Hoover's, and Thomson publish in-depth financial data about companies, markets, and industries. You can access some of this data on the web through publicly available tools, including Yahoo! Finance. Other data will be available only through a library subscription. If your library subscribes to Lexis-Nexis Academic, then you will have access to the data and analyses published by Standard & Poor's and Hoover's.

FIGURE 7.6 Searching an Online Database
Image courtesy of EBSCO Publishing.

Enter key terms ("corporate" and "e-learning") into the search box.

Check the "full text" box to limit your search to articles that have full text available in the database. For some articles, the database may include only abstracts.

The results list identifies the name of the article, authors, and other publication information. Links provide access to the full text of the article.

The database will also generate a fully formatted citation that you can cut and paste into your reference list.

Use a library or bookseller to find relevant books

Because the web contains so much information, students often neglect to search for books. However, books—like print articles—can be more valuable than online resources because books are often professionally reviewed, edited, and produced by reputable authors and publishing companies with established credibility. By contrast, anyone can post resources online about nearly anything. The drawback with books is that they may become outdated more quickly than online content, which can be updated regularly.

To find books that remain relevant and timely, your first stop may be your library's online catalog. The catalog will probably allow you to do a key word search using many of the same techniques you use for a web search. If you find one book that seems relevant to your research, check the online record to see what broader subject categories are associated with that book, and then search for other books in the same category. You may find it equally useful to browse through the library bookshelves. If you find one book that looks useful, go to its location in the library and look at other books in the same section.

The advantage of looking at books in a school library is that the librarians and faculty have determined those books are worthy of being in the library's collection. The disadvantage is that libraries rarely have the newest books since it often takes a long time for a library to acquire a book. For more recent books, try searching the websites of online booksellers like amazon.com or barnesandnoble.com. For example, a quick search for "learning management systems" at amazon.com results in several titles, including *Return on Learning: Training for High Performance at Accenture* and *iLearning: How to Create an Innovative Learning Organization.* If your library does not own the book—and you cannot buy it—you may be able to ask your library to borrow it from another library.

Follow leads in good sources

If you find a good book or article on your subject, check the bibliography or reference list to find additional resources for your research. For example, if you read an interesting article in the journal *Chief Learning Officer* about transitioning an organization from traditional to online learning, look at the article's references. If the article was valuable to your research, the references used to write the article might also be useful. As you browse through the library, check the bibliographies of the books you find. You may see references to other books and articles you should read.

Evaluate your sources for credibility

Even after narrowing your search results, you are often left with thousands of options. How do you decide which resources to use? No matter what kind of source you find—print or electronic—you must evaluate it for credibility. Is the information timely? Is it factual or opinion-based? Is any research well documented? Are the author and publisher respected by others? To determine the reliability and relevance of a source, use the *3 A's: Authorship, Accuracy, and Age.*

Authorship: Can you trust the author and publisher?

- If your source is a website, does it identify the author?
- Whether on the web, in an article, or in a book, is the author qualified or an expert in this content? Check the author's biography.
- Is the source published by a reputable press, or is the website sponsored by a reputable organization? On the web, you can generally feel confident about information that is published by the government and universities. If you are unfamiliar with an organization that publishes information you would like to use, read more about that organization to determine whether it is respected by others and considered reputable.
- Does the author provide support for claims, or is the text mostly unsupported opinions? Unsupported opinions are less credible than arguments supported by evidence.

Accuracy: Can you trust the information?

- Was the book or article peer reviewed? If a text has been reviewed by other experts before publication, the result is likely to be more accurate.
- Do others frequently cite the source? You can find out by using a citation index such as Social Science Citation Index, ISI Science Citation, or Google Scholar (scholar.google.com).
- Do other sources agree with this information?
- Does the author acknowledge and respond to opposing points of view?
- Does the author cite sources for numbers, facts, or research findings? Or does the author expect you to take his or her word for the data?

Age: Is the information current or still relevant?

- How current is this information? If you're researching a technology topic, the material needs to be very current. By contrast, if you're researching an issue in business ethics, the source may offer useful perspectives even if decades old.

- Does the source provide a last-updated date or copyright?
- Are any web links broken (often indicating an outdated page)?

Evaluating sources using these criteria—authorship, accuracy, and age—helps you decide whether a source is useful and what to use it for. FIGURE 7.7 illustrates an evaluation of three articles on learning management systems. Article 1 is a *white paper*—that is, a report produced by a company or organization to educate readers about a complex business issue, product, or technology. White papers are potentially biased because they may promote the organization's own products. In addition, this white paper is too old to cite as factual. Article 2 is more credible because it is both relatively recent and is published by a highly respected, unbiased organization. Article 3 may be worth citing because it is the very recent opinion of an acknowledged expert.

FIGURE 7.7 Evaluation of Three Articles

SOURCE	EVALUATION	DECISION
Article 1: White Paper Element K. (2003). *Learning management systems in the work environment: Practical considerations for the selection and implementation of an e-learning platform.* [White paper]. Rochester, NY: Element K.	**AUTHORSHIP** Element K—a training and development organization that implements learning solutions for its clients **ACCURACY** • Includes citations • Is cited in several peer-reviewed articles • May be biased because Element K sells learning management systems **AGE** Not a recent source	This article is too old to cite as factual on this topic, since learning management systems change quickly. In addition, the article is probably biased toward certain LMS systems. However, it may provide useful background information.
Article 2: Research Report Schooley, C. (2007, October 24). *How to select a learning management system.* [Research report]. Cambridge, MA: Forrester Research.	**AUTHORSHIP** Forrester Research, an independent research company. Forrester sells this research report for $499 **ACCURACY** • Cited in at least one peer-reviewed article • Includes citations **AGE** Published more recently than Article 1	This research report is fairly recent and probably unbiased. Forrester Research is well-respected. This is a good study to understand criteria for selecting a system. It is not a good study to compare actual systems, since the systems may have changed since 2007.
Article 3: Blog Entry Siemens, G. (2009, November 10). Future of learning: LMS or SNS. [Web log message]. Retrieved from http://connectivism.ca	**AUTHORSHIP** George Siemens, an Associate Director at the Learning Technologies Centre of University of Manitoba, author of *Knowing Knowledge*, President of Complexive Systems, Inc., a learning lab focused on assisting organizations develop integrated learning **ACCURACY** Represents the opinion of an acknowledged expert so this opinion is worth considering **AGE** Published most recently	Because Siemens is an expert in the field, his speculations about LMS systems may be worth including. It is important to acknowledge they are just speculations.

Currently, more than 195 countries and independent territories exist in the world.[3] Spread among these countries, people belong to hundreds of different cultures and speak approximately 7,000 languages and dialects.[4] With all of this diversity, preparing yourself to work internationally or in a multicultural workforce is a huge task.

You cannot anticipate all the countries and cultures you may need to know about during your career. Fortunately, the web will make this information easy to find when you need it, if you know how to look for it. Specific websites will change over the years. However, as this chapter discusses, you can find the information you need by using effective search terms.

The following table provides four sets of search terms and examples of resources you can find using these terms. These sites can help you begin your research on doing business and communicating with people around the world. Visit mybcommlab.com for links to the websites described. By using these and similar sets of search terms, you will be able to find additional resources on your own.

PEARSON
mybcommlab

For CULTURE exercises, go to Exercises 25 and 26 on page 249 and Exercise 29d on page 250 or to this chapter's End-of-Chapter Exercises at mybcommlab.com.

SEARCH TERMS: "INTERNATIONAL BUSINESS CULTURE"

RESOURCE	CREATED BY	WHAT YOU WILL FIND
Dialogin	Delta Intercultural Academy, a "knowledge community on culture and communication in international business"	Articles, discussion forums, and a knowledge base on intercultural communication
Geert Hofstede's Cultural Dimensions	Geert Hofstede, an intercultural expert	A powerful framework for analyzing cultures and helping individuals identify how to work with other cultures

SEARCH TERMS: "INTERNATIONAL BUSINESS STATISTICS"

RESOURCE	CREATED BY	WHAT YOU WILL FIND
GlobalEDGE™	International Business Center at Michigan State University and partly funded by the U.S. Department of Education	A knowledge web portal that connects international business professionals worldwide to a wealth of information, insights, and learning resources on global business activities
The CIA World Factbook	United States Central Intelligence Agency	A broad range of statistical data and information about the countries of the world produced primarily for government use but freely available to everyone

SEARCH TERMS: "GLOBAL BUSINESS COMMUNICATION"

RESOURCE	CREATED BY	WHAT YOU WILL FIND
Global Business Perspectives	Beverly Cornell, a global business consultant	A compilation of articles and podcasts on doing business globally and in specific countries
International Business Center	International Business Center, a not-for-profit organization	A series of excellent resources for international businesspeople, international business students, and teachers and professors at international business schools throughout the world

SEARCH TERMS: "INTERNATIONAL BUSINESS ETIQUETTE"

RESOURCE	CREATED BY	WHAT YOU WILL FIND
International Business Etiquette and Manners	Global Leadership MBA Graduates from University of Texas—Dallas	Analysis of business etiquette in more than 30 countries around the world
Executive Planet	International Business Center, a not-for-profit organization	A wiki where experts in specific cultures provide advice about communicating and conducting business in those cultures

How do I conduct and evaluate primary research?

Some research questions or problems require that you conduct your own original, or primary, research. Imagine that you want to know which learning management systems are used most widely in your industry. If no one else has already done this research, you may decide to compose a *survey*—or standardized questionnaire—to distribute to the head of training of each company in your industry. You may also want to *interview* content experts to get their in-depth thoughts about various systems. Finally, imagine that you want to know whether it will be difficult for new managers to learn how to use a specific learning management system for performance evaluations. Rather than ask the managers how difficult they think the process will be, you might conduct *observational research*. You could get a trial version of the software, input trial data, ask specific managers to do a task with the data, and observe them as they do this task, noting any problems that need to be addressed.

Each of the three types of research—survey, interview, and observation—is widely used in business. The sections that follow introduce you to all three methods. However, if you are working on an extensive project that requires you to become very skilled at any of these approaches, you may need to take a course or read a text in research methods.

Conduct survey research to gather information that is easy to compare

Survey research uses a predetermined list of questions, also known as a *survey instrument*, to collect a structured set of information from a selected audience. Surveys allow you to compare the number of participants who respond in specific ways.

To analyze whether survey research will be useful, you first need to determine what data you need to gather and from whom. As you'll recall from Figure 7.1 on page 219, our three main research questions about learning management systems are the following:

Research Question 1: Would a learning management system be an effective training tool for our company?

Research Question 2: If a learning management system would be effective, which one is the best option to meet our specific training needs?

Research Question 3: What will be the cost of the recommended option?

A survey asking employees and managers their opinions about Questions 1 and 2 will not be useful. Their responses would simply give you a set of vague and general opinions without any detailed explanation to help you analyze them. However, as you consider how to answer Question 2, you may decide to survey employees to learn about their prior work experiences with specific learning management systems. Such a survey can provide information about what systems are used in other companies, how they are used, and how employees respond to the systems.

To administer a survey like this, you will need to decide which people to survey, how to word the questions, how to administer the survey, and how to analyze the results.

Choose which people to survey

The audience from whom you want to collect survey responses is your **survey population**. Oftentimes, you cannot survey the entire population because there are simply too many people to contact. In these cases, you can identify a **sample** or a representative portion of your population. Different kinds of samples can be used for different purposes. For example, if you determine that it would be easier or that you would get a better response rate by surveying the employees in your building rather than all the branches across the country, you would be using a **convenience sample**—a sample selected because you have easy access to that population. However, if you do most of your training with new hires, you could survey employees who were hired within the last year, which would be a **targeted sample** restricted to that specific group. Keep in mind that your ability to generalize your findings to the larger population may be limited by using a convenience or targeted sample. If you need to generalize to everyone, the best alternative is to use a **random sample** selected broadly from all available members of the population you want to study. A sample

Survey A predetermined list of questions used to collect a structured set of information from a selected audience.

Survey population The audience from whom you want to collect survey responses.

Sample A representative portion of your population.

Convenience sample A survey population selected because you have easy access to that group.

Targeted sample A sample that consists of only specific people from the group you are studying.

Random sample A population selected broadly from all available members of the population you want to study.

is random when every member of the population has an equal chance of being selected. For example, if you want to survey all 500 employees in a company, you could generate an alphabetical list and distribute a survey to every second person on the list. A random sample increases the likelihood that the responses will be statistically valid and accurately represent the larger population.

Decide on a survey medium

To select a medium for delivering your survey questions to your participants, consider the advantages and disadvantages of the various options in FIGURE 7.8.

FIGURE 7.8 Selecting the Best Medium for Survey Research

ADVANTAGES	DISADVANTAGES
FACE-TO-FACE SURVEYS	
• Increase likelihood that participants will respond because you contact them personally • Allow participants to ask clarifying questions	• Are time-consuming to conduct • Require researcher and respondent to be in the same place at the same time • Require researcher to enter results into a spreadsheet or tabulate them manually
TELEPHONE SURVEYS	
• Increase likelihood that participants will respond because you contact them personally • Allow participants to ask clarifying questions	• Are time-consuming to conduct • Require researcher to enter results into a spreadsheet or tabulate them manually
MAIL SURVEYS	
• Project a professional image and as a result may encourage participants to respond	• Require researcher to find participants' mailing addresses and prepare mass mailing • Incur postage costs for mailing and for return mail • May be ignored by participants • Require participant to mail responses back to researcher • Require researcher to enter results into a spreadsheet or tabulate them manually
EMAIL SURVEYS	
• Are easy to disseminate and to access • Allow participants to contact researcher with questions, through a link in the email • Cost little or nothing to distribute	• Require researcher to find participants' email addresses • May be ignored by participants • Require participants to email back
WEB SURVEYS	
• Are easy to disseminate and access through emailed link • Allow participants to contact researcher with questions, through a link on the website • Cost little or nothing to distribute • Do not require researchers to enter data manually • May automatically tabulate results, analyze data, and provide easy-to-read data graphics	• Require researcher to find participants' email addresses to send link to web survey • May require researcher to pay for survey tool • May be ignored by participants

Compose effective survey questions

To determine the content of your survey questions, use your broader research questions as a guide. For example, if you want to determine which learning management system would be most effective, you might ask your survey population how satisfied they were with systems they used in the past. Once you know what you want to ask, the next step is to determine how to write questions so that you get the information you need. Avoid ambiguous questions that can be interpreted in multiple ways. For instance, don't ask, "How would you rate the learning management system?" because you will have no way of knowing what criteria the respondent is using for the rating. To fix this problem, identify the criteria for their response such as, "how would you rate the effectiveness of the online training you have taken compared to traditional face-to-face training?" To ensure your survey questions are effective, you can pilot test them with a focus group before distributing the survey.

FIGURE 7.9 shows examples of several survey question formats. Examples include questions that require respondents to select a specific response (yes or no), rate or rank

FIGURE 7.9 Five Types of Survey Questions

YES/NO
Have you used a learning management system (LMS) for training in any of your prior work experiences?
○ Yes   ○ No

MULTIPLE CHOICE
If yes, how would you rate your satisfaction with the effectiveness of the online training you have taken compared to traditional face-to-face training?
○ = More satisfied with LMS for ALL learning experiences
○ = More satisfied with LMS for MOST learning experiences
○ = Neither more satisfied nor more dissatisfied with LMS
○ = Less satisfied with LMS for MOST learning experiences
○ = Less satisfied with LMS for ALL learning experiences

LIKERT (AGREEMENT) SCALE
For each statement, indicate to what extent you agree with the statement:

If the company adopts an online LMS option . . .	Strongly Disagree	Disagree	Neutral	Agree	Strongly Agree
it would improve our company's overall training experience.	○	○	○	○	○
I might sign up for more elective training sessions.	○	○	○	○	○
I would miss the social interaction of meeting employees from other branches.	○	○	○	○	○

RATING SCALE
If you have experience with any of the following LMS systems, please rate how strongly you recommend that Ipswich Brands adopt it, on a scale of 1 to 10. A score of 1 indicates you do not recommend the product, and a score of 10 indicates that you strongly recommend the product.

If the company adopts an online LMS option . . .	Do Not Recommend				Neutral				Strongly Recommend	
A2Z	1	2	3	4	5	6	7	8	9	10
Eclipse	1	2	3	4	5	6	7	8	9	10
Teach2Me	1	2	3	4	5	6	7	8	9	10

OPEN ENDED
If you recommend an LMS based on your experience, please provide the name of the LMS: _____

listed options, or assign a value to a statement. Your survey may include a variety of question formats, or you might find that one format, such as multiple choice, works well to gather data that answer your research questions.

Many surveys also request demographic information that allows you to categorize respondents' answers in relevant ways. For example, in some surveys, you may find it relevant to ask participants about their age or where they live. For this LMS survey, however, age and location are not relevant. Instead, you might ask a question about when the participants joined the company and how many training courses they have taken.

Analyze, interpret, and evaluate results

After the survey is completed, you need to count, summarize, and analyze the responses. For each question, you will need to decide which measures to use to report responses: percentage, range, mean, median, mode, or the total count, called "n" for "number."

For some questions, percentage and total count are the most logical data to report. Consider, for example, the yes/no question in Figure 7.9:

> "Have you used a learning management system for training in any of your prior work experiences?   ○ Yes   ○ No"

You would report the percentage of people who have used a system in the past. This percentage lets you know whether most people or very few people in the population have LMS experience. You also want to know exactly how many people this percentage represents. If only 20 percent of the 130 people surveyed have LMS experience, you will have data from only 26 people. You will need this total count information to analyze the results of later questions, like the multiple-choice question in Figure 7.9 that asks,

> "If yes, how would you rate your satisfaction with the effectiveness of the online training you have taken compared to traditional face-to-face training?"

When you analyze the answers, you will need to know that only 26 people are qualified to answer this question. If you report the multiple-choice results of this question as percentages, you will need to acknowledge that these are percentages of 26, a very small number.

Other questions require data relating to averages: range, mean, medium, and mode. For example, consider the rating scale question in Figure 7.9:

> "If you have experience with any of the following learning management systems, please rate how strongly you recommend that Ipswich Brands adopt it, on a scale of 1 to 10. A score of 1 indicates you do not recommend the product, and a score of 10 indicates that you strongly recommend the product."

Assume you received responses from 26 employees, summarized in FIGURE 7.10. The different measures provide different information about the data.

According to Figure 7.10, 11 employees, or 42 percent of the total number of people who responded, indicated experience with A2Z Systems. The **range**—the span between the highest and lowest values—demonstrates that their responses varied greatly. Some people ranked A2Z poorly, but other people ranked it fairly well. The ranges for the other two products indicate a narrow distribution, indicating more consistent perceptions among the employees.

The **mean** is the average and is determined by adding all the responses and dividing the sum by the number of responses. Although Teach2Me has the highest mean, only five people (19 percent) had experience with that system. The high mean would inspire more confidence if it represented the opinion of more people. The **median** is the number that represents the middle of the responses or the most central number. Although the median and mean are the same for two of the products, the median is slightly higher for A2Z Systems, which indicates that more people responded

FIGURE 7.10 Responses to Rating Scale Question in Figure 7.9

	A2Z SYSTEMS	ECLIPSE SOFTWARE	TEACH2ME
Employee Ratings	1, 1, 1, 3, 6, 6, 7, 7, 8, 8, 9	5, 5, 5, 6, 6, 6, 7, 7, 7, 7	8, 9, 9, 9, 10
Number of Responses*	n = 11 (42%)	n = 10 (38%)	n = 5 (19%)
Range	1–9	5–7	8–10
Mean	5	6	9
Median	6	6	9
Mode	1	7	9

*Total does not add to 100% because of rounding.

above the average than below. The **mode** is the number that most frequently appears in the distribution. Although the mode is not typically calculated for survey data, you may find the mode useful to help you differentiate between items that have similar means or similar medians. For example, in Figure 7.10, the median rating for both A2Z and Eclipse is 6. However, the two programs have very different modes. For A2Z, the mode is 1, meaning that the program received more 1s or "do not recommend" than any other rating. By contrast, the mode for Eclipse is much higher, 7, reflecting a stronger recommendation for the product.

In addition to analyzing the survey results, you also need to evaluate them to determine how you can best represent them. You may not feel confident about using your survey results if you did not get enough responses or responses from the right people. Even if you feel confident about your responses, you need to evaluate what you can say about them. Assume that your company has 130 employees and you received 80 responses, with 26 responses from employees who indicated experience with the three learning management systems you are considering. Can you say 20 percent of employees (26 out of 130) have experience with one of the three systems? Or is it more accurate to say 33 percent of the employees who responded (26 out of 80) have experience with one of the three systems?

Conduct interview research to gather in-depth information

An **interview** is a discussion between two or more people, usually in a question-and-answer format. The interviewer asks questions and records the interviewee's responses. You can also conduct an interview by email, especially if you have only a few questions to ask.

Interviews have at least one significant benefit compared to surveys. While survey research gives you numbers to analyze, it does not give you the opportunity to delve deeply into the answers. By contrast, interview research allows you to get richer, more detailed information because interviewees are not limited to predefined responses. In fact, your preplanned questions are often just a starting point that can lead to discussions you might not predict. However, interviews are more time consuming than surveys. For example, it would take you a lot longer to interview each of the 80 people who responded to the LMS survey than simply distributing the survey questions.

Depending on the research questions you need to answer, consider interviewing content experts, employees, customers, or product users. Experts can include authors of the books or articles you read, columnists who publish related blogs, and people who post comments to community message boards. In many cases, authors provide their contact information or at least their email addresses. An email posing a specific question could result in a specific answer, while a conversation may allow a more in-depth discussion.

Range The span between the highest and lowest values.

Mean The average derived by adding all responses and dividing the sum by the number of responses.

Median The number that represents the middle number in a distribution or the most central number.

Mode The number that most frequently appears in a distribution.

Interview A research method involving a structured discussion between two or more people, usually in a question-and-answer format.

For the learning management systems research, interviews are a key element of the work plan illustrated in Figure 7.4 on page 223. The plan calls for you to find appropriate people in other companies and interview them about their experiences with learning management systems. If you secure an interview with someone, you will have only one chance to ask all the questions you need. Therefore, you need to plan carefully. Use the following advice for planning the interview, conducting the interview, and evaluating the results.

Planning an interview

- **Generate a list of questions.** Brainstorm as many questions as possible and record each one. Then evaluate your list to eliminate redundant or extraneous questions.
- **Organize related questions into categories.** Evaluate your long list of questions and organize them into categories. For the LMS research, these categories may include questions about how the company selected their learning management system, how the system is used at that company, how the employees perceive the system, and where additional sources of information can be found.
- **Identify sources to answer questions.** You may need to consult a variety of sources or people to answer your questions. Identify the sources for each question and create a second list of the same questions organized by source.
- **Determine how you will record responses.** Even if you tape record the interview, take notes in case a mechanical problem occurs with your recording. Also, be sure to get the interviewee's permission to make a recording.
- **Write an interview guide.** An interview guide is a plan of action for the interview that outlines the questions you will ask. Writing down the questions ensures that you do not forget something important. You may want to construct the interview guide so that you have room for taking notes. You may also want to provide the interviewees with the list of questions before the interview. Doing so allows them to organize their thoughts and possibly collect examples or additional information that they would not have readily available at your scheduled interview.

Although your interview questions will depend on the nature of your problem or decision, the Sample Interview Guide in FIGURE 7.11 provides some generic questions you can adopt to meet the needs of your research.

Conducting an interview

- **Arrive early.** You may need to set up recording equipment or review your notes to prepare.
- **Provide a foundation.** Introduce yourself, describe your research, state your purpose, and confirm the length of the interview. Even if you mentioned these things in your initial email or telephone conversation, providing this information again will set the context for the discussion and clarify expectations.
- **Be professional.** Speak clearly and be sure the interviewee understands your questions.
- **Listen carefully.** If you do not understand an answer, do not be afraid to ask for clarification. You may have to ask questions like "Why is that?" or "Can you explain that again?" to get the information you need.
- **Keep returning to the interview guide.** Responses to questions can lead to tangents that can provide useful information, but also distract you from your list of questions. Keep an eye on the time to ensure you do not run out of time before you have asked all the questions on your list. If the answers start to wander, bring the conversation back to its purpose.
- **Be flexible.** If an answer triggers a question not on the guide, ask it. For example, if the people you're interviewing comment about slow response from the technical support department of the software developer, ask if that was a pattern and how the slow response time affected the company.
- **Don't argue.** Your interviewees may make incorrect statements or state opinions as facts. Instead of correcting them or arguing their point, probe more deeply to understand why they hold their opinion. Putting them on the defensive may make

FIGURE 7.11
Sample Interview Guide

interview guide

1. Introduce yourself and the purpose of the interview. Thank the interviewee for spending time with you.
2. Questions about the interviewee:
   a. What does your organization do?
   b. Who does your organization serve?
   c. What is your position in the organization?

3. Questions about the problem:
   a. How many LMS options did you consider before selecting one?
   b. What criteria did you use to select your learning management system?

4. Questions about users and stakeholders:
   a. What do your employees think about your learning management system?
   b. How often do your employees use your learning management system?
   c. How do you update your training modules?

5. Questions about features:
   a. What are the strengths of your learning management system?
   b. What are the weaknesses of your learning management system?

6. Questions about the research:
   a. Can you suggest experts or other people?
   b. Can you suggest relevant secondary sources (books, articles, websites)?
   c. What advice can you give me as we determine the best learning management system for our company?

7. End the interview on a positive note by thanking the interviewee again.

them less willing to share their knowledge with you. For example, if an interviewee says her company decided against a specific learning management system because it was too expensive, don't argue that you know the price is much lower than comparable programs that are not as strong. Instead, you could ask if there were any other reasons why they rejected that program or why they believed the program they chose was a better value.

- **Follow up with a thank you.** Expressing appreciation at the end of an interview is important. In addition, following up with a phone call or email is good professional practice and may prompt your interviewee to provide additional feedback.

Evaluating interview results

After the interview, draft a concise, well-organized summary of the conversation. In some situations, you may decide to share your summary with your interviewee to confirm the information that you gathered is correct. Organize your findings so that key information is together. Despite having an organized list of interview questions, you may find that the interviewee's responses included tangents that were informative, but not systematically organized. That means you should not type your notes in the order in which you recorded them. Instead, you will need to organize your notes into logical categories. These categories may be different from the ones you used to organize your questions in the interview guide. Determine what additional information you now need and how to get it. The interviewee might not have been able to answer all your questions, may have suggested new questions, or may have been able to give only part of an answer.

Conduct observational research to understand how people act

For many topics, observation is an important supplement to survey and interview research. **Observational research** involves watching people perform relevant activities and then recording details about what you have observed. For example, when gathering

Observational research A research method that involves watching people perform relevant activities and recording details about what you observe.

information about learning management systems, you could ask an LMS provider if you can observe—and even participate in—another company's online training session.

Observation offers advantages over self-reported data from surveys and interviews. When people describe and evaluate their past experiences in a survey or interview, their reports may be inaccurate. They may not completely remember what happened,

 ETHICS How to Be an Ethical Researcher

When you present research in a business report or proposal, your audience has the right to expect that the information is reliable, accurate, and complete. To meet those expectations, as a researcher you have ethical responsibilities. The following six guidelines address both how to gather information and how to report it.

1. **Use reputable sources.** If you use secondary sources, take responsibility to ensure that those sources are credible using the criteria of authorship, accuracy, and age. Also ensure that their information can be verified. For example, imagine you are conducting research to help your company decide whether to use direct mail advertising sent through the U.S. mail. You want to be able to report on the environmental impact of mail that people discard. What would be the best source to cite: Wikipedia, a company that is marketing software for electronic direct mail, or the United States Environmental Protection Agency? If you originally found the information in Wikipedia, look at the reference list at the end of the article and see if you can verify the information in a more credible source. Then cite the more credible source.

2. **Cite all sources.** In business research, just as in academic research, you are responsible for citing all sources for ideas, opinions, and facts that you learned from other sources. Citing sources gives credit to the original source of the idea, gives your work more credibility, and helps your audience analyze your information. Imagine, for example, that you wanted to provide information about the unemployment rate in the United States. That "fact" may differ depending on whether you got the information from a blog on the web or from the Bureau of Labor Statistics.

3. **Ensure that all survey and interview sources provide informed consent.**[5] When you survey or interview people—especially when the survey is not anonymous—let those people know how you plan to use the information and if they may experience any negative consequences from the way you use the data. For example, imagine you are interviewing residents of a town to identify opinions for and against building a new shopping mall. In conducting this research, you need to ensure that people know you will be quoting them in a report to the city council. They also need to know that the city council will use the results to help decide whether to provide a zoning variance for a shopping mall. Once your interview subjects have this information, you need to be sure that they explicitly consent to their material being used this way.

4. **Report research accurately.** Be sure that you understand the intention of a source before reporting it. Do not take quotations out of context, report data in a misleading way, or make claims that your research cannot support. For example, if your research consisted of interviewing 10 customers about to enter a coffee store, you cannot say "According to our interviews, consumers prefer coffee over tea." You have data from only 10 people. You do not have enough data to support the larger conclusion. In addition, your sample may be biased, since you are interviewing people who are likely to be coffee drinkers. Similarly, if your data about economic growth came from a reputable source published in 2002, you cannot say, "According to the *International Economics Statistics Database*, Equatorial Guinea has the fastest growing economy in the world." That was true in 2002, but is it true now? It would be more ethical to say, "In 2002, Equatorial Guinea had the fastest growing economy in the world."

5. **Include all relevant information.** You may find it tempting to report only research that supports the position you want to argue. However, if you find information that contradicts your position, you have an ethical responsibility to address it in your report. For example, suppose you plan to argue that your company should not advertise through direct mail but instead use email advertising. You'd like to be able to show that direct mail is not environmentally friendly, since it contributes significantly to the solid waste stream. In researching, however, you find this fact: "although advertising mail accounts for almost 52 percent of total USPS (United States Postal Service) mail volume and 42 percent of the total weight, it represents only 2.2 percent of the municipal solid waste (MSW) stream."[6] Instead of ignoring this fact and maintaining your original position, choose one of these other options:

   - **Concede the fact and explain why it does not undermine your position:** "Although direct mail advertising represents only a small percentage of our solid waste stream, every bit of extra solid waste costs money for disposal and takes up valuable space in landfills."

   - **Eliminate this environmental argument** from your paper and stress other arguments against direct mail advertising.

   - **Modify your position.** You may not expect to find information that convinces you to change your point of view, but this routinely happens when people conduct thorough research.

6. **Respect intellectual property and "fair use" of other people's material.** Under U.S. copyright law and the doctrine of fair use, you may include brief quotations from others' work in your reports and presentations. However, you cannot quote substantial portions of another work in your own, even if you cite that work, because you are benefitting from that person's intellectual property.[7] If you plan to draw heavily from someone else's text, it is safest to receive written permission from the copyright owner. ■

For ETHICS exercises, go to Exercises 23 and 24 on page 249 or to this chapter's End-of-Chapter Exercises at mybcommlab.com.

mybcommlab

or they may want to give you the answer they believe you want to hear. Direct observation of actual behavior can give you much more accurate results.

When you observe, do not trust your memory. Carefully record important information about what you saw and heard as the observation proceeds, and take time immediately after you conclude the observation to make additional notes.

To get the most information from your observational research:

- **Decide what kinds of observations will be most helpful.** In other words, don't observe for the sake of observing. Ideally, observe people performing the actual activities with the actual products in the actual settings where they are normally used.
- After scheduling the observation, **plan for time before the observation to set up recording equipment**, if you are using it, as well as time after the observation to make notes or follow-up with participants.
- **Write an observation plan** that includes the day, time, and length of the observation as well as questions about features or actions and other issues relevant to your research.
- After completing your observations, **summarize the results** in writing.

Study Question 7.4

How do I organize the results of my research?

The amount and kind of research you conduct are crucial to good data gathering, but so are the ways in which you organize the research to share with others. The process of organizing research results is continual, starting from your first research effort. Use the following steps to ensure that your information will be easy to access as you begin to prepare your report or presentation.

Build your reference list as you research

As you collect sources, record all the information you need to prepare a reference list, such as authors' names, date of publication, the publication's name, the complete web address if online, volume and issue numbers, and all page numbers (not just the starting page). This information will save you time as you prepare your final report and presentation. It will also ensure that you can find the information again when you need it.

Several software programs are available to organize citations and sources, such as EndNote, RefWorks, and EasyBib. Some versions of Microsoft Word will do this also. These programs prompt you for information and then format your references in any one of several citation styles, including American Psychological Association (APA) style, Modern Language Association (MLA) style, and Chicago style, based on the *Chicago Manual of Style*. If in your research you use the same sources for multiple projects or courses, you can save the sources and reformat the references in any of the output formats.

The citation style you use will depend on the industry in which you work, the organization that is publishing your work, or your instructors' preferences. Both APA style and Chicago style are widely used in business. Although businesses rarely use MLA style, it may be required by your instructor. FIGURE 7.12 illustrates how a quotation from the same source would be formatted in APA, Chicago, and MLA style.

Appendix C and mybcommlab.com both include additional information about documentation in these styles.

Organize documents and notes for easy reference

Using a logical filing system will help you organize the information you find during your research so you can easily integrate it into your documents. If you print your sources, you can use file folders or a three-ring notebook with tabbed dividers to organize your information by topic. However, because many sources are available electronically, you may find it more effective and efficient to save your files without printing, especially if

new hires @ work

Rachel Whidden
Meetings Coordinator
American Chamber of Commerce Executives
Elon University, 2008

"I collect a lot of information to organize events and need to be able to refer to it for future events. I've learned not to throw anything away, and I've created an effective organizing system that makes it easy to find what I need."

FIGURE 7.12 Examples of Reference Citation Styles

See Appendix C and mybcommlab.com for additional discussion of formats

APA STYLE (6th ed.)	CHICAGO STYLE (16th ed.)	MLA STYLE (9th ed.)
In-text citation: . . . Moodle was used in a landmark case study analysis to demonstrate how course management systems can generate effective results (Romero, Ventura, & Garcia, 2008). This study effectively . . .	*In-text citation:* . . . Moodle was used in a landmark case study analysis to demonstrate how course management systems can generate effective results (Romero, Ventura, and Garcia 2008, 368). This study effectively . . .	*In-text citation:* . . . Moodle was used in a landmark case study analysis to demonstrate how course management systems can generate effective results (Romero, Ventura, and Garcia 368). This study effectively . . .
Reference page citation: Romero, C., Ventura, S., & Garcia, E. (2008). Data mining in course management systems: Moodle case study and tutorial. *Computers & Education, 51*(1), 368–384.	*Reference page citation:* Romero, Cristobal, Sebastian Ventura, and Enrique Garcia. 2008. Data Mining in Course Management Systems: Moodle Case Study and Tutorial. *Computers & Education* 51 (1): 368–384.	*Works Cited page citation:* Romero, Cristobal, Sebastian Ventura, and Enrique Garcia. "Data Mining in Course Management Systems: Moodle Case Study and Tutorial." *Computers & Education* 51.1 (2008): 368–384. Print.

Apply Figure 7.12's key concepts by revising a new document. Go to Chapter 7 in mybcommlab.com and select Document Makeovers.

you have several sources to evaluate before you decide to use them in your research. The following guidelines will help you organize your information for easy reference. Also be sure to back up your files so you don't lose valuable resources.

- **Create identifiable filenames.** When you download a file from the web, such as a PDF, the filename may not adequately identify the file's contents. For example, you would have to open a file labeled "DEC1202.pdf" to determine what it was. If a file has a vague name, rename it so that you will be able to quickly identify it when you skim your file list later. You may decide to save the DEC1202.pdf file with the article's title, "Overview of Open Source Learning Management Systems," or by topic and publisher, "Open Source LMS–EDUCAUSE."

- **Group similar content for easy synthesis.** On your computer, create a folder for each research project. Within that folder, create subfolders that allow you to organize the information. You can organize folders by topic as illustrated in FIGURE 7.13. Alternatively, you can organize them by type of information (for example, survey results, software reviews, etc.) or by the research questions from your work plan.

FIGURE 7.13
File Folder Organization

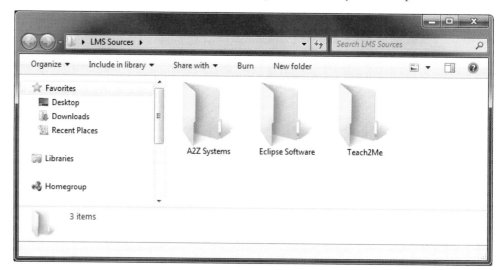

Organize your findings by research questions

Inexperienced researchers often make the mistake of organizing their research by the source of information. While you might first record information in that way, you will find it more useful to *synthesize*, or combine, information from various sources as you work through the research process.

The work plan outlined in Figure 7.4 on page 223 is one useful guide for organizing your findings within the original research questions. You may need to expand the format of the table to fit your data. FIGURE 7.14 provides an example of findings organized for the first LMS research question: "Would a learning management system be an effective training tool for our company?" Note how the information in the figure is not organized by source. Instead, the information is integrated into the work plan by research activity. If all the information about A2Z Systems were listed separately, it would be difficult to compare it to the other options. By organizing the information by question, you will be able to make good comparisons more easily.

As you continue your research, you can use the same work plan to organize your conclusions and recommendations. Simply add extra columns to the right.

FIGURE 7.14 Adding Findings to the Work Plan

RESEARCH QUESTIONS	RESEARCH ACTIVITIES	TARGET DATE	KEY FINDINGS	IMPLICATIONS/ CONCLUSIONS	RECOMMENDA- TIONS

Research Activities	Target Date	Key Findings — LMS Options		
		A2Z Systems (A2Z.com)	Eclipse Software (Eclipse.com)	Teach2Me (Teach2Me.com)
Research training and education journals, books, and websites.	Weeks 1–2	• Supports multiple platforms • Online demo only; no onsite rep support	• Requires a single platform • Online demo and onsite rep support	• Supports multiple platforms • Online demo and onsite rep support
Compare options against company's training needs.	Week 2	• Customizable modules may provide flexible training; no online support provided • Supports both stand-alone and instructor-led training	• All modules are completely customizable; online support provided • All support included	• Customizable modules must be purchased separately • Online support billed separately
Survey or interview people in other companies	Week 2	**Agrulo Interview:** • Initial learning curve was difficult; required extensive start-up training • Lack of online support frustrating • Phone support not enough • Bottom line: It's better than nothing	**Millersby Interview:** • Learning curve difficult, but manageable • Online support helpful • Bottom line: It's okay; we're still learning	**Takata Interview:** • Easy setup; user-friendly interface • No need yet for online support • Bottom line: We love it!

IN SUMMARY, the process of doing research and organizing your findings begins during the analyzing phase of the ACE process and may continue until your document or project is completed. At any stage in the process, you may develop new questions that uncover new research needs. Your ability to research efficiently and effectively depends on your having a clear research plan—knowing what you want to learn and what sources and research activities will provide the information. Organizing your research materials and findings puts you in a good position to use your research to write proposals (Chapter 8), reports (Chapter 9), and presentations (Chapter 10).

CHAPTER 7 Summary

7.1 How do I determine what information I need? *(pages 218–223)*

- **Analyze the research question and topic** to understand the information you need to gather. You may find it useful to divide your research question into several subquestions. In addition, conduct background research to understand your topic's history, context and structure, and categories.
- **Identify audience concerns and needs** by determining what the primary and secondary audiences already know and need to know.
- **Establish the scope of the research** (how broad or specific your focus will be) by considering the needs of the project and the time available to do the work.
- **Define research activities** to gather information from primary, secondary, or tertiary sources.
- **Develop a work plan** that organizes your research process and ensures that you gather information to answer all your research questions.

7.2 How do I conduct and evaluate research in print and online sources? *(pages 223–230)*

To be an effective researcher,

- **Search the web strategically.** Focus your search by using quotation marks, wildcards, and alternative wordings. You can also search for specific file types.
- **Use an online index or database to find articles and business data** such as newspapers, magazines, trade journals, and academic journals. Peer-reviewed articles have more credibility than nonvalidated web articles.
- **Use a library or bookseller to find relevant books.** Much excellent information is published only in books. However, in some fields, books can quickly become outdated.
- **Follow leads in good sources** to identify additional good sources.
- **Evaluate your sources for credibility** using the 3 As: Authorship, Accuracy, and Age.

7.3 How do I conduct and evaluate primary research? *(pages 231–239)*

Three useful research techniques to collect original data are surveys, interviews, and observations.

- **Conduct survey research to gather information that is easy to compare,** such as quantitative data that can be reported as counts, percentages, ranges, means, medians, and modes. Before conducting survey research, choose which people to survey by identifying the population and determining what kind of sample you will use (convenience, targeted, or random). Write effective survey questions, and decide on a survey medium. Following the survey, analyze, interpret, and evaluate the data.
- **Conduct interview research to gather in-depth information.** Effective researchers know how to plan the interview, what to do during the interview, and how to evaluate the interview results.
- **Conduct observational research to understand how people act.** A person's actions are often more revealing than his or her words.

7.4 How do I organize the results of my research? *(pages 239–241)*

- **Build your reference list as you research.** This will save you time as you prepare your final report and presentation and ensure you can find the information again.
- **Organize documents and notes for easy reference.** Create identifiable filenames and a useful filing system.
- **Organize your findings by research questions.** This will help you synthesize the material when it is time to compose.

PEARSON mybcommlab *Are you an active learner? Go to mybcommlab.com to master Chapter 7 content. Chapter 7 interactive activities include:*

- Customizable Study Plan and Chapter 7 practice quizzes
- Chapter 7 Simulation, How to Find, Interpret, and Use Business Data Effectively, that helps you think critically and prepare to make choices in the business world
- Flash Cards for mastering the definition of chapter terms
- Chapter 7 Video Exercise, Finding, Evaluating & Processing Information, which shows you how textbook concepts are put into practice every day
- Interactive Lessons that visually review key chapter concepts
- Document Makeovers for hands-on, scored practice in revising documents

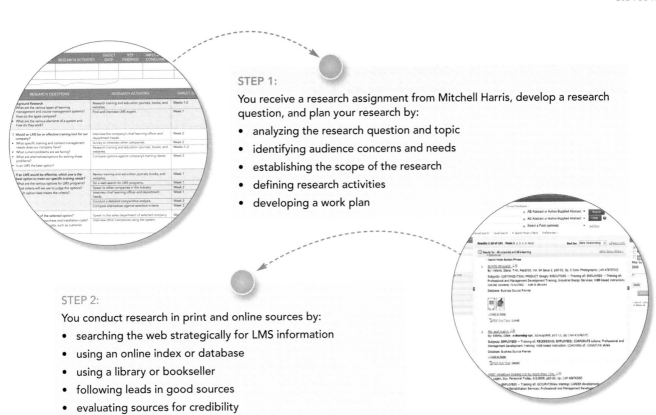

STEP 1:

You receive a research assignment from Mitchell Harris, develop a research question, and plan your research by:

- analyzing the research question and topic
- identifying audience concerns and needs
- establishing the scope of the research
- defining research activities
- developing a work plan

STEP 2:

You conduct research in print and online sources by:

- searching the web strategically for LMS information
- using an online index or database
- using a library or bookseller
- following leads in good sources
- evaluating sources for credibility

STEP 3:

You conduct primary research by:

- surveying employees
- interviewing experts and LMS users
- observing people using learning management systems

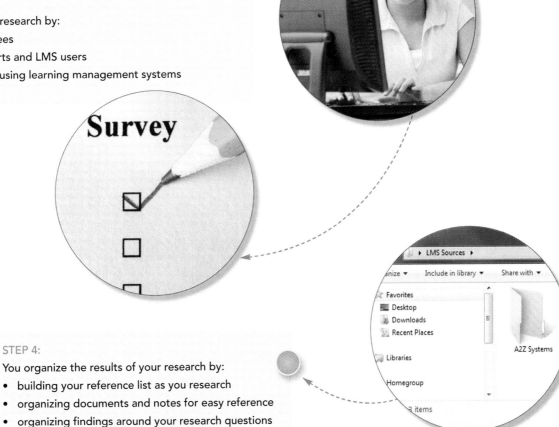

STEP 4:

You organize the results of your research by:

- building your reference list as you research
- organizing documents and notes for easy reference
- organizing findings around your research questions

KEY TERMS QUICK ACCESS REVIEW

Convenience sample *p. 231*	Primary sources *p. 221*	Secondary sources *p. 221*
Interview *p. 235*	Qualitative Research *p. 221*	Survey *p. 231*
Limitations *p. 221*	Quantitative Research *p. 221*	Survey population *p. 231*
Mean *p. 234*	Random sample *p. 231*	Targeted sample *p. 231*
Median *p. 234*	Range *p. 234*	Tertiary sources *p. 221*
Mode *p. 235*	Sample *p. 231*	
Observational research *p. 237*	Scope *p. 221*	

CASE STUDY Researching to Answer Business Questions

This case study will help you review the chapter material by applying it to a specific business situation.

Receiving a Research Assignment

Shuang Yu is a recent graduate of Milford University. She has started working in new business development at Affordable World Energy (AWE), a company that designs affordable products that generate electricity. The primary market for these products is countries with large rural populations that do not have access to electricity. As its next project, AWE is designing small-scale windmills to generate power for individual homes. The company needs to decide on the first market for this product and has narrowed the scope of its search to three countries that all have large populations without electricity: India, Kenya, and Panama. Shuang's assignment is to research which country has the best consumer base, the most suitable wind conditions, and best manufacturing infrastructure to manufacture the windmills locally.

Review Question 1: *Shuang will be presenting her findings to the company president and board of directors in a month. She needs to start structuring this research project immediately. If you were in Shuang's position, how would you proceed? Where would you look for information, what would you look for, and how would you organize this information?*

Developing a Work Plan

As a first step in planning her research, Shuang develops a purpose statement:

Purpose: To determine whether India, Kenya, or Panama is the best country in which to produce and sell small-scale wind turbines to provide power to rural homes.

She also begins to develop a set of research questions:

1. What criteria should I use to evaluate these countries? How should I weight the criteria?
2. Which country has the best market for small wind turbines?
3. What are the necessary wind conditions for wind turbines?
4. Which countries have the necessary wind conditions?
5. What government regulations may affect the production and sale of wind turbines?

6. How much can the rural population afford to spend on a wind turbine?

Review Question 2: *Are there additional questions that Shuang should add to her work plan? For all the questions, what research activities would you plan to answer the questions?*

Researching Online Sources

Shuang begins her research by trying to identify which country has the best market for small-scale wind turbines. She hopes to find this information on the web. But what should she search for?

- **Search 1:** For her first Google search, she uses the terms *"rural wind turbine market."* This search yields some interesting results, including a market study by the American Wind Energy Association titled "AWEA Small Wind Turbine Global Market Study 2008."[8] Although the research report focuses primarily on the United States' market, it does include a small section on global markets and, more importantly, a discussion of the types of regulations that prevent countries from adopting wind power. This helps answer one of her research questions.

- **Search 2:** Shuang then decides to try a second set of terms to approach the search from a different angle. She decides that one way to identify the biggest market is to identify what country has the largest population without electricity. So she uses *population "without electricity."* Much to her surprise, she finds a report published by the United Nations Development Programme that lists the number of people (in millions) without electricity for 174 countries.[9] Shuang finds that Panama has only half a million people without electricity. By contrast, Kenya has about 30 million, and India has about 500 million. By reading the source citations in this report, Shuang also learns about the International Energy Agency, which collects data about global energy needs.

Review Question 3: *Identify another research question that Shuang needs to answer and develop some alternative search terms to research this question using a general search engine, a deep web search engine, or an online article database. Which search terms offer the most useful results?*

Conducting Primary Research

Shuang has already identified at least one primary source she needs for research: her boss, the head of marketing at Affordable World Energy. As part of her research, Shuang needs to understand what criteria she should be using to evaluate the market opportunity in the three selected countries and how she should rank those criteria. Is it more important that the market is big? Or is it more important that the country has industry that can manufacture the wind turbines? Her boss will know what criteria the company believes is most important.

She wonders, though, if she should be talking with anyone else or conducting any surveys. She has only a few weeks left to complete her research.

Review Question 4: *Is there any information that Shuang could get more easily by interview than by researching secondary sources? If so, what is this information and who would you recommend she contact?*

Organizing Research Results

Because Shuang's research project is such a major undertaking, she needs to develop a systematic plan to keep track of her sources and her results. Here is what she does:

1. She starts a Word file titled "Reference list," and she includes an entry for every item she reads. She formats these according to APA style and keeps the list in alphabetical order. She keeps a separate list of everyone she talks to, with the person's name, title, contact information, and date of interview.

2. She either prints out or downloads a PDF of her web-based sources. This ensures the material will remain available to her even if the website changes. She saves the files in folders organized by research question.

3. She creates a Word file for each of her research questions and types notes from her research right in those files, being sure to provide citations to all her sources.

Review Question 5: *Do you have any additional tips and tricks you use to organize research results? If so, would they be useful for this project?*

CRITICAL THINKING

1. As a researcher, how will you benefit from taking the time to identify the problem, analyze the audience, determine the purpose, establish the scope, and develop a work plan before finding information? Wouldn't it be easier to find a lot of information about a topic and then organize the content based on what you find?

2. Some people argue that libraries are becoming obsolete because so much research material is now available on the web. Compare the kinds of resources that are freely available on the web versus the kind of resources that you can access only via a library. Based on that comparison, what value do you believe libraries offer? As a researcher, what would you use a library for?

3. Wikipedia can be a useful tool in your research. Why do researchers not consider Wikipedia a credible source for information to cite? What should you do if you find information in Wikipedia that you would like to include in your report or presentation?

4. Assume you are interested in getting a masters degree in accounting in your state or a nearby state. Design a search string for Google that will help you identify available programs. How would using quotation marks and minus signs help you in this research?

5. An Amazon.com book search reveals a book titled *Learning Management Systems Market Trends* dated September 2001. Would you include this book in your research on learning management systems? Why or why not?

6. Surveys are typically used to collect quantitative information. Explain how a researcher could use a survey to collect qualitative information also.

7. Assume that you have distributed a survey to determine what frustrates employees most about the company's current approach to training and you received only 25 responses from a population of 200 employees. How would you proceed? How could you use the information from your survey in your report? How could you get additional information?

8. If an interviewee's responses can lead to meaningful tangents, why is an interview guide useful?

9. Assume you have scheduled interviews with three different content experts on a particular topic. The second content expert provided good information and expounded on several related topics that you did not think to ask during the first interview. Would you schedule a follow-up interview with the first content expert to address the additional topics? Or, would you simply rely on your third and final interview to gather the related information? Explain your answer.

10. Assume that you work for a company that manufactures luggage. The company would like to design a new line of luggage that meets the needs of business travelers who fly frequently. You have been assigned to conduct research to identify business travelers' needs. Where could you conduct observational research? What would you be able to learn from observational research that you could not learn from survey research or interviews?

DEVELOPING YOUR COMMUNICATION SKILLS

7.1 How do I determine what information I need?

(pages 218–223)

EXERCISE 1 Analyze the research question and topic

a. Identify a problem at your school—for example, a problem concerning parking, meal plans, class registration, or credit for community service—and imagine that you are beginning a research project to identify a solution to the problem. Develop a set of research questions to guide your research.

b. What background research will help you understand your topic? Use the table in Figure 7.2 on page 220 to list a set of relevant background research questions.

EXERCISE 2 Identify audience concerns and needs

In Exercise 1, you identified a campus problem and a set of research questions. Assume you plan to conduct the research and propose a solution to the appropriate audience(s) on your campus. Answer the following questions related to this problem:

a. Who is the primary audience?

b. Who is the secondary audience?

c. Who else may be affected by this problem or decision?

d. What does the audience already know? What do they need to know?

e. What questions will your audience expect you to answer when you present the research?

f. What sources will your audience expect you to consult?

EXERCISE 3 Establish the scope of the research

Use the problem identified in Exercise 1 and the audience analysis outlined in Exercise 2 to determine a purpose statement (or statements) and research questions. Refer to the examples in Figure 7.1 on page 219 and Figure 7.2 on page 220.

EXERCISE 4 Define research activities

Use the problem identified in Exercise 1, the audience analysis outlined in Exercise 2, and the scope determined in Exercise 3 to define at least two research activities for each research question. Create a table similar to that in Figure 7.3 on page 222.

EXERCISE 5 Develop a work plan

How would you sequence the research activities identified in Exercise 4? Create a work plan like that in Figure 7.4 on page 223 and justify the order of events.

7.2 How do I conduct and evaluate research in print and online sources? *(pages 223–230)*

EXERCISE 6 Search the web strategically [Related to the Technology feature on page 226]

a. Use the same keywords to search a topic of your choice using two different online search engines, including one deep web search engine such as Biznar or Science.gov. Compare the first page of each list of results. Do differences exist between the two lists? Summarize the differences and similarities between the two lists and explain why the results were not identical.

b. Conduct a Google search for PDF documents using the search string *campus parking problem filetype:pdf.* Conduct a second search, this time for PowerPoint documents, using the search string *campus parking problem filetype:ppt.* From each of these searches, identify at least one document you might use in researching a proposal to improve parking on your campus. (If you use a different search engine, then use the advanced search feature to narrow your search to .pdf or .ppt files.)

EXERCISE 7 Use an online index or database to find articles and business data

a. Use an online database available through your school's library to find at least three articles or books related to the research topic you chose in Exercise 6a or a different topic of your choice. Of the three sources, find at least one article from a magazine or trade journal, and find at least one article from an academic journal. Compare the information in the three sources. How does the information differ? How is it similar? If you found a book also, compare the information in the articles to that in the book. What are some key differences?

b. Use the online index for your school newspaper, a local newspaper (for example *St. Louis Post Dispatch, Chicago Tribune, Los Angeles Times, Boston Globe*), or a national newspaper (*New York Times, Wall Street Journal*) to search for at least one newspaper article related to the topic you chose in Exercise 6a. Identify all the search terms you tried. If your search was successful, summarize the information you found in the article. If your search was unsuccessful, explain why you believe you could find no newspaper articles on your topic.

c. Use two online business research tools, such as Yahoo! Finance, Hoover's, or Standard & Poor's, to search for financial data on a single company that interests you. Compare the results from the two searches. Does one provide more information than the other? Is one easier to use or read than the other? Which tool would you choose to use the next time you need to research financial data about a company? Be prepared to discuss your answer in class.

EXERCISE 8 Use a library or bookseller to find relevant books

a. Assume you would like to propose that your university adopt or expand its service learning opportunities. You plan a research project to propose a new service learning model. One of your research questions is this: "How have other colleges and universities implemented service learning?" Using your college or community library online catalog, find two sources that you think would be relevant, and do the following:

- Read through all the information in the online catalog entry. Identify any information that helps you decide whether this book will be useful to your research.

- Go to the Amazon website and search for the books you found in the library. If Amazon has a listing for the books, read through the product descriptions and reviews on the page to learn more about the books.

- Using the information you found in your library catalog and on Amazon, explain whether each book would be helpful to your research and, if it would be helpful, how. Be sure to provide a reference list using the documentation style that your instructor prefers.

b. Assume you would like to expand your search for information about service learning to identify good books on the subject that your library does not own. Go to Amazon's website and search for "service learning" in the book department. Identify any books that you believe would be useful but are not in your library. Be sure to provide a reference list using the documentation style that your instructor prefers.

EXERCISE 9 Follow leads in good sources

a. Assume that in your research on learning management systems, you found the following reference in one of the articles you read: Perry, B. (2009). Customized content at your fingertips. *T+D, 63*(6), 29–31. How would you go about finding that source?

b. Assume that in your research on learning management systems, you read a white paper by the consulting company Element K, titled *Learning Management Systems in the Work Environment*. This document cites a report by the Hudson Institute stating that "By 2020, 60 percent of jobs will require skills that only 20 percent of the workforce now possesses."[10] Unfortunately, the white paper does not provide complete documentation for the Hudson Institute report. How would you go about finding that report?

EXERCISE 10 Evaluate your sources for credibility

a. Find one or both of the sources identified in Exercise 9 and evaluate it for credibility based on the 3 As: Authorship, Accuracy, and Age. Would you use this source in your research?

b. Assume you have just started a new job. Before you get your first paycheck, you would like to research how to minimize the amount of income tax you will have to pay. Conduct a web search for sources relating to minimizing or decreasing income taxes. Find at least one source that you believe is credible based on the 3 As. Find at least one source that you believe is not credible based on the same criteria. Write a brief comparison of the two sources, explaining which you would use and why.

c. Conduct a web search to find at least one blog on taxes and economics and write a brief explanation of whether you consider this source to be credible.

7.3 How do I conduct and evaluate primary research? *(pages 231–239)*

EXERCISE 11 Conduct survey research to gather information that is easy to compare

a. You and a few classmates would like to launch your own entrepreneurial business. You want to provide a product or service that will meet a need in your community. As part of your initial research, you would like to conduct a survey to get ideas about products or services people in the community

need. Write five survey questions that you believe will give you useful information. Be prepared to explain why you think these are good questions. Also, select what you believe to be the best medium for this survey. Be prepared to explain why you think this is the best medium.

b. How would you select a sample of the population for your survey in question 11a? Would you choose a convenience, targeted, or random sample? Explain why.

c. Calculate the mean, median, and mode for the following data and report your answers on a table adapted from the one in Figure 7.10 on page 235. Below your table, write a brief summary that highlights the differences among the three results.

1. Have you used a learning management system for training purposes in any of your prior work experiences?
   Yes = 25 responses
   No = 32 responses

2. If yes, how would you rate the use of a learning management system (LMS) compared to traditional face-to-face training?
   5 = more satisfied with LMS for all learning experiences
   16 = more satisfied with LMS for most learning experiences
   3 = neither more nor less satisfied with LMS
   0 = less satisfied with LMS for most learning experiences
   1 = less satisfied with LMS for all learning experiences

EXERCISE 12 Conduct interview research to gather in-depth information

As part of your research for launching an entrepreneurial business (see Exercise 11a), you would like to interview successful small business owners in your community to get their advice about how to be successful and avoid mistakes. Identify at least one person to interview and write an interview guide you can use.

EXERCISE 13 Conduct observational research to understand how people act

A large consumer products company is interested in understanding how consumers make choices about which breakfast cereal to buy. In addition to surveying and interviewing consumers, the company would like to observe people's purchasing behavior. Plan an observation session in a local supermarket. Assume that you will be standing near the cereal aisle for approximately 30 minutes, watching people make cereal decisions. What specific types of behavior will you be looking for, and why do you think that information will be useful? (For example, you might gather information about how many different cereal boxes a consumer looks at before selecting one.)

7.4 How do I organize the results of my research? *(pages 239–241)*

EXERCISE 14 Build your reference list as you research

a. In the case study at the end of the chapter (pp. 244–245), Shuang found a number of sources that she will cite in her research to identify an initial market for Affordable World Energy's small-scale windmills. Build a reference list for these sources, using the documentation style that your instructor prefers. You can find information for building reference lists in Appendix C.

b. Assume that Shuang also conducted telephone interviews with two or three experts that she will cite in her paper. What is the correct method for documenting these sources in the documentation style you are using (APA, MLA, or Chicago Style)?

EXERCISE 15 Organize documents and notes for easy reference

You are an assistant to Madelyn Dupré, the director of training at a large company. She has been asked to make an hour-long presentation to new account representatives about business etiquette issues in the four countries where your company does most of its international business: Brazil, Russia, China, and India. Madelyn asks you to help find information by gathering relevant sources. Use the search tools outlined in the chapter to find at least 10 electronic sources. Ensure the files include complete citation information, save the sources with filenames that are easily identifiable, and group them in a logical manner on a flash drive or CD to submit to your instructor.

EXERCISE 16 Organize your findings by research questions

Assume that you are researching how to minimize your income tax, as described in Exercise 10b. Brainstorm some research questions or categories you can use to organize your findings. For example, one category might be findings relating to tax credits. What other categories may be useful to your research?

WRITING

EXERCISE 17 Finding advertising information

Your neighbor, Mrs. James, recently retired after 30 years as an elementary school teacher and wants to open a knitting shop in your community. She's been finding information about available storefronts, small business loan opportunities, and suppliers, but doesn't know where to begin to advertise her business. Yesterday, she asked if you could help her gather some information about advertising opportunities and costs. Find local information about how to use the following advertising outlets, including costs for small ads.

a. Radio

b. Newspaper

c. Direct Mail

d. Coupons

e. Other . . . ?

Write a one-page summary of your findings that you will share with Mrs. James. Be sure to include necessary citations and a reference list so that Mrs. James can follow up on your research.

EXERCISE 18 Finding information to address sales issues

You work part-time at a local bookstore, The Book Nook, which has suffered declining sales over the last six months. Since no new bookstores or mega discount stores have opened recently to draw away customers, the owner, Inez Higgins, assumes more people are buying their books online rather than in her store. However, that's just a guess. She has asked you to help her find useful information on ways to increase in-store book sales. Determine what kinds of books, changes in hours, added services, and other factors might increase sales.

a. Using the search term *"increasing bookstore sales,"* conduct a web search and identify at least five sources you recommend Ms. Higgins read.

b. Using the search term *"book buying behavior,"* conduct a web search and identify at least two additional sources.

c. Experiment with different strings of search terms, conduct a web search, and identify at least two additional sources.

d. Identify at least two primary research activities you recommend that Ms. Higgins do.

Write an email or memo to Ms. Higgins listing the research sources and primary research activities you recommend she pursue. For each research source, provide the name, the URL, and a brief sentence describing why the source will be valuable. Give her advice for finding additional sources.

EXERCISE 19 Finding information to make a persuasive appeal

You are interning in the city commissioners' office this semester. The city council has developed a plan for a new bypass around the city limits to decrease the flow of traffic on local streets, especially during morning and evening rush hours. However, the bypass is dependent on the passing of a new tax. Your manager asks you to find information that would help "sell" the bypass idea (and therefore the tax) to the electorate. Where would you find the information you need to persuade people in your community? Brainstorm sources of information for your city and write a one-page summary of your ideas for collecting information that you will submit to the city commissioners.

EXERCISE 20 Finding information about corporate policies

You are interning this semester for McConnell Consulting, a newly developed consulting company in your area. The company's CEO has been so busy managing the start-up of the organization and developing a client network that he has not had time to create personnel policies. Mr. McConnell has asked you to find information about the kind of content to include, paying close attention to harassment policies that protect both employees and clients. Using the web, online databases, and a library book catalog, find at least five credible sources that relate to creating personnel policies, and outline your sources with citations in a one-page report to Mr. McConnell.

EXERCISE 21 Finding information about building modifications

You are the assistant manager for a large art gallery in a metropolitan area. The gallery has grown significantly in the last few years and has finally outgrown the building it has rented for nearly

25 years. Recognizing your need for additional space, a generous benefactor recently donated a large historical building downtown. The location is great, and the building has a lot of open spaces for showings and exhibits as well as storage areas and office space. However, it is not handicap accessible. Because the building is listed in the city's historical register, you're not sure if you can make noticeable renovations to the exterior, such as a wheelchair ramp at the entrance. Determine where you could find information about historical renovations, especially handicap-access renovations. Outline your sources with citations in a one-page report.

EXERCISE 22 Recommending a citation management software program

A friend asked you to recommend a citation management software program that stores and formats references. Compare the features of two programs and summarize your findings in a persuasive message to your friend recommending one program.

EXERCISE 23 Evaluating conflicting information
[Related to the Ethics feature on page 238]

Assume during your search for information about learning management systems, you find a lot of support for Teach2Me software. Although only five of your employees indicated prior experience with this product, all of their responses were very positive. The cost of the product, including initial start-up costs and ongoing maintenance and technical support, is less than your current travel budget for training. Your interviews with other companies who use Teach2Me have been positive. The online demo you went through impressed you more than the other two options. Therefore, you decide that in your report to your supervisor, you will recommend that your company choose Teach2Me as its learning management system.

However, as you review the information you gathered, you find a product review in a trade journal that suggests Teach2Me is not as robust as either A2Z Systems or Eclipse Software. The review indicates that Teach2Me does not offer as many features, the interface is more complicated to learn, and the tech support, though affordable, often requires long wait times.

Since this article is the only negative information you can find about Teach2Me, you consider not including it in your report to your supervisor. You are concerned that because the information does not support your recommendation, your supervisor will question your decision. However, you know that would not be ethical. Write an email message or memo to your instructor explaining how you would include the information while supporting your recommendation for Teach2Me.

EXERCISE 24 Making an ethical choice
[Related to the Ethics feature on page 238]

Suppose you are searching for secondary information to support a paper for your economics class. You find an article in a trade journal that nearly matches your assignment requirements. The headings are similar to the outline you have prepared for your paper, and you have found and evaluated many of the cited sources listed at the end of the article. Because your economics professor has listed this trade journal (although not this article) as a resource on the class website, you are concerned that she may assume you plagiarized the article. Even if you do not use any of the same wording as the article, the similarities to the outline of your paper may be interpreted as copying the author's content. How do you proceed?

a. Do you ignore the source, hoping not to draw your professor's attention to the article in case she is not familiar with it? If your wording is different enough from the article, you assume you can claim you never read the article.

b. Do you write the paper as you planned and simply cite the source?

c. Do you try to explain the problem to your professor and ask for guidance? If so, how can you document that you did not read the article prior to developing your outline?

d. Is there another step you could take?

Write an email message or memo to your instructor explaining what you would do, and outline the specific pros, cons, and ethical issues related to your decision.

EXERCISE 25 Finding secondary information sources
[Related to the Culture feature on page 230]

Your consulting company provides public relations services to a wide variety of manufacturing companies. Your headquarters are in Palo Alto, California, but branch offices are located throughout the country. Your CEO is considering opening a new office in Guangdong Province, China, where many U.S.-based firms have outsourced their manufacturing contracts. Your manager asks you to provide information about the logistics of opening a branch in the province. He also wants to know how doing business in China may differ from doing business in the United States. Where would you find this information?

Outline a purpose statement and research questions. Then determine where you could find sources of secondary information. Create a work plan similar to the ones presented in the chapter that outlines your sources. List the possible sources for each research activity using the documentation style requested by your instructor. You do not need to summarize the findings of the sources.

EXERCISE 26 Conducting primary research
[Related to the Culture feature on page 230]

Assume your business communication instructor has given your class an assignment to do primary research to develop a list of tips for effectively communicating with people from different cultures. You will present your findings in a short presentation during class in two weeks. You need to make a research plan:

a. Will you conduct a survey? If so, who will your population be and what questions will you ask?

b. Will you conduct interviews? If so, who will you interview and what questions will you ask?

Outline your sources and questions in an email message or memo to your instructor. Be sure to include names and contact information about possible interviewees.

COLLABORATING

EXERCISE 27 Finding and comparing information

A manager at your company asks your team to find information about local car dealerships that lease corporate vehicles. Use one or two search engines to assign a different dealer to each member of your team. Have the team members find information about their assigned dealer from the dealers' websites as well as external reviews by third parties. Each team member is to create a one-page document identifying the main features of his or her assigned dealer and summarizing the reviews, which should be appropriately cited.

Share your individual documents during a team meeting—either in person or electronically. Analyze the similarities and differences among the dealer options. Determine which dealer provides the most flexible leasing options and/or which one has the best reviews. Write a one-page report to your instructor identifying all the dealers considered and supporting your team's recommendation of a specific dealer. Attach the individual reports as documentation.

EXERCISE 28 Writing survey questions/comparing analyses

Your school would like to assess students' perspectives of its current course management system. They have asked your business communication class to survey students about their likes and dislikes as well as recommend possible changes to the system. In small teams, create a survey questionnaire that includes a variety of question types, including at least one qualitative (open-ended) question. Before creating a final draft and collecting data, test your survey with other members of your class to ensure the questions are worded effectively.

Each member of your team should collect at least 10 survey responses from students around campus. Be sure not to survey students enrolled in your business communication class or students who have answered a similar questionnaire from other business communication students. Have each team member analyze the data he or she received and report the range, median, mean, and mode for quantitative responses. Summarize the qualitative responses indicating any commonalities among responses.

In a team meeting, compare your individual findings. Discuss how the qualitative responses were analyzed. Then combine the data from all team members and summarize your findings in a report to your school administration.

SPEAKING

EXERCISE 29 Presenting information

Conduct research to prepare for a three- to five-minute presentation on one of the following topics. Prepare a visual aid to support your presentation. The visual should cite your source(s) using a complete reference citation (see Appendix C for examples).

a. Find two websites that provide information about a topic of your choice. One website should be a credible site based on the 3 As—Authorship, Accuracy, and Age. The second website's credibility should be questionable based on the same criteria. Present the two sources to the class, and identify how you used the 3 As to assess their credibility. Demonstrate how the questionable source lacks credibility.

b. Create a five-question survey on a topic of your choice. Use a variety of question types. Create one version of the survey that includes weak or vague wording that could possibly be misinterpreted. Create a second version of the survey that ensures measurable responses and elicits the information needed. Present the two versions of the survey to the class, explaining why the second set of questions will achieve better results.

c. Identify a specific research question you would like to answer. Search for sources using a general search engine, a deep web search engine, and an online database. Prepare a brief presentation comparing the results using the three different search tools. Identify which source gave you the most valuable results for your research, and explain why. **[Related to the Technology feature on page 226]**

d. Assume that you work for Affordable World Energy (see Case Study, pp. 244–245), and your managers have decided that India is a good market for the company's new windmill. Now, they are interested in understanding some of the cultural elements that may affect doing business in India. The managers ask you to do some research and prepare a five-minute presentation. Research Indian culture, using some of the sources identified in the Culture feature on page 230—or other sources that you find. Prepare a five-minute presentation that highlights your most important findings. **[Related to the Culture feature on page 230]**

e. Wikipedia is a convenient source for research. However, many people argue it is not a credible source and should not be cited in high quality research reports. Find and read at least two articles in the academic or popular press about Wikipedia, and develop a five-minute presentation supporting an opinion about whether a researcher should or should not avoid citing Wikipedia. Be sure to cite your sources in your presentation. For advice about how to cite sources in a presentation, see Appendix C.

GRAMMAR

EXERCISE 30 Common sentence errors:
Subject-Verb Agreement (See Appendix D—Section 1.3.3)

Rekey the following paragraph (or download a copy from mybcommlab.com) and edit, correcting the 10 errors in subject-verb agreement. Underline all your corrections.

When making a business call, being put on hold for countless minutes fray even patient people's nerves. Having to wait, as well as not knowing for how long, are upsetting. Each of us have our own way of coping with this irritant. *The Sounds of Silence* apply not only to the Simon and Garfunkle song but also to endless minutes on hold. Three minutes feel like forever to the person waiting. If you must put someone on hold, there is several things you should do. First, ask, "May I put you on hold?" and then give the caller an estimate of the probable waiting time. The person on the other end might be one of those callers who really need to know how long the wait might be. The unknown number of minutes are what drive people crazy. Data collected by Hold On America, Inc. shows that callers become frustrated after 20 seconds. After 90 seconds, 50 percent of callers hangs up.

EXERCISE 31 Common sentence errors:
Pronoun-Antecedent Agreement (See Appendix D—Section 1.3.4)

Rekey the following paragraph (or download from mybcommlab.com) and edit, correcting the 10 errors in pronoun-antecedent agreement. Underline all your corrections.

Everybody has preferences about their communication tools. A person may prefer email rather than telephone, so they might respond to a voicemail message by sending an email instead of returning the call. If you ask either of my managers, Jenny or Kurt, they will tell you that I would rather email them. Business professionals will often choose the one with which he or she is most at ease. Considering its total number of calls versus emails per month, the sales team obviously would rather talk than write. Each of these communication media has their advantages and disadvantages. Text messages and email may be best because it will be delivered whether the recipient is there or not. On the other hand, someone who leaves a voicemail message probably assumes you will call them back, not send a text. Otherwise, they would have texted you instead of calling.

8 Preparing Persuasive Business Proposals

new hires @ work

Amanda "Mimi" Bory
Special Events Coordinator
The Maryland Zoo in Baltimore
Stevenson University, 2009

IN MY JOB, I WRITE MANY SPONSORSHIP PROPOSALS FOR EVENTS. This requires me to research businesses and find ways to explain how they will benefit from sponsoring a Zoo event. Keeping up with the news has really helped me better understand how to engage businesses to partner with the Zoo. When writing proposals, I've learned to keep things specific and well organized with headings and bullet points. The more facts and figures I include, the more successful I am at securing sponsors. Businesses aren't looking for a lot of 'fluff'—they want to see the facts and the benefits clearly outlined.

Introduction

In this chapter, you'll apply what you learned in Chapter 5 about persuasive messages to a **proposal**, a communication designed to persuade a business decision maker to adopt a plan, approve a project, choose a product or service, or supply funding. A proposal needs to convince your audience that your idea or solution is feasible and will meet their needs. Depending on the proposal, you may also need to convince your audience that you are the right person to implement the solution.

Proposals can take different forms. For example, if you work for a small bookstore, you may send your manager an informal email proposing a new story hour for children. If you manage a chain restaurant and want to change the menu, you might submit to the owner a formal proposal that includes detailed information complete with a title page, table of contents, and charts and tables. If you are making an oral proposal to a client, you may deliver your proposal as a presentation.

This chapter explains how to use ACE to decide which form to use for a proposal and what content to include. The chapter also identifies three common types of persuasive proposals that you may have to write in the workplace:

- proposals for action or change
- sales proposals to provide products or services
- proposals for funding

Finally, the chapter provides guidelines for formatting formal proposals, including responses to Requests for Proposals (RFPs).

How do I use ACE to prepare an effective proposal?

■ Access this chapter's simulation entitled Persuasive Business Messages & Proposals, located at mybcommlab.com.

Preparing a **proposal** is complicated. It requires that you propose an idea that meets your audience's needs, develop a persuasive appeal, provide details on how to implement the proposal, and explain costs. FIGURE 8.1 illustrates how the ACE process can help you ask good questions when preparing a proposal.

Let's apply these questions to a specific situation. Imagine that you work for a small publishing company and one of your employees, Marina Jacobs, recently retired. To help reduce expenses, your supervisor, Doug Seaver, wants to wait six months to hire a full-time replacement. You and Doug have taken on additional work to compensate for the reduced staff. After a few weeks, you believe the additional workload is affecting the quality of your work and is distracting Doug from his main responsibilities—acquiring new manuscripts and developing online publications. To solve these problems, you want to propose that the company hire a part-time replacement. You know the university in town offers an internship program. After learning more about the program, you decide to suggest this opportunity to Doug. How will you analyze, compose, and evaluate your proposal?

Analyze: Understand purpose, context, and content

Like any other persuasive communication, a proposal benefits from in-depth analysis. You will be able to persuade your audience only if you understand the need your proposal meets (purpose), the type of proposal that is appropriate (context), and the arguments and information that will influence your audience (content).

Purpose

The first step in preparing a proposal is to develop a clear idea of your purpose: what need are you addressing and how do you propose to meet that need? In the case of the internship program, you are addressing the company's need to ensure quality work until a full-time replacement is hired. For the proposal to be successful, your supervisor must feel confident that your proposal will solve the problem without costing more than he is willing to spend.

FIGURE 8.1 Using ACE for Persuasive Proposals

- What am I proposing and why?
- What is the context of my proposal? Is it external or internal? Is it solicited or unsolicited? Is it competitive or noncompetitive?
- Will my audience already be interested, or will I need to grab their attention?
- What requirements, if any, must this proposal meet?
- How will the audience benefit from the proposal?
- What objections should I anticipate?
- Should I do any initial research before writing the proposal? What do I need to learn?

- How formal or informal should this proposal be?
- What is the best medium for the proposal?
- How can I establish credibility?
- What content must I include?
- How should I organize the content?
- How can I use a "you" perspective?
- What word choices will be most effective?

- Will the audience be convinced that the proposal addresses a real need?
- Have I stated what I am proposing?
- Have I shown that my proposal meets the need?
- Have I stressed audience benefits?
- Have I shown I am qualified?
- Have I explained the details: deliverables, costs, schedule?
- Have I asked for agreement?
- Have I used good headings and highlighted main points?
- Have I edited for style and tone?
- Have I proofread for errors?

Context

By considering the context, you can identify the level of persuasion necessary as well as the appropriate form for the proposal. Ask yourself three questions:

❶ **Is the proposal external or internal?** An *external proposal* is addressed to people outside your organization, such as a potential client or an agency that will provide funding. An *internal proposal* is addressed to people within your organization. External proposals usually take the form of a letter or a report-style document. Internal proposals can sometimes be less formal. An internal proposal may be a memo or, in some cases, just an email.

For the internship, you will be writing an internal proposal to your supervisor. It may require only a few paragraphs, so an email message would be appropriate.

❷ **Is the proposal solicited or unsolicited?** A **solicited proposal** is one your audience has asked you to submit. By contrast, an **unsolicited proposal** is one that you initiate. The distinction is important.

If a proposal is solicited, your audience has already identified a problem or need and has requested a solution. You may be responding to an official **request for proposal (RFP)**, which identifies the need and is published widely so that the organization gets multiple competitive proposals. Or you may be responding to a request that is much more informal. Solicited proposals usually take the form of a report-style document or a formal, detailed letter that uses a direct organization because your audience is expecting to hear your main idea.

If the proposal is unsolicited, your audience has not asked for the proposal and may not even be aware that a problem or opportunity exists. When you prepare an unsolicited proposal, you need to do more than just convince your audience you have a good idea. You first need to grab your audience's attention by

Proposal A communication designed to persuade a business decision maker to adopt a plan, approve a project, choose a product or service, or supply funding.

Solicited proposal A proposal that your audience has requested.

Unsolicited proposal A proposal that your audience is not expecting.

Request for proposal (RFP) An invitation for suppliers to competitively submit proposals to provide a product or service.

convincing them that they have an unmet need or can benefit from a new opportunity. In addition, if your audience doesn't know you, you will need to build your credibility as part of the proposal. You may need to explain your experience and qualifications. Unsolicited proposals usually take the form of a letter, memo, or email. The organization of these proposals is often indirect since you first need to prepare your audience for your idea.

In your internship scenario, the proposal is unsolicited, so you will need to persuade your audience that the problem is significant enough to warrant the cost of the part-time intern. You also need to convince Doug that the intern will be able to reduce your workloads.

❸ **Is the proposal competitive or noncompetitive?** In a **noncompetitive proposal** situation, your audience will not be considering any offers other than yours. In a **competitive proposal** situation, others will be competing with you for the sale, the funding, or the opportunity.

Proposals that respond to RFPs are always competitive. The RFP will outline the important criteria on which you will compete. In some situations, price will be the most important criterion. In other situations, your ability to deliver your product or service quickly may be most important. In still others, your proposal will be judged based on your ability to meet very specific requirements. When submitting a competitive proposal, you need to think carefully about what your audience is really looking for and what criteria they will use for judging.

In the internship scenario, the proposal is noncompetitive, so you do not need to prove that your idea is better than a competitor's.

Content

Once you have determined the appropriate format and necessary level of persuasion, you can begin to analyze content by considering requirements, benefits, and potential objections.

- **Requirements:** Every proposal must address audience requirements. When a proposal is solicited, the audience will explicitly state their requirements. For an unsolicited proposal, you will need to put yourself in the audience's position and brainstorm those requirements on your own. For example, in the internship proposal, you will need to determine the qualifications Doug will require an intern to have. If Doug has taken responsibility for all marketing after Marina's retirement, he may require that an intern be experienced in marketing (rather than accounting or editing).

- **Benefits:** A good proposal will go beyond the requirements and describe how your audience or organization will benefit from your proposal. Will they save money or save time? Will you be helping them produce a better product? Does your proposal help them meet regulatory requirements? Does it help them advance their mission? Develop a list of benefits that you can use when you compose the proposal. In a competitive proposal, consider the benefits you provide compared to your competition. In the internship proposal, you might mention the positive public relations your company will gain from hiring a student intern. You may also suggest that by hiring a qualified intern, you may be able to groom a future full-time employee.

- **Potential objections:** To complement your list of benefits, also consider the objections your audience may raise. Will your audience believe your proposed plan costs too much or that it will not solve their problems? As you identify possible objections, brainstorm ways to respond to those objections. If you think that hiring an intern will cost more than Doug is willing to spend, you can stress that a part-time intern will certainly cost less than a full-time employee. You can also suggest that hiring a marketing intern will give Doug more time to acquire new manuscripts and develop online publications.

As you analyze content needs, consider whether you need to conduct research to develop your proposal. Do you need to learn more about your client's industry or about competitors who may be submitting competitive proposals? Do you need to learn more about alternatives or solutions you can offer? Do you need to conduct research in order to propose realistic costs? Do you need to find evidence that your solution has been successful in other organizations? For the internship proposal, you may need to do additional research to learn how the internship program at the university works and how a company advertises for an intern.

Compose: Choose the medium, draft the content, and organize

When you prepare a proposal, you have a number of decisions to make:

- **How formal or informal should this proposal be? What is the best medium for the proposal?** Internal proposals are often informal, taking the form of an email. However, informal does not mean casual and unstructured. If you are asking your organization to invest money in a project or take a risk, you must make a convincing argument and document all your details. External proposals typically take the form of a proposal letter (sometimes attached to an email, which serves as a cover letter), or they may be structured like a formal report. In some organizations, proposals are delivered as presentations with all the details available on the slides or in an appendix.

- **What content must I include?** When readers get a proposal—whether it is a sales or action proposal—they are looking for specific types of information: statement of the problem or opportunity, your specific proposal, reasons for supporting it, implementation plans, and costs. Specific RFPs may ask you to include additional information, but the core set of information must always be present and easy to find. Section 8.2, starting on page 258, explains much of the detail you will need to include.

- **How should I organize the content?** Business readers are able to extract information more quickly from proposals that follow an easy-to-read organization with the following sections:[1]

  1. **Overview or Executive Summary:** A condensed description of the proposal that summarizes key ideas. After reading the overview or executive summary, the audience should understand your proposal's main ideas without having to read through the entire document.

  2. **Introduction:** An informative and persuasive beginning. The introduction should grab the audience's attention, convince the audience you are addressing a significant problem, and preview the content that will be included in the body of the proposal.

  3. **Body:** Distinct sections with informative headlines that help readers find material of interest, for example Problem or Opportunity, Proposed Solution and Rationale, Recommended Implementation Plans, and Costs of Implementation.

  4. **References**: A list of sources used in the document (if applicable).

  5. **Appendices:** Supplemental information (if applicable).

- **What word choices will be most effective?** In a proposal, use active voice rather than passive voice to describe the services you will provide and the activities your audience must complete. Active voice is both stronger and clearer, and it eliminates ambiguity about who must do what.

   Passive: After the internship program is approved, the internship coordinator will be contacted.

   Active: After **you** approve the internship program, **I** will contact the internship coordinator.

   Different sections of a proposal require different verb tenses. When you write about what you propose, use future tense. When you write about your capabilities, use present tense. When you write about your past experience, use a verb form that refers to the past.

> Cochran University's internship program **is** highly regarded in the local community. For the past 10 years, the program **has placed** more than 200 students per year with local businesses. To ensure a good match, the university **prequalifies** all applicants. We **will** see only candidates who meet our qualifications.

Noncompetitive proposal A proposal that has no competition because your audience will not be considering any offers other than yours.

Competitive proposal A proposal that will compete with other proposals for the same sale, funding, or opportunity.

Executive summary A condensed description of a document that summarizes key ideas.

Evaluate: Assess the effectiveness of the proposal

A proposal needs to include a structured set of information and present the information in a readable format. Use the following checklist to evaluate your proposal:

- **Introduction:** If the proposal is solicited, does the introduction clearly indicate that I understand the audience's needs and clearly state what I am proposing? If the proposal is unsolicited, will the introduction grab the audience's attention and convince them that my proposal is addressing a real need?
- **Proposal/Solution:** Have I stated my proposal clearly and showed convincingly that my proposal is a good way to meet the audience's needs?
- **Benefits/Requirements:** Have I explained clearly how the proposal will benefit the audience or how it addresses the audience's mission and priorities? Does the wording use the "you" perspective?
- **Qualifications/Feasibility:** Will the audience be convinced that I have the qualifications to perform the proposed work—or deliver the proposed services? Have I provided enough evidence? Will the audience be convinced that the proposed idea is feasible and can be implemented effectively?
- **Details:** Have I specified sufficient details: deliverables, costs (if any), schedule?
- **Call to action:** Have I specifically asked for agreement? Have I provided contact information so the audience can tell me whether to move forward with the proposal? Have I indicated a date by which I need a response, if applicable?
- **Format:** Is the proposal easy to read with good headings and key points that stand out?
- **Language:** Is the language clear, concise, and professional-sounding?
- **Proofreading:** Have I proofread the document to eliminate errors?

Study Question 8.2

How do I make a proposal persuasive?

Because a proposal is a persuasive document, it must not only provide information but also motivate your audience to act. The proposal must:

- articulate the problem, need, or opportunity
- identify the outcomes and benefits
- present a compelling recommendation
- provide persuasive supporting details that emphasize feasibility and credibility
- request action

FIGURE 8.2 illustrates one of several approaches to organize this information. You will see examples of other organizational strategies throughout this chapter.

Articulate the problem, need, or opportunity

Near the beginning of the proposal, summarize the current business problem, need, or opportunity. This summary serves three persuasive purposes. In a solicited proposal, the summary gives the audience confidence that you have listened to them carefully, truly understand what they are trying to accomplish, and are able to present an appropriate solution. It builds your credibility. In an unsolicited proposal, summarizing the problem, need, or opportunity helps convince the audience that they will benefit from continuing to read so they can learn about your proposed solution or idea. Finally, in any proposal, the initial summary is the "setup" for the final recommendation. If you articulate the problem, need, or opportunity at the beginning of the proposal, you will be able to show at the end of the proposal how your recommendation solves the problem, addresses the need, or takes advantage of the opportunity.

mybcommlab

Apply Figure 8.2's key concepts by revising a new document. Go to Chapter 8 in mybcommlab.com and select Document Makeovers.

FIGURE 8.2 Informal Persuasive Proposal

email

Doug:

I have an idea about how we can get high-quality help in the office to ease our work overload without hiring a full-time employee.

Directly introduces the outcome and benefit without identifying the actual proposal. This will capture Doug's attention.

As you know, since Marina Jacobs left Omni, you and I are both working long hours. I've been working overtime each week on manuscripts, and I've seen you work late many evenings on product marketing. I'm worried that the quality of my work is suffering. After a long day, I'm not able to double-check my work as carefully as I should, and I'm falling behind on correspondence. Your extra marketing efforts are also distracting you from working with new authors and developing new products.

Articulates the problem and explains how the problem negatively affects the business.

I know that you're not ready to hire a new full-time employee to fill Marina's spot since we need to economize right now. However, have you considered hiring one or more interns to handle the extra work? I'm attaching a description of the Cochran University Urban Interns program. Students pay tuition, work 15 hours a week for a local business for one semester (15 weeks), and take two internship-related courses. For that, students receive minimum wage from the employer and a full semester of credit from the university.

Gains credibility by showing an understanding of Doug's financial concerns. States the recommendation as a question and provides supporting details to prove feasibility.

Cochran has both an excellent writing and marketing department, and we can hire two interns to handle the two elements of Marina's job. The benefit for us is that we have smart interns for 15 weeks for a very low cost. In addition, we get good exposure for our business and may find someone who will be a good permanent employee. The benefit for the interns is that they get great hands-on experience at a publishing company.

States the recommendation more explicitly and focuses on benefits to make the proposal more compelling.

The director of the Urban Interns program is Deborah Forrest. As soon as you approve this solution to our problem, I will meet with her to get more details. I look forward to your response.

Concludes with a call to action and identifies next steps.

Thanks, Nick

Identify the outcomes and benefits

When you discuss how you will solve the audience's problem or meet their need, you are identifying the audience's *pain*. However, it is equally important in a proposal to identify how the audience will benefit—in other words, identify their *gain*. Consider two types of gain.

First, how will the audience benefit by solving this problem? Many proposals—especially those that are unsolicited—are unsuccessful, not because the audience accepts a different proposal but because the audience decides to do nothing at all. Help the audience understand why this problem deserves attention and how the benefits of fixing it will outweigh the proposed cost.

Second, how will the audience benefit by accepting your specific proposal? Most problems have several possible solutions. Why is your proposed solution particularly good? What are the benefits of your approach? What unique value does your plan offer? Be sure to highlight the key reasons for accepting your proposal. You can mention these at the beginning and again at the end of the proposal. You can also integrate the discussion of benefits with the detailed discussion of your plan.

new hires@work

Roy Dockery
Field Engineer
Swisslog Health Care Logistics
Thomas Edison State College, 2009

"In school, I learned audiences will ask WIIFM (What's in it for me), and I need to provide the answer. But I never understood the importance of WIIFM until I wrote my first proposal. It makes a huge difference in the outcome."

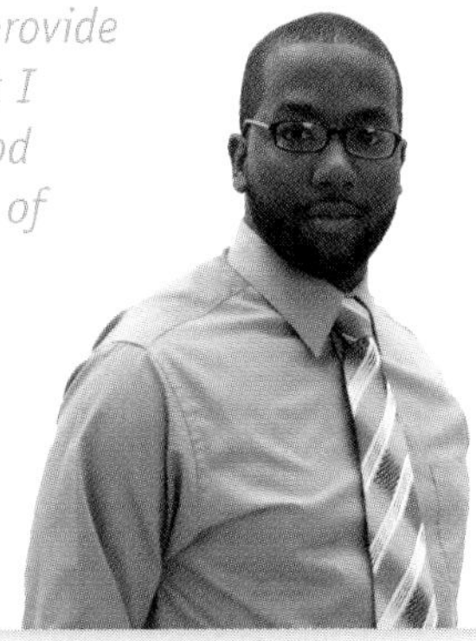

Present a compelling recommendation

Many unsuccessful proposals fail to make any recommendation at all. They simply describe a product or service. To be persuasive, a proposal should make the recommendation compelling by clearly demonstrating how it meets the audience's needs and requirements. In the analyzing stage, create a checklist of all the requirements your proposal must meet and then, when composing, show how you meet every requirement.

Provide persuasive supporting details

The details you provide must prove two things: that the plan is feasible and that you are credible. The best way to address feasibility is to present implementation plans. What is the time line for the project? When and how will the work be completed? What are the **deliverables**—the items you are agreeing to provide to the audience? What are the costs? What gives you confidence that the plan will succeed?

Establishing credibility means showing that you have the ability to deliver what you propose. Whether you are writing a sales proposal or a proposal for funding, your audience will need to have confidence that you can deliver your promises. That is why your proposal should show that you have the qualifications, facilities, time, staff, and expertise to complete the project. You can demonstrate this by including testimonials, describing similar projects you have completed, and describing resources available to you, and providing brief biographical sketches of the staff.

Request action

A persuasive proposal will look forward to next steps and request a response. Otherwise, it may be easy for your audience to forget or ignore your proposal. Solicited sales proposals often include an acceptance or authorization sheet that your audience can sign. For unsolicited proposals, however, you may want to suggest a meeting or telephone call as the next step.

Even though the proposal in Figure 8.2 (page 259) is an informal, internal proposal composed as an email, it includes all the persuasive elements described in this section. Notice that the organization of this email is indirect, which makes sense since Doug was not expecting this proposal.

Study Question 8.3

What types of business proposals should I be prepared to write?

During your career, you may need to write three types of proposals: proposals for action or change, sales proposals (either solicited or unsolicited) to provide products or services, and proposals for grants or other funding. This section provides examples of proposals in all three categories.

Proposals for action or change

If you have an idea at work that you would like to implement or a project that needs funding, a proposal may win you the support you need. In business, proposals for action are strongest when they make a **business case**—when they argue that a specific course of action is good for an organization and makes business sense. When writing a business case, you need to discuss benefits, costs, risks, and implementation plans.[2]

The proposal in Figure 8.2 was a proposal for action or change. FIGURE 8.3 on page 261 provides another example of this type of proposal, requesting funds for new equipment. You will notice that its format is more formal than the one in Figure 8.2. It also is longer because it needs to include a lot of informative and persuasive content to make a business case. However, the headings help the reader see the structure of the

FIGURE 8.3 Formal Internal Proposal for Action

proposal

Highlights four benefits with key words at the beginning of each numbered section. Focuses on how the solution benefits the company as a whole.

Benefits of Creating a Centrally Accessible Collaborative Workspace
Creating a centrally accessible collaborative workspace offers four benefits. The workspace will:

1. **Maximize team effectiveness.** The large display enables easy collaboration in a single workspace among a critical number of people. Rather than working in small groups crowded around tiny laptop screens or working in large groups with each member looking at only his or her own screen, the large screen allows teams to maximize their effectiveness.

2. **Improve work quantity and quality.** According to research [...] Ross Business School at the University of Michigan, collabor[...] like *TeamWork* are capable of improving the amount and qu[...] work. (The abstract of the research report is included as App[...] increased productivity, our teams will be able to evaluate m[...] opportunities and develop recommendations that take adva[...] members' creative thinking.

3. **Encourage teamwork in other departments.** Installing Tea[...] north conference room makes it accessible not only to the t[...] department but also to any group in company. This may en[...] departments to develop productive teamwork practices.

4. **Expand the functionality of the conference room.** In addit[...] collaboration, the Intelliboard system will display presentati[...] connected laptop. This means that the conference room ca[...] presentation room without purchase of additional projectors[...]

Provides credible detail about costs. Costs can be placed before benefits when you want to show that the cost of an item will lead to cost savings as a benefit.

Requested Budget
The IT budget for this project is $7,650, for the server, monitor,

Item	Price
TeamWork server	$ 1,600
IntelliBoard monitor	$ 4,000
TeamServe collaborative software	$ 2,050
Total	**$ 7,650**

This one-time fee includes three years of technical support and product upgrades.

Next Steps

Ends with call to action and anticipates audience's interest in a demonstration

Collaboration software and hardware are currently our departm[...] priority. We would like to install this system and have it function[...] of the year. We would appreciate the budget being authorized[...] that we can order the equipment and arrange for installation. If[...] demonstration of the hardware and software before authorizing[...] that at your convenience.

2

Proposal to Create a Computer-Aided Collaborative Workspace
Kip Koestler, Manager, Strategy and Business Development
September 1, 20XX

Begins directly with specific proposal followed by the positive outcome that will result.

The Strategy and Business Development Department (SBD) requests funding of $7,650 to create a small-group, interactive workspace in our north conference room. It will include a large interactive display that will be visible to all team members and controllable from any connected laptop computer. The space will make it easier for our project teams to collaborate and produce high-quality work.

Current Situation

Explains the problem and the need for the proposed system.

In the past 12 months, SBD has restructured its 20 employees into five work teams that are responsible for evaluating merger, acquisition, and new business opportunities. This new team structure is very effective compared to the previous structure, where each employee worked independently on his or her own projects. Our productivity has increased by 20 percent. However, our current office space is not set up to support collaboration.

Each team member has a small individual office that does not offer enough room for teams to collaborate. Our two conference rooms have sufficient space for collaboration, but they do not have appropriate software or hardware to support team activity. Current efforts at collaboration typically result in one of two outcomes. Group members either (1) crowd around a single computer where only some can view the screen and only one can control the input devices, or (2) divide the workload, then proceed to work alone on their own computers, sending results to a single person designated to compile the results. Neither situation is optimal for effective teamwork. As a result, we are not getting the full value of team thinking.

Proposed Solution: Create a Collaborative Workspace To solve this problem, we

Highlights the proposed action and specific implementation details.

propose creating a team collaboration space in the second-floor north conference room, equipped with collaboration software and hardware. We evaluated three computer-based systems and propose implementing the TeamWork system. (A full comparison of the three systems is available in Appendix A.) TeamWork facilitates collaboration through a shared desktop server and a large public display visible to all group members. The system includes the following software:

- IntelliBoard presentation software, which both displays presentations and allows team members to write directly on the screen with a digital pen and save the results,

- TeamServe collaboration software, which permits remote control of the desktop server by any of the participating collaboration members and facilitates file sharing and storage among team members.

TeamWork requires no software installation or licensing for individual laptops,

Explains rationale for choosing this specific system.

allowing anyone in the company to use it. Its total system cost is the lowest of all evaluated systems, and it is highly rated by Business Computing magazine (September 20XX) based on reliability and technical support.

1

document at a glance. You can send this report-style proposal in hard copy or electronically, as an email attachment. One advantage of sending it by email is that you can summarize the proposal in the email and request action, for example a meeting to discuss the proposal.

Solicited sales proposals

If you work in an organization that sells products or services, you may have to prepare *sales proposals* for your customers and clients. Like an action proposal, a strong sales proposal makes a persuasive case that the audience will benefit from what you propose. In addition to serving as a persuasive tool, a sales proposal often serves as a sales contract. It identifies exactly what you will deliver, at what cost, in what time frame, and under what circumstances. When your client signs the proposal, both parties have made a commitment.

FIGURE 8.4 is a sales proposal from Cronin Environmental Services (CES) to a new client, Davis College. The proposal is two pages long, so the writer chose a letter format. If the document were more than three pages, the writer might choose a report format.

Deliverables The items or services you agree to deliver to your audience.

Business case A justification for a proposal showing that the recommended course of action is good for an organization and makes business sense.

FIGURE 8.4 Solicited Sales Proposal

`letter`

CRONIN
Environmental Services, Inc.

1442 Industrial Parkway West
Rollins, MN 55555

612.555.5555
Fax: 612.555.6666
www.cronin.com

October 24, 20XX

Mr. Paul Phillips
Director of Physical Plant
Davis College
285 S. Kings Way
Rollins, MN 55555

Subject: Proposal to Update Davis College's Waste Reduction Plan

Dear Mr. Phillips:

Cronin Environmental Services, Inc. (CES) is pleased to submit this proposal to assist Davis College (DC) in preparing an updated Waste Reduction Plan as required by the Minnesota Department of Community Affairs (MDCA). CES has extensive experience producing MDCA waste reduction plans. Based on that experience, this letter identifies CES's recommended scope of work, time frame, and budget. It also provides background about CES's expertise.

The proposal starts by (1) identifying the project and reason for writing, (2) stressing CES's qualifications, and (3) previewing the structure of the proposal.

SCOPE OF WORK

To evaluate the waste composition at Davis College and prepare the required analyses and report, CES proposes to do the following:

The Scope of Work section of the proposal functions as a contract to identify what CES will do and what Davis College must do. The two sets of requirements are laid out in two easy-to-read lists. Each item in the first list begins with an action verb.

- Review waste hauling and recycling records for the past 12 months.

- Coordinate with the Facilities Management staff to schedule a representative sampling of the waste generated at the DC main campus. CES will work with the Facilities Management staff to identify a location for sorting to minimize inconvenience and, if needed, for temporarily storing the material being sorted (for less than one day).

- Conduct a sort-and-weigh using one-day's worth of waste from the campus. The sort will address all the waste components required by MDCA, including glass, aluminum containers, plastic (high-density and low-density polyethylene, and polyethylene terepthalate), and landscape waste. In addition, the sort will identify weight components of newsprint, cardboard, white and computer paper, magazines, and a mixed paper category.

- Conduct a brief walkthrough of the college to evaluate the recycling and waste reduction activities at the campus.

- Meet with Facilities Management staff as necessary to discuss questions pertinent to the report.

- Prepare a draft report for DC to review and approve.

- Prepare four copies of the Waste Reduction Plan Update, which DC can submit to MDCA, and two copies for the college's records.

(continued)

FIGURE 8.4 Continued

Mr. Paul Phillips
October 24, 20XX
Page 2

The scope of work assumes that DC will provide the following information necessary to prepare the report:

- data on procurement of recycled materials, such as paper
- waste hauling and recycling records
- data on numbers of students and employees

CES will supply the required forms to obtain this information.

PROPOSED TIME SCHEDULE
CES is able to begin the fieldwork within two weeks of the notification to proceed. The fieldwork will take three days. We can have the analysis complete within four weeks from the completion of the fieldwork, depending on how quickly DC provides the other required data for the report.

BUDGET
CES proposes a not-to-exceed budget of $9,200 to complete this scope of work. The budget is based on the time estimated to complete the work. You will be billed for only the actual time and expenses related to the project. If our time and expenses are lower, the fee will be lower.

The schedule and budget are both conditional: CES can do its part on time only if Davis College does its part on time. The budget is a maximum budget. If the work takes less time, CES will charge less. This will make Davis feel more confident that the price will be fair.

CES EXPERIENCE
CES is an engineering consulting firm with offices throughout the state, including one in St. Paul (located three blocks from the MDCA building). CES offers your company:

- **Extensive experience** conducting waste audits, performing analyses of recycling programs, and developing waste reduction plans for a diverse range of facilities, including commercial offices, elementary schools and colleges, hospitals, and other institutions. CES was recently selected by Winona County to provide waste reduction services for businesses and multifamily complexes throughout the county.
- **A track record of success.** In the past year, CES has produced waste reduction plans for 11 organizations. All of the plans were approved by the MDCA. In addition, CES has been extremely successful in helping its clients secure more than $2 million in grant funds.

Experience is one of the most important sections of the proposal because it shows CES can deliver what it promises.

An extensive client list is attached to this proposal. I have also attached a short article on CES, published in *Engineering News Record*.

The attached client list and article increase the company's credibility.

CONTRACT
Enclosed are two copies of our Standard Agreement for Professional Services. If you agree to this proposal, please sign both agreements, return one, and keep one for your records.

Mr. Phillips, we look forward to working with you on this project. With our experience in producing MDCA reports, we are confident we can produce the documentation you need with minimal disruption to campus life. If you have any questions before signing the contract, please contact me at 612-555-5555.

Sincerely,

Kim Colgate

Kim Colgate
Project Manager

Enclosures

ETHICS Does Your Proposal Demonstrate Integrity?

Companies that request proposals and those that provide proposals each have ethical obligations.

A company that requests a proposal has the obligation to read it carefully and evaluate it according to the stated requirements. In the worst-case scenario, a company may request competitive proposals but give "inside information" to a preferred competitor, allowing that person to produce a more persuasive proposal. It is unethical to ask someone to spend time and energy to produce a proposal if you know in advance you will be awarding the contract to someone else.

A company that submits a proposal also has an ethical obligation—the obligation to provide content that is honest and accurate. It is unethical to bend the truth to make the sale. Linda LaDuc from the University of Massachusetts observes some writers believe "they must make the immediate sale or gain immediate acceptance at all costs, and so they argue very persuasively, but not very honestly."[3]

As a writer, avoid these common traps that undermine the integrity of your proposal:[4]

- Do not knowingly exaggerate the benefits of your proposal or hide the costs in order to meet your audience's requirements or expectations.
- Do not overpromise what you can deliver.
- Do not ignore technical difficulties.
- Do not dismiss or suppress other viable options that your audience should consider.

Consider the following example of how to revise an overblown phrase to make it more accurate:

Inaccurate original: "Our wireless router is the most powerful on the market and can be self-installed by following the instructions in the accompanying installation manual."

Problem: The writers are leaving out the fact that the installation manual is 35 pages long and extremely technical. It is written primarily for people with significant hardware installation experience. They are making the router seem easier to install than it actually is. The writers are also making an unsubstantiated and overblown claim about the power of the router. More powerful routers exist, but they are aimed at large businesses, and this is aimed at small businesses.

More ethical revision: "Our wireless router has been rated by *PC World* as the most powerful small-business router on the market. It can also be installed easily either by your internal information technology group using the included installation manual or by our technical support staff at a nominal fee."

The revised version is more ethical because it is more accurate. Although the claims are qualified, they still stress benefits. Your audience will appreciate your honesty, and the credibility you earn may lead to a stronger long-term relationship. ■

mybcommlab

For ETHICS exercises, go to Exercise 7 on page 280 and Exercise 10 on page 281 or to this chapter's End-of-Chapter Exercises at mybcommlab.com.

Because this is an external sales proposal to a new client, the tone is formal. Notice that the proposal is structured with headings and bullets that make it easy to read. Also notice that the proposal devotes substantial space to identifying the scope and cost of what CES will deliver. This is the contractual part of the proposal.

Unsolicited sales proposals

An unsolicited sales proposal is essentially a targeted marketing letter directed to someone who you believe may benefit from your products or services. Your goal is to generate interest in your business proposal and to encourage further discussions. FIGURE 8.5 is an unsolicited sales proposal from an event planning company to the Association of Investment Professionals, an association that holds several events throughout the year. Notice how this proposal, like the unsolicited internal proposal in Figure 8.2 on page 259, devotes a lot of space to persuading the audience that there is a problem or opportunity to address. Notice, too, how the headings and subheadings highlight important parts of the message. Finally, notice that although this proposal does provide some details about implementation, it does not discuss any contractual arrangements as a solicited sales proposal would.

FIGURE 8.5 Unsolicited Sales Proposal

`letter`

SWANSON
INTERNATIONAL

5250 W. 6th Street, Reston, VA 20191
800.555.1780 I Fax: 800.555.1781 I www.swanson.com

May 11, 20XX

Ms. Eva Greenwald
Executive Director
Association of Investment Professionals
931 East 59th Street
New York, NY 11234

Dear Ms. Greenwald:

We can help your organization reduce your costs, increase your revenue, and enhance your members' satisfaction with your professional events.

Swanson International is an event registration and housing service that provides support for corporate, not-for-profit, and athletic events throughout North America. After reviewing your association's website, I noticed that AIP sponsors two annual conventions and several training events throughout the country. I also noticed that all event and housing registration for these events is done manually, through telephone or mail. I believe our services at Swanson can streamline your registration process and also increase your revenue and member satisfaction. I would like the opportunity to show you how working with Swanson can benefit AIP.

How Our System Works

Hotel planning: For each event your organization sponsors, Swanson negotiates discounted room rates with a range of hotels in the area. Your members receive an attractive set of choices to meet budget and other needs. Swanson also builds in a rebate with each of these hotels, which Swanson then shares with AIP. This will pay for all of Swanson's services and also provide revenue for AIP.

(continued)

The proposal begins with an attention-getting sentence that identifies audience benefits.

Because the proposal is unsolicited, the author provides context by explaining the services that Swanson provides. The author also personalizes the proposal by showing that she has done some initial research about the association.

Section headings and paragraph topics help the audience quickly skim the content.

The description mentions audience benefits throughout to provide persuasive evidence.

FIGURE 8.5 Continued

Ms. Eva Greenwald
May 11, 20XX
Page 2

Event and hotel registration: Swanson also builds a unique website for your event, including property pictures, directions, and room types. Through this site, participants can register for an event, register for housing, and purchase event-related merchandise (such as T-shirts and pins). For those members not willing or able to use the web, we have an in-house call center to process registration requests.

Post-event rebate collection: After your event, Swanson bills the hotel for any rebates you have been promised, using our automated invoicing system.

Benefits to Your Association

Our list of satisfied clients is growing because we provide value to our clients in three areas:

- **Reduced administrative costs:** Our online registration services eliminate many time-consuming tasks facing event organizers, thus reducing administrative costs and hassle.

- **Increased revenue:** Our event registration tool will increase your hotel-related revenue because the web-based system drives participants to your hotels through the registration process.

- **Increased member satisfaction:** Participants can register for the event and accommodations in one easy step. In addition, the selection of hotels is designed to satisfy a range of budgets.

The most attractive benefit is that there are no out-of-pocket costs to AIP.

Please consider using our services for the next event you plan.

I will be in New York on business the week of June 15. May we set up a meeting to discuss how Swanson can help AIP? I would like to learn more about how many people typically attend AIP events and the kinds of hotels your members prefer. With this information, I will be able to estimate the revenue you can expect with our services.

I will call you next week to see if you are available to meet or talk by phone. Or you can reach me at (800) 555-1780. I look forward to talking with you.

Regards,

Kathryn Nylund

Kathryn Nylund
Sales Manager
Swanson International

This section repeats the benefits from the attention-grabbing introduction, providing more detail and explanation.

The main idea is highlighted and stands alone to draw attention.

The proposal ends with a call for action and contact information. For an unsolicited sales proposal, one appropriate call for action is to request a meeting. Ideally, if the meeting is successful, the audience will solicit a more formal proposal.

CULTURE Writing Proposals for Different Cultures

The advice in this chapter is particularly relevant for business proposals intended for audiences within the United States. However, what if you need to make a proposal to a business associate or potential business partner from another country? Is it realistic to believe that you can simply write a proposal—including both persuasive elements and the terms of the agreement—and expect your audience to sign that document and abide by the agreement?

Here are some differences between the United States approach to business proposals and that of three other countries—China, Brazil, and Italy:

- **Differences in the proposal process.** According to China Trade.com, "Chinese business people will seldom make a snap decision and prefer to give a business proposal careful and measured consideration."[5] In addition, as intercultural communication expert Linda Beamer explains, the Chinese "generally consider the effect of a solution on the people and relationships involved before they take action . . . . A stress on context and relationships could explain why Chinese often want to discuss alternative procedures and plans long after their foreign counterparts have finished."[6] Because relationships are so important to Chinese businesspeople, the process of negotiating an agreement can take a long time. To propose and negotiate an agreement in China, begin with conversations and discussions where both parties can learn more about what the other party values and needs. Plan to meet face to face and involve several members of your team, at different hierarchical levels. Negotiate your proposals verbally, and then finalize them with a written contract.[7]
- **Differences in persuasive content.** In the United States, businesspeople are conditioned to think that profit and fi-

nancial advantage are the biggest benefits to stress in a business proposal. In some countries, however, other benefits are more important. For example, in Brazil many consider gains in status and power to be more important than gains in profit.[8] Therefore, in a proposal to a Brazilian company, identify the social and status benefits as well as the financial benefits.

- **Differences in attitude toward signed agreements.** For most Americans, a signed proposal or contract means a final agreement that must be honored. However, in other cultures, a signed contract signals an interest in doing business rather than a commitment. For example, in China, contracts are always open to renegotiation. This is the accepted business norm.[9]
- **Differences in attitude toward oral agreements.** For most Americans, an agreement is not finalized until it is put in writing. In other cultures—for example, Italy—it is expected that oral commitments will be honored. Signing a contract is a mere formality, reflecting the commitment between business partners.[10]

If you are proposing a business arrangement to someone from a different country or culture—even if you are both in the United States—take the time to research cultural norms and expectations. A good starting place is the book *Negotiating International Business—The Negotiator's Reference Guide to 50 Countries Around the World* by Lothar Katz, the president of the cross-cultural consultancy Leadership Crossroads. Portions of the book are available on the web.

mybcommlab

For CULTURE exercises, go to Critical Thinking Question on page 279 and Exercise 12 on page 281 or to this chapter's End-of-Chapter Exercises at mybcommlab.com.

Grant proposals and other proposals for funding

If you work for a not-for-profit organization, you may need to request funding from an external source to support one of your organization's projects. For example, a homeless shelter may need to request funding from the city to replace its roof. An arts organization may request funding from the local arts council to support an after-school arts program. An academic organization may request funding from a foundation to support a business plan competition. Receiving that funding will be essential for the project's success. Depending on the requirements of the agency, these proposals for funding, also called **grant proposals**, may be prepared as formal reports, letters, or online submissions.

Grant proposal A proposal requesting funding, typically from governmental agencies or charitable foundations.

The following guidelines will help you think effectively about how to plan, organize, and submit an effective grant proposal:

❶ **Identify a funding agency that is a good match with the project you are trying to fund.** For example, imagine that you are the business manager of a hospital's physical therapy clinic in central Oklahoma. You realize that many low-income people in rural Oklahoma are not getting the medical help they need because their communities do not have physical therapists. In addition, it is too expensive for those people to travel to your center. You would like to write a grant proposal to receive funding to subsidize the travel expenses for low-income patients within 200 miles of your center. Where can you apply for that funding?

An Internet search reveals that the Wal-Mart Foundation may be a good source. The tagline of the Wal-Mart Foundation is "Creating Opportunities So People Can Live Better." The Foundation explains its mission this way:

> The Wal-Mart Foundation strives to provide opportunities that improve the lives of individuals in our communities including our customers and associates. Through financial contributions, in-kind donations and volunteerism, the Wal-Mart Foundation supports initiatives focused on enhancing opportunities in our four main focus areas:
>
> - Education
> - Workforce Development / Economic Opportunity
> - Environmental Sustainability
> - Health and Wellness
>
> The Wal-Mart Foundation has a particular interest in supporting the following populations: veterans and military families, traditionally underserved groups, individuals with disabilities, and people impacted by natural disasters.[11]

Your project meets those criteria in three ways. First, it is a health and wellness project. Second, it serves individuals with disabilities, along with others. And third, it serves people in the same communities that Wal-Mart serves, since Wal-Mart has more than 50 stores in Oklahoma. These matching criteria will be important facts to mention in the grant proposal.

❷ **Identify a contact person at the funding organization and arrange a personal meeting.** The meeting has two goals: (1) to communicate your passion for the project, and (2) to ask the granting agency if they will accept a proposal from you for the specific amount of money that you are requesting. This ensures that you send the proposal to an appropriate agency and do not waste your time.

❸ **Draft a proposal that addresses each topic area.** FIGURE 8.6 illustrates a possible table of contents for the Wal-Mart funding proposal. Notice the section called "Evaluation." This section helps the audience measure the success of the program. Directions for formatting the major sections are provided on page 271.

❹ **Draft a cover letter.** When funding agencies review multiple proposals, they expect the cover letter to help them quickly understand who you are, what you are requesting, why the request is important, how it addresses the agency's mission, and why you believe your project is feasible. As you plan a letter using the ACE process, develop answers to these questions. Then when you compose, structure the letter to make these answers easy to find. FIGURE 8.7 illustrates a cover letter for the Wal-Mart Foundation proposal, answering all these questions.

FIGURE 8.6
Table of Contents for a Funding Proposal

FIGURE 8.7 Cover Letter for a Funding Proposal

`letter`

CENTRAL OKLAHOMA
Regional Hospital

1795 NW Highway
Edmond, OK 55555

June 15, 20XX

Ms. Earlyn Felix
Grant Administrator
The Wal-Mart Foundation
501 SW 19th Street
Moore, OK 55555

Dear Ms. Felix:

Thank you for the opportunity to meet with you Thursday and for your interest in the project, *Providing Access to Physical Therapy for Low-Income Patients in Central Oklahoma*. We believe this project will help us meet the Wal-Mart Foundation goal of improving the health and wellness of underserved populations in communities in the state. In addition, this project can be replicated in other states where Wal-Mart serves its customers.

We ask you to invest $10,000 to provide transportation and lodging to low-income patients who do not have the means to travel to our hospital for physical therapy services. Your investment will provide travel funds for up to 100 patients who live more than 100 miles from Central Oklahoma Regional Hospital. We have agreements from two bus companies and a local hotel to provide services at half price for this program.

As we discussed in our meeting, our preliminary research shows that each year physicians in the Central Oklahoma area prescribe physical therapy for more than 3,000 patients. However, many communities in Central Oklahoma do not have physical therapists nearby. The nearest comprehensive physical therapy center is in our hospital in Edmond. While the cost of the therapy is often covered by Medicare or Medicaid, the cost of transportation and lodging is not. As a result, many patients do not see a physical therapist and thus experience a lower quality of life.

Our project goal over the next 12 months is to establish a program that will allow physicians to apply for travel grants on behalf of their patients. We ask for your help in funding these grants.

I will contact you next Tuesday after you've had an opportunity to review this proposal.

Best regards,

Sean Wittwer

Sean Wittwer
Grant Coordinator

Leads with the most important point: the proposed project will meet one of the foundation's goals: to improve the health and wellness of underserved populations.

Specifically identifies the amount of money the hospital is requesting and how that money will be spent. Implies the program is feasible by showing it has community support.

Explains the need that this proposal will meet.

Further reinforces feasibility by explaining how recipients of travel grants will be chosen.

Concludes by focusing on next steps.

TECHNOLOGY Submitting Proposals Online

Proposals are most often written as letters, memos, emails, or reports. However, organizations increasingly require that proposals be submitted through an online form. For example, the State Giving Program at the Wal-Mart Foundation only accepts grant proposals submitted online through the Wal-Mart Foundation website.

The form prompts a submitter to answer a series of qualifying questions about the organization, its mission, and the funding request. The application also requires the submitter to upload files, including an Excel budget spreadsheet.

You can use the ACE communication process to help you submit effective online proposals:

- **Analyze the application in advance.** Before entering information, read the entire application to get a sense of what it requires so you can organize all the information that you need to fill in the blanks. Consider printing the online application as a reference as you gather data, noting the content you will include for each item.

- **Compose detailed content offline.** Use a word processing program to write your detailed descriptions and to determine your word and character count so you do not exceed the maximum amount allowed. Then cut and paste the text into the online application.

- **Evaluate your answers compared to the foundation's criteria and priorities before you submit.** Have you used the same language the foundation uses to describe its priorities? Have you explained well how your project meets those criteria and addresses the priorities? Have you made a good case for why the foundation should support your project, especially when so many other applicants are competing for the funding? Have you established your own credibility and the feasibility of the project? In an online application, you have only a short amount of space in every box, so use it wisely to persuade the funding agency.

mybcommlab

For a TECHNOLOGY exercise, go to Exercise 15 on page 282 or to this chapter's End-of-Chapter Exercises at mybcommlab.com.

How do I structure and format a formal proposal?

If a proposal is longer than three or four pages, you need to provide some extra structure so that readers can navigate the document and easily find the information they are looking for. This section provides guidelines for structuring formal proposals, including responses to RFPs—requests for proposals.

Structure a formal proposal like a formal report

A formal proposal looks much like a formal report. In addition to the body of the proposal itself, formal proposals include these elements: cover message (letter, memo, or email), title page, executive summary, table of contents, references or works cited, and appendices if applicable.

Cover letter, memo, or email

A **cover message** introduces the audience to the proposal. This message can take the form of a cover letter for an external proposal, a cover memo for an internal proposal, or an email to which the proposal is attached. The cover message provides the reader with an overview of the content and is itself a persuasive document that convinces your audience to read the proposal carefully and positively. The cover message tells the reader:

- what you are writing about (the subject of this proposal)
- what features and benefits the proposal offers
- what you plan to do next as a follow-up

Figure 8.7 on page 269 is an example of a cover message.

Title page

The title page provides the following content:

- title of the proposal
- name of the recipient of the proposal: company or individual
- name of the writer of the proposal: company, author, or authors submitting the proposal
- date the proposal was submitted

Executive summary

Any proposal longer than five or six pages should include an executive summary, which briefly summarizes the most important information. Executive decision makers may read only the executive summary and, based on how persuasive it is, decide whether to read the entire document. An executive summary for a proposal typically includes the following information:

- the problem necessitating the proposal
- the suggested solutions
- the benefits that will result when the proposed suggestions are implemented
- important implementation details
- the qualifications that indicate you can resolve the issue

Depending on the situation, the summary may also include:

- a project management plan and timetable
- a total project budget

Table of contents

The audience may not read each section of your proposal. A table of contents, like that illustrated in Figure 8.6, allows readers to find the material that interests them. For example, the managers who read your proposals will be interested in time frames, company history, satisfied customers, and personnel requirements. In contrast, purchasing agents will be interested in product descriptions, required equipment, and warranties. Accountants will read to verify the budget and costs.

To help readers find the material that interests them, your table of contents should be a complete and accurate listing of the headings covered in the proposal. You will need to use your judgment to decide how many levels of headings your table of contents should include. Will your audience be able to find the information that they need with only first- and second-level headings? Or will your audience benefit from having third-level headings also?

References or works cited

If you refer to other sources in your proposal, include a reference page that lists all those sources. These sources may include articles, books, reports, websites, interviews, and brochures. References add to your credibility and help your audience easily find any information they want to explore further. The format of the list may vary depending on your discipline and your audience's expectations. Appendix C describes two of the most frequently used documentation formats: APA (American Psychological Association) and MLA (Modern Language Association). Additional referencing information is available at mybcommlab.com.

Cover message A letter, memo, or email accompanying a formal report or proposal, designed to explain the document and persuade the audience to read it.

Appendices

Appendices allow you to include additional information that may interest the reader but is too detailed to include in the body of the proposal. This content may include examples of previous work you have done, biographies, testimonials, survey results, product descriptions and technical specifications, complicated work schedules, or long tables that will not fit on one page. To ensure that you include only relevant appendices, refer to each appendix at least once in the body of the proposal. For example:

> *. . . For the biographies of the consultants who will manage your project, see Appendix A . . .*
>
> *. . . We have many satisfied clients, as illustrated by the testimonials in Appendix B . . .*
>
> *. . . Appendix C includes a complete list of our products . . .*

Follow these additional guidelines for appendices:

- Put each kind of information in a separate appendix. For example, you could put biographical information in Appendix A, examples of previous work in Appendix B, and product descriptions in Appendix C.
- Arrange the appendices in the order you refer to them in the text.
- Label the appendices sequentially and give each a title, for example "Appendix A: Biographies of Key Personnel."
- List the appendices in the table of contents using the complete name of the appendix (label and title).

Follow specified guidelines when responding to RFPs

Requests for proposals typically include a very specific set of requirements that the proposer must meet. In some industries, RFPs can generate proposals that are more than 100 pages long. In most cases, though, responses are much shorter.

The key to writing an effective proposal in response to an RFP is to create a checklist of requirements and to ensure that your proposal addresses all these requirements. FIGURE 8.8 is the cover letter that accompanies a 15-page RFP sent to the Revson Communication Group. When the Revson Group received this RFP, they read through the entire document, noting the proposal requirements in the margins. Figure 8.8 shows the Revson Group's annotations on the cover letter.

The formal RFP introduced in the Figure 8.8 cover letter required Revson to prepare a formal response that includes elements of both information and persuasion. To be successful, the proposal must:

- provide a quick overview at the beginning, either in an executive summary or an introduction
- make the information easy to find, using a table of contents or other contents list
- show an understanding of the client's needs
- propose a solution that meets the needs as listed in the RFP
- provide confidence that the course designers and instructors are qualified
- propose a competitive fee
- provide the required documentation

FIGURE 8.8 Request for a Proposal with Marginal Notes

`letter`

Industries

1000 Brandywine Blvd., Wilmington, DE 19800

November 7, 20XX

Revson Communication Group
5500 Kirkwood Highway
Wilmington, DE 19808

Subject: RFP for Strategic Communications Course

I am contacting you on behalf of Linus Industries (Linus). We are requesting a proposal to assist us with a one-day Strategic Communications course for senior-level managers who communicate with all levels of the organization.

Context

Linus is a broad-based health care company that discovers, develops, manufactures, and markets products and services that span the continuum of care—from prevention and diagnosis to treatment and cure. The Strategic Communications course will be one of the final pieces in a 16-course, in-depth communications cluster as part of our Business Skills curriculum. This advanced course will help Linus do a better job of communicating strategic messages with employees and leaders within the company as well as communicating externally. An initial description of the course is included on page 3 of the RFP.

Project Purpose

This project is to establish an instructor-led course that will help senior managers create appropriate strategic messages and communicate effectively with peers and employees. Our three broad areas of interest are:

- communicating strategic messages downward within the organization.
- creating an environment where dialogue is encouraged: one-on-one or within a larger group setting.
- creating a strategic communications plan for major initiatives such as organizational changes.

Scope

The solution proposed may be an entirely new creation or customization of a current course offered by the supplier. Linus does not have a method of forecasting how many people might use this tool during a year. However, 48 to 108 users per year is a reasonable estimate.

Key Requirements:

Must be a one-day course.

Must focus on communicating strategic messages internally and externally.

Must address three key areas:.
- communicating downward
- creating an environment that encourages dialogue
- creating strategic communication plans

(continued)

FIGURE 8.8 Continued

This RFP is for development of course materials. However, please include the proposed audience size per session and the total costs of facilitating the course for a given session (excluding travel costs, which are reimbursed afterwards—see Travel & Living Expenses elsewhere in this document). Linus must approve the primary instructor, but such approval is not part of this RFP. Please include data describing potential instructors.

Critical Success Factors

The course must do the following:

- emphasize skill-building, rather than "learning about" the topic of strategic communications
- offer opportunities for practice
- be appropriate for senior-level managers who expect a high-level course and have little tolerance for basic information
- be appropriate for audiences not just within the U.S., but throughout the world
- account for cross-cultural nuances regarding either the speaker or audience
- be able to be customized to fit Linus branding standards

Material Included in This RFP

On the following pages, please find:

1. Project Charter
2. Project Milestones
3. Response Terms and Conditions
4. Response Content and Evaluation
5. Proposal Submission Guidelines
6. Supplier Evaluation Criteria
7. Confidentiality Agreement

Linus expects the utmost in professional associations with its suppliers. We strive to work together in a harmonious relationship that is beneficial for both Linus and our chosen supplier(s). This RFP is an instrument designed to enable Linus to make the best possible decision in creating a business relationship with the selected supplier(s).

For more information, please contact me at 800.555.3978 or r.sklar@linusind.com. I look forward to your proposal.

Sincerely,

Richard Sklar

Richard Sklar, Manager
Professional Development

Proposal must include:
- proposed class size
- costs of developing materials
- costs for facilitating the course
- data describing potential instructors

Description of the course must emphasize:
- skill building
- opportunities for practice
- high-level content
- cross-cultural elements
- method of customizing to branding standards

Check proposal submission guidelines and evaluation criteria.

FIGURE 8.9 shows a thumbnail view of Revson Communication Group's response. Notice how the proposal includes all the formal elements. Also notice how the section headings are designed to respond specifically to the content in the RFP.

FIGURE 8.9 Response to RFP

IN SUMMARY, proposals may be as informal as an email to your supervisor or as formal as a report-like response to an RFP. No matter what their form, all proposals are persuasive documents that share four common elements. They all:

- demonstrate an understanding of a problem, need, or opportunity.
- propose a solution that solves the problem, meets the need, or takes advantage of the opportunity.
- instill confidence that the idea is feasible and, if applicable, you are qualified to implement the idea.
- help the audience see meaningful benefits from implementing the proposal.

CHAPTER 8 Summary

8.1 How do I use ACE to prepare an effective proposal? *(pages 254–258)*

- **Analyze: Understand purpose, context, and content.** To analyze purpose, focus on the audience's needs and what you are proposing to address those needs. To analyze context, ask three questions: (1) Is your proposal external or internal? (2) Is it a solicited proposal or an unsolicited proposal? (3) Is it a competitive or noncompetitive proposal? Analyze the content by considering the requirements, benefits, and potential objections.
- **Compose: Choose the medium, draft the content, and organize.** The medium will depend on the formality of the proposal. No matter what medium you choose, organize the content so that key ideas are easy to find. For formal proposals, include an executive summary, table of contents, introduction, body, references, and appendices. Choose effective words.
- **Evaluate: Assess the effectiveness of a proposal.** Use a checklist that prompts you to think about key ideas: Have you convinced the audience there is a problem? Is your solution a good one? Have you stressed benefits? Did you include enough information about implementation?

8.2 How do I make a proposal persuasive? *(pages 258–260)*

- **Articulate the problem, need, or opportunity.**
- **Identify the outcomes and benefits** of addressing that problem or opportunity.
- **Present a compelling recommendation** that addresses the problem or opportunity.
- **Provide persuasive supporting details** and outline the deliverables your proposal promises. If the audience has published a request for proposal (RFP) with requirements, then the proposal needs to show how it meets requirements as well as how it offers benefits to the audience. Most proposals also include implementation details that show the plan is feasible and that you are qualified to do the work.
- **Request action.**

8.3 What types of business proposals should I be prepared to write?

(pages 260–270)

Three kinds of proposals are common in business. All three can be solicited or unsolicited, competitive or noncompetitive, and internal or external.

- **Proposals for action or change** are strongest when they make a business case.
- **Solicited or unsolicited sales proposals** make a persuasive case that the audience will benefit from what you are proposing to sell.
- **Grant proposals and other proposals for funding** are targeted to specific funding agencies that are a good match with the project you are trying to fund. Identify a contact person at the funding organization, and arrange a personal meeting. Then draft a proposal identifying how you meet the agency's criteria and a cover letter summarizing the main points of your proposal.

8.4 How do I structure and format a formal proposal? *(pages 270–275)*

- **Structure a formal proposal like a formal report,** with a cover message, title page, executive summary, table of contents, references or works cited, and appendices (if applicable).
- **Follow specified guidelines when responding to RFPs.** To help readers find information they are looking for, write headings that relate to the RFP requirements. Place required documentation in appendices.

PEARSON
mybcommlab™ *Are you an active learner? Go to mybcommlab.com to master Chapter 8 content. Chapter 8 interactive activities include:*

- Customizable Study Plan and Chapter 8 practice quizzes
- Chapter 8 Simulation, Persuasive Business Messages & Proposals, that helps you think critically and prepare to make choices in the business world
- Flash Cards for mastering the definition of chapter terms

- Chapter 8 Video Exercise, Writing Reports & Proposals, which shows you how textbook concepts are put into practice every day
- Interactive Lessons that visually review key chapter concepts
- Document Makeovers for hands-on, scored practice in revising documents

- What am I proposing and why?
- What is the context of my proposal? Is it external or internal? Is it solicited or unsolicited? Is it competitive or noncompetitive?
- Will my audience already be interested, or will I need to grab their attention?
- What requirements, if any, must this proposal meet?
- How will the audience benefit from the proposal?
- What objections should I anticipate?
- Should I do any initial research before writing the proposal? What do I need to learn?

- Will the audience be convinced that the proposal addresses a real need?
- Have I stated what I am proposing?
- Have I shown how my proposal meets the need well?
- Have I stressed audience benefits?
- Have I shown I am qualified?
- Have I explained the details: deliverables, costs, schedule?
- Have I asked for agreement?
- Have I used good headings and highlighted main points?
- Have I edited for style and tone?
- Have I proofread for errors?

- How formal or informal should this proposal be?
- What is the best medium for the proposal?
- How can I establish credibility?
- What content must I include?
- How should I organize the content?
- How can I use a "you" perspective?
- What word choices will be most effective?

Make the Proposal Persuasive by:

- articulating the problem, need, or opportunity
- identifying the outcomes and benefits
- presenting a compelling recommendation
- providing persuasive supporting details
- requesting action

Structure a Formal Proposal Like a Formal Report

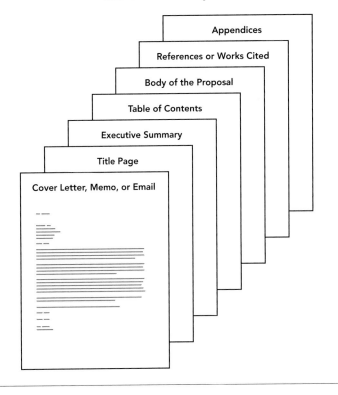

Appendices

References or Works Cited

Body of the Proposal

Table of Contents

Executive Summary

Title Page

Cover Letter, Memo, or Email

KEY TERMS QUICK ACCESS REVIEW

Business case   *p. 260*

Competitive proposal   *p. 256*

Cover message   *p. 270*

Deliverables   *p. 260*

Executive summary   *p. 257*

Grant proposal   *p. 267*

Noncompetitive proposal   *p. 256*

Proposal   *p. 254*

Request for proposal (RFP)   *p. 255*

Solicited proposal   *p. 255*

Unsolicited proposal   *p. 255*

CASE STUDY Proposing a Corporate Volunteer Program

This case study will help you review the chapter material by applying it to a specific scenario.

Craig Allen enjoys his job at Kramer Electronics. Just three years out of college, Craig received a promotion and has new responsibilities. Craig's one regret is that he doesn't have as much time to devote to community service as he did in college. During college, Craig volunteered at a local children's hospital and worked as a baseball and soccer coach at a children's camp.

One day last week, Craig saw a newspaper article about corporate volunteer programs. He read that a growing number of companies are allowing employees to take a paid day off of work to volunteer their time for special community projects. A committee within the company selects the projects based on applications from not-for-profit organizations and schools in the community.

Craig researched corporate volunteer programs and found that benefits of the programs include increased employee satisfaction and decreased employee turnover rates, as well as good public relations for the company. He became convinced that a corporate volunteer program would help both the community and Kramer Electronics.

Craig decided to do some additional research and then propose to Tom Kramer, the CEO of the company, that Kramer Electronics adopt a corporate volunteer program.

Analyzing the Context

Craig first analyzes purpose, context, and content needs using the following list of questions. Put yourself in Craig's place.

Review Question 1: *How would you answer these questions? Brainstorm some possible answers.*

- What am I proposing and why?
- What is the context of my proposal? Is it external or internal? Is it solicited or unsolicited? Is it competitive or noncompetitive?
- Will my audience already be interested, or will I need to grab their attention?
- What requirements, if any, must this proposal meet?
- How will the audience benefit from the proposal?
- What objections should I anticipate?
- Should I do any initial research before writing the proposal? What do I need to learn?

Brainstorming Content for a Proposal

As the next step in preparing his proposal, Craig creates a draft outline using the following headings, and he begins by brainstorming content for each section. His goal is both to compose the most persuasive content possible and to answer the questions he anticipates Tom will ask.

Review Question 2: *If you were brainstorming with Craig, what ideas would you consider for each of these content areas?*

1. Problem or Opportunity
2. Proposed Solution
3. Requirements
4. Benefits to Kramer Electronics and to Employees
5. Implementation Details
6. Feasibility
7. Costs
8. Next steps

To help you develop ideas, do a web or database search for corporate volunteer programs to see how other companies have structured their programs and the benefits they have enjoyed.

What to Include and What to Leave Out

As Craig was researching companies that offer volunteer programs, he found at least one company that abandoned its program, since they found employees abused it. In one company, instead of doing volunteer work, some employees took a day off. This is a risk of corporate volunteer programs. Craig wonders, "What should I do with this information? Should I mention it, or should I ignore it?"

Review Question 3: *If you were Craig, what would you do—and why?*

Deciding on a Goal and Choosing the Best Format

As Craig sat down to draft his proposal, it occurred to him that he was not sure about the form of the proposal—or even its real goal. Should he write a formal proposal with a title page, executive summary, and appendices documenting his research? Was he ready to propose a detailed plan for implementing a volunteer program? Or should he write a more informal proposal to get Tom interested in the idea and then present additional research in a meeting?

Review Question 4: *If you were Craig, what choice would you make, and why?*

CRITICAL THINKING

1. Imagine that you work for a restaurant and you want to propose to the chef/owner that he update the menu to include more low-fat options. What research would you do in the analyzing phase of ACE to support your proposal? Where would you find that information?

2. If you were going to propose an innovation or change in your college or university, what would you propose? Identify at least two benefits you could include in your proposal.

3. Imagine that you work for a painting company and you received an RFP from the city asking you to submit a competitive proposal to paint the interior of the City Hall. What research should you do before writing the proposal? Where would you find that information?

4. Assume that you are writing the proposal to paint City Hall and want to include a section about your company's qualifications. How would you decide what details to include?

5. The sales proposal in Figure 8.4 on pages 262–263 lists both what the proposer (CES) agrees to do and what the client (Davis College) must do. Why is it important in this proposal to identify specific things that the client is required to do?

6. In Chapter 5, you learned about persuasive sales letters. In what ways might an unsolicited sales proposal be different from a persuasive sales letter?

7. Many funding agencies request that you send them a letter or schedule a meeting to express interest before submitting a full grant proposal. Why do you imagine these agencies require this initial communication? How does it benefit both the funding agency and the proposer?

8. Imagine that you work for a restaurant that is just beginning to offer catering services. You receive an RFP from a nearby company requesting a proposal for catering a large corporate event of 200 people. The RFP specifies that you must supply a list of other corporate events you have catered. Since you have never offered catering services before, you cannot meet that RFP requirement. Should you decide not to submit a proposal? If you do submit a proposal, what can you say to respond to that requirement?

9. A young entrepreneur posted the following message in an online discussion forum: *"I am wondering how I would propose a business partnership with a small business owner, whom I know only through a social networking site and a few email exchanges. Should I keep researching about his business, get to know him better, establish rapport, and then propose my idea? Or should I get to the point straightaway after few mail exchanges?"* What are the pros and cons of each of these approaches?

10. According to intercultural communication experts, in China a proposal initiates negotiations. In Italy, a proposal finalizes negotiations. What are the implications of these differences for how you would approach the proposal process in these two countries? **[Related to the Culture feature on page 267]**

DEVELOPING YOUR COMMUNICATION SKILLS

8.1 How do I use ACE to prepare an effective proposal? *(pages 254–258)*

EXERCISE 1 Analyze: Understand purpose, context, and content

a. You work in the business office of Hotel Oldham, and you received an RFP from the National Sports Collectors Association (NSCA), which would like to hold its annual convention and memorabilia sale in your hotel. The planners anticipate that more than 1,000 people will attend. It's your job to write a proposal to the NSCA. How would you describe that proposal? Solicited or unsolicited? Competitive or noncompetitive? Internal or external? Identify at least one requirement that you will need to meet in your proposal. Identify one potential benefit you may want to include. Identify at least one potential objection you may have to address. What medium would you use to compose and deliver that proposal?

b. You work for SurveyKing, a company that designs customer satisfaction surveys. One of your long-time customers, a regional airline, has requested that you submit a proposal to design a customer survey to assess satisfaction with a new service. Would you consider this proposal to be solicited or unsolicited? Competitive or noncompetitive? Internal or external? Review Section 8.2 of this chapter on pages 258–260, which lists typical content for a proposal. In this situation, what content do you think will be most important for getting the sale? What content items will be less important? What medium would you choose to compose and deliver the proposal?

EXERCISE 2 Compose: Choose the medium, draft the content, and organize

Proposals rely on active voice to make clear who is responsible for each action. The following sentences, taken from draft proposals, are written in passive voice. Revise each statement to use active voice. Be sure to select the best subject and verb for each sentence.

a. The training will be conducted by EduForce.

b. To assess employee needs, 10 employees will be interviewed.

c. Before work can begin, system specifications must be sent to us.

d. As soon as the agreement is signed, interviews will be scheduled.

e. The work will be evaluated on a monthly basis and progress reports will be sent regularly.

f. Three competitive estimates will be provided by reputable roofing repair specialists.

g. All pick-ups and deliveries will be guaranteed within 30 minutes of the client's requested time.

h. First, a survey will be conducted to determine customers' perceptions of effective strategies.

i. Several data assessment techniques will be used to evaluate the information.

j. A final report will be disseminated to all stakeholders to document the project's success.

EXERCISE 3 Evaluate: Assess the effectiveness of the proposal

Assume you manage the ticket sales department of a new women's professional soccer franchise in your city. You asked three associates in your department each to propose one possible community outreach program that will help the soccer club promote ticket sales. After doing initial research, each associate wrote an introduction to a proposal with a brief problem statement and solution. Evaluate each of the following problem statements. Will the audience be convinced that the proposal is addressing a real need? Will the audience be convinced that the proposal is a good way to meet the need? Explain your answer.

a. Because our soccer club is new, we do not yet have a fan base and sufficient ticket sales. I propose that we increase ticket sales by placing posters throughout the community and advertising on local television stations. These marketing strategies will raise awareness about our team. The cost will be minimal, but the publicity will provide our team exposure to potential fans.

b. I think the real reason we are not selling tickets is that our community has never had a women's sports team. I propose

that we hold a "Dollar Day," charging only a dollar per ticket to encourage people to attend the women's soccer games and help them see how exciting women's sports can be. The cost will be minimal, since we are giving away seats that will otherwise be empty, but the free tickets will provide our team positive publicity and exposure to potential fans.

c. Interviews with general managers of five women's professional basketball teams revealed that these teams have modestly increased ticket sales each year by developing two fan bases: (1) women who are interested in fitness and participate in recreational sports and (2) young female athletes and their families. I propose that we reach out to these two audiences by sponsoring free soccer clinics for area fitness clubs and for youth soccer teams throughout the city. The cost will be minimal—only our players' time—but the clinics will provide our team positive publicity and exposure to potential fans.

8.2 How do I make a proposal persuasive?
(pages 258–260)

EXERCISE 4 Articulate the problem, need, or opportunity

You work for Organic Naturalz, a company that makes organic personal care products such as soaps, shampoos, lotions, and deodorants. Currently, the company advertises its products in traditional ways: through magazine and newspaper advertising, on television, and through in-store displays. You want to propose that the company use social media—such as Facebook, MySpace, Twitter, and Ning—to gain greater visibility among its target customers—women and men aged 16 to 30.

Conduct some web-based research on social media marketing. Based on that research and what you know from your own experience, draft a paragraph that articulates the problem or opportunity that the company can address by having a presence on social media. You may choose to focus on one particular social media tool, rather than all of them.

EXERCISE 5 Identify the outcomes and benefits

Refer to Exercise 4. Write a list of benefits that social media marketing will provide for Organic Naturalz. Be sure to provide reasoning and, if possible, evidence to support those benefits.

EXERCISE 6 Present a compelling recommendation

Refer to Exercises 4 and 5. Write a paragraph articulating a specific recommendation or proposal that you will make to your company management. What specifically will you propose that they do? Decide whether you want to propose that the company invest heavily in social media marketing or implement a pilot project. Provide compelling reasons for your recommendation.

EXERCISE 7 Provide persuasive supporting details
[Related to the Ethics feature on page 264]

You and one of your classmates plan to launch a new business after graduation: running a delivery service for dry cleaners in your town. Twice a week you will pick up dry cleaning from customers to drop off at the dry cleaner, and twice a week you will deliver cleaned clothes back to the customers. Your partner, an information technology major, has developed an online application that allows customers to pay in advance. The two of you plan to make an unsolicited sales proposal to all the dry cleaners in your town. You are concerned, however, about what to say about your qualifications. You and your classmate have no previous business experience, and you cannot truthfully say that you have delivery experience, customer service experience, or experience running an e-commerce website.

Brainstorm some ideas that you might include in your proposal to persuade your audience that you are capable of doing the job and providing the company with a real benefit. For this exercise, assume that each idea is true and could be included ethically.

EXERCISE 8 Request action

Refer to Exercise 7. Assume that you write an unsolicited sales proposal in the form of a letter to the dry cleaners in town. How will you end that letter? What action will you request?

8.3 What types of business proposals should I be prepared to write? *(pages 260–270)*

EXERCISE 9 Proposals for action or change

You work at a bank that recently reduced its workforce to save money. Tellers are handling more transactions per hour to get through the workload, so they are no longer friendly to customers. You notice that customer complaints have increased. You would like to make a proposal to management to address customer complaints. You are considering two alternatives: hiring an additional teller to reduce the workload and investing in customer service training for all tellers. You know that you will need to make a business case for any solution you propose. What will you need to research to make a business case? Create a list of questions you want to answer before making your proposal.

EXERCISE 10 Does your proposal demonstrate integrity? [Related to the Ethics feature on page 264]

Refer to Exercise 9. Assume you spoke with the teller supervisor, Anna, who agreed that both of your suggestions should be forwarded to the bank's manager. She encourages you to draft a proposal and offers the following "evidence" to include in your proposal:

- Customer complaints will continue to increase if a solution is not found quickly.
- Hiring a teller will reduce overall complaints, which will increase our customer base.
- The investment in customer service training will ensure all customers are happy and satisfied with the bank's services.
- This two-pronged approach to solving the problem is the only way to ensure the bank's success.

Although you appreciate Anna's support, you do not believe that including these statements would be ethical since they are not based on real evidence. How could you modify these statements to be more accurate?

EXERCISE 11 Solicited sales proposals

Refer to Exercise 7. Assume that you and your classmate have graduated, and your delivery service for dry cleaners is now well established. You have been working with six local dry cleaners, and you have even been able to hire two employees to help with the deliveries so you can keep up with the bookkeeping, invoicing, and marketing needs of your company. Today, you receive a call from Pam McNeely of Hoff Industries, one of the largest employers in town. Pam often uses your services for her personal needs, but today she is calling to see if you would be interested in providing corporate delivery service for employees of Hoff Industries. Of their 500 employees, 150 have indicated an interest in regular dry cleaning delivery service to/from their offices so they don't have to drive to the cleaners before or after work. Pam would like you to send her a sales proposal that she can submit to her supervisor. You are very interested in this possibility since you would nearly double your current client base. Additionally, being able to pick up and drop off orders at one location will reduce your travel costs per run. However, you need to hire at least one more driver and perhaps even purchase a van to accommodate the volume of clothing. You tell Pam you are very interested and will work on a proposal with your business partner. What headings would you include in the proposal? Identify several bullet points for each heading as a working outline of your proposal.

EXERCISE 12 Writing proposals for different cultures [Related to the Culture feature on page 267]

As a fashion industry major, you were very happy to get a job as business manager for an independent clothing designer whose clothing is sold in boutiques in Los Angeles, New York, Chicago, and Atlanta. The designer, your boss, would like to expand her distribution into international markets, starting with Japan. A trendy boutique, Parco, has expressed interest in being the exclusive outlet for her designs in Japan. Your boss is planning a trip to Japan to begin discussions with Parco. She hopes the discussions will culminate in a proposal and agreement. However, she has never done business in Japan before. She asks you to do some initial research to help her prepare to write a proposal.

As part of your research, you look at Geert Hofstede's Cultural Dimensions and learn that Japan rates high on the "uncertainty avoidance index." According to Hofstede:

> Uncertainty Avoidance Index (UAI) deals with a society's tolerance for uncertainty and ambiguity. . . . It indicates to what extent a culture programs its members to feel either uncomfortable or comfortable in unstructured situations. Unstructured situations are novel, unknown, surprising, different from usual. Uncertainty avoiding cultures try to minimize the possibility of such situations by strict laws and rules, safety and security measures. . . .[12]

Based on this research, you hypothesize that anyone writing a proposal for a Japanese audience should try to minimize uncertainty. But what does that mean? Here are some questions to discuss with your boss. What are your answers, and why?

a. When should you write the proposal: before meeting with the potential business partner to discuss at the meeting, or later?

b. Should the proposal contain very general and flexible agreements, or very detailed and specific agreements?

c. You imagine that your Japanese business partners will want to be very certain of the quality of your products before signing an agreement. What can you say in a proposal that will help your audience feel confident about product quality?

d. If you present a proposal either before or after your visit, should you expect the Japanese to sign it quickly to get the project started, or to study it and perhaps request clarification?

EXERCISE 13 Unsolicited sales proposals

You work for a web design company that is looking for new clients. In addition to advertising and sending direct mail, your company would like to send unsolicited sales proposals to small businesses with websites that need updating. Your boss has asked you to search the web to find one or two sites that would benefit from your design expertise and then develop a sales proposal to send to those businesses.

Find a small business website that you believe can be improved. Write the first one or two paragraphs of a proposal (in letter form) to that company. In this introductory material, be sure to introduce yourself and your design company, explain what you are proposing, and offer a statement persuading your audience that you can help the company solve a problem or take advantage of an opportunity. Also, be sure not to offend your potential client by saying that its current website is bad.

EXERCISE 14 Grant proposals and other proposals for funding

The Highwood Police Department plans to apply for a Community Development Grant (CDG) from the City of Highwood. Each year, the city funds more than $200,000 in grants. The city's website describes the goals of these grants in this way: Highwood uses its CDG funds to further its community development objectives, focusing on low- and moderate-income individuals, families, and neighborhoods to:

• provide decent housing
• provide a suitable living environment
• expand economic opportunities

The Police Department would like to fund a workout room in the police station. Read the introduction to the following grant proposal. Evaluate whether you think this proposal will persuade the grant committee that the proposed project meets the funding goals of the grant. Would you recommend any revisions?

> Police officers in the Highwood Police Department experience a high rate of cardiovascular and musculoskeletal problems. With more officers becoming sick and injured, fewer are available to protect public safety. To keep the officers fit for duty, the Highwood Police Department requests that the City Council authorize a Community

Development Grant to pay for a fitness center for Highwood police officers. According to research by the American Fitness Council, regular exercise will help keep law enforcement officers healthy. Project objectives include reducing by 20 percent the use of sick leave due to these problems.

Specifically, we request $32,000 to renovate the loft of the police garage as a workout room, buy exercise equipment, and train all participants. Future maintenance of the project will be possible through volunteer fund-raising efforts carried out by the Highwood Police Department Benevolent Association.

EXERCISE 15 Submitting proposals online
[Related to the Technology feature on page 270]

Use your favorite web search tool, such as Google or Bing, to find three foundation websites that offer onsite proposal submissions. Examples include the U.S. Department of Education (e-grants), the National Science Foundation, and the Bill & Melinda Gates Foundation. Identify a specific proposal opportunity from each website. Analyze the proposal requirements and compare the differences. Write a one-page summary that outlines the similarities and differences among these sites and the specific requirements for submitting proposals online.

8.4 How do I structure and format a formal proposal? *(pages 270–275)*

EXERCISE 16 Structure a formal proposal like a formal report

Refer to the informal proposal to hire an intern in Figure 8.2 on page 259. Assume the recipient, Doug Seaver, agrees with your proposal and asks you to write a formal proposal that he can share with the company executive committee for a formal vote. Describe the formal structure you would use to assemble your proposal, and explain the content you would include in each section. Identify supporting evidence you might include in appendices.

EXERCISE 17 Follow specified guidelines when responding to RFPs

Assume you work for a clothing manufacturer that specializes in law enforcement and military uniforms. You are responding to an RFP to provide uniforms for the Washtenaw County Sheriff's Department in Ann Arbor, Michigan. The RFP outlines very specific requirements for the uniforms. You can meet all the requirements except one: "The front and rear creases in the trouser legs must incorporate a permanent modified silicone crease produced by the "Lintrak™ System." Your company does not use this system but instead a competitive system called SIROSET, developed in China. You believe the SIROSET system is equally good. How will you address this issue in your proposal?

WRITING

EXERCISE 18 Writing a cover message

The proposal in Figure 8.3 on page 261 is a short, formal proposal. Assume Kip Koestler is sending that proposal as an email attachment to Leann Towner, the Director of Information Technology at his company, United Consolidated, Inc. Write a persuasive cover email for that message.

EXERCISE 19 Proposal to use social media

Refer to Exercises 4, 5, and 6 on page 280. Based on the research and analysis you did in Exercises 4, 5, and 6, write a one- to two-page memo, proposing that your company use social media as a marketing tool. Your proposal may focus on using a specific social media program, a specific type of marketing program using social media, or both.

EXERCISE 20 Proposal to recycle computers

You just heard your company is replacing all desktop computers with laptops. You recall an article about a computer recycling program to dispose of old computers in an environmentally responsible way. Write a 500- to 1,000-word proposal that justifies establishing a recycling program at your company. Choose the medium that you believe will be the most appropriate. Use the ACE process to analyze, compose, and evaluate your proposal.

EXERCISE 21 Proposal to cut costs

Your university just announced that it is increasing tuition for next year to cover increased costs. Yet, everywhere you look—in the cafeteria, in the dormitories, in the athletic facilities—you see areas where the university could cut costs. Write a letter to your university administration proposing one specific cost-cutting initiative. Do some research that will help you estimate current costs and potential savings by implementing your initiative. If your initiative will result in benefits beyond cost savings, be sure to stress those also. Use the ACE process to analyze, compose, and evaluate your letter.

EXERCISE 22 Proposal for an after-school arts program

You work as an administrator in a local elementary school in a low-income neighborhood. The school district has recently cut the school's budget for the arts, but your school would like to offer an after-school arts enrichment program for its students. Look online for an appropriate agency or foundation interested in funding education programs. Write a letter of inquiry to this agency or foundation, explaining the details of a program—for example, your school's need for $25,000 for teachers and equipment, the community the program would serve, the number of students who will use the program, and the ultimate objective of the program. To develop the details for your proposal, you can either research existing after-school art programs or use your imagination to create realistic details.

COLLABORATING

EXERCISE 23 Analyzing requests for proposals

As a team, review at least three websites that publish requests for proposals. The following websites may be helpful. You can find these sites with a web browser by typing in the name and the letters "RFP." You may also find RFPs in other places by searching just for "RFP" on the Internet.

- **FedBizOpps:** The single government point-of-entry (GPE) for federal government procurement opportunities
- **BizWiz:** A website for general business opportunities, listed under the link "RFP-Direct"
- **Network Computing:** A site requesting proposals for LANs, WANs, web management, network security, and more
- **Pollution Prevention Request for Proposal Clearinghouse:** Provides information on current and pending RFPs related to pollution prevention

- **City of Los Angeles:** Lists bids, RFPs, and grants for construction, auditing, supplies and equipment, and telecommunications
- **City of Houston, TX:** Provides downloadable bids for various services
- **City of Boston, MA:** Lists bids and RFPs

In a brief report to your instructor or presentation to the class, discuss the following questions:

a. What are some of the industries that are requesting proposals, and what types of products or services are these industries interested in?

b. What kind of information do these RFPs provide?

c. What kind of information do the RFPs request?

EXERCISE 24 Proposing a change at your school

As a team, identify a change that would benefit your school, a department within your school, or a specific course. Write a memo to the decision maker, offering a proposal for change. Your memo may include the following sections. However, you may modify the sections for your topic.

- Problem
- Proposed Solution
- Rationale and Benefits
- Implementation Suggestions
- Cost

Structure the team activity in this way, following the ACE process:

Analyze: As a team, identify the change and conduct research to learn more about the problem and to develop a feasible and effective solution. Together outline the content and develop notes for each section.

Compose: Have half the team members work as a subteam to make key composing decisions and draft the proposal.

Evaluate: Have the remaining half of the team evaluate and revise the proposal, following the evaluation checklist in Section 8.1.

Submit your notes, first draft, and revised draft to your instructor.

SPEAKING

EXERCISE 25 Making informal/impromptu presentations

a. Identify a change in graduation requirements that you would recommend for your school or major. In a two-minute presentation, identify the problem, your proposed solution, and one benefit to the school or the major.

b. Imagine that an anonymous benefactor has given your business communication class $100 to donate to one charity. In a two-minute presentation to the class, propose a charity. Provide at least two reasons why the class should select this charity.

EXERCISE 26 Executive briefings

a. Imagine you work for an organization that prepares many proposals during the year. Your supervisor asks you to eval-

uate software designed to help write or generate proposals. Search the Internet to find two programs, and prepare a five-minute executive briefing that answers three questions: (1) In what ways can proposal-generating software help an organization? (2) What are the limitations of this kind of software? (3) What specific software program would you recommend and why? Be sure to cite specific details to support your points.

b. Select the example proposal presented in either Figure 8.2, 8.3, 8.4, or 8.5. Imagine you want to present this proposal orally to a decision maker in a five-minute presentation. Prepare that presentation and deliver it to your class.

GRAMMAR

Commas: Part 1 (See Appendix D—Section 2.2)

Rekey (or download from mybcommlab.com) the following paragraph, correcting the 10 errors in the use of commas with independent clauses, dependent clauses, and phrases (see Section 2.2.1). Underline all your corrections.

Although most final job interviews are face to face telephone interviews have become common for screening interviews. Employers find that phone interviews are not only economical but they are also an effective way to determine which candidates merit a closer look. While you are on the job market a potential employer or networking contact might call, and ask, "Do you have a few minutes to talk?" Being interviewed over the phone isn't easy so you need to be prepared. What initially seems like an informal conversation about a job might actually be the first round of screening, or the first test of your communication skills. After the initial introductions and pleasantries let the caller take the lead, and guide the conversation. When you answer questions keep your responses short and to the point. The caller will ask follow-up questions if necessary, and will bring the interview to a close.

Commas: Part 2 (See Appendix D—Section 2.2)

Rekey (or download from mybcommlab.com) the following paragraph, correcting the 10 errors in the use of commas with coordinate and cumulative adjectives and with serial words, phrases, and clauses. Each missing or unnecessary comma counts as one error (see Sections 2.2.2 and 2.2.3). Underline all your corrections.

After you have sent out résumés and applied for jobs, be ready willing and able to handle a telephone interview. Keep your resume a pad and pen and a bottle of water near the phone. You will need your résumé for reference the pad and pen to take notes and the water in case your throat gets dry. Is your cell phone, service, provider reliable, or do you have to worry about dropped calls? If so, consider using a landline. Send roommates, friends, spouses, children and pets from the room when a potential employer calls. You want to be completely calmly focused and undistracted during a telephone interview.

Commas: Part 3 (See Appendix D—Section 2.2)

Rekey (or download from mybcommlab.com) the following paragraph, correcting the 13 errors in the use of commas with restrictive, nonrestrictive, or parenthetical words, phrases, or clauses. Each missing or unnecessary comma counts as one error. There are also two mistakes in the use of that, which, or who (see Sections 2.2.2 and 2.2.3). Underline all your corrections.

Anyone, who has been through an employment interview, knows it is nerve-wracking. A telephone interview which provides none of the nonverbal cues available in a face-to-face situation can be even trickier. The interviewer's word choice, tone of voice, and level of enthusiasm may therefore be important indicators. The interviewee the person that is being interviewed must listen carefully. The advice, "sit up and pay attention," certainly applies in this situation. Companies, who use telephone interviews for employment screening, have heard it all everything from bad grammar to burping.

9 Preparing Business Reports

new hires @ work

Stephanie Crim
Marketing Analyst
BP
University of Southern California, 2007

"AS AN ANALYST, I WORK WITH DETAILED INFORMATION TO REPORT ECONOMIC MODELS AND METRICS THAT SUPPORT BUSINESS DECISIONS. It is often challenging to determine the appropriate level of detail necessary to report. Too much detail can sidetrack decision makers on minor assumptions that have little impact on the overall program. Too little detail runs the risk that decision makers won't understand how the program adds up or what the key value drivers are. I've found that taking extra time to analyze the goal of the project and the needs of my audience helps me create a more effective report."

287

Introduction

Businesses run on information, and reports are designed to share that information with people who need to make decisions and solve problems. The term "report" refers to a wide range of documents and functions. Reports can take the form of emails, memos, letters, manuscripts, online submissions, or slide decks. A report may be as short as a two-paragraph email message that documents your progress on a project. Or a report may be several hundred pages long presenting the results of in-depth research and analysis about a complex business problem or technical situation.

This chapter introduces you to a variety of report types and formats, along with some key writing techniques that will help you produce reports that are clear, concise, readable, and accurate—no matter what the type or format of the report.

How do I use ACE to help me write a business report?

■ Access this chapter's simulation entitled Business Reports, located at mybcommlab.com.

All reports have one thing in common: they answer business questions. Your job in writing reports is to answer those questions with information that is useful for the audience, well organized, clear, and concise. ACE can guide you through the process of analyzing, composing, and evaluating to create a report that meets these goals. This section outlines how to apply the ACE process when writing reports.

Analyzing

- Analyze to understand the purpose and report type
- Analyze to understand audience needs
- Analyze to choose the best medium

Composing

- Compose your report to meet audience expectations
- Compose using an objective and easy-to-read style

Evaluating

- Evaluate by reviewing on your own and getting feedback from others

Analyze to understand purpose and report type

Typically, a report is either informational or analytical depending on its purpose and the key question it answers. A report summarizing what happened at a meeting or on a trip would be an **informational report**. Its main goal is to provide readers with facts that they can easily understand and refer to when necessary. By contrast, an **analytical report** helps readers draw conclusions to solve problems or support business decisions. A report that analyzes what was learned on a trip and then makes a recommendation would be an analytical report.

The first step in writing a report is to identify the question you are answering and the type of report you are writing. FIGURE 9.1 lists common business questions and the types of reports that answer them.

Analyze to understand audience needs

Report writers can find it challenging to limit the information they include in a report. When the process of research is long and involved, writers can be tempted to include everything they find. Recall the research project outlined in Chapter 7. The project involved researching and analyzing learning management systems and recommending one to the chief learning officer of Ipswich Brands. If the final recommendation report included every bit of information the writer found, the report would be extremely long.

FIGURE 9.1 Common Report Questions and Types of Reports

QUESTION	INFORMATIONAL REPORTS	ANALYTICAL REPORTS
What have you accomplished so far?	Progress Report	
What were the key results of the meeting?	Meeting Minutes	
What happened on the trip?	Trip Report	
What did your investigation reveal?	Investigation Report	
Are we complying with policies and regulations?	Compliance Report	
Is this plan feasible?		Feasibility Report
What is the better choice? Have our actions been successful?		Evaluation Report
What should we do?		Recommendation Report

To focus the report, analyze your audience to determine what information they need to make a business decision. Here are questions you might ask:

- **Is it necessary to define what learning management systems are and explain how they function?** In this case, the primary audience—and all others who will be involved in selecting a system—are familiar with learning management systems and understand how they function. So, it will not be necessary to provide general background defining learning management systems.
- **Do I need to persuade my audience to adopt a learning management system?** Persuasion is not necessary in this case, since the audience has already decided to adopt some system. The goal of this report is simply to identify good candidates to consider.
- **What information does the audience need to know—and why?** The audience needs to know the criteria you are using to evaluate systems, how the systems perform according to those criteria, and what you recommend. These questions help structure the body of the report.

Analyze to choose the best medium

A report may take the form of a memo, email, letter, formal manuscript, a **report deck** (a report document written in PowerPoint or other presentation software), or an online report. In choosing the best medium for your report, you will need to consider length, audience, the importance of the report, the way you will deliver the report, and how others will use it. FIGURE 9.2 presents the most common options.

Compose your report to meet audience expectations

When audiences read reports, they expect to find three or four kinds of information: identifying information, preview, detailed discussion, and (optionally) additional documentation.

Identifying information

In business, all reports clearly identify the author, the date, and the topic or title. Some reports also indicate the intended audience. In a memo report or in an email, this information is included as part of the heading. In a letter, the identifying information is in both the letterhead or inside address and the signature block. Also, as Figure 9.7 illustrates on page 299, letter reports usually include a subject line that identifies the type of report and the topic. More formal reports, whether written as a manuscript document or a report deck, usually have a title page that includes all the identifying information.

Informational report A report that provides readers with facts that they can easily understand and refer to when necessary. Meeting minutes, trip reports, and progress reports are types of informational reports.

Analytical report A report that analyzes information to solve a problem or support a business decision.

Report deck A report document written in PowerPoint or other presentation software.

FIGURE 9.2 Selecting the Best Medium for Reports

MEDIUM / FEATURES	ADVANTAGES	DISADVANTAGES
MEMO REPORT—See Figure 9.4, p. 295		
• Is used for short internal reports • Has standard headings (To, From, Date, and Subject—and often Copies) • Identifies the topic in the subject line • Uses content headings to signal how information is organized	• Is short and easy to read • Can include attachments that exist only in hard copy • Can be delivered securely—even hand delivered—to audience • Can be filed in hard copy or electronically for future reference	• Is appropriate only for internal audiences • Incurs costs to print or copy if it is not sent as an email attachment • Is delivered more slowly than email
EMAIL REPORT—See Figure 9.5, p. 297		
• Is used for short internal or external reports • Uses standard email headings • Identifies the topic in the subject line • Uses content headings to signal how information is organized	• Is short and easy to read • Can be distributed and received quickly • Can be filed in hard copy or electronically for future reference	• May not be a private or secure medium for reporting sensitive content • Does not offer a guaranteed way to ensure it was received • Cannot easily support tables and graphs • Cannot include attachments that exist only in hard copy
LETTER REPORT—See Figure 9.7, pp. 299–300		
• Is used for relatively short reports (less than 10 pages) for external audiences • Is printed on company letterhead • Uses traditional letter elements (date, inside address, salutation, complimentary close, signature block) • Also includes a subject line to indicate the letter contains a report • Uses content headings to signal how information is organized	• Projects a more "official" or formal image than email • Can include attachments that exist only in hard copy • Can be delivered securely to audience • Can require recipient's signature, to ensure report was received	• Is appropriate only for external audiences • Incurs costs of letterhead, printing, and postage • Takes at least a day to deliver
FORMAL REPORT—See Figure 9.8A–D, pp. 302–313		
• Is used to report the results of significant research or a project • Includes title page, table of contents, executive summary, references, and appendices (if necessary) • Is prepared on plain paper (not letterhead) • Always includes headings to signal key sections	• Can be distributed internally or externally • Projects a formal image • Can be used for very long reports • Can easily include tables, graphs, and other graphics • Provides table of contents to help audience find information • Can include supporting information as appendices • Can be produced as a PDF file to distribute and file electronically	• Incurs costs to print and deliver (if external) • Can be time-consuming to organize and format effectively
PRESENTATION REPORT DECK—See Figure 9.10, pp. 317–319		
• Is created with presentation software, such as PowerPoint • Includes much less text than traditional reports but more than traditional slide presentations • Is written to be understandable without a presenter • Conveys much of its information through graphs, diagrams, and other visual elements	• Appropriate for internal or external audiences • Replaces standard report document • Can easily include tables, graphs, and graphics • Can be used in conjunction with an oral presentation • Can be delivered to a targeted audience • Allows quick communication	• Does not provide as much detail as a formal report • If not well-written, can be difficult to understand without a presenter
ONLINE REPORT—Created with electronic tools such as online forms, wikis, and blogs		
• Online forms enable combining data from several reports into a database • Wikis are useful as a tool for reporting progress on an ongoing basis • Blogs can be used for reports that require immediate written feedback from others, such as evaluation and recommendation reports	• Allows data from several people to be combined into a master report • Provides managers with "real-time" information • Creates living documents that are never actually finished but continue to develop and grow over time	• May not be a private and secure medium for sending sensitive content • Does not ensure immediate receipt, since audience must check the website

Preview

Almost all business reports are written with a direct organization, beginning with a preview that provides readers with a quick understanding of the purpose, structure, content, and main ideas of the report. Anyone in your audience should be able to read the preview quickly and understand the main ideas. Reports provide previews in multiple ways—through introductions, tables of contents, abstracts, and executive summaries.

Every report should include an introduction that contains the following:

- **A statement about what motivated the report.** What is its purpose? What problem is it aiming to solve?
- **A brief summary of conclusions and recommendations.** These conclusions and recommendations are discussed in more detail later in the report.
- **A preview of the remainder of the report.** What does it cover and how is it structured?

In addition, formal reports also contain elements that precede the introduction and provide a quick overview of the report's structure and main ideas: a table of contents that outlines the major sections of the report and either an abstract or an executive summary.

Informational reports typically include an **abstract**—one or two paragraphs that either (a) describe the content of the report so that a reader can decide whether to read the report or (b) briefly summarize the report, including the main points, conclusions, and recommendations. An abstract should be understandable to anyone who reads the report.

By contrast, analytical reports include executive summaries designed for decision makers who may not have time to read the entire document. An **executive summary** is a separate, stand-alone mini-report inserted at the beginning of a formal report that completely summarizes the report's main ideas and recommendations. Because people may choose to read only the executive summary and not the main report, the executive summary must include all the important information. While executive summaries have no defined length, they are typically approximately 10 percent of the length of the report, up to a maximum of 10 pages.

Detailed discussion

Following the introduction, the main bulk of the report consists of detailed discussion, which is typically divided into sections that provide background information, methods, analysis of the data (including any graphs or tables that reveal insights), conclusions, and recommendations. While some writers use these generic terms as headings, the audience will better understand the report if the headings are content-focused and specific to that report. For example, as the report in Figure 9.10 illustrates on page 317, the background section of a report recommending that a company invest in one specific learning management system might be titled "Why a Learning Management System?" This heading pinpoints what type of background information the reader will find.

Supporting information

At the end of the report, you have the opportunity to add extra documentation to support your main points. In letter and memo reports, any additional documentation takes the form of an **attachment**—a supplemental document that is included with the letter or memo. Attachments might provide details that not all readers would need and that would clutter the report if included. For example, imagine you were writing a report recommending that your company hold a corporate event in a local hotel. The body of the report would include complete costs, details of what you would get for those costs, and a discussion of how this choice best meets the company's needs. Everyone who reads the report will need this information. However, in an attachment you might include complete menus for the event, the hotel site map that provides the layout of the rooms, and detailed instructions about how to reserve parking for your guests. In more formal reports and in report decks, this additional information is included in an **appendix** or in multiple appendices. Research reports that include information from secondary sources also include a **reference list** or *bibliography*.

Abstract One or two paragraphs, included at the beginning of a formal, informational report, that either (a) describe the content of the report so that a reader can decide whether to read the report or (b) briefly summarize the report, including the main points, conclusions, and recommendations.

Executive summary A separate, standalone mini-report—included at the beginning of a formal analytical report—that completely summarizes the main ideas and recommendations of the report and may be read instead of the main report.

Attachment A document that is included with a letter or memo report to provide supplementary information.

Appendix A section (or multiple sections called appendices) included at the end of a formal report or proposal that provides supplementary information.

Reference list A list of secondary research sources used in a research report.

FIGURE 9.3 summarizes where these elements appear in the various report formats. It also explains how to handle page numbering in formal manuscript reports. As you read through the chapter, notice how the example reports in the figures follow these guidelines.

FIGURE 9.3 How Elements of a Report Appear in Various Report Forms

	LETTER REPORT	MEMO OR EMAIL REPORT	FORMAL REPORT Elements	FORMAL REPORT Numbering
IDENTIFYING INFORMATION	At the beginning: letterhead or return address, inside address, date, subject line At the end: signature, distribution list	To:, From:, Date:, Subject:, Distribution:, cc:/xc:	Title Page	No number on title page
PREVIEW	Introductory paragraph: purpose, overview of the report, summary of key points	Introductory paragraph: purpose, overview of the report, summary of key points	Table of Contents List of Figures and Tables	After title page, small Roman numerals (i, ii, iii, etc.) for all other pages before the introduction
			Abstract or Executive Summary	
			Introduction	Arabic numbers (Introduction starts on page 1.)
DETAILED DISCUSSION	Paragraphs or sections that develop and support the main idea/conclusions	Paragraphs or sections that develop and support the main idea/conclusions	Sections of the report that develop and support the main idea/conclusions	Arabic numbers (The first Arabic number will appear on page 2)
SUPPORTING INFORMATION	Attachments	Attachments	Reference list Appendices	Lettered appendices (Appendix A, Appendix B); page numbers continue from body of report

Compose using an objective and easy-to-read style

The writing style of a report lends credibility to your results, which is important because reports are often used to support problem solving and decision making. For a good report-writing style, follow this advice:

- **Be objective.** For every claim you make, provide reasoning and supporting evidence. Also, be fair. Show that you have examined all sides of an issue and that you have evaluated the issue using reasonable and objective criteria.
- **Avoid narrative.** Do not waste your reader's time providing a detailed account of what you did. Instead, focus on the findings, conclusions, and recommendations

that result from your activity. Even in a progress report, focus on accomplishments rather than activities.

- **Use an appropriate tone.** While some informal internal reports may use informal language (including contractions such as *isn't, won't,* or *we'll*), reports for external audiences are typically formal.
- **Use a straightforward sentence style.** All reports benefit from a writing style that uses concise sentences and active voice. This style not only makes the report easier to read, but also makes the report easier to translate for international audiences.

Evaluate by reviewing on your own and getting feedback from others

Recall from Chapter 3 that evaluating involves both reviewing your own work and also responding to feedback from others. As you evaluate your report, ask yourself the following questions to improve your document:

- Is my report answering a clear question?
- Is the answer to my question easy to find?
- Is the title (or subject line) of the report focused and informative?
- Does the report provide a good preview in the introduction? When appropriate, does the report include a table of contents, executive summary, or abstract?
- Are the headings logical? If I read all the headings sequentially, will I understand how the report is organized?
- Is each section well organized? Is the main point of the section easy to find?
- Are the paragraphs relatively short (four to eight sentences)? Does each paragraph begin with a strong topic sentence that states the main point of the paragraph?
- Are tables, graphs, and other visuals used effectively? Are they labeled and introduced within the document?
- Are the sentences relatively short and, when possible, written in the active voice?
- Have I answered questions readers are likely to ask?
- Have I proofread carefully?

When a report is particularly important, be sure to have multiple people read it and provide feedback before you finalize the text. In fact, the most experienced workplace writers ask for feedback continually, throughout the writing process, instead of waiting until a draft is complete.[1] In that way, writers improve the effectiveness of important reports by ensuring that the reports meet audience and stakeholder needs.

The evaluating process does not end when you have delivered the report. Your audience response provides valuable feedback that can help you make better decisions the next time you write. If your report achieves your intended results, review it carefully to identify its strengths. If it does not achieve the results you intended— for example, if your analysis confused the audience or your recommendation was not approved—try to determine the cause of the problem. Did you include too much detail? Did you not provide enough support for your recommendations? Was the report so badly organized that readers had difficulty finding the information? Or was the failure caused by some external factor you could not control (for example, the budget was cut and the organization did not have the funds to implement the recommendation)? Whatever you learn from this evaluation will improve your future writing.

CULTURE   Making Reports Reader-Friendly for International Audiences

Reports often have a wider audience than typical correspondence. A useful report may be distributed broadly throughout an organization and to colleagues or clients around the world. If the report is not confidential, it may even be shared with the general public.

If you work in an international organization or an organization that disseminates information globally, you need to think about how to make your reports accessible to international audiences—even those who speak English. Although an estimated 1.5 billion people speak English worldwide, only 25 percent of those people speak English as a first language.[2] Approximately 300 million to 500 million speak English fluently as a second language, and another 750 million speak English as a foreign language.[3] Some of those people may be your coworkers or clients. Will all those readers understand long sentences and eloquent word choices? How can you make your reports as easy as possible for this audience to read?

Professionals in the field of international technical communication have developed a number of guidelines to use when preparing English documents for readers who are not native English speakers. Even if your communication is not technical, these are good guidelines to follow:

- **Use simple English.** English has more words than any other language: approximately 1 million words.[4] While this breadth of word choice makes English a very precise language, many of your readers will not be familiar with all the vocabulary. Use concrete words, avoid clichés, and check the reading level of your text when you evaluate your writing. Avoid sentences like this: "Local regulations prohibit installation of signage without a permit." Instead, say "Acme must get a permit to put up a sign."
- **Do not vary terms needlessly.** Use consistent terminology and phrases. For example, if you are writing about automobiles, consistently call them "automobiles" or "autos" rather than occasionally calling them "vehicles" or "means of transportation." This minimizes the number of terms a reader will need to remember.[5]

- **Eliminate the fat from content.** Keep your writing lean by providing only the information that people need and by eliminating extra details and words that serve no clear purpose.[6] An international audience may find it difficult to read this wordy sentence: "It is respectfully recommended that a committee be formed by A. G. Williams to conduct an investigation into potential wrongdoing by members of the executive board." They could more easily understand this leaner version: "We recommend that A. G. Williams investigate the recent actions of the executive board."

The number of English speakers is growing worldwide, and that means that the audience for your writing is growing also. In fact, Gordon Brown, the former Prime Minister of Great Britain, predicted that by 2025, "the number of English speakers in China is likely to exceed the number of speakers of English as a first language in all the rest of the world."[7]

To communicate complex ideas to those readers, choose simple language and simple sentence structure. For more advice about how to simplify your language for easy reading, review the *Plain English Handbook* published by the United States Security and Exchange Commission and available through a link on mybcommlab.com.

PEARSON mybcommlab

For CULTURE exercises, go to Critical Thinking Question 3 on page 333 and Exercise 7 on page 334 or this chapter's End-of-Chapter Exercises at mybcommlab.com.

Study Question 9.2

What types of short, routine reports are typical in business?

Most day-to-day business reports are short—less than five pages—and written in memo, email, or letter format. This section provides guidelines for three types of informational reports that are usually short: progress reports, trip reports, and meeting minutes. These reports are designed to inform others quickly about the work you have done and to provide documentation for future use. The section also provides guidelines for a short analytical report, in this case, a feasibility report.

Progress reports

If you are working on a long-term project, your supervisor may ask for a progress report that updates your status and indicates any potential problems or issues. FIGURE 9.4 illustrates a progress report written by a team of designers who work for Adaptive Living,

FIGURE 9.4 Memo-Style Progress Report

memo report

Adaptive LIVING

Interoffice Memo

TO: Rudy Glenn, VP of Fashion Products ◄--------
             Janice Kerwin, Production Manager
FROM: Eve Ireland, Lead Designer
             Niki Jantzen, Design Associate
DATE: November 22, 20XX
SUBJECT: Progress on SleekLine Adaptive Swimsuit Design

Project Summary ◄-------------
We are on schedule with the design and prototyping of the SleekLine adaptive swimsuit. The product fills an unmet market need: a swimsuit that women with rheumatoid arthritis can independently put on and take off despite their limited flexibility and range of motion. Over the past month, we have created three mockups that we have tested with potential users in a focus group. Based on the information gathered, we have narrowed our design to a tankini-style swimsuit with a top that opens in the front so that it can slip on like a shirt or jacket. The swimsuit top is secured with magnetic snaps that hold tightly but do not require finger flexibility to open or close. We are currently in the process of testing and prototyping the design.

Work Completed Since Last Report ◄------------
From October 30 until now, we have accomplished the following activities:
- Met with the occupational therapists at Central Rehabilitation Hospital to identify the specific requirements for our design
- Developed three alternative designs using three different closure systems: magnets, Velcro, and zippers
- Produced mock-ups of five designs
- Conducted two focus groups and user-tested our mock-ups with 30 women, aged 30 to 60, who have rheumatoid arthritis

Preliminary Findings (See Figure 1) ◄-------------
1. Women testing the swimsuits overwhelmingly (28 out of 30) preferred the closure to be in the front of the swimsuit.
2. The majority (19 out of 30) found magnetic closures to be easiest to use.

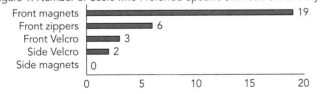

Figure 1: Number of Users who Preferred Specific Swimsuit Closure Styles

Front magnets	19
Front zippers	6
Front Velcro	3
Side Velcro	2
Side magnets	0

Work Planned for Next Two Weeks
During the next two weeks, we plan to conduct rigorous functional testing of fabric and magnets, simulating the conditions of swimming and water aerobics. Our goal is to determine the optimal strength, spacing, and polarity of magnets.

We will incorporate the results of the testing into prototypes and conduct a second round of swim tests. We will have a tested prototype by December 15.

Anticipated Problems ◄-------------
While users overwhelmingly like the magnets, users lack confidence that the magnets will hold safely and securely during water activities. Our marketing department will need to address these issues in product labeling and advertising.

Header identifies the names and titles of the recipients and the senders.

Subject line serves as the title of the report.

Opening identifies the purpose of the project and briefly summarizes the progress made.

First major section describes the work completed.

Because this progress report is addressing a research project, it is appropriate to include preliminary findings.

By discussing anticipated problems, the writers alert the reader to potential issues and allow others to start planning solutions.

new hires @ work

Bryon Creech
Logistics Manager for Well Services
Schlumberger
University of Tennessee, Knoxville, 2009

"I frequently email to our corporate office reports about the status and productivity of our vendors. These reports must be precise so information is relayed efficiently. Failure to do so results in delays."

a company that designs and sells products to help people with disabilities function independently. The team is designing a swimsuit for women with conditions such as rheumatoid arthritis that severely limit their range of motion. The team has been working on this project for several months and needs to answer two questions: How is the project progressing and when will a tested prototype be complete?

Trip reports

When you take a business trip, your manager may ask you to write a trip report to document your activities and to share what you accomplished or learned. The biggest mistake writers make in preparing trip reports is to organize them chronologically in narrative style. Instead, identify the most useful way to categorize the information—for example, by the customers you visited, by what you learned, or by the results you achieved.

In FIGURE 9.5, Warren Abbott reports on his trip to Washington, D.C., to call on current and potential clients. Notice that he organizes the report by clients visited identifying the person he met, what they talked about, and plans for next steps. The report serves a number of communication purposes. First, it gives Warren's boss, Joe Jackson, Vice President of Sales, a clear picture of potential new business. This gives Joe an opportunity to plan resources. Second, it gives Joe an opportunity to review and evaluate the follow-up plans Warren has made and to offer suggestions. Finally, the report serves as a checklist so that Warren and Joe can measure progress with the three accounts.

Meeting minutes

Minutes are written reports of meetings. The type of minutes you write will depend on the type of meeting you are summarizing and the purpose of the minutes. If you are reporting about a large group meeting that follows formal group processes, then the minutes will summarize all the discussions. Organize the minutes using the categories outlined in the meeting's agenda, such as new business, announcements, reports, votes, and decisions. People unable to attend the meeting can refer to the minutes to learn what happened.

More often, your minutes will record meetings of small committees or work teams that most members attend. Those minutes are action-oriented. FIGURE 9.6 on page 298 illustrates the minutes for a short teleconference of the Western Association of Accounting Professionals Communications Committee. The minutes briefly summarize the discussion but devote most of their space to recording specific decisions and action items resulting from the meeting. Action items can be listed in bullet format. However, a table allows you to concisely organize more detail about each of the action items.

Feasibility reports

Short analytical reports, such as a feasibility report, can also be written in letter or memo form. A **feasibility report** analyzes whether a plan can be implemented as proposed. It may also consider how to change the plan to make it feasible. A feasibility report will always include the criteria that decision makers can use to judge the proposal. The criteria may include cost, technical functionality, or potential for employees or the public to accept the proposal. Then the report will evaluate the proposal based on those criteria.

Minutes A written report of a meeting that identifies who was present, summarizes the discussion, and records specific decisions and action items.

Feasibility report A report that analyzes whether a plan can be implemented as proposed. It may also consider how to change the plan to make it feasible.

FIGURE 9.5 Email-Style Trip Report

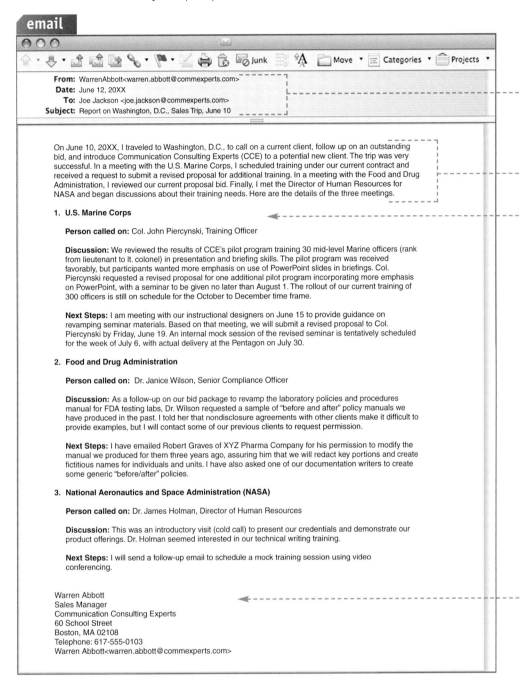

In an email report, the header provides identifying information.

First paragraph summarizes the report for a reader who does not have time for details.

Report is organized by clients visited. The most important visit—the current client—is first.

All the numbered sections present the same kind of information in the same order: organization name, employee name and title, summary of discussion, next steps.

In an email or memo report, no closing or signature is necessary. All the transmittal information is in the heading. However, for an email report you may include the signature block you usually include at the end of emails.

mybcommlab

Apply Figure 9.5's key concepts by revising a new document. Go to Chapter 9 in mybcommlab.com and select Document Makeovers.

In FIGURE 9.7 on page 299, the company Affordable World Energy (AWE) has asked Milestone Manufacturing Consultants to evaluate the feasibility of producing a small-scale wind turbine to provide household electricity to rural families in emerging countries, starting in India. The main evaluation criterion is the cost of manufacturing the turbines. AWE wants to sell this turbine for under $100 per unit. The body of this report is relatively short. However, it contains attachments that provide detailed results of Milestone's research. See the annotations for an explanation of key features of feasibility reports.

FIGURE 9.6 Meeting Minutes

meeting minutes

Western Association of Accounting Professionals Communications Committee

Meeting Minutes

Date:	April 17, 20XX
Purpose:	To address website problems and discuss methods of disseminating the new logo to the membership.
Present:	Nick Lawrence (presiding), Fiona Cray, Larry Evans, Carol Gielgud, Karla Jensen (recording), Lyle Lerner, Elaine Sears
Absent:	Susan Edwards, Vic Matthews
Location:	Teleconference
Convened:	7:30 PM CST
Adjourned:	8:15 PM CST

Heading information for minutes can include the purpose of the meeting, who attended, place, and time.

Discussion of Website Problems

Lyle Lerner reported that updating the website is cumbersome and time-consuming. To help solve this problem, Vic Matthews will update the website to a new version of Joomla, but many problems need to be identified and fixed. We discussed the best way to fix these problems and agreed to develop a requirements document and to hire a professional web developer. Nick Lawrence will ask Paul Walters about his ability to do what we need, his availability, and his fees. Carol Gielgud will also talk to Adam Earle to find out the same from him. Nick and Carol will present their findings at our June meeting.

Minutes summarize the discussion items rather than record all details.

> **Decision:** Because of problems with Joomla, we will allocate up to $2,000 to pay a professional to fix the problems with the site, earmarking $1,000 to fix the items that Lyle, Vic, and Nick identify as critical.
> **Vote:** Fiona Cray moved, Larry Evans seconded, and the motion passed unanimously.

Decisions and votes are highlighted.

Discussion of Logo

Everyone is pleased with the new, more contemporary logo. Larry Lerner will get all the associated electronic files from the designer and upload them to the intranet site. Elaine Sears will upload a simple version of the logo to the website for members to download and will send a message to the membership on the listserv informing them of this by April 25, 20XX.

Action Items

Action	Person	Goal Date	Completed Date	Follow up
Upload simple logo to website and communicate its availability to membership by email.	Sears	April 25, 20XX		
Upload all logo design files to Association intranet site for board members to use.	Lerner	April 25, 20XX		
Identify what needs to be done to make Joomla easy to work with and write up a requirements document.	Lerner, Matthews, and Lawrence	May 18, 20XX		
Contact Paul Walters to request a bid for web development.	Lawrence	May 31, 20XX		
Contact Adam Earle to request a bid for web development.	Gielgud	May 31, 20XX		
Update to current version of Joomla.	Matthews	August 15, 20XX		

When a meeting results in several action items, a table not only summarizes them but also serves as a checklist and follow-up tool to use at the next meeting.

FIGURE 9.7 Letter-Style Feasibility Report

`letter`

Milestone
Manufacturing Consultants

2245 Sherwin Parkway, Golden, CO 80401
800.555.6642 | www.milestone-consultants.com

July 23, 20XX

Mr. James Burgess
VP of Product Development
Affordable World Energy
130 West Union Street
Pasadena, CA 91103

Subject: Feasibility of Manufacturing a $100 Wind Turbine for Developing Countries   ←------

Dear Mr. Burgess:

Thank you for hiring Milestone Manufacturing Consultants to perform a feasibility analysis for manufacturing a small wind turbine to provide household electricity for rural families in developing countries. You asked us to assess the feasibility of manufacturing a turbine that can be sold for under $100. Based on our discussions with manufacturers, we believe this price goal will be feasible only if AWE can contract with a manufacturer to custom manufacture a motor that meets the specifications. The least expensive off-the-shelf motor that meets the specifications is $133 per unit. Based on this price, a more feasible selling price for the turbine is $175.

The remainder of this report outlines requirements and assumptions, presents our cost analysis, and offers specific conclusions and recommendations.

Requirements and Assumptions

Our analysis is based on the following assumptions:

1. The wind turbine must meet the specifications illustrated in Figure 1.

2. AWE will produce 50,000 units per year.

3. AWE would like to recover the capital cost for tooling within one year.

4. To keep the sales cost under $100, the total materials cost can be no more than $82 per unit, based on the assumption that nonmaterials costs (labor, assembly, marketing) will average $10 per unit and AWE's profit margin will be 8 percent, or $8 per unit.

Figure 1: Requirements for wind turbine

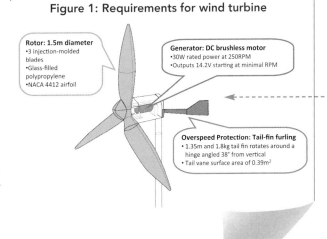

Rotor: 1.5m diameter
•3 injection-molded blades
•Glass-filled polypropylene
•NACA 4412 airfoil

Generator: DC brushless motor
•30W rated power at 250RPM
•Outputs 14.2V starting at minimal RPM

Overspeed Protection: Tail-fin furling
• 1.35m and 1.8kg tail fin rotates around a hinge angled 38° from vertical
• Tail vane surface area of 0.39m²

Letter reports always contain a subject line, similar to the subject line in a memo or email. This line substitutes for a report title.

The introductory paragraph identifies the purpose of the research and report. It also summarizes the main point about feasibility. The reader gets the answer to the question right away.

The introduction ends by previewing the organization of the report.

Figure concisely summarizes the technical specifications.

(continued)

FIGURE 9.7 Continued

letter

Mr. James Burgess
Page 2
July 23, 20XX

Cost Analysis

Injection-Molded Blades

We received three cost quotes for injection-molding the blades, summarized in Table 1. Detailed price quotations for each are available in Attachment 1.

Table 1: Cost quotations for tooling a mold and producing blades

Quote	Annual Volume	Material	Tooling Cost	Unit Cost	Mfg. Location
A	150,000	Polypropylene (quoted based on range of additives)	$74,250	$3.99 to $5.99	United States
B	150,000	Glass-filled Polypropylene	$27,360	$4.82	Shenzhen, China
C	50,000	Glass-filled Polypropylene	$31,750	$4.65	
	100,000			$4.30	Bombay, India
	150,000			$3.94	

Quantitative information is presented in tables so it is easy to understand and use for comparisons and calculations.

The most cost-effective pricing is from the manufacturer in Bombay, where the total cost per turbine will be $12.45, as shown in Table 2.

Table 2: Per-turbine cost for blades

	Calculation		Per Turbine Cost
Tooling	$ 31,750.00	per 50,000 turbines	0.63
Blades	$ 11.82	per turbine	11.82
Total			**$12.45**

Motor

We priced motors from seven manufacturers in India and China. The details are in Attachment 2. Only one motor met the specifications required for this turbine. Its price is **$133 per unit** for 50,000 units.

Additional Costs

Because AWE does not yet have detailed design specifications for the tail fin or turbine housing, we were not able to price those. On comparable wind turbines, the cost of these items is approximately 7 percent of the total unit cost. We recommend that AWE budget **$7 per unit.**

Conclusions and Recommendations

Based solely on the cost of blades and motors, we believe it will be difficult to sell the wind turbines for less than $100. One option will be to increase your price target to $175. A second option will be to negotiate with motor manufacturers for a lower-cost custom motor. Attachment 2 contains contact information for all the motor manufacturers we interviewed. To achieve the $100 price point for the turbine, AWE will need to source a motor that costs $62 per unit or less.

The conclusions section explains the main point in more detail than the opening. The section also offers options for either accomplishing or revising the plan.

We will be glad to discuss our findings with you or provide additional details.

Best regards,

Austin Nichols

Austin Nichols
Senior Consultant

Attachments (sometimes called enclosures) are listed after the signature block.

Attachment 1: Blade manufacturers: detailed price quotations, and contact information.
Attachment 2: Motor manufacturers: detailed specifications, price quotations, and contact information

How do I structure longer, formal reports?

When you are reporting on a major project or substantial research, you will most likely need to produce a formal report. A formal report may be as short as 8 to 10 pages or as long as several hundred pages. As illustrated earlier in Figure 9.3 on page 292, a formal report includes a number of elements that organize the complex material and help the reader find information easily.

The formal report divided among FIGURE 9.8A, B, C, and D on pages 302–313 illustrates these features. This report was prepared by Courtney Patterson as part of her summer internship at the Western State University's School of Management Sciences. Western State is considering expanding its business communication curriculum to include courses in social media. Courtney was assigned to conduct research on business blogging and prepare a recommendation report for the curriculum committee, addressing whether and how Western State should incorporate business blogging into its curriculum.

Create a title page for identifying information

In a formal report, the identifying information is provided on a title page like the one illustrated in FIGURE 9.8A. The **title page** of a report includes the title of the report, the name of the person or organization for whom the report was written, the name and position of the author(s), the name of the author's organization, and the date of submission.

Preview the report with preliminary sections

A formal report provides a reader with several ways to preview the report contents. FIGURE 9.8B illustrates how the blogging report incorporates these preview elements.

- **Table of Contents.** The table of contents lists all the headings in the report, along with the page numbers where the report sections begin. The table of contents serves two functions: It gives readers a quick overview of the content and structure, and it also helps readers find specific sections of the report.

  To make the table of contents easy to read, many writers connect the headings to the page numbers with spaced dots, called *leaders*. To ensure proper alignment of the leaders and page numbers, do not create the leaders by inserting periods. Instead, create a right-aligned tab for placement of page numbers, and format that tab to insert dot leaders automatically.

- **List of Figures and List of Tables.** When a report contains many figures and tables, you can help readers find specific items by including lists of figure and table titles along with their page numbers. These lists follow immediately after the table of contents.

- **Executive Summary.** An executive summary is a mini-version of the report designed to communicate the most important ideas to an audience of decision makers. An executive summary is at most 10 percent of the length of the report.

- **Introduction.** Even though a report begins with an executive summary, the introduction is written as if the reader did not read the executive summary at all. The introduction typically explains the problem or issue that motivated the report. It also summarizes key points or main conclusions and previews how the rest of the report is structured.

Develop the details within sections

The detailed discussion (sometimes called the *body*) of a formal report is always organized with headings. The structure and headings are typically content specific. For example, if you are writing a recommendation report, then the major headings may be the key recommendations. As FIGURE 9.8C illustrates, the blogging report has two major sections, each of which is broken into subsections.

Title page The first page of a formal report, which includes identifying information, such as the report's title; the name of the person or organization for whom the report was written; the author's name, position, and organization; and the date of submission.

FIGURE 9.8A Title Page of a Formal Report

INTEGRATING BLOGGING INTO THE BUSINESS COMMUNICATION
CURRICULUM AT WESTERN STATE UNIVERSITY

Prepared by
Courtney Patterson
School of Management Sciences
Western State University

August 1, 2010

Title page includes
identifying information:
title, organization,
author, and date.

FIGURE 9.8B Preview Elements in a Formal Report

Table of Contents

ii

The table of contents includes all the headings in the report and their page numbers.

Right-aligned tabs are formatted with dot leaders connecting the headings and page numbers.

All page numbers before the introduction are in small Roman numerals. The title page counts as page i, even though it is not numbered.

This report does not need a list of figures and list of tables because the report is relatively short and contains only two figures and one table.

(continued)

FIGURE 9.8B Continued

Executive Summary

Purpose of This Report

Blogging is a growing medium of communication in business. However, the Western State University School of Management Sciences offers students no instruction in blogging. The purpose of this report is to analyze the current state of business blogging and to recommend ways that Western State University can prepare business students to be better communicators with new social media.

Research and Analysis

This report is based on extensive research, including a review of key documents and books about blogging, analysis of nearly 100 small business and corporate blogs, and analysis of blogging statistics using the data provided by Technorati (2008), an organization that analyzes blogs and trends in blogging and also periodically surveys bloggers and readers of blogs worldwide.

Key Findings

- Blogging has evolved from a purely personal form of online diary into a vehicle for widespread communication.

- Blogging has grown exponentially from just a few blogs in the early 1990s to more than 130 million today.

- As of 2006, an estimated 20,000 businesses regularly used blogs to communicate.

Conclusion

Blogging has become a key way businesses communicate with customers and other stakeholders. Use of blogs in business will likely continue to grow.

Recommendations

Since Western State University does not address blogging in any of its current management communication courses, and since blogging has evolved into a serious method for business communication, this report offers four recommendations:

1) **Address blogging and social media in BUAD 287: Business Communication—** at least one class session should focus on social media, including blogging.

2) **Add an elective course, History of Social Media,** which will focus on analyzing blogging and other forms of social media. This course will take a theoretical approach.

3) **Add an elective course, Social and Technological Business Communication,** which will be designed to give students practical instruction using social media as a form of business communication.

4) **Develop a school-wide Management Sciences blog** to provide students with hands-on experience in blogging.

iii

The executive summary follows the table of contents. This summary uses subheadings to guide the reader.

The executive summary is a miniature version of the report and includes all important findings, conclusions, and recommendations.

FIGURE 9.8B Continued

Introduction

The popular social medium of blogging is a powerful tool for business and corporate communication. Blogging gives corporations a personality and human voice, enhancing their ability to reach consumers. As the blogging world, or blogosphere, has grown, the corporate world has begun to adapt to the communication style that blogging makes possible. Moreover, individual experts in the important disciplines of economics, finance, investing, law, and marketing are writing extremely influential blogs on a range of important subjects affecting business, often creating mini-essays with detailed arguments on timely issues and trends.

Given the importance of blogging—especially in business—it is surprising that Western State University does not include instruction about blogging in its business communication curriculum. As a result, business students are graduating without a disciplined intellectual understanding about how to use blogging as a business communication tool.

This report addresses the question of whether and how Western State University should integrate blogging into its curriculum. This report is based on extensive research, including a review of key documents and books about blogging, analysis of nearly 100 small business and corporate blogs, and analysis of blogging statistics using the data provided by Technorati (2008), an organization that analyzes blogs and trends in blogging and also periodically surveys bloggers and readers of blogs worldwide.

This research supports the recommendation that WSU integrate blogging into the curriculum for three key reasons:

1) Business blogging has become a significant and credible form of communication.

2) Businesses are increasingly using blogs to communicate.

3) Effective blogging requires education.

To best prepare students to communicate effectively through workplace blogging, WSU should integrate blogging in the following ways:

- Add a module on blogging/social media to BUAD 287: Business Communication.

- Add two elective courses to the curriculum, focusing on social media in general, including blogging.

- Develop a school-wide Management Sciences blog to provide students with hands-on experience in blogging.

This report explores the reasons that blogging should be integrated into the curriculum, looks at current uses of blogging in the university, and then provides detailed discussion of where blogging can fit into the curriculum.

1

The introduction provides a complete preview of the report. It begins by discussing the reason for the research and the question the report is addressing. It also briefly presents the research methods, which lends credibility to the report.

The final two paragraphs of the introduction—reasons and recommendations—summarize the report's most important ideas and preview its structure.

FIGURE 9.8C Detailed Discussion Elements in a Report

Reasons to Incorporate Blogging into the Curriculum

The first major section of the detailed discussion focuses on the reasons to incorporate blogging into the curriculum.

Reason 1: Business Blogging Is a Significant and Credible Form of Communication

In the last 15 years, business blogging has evolved into a significant and credible platform for business communication. Large and small corporations are creating and managing blogs as an important way to reach customers and stakeholders.

This section is broken down into subsections. Each subsection heading states a specific reason. These specific headings help a reader find main ideas quickly.

The birth of blogging occurred in 1994 when a student at Swathmore College, Justin Hall, launched links.net (Rosenberg, 2009). In the early years, blogs were personal websites where site creators (bloggers) could keep an online, public diary of their lives. Blogs were usually written by individuals who would write from their subjective point of view on any topic, such as their particular events in their personal lives or their individual reactions to external events. As such, the first generation of blogs were highly individualized, with the specific life and experiences of the blogger as the main source of blog content.

As the number of blogs grew very quickly, bloggers who read and followed other individuals' blogs created what amounted to a viral social network from blogging, typically by linking to other blogs and other websites of interest. Blogs oriented to political discussion emerged on the scene in 2001, prompted by the controversial election of George W. Bush in 2000 as well as the events of September 11, 2001. By 2008, blogging became so critical to reaching audiences that 95 of the top 100 newspapers had reporter blogs (Technorati, 2008).

The report documents its sources with parenthetical citations, using APA style (covered on pages 311–312).

In its 2008 *State of the Blogosphere* report, Technorati stated that it had indexed 133 million blogs since 2002. Of this 133 million, 76,000 blogs have what is known as Technorati Authority (TA), a label denoting the number of blogs linking to a website in the last six months (the higher the number, the more TA the blog has). Thus, approximately 76,000 blogs are actively linking to other blogs and websites.

At the time of that report, close to one million posts were being created every day in up to 81 languages from 66 countries (Technorati, 2008). Blogging has expanded to include genre-specific blogs, such as political commentary blogs, media blogs that use music and video posts, and corporate blogs (Rettberg, 2008). Blogging has evolved from online personal diaries to commentary and discussion on social, political, legal and economic issues by academic scholars/expert professionals. Blogging has also become a vehicle for businesses to communicate with customers and stakeholders.

As blogging has evolved, so has its credibility as a communication medium. In its survey for the 2008 *State of the Blogosphere* report, Technorati asked a statistically valid representative sample of bloggers worldwide about the credibility of the blogging world. The results suggest blogging is becoming more credible as a source of information (see Figure 1).

This last paragraph introduces Figure 1, below.

Reason 2: Businesses Are Increasingly Using Blogs to Communicate

In the early days of blogging, prominent thinkers about blogging such as Rick Levine, Christopher Locke, Doc Searls, and David Weinberger (1999) prophesied the influence blogging could have on the corporate world. In *The Cluetrain Manifesto*, Levine et al. wrote: "A powerful global conversation has begun. Through the Internet, people are discovering and inventing new ways to share relevant knowledge with blinding speed. As a direct result, markets are getting smarter—and getting smarter faster than most companies" (1999, p. 10). They knew that, in order to survive, companies would have to learn from the technological changes occurring through blogging's conversational medium.

Direct quotations require either a page number or sufficient information to allow a reader to find the original source.

2

FIGURE 9.8C Continued

Figure 1 – Response to Survey About Credibility of Blogging

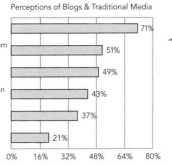

Perceptions of Blogs & Traditional Media

Blogs are getting taken more seriously as sources of information — 71%
More people will get their news and entertainment from blogs than from traditional media in the next 5 years — 51%
Blogs are just as valid media sources as traditional media — 49%
I get more of my news and information from blogs than other media sources — 43%
Blogs are often better written than traditional media articles — 37%
Newspapers will not be able to survive in the next 10 years — 21%

0% 16% 32% 48% 64% 80%
Percentage of People Responding Positively

Adapted from Technorati (2008). *State of the Blogosphere.* http://technorati.com/blogging/stateof-the-blogosphere/

Corporations heeded this advice and now have a prominent place in the blogosphere. Technorati's 2004 estimate counted roughly 5,000 corporate blogs (Sifry, 2004), a number that some experts believe had quadrupled by 2006 (Cass, 2006). The official blog for Google (http://googleblog.blogspot.com/) is so widely read and linked that Technorati Authority rated it the 13th highest ranked blog among all categories of blogs.

Table 1 shows an alphabetized list of the top 75 business blogs in 2009 as measured by the *Financial Times ComMetrics Blog Index of Corporate Blogging Effectiveness* (2009). While many of the businesses listed are Internet related, a number of traditional technology, finance, industrial, and retail corporations are also on the list, for example, Alcoa, General Electric, Wells Fargo, and Wal-Mart. For WSU business communication students, such blogs would be worth studying as examples of effective blogging in a business setting. (The Appendix lists the URLs for the top 25 of these blogs.)

Blogging in Small Businesses. Businesses typically use blogs in one of two ways: to showcase the personnel/expertise of the corporation or to engage in product-related conversations with others in a public and widely read forum. For a smaller business, a blog can be an economical way of getting attention and attaining a global reach at little to no cost.

Small business blogs are particularly effective when they focus on the company's personality and expertise instead of on marketing its products. In effect, the credibility of a small business blog depends on showing passion rather than salesmanship (Herzlich, 2009; Scoble & Israel, 2006). A blog can act as a conduit for a small company to begin conversations that build consumer trust, rather than simply serve as another avenue for marketing products.

3

Figure 1 is adapted from a source, so it needs a source citation directly below it. The citation is formatted in APA style, because that is the documentation style of the report.

This introduction to Table 1 tells the reader what the table is and also directs the reader to look for specific information.

All appendices need to be referenced in the body of the report. The reference should explicitly state what a reader will find in that appendix.

Because the discussion of Reason 2 is long, the material is divided into subsections: blogging in small businesses and blogging in large corporations.

(continued)

FIGURE 9.8C Continued

Table 1 – 75 Corporations Whose Blogs Appear in the *Financial Times ComMetrics Blog Index* of *Corporate Blogging Effectiveness*

ABB	Deutsche Bank	Johnson & Johnson	SAP
Accenture	Deutsche Telekom	Johnson Controls	Siemens
Adobe	E.ON	Kraft Foods	Sony
Alcoa	eBay	McDonald's	Swisscom
Amazon	EMC	Microsoft	Sygenta
American Express	Emerson Electric	Nestlé	Telenor Group
Arcelor Mittal	Ericsson	News Corporation	Telia Sonera
Aviva	Fedex	Nike	Telstra
Bank of America	Fiat	Nissan	Time Warner
Bayer	France Telecom	Nokia	Toyota
BBVA	General Electric	Novo Nordisk	Unilever
Berkshire Hathaway	GlaxoSmithKline	Oracle	UPS
BNP Paribas	GM	Petro Canada	Verizon Communications
Boeing	Google	Procter & Gamble	Viacom
Chevron	Henkel	Renault	Volvo
Cisco	Hewlett Packard	Reuters	Wal-Mart
Coca-Cola	IBM	Royal Bank of Canada	Wells Fargo
Daimler	InBev	Royal/Dutch Shell	Yahoo!
Dell	ING	Samsung	

Adapted from: Financial Times (2009). Powered by My.ComMetrics.com—updates available at http://FTindex.ComMetrics.com/

Thomas Mahon, for example, is a London tailor who started a blog called English Cut where he writes about the technical aspects of tailoring, such as the differences among suits and kinds of fabrics. As Figure 2 illustrates, Mahon does not primarily promote his own business. Instead, Mahon uses his blog to influence his customers' perceptions of him and his quality tailoring. His blog provides a public, yet informal place where consumers can view his life and his love for tailoring—and come to appreciate his work.

Blogs also offer small businesses the opportunity to become completely transparent with their consumer base (Halzack, 2008; Mahon, 2009; Rettberg, 2008; Scoble & Israel, 2006). For example, Honest Tea began its blog in 2005 expressly desiring openness with its consumers. Before Coca-Cola acquired a 40% share of Honest Tea, the company blogged about the decision and even responded to consumers' criticisms (Goldman, 2009). This transparency allows a company like Honest Tea to build consumer trust and credibility.

4

Table 1 also includes a source citation. The citation is formatted in APA style, because that is the documentation style of the report.

The reference to Figure 2 tells the reader what to notice in the figure.

The anecdote about Honest Tea supports the point about blogs and transparency. Instead of inserting a screen shot of the blog, the writer provides a citation, allowing the interested readers to find the original blog entry.

FIGURE 9.8C Continued

Figure 2 – Screen Shot of Thomas Mahon's Blog, EnglishCut.com

u.s. visit June 9th-16th finalised

names in a hat...

you never know who's talking...

loving home wanted...

american tour june 9th-16th

straight or crooked...

flared trousers & tailors' dens.

paris april 24th-25th

savile row's wyatt earp....

tea and biscuits

sb peaked lapel...

mr. cameron

dressing for a warm climate

no strings attached

oiling the shears...

large gentlemen, please take note...

thank you...

ARCHIVES

April 2010

March 2010

February 2010

January 2010

December 2009

November 2009

September 2009

August 2009

July 2009

June 2009

May 2009

April 2009

(myself and ethan. looking weary preparing for the USA)

It's all go here getting ready for our trip to the USA in April. Ethan's having one of the most concentrated courses in bespoke cutting as you could ever imagine.

I was recently asked some questions about the trade on Savile Row by these very nice people - mannerofman.com

I guess it gives an insight on how we see Savile Row and the craft in general. I hope you enjoy it as there's a few nice pics (not me personally) of some of us here. I'll carry on cutting but I hope you enjoy.

The illustration in Figure 2 does more than provide visual interest. It helps make the point that business blogs provide a personal face for a small business.

From: Englishcut.com

Blogging in Large Corporations. Larger companies also benefit from blogging's emphasis on personality and community. Whereas a smaller company may use a blog to inform readers of the company's qualifications and dedication to quality, an established, larger company can use blogging to rebrand itself as a more consumer-friendly, actively listening business.

Robert Scoble (2003), a Microsoft employee, used his blog to interview other Microsoft employees. By creating a personal face for a corporation nicknamed the "Evil Empire," Scoble did much to positively shift perceptions of Microsoft in less than six months. Multiple employees at Microsoft then began day-to-day blogs to provide information to customers.

Some corporations achieve this personal face by publishing blogs by their CEOs. Mark Cuban, owner of the Dallas Mavericks, writes the widely read **blogmaverick.com,** which has a Technorati Authority ranking of 837 (Technorati, 2008). Other corporations, like Wal-Mart, present the voice of the employee. In **checkoutbloggers.com,** Wal-Mart managers and associates spread the news about new gadgets, games, and Wal-Mart initiatives.

5

(continued)

FIGURE 9.8C Continued

Established corporations also use blogs to enter into existing web-based conversations about the company's products or services. Corporate bloggers search online for mentions of their company, looking specifically for misinformation, rumors, or easily answered questions. By responding to these comments online, bloggers communicate that the company is interested in being an active participant of a community, not just in selling its products (Rettberg, 2008).

Finally, corporations also use "dark blogs," which are not available to the public, for internal communication. For example, one large European pharmaceutical company uses blogs as a form of internal knowledge sharing to pool competitive intelligence (Charman, 2005).

Reason 3: Effective Blogging Requires Education ◀-- Like the discussion of Reason 2, the discussion of Reason 3 is divided into sections. In this case, it is divided into bulleted paragraphs because it offers a "list" of skills. Bullets are an appropriate format for lists.

Although blogs are a significant form of business communication, blogging requires a unique set of skills that need to be taught.

- **How to communicate professionally in informal language.** Blogs communicate information with a more personalized and individualized voice than most news, corporation, or media outlets do. Because of blogging's roots in personal journaling, blogs communicate with an informal language that typically represents the writer. Blogs are clearly authored by individuals, even if those individuals are doing so at the request of a corporation.

  This individualized voice leads to a number of advantages. Successful blogs allow corporations to connect to a wide range of consumers. The blogs also provide a forum for treating consumers as real humans through authentic conversation rather than through impersonal marketing and branding rhetoric, which is often criticized as insincere. Commentators have referred to this evolution of marketing communication as a corporate revolution (Rettberg, 2008; Scoble & Israel, 2006; Technorati, 2009).

- **How to generate consumer interest in a company without turning consumers off.** One of the easiest ways for a blog to be ineffective is if it is used as a product-advertising tool. To be effective, blogs should focus on communicating to consumers and investors information that is seen as objective as possible, without any sales pitches.

- **How to maintain transparency in writing.** Another pitfall for corporate bloggers is failing to take seriously the directive for transparency that personal communication demands. Scoble's (2003) Corporate Weblog Manifesto, posted on his blog, includes principles such as these: "Tell the truth, the whole truth, and nothing but the truth. If your competitor has a product that's better than yours, link to it" and "Post fast on both good news and bad ... The trick to building trust is to show up." As *New York Times* columnist Marci Alboher (2007) points out, this "kind of transparency is a popular reason for blogging, particularly for companies that want to be identified as mission-oriented or socially responsible" (p. 3C). However, the failure to be transparent will make the company appear evasive.

- **How to use blogging as part of a larger communication strategy.** Bloggers have to deal with an audience that must be kept interested. One important and often overlooked challenge with blogging is its commitment: a blog must be a regularly updated forum. Without consistent updates, the blog will lose its readership (Alboher, 2007; "Blogging," 2009; Thompson, 2009; Scoble, 2003). Scoble (2003) stated this need for commitment in a clear axiom: "Demonstrate passion. Post frequently" (p. 18).

6

FIGURE 9.8C Continued

Recommendations for Incorporating Blogging into the WSU Curriculum

At first glance, it may look as if business blogging is only a function of corporate communication, and thus only marketing or journalism majors need to learn how to do it. However, as channels of business communication evolve, the curriculum for all business students must evolve with them. As this report has shown, blogging offers an intellectually rich and interesting business communication channel for the following reasons:

- Even in its short history, blogging has undergone dramatic changes.
- Thousands of corporations are blogging; a rich set of examples can easily be mined for detailed theoretical and practical studies.
- Blogging continues to evolve with the speed typical of most Internet phenomena.

WSU can prepare business students to communicate well in this channel by adopting the following additions and modifications to the management science curriculum:

Recommendation 1—Address Blogging/Social Media in BUAD 287: Business Communication

At least one week of classes in this mandatory course should be devoted to reviewing social media, including blogging. This basic introduction will alert all students to the importance of blogging in business.

Recommendation 2—Add 300-Level Elective: History and Theory of Social Media

Western State should add a course focusing on the *History and Theory of Social Media*. This course would survey the past and present developments of social media, including blogging as well as other new forms of social media (such as Twitter, Facebook, MySpace, Ning) and track how media has changed in the last two decades due to Internet technology. This course would take a theoretical and analytical approach to blogging and social media.

Recommendation 3—Add 300-Level Elective: Social and Technological Business Communication

Western State should add a course focusing on *Social and Technological Business Communication*. This course would provide practical knowledge on how businesses communicate through blogging and other social media, understand the challenges and opportunities for big and small businesses, and learn how to incorporate blogging and other social media into a firm's overall business communication strategy. The course would focus on giving students practical instruction in using blogging and social media. One model for such a course is Georgetown University's Social Media in Business, Development and Government (Georgetown University, 2009).

Recommendation 4—Create a School-Wide Blog for Students

Western State School of Management Science has the opportunity to model effective blogging for students by creating its own blog to communicate with stakeholders and by encouraging students to participate and to develop their own linked blogs.

7

New sections of a report begin at the top of a new page.

This section is divided into four key recommendations, which are formatted as subsections with headings. This formatting allows the reader to skim the headings easily. It also allows Word's automatic table of contents tool to include that text in the table of contents at the start of the report.

Conclude the report with supporting information

Formal reports may conclude with two types of supporting information: reference lists and appendices. As **FIGURE 9.8D** illustrates, the blogging report contains both types of supporting information.

References. If a report uses secondary research sources, create a reference page to list the sources. Use an appropriate documentation method, such as APA (American Psychological Association), CMS (Chicago Manual of Style), or MLA (Modern Language Association). The reference section begins on its own page, immediately after the detailed discussion (or body) of the report. You can find details about these documentation styles in Appendix C and in mybcommlab.com.

FIGURE 9.8D Supporting Information Sections of a Report

References

Alboher, M. (2007, December 27). Blogging's a low-cost, high-return marketing tool. *New York Times*, p. 3C.

BLOGGING: Natural selection. (2009, January 15). *New Media Age*. Retrieved from HighBeam Research: http://www.highbeam.com/doc/1G1-192295694.html

Cass, J. (2006, March 28). Fortune 500 take lead in corporate blogging: Only 0.73% of employers blog - while 4.6% of Fortune 500 blog. [Web log post]. Retrieved from http://blogsurvey.backbonemedia .com/archives/2006/03/fortune_500_tak_1.html

Charman, S. (2005). Dark blogs: The use of blogs in business. *Corante Research Report*. Retrieved from http://www.suw.org.uk/files/Dark_Blogs_01_ European_Pharma_Group.pdf

Cuban, C. (n.d.). *Blog maverick*. Retrieved from http://blogmaverick.com

Financial Times ComMetrics blog index 2009. (2009). Retrieved from http://ftindex.commetrics.com/

Georgetown University. (2009). *Social media in business development and government*. Retrieved from https://digitalcommons.georgetown.edu/blogs/msfs-556-spring2009/course-description/

Goldman, S. (2009, August 7). *For Honest Tea, Coke is it*. [Web log post]. Retrieved from http://www.honesttea.com/blog /category/from-seth-and-barry/

Halzack, S. (2008, August 25). Marketing moves to the blogosphere; Business model shifts to engage customers online. *Washington Post*, p. D1.

Levine, R., Locke, C., Searls, D., & Weinberg, D. (1999). *The cluetrain manifesto: The end of business as usual*. New York: Basic Books.

Mahon, T. (n.d.) *English cut*. Retrieved from http://englishcut.com

Rettberg, J. W. (2008). *Blogging*. Malden, MA: Polity Press.

Rosenberg, S. (2009). *Say everything: How blogging began, what it's becoming, and why it matters*. New York, NY: Crown Publishers.

Scoble, R. (2003, February 6). *Corporate weblog manifesto*. [Web log post]. Retrieved from http://scoble.weblogs.com/2003/02/26.html

Scoble R., & Israel, S. (2006). *Naked conversations*. Hoboken, NJ: John Wiley & Sons, Inc.

Sifry, D. (2004, October 17). *Oct 2004 state of the blogosphere: Corporate bloggers*. [Web log post]. Retrieved from http://www.sifry.com/alerts/archives/000390.html

Technorati (2008).*The state of the blogosphere 2008*. Retrieved from http://technorati.com/blogging/state-of-the-blogosphere/

Thompson, L. (2009). Blogs: If used properly, an investor-friendly tool. *Compliance Week, 6*(62), p. 60.

Wal-Mart (n.d.) *Check out blog*. Retrieved from http://checkoutblog.com

8

The reference list is prepared in APA style:

- Sources are listed alphabetically by last name (or title when there is no author).
- The publication date immediately follows the author.
- In source titles, only the first words and proper nouns are capitalized.

← Educational website

← Blog message

← Newspaper article

← Book

← Company website

← Magazine article

Appendices. Following the reference list, a report may include additional supporting information in an appendix or multiple appendices. Appendices contain information that would interrupt the flow of the report but that readers may find useful—for example, raw data, calculations, large tables, or other graphics too big for the body of the report. If the report includes more than one appendix, the series is labeled Appendix A, Appendix B, and so forth. Appendices are also given a content-specific name,

FIGURE 9.8D Continued

Appendix
Ranking, Names, and URLs of the Top 25 Corporate Blogs

The 25 corporate blogs listed below received the highest rankings from The Financial Times (2009). The Financial Times ranks blogs by assessing how popular they are with Internet users or how many people are referring to them. In creating this index, The Financial Times uses the following metrics: Google PageRank, Technorati Ranking, Technorati Authority, Yahoo! InLinks, and Google Blog Search.

Rank	Company	URL
1	Google	http://googleblog.blogspot.com/
2	Viacom	http://splashpage.mtv.com/
3	Reuters	http://www.reuters.com/finance/deals
3	Yahoo!	http://www.ysearchblog.com/
3	Adobe	http://blogs.adobe.com/
6	Nokia	http://conversations.nokia.com/
7	Oracle	http://blogs.sun.com/jonathan/
8	Microsoft	http://blogs.msdn.com/ie/default.aspx
9	Dell	http://en.community.dell.com/blogs/direct2dell/
10	Amazon	http://affiliate-blog.amazon.com/
10	General Electric	http://www.gereports.com/
12	eBay	http://developer.ebay.com/community/blog/ http://www.ebaypartnernetworkblog.com/en/
13	American Express	http://www.openforum.com/
14	Cisco	http://blogs.cisco.com/gov
14	Boeing	http://boeingblogs.com/randy/
14	Time Warner	http://searchblog.aol.com/
14	Coca-Cola	http://www.coca-colaconversations.com/
14	Toyota	http://pressroom.toyota.com/pr/tms/our-point-of-view.aspx
14	GM	http://gmreinvention.com/
14	Hewlett Packard	http://www.communities.hp.com/online/blogs/csremea/default.aspx
14	Wells Fargo	http://blog.wellsfargo.com/wachovia/
14	Accenture	http://www.accenture.com/Global/Accenture_Blogs/ Accenture_High_Performance_Business_Blog/default.htm
14	E.ON	http://eon-uk.com/
14	Alcoa	http://www.alcoa.com/alcoa_recycling/en/home.asp
25	News Corporation	http://allthingsd.com/

9

Margin annotations:

This report contains only one appendix, so the appendix does not need to be labeled Appendix A.

The name of the appendix appears immediately under the label.

The table appears in an appendix rather than the body of the report for two reasons:

1. Readers do not need the information as they read the report.

2. The information is so detailed that it would interrupt the report's flow if it appeared in the detailed discussion section.

for example, *Appendix A: Map of Conference Centers within 10 Miles of Acme's Home Office.* Typically, the body of the report will refer to each appendix in the order of its placement in the report. Appendix A is the first appendix the report refers to, Appendix B is the second, and so forth. This means you may need to rearrange the appendices during the process of revising a report.

TECHNOLOGY   Using Software Features to Help Format Formal Reports

Microsoft Word and other word processing programs offer powerful features that help you format formal reports. The following features will save you time and improve the professional look of your work. To learn about other features, use your program's help files.

- **Automated styles.** Word has a number of different text styles that you can use in your report. A style consists of a font, size, color, and placement on the page. You can use one style for normal paragraphs, another for headings, a third for quotations, and a fourth for captions. One advantage of using styles rather than manually formatting paragraphs is that if you mark content as a specific style and then decide to change that style, the change occurs to all the marked text throughout the document.

- **Automated headings.** Word offers a set of styles called *Heading 1, Heading 2,* and *Heading 3*. You can customize those styles with any font and size. If you use these heading styles for the headings in your report, you can take advantage of Word's automated table of contents feature.

- **Automated tables of contents.** Many word processing applications offer an easy process to design and insert a table of contents. When you select "Insert Table of Contents" in Word, the program finds all of the headings that you have created using the built-in heading styles and copies them into a preformatted table of contents along with their associated page numbers. As you modify your report, you can continue to update your table of contents to include additional headings and changes in page numbers.

- **Formatted tab styles, including automated leaders.** Many tables of contents include dots, called *leaders*, connecting the section title and the page number. Word allows you to insert those leaders automatically by formatting your tab style, whether or not you use an automated table of contents. Simply create a tab in a docu-

ment by clicking your selected tab position on the ruler at the top of the page. Then format the tab by clicking the bottom right corner of the paragraph menu (on the Home tab) and then the Tabs button at the bottom left corner of the paragraph dialog box. Select the leader style you prefer and click OK. When you use the tab key to tab to that spot, leader dots will fill the tabbed space.

- **Automated page numbering, using both Roman and Arabic numerals.** You can control the placement of page numbers in your document by inserting headers or footers. You can further control page numbers by using Word's "insert section break" feature and formatting the page numbers differently for each section. For example, you can create a title page with no page number. Then insert a section break and use small Roman numerals for the page numbering on the table of contents page and executive summary. Insert another section break and begin the numbering again with Arabic numerals, with the introduction counting as page 1, even though sequentially it is not the first page of the file.

- **Automated footnotes, endnotes, citations, bibliographies.** Most word processing applications allow you to add and number footnotes, endnotes, and citations automatically. As you add, remove, or cut and paste text in your draft, your note numbers automatically change to reflect their new position.

- **Automated labeling of figures and tables.** You can automatically number and label figures and tables using Word's "Insert Caption" command. As you move the figures and tables in your draft, Word will automatically update the figure and table numbers.

PEARSON mybcommlab

For a TECHNOLOGY exercise, go to Exercise 10 on page 335 or to this chapter's End-of-Chapter Exercises at mybcommlab.com.

Study Question 9.4

What guidelines should I follow for writing report decks?

Increasingly, organizations are using presentation software such as PowerPoint to write reports.[8] These reports, called report decks, differ from traditional slide presentations in one key way: they are designed to substitute for a standard report document and to be understandable without a presenter. Often, the writer sends the report deck as an email attachment, and the audience reads the report deck onscreen one page at a time. Sometimes, the writer prints the report deck as a handout for participants at a meeting. Meeting attendees go through the deck slide by slide to discuss the key points. The slides may or may not also be projected. The hybrid status of a report deck—partly report and partly presentation—explains why slides in report decks contain more detail than slides in traditional presentations.

Writing a report using presentation software requires a new way of thinking about how to structure a report and how to design individual slides. To be successful, use the following guidelines.

Understand why and when to use report decks

Organizations use report decks for three main reasons. First, when the organization needs a written report and plans to present that report at a meeting, a report deck can serve both functions. Producing one document instead of two saves time and money. Producing that document in presentation software such as PowerPoint also facilitates discussion. It is easier to talk about the report if you can project specific sections than if you need to ask your audience to find "the second paragraph on page 10." Second, compared to word processing software, presentation software more easily allows you to place pictures, tables, and graphs in precise locations. Finally, many organizations use presentation software, such as PowerPoint, for report writing because employees know how to use the software well. According to John Spelich of Gateway Computers, "We use Microsoft PowerPoint for just about everything. It's remarkable how often I see it, even just for basic information we might share internally. It's become a 'go-to' software package that almost everyone feels comfortable using. We use it with employees, customers, the news media, with investment analysts, and more."[9]

Report decks can be used for any type of report. Many consulting companies and business strategy organizations use decks to report the results of analyses to their clients. Other organizations prepare progress reports as decks to be presented at monthly department meetings. Many science-based organizations use decks to report the results of technical investigations because presentation software easily allows them to include photographs and diagrams.

Design the deck effectively

Just as a traditional word-processed report needs to be well designed, so does a report written in presentation software. Save yourself time and effort by applying your design features to a master slide. Formats on the master slide will be applied to all the slides in your presentation. Follow these guidelines:

- **Use a basic solid background.** Avoid background graphics or dramatic gradations. These will compete with your text and graphics for the reader's attention.
- **Size your title box to accommodate two-line headlines, using a font that is approximately 22 to 24 points.** This will allow you to fit sentence-style headlines at the top of your slides.
- **Leave space for a "road sign" on the upper left or upper right corner of your slides.** These road signs indicate the section of the deck, like a header on a word-processed report.
- **Include a footer at the bottom of each slide.** The footer contains the page number, the name of the project and, usually, a copyright marking. A copyright on each slide is important, since your audience may extract slides and present them out of context. The copyright will indicate to future readers that the slide originally came from a report deck you produced.
- **Check to see how your master slide looks when printed in black and white.** While many people will read the report in color onscreen, those who print the report may print in black and white.

Design the deck content to be easy to follow

Because a reader should be able to follow the logic of a report deck without the benefit of a presenter's explanations, the deck needs to be very easy to read. Like any other report, a good deck will be divided into sections and begin with a preview. Some decks include executive summaries. All decks include an "agenda" or contents slide that serves as a table of contents. This slide differs from a traditional table of contents in that it usually does not list the "page" numbers of sections of the report. However, if your deck is long, you may choose to help your reader by adding page numbers. To remind your reader of the current section name while reading the report, place section titles in "road signs" at the upper right or left corner of the slide.

Individual slides also need to be easy to follow. Each slide should communicate a clear and complete point. This means that a report slide may have more text on it than a traditional presentation slide. However, this does not mean that a report deck will be text-heavy. Instead as the effective slide in FIGURE 9.9 illustrates, the headline states the main point of the slide—in much the same way that the topic sentence of a paragraph states the main point of the paragraph. Then the body of the slide provides supporting detail, usually in the form of a table, graph, diagram, or illustration, with a few short explanatory text boxes.

When designing deck slides, follow these guidelines:

- **Use short, sentence-style titles, called headlines.** Compose your headline as if it were the topic sentence of a paragraph.
- **Position headlines to the left and use sentence case.** Since headlines function as short sentences, graphically treat them like sentences, capitalizing only the first word. Do not center them or capitalize every word, as you would do with the titles in typical presentations. Although the headline functions as a short sentence, no period is required at the end. The only end punctuation that is required is a question mark if the headline is a question.
- **Develop slide content to support the headline.** Be sure that everything on the slide relates to and supports the headline. If you have too much information for one slide, then develop a second slide on the topic.

FIGURE 9.9
Designing Effective Deck Slides

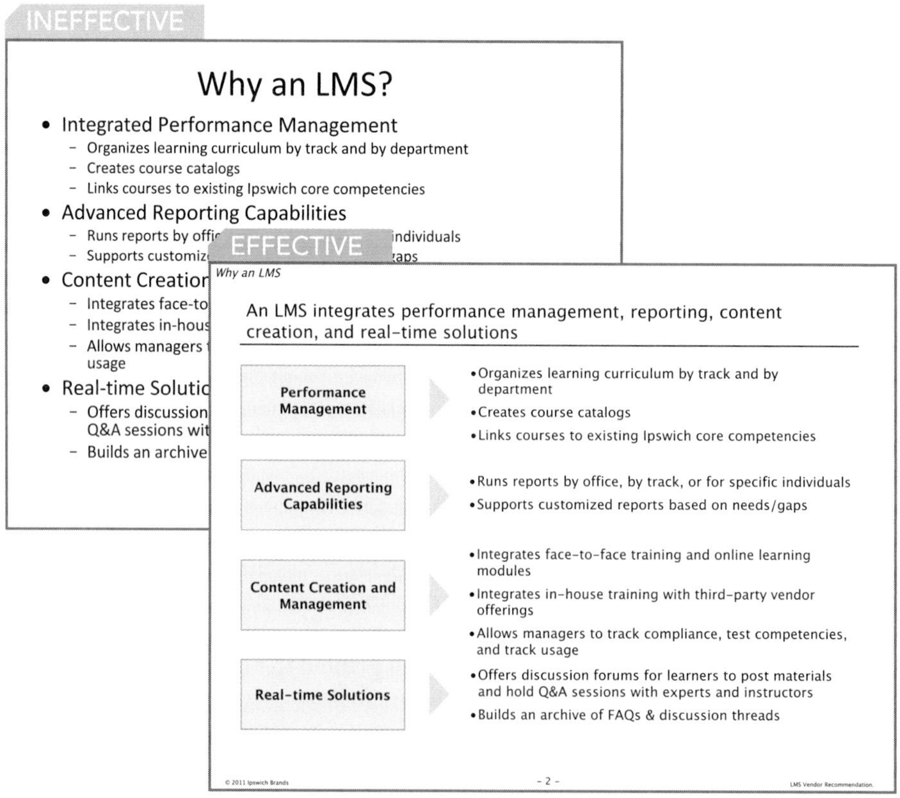

- **Leave enough blank space so that your audience can focus their vision.** It is better to write a few well-crafted, concise points than to include whole paragraphs on a slide.

- **Avoid using bullets for all your text.** Page after page of bullets can make your audience lose attention. Instead, place text in tables or in text boxes arranged to show the relationship between ideas.

- **Whenever possible, use visuals to develop ideas.** Do not rely only on words. Slides are a visual medium, so communicate your message by using graphics as well as words.

Figure 9.9 shows how to revise a traditional bullet point list into a more effective report deck page. Notice how the effective slide on the right uses a sentence-style headline to communicate its main point and places the four main advantages of a learning management system in boxes going down the left side of the slide. This format helps the audience focus on the main ideas before reading the details. Although this slide uses more text than you would include in a traditional projected presentation, the text will be easy for someone to read on a computer screen or in a printout, which is how a report deck is typically distributed and read.

Producing a report deck requires creating many slides with each designed to support a key point. FIGURE 9.10 on pages 317–319 illustrates such a report deck. Recall in Chapter 7 that you imagined yourself as Alan Cotton, Learning and Development Manager for Ipswich Brands. Ipswich Brands is considering adopting a learning management system to support the large amount of training it offers. Alan researched learning management

FIGURE 9.10 PowerPoint Report Deck

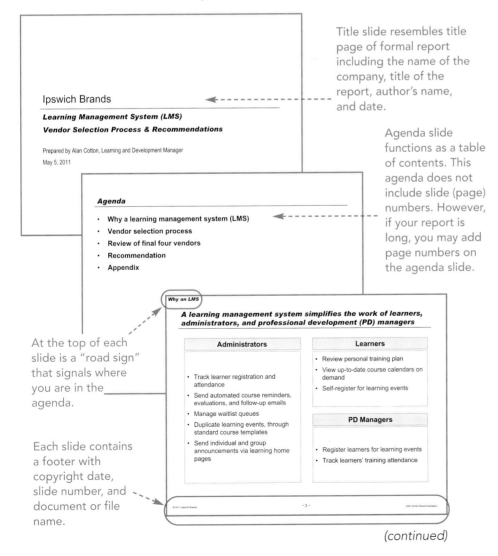

(continued)

FIGURE 9.10
Continued

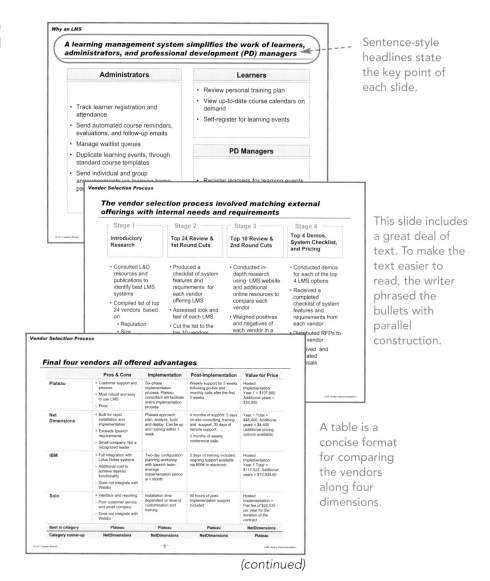

(continued)

systems following the process outlined in Chapter 7. Based on that research, he evaluated options to present to the company's chief learning officer, Mitchell Harris. Figure 9.10 is the analytical evaluation report he produced. As you read through the report, notice the sentence headlines and the different ways the slide content supports the headlines. Also note that this report does not include an executive summary, though some report decks do. This deck is unusual because it is organized indirectly. The final recommendation of potential vendors comes at the end of the report. This organization allows Alan to persuade readers that a learning management system will benefit the company before he recommends specific vendors.

Study Question 9.5

How do I integrate tables and graphs into my reports?

Business reports often rely on numbers, and **data graphics**—tables and graphs—are the best tools for communicating these numbers. Have you ever read a complicated description of information and then looked at a table or graph and thought, "Now I understand"? Well-designed tables and graphs provide a picture of data and allow you to see relationships and trends much more clearly than with text alone.

However, creating effective data graphics and integrating them into your text is not always easy. It involves a multistep process. This section provides a quick glimpse of that process so that you can begin using graphics effectively in your own documents.

FIGURE 9.10 Continued

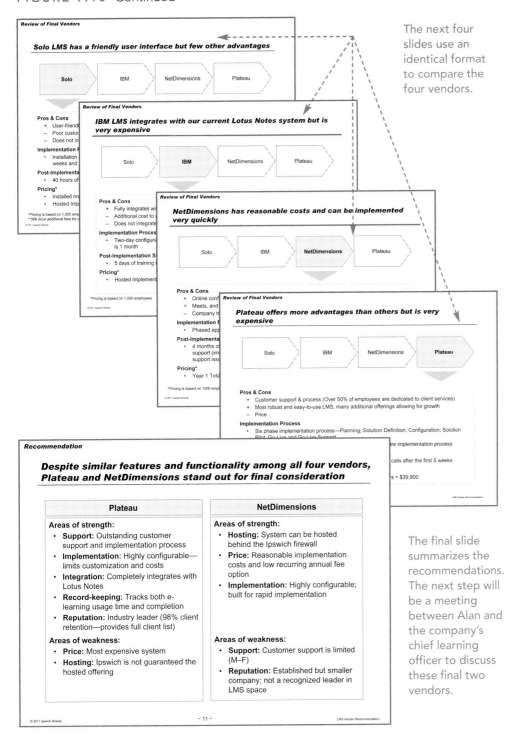

The next four slides use an identical format to compare the four vendors.

The final slide summarizes the recommendations. The next step will be a meeting between Alan and the company's chief learning officer to discuss these final two vendors.

Choose the best form of display: table or graph

Tables and graphs represent data in different ways. **Tables** arrange data in columns and rows, allowing you to read down or across to see different relationships. **Graphs** illustrate the relationship among variables or sets of data as an image or shape drawn in relationship to two axes.

Because they represent data in different ways, tables and graphs have different uses. FIGURE 9.11 illustrates the same data presented in text, graph, and table form. As you can

Data graphics Visual representations of data, in tables and graphs, that allow you to see relationships and trends much more clearly than in text alone.

Tables A graphic that arranges data in columns and rows, allowing you to read down or across to see different relationships.

Graphs A visual representation of data that illustrates the relationship among variables, usually in relationship to *x*- and *y*-axes.

FIGURE 9.11 Comparing Text, Table, and Graph Options

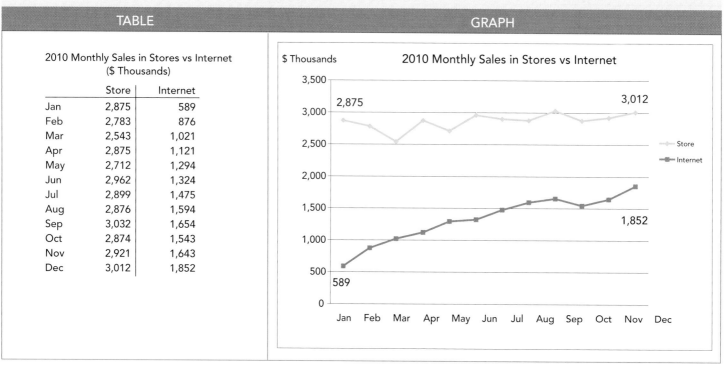

TEXT

In January of 2010, sales in our stores reached almost $2.9 million. Monthly store sales remained steady, ending at just over $3.0 million in December. By contrast, monthly Internet sales tripled over the course of the year. In January, they were only $589,000, but Internet sales climbed steadily throughout the year until they reached a monthly level of more than $1.85 million in December.

TABLE

2010 Monthly Sales in Stores vs Internet ($ Thousands)

	Store	Internet
Jan	2,875	589
Feb	2,783	876
Mar	2,543	1,021
Apr	2,875	1,121
May	2,712	1,294
Jun	2,962	1,324
Jul	2,899	1,475
Aug	2,876	1,594
Sep	3,032	1,654
Oct	2,874	1,543
Nov	2,921	1,643
Dec	3,012	1,852

GRAPH

see, it is difficult to understand the significance of numbers that are embedded in the paragraph. The table makes it very easy to find exact values. However, the table does not help you see specific patterns and trends. While the graph does not provide exact values, it highlights trends and relationships by showing the data as a shape. You should choose the form of data graphic that helps your audience most clearly see the important points you want to make about the data.

Choose the best type of graph

If you decide to represent your data with a graph, you have many types of graphs to choose from. In fact, in his comprehensive illustrated reference book, *Information Graphics*, Robert L. Harris illustrates 27 basic graph types (such as line, column, and bar). Within each graph type, Harris catalogs many different variations—for example, 18 variations of a basic bar graph.[10]

With so many options, choosing the best graph can become overwhelming. However, most business documents rely on a subset of nine types of graphs that can be created with spreadsheet or charting software, including Microsoft Excel. Each graph has a different purpose and illustrates a different relationship. FIGURE 9.12 summarizes those nine graph types. For each graph, you'll find the purpose, an illustration of the graph, examples of how to use it, and best practices for designing the graph. These best practices have developed over time as ways of helping communicators reveal meaningful information about data. You will find an explanation of the design principles in the next section.

Design graphs and tables to communicate

Whether you are designing graphs or tables, follow the core principle of Edward Tufte, one of the most famous information designers in the world. Tufte recommends that tables

FIGURE 9.12 Guidelines for Selecting the Best Graph

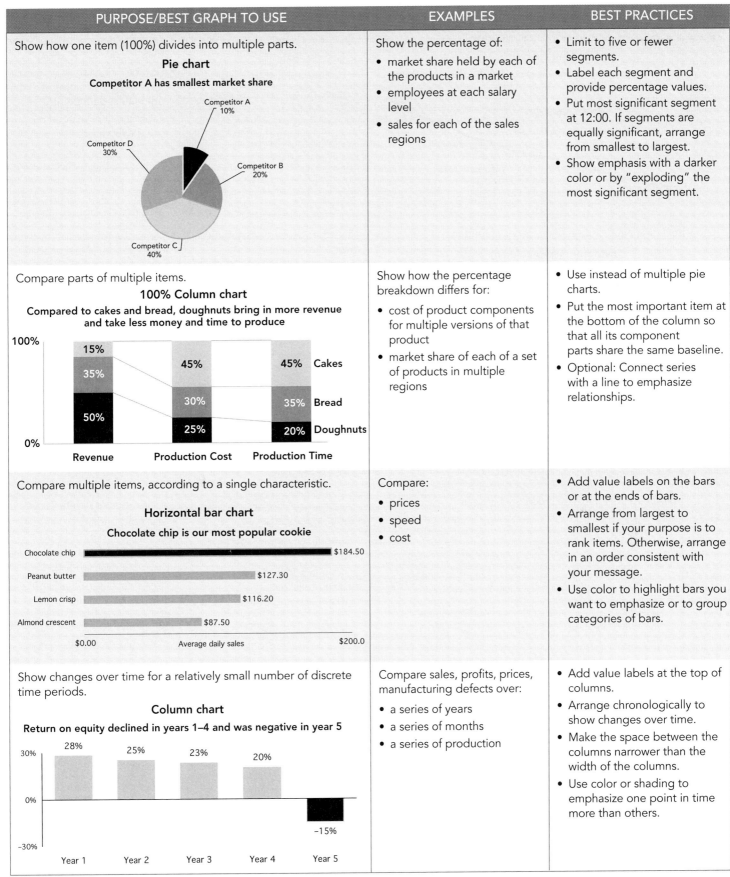

PURPOSE/BEST GRAPH TO USE	EXAMPLES	BEST PRACTICES
Show how one item (100%) divides into multiple parts. **Pie chart** **Competitor A has smallest market share** Competitor A 10% Competitor D 30% Competitor B 20% Competitor C 40%	Show the percentage of: • market share held by each of the products in a market • employees at each salary level • sales for each of the sales regions	• Limit to five or fewer segments. • Label each segment and provide percentage values. • Put most significant segment at 12:00. If segments are equally significant, arrange from smallest to largest. • Show emphasis with a darker color or by "exploding" the most significant segment.
Compare parts of multiple items. **100% Column chart** **Compared to cakes and bread, doughnuts bring in more revenue and take less money and time to produce** Revenue: 15%, 35%, 50% Production Cost: 45%, 30%, 25% Production Time: 45%, 35%, 20% Cakes / Bread / Doughnuts	Show how the percentage breakdown differs for: • cost of product components for multiple versions of that product • market share of each of a set of products in multiple regions	• Use instead of multiple pie charts. • Put the most important item at the bottom of the column so that all its component parts share the same baseline. • Optional: Connect series with a line to emphasize relationships.
Compare multiple items, according to a single characteristic. **Horizontal bar chart** **Chocolate chip is our most popular cookie** Chocolate chip $184.50 Peanut butter $127.30 Lemon crisp $116.20 Almond crescent $87.50 $0.00 — Average daily sales — $200.0	Compare: • prices • speed • cost	• Add value labels on the bars or at the ends of bars. • Arrange from largest to smallest if your purpose is to rank items. Otherwise, arrange in an order consistent with your message. • Use color to highlight bars you want to emphasize or to group categories of bars.
Show changes over time for a relatively small number of discrete time periods. **Column chart** **Return on equity declined in years 1–4 and was negative in year 5** Year 1 28% Year 2 25% Year 3 23% Year 4 20% Year 5 −15%	Compare sales, profits, prices, manufacturing defects over: • a series of years • a series of months • a series of production	• Add value labels at the top of columns. • Arrange chronologically to show changes over time. • Make the space between the columns narrower than the width of the columns. • Use color or shading to emphasize one point in time more than others.

(continued)

FIGURE 9.12 Continued

PURPOSE/BEST GRAPH TO USE	EXAMPLES	BEST PRACTICES
Show changes over time to emphasize a trend. **Line chart** **Year to date, actual revenue is exceeding budgeted revenue** 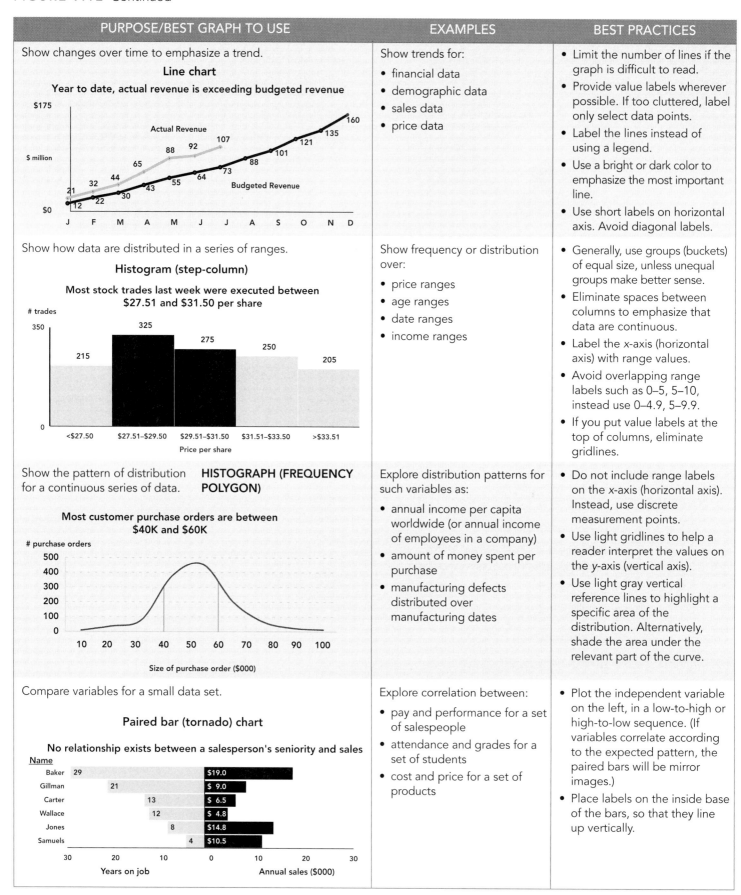	Show trends for: • financial data • demographic data • sales data • price data	• Limit the number of lines if the graph is difficult to read. • Provide value labels wherever possible. If too cluttered, label only select data points. • Label the lines instead of using a legend. • Use a bright or dark color to emphasize the most important line. • Use short labels on horizontal axis. Avoid diagonal labels.
Show how data are distributed in a series of ranges. **Histogram (step-column)** **Most stock trades last week were executed between $27.51 and $31.50 per share**	Show frequency or distribution over: • price ranges • age ranges • date ranges • income ranges	• Generally, use groups (buckets) of equal size, unless unequal groups make better sense. • Eliminate spaces between columns to emphasize that data are continuous. • Label the x-axis (horizontal axis) with range values. • Avoid overlapping range labels such as 0–5, 5–10, instead use 0–4.9, 5–9.9. • If you put value labels at the top of columns, eliminate gridlines.
Show the pattern of distribution for a continuous series of data. **HISTOGRAPH (FREQUENCY POLYGON)** **Most customer purchase orders are between $40K and $60K**	Explore distribution patterns for such variables as: • annual income per capita worldwide (or annual income of employees in a company) • amount of money spent per purchase • manufacturing defects distributed over manufacturing dates	• Do not include range labels on the x-axis (horizontal axis). Instead, use discrete measurement points. • Use light gridlines to help a reader interpret the values on the y-axis (vertical axis). • Use light gray vertical reference lines to highlight a specific area of the distribution. Alternatively, shade the area under the relevant part of the curve.
Compare variables for a small data set. **Paired bar (tornado) chart** **No relationship exists between a salesperson's seniority and sales**	Explore correlation between: • pay and performance for a set of salespeople • attendance and grades for a set of students • cost and price for a set of products	• Plot the independent variable on the left, in a low-to-high or high-to-low sequence. (If variables correlate according to the expected pattern, the paired bars will be mirror images.) • Place labels on the inside base of the bars, so that they line up vertically.

(continued)

FIGURE 9.12 Continued

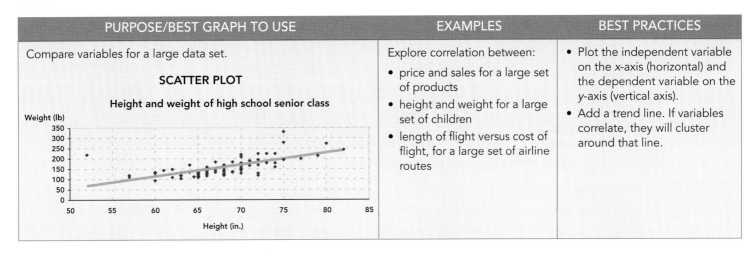

PURPOSE/BEST GRAPH TO USE	EXAMPLES	BEST PRACTICES
Compare variables for a large data set. **SCATTER PLOT** Height and weight of high school senior class	Explore correlation between: • price and sales for a large set of products • height and weight for a large set of children • length of flight versus cost of flight, for a large set of airline routes	• Plot the independent variable on the *x*-axis (horizontal) and the dependent variable on the *y*-axis (vertical axis). • Add a trend line. If variables correlate, they will cluster around that line.

and graphs be designed to communicate data effectively. Eliminate all distractions that do not help the audience understand the data.[11] For tables, this means eliminating or minimizing all unnecessary gridlines and borders. For graphs, it means eliminating anything that exists only for decoration. All the graphs illustrated in Figure 9.12 follow current best practices in designing graphs.

Checklist for effective graph design

Use **FIGURE 9.13**—which illustrates graphing terminology—and the following checklist for advice about designing graphs. The numbers on the checklist correspond to the numbered elements on the figure.

❶ **Chart title: Title all graphs.** Give every graph a title, or headline, that summarizes its data, purpose, and/or message. A succinct yet precise headline means future users of the graph will know exactly what it is about, even if the graph is reused in a different document. Use the same headline style for all the graphs in a report. They may either be topic headlines, like the one in Figure 9.11: "2010 Monthly Sales in Stores vs Internet." Or they may be message headlines like "In 2010, Store Sales Remained Flat while Internet Sales Increased." If the graph is plotting data from a specific time frame, it is good practice to indicate the time period in the title (or in a footnote). Remember that in a formal report, the graph titles will all appear in the list of figures that follows the table of contents.

❷ **Data markers: Use subtle data markers to identify specific data points.** In a line graph, data markers identify the specific data points you are connecting. For example, Figure 9.13 shows a graph that covers one year but the lines are drawn from only 12 data points (one for each month). To avoid distracting readers, keep the data markers small, no more than two points larger than your smallest font.

❸ **Axis title: Title all axes, and position the titles horizontally.** Many software programs default to the vertical position with *y*-axis titles, which requires readers to tilt their heads or the document to read. Reorient those labels so they are positioned horizontally in the manner of normal text on the page.

❹ **Axis labels: Label all axes unless it is absolutely clear what is being measured. Position all axis labels horizontally, if possible.** At times, the title of a graph will make it obvious what units are being graphed on the *x*- or *y*-axes. Usually, however, it is crucial to label both what is being measured and the units of measurement (for example, $, billion, kilograms, widgets sold). If at all possible, avoid orienting *x*-axis labels at an angle. Instead, try to establish good abbreviations that allow you to use short, horizontal labels.

❺ **Scales: Begin numerical scales at zero.** Starting the scale at a higher number distorts the information.

❻ **Tick marks: Use tick marks only when helpful.** These small dashes on the *x*- and *y*-axes are sometimes helpful to align the axis labels with data points. However, in many instances, you can eliminate them.

FIGURE 9.13 Graph Terminology

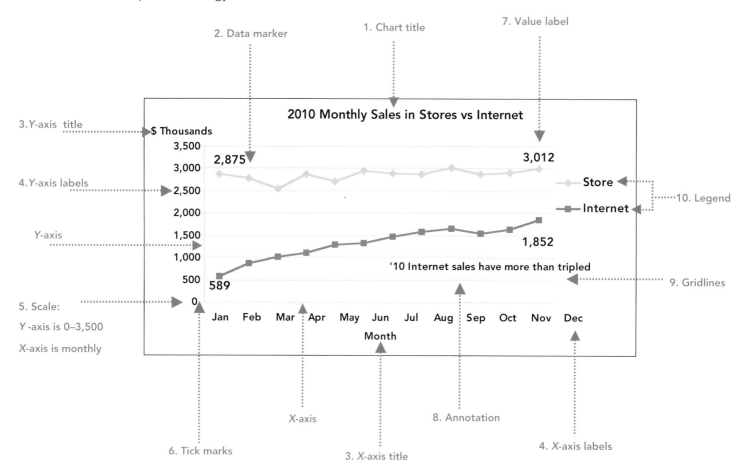

⑦ **Value labels: Place value labels on data points rather than relying only on the y-axis scale.** Value labels communicate precise, not estimated, values. If your graph contains too many labels, delete some to avoid clutter. Use only enough labels to allow readers to interpret the data. If you use value labels on data points, you can also delete many of the numerical labels on the y-axis. Minimum and maximum values are usually sufficient.

⑧ **Annotations:** Include annotations to highlight key data changes or to focus on specific data points.

⑨ **Gridlines: Use minimal gridlines.** If you must use gridlines, use light gray instead of black.

⑩ **Legends: Avoid legends when possible.** Consider using labels instead, placing them as closely as possible to the lines or bars. Legends require eye movement back and forth, which requires the audience to exert additional effort to match legend colors to the data on the graph. If you do need to use a legend, be sure distinctions are visible when viewed both in color and in grayscale.

When designing the data objects on the graph (the lines, columns, bars, etc.), follow these guidelines:

• **Use thin lines.** The human eye can distinguish lines of a half point easily, so minimize ink wherever possible. Use thin axes, bars, and arrows.

• **Avoid 3-D effects.** Three-dimensional effects make the data less precise by distorting the scale and adding extra ink. Also, avoid cross-hatching and other ink patterns. Instead choose solid colors or grayscale options with differentiation that your audience can easily see both on the computer screen and the printed page.

• **Avoid contrasting borders around objects.** An additional color as a border is unnecessary if you are graphing only a single data series (with just one color) or you have created a graph with sufficient color differentiation between data items. Borders are also unnecessary—and distracting—around legends and the plot areas of graphs.

Checklist for effective table design

Use the following checklist of advice for designing tables in a report. FIGURE 9.14 illustrates the principles in the checklist.

Certificate of Deposit Balances

CD LENGTH	DATE OPENED	RENEWABLE?	INTEREST RATE	CURRENT VALUE
Five Year	03/03/20XX	N	4.25%	$ 15,215.50
Three Year	11/01/20XX	N	3.25	10,311.73
One Year	08/13/20XX	Y	2.00	2,250.50
Six Month	06/01/20XX	Y	1.15	870.27
Total				**$ 28,648.00**

FIGURE 9.14
Effective Table Design

- **Title each table.** Give every table you produce a specific title that captures the table's content. If you would like a reader to notice something in the table, mention that in the title.
- **Label columns and rows effectively.** Review your table to ensure that readers will know exactly what is in each cell.
- **Eliminate heavy gridlines.** These are the horizontal and vertical lines that separate cells in a table. Do not imprison your data in a grid of black lines. As Figure 9.14 illustrates, tables can be easy to read if you leave sufficient space between the rows and columns. If you would like to use a grid, choose light gray lines.
- **Use shading strategically.** You can use shading to highlight data or distinguish alternate rows. Keep all shading light. Also consider whether your final document will be photocopied. Use shades of gray if your report will be duplicated in black and white.
- **Remove unnecessary repetition from cells.** You do not need to include a $ or % in all cells in a column. Put signs in the appropriate column or row header or with the first value. For example, the last column in Figure 9.14 uses a dollar sign only with the first value and the total.
- **Align numbers to the right.** Keep decimal points aligned. Use a consistent number of decimal places in all values in a column. For example, see the "Interest Rate" column in Figure 9.14.
- **Align text to the left.** For example, see the "CD Length" column in Figure 9.14.
- **Center content only if every row in that column contains the same number of characters.** Figure 9.14 illustrates three examples. In the "Renewable" column, Y and N are centered because each entry is one character long. In the "Date Opened" column, the dates are centered because they are written in identical format (two digits for the month, two digits for the day, and four digits for the year), so all entries have the identical number of characters. The text in the "Interest Rate" column could also be centered because the character lengths are identical. However, if one interest rate were 10 percent or larger, you would need to right align the numbers to make the decimal points line up.

Integrate the display with the text

In business reports, data displays and text play complementary roles. They need to work together to communicate the full message. While the graph or table presents the data, the text must contextualize and interpret the data, telling readers what they are looking at (the purpose of the data display and the source of the data) and then highlighting the key point the reader should understand from the data. Consider the graph in FIGURE 9.15, and compare two versions of text—Version A and Version B—that might accompany it in a business report.

FIGURE 9.15 Using Text
to Explain Graphics

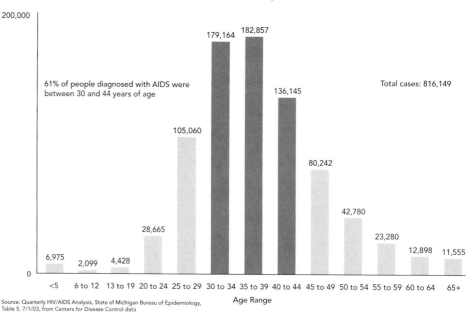

Figure 1: Age at diagnosis of all AIDS cases reported in the U.S. from 1981 to 2001

Source: Quarterly HIV/AIDS Analysis, State of Michigan Bureau of Epidemiology,
Table 5, 7/1/03, from Centers for Disease Control data

Version A As Figure 1 illustrates, between 1981 and 2001, more than 362,000 people in their 30s were diagnosed with AIDS. By contrast, only 11,555 people 65 years or older were diagnosed.

Version B We recommend that AIDS prevention efforts be targeted to people in their 20s and 30s. According to data from the Centers for Disease Control (Figure 1), between 1981 and 2001, more than 61 percent of people who were diagnosed with AIDS were between 30 and 44 years old. Since the mean incubation period for AIDS in adults is approximately nine years, it is likely that 61 percent of AIDS patients contracted the disease in their 20s and early 30s. This is not surprising since the 20s and 30s are ages of high sexual activity as well as ages where experimentation with intravenous drugs occurs. Sexual activity and intravenous drug use are the two most significant means of AIDS transmission.

Version A simply repeats data that can be seen in the graph itself. Version B, by contrast, generalizes from the data and identifies significant patterns. It also integrates the data into an argument.

To integrate verbal and visual elements of a text, follow these steps:

- **Label and number figures and tables sequentially throughout the report.** You may either number figures and tables in their individual sequences (Figure 1, Figure 2, Table 1, Table 2), or you may combine tables and figures into one list, calling them Exhibit 1, Exhibit 2, Exhibit 3.

- **Refer the reader to the graphic within the text.** Refer to the graphic by figure or table number, as illustrated in the Version A and Version B paragraphs—and as illustrated throughout this book.

- **Place the graphic as close as possible after the first reference.** Do not place graphics before the text mentions them, as this will confuse readers.

- **Tell the reader what to notice in the graphic.** In a data graphic, what are the important findings or trends? In a picture or illustration, where should the audience focus their attention? In a diagram, how should the audience read the illustrated relationships? Answer these questions in the text that accompanies the graphic.

- **Be sure to design the graphic to support the message in the text.** Ask yourself if readers will be able to see what you want them to see.

- **Finally, although the text and graphics are interdependent, design the graph to be self-explanatory.** Provide enough labeling on the graphic and enough description in the figure name and caption so that readers can understand what they are seeing without reading the accompanying text. This allows readers to scan the document and derive a good deal of information by looking solely at the graphics.

ETHICS When Telling the Truth Is Not Good Enough

Because businesses often rely on reports to make informed decisions, reports must be complete, accurate, and honest. If a report omits important data or represents the data incorrectly, decision makers can draw the wrong conclusions. Consider these two cases of true but misleading information, based on actual business scenarios.

1. CustomResearch.com is a company that produces custom-written term papers for students. The company has been growing and would like to attract investors. It puts together a report that not only includes the company's impressive financial data, but also aims to show that the company is well respected. To support this claim, the report includes this sentence: "CustomResearch.com is the only company in the industry that has been featured on national television news."

   What impression does this statement give of the company's reputation? Does this statement accurately inform potential investors? Would it change your impression of the company to learn that, although it is true CustomResearch.com was featured on ABC news, the news story portrayed CustomResearch.com as an unethical organization that promotes plagiarism? The statement in the report is true, but misleading.

2. A report on the financial condition of Acme Tire Company includes this statement supported by the following graph: "As a sign of our financial strength, this year we experienced the greatest growth in earnings per share in our four-year history." This statement is true. Coupled with the graph, though, is it misleading?

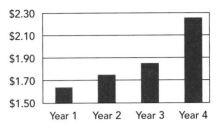

Earnings Per Share

A glance at the graph above suggests that earnings per share doubled (grew 100 percent) between Year 3 and Year 4. A reader must look very carefully to see that the graph starts at $1.50. Earnings were $1.80 per share in Year 3 and $2.20 per share in Year 4. Earnings grew not 100 percent but instead 22 percent. A more accurate graph would look like this one, which starts at $0.00.

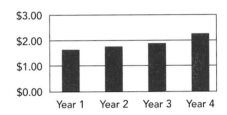

Earnings Per Share

In reports, as in all business communication, a partial truth is unethical, especially if it encourages a reader to draw the wrong conclusion. ■

PEARSON **mybcommlab**

For an ETHICS exercise, go to Exercise 14 on page 336 or to this chapter's End-of-Chapter Exercises at mybcommlab.com.

For an ETHICS exercise, go to Exercise 14 on page 336

Study Question 9.6

How should I document my research?

Documenting—or citing your sources—is a key part of all writing in academia and most professional writing. Appropriate documentation serves many functions.

- **It adds credibility to your writing.** Many writers assume that they will seem smarter if they make their ideas appear original. In fact, the opposite is true. Your writing will be more impressive if it shows that you are well informed by having read relevant texts or talked to key people.

- **It strengthens your argument.** Most report writing relies on up-to-date and accurate data. By providing appropriate citations, you can give your audience confidence in the strength of your data.

- **It helps your audience locate information mentioned in your report.** Your audience may want to read more deeply into your topic. They will rely on your reference list to give them direction.

- **It helps demonstrate that you are ethical.** If you acknowledge all your sources, no one will accuse you of **plagiarism**, which is presenting others' ideas as your own.

To ensure good documentation, use the advice that follows.

Plagiarism Intentionally or unintentionally failing to acknowledge others' ideas in your work.

Determine what needs to be documented

You need to document—or give credit for—any information or opinion that you originally found in another source. Specifically, you need to document the following:

- **Exact quotations. Quotations** are any phrases, sentences, paragraphs—even single, distinctive words—that you take from any of your sources. When you include a source's exact wording in your text, you need to enclose it in quotation marks or, if it is a long quotation, you omit the quotation marks and instead indent and single space the quotations as a block of text. In addition, you need to cite the original source. You can use footnotes, endnotes, or parenthetical citations—in other words, inserting in parentheses the author's last name, year of publication, and page number where the quotation can be found in the original source.

    If you find that more than 10 percent of your content consists of quotations, then you are relying too heavily on your sources and not adding enough analysis, critique, or explanation of your own. Most business reports contain very few direct quotations. More often, writers choose to paraphrase or summarize the content. Reserve quotations for the following situations:
    - When you want to present someone else's point of view in that person's own words
    - When you are citing an authority whose exact words are well phrased and powerful
    - When you want to comment on what someone else has said
    - When you need to be very precise and the exact wording allows you to do so

- **Paraphrase.** A **paraphrase** is a version of what someone else says but in your own words and with your own emphasis. A good paraphrase will have a completely different sentence structure than the original, not just a few replaced words. Paraphrased content also needs to be cited appropriately with the author's name and year of publication.

- **Summary.** A **summary** is a very brief version of another person's point of view. When you summarize, you still need to acknowledge the source of those ideas by using some form of citation.

- **Specific facts and data.** You also need to cite every piece of information that is not common knowledge or the result of your own primary research. This includes opinions, arguments, and speculations as well as facts, details, figures, and statistics. Writers are often confused about what is common knowledge. Simply put, common knowledge includes things that most people know. For example, most people know that Paris is the capital of France. You would not need to cite a source for that. By contrast, most people do not know that the population of Paris was approximately 2.2 million people in 2009. For that data, you would need to cite the French National Institute of Statistics and Economic Studies.[12] This citation adds credibility to your statement and helps readers identify where to look for more information.

- **Tables, graphs, photographs, and other graphics.** If you copy a visual from another source and place it in your document, you need to cite the source for that visual. You do this by including the citation in your caption or directly under the visual, as illustrated in FIGURE 9.16, which uses the APA format for citing graphics.

Prepare the documentation

In a formal report, appropriate acknowledgment of sources happens in three ways. You must use all three of these acknowledgments in a report.

- **Citations.** Every time you use material from another source in your text, add a citation. Your citation may be in the form of a footnote, endnote, or parenthetical citation inserted directly after your reference. The form you use will depend on the requirements of your organization or school. The three most common formats or styles of documentation are:
    - APA (American Psychological Association), frequently used in social sciences and business
    - MLA (Modern Language Association), commonly used in the humanities
    - CMS (Chicago Manual of Style) frequently used in business, history, and some social sciences.

    For details about these styles, see Appendix C.

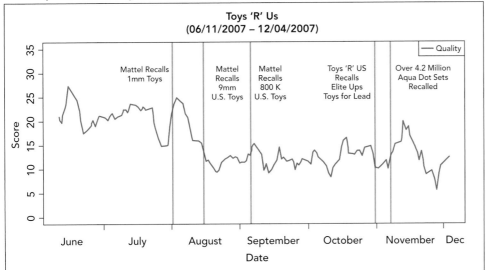

Impact of Mattel Toy Recalls on Consumer's Perception of Product Quality at Toys 'R' Us

From YouGovPolimetrix (2008). *Understanding people: Case study Toys 'R' Us.*
http://www.polimetrix.com/documents/ToysRUs.pdf. Copyright 2008 by Polimetrix.

FIGURE 9.16
Adding an APA Source Citation
to Graphics

- **Text references.** Do not rely exclusively on citations to orient readers to your sources. Instead, introduce cited material by explicitly referring to the source within your text:

  > According to the INSEE (2009), the population of Paris exceeded 2.2 million people in January 2009.

  > or

  > The French National Institute of Statistics and Economic Studies reported that population of Paris exceeded 2.2 million people in January 2009 (INSEE, 2009).

- **Reference list or bibliography.** Provide a list of sources at the end of every research report. Each item in the list must include enough information for readers to find that document on their own. APA, MLA, and University of Chicago each have different names for this list:
  - APA titles the page *References*
  - MLA titles the page *Works Cited*
  - CMS offers two options. It titles the page *Bibliography* if you are using footnotes or endnotes, and it titles the page *References* if you are using parenthetical citations.

  In addition, each documentation style follows different rules about the kind of material to include in the list and how to format that material. For details and examples, see Appendix C.

Write the citations, text references, and bibliographic entries as you work on your report. Do not wait to add them until after you've written your entire draft. Waiting to document leads to two problems. First, if you don't document as you gather your research and take notes, you may omit required information that will be hard to find later (and will lead to a waste of time). Second, if you don't add citations as you draft your documents, you may forget what you've quoted and unintentionally plagiarize material.

IN SUMMARY, no matter what business you enter, you are likely to write reports. The term "report" refers to a wide range of documents that provide information or analysis to answer business questions. Whether written in the form of a memo, letter, email, formal manuscript, or report deck, reports share a number of features, including an objective style and a structure that makes information easy to find. Many reports also include tables, graphs, diagrams, and documentation of research. The guidelines in this chapter will help you manage all this material and present it in ways that will be clear to your audience whether they read the report now or in the future.

Quotations Any phrases, sentences, paragraphs—even single, distinctive words—that you take from any of your sources.

Paraphrase A version of what someone else says, but in your own words and with your own emphasis.

Summary Very brief version of text, using your own words.

CHAPTER 9 Summary

9.1 How do I use ACE to help me write a business report? *(pages 288–294)*

- **Analyze to understand purpose and report type.** Some reports are informational, others are analytic.
- **Analyze to understand audience needs** and determine what content to include.
- **Analyze to choose the best medium.** Email, memo, and letter reports are usually short. Formal reports are often longer. Report decks are effective for any length.
- **Compose your report to meet audience expectations.** Include identifying information, a preview, detailed discussion, and supporting information. Most reports are organized directly.
- **Compose using an objective and easy-to-read style** by focusing on facts and analysis.
- **Evaluate by reviewing on your own and getting feedback from others** to ensure you are meeting audience and stakeholder needs. Use an evaluation checklist to review your report (see page 293).

9.2 What types of short, routine reports are typical in business?

(pages 294–300)

- **Progress reports** provide information about the status of a long-term project.
- **Trip reports** document activities during business trips and outline accomplishments.
- **Meeting minutes** document discussion and decisions at meetings.
- **Feasibility reports** analyze whether a plan can be implemented as proposed.

9.3 How do I structure longer, formal reports? *(pages 301–314)*

- **Create a title page for identifying information** including the title of the report, who the report was written for, the author (including the person's organization), and the date of submission.
- **Preview the report with preliminary sections** including a table of contents, list of figures and/or tables (if applicable), an executive summary, and introduction.
- **Develop the details within sections** using headings to organize the content of the report.
- **Conclude the report with supporting information,** such as references and appendices.

9.4 What guidelines should I follow for writing report decks?

(pages 314–318)

- **Understand why and when to use report decks.**
- **Design the deck effectively** by using a solid background, appropriate font sizes, "road signs" to identify sections, and footers.
- **Design the deck content to be easy to follow** by using sentence-style headlines that summarize the main point of the slide and by designing the slide to support and explain the headline.

9.5 How do I integrate tables and graphs into my reports? *(pages 318–327)*

- **Choose the best form of display: table or graph.** Tables arrange data in columns and rows to demonstrate relationships. Graphs use images or shapes to illustrate relationships among variables or data.
- **Choose the best type of graph** by considering the purpose and relationship of the data.
- **Design graphs and tables to communicate.** Use titles, axes labels, thin lines, visible data markers, and annotations. Avoid 3-D, contrasting borders, gridlines, tick marks, and legends.
- **Integrate the display with the text.** Help readers focus on the display and understand it.

9.6 How should I document my research? *(pages 327–329)*

- **Determine what needs to be documented.** Document all content taken from other sources.
- **Prepare the documentation** by introducing sources in the narrative, providing citations in the text, and preparing a reference list as you compose.

PEARSON
mybcommlab™
Are you an active learner? Go to mybcommlab.com to master Chapter 9 content. Chapter 9 interactive activities include:

- Customizable Study Plan and Chapter 9 practice quizzes
- Chapter 9 Simulation, Business Reports, that helps you think critically and prepare to make choices in the business world
- Flash Cards for mastering the definition of chapter terms

- Chapter 9 Video Exercise, Completing Reports & Proposals, which shows you how textbook concepts are put into practice every day
- Interactive Lessons that visually review key chapter concepts
- Document Makeovers for hands-on, scored practice in revising documents

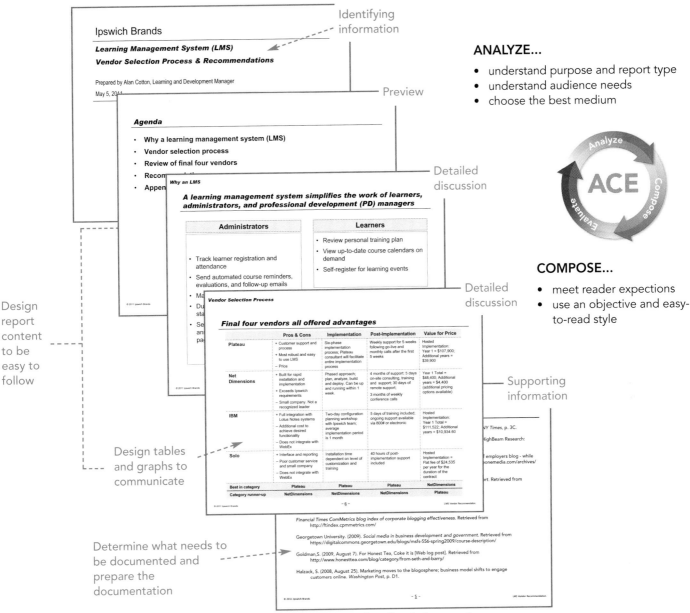

ANALYZE...

- understand purpose and report type
- understand audience needs
- choose the best medium

COMPOSE...

- meet reader expectations
- use an objective and easy-to-read style

Identifying information

Preview

Detailed discussion

Detailed discussion

Supporting information

Design report content to be easy to follow

Design tables and graphs to communicate

Determine what needs to be documented and prepare the documentation

EVALUATE by reviewing on your own and getting feedback from others...

- Is my report answering a clear question?
- Is the answer to my question easy to find?
- Have I included all the information my readers will need?
- Is the title (or subject line) of the report focused and informative?
- Does the report provide a good preview in the introduction and, when appropriate, in a table of contents, executive summary, or abstract?
- Are the headings logical? If I read all the headings sequentially, will I understand how the report is organized?

- Is each section well organized? Is the main point of the section easy to find?
- Are the paragraphs relatively short (four to eight sentences)?
- Does each paragraph begin with a strong topic sentence that states the main point of the paragraph?
- Are the sentences short and, when possible, written in the active voice?
- Are the tables, graphs, and other graphics used effectively? Are they well labeled and introduced within the document?
- Have I provided sufficient documentation?

CASE STUDY Reporting Results to a Client

This case study will help you review the chapter material by applying it to a specific scenario.

When Jeff Ellis graduated with a degree in civil engineering, he pictured himself designing buildings and bridges and managing construction teams. He never imagined himself behind a computer writing reports.

However, that is exactly where Jeff finds himself today. He has just finished his first major project at Schuyler Engineering, an environmental assessment of a plot of land on which a client wants to build an office park. Emily, the senior engineer on the project, has asked Jeff to write the client report. When Jeff asked Emily if she could give him a model to follow, Emily pointed to the file cabinet and said, "Sure, you'll find lots of reports in there."

Jeff did find a lot of reports: long ones, short ones, letter reports, and very formal reports. The diversity confused him and left him asking "What is the best approach to take?" Jeff is glad he saved his business communication text from college. That may give him some better ideas for how to structure a professional report.

Writing a Report Introduction

Jeff begins writing his report with the first step of the ACE process: analyzing to determine the purpose, audience, and medium. His audience, the CEO of Halvorson Properties, wants to know whether it is safe to build an office park on the property he owns. Because this decision has significant financial and environmental effects, Jeff decides to write a formal letter report that clearly communicates the message that the property is safe. His research indicated that it has not been affected by hazardous waste or contaminated groundwater. He will provide enough details about his methodology and findings to give Mr. Halvorson confidence in this assessment.

With those decisions in mind, Jeff sits down to write the report's introduction. After writing his first paragraph, he emails it to Emily, who revises it.

Review Question 1: *Compare Jeff's draft of the introduction with Emily's revision. What key differences do you notice between the two openings? Which opening would you choose?*

Jeff's first draft:

Dear Mr. Halvorson: At your request, we have conducted an investigation of the site defined by the attached survey

map for the purposes of rendering an opinion as to whether the site contains hazardous waste or is being impacted by contaminated groundwater. Our investigations consisted of making soil borings and visual observations of the ground surface, vegetation, and drainage patterns and laboratory testing of soil samples. The testing included physical properties testing and chemical testing of the water extracted from the soil. In addition, we have examined various maps and aerial photos, contacted various government agencies, and contacted the power company in our efforts to determine whether hazardous waste is known to have impacted the site. Our findings are as follows.

Emily's revision:

Dear Mr. Halvorson:

At your request, we have investigated the site defined by the attached survey map to determine (1) how the site was used, (2) whether the site contains hazardous waste, and (3) whether it is affected by contaminated groundwater. Our investigation is complete except for the results of governmental and power company records searches.

Assuming that these searches support our findings, it is our professional assessment that the site has not been impacted by hazardous waste or groundwater contamination that would render it unsuitable for development as an office park.

This letter describes our methodology and reports our findings.

Structuring the Report's Findings

As Jeff develops his investigation report, he decides that the detailed discussion of the report will include the specific findings of his investigation. Here is the first draft he produced:

Our investigations indicate that nearly all of Parcel 1 has been idle for at least 10 to 15 years. An old house foundation exists near the south central portion of Parcel 1. Parcel 2 appears to have been idle for many years. However, recent dumping of construction debris and fill is apparent primarily along the eastern property line. Parcel 3 is vegetated with an old orchard near the center of the property, and remnants of abandoned residences are apparent. Parcel 3 also has been impacted with piles of construction debris and dumped fill along its easternmost side. Parcel 4 is primarily a protected wetlands area identified by the U.S. Army Corps of Engineers. Some filling has occurred along the eastern and southern border of Parcel 4.

On the basis of soil borings, laboratory test results, and our observations of the previously referenced site, in our opinion it is unlikely that any storage, disposal, or release of oil, fuels, gases, chemicals, trash, garbage, or other solid or hazardous materials has taken place on this property. Only trace amounts of these materials are present, as associated with the residential occupancy and the relatively recent illegal dumping of debris. We have requested a letter from People's Electric certifying that the site is not presently served by transformers containing PCBs nor is the site known to have been impacted by spills of PCBs. Except for the possibility of old heating oil tanks or septic tanks associated with the previous homes, there are no buried tanks on the site. Considering the soil types encountered in the borings, it is extremely unlikely that fuel oils, even if they were present, could migrate more than a few inches. Therefore, we do not consider this site to have been affected by an oil spill or buried tanks or pesticides other than those associated with residential occupation and farming operations.

As Jeff reviews his draft, he realizes that the main ideas are not easy to find. This time, instead of giving his draft to Emily to review, he writes a new outline of the findings section on his own. His goal is to design the page so that the main ideas stand out, using both headings and good topic sentences of paragraphs.

Here is his outline:

Findings about land use

1. Parcel 1:
2. Parcel 2:
3. Parcel 3:
4. Parcel 4:

Findings about contamination

1. Our investigations indicate it is unlikely that this property has been contaminated by any storage, disposal, or release of oil, fuels, gases, chemicals, trash, garbage, or other solid or hazardous materials.

2. It is also unlikely that the groundwater or soil on the site has been contaminated by activities on the adjacent sites.

Review Question 2: *Using these headings, subheadings, and topic sentences, how would you complete the findings section of the report? Where would you place the supporting details from his draft?*

Phrasing a Conclusion Accurately

As Jeff completes his report, he wonders how he should phrase the conclusions he reaches in his report. Here are two statements he is considering:

Option 1: It is our professional opinion that the site has not been impacted by hazardous waste or groundwater contamination that would render it unsuitable for development as an office park.

Option 2: It is our professional opinion that the site has not been impacted by hazardous waste or groundwater contamination and thus the site is safe for an office park.

Review Question 3: *Which do you think is the better option, and why?*

CRITICAL THINKING

1. What are the advantages of writing a report using a direct organization rather than an indirect organization? Are there any situations where an indirect report organization may be more effective?

2. Imagine that some of your coworkers complain that trip reports are just busywork and a way for management to make sure employees are conducting business and not just having a good time. How might you counter that argument? What are some of the real business purposes of a trip report?

3. The Culture feature on page 294 offers three suggestions for writing reports for international audiences who will read the report in English. Imagine that your report will be translated into another language, for example Spanish or Japanese. Would this same advice make the document easier to translate? In what ways? Based on your knowledge of other languages, what other advice would you give writers who are preparing reports that will be translated?

4. Formal reports contain a number of features that help readers navigate: a table of contents, lists of figures and tables, executive summaries, informative headings, and appendices for supplementary information. Why is it useful to include all rather than just some of these features?

5. Imagine that a classmate or coworker argues that it is redundant to include both an executive summary and an introduction in a report. How would you explain the different functions of an executive summary and introduction—and the reason for including both?

6. Figure 9.12 on pages 321–323 suggests using a horizontal bar chart to rank and compare items. Some writers use column charts for that purpose also. What are the pros and cons of using bars versus columns for graphs that compare items?

7. According to the old saying, "A picture is worth 1,000 words." If that is the case, then why is it important to explain all graphics within the text of your report, rather than assuming the graphics will speak for themselves?

8. A letter report is a hybrid between a regular business letter and a formal report. What features does a letter report share with a business letter? What features does it share with a formal report?

9. Imagine that you were asked to write a type of report not illustrated in this chapter, for example a compliance report. How would you go about learning the key features of a compliance report and the type of content that is required?

10. Some organizations are asking employees to post information in wikis rather than write traditional reports. What would be the advantages and disadvantages of reporting information on an internal corporate wiki?

DEVELOPING YOUR COMMUNICATION SKILLS

9.1 How do I use ACE to help me write a business report? *(pages 288–294)*

EXERCISE 1 Analyze to understand purpose and report type

For each of the following questions, identify the type of report you would write. Is it primarily informational or analytical? Refer to the report names in Figure 9.1 on page 289.

a. Has our new marketing plan met our sales objectives?

b. Why are so many of our widgets being returned as defective?

c. Are we on track with our project?

d. Can our client, Rose's Bakery, afford to open a new store next year?

e. Who is responsible for the property damage in our client's building? The construction crew? The painters? The tenants? The maintenance staff?

f. What new sales leads did you develop at the trade show?

EXERCISE 2 Analyze to understand audience needs

For each of the questions listed in Exercise 1, how would you analyze to understand the audience's needs? Identify at least two questions you would ask for each scenario.

EXERCISE 3 Analyze to choose the best medium

For each of the questions listed in Exercise 1, decide what medium you would use to write the report. Pick a medium and explain why it is a good choice.

- Memo report
- Letter report
- Email report
- Formal report
- Report deck

EXERCISE 4 Compose your report to meet audience expectations

Search the Internet for a report produced by a government agency. (One good example is the report *To Read or Not to Read* by National Endowment for the arts: http://www.nea.gov/research/toread.pdf). Quickly review that report and identify where and how it provides identifying information, a preview, detail discussion, and supporting information. Are the techniques that the report uses effective? Would you recommend any changes? Summarize your findings and conclusions in an email message to your instructor. Be sure to provide a complete citation for the report you are analyzing. For the information to include in a reference list citation, see Appendix C.

EXERCISE 5 Compose using an objective and easy-to-read style

Anya James works for AquaSafe Product Design, a company that designs and installs aquariums in homes and offices. Anya has been assigned to the new product development team. The team's job is to research and develop new product ideas. Currently, the team is exploring the idea of an interactive aquarium that allows users to engage more with the fish. At the end of the first three weeks on the project, Anya's manager has asked for a progress report.

Review Anya's first draft on page 335. Evaluate this progress report:

- Is the style objective, focusing on the project? Or does it focus on the team's activities?
- Is the report sufficiently factual and detailed?
- Should the report contain any additional information?

Based on your analysis, recommend at least two changes to the report.

EXERCISE 6 Evaluate by reviewing on your own and getting feedback from others

Using the questions on page 293, evaluate the formal report in Figures 9.8A, B, C, and D. Write a memo to your instructor identifying what you believe is good about the report and what changes, if any, you would recommend to improve it.

EXERCISE 7 Making reports reader-friendly for international audiences [Related to the Culture feature on page 294]

The following well-written paragraphs come from the executive summary of a report titled *The State of the Paper Industry: Monitoring the Indicators of Environmental Performance*. Imagine that this report was being read by someone from another country who speaks English as a second or third language. What words, phrases, or sentences do you think would be challenging for that reader to understand? What revisions would you suggest?

> Despite predictions that the digital revolution would make paper as obsolete as the typewriter, paper remains central to our lives. Yet most of us, most of the time, give little thought to how much we depend on paper products. Think of the hundreds of times a day we touch paper—newspapers, cereal boxes, toilet paper, water bottle labels, parking tickets, streams of catalogs and junk mail, money, tissues, books, shopping bags, receipts, napkins, printer and copier paper at home and work, magazines, to-go food packaging. The list could fill a paperback.
>
> What's more, few people pay much heed to the ways in which our use of paper affects the environment. Yet the paper industry's activities—and our individual use and disposal of paper in our daily lives—have enormous impacts. These include loss and degradation of forests that moderate climate change, destruction of habitat for countless plant and animal species, pollution of air and water with toxic chemicals such as mercury and dioxin, and production of methane—a potent greenhouse gas—as paper decomposes in landfills, to name just a few.[13]

report

TO: Ryan Leffler, Project Manager

FROM: Anya James, New Product Development Team

DATE: March 16, 20XX

SUBJECT: Progress Report

For the past three weeks, we have been researching the interactive aquarium concept and have developed five concepts we plan to test. The Interactive Aquarium presents a unique problem to the design team. We began with a completely blank slate, since this project is based on an innovative idea and has very few comparable existing products. We had to consider a very delicate group of users (fish) when making decisions about the requirements of our design concepts. It was important for us to balance the goals of our company with the needs of the animals and the desires of the users.

Research
We began by researching fish behavior and learned interesting facts that will influence our design. We then had a productive brainstorm session in which we were able to generate design ideas. From there, we have identified five major design areas we would like to test.

Design Requirements
Based on our research and discussions with users, we developed a set of design requirements numbered and listed in Table 1. We rated these requirements by importance (5 is most important and 1 is least important).

Table 1: Design Requirements

REQUIREMENT #	REQUIREMENT	IMPORTANCE RATING
1	Child safe	5
2	Child friendly	3
3	Interesting	3
4	Animal safe	5
5	Animal friendly	5
6	Can be used in/around water	5
7	Environmentally sound	4
8	Durable	4
9	Easily cleaned	2
10	Easily accessible	3
11	Not too complicated to operate	1
12	Not too heavy	1
13	No complicated assembly	1

Plan
In the next two weeks, we plan to evaluate our five ideas according to these requirements.

Accompanies Exercise 5

9.2 What types of short, routine reports are typical in business? *(pages 294–300)*

EXERCISE 8 Progress reports, trip reports, meeting minutes, feasibility reports, and evaluation reports

Use a web search engine or business portal like Biznar to find an example of one of the following types of reports:

- Progress report
- Trip report
- Meeting minutes
- Feasibility report
- Evaluation report

Evaluate the report in relation to the guidelines presented in this chapter. Write a memo to your instructor identifying what you believe is good about the report you found and what changes you recommend to improve it.

9.3 How do I structure longer, formal reports? *(pages 301–314)*

EXERCISE 9 Reviewing report structure

The United States Government Accountability Office (GAO) prepares hundreds of reports each year, usually in response to requests from the Senate, Congress, or other government sources. You can find these reports on the GAO website if you browse by topic.

Select a report that interests you and download it. Review the report and answer the following questions in a memo or be prepared to discuss them in class:

a. What information is provided on the title page?

b. How is the executive summary (called Highlights) structured? Where does it summarize the purpose of the report, the methodology, the findings, and recommendations?

c. After the table of contents, most GAO reports contain a list of abbreviations. Why do you think the reports provide a separate list rather than just define the terms the first time they appear in the report?

d. The first headline in most GAO reports is "Background." What kind of information is included in that section?

e. The GAO reports are designed with the headlines in the left margin. Do you see benefits to that page design? Do you see disadvantages?

f. Most headlines are phrased as short, complete sentences that express a main point. Do those headlines help prepare you to read the details in the section?

g. Most GAO reports contain many appendices. What kinds of information are in the appendices? Why do you think information about the report's scope and methodology is in an appendix rather than in the body of the report?

EXERCISE 10 Using software features to help format formal reports [Related to the Technology feature on page 314]

Download the "sample report" file for this exercise from mybcommlab.com. This file includes unformatted text for a formal report. The following elements are obvious based on their content: title page, location for the table of contents, executive summary, introduction, body of the report (including headings), conclusions, recommendations, references, and appendices. Use your word processor's features to make the following formatting changes:

- Apply appropriate heading styles to section titles and headings.
- Create section breaks so the title page is not numbered and the table of contents and executive summary are numbered with small Roman numerals (ii and iii). Starting with the introduction, page numbering should use Arabic numerals (1).
- Create a footer to add page numbers to the entire document, except the title page as noted above.
- Generate an automated table of contents to appear after the title page.
- Add automated captions for figures and tables throughout the report.

Save the file, adding your name to the end of the filename. Submit the file electronically to your instructor.

9.4 What guidelines should I follow for writing report decks? *(pages 314–318)*

EXERCISE 11 Understand why and when to use report decks

Report decks are very different from traditional presentation files used to support oral presentations. Search for deck-style presentations at SlideShare or a similar website. You may also search for the report decks included in the reference list at the end of this chapter (see note 8). Select a file that does not include an audio voice-over. Read the file. Who is the intended audience? Is the content organized logically? Is the content understandable without a presenter? Could the file double as a report *and* a presentation? Summarize your findings in a short email message to your instructor. Attach the report file to the email.

EXERCISE 12 Design the deck effectively

Refer to the report deck you selected for Exercise 11. Evaluate the design of that deck. Is it on a plain and readable background? Does it include a table of contents or agenda? Does it use sentence-style headlines? Does it include a footer or header? How does the deck design help you read the deck effectively? Summarize your findings in a short email to your instructor. Attach the report file to the email.

EXERCISE 13 Design the deck content to be easy to follow

Imagine you were asked to create a report deck instead of the formal report in Figure 9.8 on pages 302–313. Refer to the following set of slide headlines for that report. On a piece of paper, write the headlines and then roughly sketch what you would put on that slide.

- **a.** An estimated 20,000 corporations now communicate to customers and stakeholders through blogging.
- **b.** Not just Internet companies but traditional firms in manufacturing, retail, finance, and technology have business blogs.
- **c.** Small-business blogs are most effective when they concentrate on the company's personality and expertise, not products.
- **d.** Effective business blogging depends on a steady flow of new and updated information.

- **e.** A 2008 survey from Technorati suggests that blogging is becoming a reliable and credible source of information.

EXERCISE 14 When telling the truth is not good enough [Related to the Ethics feature on page 327]

Evaluate the following statements. Assume that each is literally accurate. What might be misleading about it?

- **a.** Reveal, Inc., founded in 2001, is a leading provider of background screening and substance abuse testing both domestically and internationally. Reveal has been in business for more than 10 years and its management team possesses over 100 years of experience.
- **b.** We recommend using Acme widgets. Acme is a nationally recognized, award-winning manufacturing organization.
- **c.** In a survey of all company employees, more than half the respondents indicated that they prefer online training over face-to-face training.

9.5 How do I integrate tables and graphs into my reports? *(pages 318–327)*

EXERCISE 15 Choose the best form of display: table or graph

Create a table based on the following paragraph. Then create a graph. Explain the differences and justify which would better represent the data. Submit both visuals and your justification in a one-page memo report to your instructor.

Jamison Lumber Company has four regional branches: North, South, East, and West. Last year, the branch sales were as follows: North = $1.23 million, South = $1.57 million, East = $2.26 million, and West = $2.10 million. This year, the North and South branches recorded a 2.5 percent and 3.4 percent increase, respectively. However, the East and West branches experienced decreases of 1.3 percent and 0.7 percent, respectively.

EXERCISE 16 Choose the best type of graph

For each of the following business messages, what type of graph will be most effective? Sketch a version of that graph and explain why your choice is the best option.

- **a.** Gadget sales have tripled since 1995.
- **b.** Of the four companies in the industry—Acme, Apex, Giant, and Excel—Acme has the smallest share of industry sales.
- **c.** Sales of Product A exceed sales of Product B and Product C.
- **d.** Earnings per share have decreased every year since 2003.
- **e.** There is a strong relationship between the number of training courses a salesperson has completed and the amount of that person's annual sales.

EXERCISE 17 Design graphs and tables to communicate

What changes would you make to the table on page 337 to follow the table design guidelines on page 325?

EXERCISE 18 Integrate the display with the text

As a member of the Acme Electric Safety Committee, you have been asked to write the committee report to the CEO answering the question "Does our electrical equipment comply with safety

YTD International Revenue							
Product	Jan	Feb	Mar	Apr	May	Jun	Total
Disk Drives	$93,993.00	$84,773.00	$88,833.00	$95,838.00	$93,874.00	$83,994.00	$541,305.00
Monitors	$87,413.00	$78,838.00	$82,614.00	$89,129.00	$873,020.00	$78,114.00	$1,289,128.00
Printers	$90,035.00	$2,120,400.00	$85,093.00	$91,803.00	$899,210.00	$80,457.00	$3,366,998.00
Computers	$92,736.00	$83,640.00	$87,645.00	$94,557.00	$92,619.00	$82,871.00	$534,068.00
Memory Sticks	$3,624,500.00	$77,785.00	$81,510.00	$87,938.00	$86,136.00	$77,070.00	$4,034,939.00
Sound Cards	$88,832.00	$80,118.00	$83,956.00	$90,576.00	$88,720.00	$79,382.00	$511,584.00
Video Cards	$82,614.00	$74,510.00	$78,079.00	$84,236.00	$82,509.00	$73,825.00	$475,773.00
RAM	$85,092.00	$76,745.00	$80,421.00	$86,763.00	$84,985.00	$76,040.00	$490,046.00
Scanners	$87,645.00	$79,048.00	$82,834.00	$89,366.00	$87,534.00	$78,321.00	$504,748.00
Input Devices	$90,275.00	$81,419.00	$85,319.00	$920,470.00	$90,160.00	$80,671.00	$1,348,314.00
Total	$4,423,135.00	$2,837,276.00	$836,304.00	$1,730,676.00	$2,478,767.00	$790,745.00	$13,096,903.00

Accompanies Exercise 17

standards?" You write the introduction to the report and decide to summarize the detailed findings in a table. However, you are unsure how to structure that table. Analyze the following introduction and three options for structuring the table (listed on page 338). What are the advantages and disadvantages of each option? Which table design would you choose?

TO: George DiLeonardo, CEO
FROM: Acme Safety Review Committee
             (Devon Rasheed, Kevin Carroll, Risa Policaro,
             and Eric West)
DATE: February 12, 20XX
SUBJECT: Acme's Compliance with Safety Standards

Purpose of the Study
Over the past month, the Acme Safety Committee has conducted a thorough review of all the safety codes and standards that apply to Acme Electric's Belmont facility. These include two sets of mandatory standards that Acme must comply with and one set of voluntary standards.

Mandatory
- OSHA (Occupational Safety and Health Administration) standards
- NEC (National Electric Code) standards

Voluntary
- UL-1950 standards for information technology equipment, including electrical business equipment.

We have also reviewed all the wiring schematics and the equipment in the facility to identify all gaps in compliance.

Results of the Study
Although Acme's equipment is properly designed for electrical load/capacity, several design details do not comply with the codes and widely used standards. Some standards apply

only to building wiring and other parts include equipment. These gaps compromise the safety of our employees and will put us at risk during regulatory inspections.

Table 1 summarizes the places where our equipment and wiring do not comply with applicable standards and offers recommendations for addressing the problems.

Accompanies Exercise 18

Evaluate the options for Table 1 (listed on page 338). Which table would you include in your committee report to the CEO and why?

9.6 How should I document my research?

(pages 327–329)

EXERCISE 19 Determine what needs to be documented

For each of the following situations, imagine that you are writing a report and need to decide whether you must provide documentation to give credit to a source. If you would document the source, how would you document it? Would you refer to the source in the text itself, use parenthetical citation (or footnotes), use quotation marks, or include an entry in a reference list? Indicate as many options as apply. If you would not document the source, explain why not.

a. In your report, you are arguing against an opinion column in the local newspaper.

b. You are providing evidence from your own experience.

c. You are including a story that one of your coworkers told you.

d. In your research, you find a phrase that you really like and decide to use it.

e. You want to quote something from a source but the quotation is too long so you change it a bit and leave out a few words.

f. You are writing a report analyzing the environmental issues relating to the U.S. newspaper industry, and in your research you

Option 1

Regulator	Rule	Affected Area	Violation	Recommendation
OSHA	Rule A Rule B Rule C			
NEC	Rule 1 Rule 2 Rule 3			

Option 2

Equipment	Rule	Violation	Recommendation
Generator 1	OSHA Rule A NEC Rule 1 Local Rule A		
Junction Box 65	OSHA Rule B NEC Rule 2 Local Rule B		

Option 3

Priority	Affected Area	Violation	Rule	Recommendation
High	Generator 1 Juntion Box 65 Conduit 64-65			
Medium	Main Bus B Riser Pipe 37 Conduit 33-34			

Accompanies Exercise 18

come across some facts about how many trees are cut down each year for paper manufacture. You want to use these facts.

g. You mention that the majority of students on your campus did not vote in the last presidential election.

h. You want to prove that your company has been complying with a certain regulation, so your reader will need to know what the regulation says.

i. You are presenting the results of a survey you conducted.

j. You are summarizing information that you learned from an interview with an expert.

EXERCISE 20 Prepare the documentation

For each of the following questions, find an appropriate source that you could use in a research report and prepare a reference list entry for that source. Use APA style, unless your instructor asks you to use a different style. (For a review of how to find good, credible sources, see Chapter 7.)

a. What is the current unemployment rate in the United States? How has the unemployment rate changed over the past 10 years?

b. What is the employment outlook for the career or profession you plan to enter?

c. What are some interesting facts about the history of your college or university?

d. Does your college or university president perceive your school's graduation rate as high or low?

e. What are some key facts about migrant farm workers in the United States?

f. How should a person calculate the amount of life insurance he or she needs?

WRITING

EXERCISE 21 Developing a mobile phone app

On-the-Go Software, a startup company in your community, would like to develop a new mobile phone app that will be profitable. As part of the company's preliminary planning, the CEO, Etta Hawkins, has hired you to research the most popular apps for iPhones and other mobile devices and to analyze why you believe these apps are successful. As you research, identify who is buying these apps and hypothesize why. Also identify features that have received positive comments and hypothesize why these features are important.

Write a three- to five-page letter report to present the results of your research. In addition, include a list of references as an attachment. You may include other attachments if you believe they will be helpful.

Address your report to Etta Hawkins, On-the-Go Software, 1111 Main Street, Mytown, MyState, MyZip.

EXERCISE 22 Recommending survey software

Your company (or your class) is planning to conduct survey research and needs to select an online survey tool to use. Your manager (or instructor) would like a program that meets these criteria:

- allows an unlimited number of survey questions
- allows an unlimited number of surveys
- can be integrated into the company (or class) website
- produces surveys that look professional rather than unformatted or poorly designed
- is easy to use when writing questions
- is easy to use when answering questions
- gathers all the survey results into an easy-to-use database or spreadsheet
- automatically produces graphs that can be used in research reports
- is the most cost-effective option

Your job is to identify three programs that might be suitable, evaluate them, and write a recommendation report to justify a specific program. Write the report in memo form, and keep the body of the report to a maximum of three pages, though you may add attachments.

EXERCISE 23 Evaluating and assessing the feasibility of sustainability initiatives

Your school is considering a number of sustainability initiatives that will make it a more "green" organization. Here are some of the initiatives the administration is considering:

- installing compact fluorescent light bulbs in residences, classrooms, and offices
- installing low-flush toilets throughout building(s)
- installing low-flow faucets and shower heads
- purifying waste vegetable oil from the food service to fuel campus shuttles
- installing a wind turbine on campus to generate electricity
- implementing "trayless dining" in the dining halls (to reduce the amount of wasted food)

You receive one of the following assignments:

a. Research sustainability initiatives at five other campuses and write a report evaluating which initiatives have been most successful. You will need to identify—and justify—specific criteria for success. (As a starting place for your research, visit the website of the Association for the Advancement of Sustainability in Higher Education. You may also search the websites of various colleges and universities.)

b. Select one of the sustainability initiatives listed previously and assess the feasibility of implementing that initiative at your school. Consider the costs, the environmental benefits, and any financial benefits. Are there any obstacles that would make the chosen initiative particularly difficult? You do not need to recommend the option. You only need to report whether your research shows it would be feasible to implement the initiative at your school.

Depending on your instructor's requirements, you may prepare your report as either a formal report or as a report deck.

EXERCISE 24 Evaluating SOS: An employee suggestion program

For the past two years, you have worked in the Human Resources Department of MetCo Manufacturing, a company that employs approximately 2,800 employees in the design and manufacture of small household products. MetCo's CEO believes that satisfied employees are crucial to the company's success and that the best solutions to problems often come from employees. You were hired to design and implement a program that encourages employees to make suggestions and register complaints, called SOS (Suggestions for Organizational Satisfaction). As the SOS coordinator, you collect all the suggestions and complaints, send the suggestions to the appropriate departments, and confidentially investigate complaints.

SOS has been operating now for one year, and your CEO wants you to evaluate it. Specifically, she wants to know how extensively the program is being used, whether it is being used more for suggestions or complaints, what types of employees are using it and what types are not, and whether employees are satisfied with the program.

As a first step, you review data about the number of complaints and suggestions received each month for the past year. These data are presented in Table 1. Then you conduct a survey of all 2,800 employees. The results are in Tables 2–6 on page 340.

Write a report in memo format analyzing the data and presenting results and conclusions. Be sure to:

- create a subject line that serves as a title for the report
- write a good introduction
- identify the research questions you are aiming to answer
- identify the most important conclusions you can draw and back each of them up with data
- use informative headings
- include tables and graphs that help illustrate and explain the data

TABLE 1 Monthly Submissions to SOS

	Jan	Feb	Mar	Apr	May	June	July	Aug	Sept	Oct	Nov	Dec
Suggestions	57	61	157	102	107	94	98	82	90	72	66	62
Complaints	332	428	496	502	553	503	466	417	381	365	332	319

Note: In March, Human Resources sponsored a "Make a Suggestion" program, with a $100 cash prize for the best suggestion.

Accompanies Exercise 24

TABLE 2   Have you ever used the SOS program?

No	369
Once	601
More than Once	1,003

TABLE 3   Classifications of the 369 people who have not used the program

Age	Number not using the program/total number of respondents in that age group
Under 25	127 / 458
25–40	51 / 731
41–55	87 / 542
Over 55	104 / 242
Gender	
Male	125 / 1227
Female	244 / 746
Rank	
Nonmanagement	227 / 1517
Management	142 / 456

Accompanies Exercise 24

TABLE 4   How satisfied were you with the response you received?

	Completely satisfied	Partially satisfied	Dissatisfied
Used SOS once	183	349	70
Used SOS more than once	692	272	39

TABLE 5   How confident are you that your question or complaint reached the right person?

	Confident	Not Confident
Used SOS once	196	405
Used SOS more than once	822	181

TABLE 6   Do you intend to use the SOS program again in the future?

Yes	1,331
No	82
Undecided	191

COLLABORATING

EXERCISE 25 Reporting on consumer attitudes

Consumer Research, Inc., has hired your team to conduct a survey to learn how the public responds to direct mail advertising sent by email. Research indicates that responsiveness to direct mail sent through the Internet is growing.[14] Consumer Research wants to know if responsiveness continues to be strong. Select an age group to survey and develop a set of questions to ask. For example, you could ask:

- How often do they open advertising they receive through email?
- What influences their decision to open the email? Is it the subject line, the sender, or something else?
- How often do they click through to a website?
- How often do they purchase something as a result of the email advertising?

Conduct your survey and then write a short report to Consumer Research, presenting your results. If possible, draw conclusions about the effectiveness of email marketing to the age group you have researched.

EXERCISE 26 Evaluating fast food restaurants

Your team works for a fast food restaurant company that is planning to open a restaurant in your area. The district regional manager wants to know more about the competition. What are the strengths and weaknesses of the competitive restaurants? Is there opportunity for a new restaurant in the neighborhood?

As a team, choose three fast food restaurants in the area and observe each restaurant for an hour at least three times within the next two weeks. Vary the day of the week and the time of day for each visit. During each visit, observe and collect data on the appearance of the restaurant, how many customers entered during that time period, the length of wait to place an order, the length of wait to receive an order, the quality of service, and the quality of food. During each visit, make a qualitative judgment about how happy the customers seem to be, and support your judgment with specific observations.

At the end of the two-week observation period, write a report to your district manager evaluating the competition and making recommendations about how your new restaurant can provide better service than the competitive restaurants you have studied.

EXERCISE 27 Writing minutes for a team meeting

If you have been working as a team on any project this term, submit to your instructor the minutes of any team meeting. Write the minutes so that they are a useful reference for team members and are informative for your instructor.

SPEAKING

EXERCISE 28 Making informal/impromptu presentations

a. Randomly select one of the critical thinking questions on page 333 and give a one-minute oral response. Provide a direct answer and give compelling support for your answer.

b. Give a brief report about your progress in your business communication course. What do you believe are your current communication strengths, what are your weaknesses, and how do you plan to address them?

c. Imagine you were assigned to write a feasibility report about a plan you are making for your life. (The research question would be: "Will it be feasible for me to . . ."?) What would you write about and why?

d. Imagine you were asked to evaluate two fast food restaurants in your area. What criteria would you use for evaluating them, and why?

e. How do you spend your time on a typical day or typical week? Quickly sketch a pie chart that divides your time into three or four major categories, with appropriate percentages for each. Present this pie chart and explain whether you are satisfied with this division of time or if you'd like to make some changes.

EXERCISE 29 Executive briefings

a. If you are working on a multiweek project in your class, prepare a written progress report for your instructor. Then plan a five-minute executive briefing to present this progress report to your instructor.

b. Prepare a five-minute executive briefing based on the feasibility report in Figure 9.7 on pages 299–300.

c. Search the Internet to find a report that you believe is well designed and easy to read. (Look for a report that you can download as a PDF or Word document, so that you can focus on the design.) Prepare a five-minute briefing on key features of the report design that you believe are effective. Conclude your briefing with a recommendation: would you recommend that your class or your company adopt this report design for their work? Why or why not? Be sure to prepare at least one visual aid for your briefing.

d. Search the Internet, newspapers, or magazines to find one data display (table or graph) that you believe is effective. Create a visual aid of that data display and present it to the class. Explain the context in which you found it, the main point or purpose of the data display, and why you believe it communicates effectively.

e. Search the Internet, newspapers, or magazines to find one data display (table or graph) that you believe is *not* effective. Create a visual aid of that data display and present it to the class. Explain the context in which you found it, the main point or purpose of the data display, and why you believe it does not communicate effectively.

GRAMMAR

Semicolons and colons (See Appendix D—Sections 2.3 and 2.4)

Rekey (or download from mybcommlab.com) the following paragraph, correcting the 10 errors or omissions in the use of semicolons and colons (see Sections 2.3 and 2.4). Underline all your corrections.

> In the online article "How to Give a Professional Voicemail Greeting The Business Etiquette of Voicemail Greetings," author James Bucki asks, "What would I want to know from the voicemail greeting?" The greeting may be perfectly clear to you however, the caller may be mystified. His advice create the greeting as if you were the listener at the other end. As a general rule, the length of a voicemail greeting should be: no longer than 20–25 seconds. Some of the most annoying greetings are: long introductions, greetings that are too casual or personal, and background music of any kind (especially music that drowns out the message). Avoid endings that are not business related (such as "have a blessed day"); because they may strike customers and clients as presumptuous. Here is an example of a bad voicemail greeting; "Hi. This is Accounting. Leave me a message." Callers have no idea whether they have reached the right person; nor do they know if they even have the right company. Too little information is bad, conversely, so is too much information.

> Business callers don't want personal details, including: the fun spot where you are vacationing; or that you are out sick with the flu.

Quotation marks and italics (See Appendix D—Section 2.5)

Rekey (or download from mybcommlab.com) the following paragraph, correcting the 10 errors or omissions in the use of quotation marks and italics. Count pairs of quotation marks as one (see Sections 2.5.1 and 2.5.2). Underline all your corrections.

> It's a *good* idea to review the voicemail greeting on your personal phone, especially if potential employers might call. As part of his greeting, my friend Joe recorded John Cleese speaking lines from the *Dead Parrot Sketch* from the British television comedy "Monty Python's Flying Circus." His friends all thought it was really funny, using the words hilarious and clever to describe the greeting. One afternoon he retrieved a phone message that said, You really should use a more professional greeting. The voice continued, I called to offer you a job interview, but I've changed my mind. Joe thought, 'I wouldn't want to work for someone who didn't understand the humor in the "Dead Parrot Sketch", anyway. Sounds like this guy just doesn't get it.' Maybe not, but Joe's chances with that company are kaput.

10 Preparing and Delivering Business Presentations

Rathi Suresh
Management Consultant
ZS Associates
Columbia University, 2007

" MY PRIMARY RESPONSIBILITY IS TO ENSURE THE SMOOTH EXECUTION OF A PROJECT. This includes communicating results and insights to clients in a compelling manner. We often communicate our findings through presentations. The biggest difference in the way I currently use PowerPoint is the overall structure of a presentation deck. In school, we were taught to present the evidence through a series of slides to ultimately arrive at a conclusion. However, at work we structure presentation decks and individual slides to state the answer first and then provide the supporting evidence for that answer. "

Introduction

Employers consider oral communication to be the most important skill for a new hire.[1] Yet, according to human resource directors, only a small percentage (24 percent) of the graduates entering the workforce actually excels in oral communication.[2] Chapter 2, "Working with Others," suggested strategies to help you communicate orally and stand out among your peers. This chapter continues the discussion, focusing on one of the most challenging forms of oral communication at work: business presentations.

All business presentations have one thing in common: they are designed to accomplish a business goal. They may present analysis and recommendations. They may update the audience on a project or report final results. They may motivate an audience to act in a certain way or simply provide people with the information necessary to perform a task or make a decision.

Preparing an effective presentation begins long before the day you deliver it. This chapter helps you develop and deliver effective presentations by:

- analyzing your purpose, audience, setting, and medium options
- planning and organizing your key points
- composing visual support materials including slides and handouts
- evaluating your presentation by practicing
- delivering the presentation effectively
- evaluating audience response

Study Question 10.1

What do I analyze when planning a business presentation?

In school, an instructor may give you a topic to research, such as business trends in China or the pros and cons of business outsourcing to India, and ask you to develop a presentation on that topic. Similarly, in business your manager may ask you to give a presentation on a specific topic. For example, you may need to present background information about a new client company and its industry, or update your managers about new technologies that can benefit your company.

More often, however, a business presentation emerges from a specific business question. This chapter is structured around a business scenario that poses such a question. As you read the chapter, you will follow the ACE process to develop a presentation that answers this question, and you will learn important techniques for composing and delivering the presentation.

Assume that you work for the human resources department of Rowland-Grey, a large company that owns six department store brands located throughout the United States. Your job is to study the work environment in individual stores and to recommend changes that will improve worker satisfaction and productivity. One day, your supervisor asks you to analyze the personnel problems in the company's computer call centers, which handle both online orders and customer feedback. The manager of the Midwest call center has been complaining that his unit is experiencing high rates of sales staff turnover and absenteeism and low rates of productivity. Your supervisor gave you exit interviews from 10 online sales clerks, all of whom quit due to headaches and eyestrain. Based on the exit interviews and additional research, you learn the following information:

■ Access this chapter's simulation entitled Business Presentations, located at mybcommlab.com.

- The annual turnover rate for employees who work in the call center is 55 percent, while the turnover rate for employees on the sales floor is 40 percent.
- The excess turnover in the call centers costs the company $660,000 a year in new employee training.
- Exit interviews show that people working in the call center routinely complain about headaches.
- The type of computer monitors combined with the lighting in the call centers lead to glare, which may be contributing to the headaches.

In a meeting, you report your findings to your supervisor and suggest that Rowland-Grey conduct a pilot program to see if purchasing new computer monitors will reduce turnover and increase productivity. Your supervisor likes the idea and asks you to make a presentation to Carolyn Reese, Senior Vice President of Planning and Development, to get funding for this pilot program. The business question you will address is this: What is the cause of high turnover and low productivity, and what can be done about it? Using the ACE process, you can plan your presentation by analyzing your purpose and outcome, audience, setting, and medium options.

Analyze your purpose and outcome: Why?

Every good business presentation has a specific objective or intended *outcome*. Ask yourself, *"Why am I delivering this presentation, and what do I want to have happen as a result?"* FIGURE 10.1 lists four general outcomes for presentations, along with specific examples of each that might apply in the Rowland-Grey scenario.

Although you may start with a general purpose like those in the left column, always move to a more specific outcome, like those in the right column. The more specific your objective, the easier it is to create an effective presentation.

FIGURE 10.1 Four General Outcomes for a Presentation

DO I WANT MY AUDIENCE TO . . .	THEN MY PRESENTATION WILL BE . . .	FOR EXAMPLE, AS A RESULT OF MY PRESENTATION, MY AUDIENCE WILL . . .
know something?	informational.	know why the call center turnover is so high and understand how glare leads to headaches.
believe something or do something?	persuasive.	implement a pilot program and purchase new monitors for the call center.
know how to do something?	instructional.	know how to install new monitors.
work together with me to reach an answer?	collaborative.	discuss the pros and cons of purchasing new monitors or lighting sources.

For this scenario, the Rowland-Grey presentation clearly needs to be persuasive. The objective is to convince Carolyn Reese, the senior VP, to approve the plan and fund a pilot program to purchase 100 new computer monitors that will reduce glare. With this specific objective in mind, you can analyze the audience: What will Ms. Reese need to know and believe to be convinced?

Analyze your audience: How many and who?

Analyzing your audience helps you make good decisions about your presentation style. Consider all the people who will attend your presentation. Size matters. With a small audience, be prepared for a more interactive presentation since your audience may interrupt you with questions. By contrast, if you are speaking to a large audience, it's likely that you can get through your presentation without someone interrupting you with a question.

Analyzing your audience also helps you develop content. If you know the people who will be in your audience, especially the decision makers, you can anticipate their needs, interests, attitudes, and possible biases. If you do not know your audience, imagine how they might respond. FIGURE 10.2 is an audience analysis worksheet you can use in planning presentation content. Analysis categories are on the left. The column on the right includes analysis notes for the Rowland-Grey presentation.

Analyze your setting: When and where?

People often create presentations without thinking about when and where they will be presenting. Use the following checklist to analyze your setting before composing your business presentations.

When am I presenting?

- **What time of day am I presenting?** Your audience may be more alert in the morning and more sluggish in the afternoon. Afternoon presentations—especially right after lunch—will benefit from a lively introduction and interactive elements to keep the audience engaged.

FIGURE 10.2 Audience Analysis Worksheet

WHAT DO I KNOW ABOUT THE AUDIENCE?	HOW CAN I USE THIS INFORMATION ABOUT THE AUDIENCE IN MY PRESENTATION?
Names and titles or profile of the group	
Main audience: Carolyn Reese, Senior Vice President of Planning and Development	Include this information on the title slide. Also mention the goals of the Planning and Development Department as part of the argument.
Relevant personal information about the audience	
Ms. Reese is the person who originally developed the call center eight years ago. She wants to see it succeed.	Mention the importance of the call center in the strategic plans of the company.
Audience needs and interests	
Ms. Reese is very interested in costs and cost savings. She is skeptical about big promises. She values proposals that are supported by logic and research.	Show that I have done research and show the calculations to support my claim that new monitors may save money. If proposing a pilot program, provide a way to measure its success.
Audience attitudes and biases	
Ms. Reese does not accept arguments based solely on employee happiness or unhappiness. She is not a big supporter of the Human Resources Department.	Minimize discussion of employee unhappiness and morale. Instead, focus on cost savings.
Audience familiarity with topic and jargon	
She is very familiar with all language having to do with finances and employees. She may not be familiar with language having to do with computer technology.	Avoid long technical explanations about why the new monitors may solve the headache problems.
Audience decision-making authority and process	
She can authorize funds for a pilot program.	Ask for authorization at the beginning and end.
Additional information I need about the audience	**Where to look for the information**
Does Ms. Reese already have any plans to replace computer monitors? Is she working on any initiatives right now that might coincide or conflict with this one? Does this proposal relate to any ideas in the strategic plan?	• Read the company's five-year strategic plan. • Ask my boss.

- **How long is my presentation, and how will I allocate my time?** How much time will you devote to presenting, and how much time will remain for questions and discussion? In a class presentation, your instructor may expect five minutes devoted to questions and answers at the end of your presentation. In a business meeting, you will probably need more time for discussion, so your presentation will be shorter.

  Also, if you are presenting slides with programs such as PowerPoint, Keynote, Impress, or Prezi, how many slides should you plan to present? Typically, 20 minutes of presentation time translates into 15 to 20 slides, if you present the slides at the rate of about one slide per minute or so. If your presentation is more interactive, you must plan for fewer slides.

- **How will I adjust if I am given more or less time than planned?** You may plan a 20-minute presentation and then find that the primary decision maker needs to leave in 15 minutes. You will be wise to mark the crucial slides of your presentation, so that you can go directly to them, leaving additional support until later.

Where am I presenting?

- **Will you be presenting in an unfamiliar room?** If possible, practice your presentation in that room or a similar room. That way you will know whether you are able to stand next to your slides and point to elements in them or whether you will have to stand at a microphone behind a podium. You will also know how loudly you will need to speak.

- **Will you be speaking with a microphone?** If so, you may need to remain in front of the microphone during the presentation. If not, you will have more ability to move around the room, interacting with both your audience and your slides.
- **Will a computer and projector be available?** Can you use your own laptop, or will you need to use equipment that is already in the room? If you are using other equipment, be sure that it projects your material correctly and that all fonts, images, video, and audio perform as planned. How far away from the screen will the audience be sitting? Be sure any projected materials are easy to read at that distance.
- **Will my audience be in the same room, or will they be participating via telephone, video, or web?** If your audience is not in the room with you, you will need to consider how they will see any slides you present, how they will ask questions, and how you will interact with them.

Analyze your medium options: How?

When you deliver a business presentation, you are not restricted to only one medium. You can combine multiple options. For example, many people choose to project slides and also provide the audience with a hardcopy handout. You can embed video or audio files with your slides, or use a document camera to project a paper document while making notes about it on a flipchart. Choosing the best medium depends on your purpose, audience, content, and setting. Consider the criteria listed in FIGURE 10.3.

FIGURE 10.3 Selecting the Best Medium for Presentations

IF YOU WANT TO:	FLIPCHARTS, WHITEBOARDS	SLIDES	VIDEO, AUDIO, PODCASTS	DOCUMENT CAMERAS	PROPS	HANDOUTS
Purpose- and content-related criteria						
Encourage the audience to collaborate, interact, and create content	■				■	■
Encourage the audience to listen and look carefully		■	■	■		■
Communicate complex material that people need to look at carefully		■				■
Share content that is not in electronic form				■	■	■
Present lengthy content that could not easily be seen in slide form						■
Provide a demonstration					■	■
Have an electronic record of the material		■	■			■
Audience- and setting-related criteria						
Present to a large audience in a large room		■		■		■
Present to a small audience in a small room	■	■			■	■
Present to one or two people in an office or conference room	■	■			■	■
Present to a distant audience accessible by computer technology		■	■			■
Have the presentation available to people at a later time		■	■			■

Study Question 10.2

How do I compose the presentation?

For many business presentations, content is composed and delivered with programs like PowerPoint, Keynote, Impress, and Prezi. When used effectively, slide presentations offer a number of advantages: they help organize the logic and flow of the presentation, engage the audience and keep them focused, keep you on track during your presentation, and provide a written record of the main ideas.

Unfortunately, because presentation programs are usually user-friendly applications, many people believe they can put their slides together quickly. However, to be effective, presenters need to compose the presentation carefully so that the slides support the presentation without boring, distracting, or confusing the audience. This section explains the seven-step process illustrated in FIGURE 10.4 for developing effective slide presentations.

FIGURE 10.4 Process for Designing Slide Presentations

| Identify the type of presentation | Organize the content | Create a storyboard | Develop a template | Design individual slides | Evaluate in a practice session | Create effective handouts |

Identify the type of presentation

Before you begin to develop your slides, you need to identify how you plan to use the presentation. Typically, you will choose between two different types of presentations with two different uses: stand-alone presentations or visual aid presentations.

Stand-alone presentations

Many business presentations require that your **slide decks**—that is, the set of slides you prepare for the presentation—serve as reference documents after the presentation and even be shared with people who didn't attend the presentation. These presentations need to make what managerial communication expert Mary Munter calls "stand-alone sense."[3] This does not mean that the slide deck needs to be comprehensive or include every word you plan to say. Instead, it means the presentation needs to make sense to anyone who reads it without the benefit of the presenter to explain the information. In addition, each slide needs to make sense to someone who enters the room midway through the presentation.

A **stand-alone presentation** is distinguished by three key features:

- an agenda slide that communicates the main ideas and logic of the presentation
- **message headlines** that summarize the key point, or message, of each slide
- support material on the body of the slide that develops and explains the headline

FIGURE 10.5 illustrates a slide from a stand-alone presentation.

Visual aid presentations

In presentations where the speaker's words carry the main story of the presentation, the slides primarily provide illustration and backup. These **visual aid presentations** ideally devote much more space to various forms of illustration that focus the discussion and demonstrate the points. The slide in FIGURE 10.6 is from a presentation promoting a culinary tour of France. The slide is visually appealing, but a presenter needs to explain the main point orally.

Organize the content

Assuming that you have done sufficient research, as described in Chapter 7, and know your material, you will have enough content to accomplish your goals in your allotted time. But how will you organize that content into a compelling presentation? As you plan

FIGURE 10.5 A Stand-Alone Slide with Message Headline

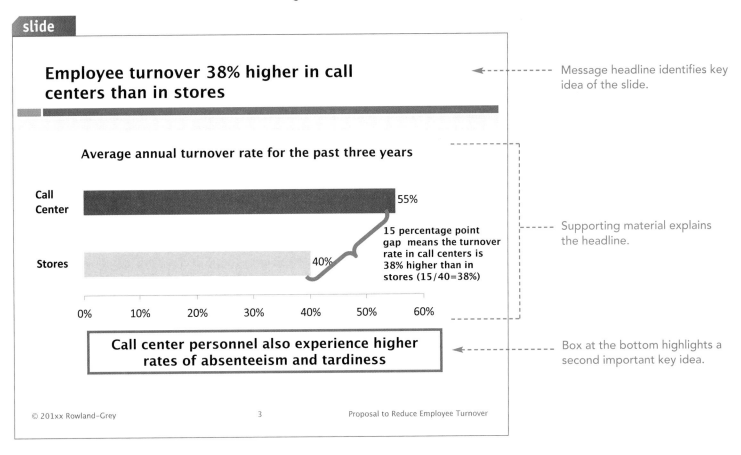

slide

Employee turnover 38% higher in call centers than in stores

Message headline identifies key idea of the slide.

Average annual turnover rate for the past three years

Call Center   55%

15 percentage point gap means the turnover rate in call centers is 38% higher than in stores (15/40=38%)

Stores   40%

0%   10%   20%   30%   40%   50%   60%

Supporting material explains the headline.

Call center personnel also experience higher rates of absenteeism and tardiness

Box at the bottom highlights a second important key idea.

© 201xx Rowland–Grey   3   Proposal to Reduce Employee Turnover

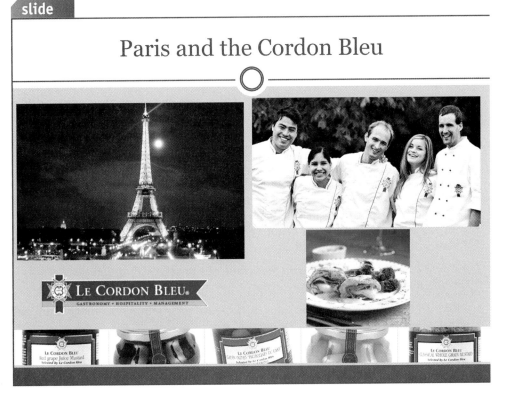

slide

Paris and the Cordon Bleu

LE CORDON BLEU®
GASTRONOMY · HOSPITALITY · MANAGEMENT

FIGURE 10.6
A Visually Appealing Slide That Does Not Stand Alone

Slide deck A set of slides used for a presentation.

Stand-alone presentation A slide deck that makes sense without the benefit of a presenter.

Message headlines Slide headlines that summarize the key message of each slide.

Visual aid presentation A presentation in which the speaker's words carry the main story of the presentation, and the slides provide illustration and backup.

the beginning, middle, and end of your presentation, remember the old saying "Tell them what you're going to tell them, tell them, and then tell them what you told them." A good presentation will follow that guideline as well as the guidelines described next.

Compose an opening that captures audience interest

Imagine your audience at the beginning of your presentation. Perhaps people are coming into the room, looking for coffee or water, or chatting with the person next to them. They are not yet focused on you. When your presentation begins, your first job is to get their attention with a strong introduction. The introduction of a presentation has three main goals: (1) establish rapport with your audience, (2) motivate your audience to care about your presentation, and (3) preview the organization of your presentation.

Establish rapport. Depending upon your audience, establishing rapport may require you to introduce yourself. If you do not already have credibility with the audience, this is a good time to earn it. However, assuming that the audience knows you, you can establish rapport with your audience by piquing their interest: state a relevant fact, share an anecdote, use a quotation, or ask a question. Not every approach is good for every situation. The following examples relate to the Rowland-Grey presentation. Which would be most effective—and most comfortable—for you?

- **State a fact.** A startling fact can capture audience attention. Even a mundane fact can be effective if it gets people to nod in agreement. For example, *"Next to payroll, annual employee training represents the single largest cost in Rowland-Grey's computer call centers."*

- **Tell an anecdote.** An anecdote is a very short story, usually a true one, that can bring a subject to life. An anecdote is one of the most powerful ways to begin a presentation. Consider this example:

  "A few weeks ago, I was driving my car from Albuquerque to Flagstaff and made the mistake of forgetting to bring sunglasses. Within about 10 minutes, the glare on the windshield was blinding, my eyes were squinting, and I had the beginnings of a major headache. Fortunately, I was able to get off the road and buy some sunglasses at a service station. But the experience gave me a new perspective on the exit interviews I had been reading from employees who left our computer call center. Many said they left because the computer glare caused headaches. I can say, I know how they feel."

- **Quote someone well known, or quote a familiar saying.** If you can find a quotation or saying that relates to your point, you can use it—or a variation of it—to get people to think. Here's an example:

  "As the old saying goes, you need to spend money to make money. It's also true that you sometimes need to spend money to save money. Today I'm presenting a proposal to spend money updating equipment, an expenditure that has the potential of saving us hundreds of thousands of dollars in costs related to employee turnover."

- **Ask a question.** Questions immediately involve your audience and get them thinking about your presentation. Your question can be a genuine one that you'd actually like members of your audience to answer, either in words or by a show of hands. Or, your question can be a rhetorical question that you plan to answer yourself. For example, you could begin your Rowland-Grey presentation to Carolyn Reese with one of these questions:

  "Would you be surprised to learn that employee turnover for online sales clerks is costing Rowland-Grey $660,000 a year?"

  "Why do Rowland-Grey online sales clerks leave their jobs more quickly than any other category of clerks in the company?"

  Starting with a question may be risky because your audience may consider it an invitation to provide an answer that takes the presentation off track. The key is finding the right question to engage your audience and to set up the remainder of your introduction.

Motivate your audience to care. An audience will care about your presentation if they believe it is valuable to them. Does your audience have a problem that you will solve? Is there a need for change? Are you identifying an opportunity that they can take advantage of? Is there a specific way that your audience will benefit?

For example, the proposal to replace computer monitors at Rowland-Grey offers employees the benefit of a more comfortable working environment and better health, and it offers managers the benefit of improved employee productivity. However, neither of these benefits is of primary importance to your audience, Carolyn Reese. She is probably more concerned with cost savings. As a result, the opening that you choose needs to focus on that benefit. You might say that your plan will save the company money or be even more specific, stating that Rowland-Grey's computer call centers are suffering from excessive turnover and associated training costs and that you will be proposing a solution to that expensive problem.

Preview the presentation's organization. At the end of your introduction, make a connection between the opening and the remainder of the presentation. How will you be addressing the problem you have identified or organizing the information your audience needs to know? What is the flow of the presentation, and why is that flow logical? Preview the presentation for the audience before discussing your points. In other words, "tell them what you're going to tell them."

Organize your content using a logical pattern

If the introduction "tells them what you're going to tell them," how do you organize the main part of the presentation—what you are actually telling the audience? As you plan the organization, consider these common patterns:

- **Categorization.** Group the content under key categories, for example, four reasons, five steps, or three options. Although the number of parts will depend on the content and purpose of your presentation, your audience will find it easier to follow your organization if you limit the number of parts to five or fewer. You will need to decide the order in which to present this content: most to least important? Most to least likely? Be sure to choose an order that makes sense.

- **Component parts.** To help your audience understand details, you can break a topic into its component parts. If you are discussing the problems in the company, you may divide the discussion into the component regions—for example, you may talk about the problems in the Northeast region, then Southeast, the Midwest, and the Southwest. Similarly, if you are talking about proposed changes to an automobile, you may present changes to the body, the engine and mechanical components, the chassis, and the interior.

- **Chronological order.** Will you organize the presentation according to the order in which activities happened or will happen? Chronology works well, for example, if you are presenting a time line for a project or the phases to implement a new computer system.

- **Conceptual order.** For some presentations, you might find it useful to develop a model or diagram that illustrates the relationship between ideas you plan to present and then use that visual to organize your presentation. For example, if you were delivering an informative presentation about the ACE process, you might organize it by the three elements represented in the ACE diagram: Analyze, Compose, and Evaluate, as illustrated in FIGURE 10.7. In fact, you might even use this diagram as an agenda for the presentation.

- **Problem/solution.** Because business presentations often aim to solve problems, organizing the content by problem/solution can be very useful. The main challenge is to determine how to weight the two parts. Some business presentations fail to achieve their goal because they spend so much time on the problem that they never get to the solution. In a business presentation, the solution usually deserves the most weight.

- **Opportunity/action.** In this organization, rather than focusing on the problem, you emphasize an opportunity that will be valuable to your audience and then show how you can help your audience take advantage of this opportunity.

FIGURE 10.7
Presentation Organized by Model

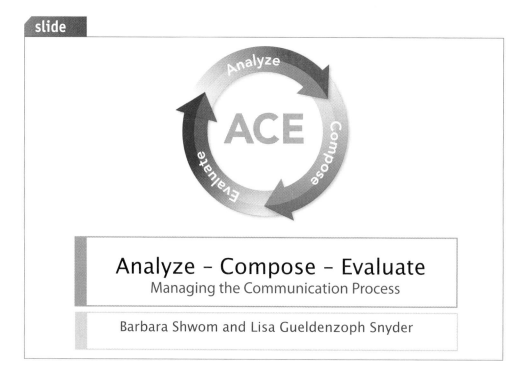

- **Questions/answers.** If you have done a good job analyzing your audience, you may be able to imagine the questions that will be on your audience's minds when they attend the presentation. These questions can help you organize the presentation. For example, if you are delivering an informational presentation about a new dental insurance option available to employees, you might organize the presentation around questions such as these:
  - Why did Acme add a new dental plan option?
  - What are the key features of each available option?
  - How can I choose between them?
  - How do I sign up for my preferred plan?
  - Can I change plans during the year?

  If you choose a question/answer structure, then the questions themselves become the agenda for your presentation.

Which of these structures will work best for the Rowland-Grey presentation? Although a number of approaches are feasible, perhaps the best one is problem/solution, since this is likely to be the one that will best motivate the audience. Whether you choose one of these organizational patterns or a different one, be sure it fits your objective and the material you need to present. Remember that you will need to explain to your audience the reason for this structure.

Compose a memorable conclusion

The end of a presentation is as important as the beginning. Because the conclusion is the last thing the audience hears, it may be the first thing the audience remembers days or weeks after your presentation. Take advantage of this powerful moment in your presentation by using at least one of the following strategies. The best endings typically use all four.

- **Summarize your main message.** All presentation guidelines recommend summarizing at the end. In other words, "Tell them what you told them." However, a good summary does more than just say *"I've talked about our turnover problem and a proposed solution."* Remind the audience why you talked about those topics. What makes them important to you and to the audience? What impact will they have? What are the benefits? How should the audience use the information or respond to it? Audiences need to hear again, "What's in this for me?"

- **Ask for what you want.** What do you want the audience to do? Send you information? Schedule a meeting with a decision maker? Approve your proposal? Act on your recommendations? You'll need a call to action with specific, clear, and tangible tasks. As salespeople say, "Make the ask!"
- **Visualize the outcome for the audience.** Paint a picture of the audience's world when your plans, product, or recommendations are in place. What will be more efficient, less costly, more comfortable, or more competitive? What kind of satisfaction will they experience?
- **Make next steps clear.** If your presentation leads to future action, outline the next steps and identify who is responsible for what. A simple checklist or time line can effectively display the content and provide a visual reference.

Create a storyboard

The concept of a storyboard comes from the film industry. Traditionally, a filmmaker will map out the film, scene by scene, sketching the vision for the scene and including notes for direction and filming. Applied to a presentation, a **storyboard** is a slide-by-slide sketch that helps you take the organization you have developed and create a story flow. The storyboard also helps you see the big picture of the presentation before you get too involved in creating individual slides.

To create a storyboard, sketch boxes for your slides (or use Post-it notes) and write a headline in each box. Then sketch your vision for the body of the slide. How will you support that headline and illustrate that key idea? FIGURE 10.8 illustrates a storyboard for the Rowland-Grey presentation.

Develop a template

In business communication, the presentation slide design should always be secondary to your message. You don't want your audience to focus more on the pattern in the borders than on the message itself. The best approach is to keep your slide design simple so your readers can concentrate on the content you are trying to convey. Fortunately, slide programs like PowerPoint and Keynote allow you to create your own slide templates (PowerPoint templates are saved in the Microsoft template folder as .pot files). The following fundamental design guidelines will help you develop a template that supports effective visual communication.

- **Design your template on master slides.** A **slide master** is a presentation software tool that allows you to apply design features to all of your slides in that file. This tool will enforce consistency in your visual elements: colors, fonts and font sizes, bullets, headers, footers, and margins will remain consistent from slide to slide. Using this tool also saves you time since you won't need to make these changes on every slide you add. FIGURE 10.9 on page 355 illustrates how you might set up elements on a slide master for a report-like standalone presentation.
- **Use a simple look.** Avoid frequently-used templates that immediately communicate a lack of originality. Also avoid templates with decorative, nonfunctional graphics. These graphics often take up a good deal of space that can be better used for content relevant to your message. Slides work best when they have sufficient space for message content and when all graphics support that content. If you want to include a thematic graphic that relates to your presentation content, put it on the title slide. If you would like a logo or other corporate identity item on each slide, reduce the size and put it in the footer where it will be visible but will not detract from the message.
- **Use basic, solid backgrounds.** Avoid dramatic color gradations or fill effects on backgrounds. These will often conflict with the color of the font you choose—at least on part of the screen. Light backgrounds work best for presentations intended to be read on a computer, projected in a small or well-lit room, or printed for your audience. Dark backgrounds usually work better in dark or large rooms. If you choose a dark background, be sure to check whether your presentation prints well in black and white.

Storyboard A slide-by-slide sketch of the presentation that is used as a tool for organizing the flow of the presentation.

Slide master A tool within presentation software that allows you to select design features that will apply to all slides.

FIGURE 10.8 Presentation Storyboard

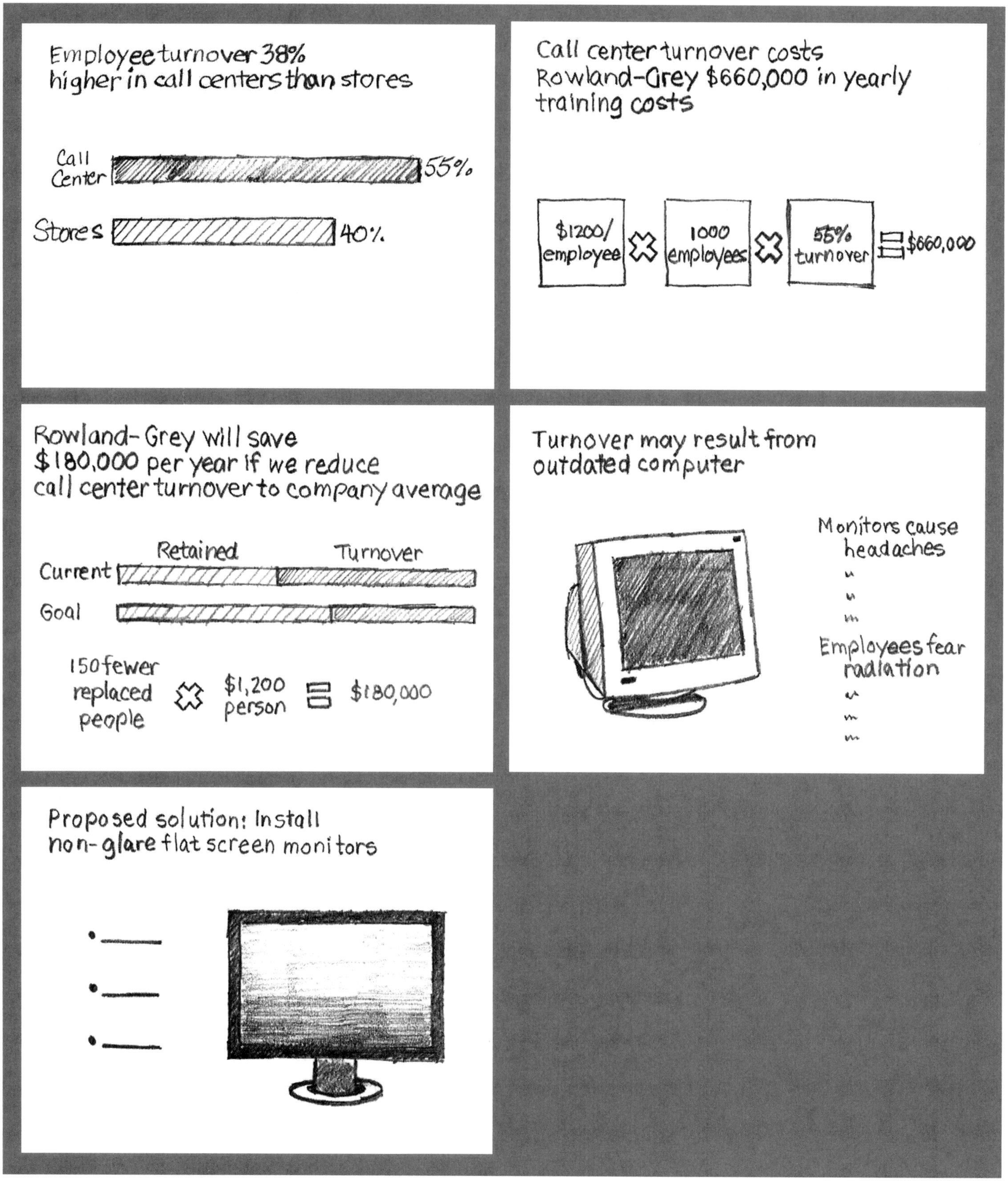

FIGURE 10.9 Slide Master for a Title Slide and Body Slides
(Font size in these slides was reduced so they would fit on one page.)

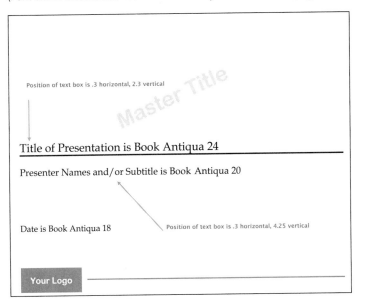

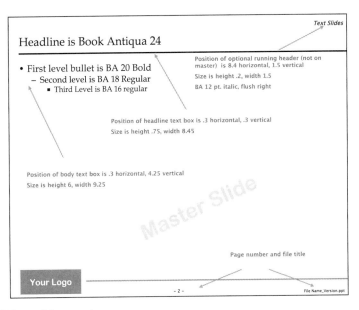

- **Use contrasting color for text.** If you are planning to project slides with a projector, test your color combinations to make sure that the headlines and text contrast sufficiently with the background. If possible, test the slides in the room where you will present.

- **Use a consistent color palette.** Choose an effective set of colors to use for graphs, tables, and emphasis in text. Most presentation software offers you a range of good choices.

- **Use simple bullets.** Opt for bullets like this ■ and avoid overly ornate dingbats and arrows such as → that detract from your content and may not project or print correctly.

- **Use a coherent set of fonts.** Fonts can be categorized into two types: *serif* and *sans serif*. Serif fonts such as Book Antiqua and Georgia have extra "tails" at the end of each character. Sans serif fonts such as Verdana and Arial do not have extra tails. Sans serif fonts are often easier to read, especially when projected. However, serif fonts are acceptable if they are clear and legible. Presentations typically use a single font along with variations in its style such as italic and bold. You can also combine fonts within one family such as the Franklin Gothic family (Franklin Gothic, Franklin Gothic Demi, and Franklin Gothic Heavy) or the Arial family (Arial Regular, Arial Black, and Arial Narrow). If you use fonts that are outside the standard set included in Microsoft Windows, be sure to save your file with the fonts embedded. This will allow you to project your file on any other Windows-based computer (though not Macintosh computers).

- **Keep your font sizes consistent on all slides.** Do not shrink the font size on occasional slides to fit more text. Depending on how the presentation will be given and whether you are creating a stand-alone or visual aid presentation, font sizes for headlines may range from 24 to 48 points. Font size for text may go as low as 18 points if your audience will be sitting at close range. Use larger font sizes for presentations given in large rooms, so people seated in the back will be able to read your slides.

- **Position headlines appropriately.** If you are using very short headlines, center them at the top of the slide. However, if you are using message headlines, begin them at the left margin.

- **Include slide numbers.** Slide numbers can be as important in presentations as page numbers are in a traditional report. If you've provided handouts that replicate the slides, page numbers allow your audience to refer easily to a specific slide during a question-answer session or a follow-up telephone call. Page numbers also help you direct your audience to the right slide if they are navigating through your deck during an online presentation.

Design individual slides

Once you have a template, you can begin designing and composing individual slides. Use the guiding principle of "less is more." Too many people use slides as their speaking script, crowding out all white space with detailed text. With so much content on the slide, your audience can focus on nothing. Ironically, if the slide contains less information, your audience will absorb more. This "less is more" principle applies both to text slides and data slides.

Text slides

The bullet point layout is the default layout for new slides in most presentation software, including PowerPoint. This may be one reason why writers overuse bullet points rather than using other means of structuring text. As FIGURE 10.10 illustrates, bullets are certainly a better choice than dense paragraphs of text, because bullets can help the audience see the relationship among ideas at a glance.

FIGURE 10.10 "Less Is More" Text Slide

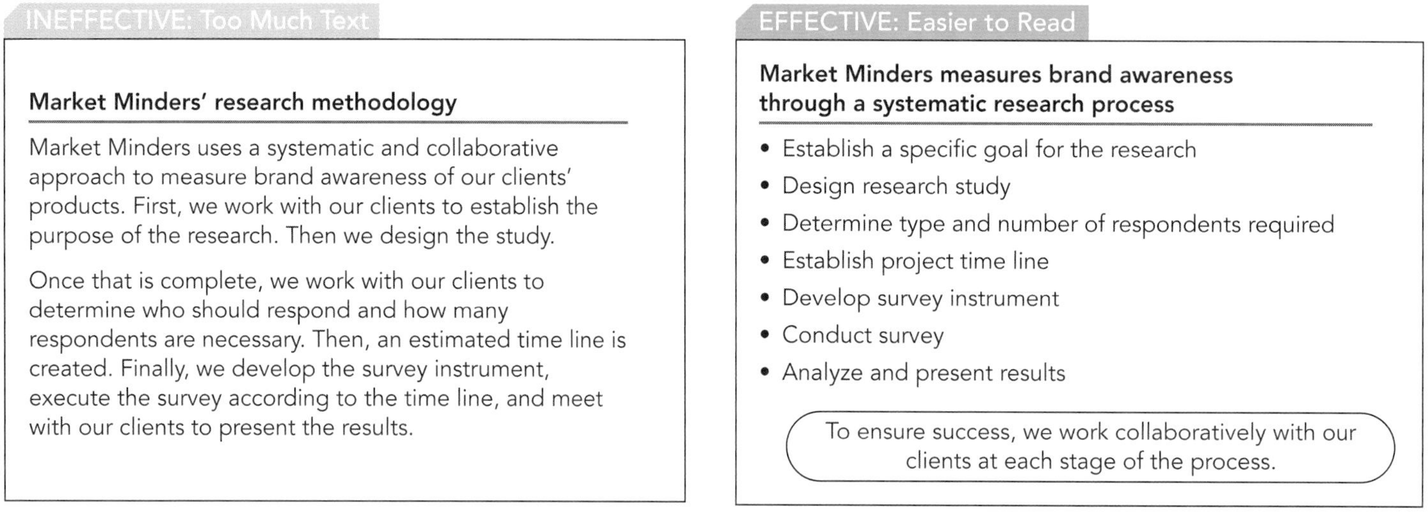

INEFFECTIVE: Too Much Text

Market Minders' research methodology

Market Minders uses a systematic and collaborative approach to measure brand awareness of our clients' products. First, we work with our clients to establish the purpose of the research. Then we design the study.

Once that is complete, we work with our clients to determine who should respond and how many respondents are necessary. Then, an estimated time line is created. Finally, we develop the survey instrument, execute the survey according to the time line, and meet with our clients to present the results.

EFFECTIVE: Easier to Read

Market Minders measures brand awareness through a systematic research process

- Establish a specific goal for the research
- Design research study
- Determine type and number of respondents required
- Establish project time line
- Develop survey instrument
- Conduct survey
- Analyze and present results

To ensure success, we work collaboratively with our clients at each stage of the process.

However, bullets are not appropriate for all text. They work best for lists: items that can be labeled as members of one category, such as reasons, examples, results, solutions, steps, implications, or conclusions. To make the bullets easy to read, be sure they are both logically and grammatically parallel. In other words, all the items should begin with the same part of speech (such as the verbs in Figure 10.10) and be phrased the same way. FIGURE 10.11 illustrates a before and after version of a slide that has been revised for parallelism.

As a general guideline, limit the number of bullets on a slide to six or seven at most. For visual aid presentations, limit the number of words per bullet to six or seven also. For stand-alone presentations, you may need more words.

For text that is not a list, eliminate bullets altogether, and present the content in text boxes, shapes, and diagrams. If you choose to present text in the form of a diagram, be sure to choose a shape that reinforces the content. Avoid diagrams that are chosen only for visual appeal and that do not help your audience better understand the information. As FIGURE 10.12 illustrates, a good diagram will help your audience see the relationships among ideas at a glance.

FIGURE 10.11 Bullet Slide Revised for Parallelism

INEFFECTIVE: No Parallelism

Four potential coatings for the new lenses

- Polylight two-stage CC coating (the newest Polylight)
- Polylight two-stage BB coating (which we use on our current lenses)
- Two single-stage coating systems from different manufacturers
  - Kefvue
  - Reflezene
- Single-lot data has been collected for the BB and CC coatings and multiple-lot data has been collected for the single-stage systems.

At first glance, the four bullets on the "ineffective" slide appear to represent four coating systems. However, the final bullet does not present a coating system at all. Instead, it discusses data collected about those systems.

EFFECTIVE: Better Grouping and Parallelism

Four potential coating systems for the new lenses

- One-stage coating systems
  - Kefvue
  - Reflezene
- Two-stage coating systems
  - Polylight BB coating (used on our current lenses)
  - Polylight CC coating (the newest polylight coating)

We have collected multiple-lot data for the one-stage systems and single-lot data for the two-stage systems.

In the revised slide, the four coatings are divided into two categories and phrased in similar ways. The point about data collection remains on the slide but has been moved to a text box at the bottom of the slide.

FIGURE 10.12 Diagram Slide Revised to Show Relationships

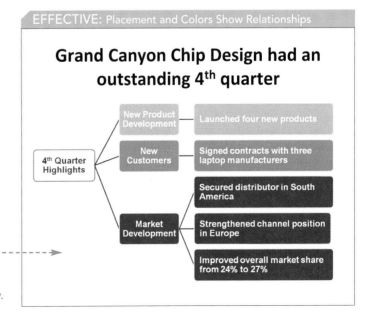

INEFFECTIVE: Does Not Help Audience See Relationships

Grand Canyon Chip Design had an outstanding 4th quarter

Although this circular diagram would be effective for content that is evenly distributed, in this case it implies the fourth-quarter highlights are separate and unrelated.

EFFECTIVE: Placement and Colors Show Relationships

Grand Canyon Chip Design had an outstanding 4th quarter

This diagram helps the audience see at a glance that fourth-quarter highlights fell into three groups: new product development, new customers, and market development. Market development is the biggest category.

Data slides

In business presentations, you will often need to represent numerical data on slides. As FIGURE 10.13 illustrates, graphs typically do a better job than tables of showing the relationships between numbers and the meaning of the data. For more information about developing good graphs, see Chapter 9.

FIGURE 10.13 Quantitative Data Represented as a Table and a Graph

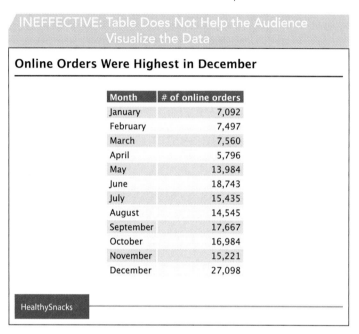

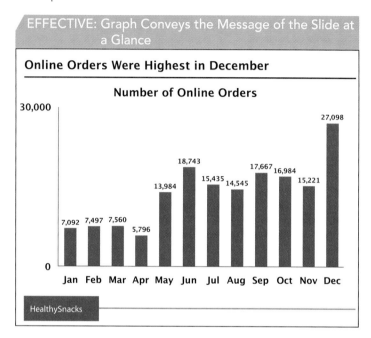

Evaluate your slides in a practice session

As you design your slides, you may be focusing more on how the slide looks than on how you can present the slide. That is why it is important to practice presenting each slide and then to revise the slides to make them easier to present. As you evaluate your slides, consider both the arrangement of content and the animations.

Are the slides easy to present?

For example, consider the ineffective slide in FIGURE 10.14, which presents data about the potential number of total prescriptions for a medication (TRxs), organized by region. The slide is clean, clear, and easy to read. However, it would not be easy to present. What message do you see in the slide? What would you want to say about market potential? Because the regions are ordered geographically, from east to west, no clear message stands out.

By contrast, the effective slide in FIGURE 10.14 is much easier to present. A presenter could look at the slide and say the following: *"While there is substantial sales potential for our product throughout the country, that potential is not divided evenly throughout the sales districts. The graph on this slide is organized by size of potential. As you can see, the West district has over seven times more market potential than the New York Metro District."*

Are animations effective?

Practicing not only allows you to evaluate individual slides, but it also helps you make good decisions about whether to use slide **animations**—software effects that control when and how elements appear on your slides while you present. As a general guide-

FIGURE 10.14 Creating Graphs That Are Easy to Present

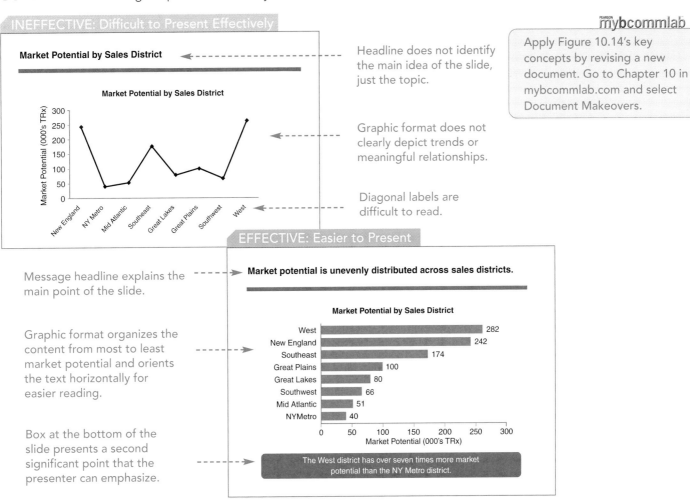

line, use animation only if it helps you present a slide effectively and if you believe it will help your audience better understand your points.

Some presenters like to animate all bullet point lists, making the points appear on the slide one by one. Animating bullet points lets you move sequentially through every point on your slide, discussing each in order of appearance. This technique can be useful to focus your audience's attention on each idea and prevent your audience from spending time reading the slide rather than listening to you.

However, animating bullets can also cause problems. First, the animation requires you to move sequentially through every point on your slide, discussing each one in order of appearance. If your list includes items that you do not want to discuss in detail, the animation calls unnecessary attention to that fact. By contrast, if the entire list appears at once, you can easily introduce it by saying that certain items in the list are most important and you want to focus on those. Second, animations become awkward if you need to return to an earlier slide. You will need to repeat every click going backward and forward, which can be tedious for the audience. Finally, this technique of gradually revealing your points will prevent your audience from seeing the "big picture" of your slide. This can hinder comprehension.

To prevent these problems, animate bullet lists only if you believe the audience will better understand each bullet if it is revealed separately. Similarly, animate diagrams only if the animation helps you present a process or a concept more effectively. For example, if you wanted to present the ACE diagram in a presentation, you might have the Analyzing portion appear first, then Composing, then Evaluating, discussing each part in turn as

Animations Software effects that control when and how elements appear on your slide when you present.

shown in FIGURE 10.15. By the end, the circle would be visible, and you would discuss why ACE is a circular process. In this case, the animation would support your discussion.

FIGURE 10.15 Using Animation to Present Parts of a Diagram

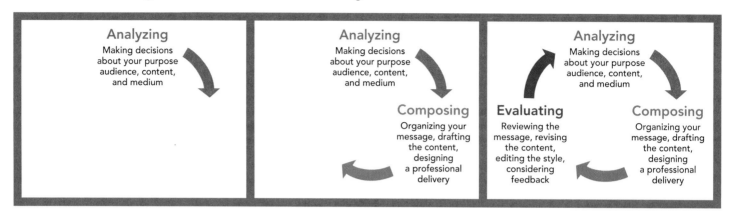

If you choose to use animations in any presentation, follow these guidelines:

- **Be consistent within the presentation.** Use only one technique (for example, *appear, dissolve, fade in)* anywhere you animate entrances and exits within the presentation.
- **Be conservative.** You may think it is entertaining to have items fly in from the left and right. However, this movement will not enhance your content. It will simply distract your audience.
- **Practice.** Presenting an animated slide is more difficult than presenting one without animation. Practice delivering the slide so that you know how to take advantage of the animation. If you find the animation difficult to present, remove it from the slide.

The slide presentation in FIGURE 10.16 incorporates all the ideas from this section. This is the final presentation prepared for Carolyn Reese, Senior Vice President of Planning and Development of Rowland-Grey. A slide presentation is a good medium choice for this scenario. You will be meeting with Ms. Reese and your supervisor in a small conference room that has a projector. While you considered preparing just a handout with no slides, you decided it would be easier to present the problem and solution if you had a visual aid to project in front of the room, to focus your audience's attention. The paper copy of the slides will serve as a handout and will help Ms. Reese justify her decision to support the pilot program.

Create effective handouts

Handouts—documents distributed to the audience during or after a presentation—can take many forms. Standard formats for handouts include slide miniatures, slides with "notes" pages, and supplementary information. Sample handouts are shown in FIGURE 10.17 on page 365.

When creating handouts, use these guidelines:

- **Select a format that best fits your content.** Making handouts of presentation slides is very convenient. However, your presentation may benefit from other types of handouts. For example, if you are making a detailed sales presentation or client proposal, your handout may include product specification sheets or spreadsheets that would be too detailed to read on a screen. Providing that material in handout form is more effective. If you have several resources to share—such as forms, sample designs, or documentation—you can use folders, report covers, or binders to organize your handout materials.
- **Choose an effective format for note taking.** Consider the needs of your audience. Will they want to make notes on your handouts? If so, avoid slide miniatures that fill the entire page with no room for notes. Be sure to leave ample margins or provide other blank space.

FIGURE 10.16 Rowland-Grey Slide Presentation

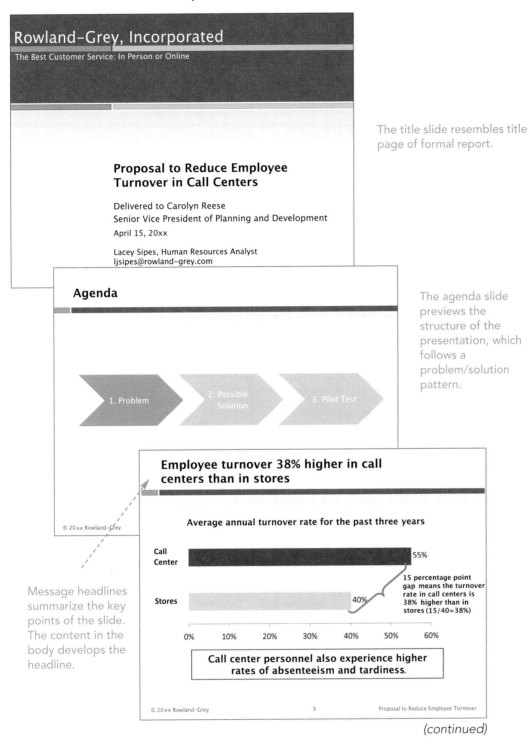

The title slide resembles title page of formal report.

The agenda slide previews the structure of the presentation, which follows a problem/solution pattern.

Message headlines summarize the key points of the slide. The content in the body develops the headline.

(continued)

FIGURE 10.16 Continued

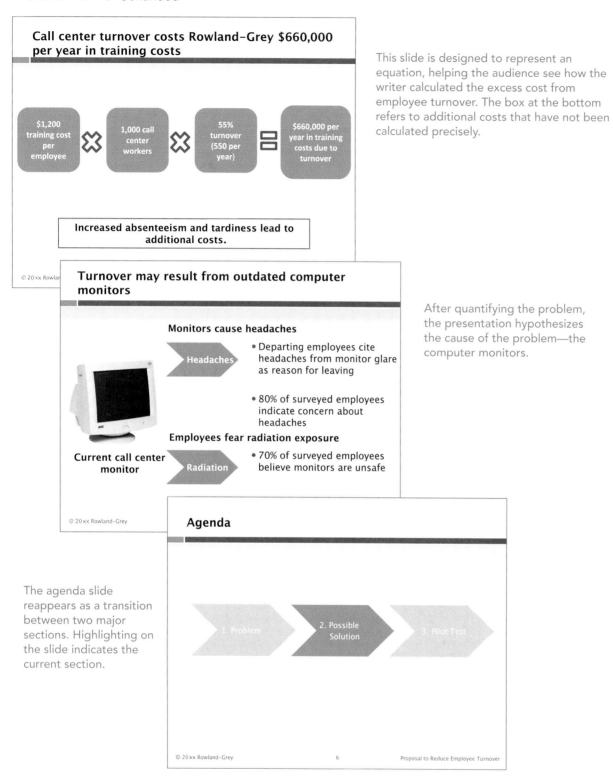

This slide is designed to represent an equation, helping the audience see how the writer calculated the excess cost from employee turnover. The box at the bottom refers to additional costs that have not been calculated precisely.

After quantifying the problem, the presentation hypothesizes the cause of the problem—the computer monitors.

The agenda slide reappears as a transition between two major sections. Highlighting on the slide indicates the current section.

FIGURE 10.16 Continued

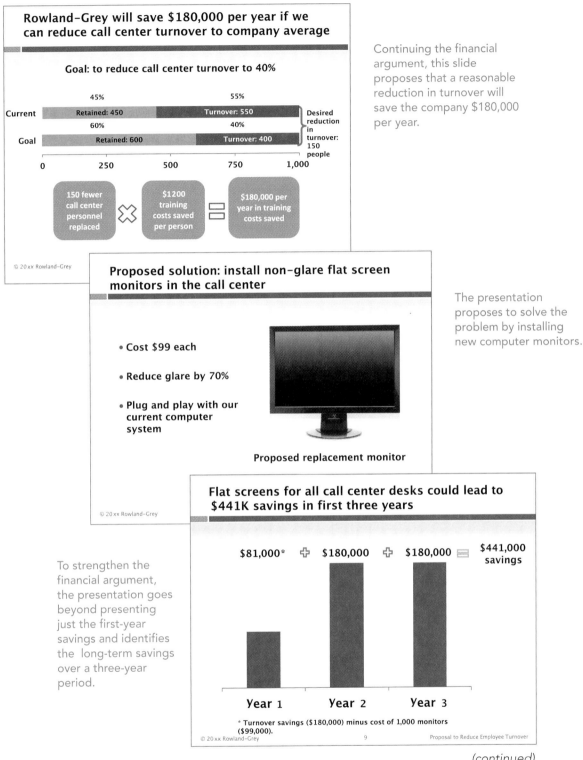

Rowland–Grey will save $180,000 per year if we can reduce call center turnover to company average

Goal: to reduce call center turnover to 40%

Current — 45% Retained: 450 | 55% Turnover: 550

Goal — 60% Retained: 600 | 40% Turnover: 400

Desired reduction in turnover: 150 people

0   250   500   750   1,000

150 fewer call center personnel replaced ✕ $1200 training costs saved per person = $180,000 per year in training costs saved

© 20xx Rowland–Grey

Continuing the financial argument, this slide proposes that a reasonable reduction in turnover will save the company $180,000 per year.

Proposed solution: install non–glare flat screen monitors in the call center

• Cost $99 each

• Reduce glare by 70%

• Plug and play with our current computer system

Proposed replacement monitor

© 20xx Rowland–Grey

The presentation proposes to solve the problem by installing new computer monitors.

Flat screens for all call center desks could lead to $441K savings in first three years

$81,000* ✚ $180,000 ✚ $180,000 ═ $441,000 savings

Year 1   Year 2   Year 3

* Turnover savings ($180,000) minus cost of 1,000 monitors ($99,000).

© 20xx Rowland–Grey   9   Proposal to Reduce Employee Turnover

To strengthen the financial argument, the presentation goes beyond presenting just the first-year savings and identifies the long-term savings over a three-year period.

(continued)

FIGURE 10.16 Continued

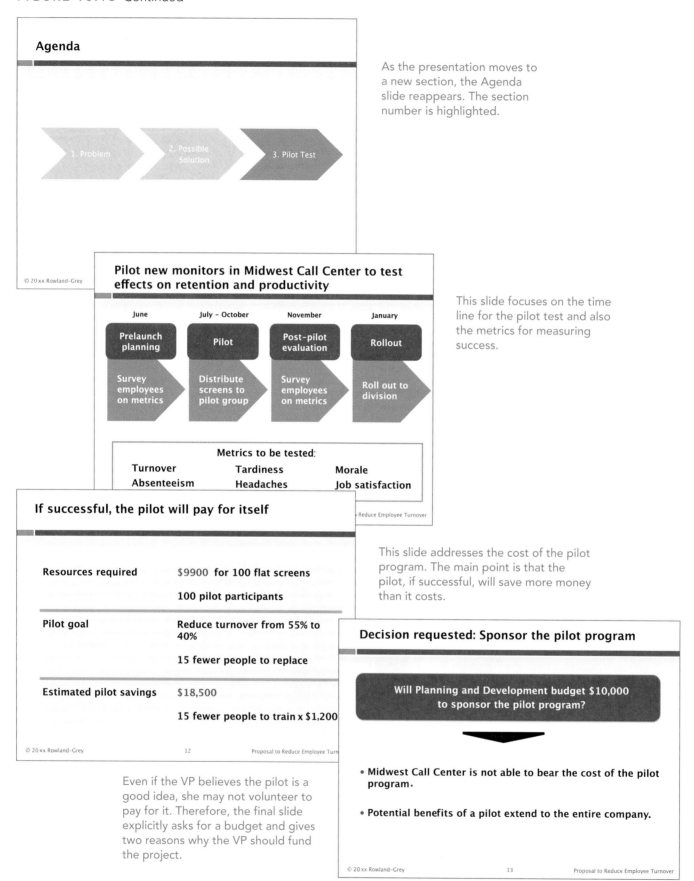

Agenda

1. Problem   2. Possible Solution   3. Pilot Test

© 20xx Rowland-Grey

As the presentation moves to a new section, the Agenda slide reappears. The section number is highlighted.

Pilot new monitors in Midwest Call Center to test effects on retention and productivity

June	July – October	November	January
Prelaunch planning	Pilot	Post-pilot evaluation	Rollout
Survey employees on metrics	Distribute screens to pilot group	Survey employees on metrics	Roll out to division

Metrics to be tested:

| Turnover | Tardiness | Morale |
| Absenteeism | Headaches | Job satisfaction |

Reduce Employee Turnover

This slide focuses on the time line for the pilot test and also the metrics for measuring success.

If successful, the pilot will pay for itself

Resources required	$9900 for 100 flat screens
	100 pilot participants
Pilot goal	Reduce turnover from 55% to 40%
	15 fewer people to replace
Estimated pilot savings	$18,500
	15 fewer people to train x $1,200

© 20xx Rowland-Grey   12   Proposal to Reduce Employee Turn

This slide addresses the cost of the pilot program. The main point is that the pilot, if successful, will save more money than it costs.

Even if the VP believes the pilot is a good idea, she may not volunteer to pay for it. Therefore, the final slide explicitly asks for a budget and gives two reasons why the VP should fund the project.

Decision requested: Sponsor the pilot program

Will Planning and Development budget $10,000 to sponsor the pilot program?

- Midwest Call Center is not able to bear the cost of the pilot program.

- Potential benefits of a pilot extend to the entire company.

© 20xx Rowland-Grey   13   Proposal to Reduce Employee Turnover

FIGURE 10.17 Sample Handout Formats

Slide Miniature Handouts
- Replicate the slides in reduced form
- Are used for stand-alone and report deck presentations
- May not be legible if font sizes are small

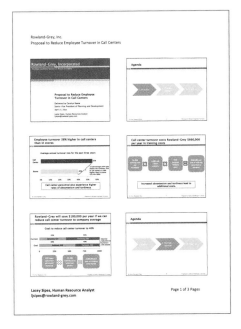

Slides with Notes Pages
- Replicate one slide per page
- Include additional notes for each slide
- Are used for presentations that require explanation

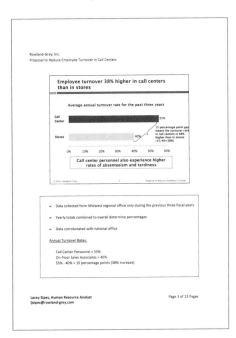

Supplementary Information Handouts
- Many include additional detailed tables, spreadsheets, appendices, or resources
- Are used for presentations that benefit from additional documentation

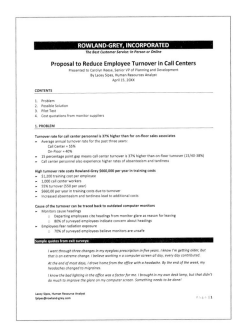

All Handouts Include . . .
- Header with title and name
- Contact information
- Page numbers

- **Consider the impact of color.** Handouts printed in color may be perceived as more impactful than black-and-white documents. However, they are more expensive to produce. Printing handouts in grayscale provides contrast without additional expense.
- **Proofread carefully before copying.** You can easily make changes to your electronic files before your presentation. However, if you find an error after you copy your handouts, printing and recopying them will cost extra time and money.
- **Make extra copies.** Even if you think you know how large your audience will be, make 10 percent more handouts in case extra people show up or someone wants to share copies with colleagues who couldn't attend your presentation.
- **Decide when to distribute your handouts.** In some situations, you may want to distribute your handouts as your audience enters the room. They can preview the topic and begin to think about your information before the presentation begins. In other cases, you may want to distribute the handouts right when you begin. Having handouts during the presentation allows the audience to make notes and identify question areas as they follow along. If you do not want your audience to read a handout while you are presenting, you may decide to provide handouts only at the end as take-aways.

TECHNOLOGY
Using Hyperlinks in Presentations

At first glance, slide presentations appear to be very linear, forcing a presenter to march forward slide by slide, taking no detours. However, presentation programs like PowerPoint offer the ability to present slides out of order, link to other presentations, launch other programs, and even load up a website through the use of hyperlinks.

When Would You Use a Hyperlink?

- To link to a detailed appendix slide containing a complex table or spreadsheet that you don't intend to present unless someone asks. During the presentation, if someone asks for this information, you can jump to the appendix and go into more detail.
- To create a "home" link at the bottom corner of every slide that returns you to a navigation or index page containing links to the various sections of your presentation. This approach gives you the option of presenting slides in the order that most interests your audience.
- To link to a website you are describing in your presentation.
- To launch another file, such as a Word document, spreadsheet, or a slide in another presentation.

- To create a multiple choice or yes/no option for your audience. By clicking the "Yes" link, the presentation displays a different slide than if you had clicked the "No" link.

Hyperlinks help you create interactive presentations and give you the ability to navigate through your presentation in any way you like. To insert a hyperlink in PowerPoint, use the following instructions. If you use different presentation software, explore the help files to find similar instructions.

1. Use your cursor to select text, an autoshape, or an image (note: you cannot insert a hyperlink on a blank slide).
2. Go to *Insert* on the menu bar.
3. Select *Hyperlink*—the Insert Hyperlink menu will be displayed.
4. Select the object you want to *Link to*.
5. Enter the *Text to display*.
6. Click *OK*, and the hyperlink will be created.

Note that the hyperlink is active only in the Slide Show mode of PowerPoint. Also, when you click on a hyperlink that moves you to another slide in the presentation, you can return to the previous slide by right-clicking on the slide and selecting *Last Viewed*.

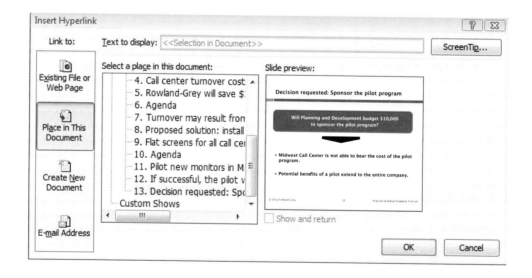

Shrinking the Size of Presentation Files

Presentation files can become quite large, making them difficult to email and share. Here are some technology tips you can use to shrink your files in PowerPoint. If you use different presentation software, check that program's help files for similar tips.

- **Compress your pictures.** Picture files are often very large, and when you place those pictures into your PowerPoint file, the size of your PowerPoint file also will get larger. Fortunately, PowerPoint gives you the option to compress pictures, decreasing their file size while not decreasing resolutions. Here's how you do it:

  1. Select the picture so the Picture Tools menu is active, and then click *Compress Pictures* on the menu bar.
  2. Under "Apply compression settings now," do one of the following:

     To compress just the current picture, check *Apply to selected picture only*.

     To compress all the pictures in your presentation, leave the checkbox blank.
  3. Click the "Options," button and select both check boxes to "Automatically perform basic compression on save" and "Delete cropped areas of pictures." Under "Target output," select the format you will use: printouts, screen displays, or email attachments.
  4. Click *OK*.

  5. If prompted, click *OK* in the "Compress Pictures" dialog box.

- **Use Insert to bring in images.** Don't copy and paste or drag images into PowerPoint. Instead, include images in PowerPoint files using the Insert function. When you copy and paste (or drag) an image into PowerPoint, PowerPoint may create an embedded object that is much larger than an inserted picture. To insert an image, on the Insert menu, point to "Picture," and then click *From File* and browse to that image.

- **Turn off Fast Saves.** In older versions of PowerPoint, "Fast Saves" save presentations with extra data. To turn off Fast Saves in versions before PowerPoint 2007, go to the *Tools* menu, click *Options*, click the *Save* tab, and then clear the *Allow fast saves* check box. Doing this forces PowerPoint to remove excess data from your presentation file each time you save. After turning off Fast Saves, save your presentation again under a new name. On the File menu, click *Save As*, type a name for the new version of your presentation in the File name box, and then click *OK*.

PEARSON
mybcommlab

For a TECHNOLOGY exercise, go to Exercise 14 on page 385 or to this chapter's End-of-Chapter Exercises at mybcommlab.com.

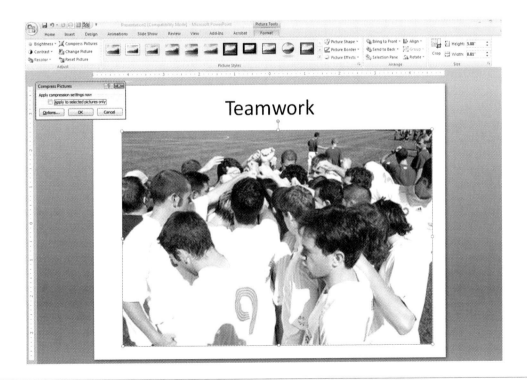

How do I deliver and evaluate the presentation?

Many people get nervous when making presentations. Their minds go blank, their hands shake, or they talk too quickly or too softly. Even if you don't suffer from these problems, you can enhance your oral communication skills so you can stand out among your peers. The only way to become a good presenter is to practice. This section offers you proven tips for presenting effectively. Pick one or two specific items to work on each time you practice your presentation. In time, you will incorporate all of them into your presenting technique.

new hires @ work

Rasheite Radcliff

Substitute Teacher

Greeley Alternative School

The University of South Florida, 2008

"I've found the more I practice, the more comfortable I am during a presentation and the more at ease I look, which leads to a successful presentation and an attentive audience."

Set the stage

- **Practice (out loud).** It's easy to feel nervous when you are not well prepared. Presenting is like an athletic performance. A presenter needs to get ready—just as an athlete would practice regularly and then stretch to warm up. Practice means saying the words out loud, not merely going over them in your head, to create a "sound image" to recall during your actual presentation.

- **Dress for the part.** For formal presentations, wear business-formal clothing, similar to what you would wear to a job interview (see Chapter 12 for a description of business formal). Even in less formal presentations, dress with care. Wear clothing that looks neat and allows you to move comfortably. You want people to pay attention to you, not your clothing. Empty your pockets of keys or loose change that can jingle when you move. Avoid distracting jewelry—and, of course, turn off cell phones.

- **Arrive early and warm up.** Warming up can take several forms. Greet your audience, introduce yourself, and get used to talking with them. Use relaxation techniques to focus your mind and relieve stress. Breathe deeply from your diaphragm to control the adrenaline and relax the neck and jaw muscles. This will help you project your voice. Take a quick look at your notes, and review your opening and closing remarks to refresh your memory. Double-check handouts and equipment to give yourself peace of mind.

- **Set up all equipment and props.** If you plan to use presentation slides, turn on the projector and have the title slide in place when the presentation begins. If you prefer to begin with a dark screen and display the title slide later, in PowerPoint you can strike the letter "B" to blacken the screen. Striking "B" again will make your slide appear. If you're using flipcharts, a whiteboard, or props, make sure they are positioned to be easy to reach during your presentation.

- **Decide where you will stand.** Whenever possible, avoid standing behind lecterns and large desks or tables because they create a barrier between you and the audience. If you are using a projector, position yourself on one side of the screen so that you do not have to walk between the screen and the projector's light. Clear space around the projector and other equipment so that you have plenty of room to move around comfortably and approach the audience. Using a remote control to change slides can help you navigate your presentation space.

- **Keep the lights up and attention on you.** If you choose a technology that requires low light, plan to begin speaking with the lights on. This guarantees that attention will be where you want it—on you and your message. It can be very effective to start your presentation before projecting any visuals. Connect with the audience and then move to the slides.

- **Have water available.** If you are speaking for a long time, you will need to drink water to prevent your mouth from drying out and your vocal cords from being constricted.

Control your body

- **Start from a ready position to control body movements.** Before you begin to speak, get your body into position, just as you would get into position to swing a bat in baseball or make a jump shot in basketball. Try this stance:
  - hands loose at your side
  - knees and elbows relaxed

- weight balanced on both feet
- feet shoulder width apart

  If this does not feel comfortable to you, find a position that does. Once you're in that comfortable and confident position, your gestures and movements will feel more natural.

- **Maintain good eye contact with your audience.** Keeping eye contact is critical for success. If you are using slides or a white board, you may be tempted to move away from the audience and turn toward your visual. However, the only way to keep your audience involved is to face them and look them in the eye. Hold contact with one person for two or three seconds, and then move to another. Engage everyone in your audience, not just the decision makers or those who are sitting front and center.

- **Smile.** Like eye contact, smiling is a must. A smile projects energy and makes you appear happy to be presenting. It also relaxes facial muscles to help you get the most from your speaking voice. Finally, it encourages your audience to smile in return, which will make them more receptive to your presentation. They will find it hard to argue with a smiling person.

- **Animate with body language.** Rather than standing in one position, let your body move. Move away from the projector and screen, lean forward, and walk toward your audience. Use natural hand gestures to punctuate your points, just as you would in conversation. Do not think too much about gesturing. Just take your hands out of your pockets, unclasp them, and let them work naturally.

Use your voice effectively

- **Speak to the back of the room.** Speaking to the back of the room will help you adjust your volume so that you project your voice effectively. When you make eye contact with people in the front of the room, maintain the same level of volume so that people throughout the room can hear you. Too often, speakers lower their voices when they answer questions from people in the front of the room. Even in a small room, the person who cannot hear you will feel left out.

- **Speak slowly, especially at the beginning of the presentation.** Your audience may need a few minutes to get used to your way of speaking. You can help them by speaking slowly and enunciating clearly, especially at the beginning of your presentation.

- **Modulate your voice.** Nothing destroys audience attention more than a monotone presenter. One technique for animating your voice is to emphasize important words and phrases. If you are using slides, take your cue from the words you emphasized on the slides with color contrast or boldface.

- **Minimize verbal tics.** Many people unconsciously use certain words as fillers—for example, *"like," "okay,"* and *"you know."* Be aware of your own speaking habits, and practice eliminating them in your speech.

- **Use pauses—a remedy for the "ers" and "ums."** Pausing intentionally is one of the best ways to prevent *"ers"* and *"ums"* because you give yourself permission to be silent. Silence can be a speaker's ally, not enemy. A quiet moment gives the audience time to process your information and signals that something new is coming.

Present your visuals effectively

- **Introduce each visual by explaining your intended point.** One picture may be worth a thousand words, but people are likely to interpret the picture in their own words, which may be different from yours. To be sure that the audience sees what *you* intended, introduce the slide as soon as it appears. For text slides, do not read the slide word for word. Just explain the purpose or main point of the slide, and then give the audience a few moments to look at it before you launch into your discussion. For tables, identify how the table is organized and what appears in the columns and rows. For graphs, identify what the graph is depicting, what each axis is measuring, and the key point.

  For example, if you were presenting the slide shown in FIGURE 10.18 from the Rowland-Grey presentation, you might say something similar to the quoted text in the annotation.

- **Direct attention to visuals with hand gestures and words.** Visuals need your help to make a point. The best practice is to refer directly to material on a slide. You can move

FIGURE 10.18 Introduce Visuals

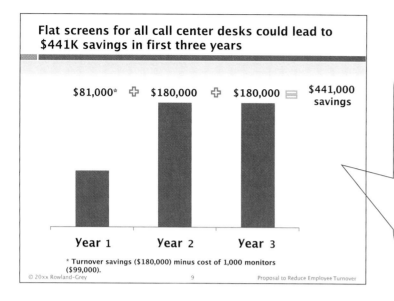

toward the side (but not turn your back on the audience), gesture to the screen, and direct your audience's attention with words: *"Moving from left to right . . ."* or *"At the center of the chart . . ."* If you place arrows and other highlighting marks directly on your slides, you can refer to those. Laser pointers help indicate a particular spot on the slide, but use them quickly to direct the audience's attention, and then turn them off.

- **Take cues from your visuals and avoid a handful of note cards or a word-for-word script.** You may want to have notes available as a backup. But taking cues from visual aids is more effective than holding a deck of note cards or following a presentation script. Reading from notes or a script does not build rapport with your audience. In addition, holding on to cards or paper prevents natural gestures and makes you look like a student in a speech class rather than a professional in a business setting. If you need more memory cues than your visuals provide, try penciling notes on a flipchart or glancing discreetly at notes placed on a nearby table.

- **Do not apologize for nervousness or mistakes.** If you forget what you plan to say or make a mistake, do not apologize. This takes attention away from your content. Just take a deep breath, regroup, and move ahead.

Coordinate with your team

If you are presenting as a team, follow these guidelines.

- **Take advantage of everyone's strengths.** In a class, your instructor may require that everyone on your team participate equally in the presentation. However, in business, the only reason to plan a team presentation is to take advantage of each person's strengths and knowledge. Ensure that everyone who is presenting has a defined role in the presentation and that the team projects a unified and confident image. The whole should be greater than the sum of the parts.

- **Decide how you will handle introductions.** Will the first presenter introduce everyone at the beginning? Or will people introduce themselves? This may seem like a minor point, but unless you have planned this, the team members may start talking over each other.

- **Practice transitions from person to person.** During team presentations, each speaker needs to make a connection between his or her content and the next speaker's. As you finish speaking, introduce the next speaker and topic making that connection. For example, *"Now that I've outlined the budget issues, Marla Whitt from IT will discuss implementation plans."* These transitions help the audience follow the flow of your presentation.

- **Let your teammates speak.** If your teammate forgets to mention a point or presents material differently from the way you'd like it explained, do not interrupt to expand on the answer. Doing that will damage the image of your team and undermine your teammate. Allow your teammate to finish. You can come back to the point later.

- **Correct a teammate only when necessary.** If your teammate fumbles or says something wrong, do not jump in to correct, especially if the point is not very important. If it is an important point that must be clarified, make the correction very politely and considerately.
- **Be prepared to present other teammates' slides.** Emergencies arise and teammates may be late to a presentation, or they may not come at all. Be sure that you are able to present every slide in the presentation in case you need to step in at the last moment.

Evaluate the audience's response

During the presentation, "listen" to the audience's feedback. Are they nodding in agreement with you or nodding off from boredom? Do they look interested in your content or confused by it? Listening while you present can be challenging, since you are also trying to think about what to say, navigate your slides, and maintain good eye contact. However, if you can gauge your audience's response as you are speaking, you have the opportunity to revise and adjust. Consider the following strategies to "listen" while you present.

- **Pause between sections.** Scan the audience during transitions between slides or between major ideas. Do they seem attentive and interested?
- **Ask questions.** Unless you want to open the floor to a Q&A session, limit questions during your presentation to close-ended inquiries that assess the audience's participation. For example, if you see someone looking confused, you could say, "I know this process is complicated. Does anyone need additional explanation?"

After the presentation, reflect on your audience's overall response:

- Were there points in the presentation where the audience nodded in agreement?
- Did anything confuse or amuse the audience?
- Did you get the kinds of questions you expected?
- What surprised you?
- Could you have prevented any confusion or disagreement by presenting something differently?

By answering these questions, you can evaluate your approach and your performance—and plan what to repeat or what to change the next time you present.

Adapt your approach for online presentations

Not all presentations are delivered face to face. Given the expense of traveling and the ease of connecting with others on the Internet, you may be asked to present your material to distant audiences online using one of the many available online presentation tools such as WebEx, Go To Meeting, Yuuguu, or even Skype. Or you may choose to upload your presentation to Slideshare so that your audiences can access it during a telephone meeting.

Delivering presentations over the web presents a different set of challenges than presenting face to face in a small meeting or larger group setting. You will need to address each of these challenges to be a successful online presenter.

- **Ensure your audience has connectivity.** When you make a presentation face to face, you are the only one who has to worry about technology—does your computer work? Can it connect to the projector? In contrast, when you deliver a presentation online, you need to confirm with your audience that they are connected and can see the presentation. Did they get the link you sent them? Can they log on to any special software you are using? Wait for them to confirm they can see your presentation document on their own screen before you begin.

- **Make a plan for controlling what your audience sees on their screens.** Some online presentation software allows you to "share your screen," which means the audience sees on their screen exactly what's on your screen. As the presenter, you can control what they see and move forward from slide to slide at the pace you want. In this case, the online presentation resembles an in-person meeting. Other presentation technologies require the audience to have a copy of the presentation on their screens, which they control independently (equivalent to having sent them an email attachment that they can open on their own machine). When your audience can move through the slides independently, you need to provide cues about where you are in the presentation. For example, you can say, *"Here on slide 3, you can see . . . On the next slide, slide 4 . . ."* For this reason, it is important to remember to number your slides. If you direct the audience to the specific slide number, they will more likely focus on what you want them to see when you want them to see it rather than click ahead (or lag behind) in the presentation.
- **Open the meeting early and put a welcome slide on your computer screen,** confirming meeting details if you are using a screen-sharing program such as WebEx. This early start will allow those new to the technology to become familiar with the interface while they wait.
- **Use a webcam or provide a picture** to help establish rapport with attendees. If you are using a webcam, look frequently at the camera (rather than at the screen) so that remote people feel that you are making eye contact with them. If you are not using a webcam, you can display a picture of yourself on the welcome slide to help the audience visualize you.

ETHICS Avoiding Plagiarism in Presentations

In Chapters 7 and 9, you learned rules for avoiding plagiarism in research reports. But what about in presentations? Do the same rules apply?

1. **Is it acceptable for your presentation to include a photo found on the Internet? Do you need to acknowledge the source?** If you use a photo published on the Internet or in any other publication, you must acknowledge the source in your presentation. You can include a source citation directly below the photo. However, if you are using your presentation for any commercial purposes—or if you are distributing it widely—for example, on Slideshare or in customer meetings—just acknowledging the source is not enough. You must get permission from the original owner of the photo to use it. For example, if you create a presentation to persuade firms to invest in India and want to use a photo of new skyscrapers in India to communicate economic growth, you must acquire the rights to use that photo by contacting the photographer or other copyright holder. As the U.S. Copyright office says: "Acknowledging the source of the copyrighted material does not substitute for obtaining permission."[4]

2. **If you purchase a license to use a presentation photo from a digital media source such as Getty Images or Corbis Images, do you need to acknowledge the source?** If you purchase a license to use a professional photograph—or you commission a custom photograph—you do not need to acknowledge the sourse and you may use the photo in your presentations in any way allowed by the terms of the license. Some photos are "royalty free." This means you can use them multiple times for a single fee. Other photos come with more restrictions.

3. **If other people in your company or organization have created effective slides, is it acceptable to use those slides in your business presentation? Do you need to acknowledge the source?** Within an organization, it is usually acceptable to share slides to use in presentations made on behalf of the organization. In fact, some companies create slide libraries to encourage employees to use slides that have been pre-approved, especially for customer and other public presentations. Since your company "owns" the slide you are borrowing, you do not have to acknowledge the source.

4. **If you find a slide template that you like on the web, is it acceptable to copy that slide template if you don't copy any of the content?** Graphic designs can be copyrighted in the same way content is copyrighted. If someone is selling a slide template design through the Internet, you may purchase and use it. However, if you simply download a presentation file from the Internet and decide to use it for your presentation, you may be violating someone's copyright.

5. **If you include other people's work in your presentation—for example, data from another source—how do you acknowledge it?** Typically, you will acknowledge a data source under the graph or table that uses the data. Similarly, if you "borrow" concepts or ideas from another author, acknowledge it right on that slide. In business presentations, many slides contain "footnotes" that acknowledge information sources. For examples of acknowledging sources on presentation slides, see Appendix C. ■

PEARSON **mybcommlab**

For an ETHICS exercise, go to Exercise 20 on page 385 or to this chapter's End-of-Chapter Exercises at mybcommlab.com.

- **Use good telephone etiquette.** Online presentations are like phone calls, so good phone etiquette applies. This means you need a good connection and good equipment so your audience can hear you. Speakerphones can work if you want to be hands-free, but you may hear occasional static. Good headsets can also work, but test them first. Whether you use a traditional land-line service or Internet-based telephony such as Skype or Google Talk, establish your voice connection before you have your audience look at the presentation document.
- **Engage the audience with voice and screen movement.** With an online presentation, you cannot use body language, but you can engage the audience with excellent vocal delivery. To further engage the audience, plan for motion on the screen. Provide annotations on slides or use pointers to draw your audience's attention.
- **Invite questions frequently.** When you make an online presentation, you can't get visual feedback from your audience. As a result, it's important to hear from them frequently. If the audience remains silent, you may not know if they are confused or if they have fallen asleep. Ask for specific questions after each major point to ensure understanding.

Study Question 10.4

How do I handle questions and answers?

During a presentation, a question-and-answer (Q&A) session offers many benefits.

- The most effective presentations are interactive. You can make your presentation interactive by asking for questions.
- As a presenter, you are likely to learn something important from questions, especially how well your audience understands your points.
- Questions also give you a chance to emphasize and expand important points.
- An exchange with the audience helps build your credibility by demonstrating your expertise and openness.
- Skillful replies help you diffuse criticism and objections.

Answering questions during a presentation is a form of **impromptu speaking**, speaking without advance knowledge of the topic or question. People often get nervous when required to speak spontaneously. This section offers advice about how to plan in advance for a Q&A session and how to structure good answers to questions.

Plan for a question-and-answer (Q&A) session

Anticipate questions and plan short answers. The main problem people face in impromptu speaking is the temptation to ramble. In other words, people talk aimlessly until they discover the point they want to make. The following advice will help you avoid that problem.

- **Anticipate.** Think in advance about questions your audience is likely to ask and plan short answers.
- **Map out an answer in your head.** Though it may be difficult to organize your impromptu thoughts, mentally note or write down a few key points you want to cover to keep on track.
- **Keep your answers short.** Begin with the shortest possible version of the answer and then stop. If people require additional information, they'll ask follow-up questions.

Decide how your team will handle questions. In a team presentation, you will want to avoid having team members look at each other blankly, waiting for someone else to answer. You will also want to avoid having multiple members trying to answer a question at the same time. Consider one of the following options for handling questions as a team. Both options depend on the team making a plan in advance about who will answer what kind of question.

new hires @ work

Anthony Boney
Mortgage Specialist
Bank of America
North Carolina A&T State University, 2008

"I'm a good presenter, but the tricky part is the Q&A. Thinking on your feet is tough when important decision makers are there. I try to keep the big picture in mind so I don't get lost in the details."

Impromptu speaking Speaking without advance knowledge of the topic or question.

- **Assign one team member to facilitate the Q&A session.** That team member will ask for questions and "assign" them to the team member designated to answer that kind of question. The facilitator may also answer questions, but must be careful not to answer too many. Otherwise, he or she will seem to be claiming the spotlight.
- **Allow team members to decide whether a question falls under their designated area.** For this option to work well, the team member should not just launch into the answer. Instead, identify that you plan to answer it by saying something like, *"I'll take that question."* This signals to the rest of the team that the question is covered, and it prevents two people beginning to answer at the same time.

Set up the Q&A session in your introduction. Tell the audience what to expect. Should they ask questions as you go? Or save them to the end? Even if you ask your audience to hold questions until the end, you will need to be prepared for the audience member who wants to ask questions during your presentation. In that situation, the best way to stay on track is to provide a brief answer and to promise to provide more detail at the end of the presentation. When you're ready for questions, do not ask, *"Are there any questions?"* Encourage participation by asking, *"What questions do you have?"*

Answer questions skillfully

Give a three-part answer. A good answer has three parts. First, restate or summarize the question to be sure everyone heard it and that you understand it correctly. Repeating also gives you time to think of an answer. Second, respond in headlines or lead sentences. Give the main point of your response at the beginning and then follow up with details. Otherwise, you may appear to be disorganized or evasive. As you answer, avoid looking only at the person who asked the question. You will want to get the entire room involved in caring about—and understanding—your point. Finally, return to the original questioner to verify that you have provided a sufficient answer.

Break long and complex questions into parts. If you get a complex question that is difficult to answer, try breaking it into parts by listing the segments on a flipchart or whiteboard. Then answer each part separately, referring back to your list.

Be honest. If someone asks a question you cannot answer, don't be afraid to say, *"I don't know."* Credibility disappears when a speaker gets caught making up an answer. Just admit that you need to find the answer and then follow up with the questioner as soon as possible.

Avoid being defensive or dismissive. Some types of questions tempt presenters to defend themselves or dismiss the audience's concerns. These types of questions require especially skillful answers:

- **A hostile question.** If a questioner seems antagonistic, be careful not to become defensive. First, reframe the question, stating it in a way that seems less hostile and more objective. Then acknowledge the other person's position and try to identify the source of the objection. Work on creating a mutual understanding of the issue rather than trying to be "right."
- **A question you plan to answer later.** If you plan to answer the question later, don't dismiss the question by saying *"I'll get to that later."* Instead, give the questioner a short answer immediately and then mention that more detail will follow. That should satisfy that person's need to know and keep him or her paying attention.
- **An idea that you've already rejected.** If someone raises an alternative you have already rejected, don't be too quick to dismiss the idea. The person could get defensive. Acknowledge the possible value of the alternative, and then explain objectively the reasoning that led you to reject it.
- **A question that takes the presentation off track.** If someone uses a question to try to take over the meeting, look for an opportunity to regain control of the discussion. Don't dismiss or insult the questioner by indicating that the question is irrelevant or off point. Instead, refer to the meeting agenda or the map of the presentation to get back on track.

CULTURE Meeting Audience Expectations

If you have the opportunity to deliver a business presentation in a cross-cultural setting, you may need to adjust some of your presentation habits to meet audience expectations. The following examples illustrate some changes you may need to adopt:

Feature of the Presentation	Presenting to U.S. Audiences	Presenting to Audiences from Other Cultures
Introductions	After introducing themselves, presenters often go directly to the content of their presentation.	In more formal and more hierarchical cultures, politeness dictates that presenters acknowledge and thank the senior members of their audience for attending before beginning the presentation.
Speed	U.S. audiences often prefer a fast-paced presentation style that quickly gets to the point.	In Europe and Asia, audiences often prefer presentations that are slower and offer them an opportunity to think carefully and process information.
Body Language	U.S. audiences appreciate lively presenters who use expressive body language.	In other cultures, presenters are more reserved and calm. To determine the appropriate use of hand gestures and expression, pay attention to other presenters from that culture. You can often find examples on YouTube and other media sites.
Vocabulary	When presenting to U.S. audiences, you can feel confident people will understand your vocabulary if you use plain business language. Using synonyms for words will typically not confuse your audience.	Though many people in other cultures do speak English, you can help them understand you better by speaking slowly and clearly and by using relatively simple words—for example, avoid "ubiquitous" and instead say "widespread." Remember, too, that some words have different meanings in different cultures. For example, in the United States, the word "billion" means a thousand million. In the United Kingdom, it means a million million. That is a huge difference.
Eye Contact	In the United States, presenters are trained to make eye contact with all members of the audience—and expect the audience to make eye contact in return.	In some Asian cultures, people are uncomfortable with direct eye contact and may look down or away rather than directly at the presenter. In these cultures, lack of eye contact may be a sign of respect.[5]
Reading the Audience	In the United States, if audience members are nodding, that usually means they agree with the presenter. Presenters also look for smiles as signs of agreement.	In some cultures—for example Japan—head nodding means only that the audience understands what the presenter is saying, not that they agree.[6] In some eastern European cultures, such as the Russian culture, smiling is reserved for friends and relatives, people you know well.[7] Stony stares from an Eastern European audience means they are paying attention, not that they are angry.

PEARSON
mybcommlab

For a CULTURE exercise, go to Exercise 25 on page 386 or to this chapter's End-of-Chapter Exercises at mybcommlab.com.

IN SUMMARY, business presentations offer you the opportunity to address a business issue and to impress your audience with your analytic, persuasive, and speaking skills. Using the ACE communication process helps you develop well-organized and targeted content. To communicate that content well, design effective slides, practice both your presentation skills and the specific presentation so that you know how to make each point, and present each slide. Building a confident and professional presentation style offers benefits beyond just improving your business presentations. Being a confident presenter will also help you sell your strengths during job interviews and increase your chances for promotion to leadership positions.

10.1 What do I analyze when planning a business presentation? *(pages 344–347)*

- **Analyze your purpose and outcome: Why?** What do you want to have happen as the outcome of the presentation? Do you want your audience to know something (informational presentation), believe or do something (persuasive presentation), know how to do something (instructional presentation) or work with you during the presentation (collaborative presentation)?
- **Analyze your audience: How many and who?** Understand who they are and what they need to know so you can achieve your outcome.
- **Analyze your setting: When and where?** Consider any constraints or opportunities your setting offers.
- **Analyze your medium options: How?** Identify the medium choices that best fit your needs (and your audience's). Possibilities include slides, handouts, video, audio, podcasts, flipcharts, posters, whiteboards, and props.

10.2 How do I compose the presentation? *(pages 348–367)*

- **Identify the type of presentation.** Slide presentations may be designed to stand alone without a speaker or to serve as a visual aid that requires a speaker to explain. Stand-alone presentations typically use message headlines and more complete content support than visual aid presentations.
- **Organize the content.** Compose an opening that captures audience interest, organize content using a logical pattern, and plan a memorable conclusion.
- **Create a storyboard** before writing detailed slides. A storyboard helps you take the organization you developed and create a story flow.
- **Develop a template.** Choose a simple slide design that will not compete with your content, and create a master slide that uses a consistent set of fonts and design features.
- **Design individual slides** to be easy to understand at a glance. Slides will be more effective if they are not crowded with content. Text can be presented in grammatically parallel bullet points, in text boxes, or in shapes. Diagrams should effectively show relationships. Data slides should make their point clearly. Animations should facilitate the presentation rather than make it more cumbersome.
- **Evaluate your slides in a practice session.** If a slide is not easy to present, redesign it. Determine whether animations will help or hinder your presentation.
- **Create effective handouts.** Select a format that best fits your purpose and your audience's needs.

10.3 How do I deliver and evaluate the presentation? *(pages 368–373)*

- **Set the stage** for a great presentation by warming up before the presentation and by dressing for the part. Arrive early to ensure that all equipment is functioning and to begin establishing rapport with your audience as they arrive.
- **Control your body.** Stand comfortably and confidently, use engaging body language, maintain eye contact with your audience, and smile.
- **Use your voice effectively.** Control your volume by speaking to the back of the room. Speak clearly, enunciate your words, use your voice to emphasize key ideas, and pause (or keep silent) as you are thinking rather than fill the air with "ers" and "ums."
- **Present your visuals effectively.** Introduce each visual by explaining your point, direct attention to visuals with gestures and words, and use visuals as cues rather than referring to note cards or scripts.
- **Coordinate with your team.** Plan speaking roles, transitions, and responsibilities for answering questions.
- **Evaluate the audience's response** by "listening" to the audience's nonverbal feedback.
- **Adapt your approach for online presentations.** Ensure your audience has connectivity, control what the audience sees, open the meeting early, use good telephone etiquette, engage the audience, and invite questions frequently.

10.4 How do I handle questions and answers? *(pages 373–375)*

- **Plan for a question-and-answer (Q&A) session.** Anticipate questions, plan short answers, and begin the presentation by telling the audience when you would like to address questions.
- **Answer questions skillfully,** using a three-part structure: repeat the question, give a short direct answer, and confirm the answer with the original questioner. Be prepared for challenging questions and plan strategies in advance.

PEARSON mybcommlab *Are you an active learner? Go to mybcommlab.com to master Chapter 10 content. Chapter 10 interactive activities include:*

- Customizable Study Plan and Chapter 10 practice quizzes
- Chapter 10 Simulation, Business Presentations, that helps you think critically and prepare to make choices in the business world
- Flash Cards for mastering the definition of chapter terms
- Chapter 10 Video Exercise, Developing Oral & Online Presentations, which shows you how textbook concepts are put into practice every day
- Interactive Lessons that visually review key chapter concepts
- Document Makeovers for hands-on, scored practice in revising documents

WHAT DO I ANALYZE?

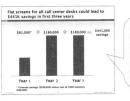

- What is the purpose of my presentation?

- Who is my audience and what do they need to know?

- When and where am I presenting?

- What medium options should I use: slides, a flip chart, white board, video clips, handouts, props?

HOW DO I COMPOSE?

- If I am composing slides, should they be able to stand alone, or are they visual aids?

- How should I organize the presentation? Beginning, middle, and end?

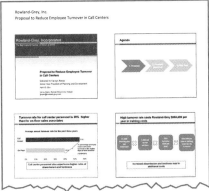

- How do I design individual slides to be clear and easy to understand?

- What handouts do I need?

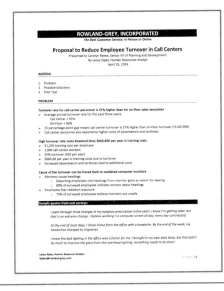

HOW DO I DELIVER AND EVALUATE?

Evaluate while you practice:

- Practice your opening: Is it smooth?

- Practice presenting each slide: If a slide is hard to present, revise it.

- Practice your delivery: Are you speaking loud enough for your audience to hear? Are you comfortable standing in the front of the room?

- Practice coordinating with your team: How will you transition from one person to the next?

- Practice questions and answers: Have you anticipated questions? Did you remember the guidelines for answering questions?

Evaluate while you deliver:

- During the presentation, "listen" to the audience's feedback and adjust your presentation to meet their needs.

- After the presentation, reflect on your audience's overall response and plan what to repeat or change the next time you present.

KEY TERMS QUICK ACCESS REVIEW

Animations *p. 358*

Impromptu speaking *p. 373*

Message headlines *p. 348*

Slide deck *p. 348*

Slide master *p. 353*

Stand-alone presentation *p. 348*

Storyboard *p. 353*

Visual aid presentation *p. 348*

CASE STUDY Culinary Adventure Tour Presentation

This case study will help you review the chapter material by applying it to a specific scenario.

Planning a Presentation

Stephanie Lo graduated from college with a major in French and a minor in communication. She was very happy to get a job with JourneyFree, LLC, a company that specializes in organizing educational tours for students, professionals, and other groups. Ultimately, Stephanie would like to become a tour leader, but for now she is the assistant to the vice president of tour operations, Rachel Jones. Stephanie's role is to work on marketing communications.

Stephanie's first project called on all her strengths—developing communications to market JourneyFree's newest product, a culinary tour of France, specifically designed for culinary arts and nutrition teachers in high schools and trade schools. In addition to advertising online and sending brochures to high schools, Stephanie's supervisor, Rachel, plans to visit school districts in major cities and present the program to superintendents, principals, department chairs, and teachers. She will give a brief and colorful slide presentation and offer samplings of the French food that culinary arts teachers will experience on the tour.

Thirty culinary arts teachers have invited Rachel to give a presentation next week, so she needs a slide presentation fast. She asks Stephanie to design and develop a draft of the presentation. Together they work out the following outline:

- The Educational Experience
- Trip Overview
- Trip Logistics and Costs
- About JourneyFree, LLC
- Q&A

Rachel and Stephanie also discussed the audience and key selling points to make in the presentation. The next day, Stephanie puts together a draft of presentation slides. She is planning to meet Rachel to review the slides and to discuss the talking points that will go with the slides.

Stephanie would like your help in analyzing the audience, evaluating the presentation, and composing the content for the presentation. After the slides, you will find questions designed to help you think systematically about the presentation, using the ACE approach. Answer the questions to review the key concepts in the chapter.

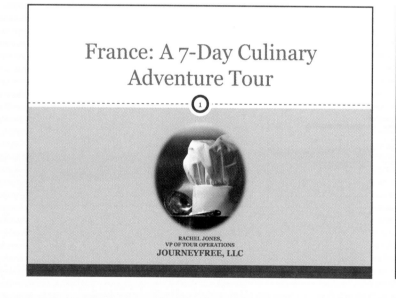

France: A 7-Day Culinary Adventure Tour

①

RACHEL JONES,
VP OF TOUR OPERATIONS
JOURNEYFREE, LLC

Why this tour will help culinary teachers

②

- Explore range of French culinary arts over a fun-filled seven-day journey through France
- Diversify and expand knowledge of culinary teachers in your vocational high schools
- Foster a stronger connection between teachers and French gastronomic culture

Slide 3 — Today's Itinerary

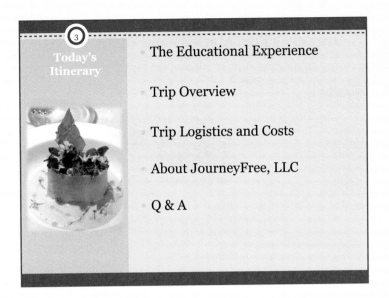

Today's Itinerary

- The Educational Experience
- Trip Overview
- Trip Logistics and Costs
- About JourneyFree, LLC
- Q & A

Slide 4 — The Educational Experience
Why do teachers need this trip?

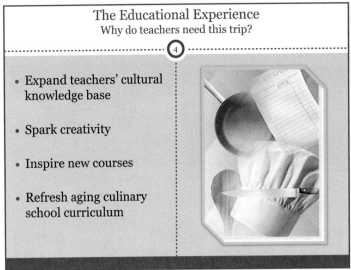

- Expand teachers' cultural knowledge base
- Spark creativity
- Inspire new courses
- Refresh aging culinary school curriculum

Slide 5 — The "Educational Vacation" Experience

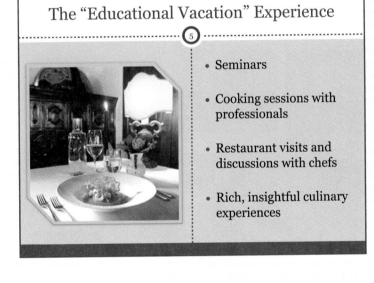

- Seminars
- Cooking sessions with professionals
- Restaurant visits and discussions with chefs
- Rich, insightful culinary experiences

Slide 6 — Today's Itinerary

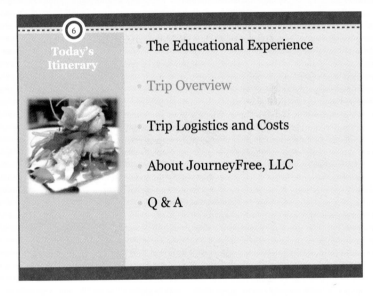

Today's Itinerary

- The Educational Experience
- Trip Overview
- Trip Logistics and Costs
- About JourneyFree, LLC
- Q & A

Slide 7 — Why France?

- The cooking capital of the world
- Each region offers new culinary wonders
- Less costly than one might think

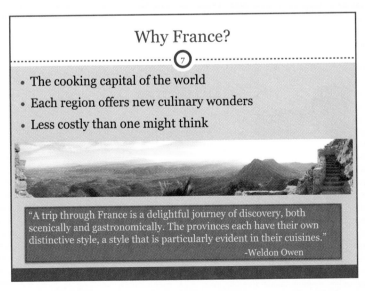

"A trip through France is a delightful journey of discovery, both scenically and gastronomically. The provinces each have their own distinctive style, a style that is particularly evident in their cuisines."

-Weldon Owen

Slide 8 — An Overview of the Trip
A Seven-Day Journey

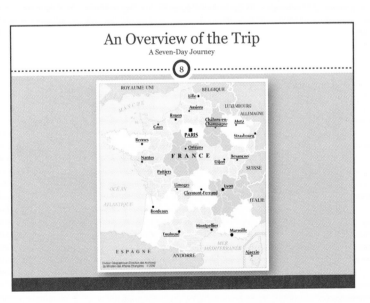

Paris and the Cordon Bleu

Brittany's Fish Markets and Pastry Shops

The Loire Valley Chateaus

The Bordeaux Region and Its Vineyards

The Markets of Marseille and Gastronomy of Provence

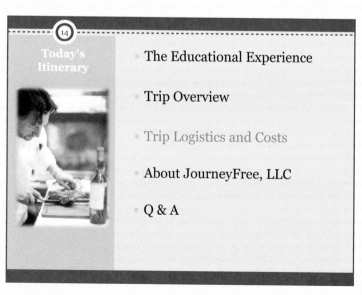

Today's Itinerary

- The Educational Experience
- Trip Overview
- Trip Logistics and Costs
- About JourneyFree, LLC
- Q & A

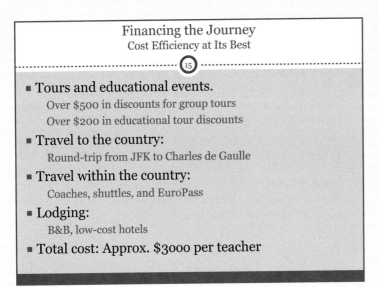

Financing the Journey
Cost Efficiency at Its Best

15

- **Tours and educational events.**
  - Over $500 in discounts for group tours
  - Over $200 in educational tour discounts
- **Travel to the country:**
  - Round-trip from JFK to Charles de Gaulle
- **Travel within the country:**
  - Coaches, shuttles, and EuroPass
- **Lodging:**
  - B&B, low-cost hotels
- **Total cost: Approx. $3000 per teacher**

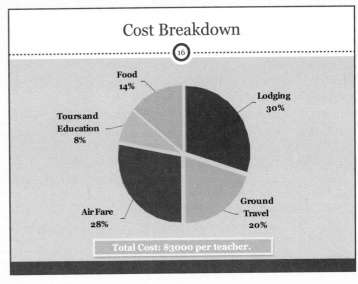

Cost Breakdown

16

Food 14%
Lodging 30%
Tours and Education 8%
Ground Travel 20%
Air Fare 28%

Total Cost: $3000 per teacher.

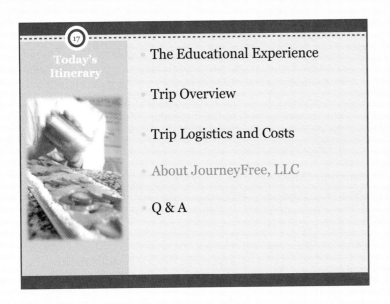

17

Today's Itinerary

- The Educational Experience
- Trip Overview
- Trip Logistics and Costs
- About JourneyFree, LLC
- Q & A

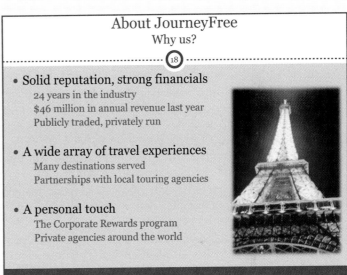

About JourneyFree
Why us?

18

- **Solid reputation, strong financials**
  - 24 years in the industry
  - $46 million in annual revenue last year
  - Publicly traded, privately run
- **A wide array of travel experiences**
  - Many destinations served
  - Partnerships with local touring agencies
- **A personal touch**
  - The Corporate Rewards program
  - Private agencies around the world

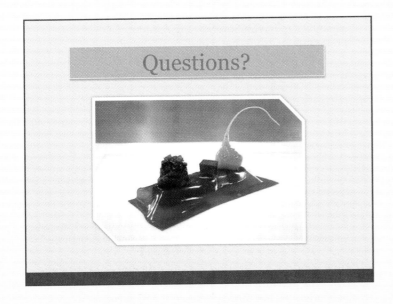

Questions?

Questions for Reviewing the Culinary Adventure Tour Presentation

Analyzing Purpose and Audience

1. What is the purpose of this presentation? Is it primarily informative or persuasive?

2. The ideal outcome of the presentation is that teachers sign up for the trip—or schools fund teachers for the trip. Should the slides end by asking for a "sale"? Or should the presenter do that orally? Or should the presenter leave the audience to think about the content and follow up later to sign up?

3. Imagine yourself as the target audience: high school teachers and administrators. What questions do you think they will have? Does this presentation leave any important questions unanswered?

Reviewing the Structure and Composing Oral Content

4. The slides themselves do not begin with a compelling opening. Brainstorm what Rachel could say as she begins her presentation.

5. The presentation is divided into five parts. Do you think this is an effective structure? If so, why? If not, why not?

6. Between each section of the presentation, a transition slide appears to indicate the new section. Are the transition slides effective?

7. The end of the presentation simply asks for questions and answers. Consider the advice for endings given in this chapter:
   • Summarize your main message.
   • Visualize the outcome for the audience.
   • Ask for what you want.
   • Make next steps clear.

Brainstorm what Rachel could say at the end of the presentation in all four of these categories. What do you recommend that she say?

Evaluating the Presentation Slides

8. This presentation is not designed to stand alone. It needs a presenter. In this case, would a stand-alone presentation be a good or bad idea? Explain your answer. Should Rachel bring handouts, brochures, or other written material to leave behind?

9. This presentation uses a consistent visual style and template. In your opinion, does it work well with this presentation? If so, why? If not, why not?

10. This presentation includes a number of bullet point slides. Are the bullets parallel? Are any slides too crowded? Are there any slides you would recommend revising?

11. This presentation includes only one data graphic: the pie chart on Slide 16. Is that pie chart appropriate and easy to read? If not, how would you revise it?

12. Slides 9 through 13 present attractive pictures of the areas of France the tour will visit. To be effective, the pictures should be similar. All the headlines mention some food or beverage-related term—except for one headline. How could you revise that headline?

13. The final slide asking for questions features a picture of pastry. Assume that you'd like a picture that will help spark interesting questions. What picture(s) or text could the slide contain, instead of a picture of pastry?

14. As Stephanie evaluates whether the slides will be easy to present, she considers using animation on various slides. Perhaps the bullets should come up one by one. Perhaps the pictures of the French regions should appear gradually, instead of all at once. Identify which slides—if any—would be more effective if they revealed content gradually rather than all at once.

15. As a final step in reviewing, Stephanie should proofread all slides for correctness and consistency. Consider typing errors, spelling, font size, consistent punctuation, consistent heading sizes, and consistent bullet points. Do you see anything that needs to be changed?

Delivering the Presentation

16. Slides 9 through 13 include no text. Rachel will need to talk through the key points on these slides. What kinds of information should she provide when she projects these slides?

17. Rachel intends to serve regional food at this presentation. Should she serve it at the beginning of the presentation? At the end? Or as she discusses each region? What is the rationale for your answer?

Handling Questions and Answers

18. Should Rachel plan to take questions throughout the presentation or just at the end? What is the rationale for your answer?

19. What questions should Rachel anticipate? Should she address any of those questions in the presentation itself?

CRITICAL THINKING

1. Public speaking makes many people nervous. What do you think are the main reasons public speaking causes fear? What makes you nervous about making presentations? What do you currently do to make yourself less nervous? What additional tips in this chapter can help you feel more comfortable presenting?

2. Research has shown that public speaking ability is a key predictor of career success. Why do you think that is the case?

3. Imagine that you are presenting quarterly financial results at a meeting. You need to decide whether to present the key figures in a handout that the audience can look at as you present, to project the key figures in a slideware presentation, or do both. What are the pros and cons of each option? What would you decide?

4. Imagine that you are making a sales presentation and you brought a few examples of the product you are selling to share with the audience. You wonder whether there is any advantage to having images of the product in a slide show presentation also. What would be the advantage of having projected images in addition to examples of the product to pass around?

5. During a presentation's question-and-answer session, it is a good practice to repeat a question to the entire audience before you answer it. Name at least three advantages you gain by repeating the question.

6. Why is it important to practice presenting a slide as part of the evaluating/revising process?

7. If you are presenting to people in a different culture, how can you learn about that culture's preferences and expectations?

8. How would you describe the key differences between a business presentation and a speech? Why do you think presentations are more common than speeches in business?

9. Imagine that you have a teammate who is a poor presenter. That person is required to participate in a class presentation. What are some options to ensure a valuable contribution from that presenter?

10. Teams often divide the work of creating presentation slides so that work is equally divided. What are the potential problems of this approach? How can you address or avoid those problems?

DEVELOPING YOUR COMMUNICATION SKILLS

10.1 What do I analyze when planning a business presentation? *(pages 344–347)*

EXERCISE 1 Analyze your purpose and outcome: Why?

For each of the following scenarios, determine the purpose and intended outcome of the presentation.

a. A presentation to a group of potential customers explaining various types of investment instruments

b. A presentation to a group of potential customers explaining why they should use your company as an investment firm

c. A presentation to your supervisor explaining how to implement a process you have developed

EXERCISE 2 Analyze your audience: How many and who?

Select one of the following scenarios and identify a real person whom you know to be the audience. For your chosen scenario, fill out an audience analysis worksheet as shown in Figure 10.2 on page 346, analyzing the specific audience you identified.

a. A professor you know well is the executive director of your school's Young Entrepreneur's Club. You and a few of your classmates have an idea for an entrepreneurial business you would like the club to fund. Funding is competitive, and this professor makes the funding decisions. Identify your entrepreneurial idea, and complete an audience analysis form, analyzing this professor as your audience.

b. Your family members or friends are debating where to go for a group vacation. The group decided that each person with a preferred location would develop a brief presentation to persuade the others. Identify your preferred location and specific audience members, and fill out an audience analysis worksheet.

c. Your business communication class is planning a fundraiser and is in the process of planning where to donate the money. Your instructor invites people who are interested in proposing a charitable organization to give a persuasive presentation in class. Fill out an audience analysis worksheet to analyze your instructor and classmates as your audience.

EXERCISE 3 Analyze your setting: When and where?

Prepare a written response for each of the following scenarios.

a. Imagine you are planning to give a presentation in the same setting where you hold your business communication class or some other specific classroom at your school. What key features of that setting should you keep in mind as you plan your presentation?

b. Imagine you are planning to give the same presentation over the internet (via WebEx or some other technology), with each person looking at your slides on his or her own computer and listening to you via telephone. What are some key differences between this setting and the classroom setting? What will you do differently as you prepare your presentation?

c. Imagine that instead of giving your presentation live, you will be video-recording it and posting it on YouTube or some other site for people to watch at their own convenience. What will you do differently for that setting?

d. Imagine that instead of video-recording your presentation, you will simply be posting your presentation slides for people to read. What will you do differently in that setting?

EXERCISE 4 Analyze your medium options: How?

For each of the scenarios in Exercise 2 (Analyze Your Audience: How Many and Who?), explain which medium option(s) you would use and why. Also explain what medium options would not be appropriate and why.

10.2 How do I compose the presentation?
(pages 348–367)

EXERCISE 5 Identify the type of presentation

Conduct an Internet search with the advanced search function of Google, Bing, or some other web browser, looking specifically for PowerPoint files. Find a slide deck and identify whether the slides are comprehensible on their own or whether they require a presenter. Identify at least one slide from the deck that you can share with your class in order to support your evaluation.

EXERCISE 6 Organize the content: Planning an opening

Select one of the scenarios in Exercise 2 (Analyze Your Audience: How Many and Who?) and plan two different openings, using two of the following four techniques:

a. State a fact.

b. Tell an anecdote.

c. Quote someone well known or quote a familiar saying.

d. Ask a question.

EXERCISE 7 Organize the content: Planning your structure

For each of the options in Exercise 1 (repeated here) how would you structure the presentation?

a. A presentation to a group of potential customers, explaining various types of investment instruments

b. A presentation to a group of potential customers, explaining why they should use your company as an investment firm

c. A presentation to your supervisor, explaining how to implement a process you have developed

EXERCISE 8 Organize the content: Planning your ending

For each of the options in Exercise 1 (Analyze Your Purpose and Outcome: Why?) and Exercise 2 (Analyze Your Audience: How Many and Who?), choose one or more of the following as an appropriate ending. How would you justify your decision?

- Summarize your main message.
- Visualize the outcome for the audience.
- Ask for what you want.
- Make the next steps clear.

EXERCISE 9 Create a storyboard

Imagine that a prospective employer has asked you to submit a slide deck along with your application. In five slides, you are to demonstrate why you are a good candidate for the job. Prepare a storyboard for this slide deck. The storyboard will consist of five rectangles, each representing a slide. For each "slide," write a clear headline and sketch the content of the slide body—or write notes about what you will include.

EXERCISE 10 Develop a template

a. Many sites on the web offer downloadable PowerPoint templates. Conduct a search using the terms "PowerPoint templates," and find at least one template that you believe would be appropriate for a business presentation and one that you believe is not appropriate. Be prepared to share your findings with your class.

b. Select a template that you believe is acceptable and create an alternative version of that template by changing key features on the slide master. Change the fonts, the font sizes, the shape of bullets, and the colors. Compare the two versions and write a memo to your instructor explaining which you like best and why.

EXERCISE 11 Design individual slides

a. Select one slide from your storyboard in Exercise 9 (Create a storyboard), and design two versions of the slide: one that uses bullets and one that does not.

b. The slide at the bottom of the page describes the target market of the grocery store chain Trader Joe's. What changes would you make in the design and wording of this slide? In addition, proofread the slide to catch any errors.

EXERCISE 12 Evaluate your slides in a practice session

a. Review the JourneyFree culinary tour presentation in the case study on pages 378–382. Imagine yourself presenting slides 7, 15, 16, and 18. Your job will be to present these slides without simply reading the bullet points. Select two of these slides and write a "script" of what you would say. Consider whether you would change these slides in any way to make them easier to present.

b. Publicly traded companies typically make their investor presentations available on their websites. These presentations are created as slides, which are often saved as PDF files. Go to the websites of the companies in the following list (on page 385) to find investor presentations, or search the Internet to find an investor presentation from any other company that interests you. (Hint: use a web browser and type in <*Investor presentations [company name]*>.) You may have to do a bit of exploration to find presentations on the company's website.

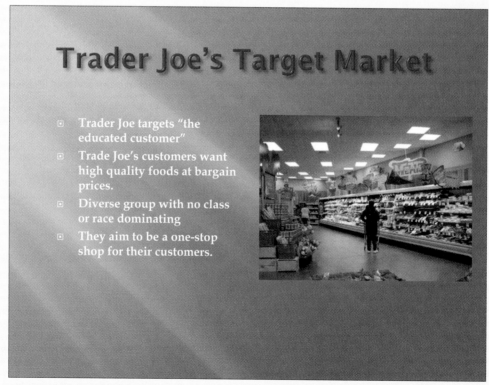

Accompanies Exercise 11

- eBay
- General Electric
- Google
- IBM
- Johnson & Johnson
- JP Morgan Chase
- McDonald's
- Microsoft
- Verizon
- Wal-Mart
- Wells Fargo

Select a brief presentation of 10 to 15 slides, or select a portion of a longer presentation. Review and analyze the selected slides, answering the following questions:

- Do the slides follow the principles of good slides in this chapter? Describe how the slides do or do not follow these principles.
- Can you read and understand the slides as an independent document without a speaker? Why or why not?

Make sure you attach the presentation to your answers.

EXERCISE 13 Create effective handouts

Refer to Exercise 1 (Analyze Your Purpose and Outcome: Why?) on page 383. For each of the scenarios, decide which handout format would best support the presentation. Identify the pros and cons for each of the following options: slide miniatures, slides with notes pages, or handouts with supplementary information. Summarize your explanation in a memo to your instructor.

EXERCISE 14 Using hyperlinks in presentations [Related to the Technology feature on pages 366–367]

Your company, Beautiful Hair, is planning to launch a new advertising campaign for its women's hair care products. Managers are considering two directions. One campaign features thin, young, glamorous models. The other features models that look like "real women." Your supervisor has asked you to research current attitudes toward presenting women in advertising and make a presentation recommending an approach to the marketing department. Your supervisor expects you to include images from competitive products' advertising campaigns in your presentation. She also expects you to document your research. Prepare a slide presentation supporting and explaining your recommendation. If useful, include hyperlinks to videos of competitive advertisements.

If your instructor asks you to make this presentation in class, practice in advance, working on all the delivery skills you learned in Section 10.3 of this chapter. Your instructor may ask classmates to provide you feedback on your presentation delivery.

10.3 How do I deliver and evaluate the presentation? *(pages 368–373)*

EXERCISE 15 Set the stage

Think about the last slide presentation you delivered, either in a class or your job. Explain how you used the following presentation techniques to set the stage for your presentation: practice, dress for the part, arrive early and warm up, set up the slides and projector, decide where you will stand, keep the lights on so that attention is on you, and have water available. If you didn't use a technique, explain why not or whether it would have improved your presentation experience.

EXERCISE 16 Control your body

Many people are not aware of the body movements they make during a presentation. Use a webcam or video camera to record your-self making one of the impromptu presentations in Exercise 34. Play the recording and evaluate your body language, eye contact, and facial expressions. Summarize your evaluation in a memo to your instructor.

EXERCISE 17 Use your voice effectively

Refer to Exercise 16 (Control Your Body). Evaluate your presentation recording based on the techniques outlined in this section. Did you speak to the back of the room? Did you speak slowly, especially at the beginning of the presentation? Did you modulate your voice and minimize verbal tics? Did you use pauses instead of *ers* and *ums*? Summarize your evaluation in a memo to your instructor.

EXERCISE 18 Present your visuals effectively

Go to mybcommlab.com to view one of the sample presentations linked to this chapter. In a memo to your instructor, summarize your evaluation of the presentation based on following criteria:

Did the presenter:

- Introduce each visual by explaining the intended point?
- Direct attention to visuals with hand gestures and words?
- Take cues from the visual aids rather than using note cards or a script?
- Avoid apologies for nervousness or mistakes?

EXERCISE 19 Coordinate with your team

Think about the last team presentation you gave. In a memo to your instructor, describe the setting (when, where, and what) and then explain how your team used the guidelines outlined in this section to coordinate your group effort. If your team did not integrate one (or more) of the guidelines, identify if a negative result occurred.

EXERCISE 20 Avoiding plagiarism in slide design [Related to the Ethics feature on page 372]

The following questions relate to the Trader Joe's slide in Exercise 11 (Design Individual Slides).

a. The slide uses a picture of Trader Joe's found on the website Wikimedia Commons. The photographer and picture owner is Sage Ross. Under the picture, the website includes this licensing notice:

> I, the copyright holder of this work, hereby release it into the public domain. This applies worldwide. In case this is not legally possible: I grant anyone the right to use this work for any purpose, without any conditions, unless such conditions are required by law.

Is it legal and ethical to use this picture in a presentation? Is a citation required?

b. The first bullet in the slide includes a quotation that came from an article published in the *Seattle Times* on August 30, 2003: "Trader Joe's Targets 'Educated Buyers.'" The article was quoting the founder of Trader Joe's, Joe Coulombe. How would you cite this in your presentation?

c. The template of this presentation is one of the many offered in PowerPoint. Would it be considered plagiarism to use this template?

Summarize your answers to these questions in a memo to your instructor.

EXERCISE 21 Evaluate the audience's response

Attend a presentation on campus or in your community. Pay attention to the audience and evaluate their responses. What signs do you see that the audience is engaged? What signs do you see that the audience is bored? Summarize your observations in an email to your instructor or be prepared to discuss them in class.

EXERCISE 22 Adapt your approach for online presentations

Imagine that you are presenting the Rowland-Grey presentation (Figure 10.16) online to Carolyn Reese, who is out of the office. Select one slide and plan how you would present that slide to her if she is viewing it on a computer in a different location.

10.4 How do I handle questions and answers?
(pages 373–375)

EXERCISE 23 Plan for a question-and-answer (Q&A) session

a. Review the Rowland-Grey presentation in Figure 10.16. What questions should you anticipate from the audience?

b. Review the JourneyFree culinary tour presentation on pages 378–381. What questions should you anticipate from the audience?

c. For each of the presentations in **a** and **b**, would you recommend that the presenters invite questions at any time or ask the audience to hold questions until the end? Justify your answer.

EXERCISE 24 Answer questions skillfully

Imagine that Rachel Jones is giving the JourneyFree presentation (pages 378–381), and she receives the following questions. Plan answers to the questions:

a. **A hostile question:** *"You say the tour is only $3,000, but that is a huge amount of money for underpaid teachers. How can we afford that?"*

b. **Question to which you do not know the answer:** *"Where can we apply for external funding for these kinds of educational experiences?"*

c. **An idea you have already rejected:** *"Wouldn't Japan or China be a better location, considering the importance of those cuisines for today's cooking?"*

d. **A question that gets the presentation off track:** *"I'm glad you're organizing this trip to France because France is my favorite country. I've been there five times, and each time I learn something new. In fact, the last time I was there . . ."*

EXERCISE 25 Meeting audience expectations [Related to the Culture feature on page 375]

When you present to audiences in other cultures, it is important to follow that culture's rules of business etiquette. On YouTube (or other video-sharing site), find a video about business etiquette in a country other than the United States. Show your video to the class and then, as a team, facilitate a class discussion about how to apply those etiquette principles if you were delivering a business presentation in that culture.

WRITING

EXERCISE 26 Presentations recommending a purchase

You work for the information technology department at Reynolds Media and Marketing, a small public relations company with 30 employees. The company has budgeted $75,000 for this year to replace all desktop computers with notebook computers. For efficiency, the company would like everyone to have the same model of computer. However, employees can't agree on the best model. Some employees would like to switch to Macs. Others prefer PCs. The graphics staff want big screens. Those who travel prefer laptops rather than desktops.

Your manager asks you to select three good alternatives, evaluate them, and recommend one. Research computer alternatives and prepare a persuasive slide presentation, recommending one particular model. If your research leads you to believe the company should support two different models to meet the needs of different employees, recommend that in your presentation, supported by persuasive reasons. Include a hyperlink to the appropriate product page on each computer manufacturer's website.

If your instructor asks you to deliver this presentation in class, practice in advance, working on all the delivery skills you learned in Section 10.3 of this chapter. Your instructor may ask classmates to provide you feedback on your presentation delivery.

EXERCISE 27 Preparing a training presentation

Take any topic from this textbook and prepare a three- to five-minute presentation to teach the topic to students who are not enrolled in a business communication course. Begin with an opening designed to engage your audience and convince them of the importance of the topic (what's in it for them). Prepare a few slides to teach key points. Conclude with "next steps," providing advice about how your audience can continue learning about the topic.

If your instructor asks you to deliver this presentation in class, practice in advance, working on all the delivery skills you learned in Section 10.3 of this chapter. Your instructor may ask classmates to provide you feedback on your presentation delivery.

EXERCISE 28 Evaluating your presentation delivery skills

Prepare a three-minute "icebreaker" presentation about yourself to deliver to your classmates. Focus on your life, your hobbies and interests, your job, your family, your travel, your recent reading—or any combination of these. Here are four ideas for how you can organize this presentation:

a. Chronological: Present three or four events in your life that have been important to you and made you the person you are today.

b. Topical: Provide a sample of your life, telling your audience a little bit about different topics such as your family, your education, and your hobbies.

c. Common thread: Identify a common thread that runs through several events in your life, and provide examples.

d. Key event: Focus on one defining event that set your life on its current path.

If your instructor arranges for students' presentations to be video-recorded, watch the video and evaluate your presentation delivery skills, based on the advice in Section 10.3. Submit to your instructor a memo with your evaluation and a list of key presentation skills you will work on in the class.

EXERCISE 29 Evaluating the presentations skills of others

Evaluate the presentation skills of a business presenter based on a presentation or speech you find on the Internet. Options include a speech by the head of a business, such as Steve Jobs, your state senator, or your favorite writer.

Where can you find such talks and presentations? In addition to YouTube and GoogleVideo, you can find presentations and speeches on websites of the following organizations:

- American Enterprise Institute
- Brookings Institution
- Center for Strategic and International Studies
- Council on Foreign Relations
- CSPAN
- FORA-TV
- Heritage Foundation

After you watch the presentation, write a memo to your instructor answering the following questions:

- Did the speaker read a speech or talk extemporaneously?
- Did the speaker use visual aids? Were they effective?
- What was the speaker's main point? Summarize it in a few sentences.
- How was the presentation organized?
- What were the main claims of the presentation? Were the claims credible? Why or why not?
- Do you consider this presenter to be a good speaker? Provide evidence to support your point of view.
- Do you have any recommendations for the presenter? Explain them.

COLLABORATING

EXERCISE 30 Developing presentation skills

a. Working with a team of classmates, develop a five-minute presentation-related activity for your class. It can be a brief ice-breaker for the beginning of a class session, an exercise to evaluate and revise a slide, an exercise to practice body-language and other presentation skills, or your own creative idea. Summarize your activity and provide directions on one or two well-designed slides for your instructor to evaluate.

b. As a team, prepare a five-minute presentation on some aspect of business communication that you find challenging (or that your instructor assigns). After the presentation, conduct a question-and-answer session with the class.

EXERCISE 31 Delivering a slide presentation

Imagine that you and two teammates are presenting either the Rowland-Grey (pages 361–364) or the JourneyFree presentation (pages 378–381). Download the presentation file from mybcommlab .com. Practice the presentation, working on all the delivery skills you learned in Section 10.3 of this chapter. Deliver this presentation in class. Your instructor may ask classmates to provide you feedback on your presentation delivery.

EXERCISE 32 Reporting on consumer attitudes

Consumer Research, Inc., has hired your team to conduct a survey to learn how the public responds to direct mail advertising sent by email (sometimes called "junk email"). Research conducted in 2007 indicated that responsiveness to this type of advertising was growing.[8] Consumer Research wants to know if responsiveness continues to be strong. Select an age group to survey and develop a set of questions to ask. For example, you could ask:

- how often they open advertising they receive through email
- what influences their decision to open the email (the subject line? the sender?)
- how often they click through to a website
- how often they purchase something as a result of the email advertising

Refer to Chapter 7 (Study Question 7.3) to review strategies for creating effective surveys. Conduct your survey and then prepare a presentation to Consumer Research that outlines your results. If possible, draw conclusions about the effectiveness of email marketing to the age group you have researched.

If your instructor asks you to deliver this presentation in class, practice in advance, working on all the delivery skills you learned in Section 10.3 of this chapter. Your instructor may ask classmates to provide you feedback on your presentation delivery.

EXERCISE 33 Evaluating fast food restaurants

Your team works for a restaurant chain that is planning to open a restaurant in your area. The district regional manager wants to know more about the competition. Are the competitive restaurants excellent? Or is there room for a good new restaurant in the neighborhood?

As a team, choose three restaurants in the area and observe each restaurant at least three times within the next two weeks. Vary the day of the week and the time of day for each visit. During each visit, observe and collect data on the appearance of the restaurant, how many customers entered during that time period, the length of wait to place an order, the length of wait to receive an order, the quality of service, and the quality of food. During each visit, make a qualitative judgment about how happy the customers seem to be, and support your judgment with specific observations.

At the end of the two-week observation period, prepare a slide presentation to deliver to your district manager, evaluating the competition and making recommendations about how your new restaurant can provide better service than the competitive restaurants you have studied.

If your instructor asks you to make this presentation in class, practice in advance, working on all the delivery skills you learned in Section 10.3 of this chapter. Your instructor may ask classmates to provide you feedback on your presentation delivery.

SPEAKING

EXERCISE 34 Impromptu speaking

In a one- to two-minute presentation, answer one of the following questions. Be sure to begin your presentation with the short version of the answer and then elaborate:

a. What advice would you give students graduating from your high school this year and planning to attend your college?

b. What is your ideal job when you graduate?

c. If you could travel anywhere, where would it be?

d. What is the most valuable course you have taken thus far in college?

e. What one change would you recommend to the president of your college?

EXERCISE 35 Executive briefings

a. If you are working on a long-term project, prepare an oral progress report for your instructor. See Chapter 9 to review information about progress reports.

b. Assume that the business communication faculty at your school is trying to decide whether all students in business communication courses should be required to learn a presentation program, such as PowerPoint, Keynote, Impress, or Prezi. They have asked five current business communication students, including you, to present their views at a department meeting. You will have only three minutes to speak. Prepare a brief presentation to the faculty. Support your presentation with some form of visual aid.

GRAMMAR

Apostrophes (See Appendix D—Section 2.6)

Rekey (or download from mybcommlab.com) the following paragraph, correcting the 10 errors or omissions in the use of apostrophes. Underline all your corrections.

Practicing for a telephone interview will give you confidence that you wont blow the real thing. Ask one of your parents' or a friend to conduct a mock interview with you. Have him or her phone you and ask an interviewers questions. Its also helpful to get a spouses' or father's-in-laws critique of your answers. Ask one of them to listen in, or, whats even more useful, tape record the mock interview for later analysis. Pay attention not only to the content of your answers, but also to the vocal quality; is your's clear, without too many "uhm's" "you knows," and "likes"? The practice sessions payoff is your improved interviewing skills.

Parentheses, dashes, brackets, and ellipses (See Appendix D—Section 2.7)

Rekey (or download from mybcommlab.com) the following paragraph, inserting parentheses, dashes, brackets, and ellipses where required. There are 10 omissions. Consider pairs of parentheses or brackets as a single omission. Underline all your corrections. In cases where there is more than one possibility, be ready to explain your choice.

The time to research a potential employer is before not after the job interview. Interviewers expect job applicants to know something about a company's products goods or services its markets local, national, international and its operating locations. Job applicants can begin their research on an Internet search engine Google or Bing. Career advisor Martin Reis writes on his blog, "A company's URL Uniform Resource Locator is the gateway to a wealth of information new products, financial statements, press releases, the corporate mission statement . . ." There is something else a company's website may reveal its corporate culture. Web page photos can provide clues about dress standards casual or traditional, employee diversity ethnicity, gender, age, and community involvement.

11 Creating Résumés and Cover Letters

new hires @ work

Roy Dockery
Field Service Engineer
Swisslog Healthcare Solutions
Thomas Edison State College, 2009

"**MY FORMAL EDUCATION EQUIPPED** me with essential interviewing and résumé-building skills that resulted in multiple job offers. Focusing on the employer's needs really made a difference when I was competing with more experienced candidates for the same job. To do this, I made a list of the keywords in a job advertisement and ensured those words were effectively woven into both my cover letter and résumé. You can't simply state that you have these skills, though. You have to demonstrate *how* you got them."

Introduction

Your employment search may be your initial—and potentially most critical—opportunity to use all the knowledge and skills gained throughout your college education. How you communicate your abilities—starting with your résumé and cover letters—will determine your career opportunities. Earning a degree does not guarantee that you will find the job of your dreams. Applicants who hastily put together a generic résumé and cover letter and send the same documents to every job they apply for, without customizing, don't get many interviews. To persuade an employer to interview you, your cover letter and résumé need to be tailored to meet the specific needs of the employer. The ACE process will help you do that.

Analyze **Compose** **Evaluate**

This chapter shows you how to:

- **analyze** your career goals and the needs of potential employers to determine what industries and companies to target for your job search

- **compose** targeted cover letters and résumés that communicate your strengths at a glance

- **evaluate** your application materials to ensure they are effective, and deliver employment materials in a professional manner

What should I analyze before composing résumés and cover letters?

Beginning a job search requires a significant amount of analysis. Analyzing your own career interests and goals will help you decide what employment opportunities to pursue. Analyzing your strengths and skills will help you determine whether they match your goals or whether you need to expand your capabilities. Analyzing options for identifying job openings will expand your opportunities. Finally, analyzing your professional image will help you present your skills and abilities effectively in your résumés and cover letters.

Analyze your career goals

Many college students choose a major based on their interests or academic strengths, such as English or math. Others choose a major based on specific career goals, such as accounting or law. Regardless of your major, you need to decide what you want to do after graduation. You could decide to look for a job or pursue a graduate degree. The following activities will help you clarify your career goals.

Gain experience with internships and summer jobs. Internships and summer jobs can help you determine if you are truly interested in pursuing a career in a particular field. Internships are an opportunity for you to "test drive" a company and career path. For example, if you're an English major, an internship at a publishing company or local newspaper can help you decide whether you would like to be an editor or writer. Internships are also an opportunity for an employer to determine if you are a good fit for the company. Students who do well in their internships may receive job offers for full-time positions upon graduation. In fact, the National Association of Colleges and Employers reports that employers convert more than 50 percent of eligible interns into full-time employees.[1]

If you're not able to move to a new location for an internship opportunity, consider researching virtual internships that allow you to work for a company online. Like online classes, virtual internships will let you take advantage of technology tools, such as web-based teleconferencing, to communicate, share information, and submit work. The number of virtual internships are increasing due to improved technology and growing social media outlets. The *Wall Street Journal* reported that a quarter of the postings at Urban Interns were virtual internships, many of which were for positions in research, sales, marketing, and social media development.[2] You can find information about virtual internships at corporate websites and on internship clearinghouse websites (see mybcommlab.com for links).

Gain transferrable skills by volunteering. You can gain additional experience and skills by volunteering a few hours a week. In addition to participating in clubs and organiza-

■ Access this chapter's simulation entitled Cover Letters and Résumés, located at mybcommlab.com.

tions related to your major, you can volunteer for nonprofit organizations. For example, accounting students might volunteer with the IRS's Volunteer Income Tax Assistance (VITA) Program or the Tax Counseling for the Elderly (TCE) program. Engineering students could volunteer with Habitat for Humanity. IT students could volunteer to build or manage websites for charitable organizations. Volunteer experiences not only give you an opportunity to explore working in a specific field, but they also enhance your résumé and help you develop *transferrable skills* that relate to your career goals.

Narrow your focus by identifying preferences. Even within a career field, several different kinds of jobs exist. For example, if you want to be an accountant, do you want to work for a government agency or a private company? If you want to be a lawyer, do you prefer criminal law or corporate law? If you are not sure which employment options are right for you, identify your strengths and preferences by considering the following questions:

- Do you prefer to work collaboratively with other people or on your own?
- Would you enjoy a creative position or a more procedural job?
- Do you see yourself working for a large or small company? In a large or small city?
- Would you enjoy a job that requires travel?
- Do you want to start your own business to promote a new product or service?

Research your career options. Once you have a better understanding of your interests, learn about your career options by researching different positions. The U.S. Bureau of Labor Statistics produces the *Occupational Outlook Handbook*, which provides detailed information about hundreds of jobs in a wide variety of categories. You can search by profession or job title to learn about educational requirements, salary ranges, projected job prospects, the nature of the work, and working conditions.

Keep an open mind about possible jobs and job locations. If you are flexible, you may find a perfect job in an unexpected location. As Frank Tortorello, a former manager of college recruiting for Merrill Lynch, explains, "If you listen to common wisdom, finance is dead. . . . Maybe finance on Wall Street is dead, but lots of companies still need help in this area."[3]

Create a plan for your future. Think about what your career goals might be five or ten years from now. What do you want to accomplish? Your career goals may change as your work experience develops, but having a plan for your career progression helps you narrow your employment options now and market yourself for your future. For example, a marketing major may apply for sales trainee jobs leading to a career path in sales management. Alternatively, the marketing major could choose to apply for jobs as a marketing analyst leading to a career path in marketing or market research.

Analyze your strengths and skills

Analyzing your strengths and skills helps you accomplish two goals. First, you can determine which jobs you are best qualified to pursue. Second, your analysis will help you build evidence of your skills to use in your cover letters, résumés, and interviews. The following steps can help you prepare to sell yourself to a potential employer.

Outline your experiences. Make a list of all your work experiences, even if they do not directly relate to the focus of your current job search. For each job you've had, create three to five bullet points that identify the specific skills you developed on the job and the specific results you achieved. The following list is based on an internship experience with a financial management company. Note how each bullet item begins with an action-oriented verb:

- Gained problem solving and interpersonal skills while providing personal customer service to a diverse client base
- Improved data management by organizing client records, inputting data, and designing reports in the client database
- Analyzed spreadsheets to create effective charts and graphs to support persuasive client presentations
- Gathered information, evaluated content, and wrote articles for a monthly newsletter that provided financial management advice to clients

Identify areas of expertise. In addition to your work experiences, you may have developed areas of expertise from coursework, extracurricular activities, and hobbies. For example, you may have learned how to program Java applets in a computer class or taught yourself how to design web pages. These areas of expertise may be assets even in nontechnical fields, such as management and marketing. Having a wide variety of talents will make you more marketable.

List your sellable qualities. Sellable qualities are abilities that make you an asset to a company. Even if you do not have work experience or related hobbies, you most likely have developed workplace qualities that employers value. For example, you may have gained interpersonal skills as a youth soccer coach or leadership skills as the president of a student organization. Rather than merely listing your skills and traits, identify how, where, or to what extent you develop them:

- Wrote and presented role-playing scenarios for SADD awareness events at local high schools
- Developed leadership skills as president of the campus Business Club; initiated two successful fundraising events, led meetings, and delegated duties
- Gained collaboration and negotiation skills working with parents and children as a youth soccer coach for four years
- Participated in state, regional, and national SiFE team competitions; placed in top three rankings at all levels

Recognize your weaknesses. As you analyze your strengths, also consider your weaknesses. Being aware of your weaknesses is beneficial for two reasons. First, once you identify skills you don't have, you can work on improving them, especially if they are often required for jobs in your field. Second, you can avoid applying for positions that require skills you do not have.

Update your list frequently. As you gain experience—both in school and at work—update your lists of experience, expertise, and sellable qualities. Maintaining an ongoing "skill inventory" will help keep your résumé current and tailor your résumé to present your qualifications for different jobs.

Analyze your options for finding job opportunities

Once you know your career goals and what you offer an employer, you will be in a good position to identify employment opportunities that match your goals and take advantage of your strengths. The following activities will increase the number of job opportunities available to you.

Register with career centers. Many colleges and universities have career centers that provide career counseling services, résumé assistance, mock interviews, and workshops that focus on employability skills. These centers also help students obtain internships or service learning opportunities, such as volunteering to do office work for a charity organization. Some career centers continue to offer services to alumni, so you may want to bookmark their websites for future reference. For graduates with several years of industry experience, other resources include employment agencies or head-hunting firms that specialize in matching employers with qualified job applicants.

Register with job banks and search employment advertisements. Searching for jobs through job banks and advertisements not only helps you find openings, it also helps you learn which skills employers require for your ideal jobs. Check print sources, such as newspapers and trade journals, as well as online resources, such as Monster and HotJobs. Don't limit yourself to your comfort zone. Although you should respond only to job advertisements for which you are qualified, keep an open mind about opportunities that do not match your "ideal job." You may not think you are interested in moving across the country or working for a waste management company, but how will you know until you see the city or find out more about the job? Accepting an invitation to interview does not require you to accept the job if it is offered to you.

Many online job banks also provide services and opportunities for job seekers, such as those illustrated in FIGURE 11.1. For example, you can set up email alerts based on your search parameters to review postings that match your interests, and you can also post résumés. If you choose to post your résumé through an online job bank, identity theft experts recommend that you create an online version that reveals no personal information: use your first initial and last name instead of your full name, specify an alternate email address, include only a cell phone number that is not listed in any directory, use a post-office box as your address, and provide only limited information about your school affiliations and past employers.[4] To make your résumé easier for employers to find, add powerful keywords to your online posting. Maureen Crawford Hentz, a talent acquisition manager for Osram Sylvania, says that she checks up to 16 websites a day to find the right candidates and relies on keyword searches. She recommends using the specialized language of your field as well as key synonyms that will help a human resources professional target your résumé.[5]

FIGURE 11.1 Example of an Online Job Bank

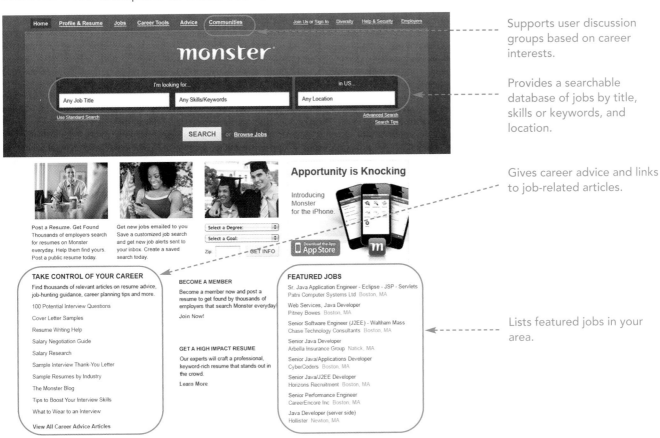

Reprinted with permission from Monster Worldwide, Inc.

Develop professional and personal networks. Your **network** is the circle of people you know who are aware of your career goals. Your network includes fellow students, friends, coworkers, faculty, staff, business contacts, and family members. Word of mouth—telling everyone in your network that you're looking for a job—is one of the most effective ways to learn about employment opportunities, many of which are not posted in job advertisements or company websites. The larger your network, the more likely you are to hear about open positions. You can expand your network by exploring alumni databases, attending job fairs, and participating in campus workshops or presentations sponsored by companies in your area.[6]

Network The people you know who are aware of your career goals and can help you learn about career opportunities.

Use social networking outlets. Another effective way to develop your professional network is to use social networking tools. Job recruiters find professional sites like LinkedIn and Zing to be great resources in finding job candidates.[7] A good profile on a professional networking site will include detailed descriptions of your expertise and job history and also will include keywords that help recruiters find you. The profile illustrated in FIGURE 11.2 also provides a photo, although opinions are mixed about whether that is a wise idea. Mark Jaffe, president of a headhunting firm, offers the following advice about including a photograph as part of your profile:

> If it's a solid asset, great, use it—as long as you're absolutely certain that it projects the soul of professionalism. But keep in mind you may be dismissed from consideration regardless of your credentials—which quite possibly will never be examined—because you're bald, overweight, too young, too old, wearing the wrong suit or, cruelest and most unreasonable of all, too beautiful for your own good.[8]

FIGURE 11.2 Functions Available through a Social Networking Tool

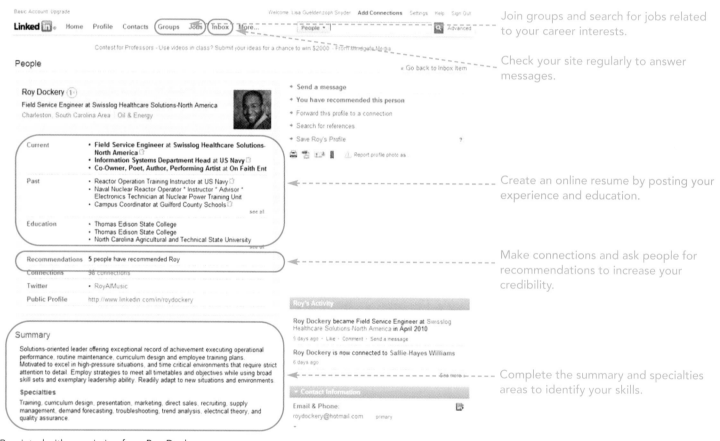

Reprinted with permission from Roy Dockery.

Although informal social networking tools—such as Facebook, Twitter, and Bebo—are designed primarily to share personal information and photos, they also play an important role in a job search. You can actively use these sites to let your friends know you are looking for a job. This can be an effective way to find unadvertised employment opportunities. However, you should also expect that employers will research you through your social media sites and connections. In fact a survey conducted by Career-Builder found that more than 50 percent of employers research job candidates through social networking sites, with 30 percent of employers searching Facebook.[9] Even if you've made your social networking sites private, employers may be able to access information about you through your friends' unprotected pages.

To ensure that your social media sites do not hurt your chances of receiving a job offer, be sure to clean them up before launching a job search. Remove any pictures and information you would not want a potential employer to see, and ask your friends to remove from their Facebook or MySpace pages any images of you—or at least your identification—that may be perceived as unprofessional. Employers surveyed by CareerBuilder cited the following kinds of content on social networking sites that caused them not to hire a candidate: inappropriate photographs or information, discussions of drugs and drinking, negative comments about previous employers, and poor communication skills. Inappropriate comments can cost you, even after you are employed. For example, Brixx Pizza fired a waitress for posting negative comments about a customer's tip on her Facebook page.[10] After you've cleaned up your existing social media sites, Google yourself and also search within social media sites to see what others can find about you online.

Join professional organizations. To enhance your network while gaining valuable skills, determine which student clubs at your school relate to your career goals. Some organizations may be social clubs, but many others focus on specific academic disciplines, such as the Society for Human Resource Management (SHRM), or professional development, such as Toastmasters.

Target specific employers. If you are interested in working for a specific company because of its location or leadership in your field, research the company to familiarize yourself with its mission, products or services, corporate culture, and financial health. Do not limit yourself merely to reading the company's website. Research its current challenges and reputation with GoogleNews, study its stock history with Yahoo! Finance, read past articles about its performance in *Fortune Magazine*, and talk to current or former employees. Professional networking websites like LinkedIn also provide company profiles. The information you gather gives you content to discuss during your job interview (see Chapter 12) and helps you assess the company's financial future. If you like what you find, research the company's requirements for submitting résumés so you are prepared when you are ready to apply.

Analyze your professional image

When you apply for a job, you are marketing yourself to an employer and portraying an image. You communicate that image verbally in the wording of your cover letter and résumé, as well as nonverbally in the promptness with which you return messages and the way you dress for interviews. Think of that image as your personal brand—the thing that makes you stand out compared to other applicants. As you prepare for a job search, analyze and build your image to ensure that it is professional and consistent. Ask yourself the following questions:

Is your email image professional? To improve your email image, do the following each time you send an email:

- **Use a professional-sounding email address.** Although college students usually have school-based email accounts, students often choose not to use them when applying for jobs because the accounts may be disabled a few months after graduation. Any email service is acceptable to use during an employment search, as long as you choose a professional username that represents your actual name, not your nickname or personality. Consider the different images these email addresses communicate: "2cool4school@gmail.com" or "jon.swartz@gmail.com."

- **Evaluate the content and structure of your message to ensure it is concise, clear, and easy to read.** Ask someone to proofread it for you.

- **Include a professional email signature block.** Adding a professional signature block to your email messages is an effective way to provide your contact information. As FIGURE 11.3 illustrates, a signature block can also help you sell your strengths.

Do you have professional business cards? As you build your personal network at job fairs or workshops, share your business cards to help the people you meet remember you. Some schools allow students to order business cards. However, you may prefer to design your own so that you may continue using them after you graduate. Keep the design professional, and list your major, professional memberships, and contact information. If you create a web résumé, video résumé, or online portfolio to support your job search, include the URL.

Is your telephone image professional? You can demonstrate your professionalism by the way you speak on the phone and how you record your voice mail greeting. When

FIGURE 11.3 Professional Email Signature Blocks

Including graphics such as your school logo adds visual interest and professionalism to your email communication.

Jana C. Smithers Business Management Major NEW STATE UNIVERSITY SCHOOL OF BUSINESS BELVEDERE, MI 49720 http://www.nsu.edu/jcsmithers.htm jcsmithers@gmail.com 204.555.4432	**Jorge Vargas** Finance and Economics Major President, Students in Free Enterprise Member, Beta Gamma Sigma Mailbox #14223 City College at Pembroke Pembroke, Virginia 24136 jvarga@att.net Cell: 612-555-8849

Listing your memberships, especially those that relate to your degree, can enhance your professional networking possibilities.

potential employers call to schedule an interview and you are not available to receive the call, what will they hear? During your employment search, ensure your greeting clearly states your name, requests callers to leave their name and number, and identifies that you will return the call as soon as possible. Avoid distracting background music or cute sayings, and evaluate your greeting to ensure it is clear, concise, and complete. During your employment search, check your email and voice mail messages every day and respond within 24 hours, if not sooner, to promote a positive professional image.

Does your online image reflect your brand? Go beyond cleaning up your social networking sites, and create content that supports the image you want to project. Consider these questions: What are you known for? What do you want people to remember when they think about you? Keep these things in mind—and project that image—when you communicate in any medium, including social media such as Twitter and Facebook. If you Google yourself and find things that don't support the image you want to portray, delete them, if you can, and replace them with powerful examples of your professional brand.

StudyQuestion 11.2

How do I write an effective résumé?

new hires@work

Kalani Miller

Co-Owner

Mikoh Swimwear

University of California — Santa Barbara, 2009

"Persuading an employer to call you for an interview requires that your résumé and cover letter fit the employer's specific needs. It's all about what you can do for them, not what you want from them."

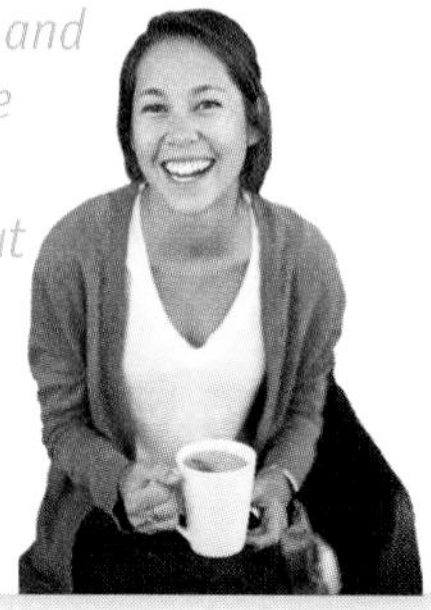

Most employers spend less than a minute to review a résumé.[11] In fact, according to résumé expert Michelle Dumas, "Unless your résumé captures immediate attention through an eye-appealing design and succinct, compelling language, your résumé will be screened out after just 15 seconds."[12] Since the goal of an employer's first review of a résumé is to narrow the pool of candidates to the best, make sure your résumé doesn't include anything that will make it easy for the reviewer to throw it away.[13,14] Instead, communicate the information and professionalism that will make you stand out among other candidates. The following guidelines will help you compose a highly effective résumé.

Select an effective résumé design and format

No single résumé format or style is perfect for all résumés. In fact, you may need to create two or more versions of your résumé to fit different submission requirements and career interests. To ensure that all versions of your résumé project a positive and professional image, use the guidelines that follow.

Use templates as guides, not absolutes. You can use professional résumé templates and online examples as good style guides. However, copying templates or examples is rarely the best way to represent your unique set of skills and experience and to set yourself apart from the competition. Instead, use the best elements from several examples as guides to develop your own uniquely—yet professionally—designed résumé that highlights your strengths and persuasively sells your skills to employers.

Enhance your image with professional page layout and design techniques. Most employers prefer a one-page résumé,[15] so create a design that is easy to read, looks professional, and fits on one page. You can accomplish this in Microsoft Word as well as other word processing and page design programs. FIGURE 11.4 compares a plain text and designed version of a résumé with identical content. To achieve a professional look, like the designed sample in Figure 11.4, you can use a contemporary looking font like Arial, Verdana, or Calibri. In addition, you can use a larger font size or bold for headings, separate sections with lines or borders, and create columns with aligned tabs rather than spaces.

FIGURE 11.4 Using a Professional Design for Your Résumé

PLAIN TEXT

Shavon D. Alkins
Box 3106, Robbins, MD 21214
sdalkins@gmail.com / (338) 555-7959

EDUCATION

Bachelor of Science in Business Administration, May 2011
Concentration in Management and International Business
Minors in Accounting and Spanish
Campus University, Robbins, MD

Study Abroad Experiences:
Philippines, January 2010
Italy, Spain, Summer 2008
Honors:
Dean's List, 2009-2011
Phillips-Perry Academic Excellenc[e]

RELEVANT SKILLS

Leadership - As treasurer of the S[panish]
service to a diverse membership
Communication - Communicate d[aily]
Read, write, and speak Spanish flu[ently]
Computer Skills - Skilled in Micros[oft]

WORK EXPERIENCE

Sales Associate, October 2011–Pr[esent]
Target Corporation, Robbins, MD
Use interpersonal skills to greet a[nd]
Assist with cashier functions and [other]

Cashier/Sales Associate, August 2[010]
Food Lion, LLC, Robbins, MD
Interact with customers, facilitate [transactions]

Bilingual Grade Classroom Assist[ant]
Eastlawn Elementary, Middletown[, MD]
Worked with 5th grade children to[...]

Language Lab Assistant, August 2[007]
Campus University, Robbins, MD
Prepared lab coursework activities

Cashier/Sales Associate, Septemb[er]
Family Dollar Inc., Pensacola, FL
Managed front-end sales and pro[vided]
Performed store setup tasks

Notice how the content in the two résumés is the same—only the format is different.

DESIGNED

Shavon D. Alkins
Box 3106, Robbins, MD 21214
sdalkins@gmail.com / (338) 555-7959

EDUCATION

Bachelor of Science in Business Administration, 3.87 GPA   May 2011
Concentration in Marketing and International Business
Minors in Accounting and Spanish
Campus University, Robbins, MD

Study Abroad Experiences:
- Philippines   January 2010
- Italy, Spain   Summer 2008

Honors:
- Dean's List, School of Business & Economics   2009–2011
- Phillips-Perry Academic Excellence Award   May 2010
  (presented to the study abroad student with the highest GPA every year)

RELEVANT SKILLS

Leadership
- As treasurer of the Spanish Club, managed budgets and funds while providing effective customer service to a diverse membership

Communication
- Communicate daily with customers while performing sales associate duties
- Read, write, and speak Spanish fluently

Computer Skills
- Skilled in Microsoft Office (Word, Excel, PowerPoint, and Outlook)
- Proficient in Microsoft Access and Adobe Dreamweaver

WORK EXPERIENCE

Sales Associate   October 2011–Present
Target Corporation, Robbins, MD
- Use interpersonal skills to greet and assist customers courteously and efficiently
- Assist with cashier functions and other duties as assigned

Cashier/Sales Associate   August 2010–October 2011
Food Lion, LLC, Robbins, MD
- Interacted with customers, facilitated transactions, and maintained cash drawer

Bilingual Classroom Assistant   August 2008–May 2011
Eastlawn Elementary, Middletown, MD
- Worked with 5th grade children to develop their literacy skills and recognize word sets in Spanish and English

Language Lab Assistant   August 2007–May 2008
Campus University, Robbins, MD
- Prepared lab coursework activities

Cashier/Sales Associate   September 2006–July 2007
Family Dollar Inc., Pensacola, FL
- Managed front-end sales and provided excellent customer service
- Performed store setup tasks

Create a second plain text version of your résumé. Many companies require résumé content to be typed or pasted into online forms that are connected to web-based databases, called Applicant Tracking Systems. The systems store candidates' information for easy search and sorting. In addition, a very small percentage of companies (only 3 percent) request unformatted résumés that they can scan themselves into their databases.[16] You can meet the needs of both sets of employers by creating a second version of your résumé. Remove all of the formatting codes, so your résumé looks like the plain text version in Figure 11.4. To help employers search your résumé effectively, ensure that it integrates key words from the job announcement.

1. Open your résumé file
2. Select all the content (use CTRL+A in Word)
3. Copy the contents (use CTRL+C in Word)
4. Open a new blank file
5. Using the Paste Special feature, select "Unformatted Text" and paste the text
6. Select all the content (CTRL+A)
7. Change line spacing to single (with no extra spaces before or after paragraphs)
8. Remove any lines, symbols, and tabs
9. Use ALL CAPS to indicate headings. Add line spaces where necessary to separate categories
10. Save the plain text file with a new filename (such as Jane_Doe_Resume_Unformatted)

If you use a different word processing program, similar options should be available. Online submissions are discussed in more detail in the Technology feature on page 416.

Choose a format that allows you to highlight your strengths

You can choose among three standard résumé formats—chronological, functional, and combined. Use the format that best emphasizes your strengths and presents you as a desirable candidate for the job.

Use the chronological résumé format to emphasize work experience. The **chronological résumé** is a traditional format that lists contents in sequential order, starting with the most recent and working backward. It highlights education and work experience as the primary assets of the applicant. This format is most appropriate for applicants who have work experience that explicitly qualifies them for the new position. For example, assume that Brendan Neilly worked as a lifeguard for Oceanfront Properties last summer. He recently saw that company's advertisement for a head lifeguard position and decided to apply. FIGURE 11.5 on page 401 shows the job description and Brendan's résumé. He chose a chronological format to emphasize his work experience.

Use the functional résumé format to emphasize skills. The **functional résumé** emphasizes the skills that qualify you for the position. This format is more appropriate than a chronological résumé for applicants who have limited work experience related to the position. For example, students pursuing internship or professional positions immediately after graduation may want to highlight their skills instead of their unrelated work experience. FIGURE 11.6 on page 402 illustrates the résumé that Brendan Neilly designed to apply for a different summer job that he found on his college's career services website: an internship in financial management. Because he has no related work experience, he reorganized the content to focus on skills before experience. Notice that he also includes different skills than he included in the lifeguarding résumé.

Use a combined résumé format to balance experience and skills. The **combined résumé** highlights the strengths of applicants who have both relevant experience and skills. This format is most appropriate for applicants who have worked in positions closely related to the one they are applying for and who also want to emphasize the advanced skill sets required for the new position. For example, assume Shavon Alkins is applying for a senior sales associate position she found advertised on Oscasco Services' website. Shavon's résumé, shown in FIGURE 11.7 on page 403, demonstrates a balance of skills and experience by highlighting the required skills listed in the job posting (leadership, communication, and computer skills) and also documenting sales experience with several companies.

Chronological résumé A traditional résumé style that lists content sequentially, starting with the most recent experience.

Functional résumé A contemporary résumé style that emphasizes categories of skills rather than job experience.

Combined résumé A résumé style that takes advantage of both the chronological and functional methods of organizing content by highlighting work experience by date and skill sets by category.

FIGURE 11.5 Chronological Format: Focuses on Experience

WANTED: Head Lifeguard. Supervise 15 guards, create schedules, oversee scheduled events, and maintain guard equipment inventory. Lifeguarding experience and certification required. Leadership and teamwork skills needed. We serve a diverse clientele including international tourists; global appreciation and cultural awareness a plus. Send your résumé to: Oceanfront Properties, 1 Oceanfront Blvd., Barnstable, MA 02630.

Brendan G. Neilly
(508) 333-0210 / bgneilly@yahoo.com

HOME ADDRESS
188 Birch Road
Sidney, MA 02515

CAMPUS ADDRESS
8239 Riverside, Apt. 3B
Piedmont Valley, MI 49494

OBJECTIVE
To provide effective leadership and model exceptional safety and customer service skills in the position of head lifeguard for Oceanfront Properties.

EDUCATION
Bachelor of Science in Business Administration, May 2014
Concentration in Finance, Minor in Economics, GPA: 3.6
Piedmont College, MI

EXPERIENCE
Lifeguard
Oceanfront Properties, Barnstable, MA, June–August 2011
- Fulfilled professional lifeguarding duties while maintaining an environment conducive to teamwork and safety
- Supervised weekly drills and assessments
- Communicated effectively with coworkers and diverse clientele

Sales Representative
Banana Republic, Natick, MA, May 2009–May 2010
- Offered exceptional customer service as a shoe and accessory salesperson
- Processed financial transactions including sales and returns

Shaw's Supermarket, Medfield, MA, November 2008–April 2009
- Greeted customers, bagged groceries, and maintained orderly working environment

SPECIAL RECOGNITIONS
- Acceptance into Piedmont Business Fellows Program, 2011
- Member of Piedmont Periclean Scholars, a competitive service learning program, 2011–Present

SKILLS, ABILITIES, & CERTIFICATIONS
- Lifeguard Management Certification, American Red Cross, January 2012
- Waterfront Lifeguard Certification, American Red Cross, May 2011
- Professional Rescuer CPR & First Aid Certification, YMCA (Piedmont Valley, MI), March 2011
- Leadership Skills (Cross Country Captain, Religious Education Instruction)
- Teamwork Skills (Intramural Sports, Group Projects, Habitat for Humanity)
- Microsoft Word, Excel, PowerPoint, Internet Research Skills

EXTRACURRICULAR CLUBS AND ACTIVITIES
- Delta, Delta, Delta Fraternity, 2011–Present
- Club Lacrosse, 2011–Present
- Habitat for Humanity, 2009–2011

SUMMER FOREIGN EXCHANGE PROGRAM
France, lived with an exchange family and was immersed into French culture, Summer 2010

Objective is to secure a summer lifeguard position, which relates closely to work experience.

Education and **work experience** are listed in chronological order, beginning with the most recent position.

Skills and certifications are listed below work experience, with the most relevant qualifications for the position at the top of the list. Additional skills that are not explicitly applicable—such as computer knowledge—are listed last.

Supplemental information includes involvement in **extracurricular clubs and activities**, which support experience with group interaction and teamwork. **Study abroad** experience suggests cultural awareness.

FIGURE 11.6 Functional Format: Focuses on Skills

Financial Management Internships

Local financial management company seeks summer interns for 10-week, full-time, paid position. Rising junior and senior finance and financial management majors only. Analytical and communication skills required. Computer skills expected. Submit your résumé and letter of interest to Daniel Shaw, Career Services, Piedmont College, by February 1. Three letters of reference required.

mybcommlab

Apply Figure 11.6's key concepts by revising a new document. Go to Chapter 11 in mybcommlab.com and select Document Makeovers.

Brendan G. Neilly

(508) 333-0210 / bgneilly@yahoo.com

HOME ADDRESS	**CAMPUS ADDRESS**
188 Birch Road	8239 Riverside, Apt. 3B
Sidney, MA 02515	Piedmont Valley, MI 49494

OBJECTIVE

To obtain a summer internship with a financial firm that requires analytical detail and excellent communication skills.

EDUCATION

Bachelor of Science in Business Administration, May 2014
Concentration in Finance, Minor in Economics, GPA: 3.6
Piedmont College, MI

SKILLS AND ABILITIES

- Financial: created a business plan for a nonprofit company as a fraternity service project, 2012
- Analytical: prepared expenses and income (fundraising) statements for lacrosse team, 2012
- Communication: effectively met needs of a diverse clientele (Banana Republic), 2009–2010
- Desktop Publishing: created professional flyers and brochures (Habitat for Humanity), 2010
- Computer: effectively use Microsoft Word, Excel, PowerPoint, Internet Research Skills

SPECIAL RECOGNITIONS

- Acceptance into Piedmont Business Fellows Program, 2011
- Member of Piedmont Periclean Scholars, a competitive service learning program, 2011–Present

EXPERIENCE

Lifeguard
Oceanfront Properties, Barnstable, MA, June–August 2011
Performed professional lifeguard duties and supervised weekly drills and assessments

Sales Representative
Banana Republic, Natick, MA, May 2009–May 2010
Processed financial transactions including sales and returns

Shaw's Supermarket, Medfield, MA, November 2008–April 2009
Greeted customers, bagged groceries, and maintained orderly working environment

EXTRACURRICULAR CLUBS AND ACTIVITIES

- Delta, Delta, Delta Fraternity, 2011–Present
- Club Lacrosse, 2011–Present
- Habitat for Humanity, 2009–2011

STUDY ABROAD EXPERIENCE

France, lived with an exchange family and was immersed into French culture, Summer 2010

Objective targets the position and highlights applicable skills.

Education is listed first since Brendan's major qualifies him for the internship.

Related skills are emphasized before the work experience, which does not specifically qualify the applicant for a financial internship. Note that the lifeguarding and CPR certifications are not included since they are not relevant to the internship.

Work experience is documented, but does not include a description of job duties because they do not support the applicant's objective of obtaining a summer internship at a financial firm.

FIGURE 11.7 Combined Format: Focuses on Balance of Skills and Experience

Senior Sales Associate. Minimum three years sales experience required. Leadership, communication, and computer skills a must. Preference given to candidates with demonstrated interpersonal skills, appreciation for a diverse clientele, and fluency in Spanish. Submit your résumé online at www.osasco.com.

This résumé does not include an **objective**. For tips on whether to include an objective, see page 404.

Shavon D. Alkins
Box 3106, Robbins, MD 21214
sdalkins@gmail.com / (338) 555-7959

EDUCATION

Education is listed with related study abroad experiences and honors.

Bachelor of Science in Business Administration, 3.87 GPA   May 2011
Concentration in Marketing and International Business
Minors in Accounting and Spanish
Campus University, Robbins, MD

Study Abroad Experiences:
- Philippines   January 2010
- Italy, Spain   Summer 2008

Honors:
- Dean's List, School of Business & Economics   2009–2011
- Phillips-Perry Academic Excellence Award   May 2010
  (presented to the study abroad student with the highest GPA every year)

RELEVANT SKILLS

Relevant skills are organized by the keywords in the job advertisement.

Leadership
- As treasurer of the Spanish Club, managed budgets and funds while providing effective customer service to a diverse membership

Communication
- Communicate daily with customers while performing sales associate duties
- Read, write, and speak Spanish fluently

Computer Skills
- Skilled in Microsoft Office (Word, Excel, PowerPoint, and Outlook)
- Proficient in Microsoft Access and Adobe Dreamweaver

WORK EXPERIENCE

Work experience is documented and includes a description of job duties because many of them support the applicant's objective of securing a senior sales associate position. The dates show that she has the required three years of sales experience.

Sales Associate   October 2011–Present
Target Corporation, Robbins, MD
- Use interpersonal skills to greet and assist customers courteously and efficiently
- Assist with cashier functions and other duties as assigned

Cashier/Sales Associate   August 2010–October 2011
Food Lion, LLC, Robbins, MD
- Interacted with customers, facilitated transactions, and maintained cash drawer

Bilingual Classroom Assistant   August 2008–May 2011
Eastlawn Elementary, Middletown, MD
- Worked with 5th grade children to develop their literacy skills and recognize word sets in Spanish and English

Language Lab Assistant   August 2007–May 2008
Campus University, Robbins, MD
- Prepared lab coursework activities

Cashier/Sales Associate   September 2006–July 2007
Family Dollar Inc., Pensacola, FL
- Managed front-end sales and provided excellent customer service
- Performed store setup tasks

Compose effective résumé content

Many job applicants incorrectly assume an all-inclusive list of skills and experience on a résumé helps them be everything to every employer. However, résumés with long lists require prospective employers to hunt to find the qualifications they're seeking. In successfully persuasive résumés (and cover letters), all the content is targeted to the position and is organized within many of the following content categories.[17]

Heading and contact information

Place your name at the top of the résumé in a bold font sized four to eight points larger than the rest of the résumé text. You do not need to include a document title such as "résumé" or "curriculum vitae." List just the one professional email address that you are using for your job search and one phone number that has a professional voice mail greeting. Traditionally, résumés have included both a present and permanent address. However, since most employers rely on email addresses and telephone numbers to communicate with applicants, it is acceptable to use only one address, assuming that you can be quickly notified if you receive mail there.

Objective

Composing a good objective statement can be challenging. In fact, many employers indicate that objective statements aren't necessary if you are responding to a specific job advertisement mentioned in your cover letter. Other employers indicate objectives are appropriate only for internship or entry-level positions. If you choose to include an objective statement, avoid overused phrases such as "to obtain a challenging position with a progressive company that offers excellent growth opportunities." This statement is too vague to help an employer, and it doesn't persuasively sell your strengths for the position. Use a concisely worded and direct objective statement about what you can do for the company, not what you want from them or your hopes and dreams.

As an alternative to an objective statement, consider creating an audience-focused qualifications summary or a professional profile that targets employer needs and demonstrates that you are a good fit for the job. A qualifications summary works well for new graduates who have strengths and skills that qualify them for the position but little, if any, related work experience. Professional profiles are more often used by applicants with well-established work histories and more professional experience to offer. A professional profile is more detailed than a qualifications summary and includes specifics about achievements that make you stand out as a candidate. FIGURE 11.8 compares a traditional objective statement, a qualifications summary, and a professional profile.

Education

List educational information near the top of a résumé because a degree is one of the primary qualifications for many positions. Although you have some flexibility about the order of your résumé content, don't make a potential employer search for standard information. Consider the following do's and don'ts as you compose the education section of your résumé.

List only schools from which you have received (or will receive) a degree. If you are a transfer student, do not list a school where you earned credits, but did not graduate. Employers are interested in your degree and the school that conferred it. Further, if you have several stops and starts in pursuit of a single degree, list only the final institution from which you will graduate. Otherwise, employers may assume you are unfocused. However, you may choose to include a second school on your résumé if you completed courses there that specifically support your career goals.

Include your grade point average. If you have less than five years of work experience following college, include your grade point average (GPA), even if it is not as competitive as you would prefer.[18] Some hiring managers have indicated they assume the ap-

FIGURE 11.8 Sample Résumé Statements

Traditional Objective:	Qualifications Summary:
To secure a challenging financial management position that allows me to use my strong analytical, interpersonal, and communication skills to help investors achieve their financial goals.	Financial management major with experience: • Analyzing detailed income and profit/ loss statements • Explaining complicated tax requirements to clients • Managing Microsoft Dynamics, Quicken, and ERP application systems.

Professional Profile:

Professional financial manager with 12 years of experience in asset management and risk analysis. Proven leadership in directing a $28 million business (110 employees) where responsibilities included controlling costs and growing profits by developing strategic financial plans, inventory control systems, and profit/loss management procedures. Implemented and evaluated ongoing assessment strategies to enhance short- and long-term budgeting goals. Seasoned know-how in interpersonal communication and collaboration. Recent industry certifications demonstrate advanced skills in financial management (CFM), analysis (CFA), and planning (CFP).

plicant's GPA is very low (perhaps lower than it actually is) if it's not included. In many cases, employers will request applicants' transcripts to verify degrees, so they eventually will see your GPA anyway. If your overall GPA is low, consider including your major GPA (an average of the courses specific to your major), but make sure you label it correctly so as not to misrepresent your qualifications. Never round up your GPA. A 2.95 is not the same as a 3.0.

List related educational information. In the education category, you can also include your honors, awards, scholarships, service learning, and study abroad experiences. For each item, list the date. If the title of an honor or award is vague, provide more detailed information. For example, the "Phillips-Perry" award listed as an honor in Figure 11.7 on page 403 would not be as effective without the explanation that the award is for the study abroad student with the highest GPA.

Do not list high school information unless you attended a prestigious school that demonstrates your unique qualifications for the job. For example, if you attended a performing arts high school and are applying for a marketing position at a theater, your high school information would be relevant. Otherwise, employers assume that college students have a high school degree or equivalent.

Do not list coursework unless it separates you from the rest of the competition. For example, if you are a business major, do not list business courses you were required to take. Employers assume you have taken these courses. However, you can include elective courses that give you valuable workplace skills, such as interpersonal communication, industrial psychology, foreign languages, or website development.

Work experience

In this section, show the employer that you have experience that qualifies you for the job. You can label the category "work experience," "related employment," or "work history." The label you use is not as important as the content you include in this section.

Highlight targeted experience rather than providing an all-inclusive list of jobs. Your résumé should highlight the experiences that qualify you for the position. List unrelated jobs—such as waiting tables—without providing bulleted details about your job duties. Additionally, your résumé does not need to include supervisors' information, salaries, or reasons for leaving past employment unless the potential employer specifically requests that information.

Include internships as work experience. The experiences you've gained from internships are important, even if they were volunteer jobs. Identify them in your work experience section, using the same format as the rest of your jobs. If your title was "intern," provide information about the department or unit you worked in.

Provide consistent information for each entry. When highlighting relevant experience on your résumé, list the position first, then the company followed by city and state (street addresses and zip codes are not required). Identify dates of employment with months and years (specific dates are not necessary). Be consistent with the format of job titles, company names, dates, and bulleted text. If aligning text (such as dates) at the right margin, use right-aligned tabs rather than spaces.

Use bulleted lines rather than paragraphs to describe your job duties and skills. Do not begin the items with the personal pronoun "I," which would be repetitive. Instead, begin each item with an action verb that highlights your skills. Use past tense verbs for previous jobs and present tense verbs for current jobs.

Be specific about capabilities. When listing your job experience, avoid vague, generic phrases and instead focus on the specific qualifications you can provide a potential employer. For example, rather than merely mentioning that you supervised employees, indicate that you supervised an eight-person crew during high-volume customer traffic while maintaining a positive working environment. FIGURE 11.9 provides examples of replacing vague, generic phrases with specific capabilities. Notice how the items in the "effective" column begin with an action-oriented verb, such as "supervised," "wrote," and "collaborated." Your school's career center may be able to suggest action words or phrases specific to your major. For example, accounting majors may use words like "compute" and "analyze." Economics majors may use phrases such as "built economic models" and "forecast sales growth." Students in fashion merchandising may use phrases such as "developed and executed designs for window and interior displays in five stores." The specific words and phrases you choose should clearly and accurately reflect your strengths and skills. As discussed in the Ethics feature on page 407, you will likely run into problems if you exaggerate your capabilities.

Target prospective employers' needs using keywords. Instead of sending the same version of your résumé to every employer, modify your résumé to meet specific employers' needs. Select keywords from job advertisements you reply to, and use them to describe your skills or your job duties. Human resource professionals will use Applicant Tracking Software (ATS) to search submissions, looking for candidates who best match the job. If your résumé doesn't include the right keywords, it won't make the

FIGURE 11.9
Using Specific Language to Describe Work Skills

INEFFECTIVE	EFFECTIVE
• Responsible for the night crew at Arby's	• Supervised an eight-person night crew • Handled all customer and worker complaints
• Experience with general office duties	• Typed and filed confidential correspondence • Formatted fliers, brochures, and newsletters
• Worked as a packager on an assembly line	• Learned the value of precision and teamwork while working as a packager on a fast-paced assembly line • Received Employee-of-the-Month award during first year
• Developed excellent communication skills	• Wrote a comprehensive policy and procedures manual for new interns
• Effective team player	• Collaborated on a successful client proposal that combined product design, marketing, and manufacturing personnel
• Detail oriented	• Developed monthly and yearly sales and budget forecasts

cut.[19] For example, if the job description says an applicant must have good communication, interpersonal, and leadership skills, integrate those three qualities into your résumé (assuming you have those skills) to demonstrate that you are specifically qualified for the position. If you cannot include the keywords, you probably are not qualified to apply for the position.

In addition to incorporating keywords from the job ad as you list your job duties, make sure you target skills that align with the company's culture. That requires doing your homework about the prospective employer. Imagine, for example, that you are applying for an information technology job at a private school that has this mission statement: "We are dedicated to creating a collaborative environment that allows each student to reach his or her own full potential." The culture of this organization clearly is collaborative, so you should identify your collaborative skills in your résumé, even if they were not listed as specific requirements for the position.

Include volunteer and extracurricular activities if you do not have related work experience. If you do not have actual employment that relates to the job, you can include a "related experience" section that focuses on other activities that helped develop your qualifications. If you want to document your leadership ability, you can describe your activities with student clubs in which you held a leadership role. Be specific about what you accomplished in these positions. How many people were in the organization? What happened under your leadership? What is the evidence of your success?

ETHICS   Exaggerating Your Résumé Is Dangerous

Your résumé can make or break your job search because it is the first impression you give to a potential employer. When the stakes are high and there are many applicants, you may be tempted to enhance your résumé by listing job duties you did not perform or stretching your responsibilities to include qualifications that you do not actually have. It may seem obvious not to lie on your résumé, but potential employers can perceive even slight exaggerations of your accomplishments as lies. The Society for Human Resource Management reports that increases in résumé lies have led managers to check the accuracy of candidates' résumés with greater detail than they had in the past.[20]

Even if you make it through the screening process and have proven yourself as a valuable employee, lying on your résumé can cut your career short. Patrick Imbardelli—the former head of the InterContinental Hotel's Asia Pacific chain—was forced to resign when the company discovered that he had lied about his academic qualifications on his résumé. He listed degrees from institutions he had attended, but from which he never actually graduated.[21]

In addition to lying about college degrees, other common errors include changing dates of education or employment, increasing previous salary amounts, inflating titles and job responsibilities, and padding grade point averages. Potential employers can easily check all of these facts. Rounding up your grade point average (GPA) or listing a "major" GPA without labeling it as such will certainly be perceived as lying.

Examples of How Exaggerations Can Happen and What Can Result

The following examples are based on actual—and unfortunate—student experiences.

- **Blatant exaggerations.** As an accounting major, Perry attended several of the Accounting Club's workshops and seminars on career development but never joined the club. When he updated his résumé his senior year, he decided to list membership in the club as an extracurricular activity. He also listed his favorite professor (who also served as the club's advisor) as a reference. When employers called the professor to ask about Perry's qualifications, both the professor and the employer were disappointed that Perry misrepresented his membership.

- **Content copied from résumé examples.** Sarah researched several different résumé templates, asked friends for copies of their résumés, and downloaded online résumé samples to help her create a résumé that successfully communicated a professional image and emphasized her strengths. She was particularly impressed with a friend's six-bullet item description of her skills and capabilities. Sarah cut and pasted the section from her friend's résumé to her own, not realizing that they might be applying for several of the same internships at their school. Later that semester, two employers complained to the school's career counseling center that students were submitting plagiarized résumés, and both Sarah and her friend were denied further access to the career center's services.

- **Unfulfilled intentions.** Jayne had every intention of filing the paperwork for her minor in psychology to complement her human resources major. Unfortunately, she missed the deadline to file the paperwork before graduation. Although her transcript would list the classes, they would not be documented as an official minor. Since she fulfilled the requirements, she decided to list the minor on her résumé anyway. Six months later and after applying for dozens of jobs without getting any interviews, she learned that potential employees discarded her résumé when they couldn't verify her "minor" on her transcript. ∎

For an ETHICS exercise, go to Exercise 12 on page 428 of this chapter's End-of-Chapter Exercises at mybcommlab.com.

mybcommlab

Capabilities and skills

Depending on the content you plan to include, you can label this section several different ways—for example, "capabilities and skills," "qualifications," or "achievements." Regardless of the label, the purpose of this section is to highlight qualities that make you an appealing candidate for the job. You can highlight those qualities in two ways.

First, use keywords that target the prospective employer's needs. Refer to the résumé in Figure 11.7 on page 403. In this example, Shavon is responding to a job advertisement that requires leadership, communication, and computer skills. Assume she found another job advertisement, illustrated in FIGURE 11.10, that emphasizes collaboration, technical competencies, and analytical skills. Note how in the résumé for that job, also illustrated in Figure 11.10, she modified her relevant skills section to use keywords from the job advertisement.

FIGURE 11.10 Targeting a Prospective Employer's Needs

Manager Needed

Sparrow Associates, a leading management consulting company in the Baltimore area, seeks an enthusiastic and professional office manager to join our team. Effective collaboration is a must. Technical competencies in Microsoft Office software required. Analytical skills—especially as related to budget data—are highly valued. Online applications accepted through June 15 only at www.Sparrow.Associates.com.

Relevant Skills

Collaboration
- Participated in several committees and fund-raising initiatives as an active member and treasurer of Spanish Club— a campus-based student organization

Technical Competence
- Skilled in Microsoft Office (Word, Excel, PowerPoint, and Outlook)
- Proficient in Microsoft Access and Adobe Dreamweaver

Analytical Skills
- Analyzed operating budget of a local not-for-profit organization and made recommendations for cost savings and made recommendations for modifying a store's product line as part of a 60-hour service-learning requirement for a managerial accounting course

Second, rather than repeating skills already identified in your description of job duties, focus on other skills that relate to the position you are applying for, such as these:

- ability to work well with others
- effective oral and written communication skills
- competence and good judgment
- innovation and creativity
- proficiency with Microsoft Office Suite
- fluency in Spanish
- reliability and trustworthiness
- enthusiasm and responsibility

Do not just list the terms. Provide credibility by including supporting details or evidence. For example, if you list proficiency with Microsoft Office, you might include these additional details:

- Produced a user-friendly, searchable, cross-referenced database with Microsoft Access
- Develop complex timelines for team projects with Microsoft Project
- Organize schedules, contacts, and communication with Microsoft Outlook

For each skill you include, be prepared to provide additional details during a job interview. For example, if you list your ability to work well with others on your résumé, be ready to provide examples of your collaborative skills. Chapter 12 provides examples of how to demonstrate these qualities in an interview.

Activities and/or Accomplishments

The goal of this section, which you may label "Activities," "Accomplishments," or "Activities and Accomplishments," is to identify your achievements, especially as they relate to your ability to succeed on the job. List extracurricular activities, volunteer work, organizational memberships, and leadership positions. Items in this category not only document your professional development and interests, but they also demonstrate your ability to balance schoolwork with other activities. Include dates of participation and provide descriptions of organizations that will be unfamiliar to your audience. For example, if you volunteered as an "Aggie Ambassador," describe what that position entailed. You can also list honors, awards, and scholarships in this category if you did not list them with your education.

References

Avoid including your references in the body of the résumé. References become relevant at a later stage of the job search. Instead, create a separate page of professional references that you can provide when it is requested. To create a unified look between your résumé and reference list, duplicate your résumé heading (name, address, email, and phone number) using the same formatting and font styles. Consider the following guidelines as you prepare your reference information.

Choose professional references who can speak about your skills. The people you ask to serve as references for your résumé are not character references. Do not include family members, friends, or religious leaders. The best choices are former employers, work supervisors, and instructors or staff who know your strengths and can explain your skills.

Ask your references for permission to include their contact information. Do not assume that the people you want to list as references will provide good recommendations for you. Ask their permission to use their name, and ask what contact information they would prefer you use.

List complete contact information for each reference. If you use a personal title (such as Mr., Ms., or Dr.) for one reference, be sure to list appropriate titles for all references. Include first and last names (double checking their correct spelling), job titles, company names, telephone numbers, and email addresses. Your list does not need to include complete mailing addresses, but you should have that information available in case it is requested. If it's not obvious how the references know you, or if they're no longer at the same company, specify the relationship, such as "former manager at McDonald's."

Provide your résumé to your references. and keep them informed about the progress of your job search. This information refreshes their memory if it's been awhile since they last worked with you and helps them target your skills when a prospective employer contacts them.

Evaluate your content and design

As part of the ACE process, use the following guidelines to evaluate your résumé and ensure that it communicates a professional image.

Is the content clear, complete, and concise? Ask someone who is not familiar with your school or work experience to review your content to ensure the wording is clear. If your reviewer doesn't understand something, it is likely that an employer won't either. Reword or explain any vague content. To check for completeness, carefully review your content to ensure you aren't forgetting relevant experiences, and make a point of updating your résumé on a regular basis. Finally, to ensure the résumé is concise, remove any irrelevant content or redundancies, such as listing the same job duties for different jobs.

Does the content specifically use keywords from the job you are applying for? Check to see that your objective statement relates to the job description and that you use keywords from the job advertisement.

Is the most important information emphasized? In earlier chapters, you learned about using the direct organizational plan in your business messages. When preparing a résumé, use this approach by placing the most important information—what qualifies you for the

new hires @ work

Travis English
Sales Supervisor
Best Buy
North Carolina A&T State University, 2008

"I keep a 'Show Me Binder' where I organize documentation of all my skills and accomplishments including employment evaluations, letters of recognition, awards, and evidence of coaching and training."

job—at the beginning of your résumé. This positioning will grab the attention of prospective employers who often quickly scan résumés to find the content they need to make interview decisions.

Is the résumé designed well and spaced to fit the page? Aim for a one-page résumé. If your résumé does not fill one full page, use extra spaces between sections or increase the line spacing throughout the page to fill a single standard 8½" × 11" page with balanced margins. If your résumé is longer than one page, do not compress it by minimizing side margins. Employers appreciate margin space for making notes. Instead, evaluate the content. Most recent college graduates, and even people with a few years of experience, should be able to condense their résumés to one page. However, if you have enough relevant and concisely worded content to require a two-page résumé[22], make sure you have balanced amounts of text on both pages.

Are alignment and style consistent? If you right aligned the dates in one section (such as education), use the same format for dates in other sections. If you used bold italics for a job title in one of your work experiences, make sure you used the same format for the rest of your job titles.

Is the résumé carefully proofread for spelling and typos? Spelling mistakes and typos on a résumé provide a quick way for an employer to eliminate the résumé from the stack of applicants. Errors suggest to an employer that you are not detail oriented or that you didn't invest the time and effort to produce high-quality work. As you proofread, double check dates, names and locations of companies, and the spellings of any names (such as awards, scholarships, and references) to ensure they are correct. Errors in numbers and proper names are often overlooked during proofing scans unless you specifically target them. In addition to conducting your own complete evaluation, ask people in your network to help you proofread your résumé.

Have you obtained sufficient feedback? In addition to evaluating your résumé and asking someone not familiar with your school or work to evaluate it, ask people in your network to evaluate your résumé. Provide them with a copy of the job advertisement so they can assess whether you have met the needs of the employer. Get feedback from

 CULTURE   Selling Your Cross-Cultural Skills

Imagine that you would like to work internationally after you graduate—such as in London, Tokyo, or Mexico City. You will probably not need to prepare a country-specific resume since most entry-level international jobs open to North American graduates are with employers who expect a North American-style résumé. However, your résumé will need to convince the employer that you will be effective in an international work environment. You need to sell your cross-cultural skills. You can accomplish this goal in two ways.

First, add a section to your resume called "International Expertise and Understanding."[23] Include all cross-cultural and international experiences gained from jobs, internships, or volunteer experiences. Also include any relevant academic courses, multicultural academic experiences, language abilities, and international travel. Grouping this material in one section increases its impact and decreases the chance that employers will miss it when reading your resume.

Second, in your skills and abilities section, stress the skills required to succeed when working in another culture. For example, include bullet points like these:

- Relate well to people with different personalities and backgrounds
- Able to adapt to change and new environments
- Adept at learning languages quickly
- Appreciate different work styles
- Experienced in working on multicultural student teams

Phrases such as these signal to an employer that you are aware that working in a cross-cultural environment requires a special set of skills.

PEARSON mybcommlab

For a CULTURE exercise, go to Exercise 14 on page 428 or to this chapter's End-of-Chapter Exercises at mybcommlab.com.

a variety of different perspectives, such as instructors, career counselors, and previous employers or supervisors. If you receive conflicting advice, consider the suggestions from the potential employer's perspective.

Study Question 11.3

How do I write an effective cover letter?

A cover letter—also sometimes called a letter of application—plays a critical role in your employment communication. A **cover letter** is a persuasive message that sells your résumé to the employer. A well-written cover letter can set you apart from the competition by conveying your professional personality and demonstrating your writing skills.

A cover letter typically includes a standard set of information. It introduces you and your résumé, specifies the position you are applying for, highlights your qualifications for that position, and requests an interview. Although all cover letters contain this basic information, an effective cover letter will be tailored to meet the needs of the employer by describing how you are qualified for the specific position. ACE will help you develop the appropriate, tailored content.

Analyze the position requirements

When you find a job advertisement that interests you, analyze the advertisement to identify the keywords that outline the job duties and requirements. Read the example in FIGURE 11.11. Which words would you highlight?

FIGURE 11.11
Sample Job Advertisement

DOVER
INDUSTRIES

Assistant Sales Manager–Dover Industries, Plymouth, Michigan
This position is responsible for assisting the sales manager of a regional chain of department stores. The role requires leadership skills to manage collaborative processes, effective communication skills to ensure deadlines are met, and efficient computer skills to coordinate and manage large volumes of data. The assistant sales manager develops and maintains positive working relationships with store managers, develops promotional strategies, executes promotional activities, reviews market strategies to identify potential customers and new business opportunities, conducts competitive research, prepares sales analysis reports, and helps store managers achieve sales and profit goals.

Job Requirements:
- Undergraduate degree in business administration or related field
- Minimum two to five years of general business experience; project management experience preferred
- Outstanding interpersonal, written communications, and presentation skills
- Effective collaboration in diverse team environments to achieve business results
- Travel requirement of 10 to 15 percent

If you were applying for the position described in Figure 11.11, you might include the following keywords in your cover letter and résumé: management, leadership, collaborative, communication skills, computer skills, business experience, project management, interpersonal skills, written communications, presentation skills, collaboration, and travel. However, you must go beyond simply listing these. Indicate how you exemplify these traits or characteristics by describing how you gained the experience or mastered the skills.

Cover letter A persuasive letter or email sent to a prospective employer along with a résumé that "sells" your résumé to the employer.

To customize your letter even more, analyze the company's website to learn about its mission, goals, and past performance. Search for news items about the company and its industry to become familiar with current events and trends. The more you know about the company, its products or services, and the specific job you want, the better you can align yourself as a viable candidate in your cover letter. Bookmark the website or print the documentation so you can easily reference this material later to prepare for the interview.

Compose persuasive content

Although cover letter samples are available in books and online resources, use them only as guides to help you create your own customized cover letters. Too often, job applicants cut and paste sample letters from websites to their word processors, changing only the name and job position before sending it to a potential employer. This practice is problematic for two reasons. First, it deceives the potential employer, who has a right to expect that you wrote the material you sent. Second, it doesn't help you sell your strengths for a specific job. Instead of copying, create a customized cover letter that persuasively sells your strengths and qualifications. This letter can become your own personal template, which you can modify for each new job application.

Chapter 5 recommended using **AIDA**—**A**ttention, **I**nterest, **D**esire, and **A**ction—to create persuasive messages about products and services. You can use AIDA in your cover letters as well to sell yourself to an employer. The following guidelines will help you compose persuasive cover letters.

Gain attention in the first paragraph

Gaining attention is relatively easy when you write a *solicited cover letter*—your reply to an employment advertisement or posting that requests applications. The audience is actively looking for someone to fill the job, so all you need to do is name the position you are applying for and motivate the audience to read further. For example, you can explain why you believe you would be a good fit for the job or you can demonstrate relevant knowledge about the company. If during your research on the company you find interesting information, you may be able to include something like this: "I'm targeting companies who know how to take good care of their clients, and the recent article in the *Chicago Tribune* spotlighting your efforts to reward your most customer-focused employees grabbed my attention."

In an *unsolicited cover letter*, gaining attention is more challenging. Because the company did not request applications, you need to persuade the audience to read your letter rather than throw it away. One approach is to send the letter to someone in the company with whom you have a connection through your network. That person is likely to read the letter and perhaps pass it on to the Human Resources department or a hiring manager. In that case, you need to convince your audience that you have enough interest or knowledge to be worth considering the next time an opening occurs.

Build interest/desire with keywords

The middle paragraph(s) of your cover letter should outline what specifically qualifies you for the position. Use the keywords outlined during your analysis of the job position to identify how you fit the employer's needs. Rather than simply restating the content of your résumé, demonstrate your knowledge of the company by showing how your abilities match the mission or goals of the potential employer. If you do not have a skill or qualification listed in the job advertisement, do not exaggerate your abilities. In some cases, you can reduce resistance to your persuasive appeal by subordinating this information—for example, "Although my full-time work experience is less than three years, my three internships in banks and brokerage firms provided me a diverse understanding of the financial services industry." Finally, do not make boastful statements. A comment such as "I am the best candidate for the position" is never appropriate since you do not know the other candidates applying for the job.

AIDA An acronym used in marketing to suggest the organization of sales communication: Attention, Interest, Desire, Action.

Motivate action in the closing

End your cover letter by requesting an interview. Avoid weak wording, such as "I hope you will contact me." Be confident, but not presumptuous. A statement such as, "I know you will want to interview me for this position" does not motivate action. The sample cover letters in FIGURES 11.12 and 11.13 illustrate different ways to motivate action. Providing your contact information at the end of the letter, even if it also appears in your letterhead or email signature block (email), can also help motivate the employer to contact

FIGURE 11.12 Sample Cover Letter (Email Format)—Solicited Message

email

FROM: sdalkins@gmail.com
TO: jw.herrick@dover.com
SUBJECT: Application for Assistant Sales Manager Position

Dear Mr. Herrick:

Thank you for the opportunity to apply for the Assistant Sales Manager position at Dover Industries. I was very pleased to learn from Monster.com that you are currently hiring. I first became interested in working for Dover when we studied the company's Quality Care program in my marketing class last year. Since then I've been following Dover Industries and have been particularly impressed by the company's ability to promote its mission to "be the preferred shopping experience for a diverse clientele by providing quality products and services."

As my attached résumé indicates, I can bring to Dover over three years of sales associate and customer service experience, most of which I gained while a full-time student. This experience, along with academic work in marketing and other business concentrations, has helped me develop the leadership, communication, and collaboration skills required to be a valuable member of your management team. I had an opportunity to develop those skills further during my junior year study-abroad term in the Philippines, where I played a leadership role on an international and interdisciplinary team of students working on an intense, month-long market research project about reaching underserved populations. I was also one of the team members chosen to return to the Philippines to present our results at the Philippine Business Conference and Expo in Manila. More recently, I had the opportunity to demonstrate my abilities as one of the team leaders in our local Target's Customer Comes First Campaign, which significantly increased our customer satisfaction ratings.

I am enthusiastic about working at Dover and would appreciate the opportunity to meet with you to discuss how I can use my experience to exceed your customer care goals. Please contact me by phone (338-555-7959) or email (sdalkins@gmail.com) at your earliest convenience to arrange an interview.

Thank you for your time and consideration.

Sincerely,

Shavon Alkins

Shavon D. Alkins
Box 3106
Robbins, MD 21214
sdalkins@gmail.com
(338) 555-7959

NOTE HOW THIS LETTER USES AIDA TO PERSUADE THE AUDIENCE:

Gains **attention** in the first paragraph by expressing a long-term interest in and knowledge about the company that goes beyond the information in the job advertisement.

Builds **interest/desire** by relating education and experience to the job requirements and providing two examples that demonstrate skills.

Motivates **action** by expressing enthusiasm, requesting an interview, including contact information, and mentioning a benefit to the employer.

FIGURE 11.13 Sample Cover Letter—Unsolicited Message

mybcommlab

Apply Figure 11.13's key concepts by revising a new document. Go to Chapter 11 in mybcommlab.com and select Document Makeovers.

letter

Shavon D. Alkins
Box 3106, Robbins, MD 21214
sdalkins@gmail.com / (338) 555-7959

October 15, 2012

Ms. Margaret Beckstein
Director of Sales
Baylin Technologies, Inc.
526 Industrial Parkway
Hanover, MD 21182

Addresses the letter to a specific person, preferably to someone in your network who can connect you with human resources.

Dear Ms. Beckstein:

Your assistant director, Robert Taylor, suggested I contact you about any management positions that may become available soon. I met Mr. Taylor at a Campus University alumni event and was very excited when I learned he was with Baylin Technologies. I am particularly interested in becoming a member of your international mobile technology team, and am enclosing my résumé for your consideration.

Gains attention by stating the purpose of the message, mentioning a mutual contact, and indicating a specific reason for interest in this company.

I first began following Baylin Technologies during my junior year study abroad experience in the Philippines. During that term, I worked with an international and inter-disciplinary team of students on a research project to provide wireless technologies to underserved populations. In that project, which we presented at the Philippine Business Conference and Expo in Manila, we researched Baylin's Southeast Asia initiative. I was impressed with the company's leadership in providing both technology and customer service in rural areas around the world. I would like to contribute to that mission.

Builds interest/desire by demonstrating knowledge about the company and highlighting experience that relates to Baylin's global focus.

As a recent business administration graduate with concentrations in both marketing and international business and a minor in Spanish, I believe I have the knowledge, skills, and interest to make a valuable contribution to your team. I am also well equipped to work with a diverse clientele based on more than three years of sales associate and customer service experience.

Continues to build interest and desire by highlighting education and relating coursework to skills and company needs.

Even if you have no specific job openings at the moment, I would value the opportunity to meet with you and discuss how I can best prepare myself for a future opening at Baylin. Please contact me by phone (338-555-7959) or email (sdalkins@gmail.com) to schedule an interview.

Motivates action by providing contact information and a reason for an interview, even if no current opening is available.

Regards,

Shavon Alkins

Shavon Alkins

Enclosure

The "enclosure" notation tells the audience to look for additional pages in the envelope.

you. To further motivate action, you can either indicate that you are eager to discuss your qualifications or request more information to stimulate a response. Figure 11.12 provides an example of a solicited cover letter in response to an advertisement, and Figure 11.13 is an example of an unsolicited cover letter to a company not currently requesting applications.

Evaluate content and format

Like all other correspondence, cover letters benefit from critical evaluation and revision. Use the following guidelines to evaluate the content and format of your cover letters to ensure they will catch the attention of the audience and persuade employers to contact you to schedule an interview.

Is the message clear, complete, and concise? Read the message aloud to ensure the wording is clear. To evaluate for completeness, review the job advertisement. Did you provide all requested information? Finally, to be concise, try to keep your cover letters to one page. Your résumé provides the detailed information that the employer will need to evaluate your qualifications. The purpose of the cover letter is to highlight your relevant skills and request an interview, not repeat the contents of your résumé.

Does the content use keywords to target the specific employer? Read your message from the employer's perspective. Did you include all the relevant keywords? Do you show how you meet the company's needs? If not, revise your message.

Can you reduce the "I" strain? Although the content of your cover letter is about you, try not to begin every sentence with "I." That leads to a monotonous piece of writing. When appropriate, modify the sentence structure to use introductory (dependent) phrases that emphasize skills or qualifications.

Did you mention your résumé was attached or enclosed? And did you actually attach or enclose your résumé? Double check email attachments before sending not only to ensure you've included them, but that you've given them meaningful filenames. For example, do not save your résumé files as "Shavon'sRez.doc" or "resume.pdf". Instead, ensure that your filename includes your full name: "Shavon_Alkins_Resume.pdf".

Is the message formatted professionally? Use the standard letter or email formats presented in Chapter 3 (other formatting guidelines are provided in Appendix B). To help your documents look consistent, use the same heading at the top of your cover letter that you use on your résumé. You will see an example of this technique if you compare Shavon Alkins' résumé in Figure 11.7 (on page 403) with her cover letter in Figure 11.13 (on page 414). The header blocks at the top of these documents are identical in information, font style, and size. If communicating via email, use an appropriate subject line that identifies the job title. Rather than vague subject lines, such as "Job Application," be specific. Notice Shavon Alkins' subject line in Figure 11.12—"Application for Assistant Sales Manager Position." In some cases, the job listing will indicate specific content for the subject line, such as a job code. Additionally, don't mark the email as high priority. Your job application may be a high priority for you, but it is not high priority for the prospective employer.

Are there typos or misspellings? Proofread your message several times, but pay additional attention to the spelling of names and double check the accuracy of numbers.

Have you obtained sufficient feedback? Finally, ask your instructors, advisors, and career counselors to help you evaluate your cover letters. Provide them with a copy of the job advertisement and your résumé as well. When possible, also get input from professionals in the field. If you do not yet have professional contacts in your network, take advantage of guest speakers in your classes, alumni of your school, colleagues of your parents, or your friends' parents. The more you revise your writing in response to feedback, the more competitive your employment communication will be.

TECHNOLOGY   Web Résumés, Video Résumés, and e-Portfolios

Although all job seekers need to have a traditional résumé, technology makes it possible to produce enhanced résumés and portfolios that help you "show" as well as "tell" about your qualifications. You can increase your job opportunities by creating web résumés, video résumés, and e-portfolios.

Web Résumés Enhance Your Online Image

Publishing your résumé on your personal website offers you a number of advantages. First, it allows you to update your résumé quickly and share it with your network by emailing the URL. It also allows recruiters to find you using a search engine like Google or Bing, especially if you include job-specific keywords. Finally, it allows you to create links from your web résumé to supporting material, including things you have written or produced. You can also include a link to a PDF version of your résumé that your readers can print. As a best practice in web résumés, always keep the material completely up to date and include a "last updated" date in a prominent place so recruiters and others who find your résumé will know that it is current.

Video Résumés Give You an Opportunity to Perform

If you are pursuing a career in which professional presentation skills are important—such as sales, public relations, or training—you might consider creating a video résumé. Videos should be short (no longer than three minutes), professional, and include only career-related content. A quick look at many of the video résumés posted to YouTube suggests that most of these will detract from, rather than support, a candidate's application. Additionally, some employers won't accept video résumés because of potential discrimination issues based on knowing the applicant's age, gender, and ethnicity.[24] If you do create a video résumé, keep the following tips in mind.[25]

- Record yourself in a professional setting and choose a background that is not distracting.
- Look professional. Dress as you would for a job interview.
- Ensure that the quality of the video is good, with clear pictures and sound and a professional look.
- Develop substantive content. Have a pitch to grab attention, and then talk about your objective, history, skills, and education.
- Rehearse your "speech" but do not read to the camera. Maintain eye contact with your audience, and avoid "ums" and "ahs."
- Stand out from the crowd. Let your character and creativity show. Allow your viewers to get to know you.
- Consider including references—credible and respected people who provide brief recorded testimonials.
- Conclude by thanking the audience and providing your contact information.

E-Portfolios Can Demonstrate Your Projects and Samples

Given the flexibility of web page layouts, you can easily turn your online résumé into an electronic portfolio including your writing samples, presentation samples, other work you have created, evaluations or certificates, and letters of recommendation. The more documentation you can provide to sell your skills and strengths—as long as it is well organized and not overwhelming—the better you can sell your personal brand.

mybcommlab

For a TECHNOLOGY exercise, go to Exercise 18 on page 429 of this chapter's End-of-Chapter Exercises at mybcommlab.com.

Used with permission from Robert Bostick's Video Résumé.

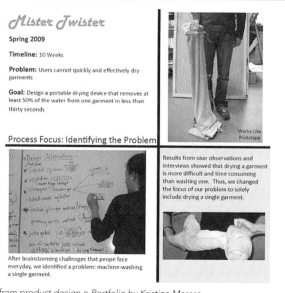

Excerpt from product design e-Portfolio by Kristina Marero, Northwestern University 2009.

How do I evaluate and submit my employment materials?

This section offers a general checklist for finalizing your documents, advice about how to submit your employment materials, and a method to track your communications during your employment search.

Finalize your employment materials

Although you evaluated your cover letter and résumé after you composed them, take a final look at your employment materials to evaluate their overall effectiveness. The following checklists will help you finalize your documents:

Cover letter

Persuasive Content

1. Does the first paragraph:
   - indicate the name of the position you want and where you found the job advertisement?
   - gain attention (by asking a question, stating a fact, or selling your skills)?
2. Does the second paragraph build interest and highlight the skills the employer needs?
3. Does the last paragraph motivate action (by asking for an interview and providing contact information)?
4. Does the letter mention your attached (or enclosed) résumé?

Organization

1. Is your heading information complete (name, address, telephone, email address)?
2. Is your email username professional, and is the hyperlink removed?
3. Is the date included and correct?
4. Did you proofread the inside address to double check the spelling of names and numbers?
5. Did you use an appropriate title (Mr., Ms., Dr.) in the inside address *and* on the salutation?
6. Does the salutation match the name in the inside address?
7. If you did not learn the name of the hiring manager from the job advertisement or your research, did you include an appropriate salutation (such as "Dear Human Resource Director" or "Dear Hiring Manager")?
8. Did you sign the letter (or use an electronic signature)?
9. Is an attachment (or enclosure) notation double spaced under your signature block?
10. Did you proofread aloud for correct wording and to eliminate typos and grammatical errors?

Page Design

1. Is the heading information (letterhead) at the top margin?
2. Is the font size of the name larger than the rest of the heading?
3. Is the heading text aligned correctly (no extra spaces)?
4. Is the letter centered top-to-bottom from the dateline down?
5. Does the salutation use a punctuation style consistent with that of the closing?
6. Are the paragraphs left-aligned?
7. Does the signature block begin with an appropriate closing and use a punctuation style consistent with that of the salutation?

Shavon D. Alkins
Box 3106, Robbins, MD 21214
sdalkins@gmail.com / (338) 555-7959

EDUCATION

Bachelor of Science in Business Administration, 3.87 GPA — May 2011
Concentration in Marketing and International Business
Minors in Accounting and Spanish
Campus University, Robbins, MD

Study Abroad Experiences:
• Philippines — January 2010
• Italy, Spain — Summer 2008

Honors:
• Dean's List, School of Business & Economics — 2009–2011
• Phillips-Perry Academic Excellence Award — May 2010
  (presented to the study abroad student with the highest GPA every year)

RELEVANT SKILLS

Leadership
• As treasurer of the Spanish Club, managed budgets and funds while providing effective customer service to a diverse membership
Communication
• Communicate daily with customers while performing sales associate duties
• Read, write, and speak Spanish fluently
Computer Skills
• Skilled in Microsoft Office (Word, Excel, PowerPoint, and Outlook)
• Proficient in Microsoft Access and Adobe Dreamweaver

WORK EXPERIENCE

Sales Associate — October 2011–Present
Target Corporation, Robbins, MD
• Use interpersonal skills to greet and assist customers courteously and efficiently
• Assist with cashier functions and other duties as assigned

Cashier/Sales Associate — August 2010–October 2011
Food Lion, LLC, Robbins, MD
• Interacted with customers, facilitated transactions, and maintained cash drawer

Bilingual Classroom Assistant — August 2008–May 2011
Eastlawn Elementary, Middletown, MD
• Worked with 5th grade children to develop their literacy skills and recognize word sets in Spanish and English

Language Lab Assistant — August 2007–May 2008
Campus University, Robbins, MD
• Prepared lab coursework activities

Cashier/Sales Associate — September 2006–July 2007
Family Dollar Inc., Pensacola, FL
• Managed front-end sales and provided excellent customer service
• Performed store setup tasks

Shavon D. Alkins
Box 3106, Robbins, MD 21214
sdalkins@gmail.com / (338) 555-7959

REFERENCES

Mr. William R. Smith, Manager
Target Store #5603
500 Valley Ridge Road
Robbins, MD 21216
Wrsmith2@targetstores.com
(338) 555-9000

Dr. Davis Archer, Dean
School of Business and Economics
Campus University
Robbins, MD 21215
darcher@campus.edu
(338) 555-7657 Ext. 3000

Ms. Melody Hamilton, Teacher
Eastlawn Elementary
326 Ravenswood Drive
Middletown, MD 21230
melody_hamilton@middletown-schools.md.us
(338) 444-5731

Résumé

Persuasive Content

1. Does your objective, qualifications summary, or professional profile focus on what you can do *for* the employer rather than what you want *from* the employer?
2. For a chronological résumé:
   • are your most recent degrees listed first (oldest last)?
   • are your most recent work experiences and activities listed first (oldest last)?
   • within your job descriptions, are the duties and responsibilities most relevant to the job listed first?
3. For a functional résumé:
   • do you include all skills relevant to do the job, along with how you developed them?
   • are your most relevant skills listed first?
4. Does the résumé use key words that target the employer's needs?

Key Elements

1. Is the heading information consistent with the cover letter?
2. Is your educational degree, date of graduation, and GPA listed?
3. Are only the institutions from which you received (or will receive) degrees listed?
4. Is all high school information removed?
5. If courses are listed, do they separate you from your competition?
6. Do key items begin with verbs rather than first person pronouns (I, my)?
7. Do your extracurricular activities include dates (years)?

Page Design

1. Is the font style consistent with the cover letter?
2. Are the locations and alignment of dates consistent throughout?
3. Is text aligned with tabs, not spaces?
4. Are all bullet items consistently aligned?
5. Are the dash styles between dates consistent throughout?
6. Does your résumé fill the page?
7. Did you proofread aloud to check for correct wording and eliminate all typos or grammatical errors?

References

1. Is the heading information and format consistent with your cover letter and résumé?
2. Is the font style consistent with your cover letter and résumé?
3. Does each reference include complete information (name, position title, company, email, phone number)? Have you been consistent about using or omitting complete mailing addresses?
4. Is the document formatted professionally and aligned evenly on the page?
5. Did you proofread names and numbers to ensure no typographical errors?

Choose a delivery method

Over the last decade, methods of delivering job applications have evolved as technology has improved. Very few employers currently request résumés and cover letters on paper. Instead, they prefer email submissions.[26,27] However, unsolicited letters may get more attention if sent by postal mail because unsolicited email often goes unread. This section offers advice about submitting job applications by email as well as by postal mail and in person.

Email

Before you email your résumé, think about how you will package your material and how you will follow up with your audience.

Decide whether to attach the cover letter as a separate file or include it within the body of the email message.
- Attached cover letters are more formal, but they can be inadvertently overlooked. If you attach your cover letter, include a short but formatted email message indicating which position you are applying for and what application documents are attached. If you combine both your cover letter and résumé into one file, ensure that each document remains well-formatted. Alternatively, you can attach your résumé and cover letter as two separate files.
- Cover letters included in the body of an email message may be problematic for recipients who read their email on mobile devices. If you decide to include your cover letter content in the body of the email message, use a standard email format rather than a formal letter style, and mention that your résumé is attached.

Use portable document file attachments and appropriate filenames. Some job advertisements may request specific file types, such as Word files or .rtf formats. If not specified, consider saving your attachments as PDF (Portable Document Format) files. PDF files maintain their formatting and are accessible by both MAC and PC computers. Be consistent with your résumé and cover letter filenames, for example, "Shavon_Alkins_Resume.pdf" and "Shavon_Alkins_Cover_Letter.pdf."

Confirm your message was received. You may use a return-receipt feature with an email submission, which offers two benefits: it communicates to the recipient that the message is important, and it provides you documentation that your message was received. If your email system does not support return receipts or if you do not receive an email response confirming receipt of your documents within a week, send a follow-up email requesting confirmation. Keep the wording of your message simple, such as "I am writing to ensure you received my cover letter and résumé sent May 14 in response to your advertisement for the open marketing manager position. Please confirm that you received my application and let me know if you need additional information. I look forward to hearing from you."

Follow up with postal mail submissions. Consider mailing duplicates of your cover letter and résumé, unless the job advertisement indicates that the company will not accept mailed copies of cover letters and résumés. Career counselor Katie Piotrowski recommends attaching a handwritten note indicating "Second submission. I'm very interested."[28] When appropriate, this additional effort can make a positive impression and increase your chances of being considered for an interview.

Postal mail

Use the following guidelines if you are asked to mail your résumé to a potential employer.

Ensure consistent font/style among all documents, including the envelope. Your cover letter, résumé, and envelope should complement each other by using the same paper quality, font, and formatting features. Consider creating business cards with the same format as well. Your business card stock should match the paper color and style of your cover letter and résumé.

Print your cover letter and résumé on quality paper. Most office and large department stores carry paper appropriate for job search documents. Use high quality bond paper in a professional color, such as white or buff. Avoid gray or patterned paper that does not photocopy well. Also, look for paper that has a watermark—a barely visible logo that can be seen only when the paper is held to the light. Good paper can subtly set your cover letter and résumé apart from the stack of copy paper used by your competition. Print your documents on a laser-quality printer and load the paper tray so the watermark is right side up.

Portray a professional image. Your handwritten signature provides a nonverbal message about your personality and professionalism. Use a readable cursive writing style and stay within the boundaries of the signature block. Sloppy or wildly artistic signatures can be perceived as flamboyant and inappropriate for business correspondence. Mailing your documents in a large mailing envelope rather than folding them into a standard envelope also presents a professional image. Regardless of which envelope size you select, print a label or feed the envelope through the printer rather than hand printing the return and recipient's addresses on the envelope.

Consider a return receipt. Before mailing your cover letter and résumé, consider purchasing a return receipt or tracking option so you receive confirmation that the envelope was delivered. A return receipt can also send the message that you paid extra attention to the mailing because you are eager about the position.

In person

On rare occasions, you may have the option of providing your application materials in person. In these cases, dress professionally and be polite. Don't assume you will simply drop off your documents with a receptionist and leave unnoticed. The employer could consider the receptionist's impression of you. In addition, even if you have not made an appointment, you may have the opportunity to meet with someone to discuss the position. Prepare for possible discussions by reviewing the interview strategies in Chapter 12. In-person submissions do not require a return receipt to ensure that the company receives your material. However, if the company does not respond to your application within two weeks, you can contact them to follow up.

Track your employment communication

Keep records of all your employment communication by using a tracking sheet like the one in FIGURE 11.14. Review your tracking information regularly so you can follow up with employers. If you have not heard from an employer a week or 10 days after the application submission deadline, you can contact the employer to inquire about the status of your application. Follow up by phone or email, whichever medium is more comfortable for you. Use the opportunity to further sell your fit for the job and mention any recent training or accomplishments. See FIGURE 11.15 for an example of a follow-up message.

IN SUMMARY, use the ACE communication process to create targeted cover letters and résumés that meet employers' needs. The guidelines you learned in this chapter will help you analyze, compose, and evaluate your employment materials to position yourself as a well-qualified applicant. As you learn new skills during your college career, regularly update your résumé so you will be ready at a moment's notice if the "perfect" job opportunity presents itself.

Create a separate page for each submission and organize your submissions by company name for easy retrieval when you are contacted by the employer to schedule an interview.

FIGURE 11.14
Tracking Sheet for Job Application Submissions

Name of Company: _____
Position/Job Title: _____
Contact Person: _____
Contact Information:
     Email: _____
     Address: _____
     Telephone: _____
     Fax: _____
     Website: _____
Position Advertised: _____
Position's Keywords: _____
Submission Deadline: _____
Date Submitted: _____
Date of Return Receipt: _____
Date of Contact: _____
Materials Submitted (Copies Filed/Attached)
    ☐ Cover Letter _____
    ☐ Résumé _____
    ☐ References _____
    ☐ Letters of Recommendation _____
    ☐ Transcripts _____
    ☐ Other: _____
Date of Follow-up: _____
Interview Scheduled: _____
Notes: _____
    _____
    _____
    _____

FIGURE 11.15
Job Application Follow-Up Message

email

FROM: Shavon Alkins <sdalkins@gmail.com>
TO: jw.herrick@dover.com
SUBJECT: Confirmation of Job Application

Dear Mr. Herrick:

I am writing to confirm you received my October 15 application for the Assistant Sales Manager position that was advertised on Monster.com. Dover's Quality Care program was a strong influence for the Customer Care campaign I worked on at Target, and I am very interested in becoming a part of the Dover team.

Please let me know if you need additional information. I look forward to hearing from you. Please call me at (338) 555-7959 or reply to sdalkins@gmail.com to arrange an interview.

Sincerely,
Shavon Alkins

Shavon D. Alkins
Box 3106
Robbins, MD 21214
sdalkins@gmail.com
(338) 555-7959

Address the hiring manager or contact person by name.

Indicate the position you applied for and when you sent your resume.

Briefly identify your knowledge of the company and your interest in a long-term career with the company.

Ask if additional information is required.

Request an interview and provide your contact information.

Close on a positive, forward-looking note.

CHAPTER 11 Summary

11.1 What should I analyze before composing résumés and cover letters? *(pages 392–398)*

- **Analyze your career goals.** To formulate your career goals, gain experience through internships, summer jobs, and volunteer experience. Narrow your career focus by analyzing your personal strengths and preferences and researching your career options. Chart a path for your career, but keep an open mind so you do not limit your opportunities.
- **Analyze your strengths and skills** by identifying areas of expertise, listing your sellable qualities, and recognizing your weaknesses.
- **Analyze your options for finding job opportunities** by registering with career centers and job banks, searching advertisements, developing professional and personal networks, using social networking tools, joining professional organizations, and targeting specific employers.
- **Analyze your professional image,** or how you will appear to employers, by reviewing the professionalism of your emails, business cards, telephone image, and online image.

11.2 How do I write an effective résumé? *(pages 398–411)*

- **Select an effective résumé design and format.** To design your résumé, use templates only as guides, and enhance your image with professional page layout and design techniques. Always keep an updated plain text version of your résumé that you can paste into online résumé submission forms. Depending on your strengths for the job, choose one of three formats: chronological to emphasize experience, functional to emphasize skills, or combined to balance skills and experience.
- **Compose effective résumé content** beginning with the heading and contact information. If you include an objective, focus on what you can do for the employer. Education and work experience are standard categories that can include or be followed by a separate section on capabilities and skills that are targeted to the employer's needs. Also include activities and accomplishments that highlight your strengths. Develop multiple résumés, if necessary, for different types of jobs. Ensure that your content is honest. Blatant exaggerations and content copied from résumé samples can quickly lead to rejection.
- **Evaluate your content and design.** Is it clear, complete, and concise? Does it use keywords from the job listing and emphasize information important to the job? Is it well designed? Is it proofread? Ask others to read your résumé and provide feedback.

11.3 How do I write an effective cover letter? *(pages 411–416)*

- **Analyze the position requirements** before drafting a cover letter to ensure you target the needs of the employer and identify keywords to include.
- **Compose persuasive content** by using AIDA: gain attention in the first paragraph, build the employer's interest and desire in the middle paragraph(s), and motivate action in the last paragraph. Letters for unsolicited applications—and letters for jobs where you are not a perfect fit—require more persuasion than solicited responses for jobs that are a perfect match for your qualifications.
- **Evaluate content and format** by reducing "I" strain, assessing the format, and proofreading carefully.

11.4 How do I evaluate and submit my employment materials? *(pages 417–421)*

- **Finalize your employment materials** using comprehensive checklists and feedback from others to ensure your audience (the employer) has a positive first impression of you.
- **Choose a delivery method** by weighing the options of email, postal mail, and in-person communication. Use appropriate follow-up techniques to ensure the employer received your documents.
- **Track your employment communication** by keeping records of the details of all your applications.

PEARSON mybcommlab *Are you an active learner? Go to mybcommlab.com to master Chapter 11 content. Chapter 11 interactive activities include:*

- Customizable Study Plan and Chapter 11 practice quizzes
- Chapter 11 Simulation, Cover Letters and Résumés, that helps you think critically and prepare to make choices in the business world
- Flash Cards for mastering the definition of chapter terms
- Chapter 11 Video Exercise, Building Careers & Writing Résumés, which shows you how textbook concepts are put into practice every day
- Interactive Lessons that visually review key chapter concepts
- Document Makeovers for hands-on, scored practice in revising documents

How do I write an effective résumé?

Select an effective résumé design and format
- Use templates as guides, not absolutes.
- Enhance your image with professional page layout and design techniques.
- Create a second plain text version of your résumé.

Choose a format that allows you to highlight your strengths
- Use a chronological résumé to emphasize work experience.
- Use a functional résumé to emphasize skills.
- Use a combined résumé to balance experience and skills.

Compose effective résumé content
- Highlight experience rather than providing an all-inclusive list of jobs.
- Target prospective employers' needs using keywords.
- Be specific about capabilities.
- Include internships as work experience.
- Include volunteer and extracurricular activities.
- Provide consistent information for each entry.
- Use bulleted lines rather than paragraphs.
- Choose professional references, list complete information, and ask permission.
- Give your references a copy of your résumé.

Evaluate your content and design
- Is the content clear, complete, and concise?
- Does the content use keywords from the job ad?
- Is the most important information emphasized?
- Is the résumé designed well and spaced to fit the page?
- Are alignment and style consistent?
- Is the resume carefully proofread for spelling and typos?
- Have you obtained sufficient feedback?

Shavon D. Alkins
Box 3106, Robbins, MD 21214
sdalkins@gmail.com / (338) 555-7959

EDUCATION

Bachelor of Science in Business Administration, 3.87 GPA — May 2011
Concentration in Marketing and International Business
Minors in Accounting and Spanish
Campus University, Robbins, MD

Study Abroad Experiences:
- Philippines — January 2010
- Italy, Spain — Summer 2008

Honors:
- Dean's List, School of Business & Economics — 2009–2011
- Phillips-Perry Academic Excellence Award — May 2010
  (presented to the study abroad student with the highest GPA every year)

RELEVANT SKILLS

Leadership
- As treasurer of the Spanish Club, managed budgets and funds while providing effective customer service to a diverse membership

Communication
- Communicate daily with customers while performing sales associate duties
- Read, write, and speak Spanish fluently

Computer Skills
- Skilled in Microsoft Office (Word, Excel, PowerPoint, and Outlook)
- Proficient in Microsoft Access and Adobe Dreamweaver

WORK EXPERIENCE

Sales Associate — October 2011–Present
Target Corporation, Robbins, MD
- Use interpersonal skills to greet and assist customers courteously and efficiently
- Assist with cashier functions and other duties as assigned

Cashier/Sales Associate — August 2010–October 2011
Food Lion, LLC, Robbins, MD
- Interacted with customers, facilitated transactions, and maintained cash drawer

Bilingual Classroom Assistant — August 2008–May 2011
Eastlawn Elementary, Middletown, MD
- Worked with 5th grade children to develop their literacy skills and recognize word sets in Spanish and English

Language Lab Assistant — August 2007–May 2008
Campus University, Robbins, MD
- Prepared lab coursework activities

Cashier/Sales Associate — September 2006–July 2007
Family Dollar Inc., Pensacola, FL
- Managed front-end sales and provided excellent customer service
- Performed store setup tasks

FROM: sdalkins@gmail.com
TO: jw.herrick@dover.com
SUBJECT: Application for Assistant Sales Manager Position

Dear Mr. Herrick:

Thank you for the opportunity to apply for the Assistant Sales Manager position at Dover Industries. I was very pleased to learn from Monster.com that you are currently hiring. I first became interested in working for Dover when we studied the company's Quality Care program in my marketing class last year. Since then I've been following Dover Industries and have been particularly impressed by the company's ability to promote its mission to "be the preferred shopping experience for a diverse clientele by providing quality products and services."

As my attached résumé indicates, I can bring to Dover over three years of sales associate and customer service experience, most of which I gained while a full-time student. This experience, along with academic work in marketing and other business concentrations, has helped me develop the leadership, communication, and collaboration skills required to be a valuable member of your management team. I had an opportunity to develop those skills further during my junior year study-abroad term in the Philippines, where I played a leadership role on an international and interdisciplinary team of students working on an intense, month-long market research project about reaching underserved populations. I was also one of the team members chosen to return to the Philippines to present our results at the Philippine Business Conference and Expo in Manila. More recently, I had the opportunity to demonstrate my abilities as one of the team leaders in our local Target's Customer Comes First Campaign, which significantly increased our customer satisfaction ratings.

I am enthusiastic about working at Dover and would appreciate the opportunity to meet with you to discuss how I can use my experience to exceed your customer care goals. Please contact me by phone (338-555-7959) or email (sdalkins@gmail.com) at your earliest convenience to arrange an interview.

Thank you for your time and consideration.

Sincerely,

Shavon Alkins

Shavon D. Alkins
Box 3106
Robbins, MD 21214
sdalkins@gmail.com
(338) 555-7959

How do I write an effective cover letter?

Analyze the position
- Research the company.
- Customize your letter to meet their needs.

Compose persuasive content
- Gain attention in the first paragraph.
- Build interest/desire with keywords and details.
- Motivate action in the closing.

Evaluate the content and format
- Is the message clear, complete, and concise?
- Does the content use keywords from the job ad?
- Can you reduce the "I" strain?
- Did you mention your résumé was attached or enclosed?
- Is the message formatted professionally?
- Are there typos or misspellings?
- Have you obtained sufficient feedback?

AIDA *p. 412*

Chronological résumé *p. 400*

Combined résumé *p. 400*

Cover letter *p. 411*

Functional résumé *p. 400*

Network *p. 395*

CASE STUDY Starting an Employment Search

This case study will help you review the chapter material by applying it to a specific scenario.

Raymond Varga completed a summer internship at Metrix Manufacturing after his junior year at Middleton College and was happy to receive a job offer from the company. Raymond had a sense of security as he started his senior year knowing that he had a job when he graduated.

The job proved to be all that Raymond expected. During his first year, he worked on several challenging projects that offered him the opportunity to expand his skills and apply the strategic management concepts he had learned during his last year of college. He liked his coworkers and was happy in his position. Therefore, he is surprised when his manager, Marilyn, explains to him today that due to the company's pending merger with their leading competitor, they would be eliminating redundant positions and managing their reduction in force based on a LIFO (last in, first out) plan. As a recent hire, Raymond would certainly be let go within the next month. Marilyn wanted to give him a "heads up" so he could start his career search while he was still employed with Metrix.

As Raymond returns to his desk, he feels overwhelmed. What does he do? He never searched for a job during college because he learned about the Metrix internship at a career fair. He never wrote a cover letter because Metrix required him to apply online and did not offer the option of uploading a cover letter along with his résumé. And he never updated his résumé after his junior year. Metrix offered him a job as soon as he completed his internship. Raymond isn't sure where to begin.

résumé

Raymond Ramón Varga

1484 Vista Ridge, Apt. 2B, Middleton, OH 43433

Phone: 419-224-4250 / Cell: 419-225-5503 / email: rvarga@metrix.com

EDUCATION

Business Administration Degree, Middleton College, OH, May 2012

WORK EXPERIENCE

May 2012–Present
Asst. Regional Sales Manager, Development Office, Metrix Manufacturing, Middleton, OH
Currently serve in an entry-level managerial position where I provide assistance to the regional manager as he develops and coordinates projects for our Midwest clients.

Summer, 2011
Internship, Development Office, Metrix Manufacturing, Middleton, OH
Provided general office duties, temped for the receptionist, routed correspondence, made photocopies

CAPABILITIES AND SKILLS

- Professional communication skills and dedicated work ethic
- Attention to detail and extremely organized
- Works well with others and possess exceptional interpersonal skills

PROFESSIONAL ORGANIZATIONS & VOLUNTEER ACTIVITIES

- Toastmasters International, 2011–Present
- Big Brothers, 2012–Present
- Habitat for Humanity, 2010–2012

Accompanies Case Study (see "Updating a Résumé," Review Question 2, on page 425)

Expanding the Possibilities

Raymond considers his employment options. He would like to find a job in the same city so he doesn't have to move. He also hopes to find a similar position where he can manage manufacturing projects for large customer orders. In just a year, Raymond has gained valuable experience at Metrix. Most of his work involved assisting the regional manager in developing contracts with clients and coordinating their projects. In the process, he has learned about many of the larger manufacturing companies in the Midwest. In addition to managing projects, he created an orientation workshop for new interns and coordinated a new database that tracked customers by demographics and sales volume. The database project required a significant amount of detailed research into past purchase orders as well as follow-up calls with purchasing agents. Raymond is confident that his communication skills have significantly improved and that he will be able to apply these strengths to a new job. Now he has to research career options and chart a path to his next position. He would like to build upon what he has learned on the job. However, he knows that limiting himself to his comfort zone will also limit his opportunities.

Review Question 1: *How can Raymond expand his possibilities?*

a. *Given his skills and work experience, what industries besides manufacturing could Raymond explore?*

b. *How should Raymond let his personal and professional network know he's looking for a new job? Who should he contact? What should he say?*

c. *How can Raymond use social networking sites such as LinkedIn, Plaxo, and Facebook to communicate he is looking for a job? Is this a good idea in Raymond's case?*

d. *How can he expand his current professional network?*

e. *While networking, Raymond will need to explain in a positive way why he is looking for a job. Suggest some phrasing he can use.*

Updating a Résumé

After contacting people in his professional network and creating a profile with the career center at his college, Raymond spends the next evening composing the content for his résumé, shown on page 424.

Review Question 2: *Carefully evaluate the content, keeping in mind that Raymond has not yet formatted his résumé or targeted a specific position. What does Raymond need to change, add, or remove? Itemize your suggestions providing a rationale for each, or create a formatted version of Raymond's content using your suggestions.*

Drafting a Cover Letter

Assume Raymond wants to apply for the job advertised in Figure 11.11 on page 411.

Review Question 3: *Refer to his résumé on page 424 and draft a cover letter using the AIDA format. Evaluate your draft using the guidelines described in this section.*

CRITICAL THINKING

1. Having a career plan is important, though experts suggest keeping an open mind about what you might want to do and where you might want to work. Describe your "perfect" job after graduation. Then identify jobs that may lead to that "perfect" job in a few years.

2. A professional image can be critical to your job search. If you were to begin a job search today, what changes to your email address, signature block, voice mail greeting, and communication habits would you need to make to ensure a professional image? Provide specific examples.

3. Which résumé format—chronological, functional, or combined—best fits your strengths and experiences? Explain why and provide three specific examples of how you would organize your résumé content based on this format.

4. Experts recommend not using personal pronouns in résumés. What do you think is the rationale behind this recommendation? Do you agree? What kinds of phrasing will you use in various parts of the résumé to avoid these pronouns?

5. Many employers list effective communication, collaboration, and interpersonal skills as job requirements. Draft at least one bullet point that explains your capabilities in each of these areas. Don't merely mention that you have these skills. Provide specific evidence that demonstrates your skills. Use Figure 11.9 on page 406 as a reference.

6. Candidates sometimes produce video résumés in order to stand out from the crowd. What are the pros and cons of sending a video résumé to a potential employer?

7. Creating a unique but consistent résumé and cover letter format is one method of demonstrating your skills with word processing and page design applications. How else might you demonstrate specific skills through your employment communication?

8. Assume you are interested in a job advertisement for an internship with a company near your college campus. The advertisement indicates the company accepts mailed and emailed applications. What are the advantages and disadvantages of mail versus email for submitting your application materials?

9. Career experts say that job recruiters spend only a few seconds glancing at a résumé before deciding to read it carefully or discard it. How can you ensure your résumé will receive serious consideration?

10. Assume you received an automated reply in response to your return receipt when you emailed your cover letter and résumé to a potential employer. However, you did not receive an individual response. Three weeks later, you still have not heard from the employer about the status of the position. What would you do to follow up? Since you know your materials were received, what content would you include in your follow-up message?

DEVELOPING YOUR COMMUNICATION SKILLS

11.1 What should I analyze before composing résumés and cover letters? *(pages 392–398)*

EXERCISE 1 Analyze your career goals

Even if you think you know what you want to do with your career, identifying your strengths and preferences can help you narrow your focus. Answer the following questions and support your responses with examples, evidence, or explanation:

- Do you prefer to work collaboratively with other people or on your own?
- Would you enjoy a creative position or a more procedural job?
- Do you see yourself working for a large or small company? In a large or small city?
- Would you enjoy a job that requires travel?

Based on your strengths and preferences, what kind of jobs related to your major would you be interested in pursuing after graduation? Provide your responses in a one-page summary.

EXERCISE 2 Analyze your strengths and skills

Even if you do not have any full-time work experience, you most likely have strengths and skills that can translate into assets for a potential employer. Create a one-page summary based on the following four-part analysis. Be as specific as possible about your skills and word them to relate to your chosen career path.

- Outline your experiences.
- Identify areas of expertise.
- List your sellable qualities.
- Recognize your weaknesses.

EXERCISE 3 Analyze your options for finding job opportunities: Virtual internships

Although your campus career center most likely provides a wide variety of traditional internship experiences, they may also list virtual internship opportunities for students who are not able to relocate. You can also find virtual internships online. Using either your campus career center or your favorite online search tool, find three virtual internship opportunities related to your career goals. (Hint: Use the search phrase "virtual internship" with your career field. For example "virtual internship" and "sales.") Evaluate your interest in and eligibility for these positions in a one-page summary and submit it to your instructor for evaluation.

EXERCISE 4 Analyze your options for finding job opportunities: Your dream job

Use at least three different websites that list job advertisements to search for your "dream job" after graduation. You can search Monster and HotJobs or websites tailored specifically to your field. Using the same search criteria, select a job advertisement that interests you from each site. Choose positions you will be eligible to apply for immediately after graduation rather than five or ten years later. What skills are listed in all three postings? Are any skills required for one position, but not the rest? Are there any other differences among the positions? Will you be qualified for these positions after graduation? If so, list the strengths you would emphasize in a cover letter or résumé to persuade the employers

to schedule an interview with you. If not, describe how you will equip yourself with the skills you will need. Summarize your findings in a one-page message to your instructor.

EXERCISE 5 Analyze your professional image

Assume you will not be able to use your school email account for more than a few months after graduation. You decide to create a new email address now to communicate with your professional network and define your professional image. Provide the following information to your instructor in a one-page summary:

- email address
- signature block (that includes contact information, and, if appropriate, a school logo and memberships or activities that would be meaningful to an employer)
- script for your voice mail greeting

11.2 How do I write an effective résumé? *(pages 398–411)*

EXERCISE 6 Select an effective résumé design and format

Which résumé format—chronological, functional, or combined—would you recommend for the following scenarios? Explain your choice for each scenario and explain how the applicants should highlight their strengths on their résumés.

a. Sally is a junior applying for an internship with a company that is looking for business students with proven analytical skills and attention to detail. Sally hasn't had any related work experience, but she has completed two service learning volunteer projects: one in a nursing home where she helped plan activities and the other for the local public television station where she prepared financials for grant applications.

b. George is applying for an entry-level managerial position with a manufacturing company. George spent five years working full time as a loader in the warehouse of a large manufacturing company while he put himself through college. However, he does not have any managerial experience.

c. Tamara has 10 years of clerical experience working as an administrative assistant in one of the academic offices on her campus. While working, she has taken classes part time and is finally ready to graduate with a degree in business administration. She is applying for a position as an office manager for a Fortune 500 company.

EXERCISE 7 Compose effective résumé content: Objective statements

Assume you are applying for an internship to gain experience related to your major. The position advertisement indicates the company prefers students with effective oral and written communication skills who are able to work efficiently in both individual and team environments. Based on your experience, draft an objective statement, qualifications summary, or professional profile for this position. Submit your information to your instructor for evaluation.

EXERCISE 8 Compose effective résumé content: Extracurricular activities

Harry is a friend you've known for several years. You are both first-semester juniors with the same major. Although you have been very involved in clubs and organizations on campus, Harry has not yet participated in any extracurricular activities. After reading this chapter, you know how important educational experiences and activities can be when applying for jobs. To help Harry prepare for his employment search, suggest at least three clubs, activities, or related opportunities on your campus that he could pursue that would help him prepare for his profession and would enhance his résumé. For each opportunity, list the requirements and costs to join, when and how often they meet, and the benefits of membership. Submit the information to your instructor for evaluation.

EXERCISE 9 Compose effective résumé content: Work history

Although your résumé should highlight your experience that specifically qualifies you for a position, maintaining a comprehensive work history provides you with a database of your experiences for future reference. Create a document titled "Complete Work History" or something similar. List in chronological order (beginning with your most recent job), every position you have held, including both paid and volunteer jobs. Use a professional format that highlights job titles, company names, locations, supervisors' names and contact information, dates of employment, beginning and ending salary information, specific job duties, and reasons for leaving. For example, a job may have been seasonal work or you may have relocated for school or family reasons. Proofread carefully, and submit the document to your instructor for evaluation.

EXERCISE 10 Compose effective résumé content: Work experience

Your roommate asked you to evaluate her résumé, which includes descriptions of her work experience in paragraph form using first-person pronouns. You know employers will find it easier to read bulleted items beginning with verbs. Transform the three paragraphs in the top of the next column into bulleted lists, maintaining the heading information for each one.

EXERCISE 11 Compose effective résumé content

Assume your friend Estelle asked you to help her with her résumé. She wants to apply for an internship program at the CIA she read about on the CIA website. Estelle is majoring in general business, but is in the process of changing her major to

---

Community Development and Outreach Intern   May 20XX–Present
Guilford Green Foundation, Sykesville, TN
During this summer internship experience, I orchestrated several campus outreach campaigns with the general public, which included recruiting donors, volunteers, and aids. I also assisted in event planning.

Sales Lead and Merchandising Manager   October 20XX–May 20XX
Ann Taylor Loft, Millersburg, TN
As a part-time sales lead and merchandising manager, I marketed our brand awareness and built a clientele base in a new area. This involved initiating networking programs with local businesses to increase traffic.

Assistant Office Manager   June 20XX–August 20XX
Iris Fashions, Sykesville, TN
This full-time summer position provided a unique perspective of helping to run a start-up fashion company. I was tasked with producing an operational structure for the franchise, managing inventory demands and maintaining accounts. I also developed unique systems tailored to the company and created PR and marketing materials to promote the emerging name.

Accompanies Exercise 10

JOB ADVERTISEMENT

HeymanCIA Part-Time Internship Program
If you are a promising undergraduate senior or graduate student currently enrolled at a university or college within the Washington, DC, metropolitan area, we'll give you practical work experience between classes. Interns become familiar with the CIA and Intelligence Community by participating in a range of meetings and projects. The program allows participants and the Agency to assess opportunities for a permanent employment following completion of undergraduate and/or graduate school.

Minimum requirements: We are looking for students with a variety of majors, including international affairs, non-romance languages, area studies, economics, geography, physical sciences, or engineering. Students selected for this program must have completed three full years of undergraduate studies or be enrolled in graduate school and be continuing school on a full-time basis following this assignment. Students must be enrolled in a College or University in the Washington/Metropolitan area at time of application and for the duration of the internship. Interns generally are required to work two semesters (depending upon University's schedule). A GPA of 3.0 or better is required.

Because of CIA's national security role, all applicants must successfully complete a thorough medical and psychological exam, a polygraph interview and an extensive background investigation. The CIA is America's premier intelligence agency, and we are committed to building and maintaining a workforce as diverse as the nation we serve.

An equal opportunity employer and a drug-free workforce.
For more information and to apply, visit www.cia.gov.

Source: Central Intelligence Agency.

Accompanies Exercise 11

economics. When you ask why she's interested in the internship, she says she reads a lot of spy novels and thinks the CIA is her "dream job." She would enjoy being a CIA operative because she is good with people and fits in easily in new situations. In her study abroad, she got along well with her host family and participated in a volunteer program at a local hospital. She would enjoy being a CIA analyst because she has a lot of computer experience. Even though she's not majoring in MIS, she has almost enough courses for a minor. Read the job advertisement and then determine if the preliminary content Estelle has gathered is effective. Is it tailored to this position? Does it focus on the employer's needs? Does it reflect her skills and abilities? Estelle knows she needs to expand her résumé and asks for your input. Use the information presented in the résumé guidelines section of this chapter to provide a comprehensive list of suggested improvements and additional content for Estelle's résumé.

EXERCISE 12 Exaggerating your résumé is dangerous [Related to the Ethics feature on page 407]

Assume that four other friends, besides Estelle, are interested in the CIA internship advertised in Exercise 11. Each friend fails to meet at least one requirement. What advice would you offer to help them ethically represent their experience on their résumés and still have a chance at being considered?

a. Mary is a third-year student at college, but she is only in her second year of actual undergraduate studies. She entered school with advanced placement credits. Thus, she will not quite meet the requirement of three years of full-time undergraduate studies.

b. Ryan has always wanted to work for the government, and the CIA is appealing to him because he is very analytical and he loves the idea of working internationally. He is majoring in French, which is not one of the CIA's preferred majors. His minor is Middle Eastern Studies, and he has begun to take a course in Arabic, but he is not fluent. He has also taken a number of economics and international relations courses.

c. Larry believes the CIA internship would position him very well to get a full-time job after graduation in the consulting industry. He is not interested in a full-time job with the CIA. However, the CIA is interested in evaluating their interns as potential full-time employees.

d. Your friend Kendra is currently studying at another school outside the geographical area specified by the job advertisement, but she wants this internship so strongly that she has applied to transfer to your school, which is in the geographical area, so that she can qualify. The CIA application is due now, and she has not yet been accepted to your school.

ESTELLE GANT
526 Maple Leaf Way, Rockville, MD 20851, 240.555.7837, e.gant@yahoo.com

CAREER OBJECTIVE
Part-time intern for the CIA

EDUCATION

Bachelor of Science, Morgan State University, GPA: 3.01	In Progress
Study Abroad Experience: Ghana: Social Transformation and Cultural Expression program	Fall 2010

WORK EXPERIENCE

Teller, Bank of America, Rockville, MD   2011–Current
- Greet customers and process banking transactions
- Analyze daily drawer reports and troubleshoot discrepancies

EXTRACURRICULAR ACTIVITIES
- Volunteer, Rockville Memorial Hospital   2012–Current
- Member, Technocrats   2011–Current

REFERENCES
Available Upon Request

Accompanies Exercise 11

EXERCISE 13 Evaluate your content and design

If you have not updated it recently, evaluate your résumé based on the guidelines outlined in this chapter. Is your content clear, complete, and concise? Does it emphasize the most important information? Is it well-designed to fit the page? Does it look professional? Are alignment and style consistent? Critically evaluate your résumé and make a list of changes you will incorporate to improve the overall content and format. Submit your list of changes to your instructor in an email message or memo. Your instructor may also ask you to provide before and after versions of your résumé based on your evaluation.

EXERCISE 14 Selling your cross-cultural skills [Related to the Culture feature on page 410]

Assume that you are interested in applying for an international job. Create a section for your resume titled "International Expertise and Understanding." Based on the advice in the Culture feature, write a set of bullet points that you can include in this section. In addition, write a second set of bullet points that you could include in your "Skills and Abilities" section, highlighting skills that will help you work effectively in a cross-cultural environment. Be honest about those skills. Remember that you may be asked to explain them in detail in an interview.

11.3 How do I write an effective cover letter?

(pages 411–416)

EXERCISE 15 Analyze the position requirements

Find an advertisement for an internship or full-time position that interests you and for which you are an eligible candidate. Analyze the job description and make a list of keywords you would highlight in your cover letter to communicate that you are qualified for the position. For each keyword, draft a sentence that you could include in your cover letter. Print the job advertisement and submit it with your keyword sentences to your instructor for evaluation.

EXERCISE 16 Compose persuasive content

Refer to Exercise 11. Assume Estelle Gant needs to draft a cover letter to accompany her résumé for the CIA internship. You advise her to gain attention in the first paragraph, build interest and desire in the middle paragraph(s), and close by motivating action. She looks at you blankly and asks you to help her draft the content. Based on the information you learned about Estelle in Exercise 11, create an outline of possible content for each paragraph.

EXERCISE 17 Evaluate content and format

The text at the top of the next column was emailed as a cover letter in response to an advertisement for a part-time accounting clerk for your college's financial aid office.

The position requires accounting majors in good standing who have detailed analytical skills and respect for confidentiality. Evaluate the cover letter based on the following guidelines presented in this chapter:

a. Does the first paragraph grab the audience's attention?

b. Does the content target the specific employer?

c. Will the wording pique the audience's interest or desire to contact the applicant?

d. Can the "I" strain be reduced?

e. Does the message indicate a résumé was attached or enclosed?

f. Does the last paragraph motivate action?

g. Is the message formatted professionally?

h. Is the message clear, complete, and concise?

i. Are all typos and misspellings corrected?

Summarize your analysis of the cover letter and suggest revisions in a one-page message to your instructor.

EXERCISE 18 Web résumés, video résumés, and e-portfolios [Related to the Technology feature on page 416]

a. Use a free web-hosting service to create an online version of your résumé. Design a professional format, using either an html template or your own web-design skills. Consider ex-

---

Dear Human Resources Director:

I am replying to your position announcement for a part-time accounting clerk in the financial aid office. Attached is my résumé.

I am a junior accounting major and president of our Accounting Club. I will graduate next year and pursue my master's degree in accountancy with a focus on public accounting. I have one summer of related experience providing bookkeeping duties for a summer camp. I know I am well qualified for this position and look forward to hearing from you about the status of my candidacy.

Sincerely,

Accompanies Exercise 17

panding your résumé content to become an electronic portfolio by including samples of documents you have written, presentations you have created, letters of recommendations, and other documentation.

b. Create a video résumé using the suggestions provided in the chapter. Keep the video short, but professional. Post your video to YouTube, Yahoo Video, or Hulu and share the URL with your instructor.

11.4 How do I evaluate and submit my employment materials? *(pages 417–421)*

EXERCISE 19 Finalize your employment materials

Print a recent cover letter and résumé (and references, if you have them) that you sent to a potential employer. Use the checklists on pages 417–418 to evaluate your documents. In a memo to your instructor, identify how your documents conform to the listed criteria and what you can do to improve them. Attach your documents to your memo.

EXERCISE 20 Choose a delivery method: Email

Enhance your current résumé or draft a résumé based on the content presented in this chapter. Using your favorite search engine, investigate options for creating a PDF file by downloading a free PDF conversion application. Or, if possible, use your word processing program to save your résumé as a PDF file. Be sure to follow the advice in the chapter about naming files. Email your résumé to your instructor with a draft of your cover letter in the body of the email.

EXERCISE 21 Track your employment communication

Review the sample tracking form in Figure 11.14 on page 421. Create a similar form, adding additional criteria you might want to record (such as the results of your follow-up communication). Complete the form with sample data and submit a printed version to your instructor.

WRITING

EXERCISE 22 Formatting a professional résumé

Select a job advertisement or internship listing that interests you and create (or modify) your résumé to apply for that job using the guidelines presented in this chapter. Use the résumé format—chronological, functional, or combined—that bests suits your experience. Submit the advertisement and your résumé to your instructor for evaluation, either in hard copy or PDF form.

EXERCISE 23 Creating a plain text résumé

Transform the résumé that you created in Exercise 22 into a plain text version that you can easily cut and paste into a web-based form or the body of an email message. Submit your résumé by email to your instructor for evaluation.

EXERCISE 24 Writing a persuasive cover letter

Find a job advertisement for a position you are qualified for. Print the advertisement and circle the keywords. Write a persuasive cover letter based on the guidelines presented in this chapter.

Evaluate the effectiveness of your letter and proofread carefully before submitting it and the advertisement to your instructor. If you have previously designed a résumé, ensure that the cover letter coordinates well with the résumé in content and visual style.

EXERCISE 25 Compiling effective references

Brainstorm the people you know who can be part of your professional network. Make a comprehensive list noting your relationships, their contact information, and professional affiliations, if applicable. From that list, select three to five professional people who can serve as professional references for you. Format a reference sheet with a heading similar to your résumé and an appropriate title listing your references and their contact information.

EXERCISE 26 Designing business cards

Design a business card that complements the format or style of your cover letter and résumé. Include your name and contact information. Consider including your major and institutional affiliation as well.

COLLABORATING

EXERCISE 27 Peer-reviewing résumé content/formats

Update your résumé, if necessary, or create a résumé based on the information presented in this chapter. In small groups, share and review copies of group members' résumés. How do the formats and content differ among the group members? Do the styles support the strengths of the students' qualifications? If the members of your group were competing for the same job, which résumé would be considered the strongest? Provide feedback to your group members, indicating both the strengths and potential weaknesses of their résumés. Individually, summarize your feedback in a message to your instructor. Organize the content by summarizing the strengths and weaknesses of each person's résumé along with the suggestions you shared with that person.

EXERCISE 28 Comparing companies' résumé submission requirements

In a team, brainstorm a list of companies within a specific industry, for example, sports-related (Nike, Reebok, Adidas), or technology-related (Microsoft, Intel, Google), or financial services (Citibank, Bank of America, Wells Fargo) companies. The number of companies you list should equal the number of people in your team. Assign one company to each team member. Visit the companies' websites to determine the employment opportunities they provide. How do they request applicant information (for example, web-based submissions, emailed résumés, or hardcopy mailings)? Discuss the similarities and differences among the companies and collaboratively write a one-page memo that summarizes your findings.

SPEAKING

EXERCISE 29 Making informal/impromptu presentations

a. What are your career goals? What is your "dream job"? In a one- to two-minute presentation, identify the kind of job you hope to obtain immediately after graduation as well as the job you hope to achieve 10 or 15 years later. Explain what you will do during that time to prepare yourself for your dream job.

b. What skill or strength do you currently possess that will help you secure a job related to your major after graduation? In a one- to two-minute presentation, describe the skill, when you obtained it, and how it will benefit your career.

c. What skill do you need to develop or enhance before you begin your job search? In a one- to two-minute presentation, describe the skill, when and how you plan to develop it, and how it will benefit your career.

d. Imagine you could write the job description for your "perfect job." Identify the job title and summarize the specific duties in a one- to two-minute presentation.

e. Identify five capabilities and skills you currently possess that you could highlight on your résumé. Describe specific evidence to support each ability. For example, you could support your ability to work well with others by citing your leadership during a two-day car wash fundraiser last semester when you successfully organized 25 volunteers.

EXERCISE 30 Briefing your class about job search resources

a. Research the student organizations your school supports. How many are there? How many of the organizations focus on students' academic or professional development? Which ones would help prepare you for your career goals? Identify three organizations and describe their goals, benefits, and (if applicable) any membership requirements. Prepare a visual aid that outlines this information, and describe your findings to your audience in a three- to five-minute presentation.

b. Research three different websites that provide résumé writing tips. Compare their suggestions for creating professional résumés and identify what you perceive to be the three most important tips that all three recommend, as they will relate to your job search. Prepare a visual aid, such as a slide or handout, that outlines these three tips, and describe your findings to your audience in a three- to five-minute presentation.

c. Use the U.S. Bureau of Labor Statistics' *Occupational Outlook Handbook* to learn about a specific job related to your major. List up to five things you read that you already knew about this position and identify where you learned about them. Then list up to five things you read that you did not know about this position. Prepare a visual aid to support a three- to five-minute presentation that describes your findings.

d. Select a specific company for which you would like to work. Research its website to familiarize yourself with its mission, products or services, corporate culture, and financial outlook. Summarize your findings in a three- to five-minute presentation during which you display either selected pages from the company's website or other visual aids you have prepared. Throughout your presentation, indicate why the information persuades you to want to work for this company.

e. Research international internship opportunities. In a three- to five-minute presentation, outline where students can find international internship opportunities and the skills they required to be competitive candidates. Prepare a one-page handout summarizing this information to support your presentation.

GRAMMAR

Capitalization (See Appendix D—Section 3.1)

Rekey (or download from mybcommlab) the following paragraph, correcting the 30 errors or omissions in the use of capital letters. Underline all your corrections.

Robin thompson, owner of etiquette network and Robin Thompson charm school, says, "personal phone calls are fine, so long as you limit them and choose the appropriate time." She also believes cell phones should be turned off at work; If you are at work, that means you have a desk phone and can be reached at that number most of the time. Cell phones and pagers don't belong in business meetings, either, she says. Would you interrupt your Vice President to answer your cell phone? (you wouldn't if you want to keep working for the Company.) Of course, when you are flying to Corporate Headquarters on the West Coast from the Regional Office in north Dakota, a cell phone can be a life saver. Because you had to take your daughter to her spanish lesson, you've missed your plane. The head of the division of specialty products wants that report by 5 P.M., president McMillan is expecting you for lunch, and your son forgot to order his date's corsage for the High School prom tonight. Note to self: text son about picking up tuxedo. Instead of a Master's Degree in business, you're thinking maybe you should have majored in Emergency Management. Thank heavens you have a blackberry.

Numbers (See Appendix D—Section 3.2)

Rekey (or download from mybcommlab) the following paragraph, correcting the 15 errors in the use of numbers. Underline all your corrections.

20 years ago mobile phones were novel and expensive. In the nineteen-eighties cellular telephones, luxury items used only by top executives, cost almost $4000 and weighed more than 2 pounds. Today, of course, even ten-year-olds have them, and the lightest ones weigh two.65 ounces. Some people have more than one mobile phone; imagine carrying 2 2-pound phones in your purse. The International Telecommunications Union estimates that there are approximately 4,6000,000,000 mobile telephones in use worldwide. That amounts to about sixty percent of the world's population. China ranks number 1 with a little over 57 percent of Chinese using cellular telephones. India ranks 2nd, adding more than six (6) million subscribers a month. According to The Washington Post, nearly 1/2 of the Indian population has wireless service—3 times the number of landlines in the country. The United States ranks third, with 91% of us using cell phones.

12 Getting the Job— Interviewing Skills

new hires @ work

Chris Chow
Analyst Consultant
Accenture
Northwestern University, 2010

"WHAT HELPED ME MOST BEFORE INTERVIEWS was to make an exhaustive list of questions and practice answering them until I felt comfortable. I also suggest researching the company and job thoroughly and bringing a list of questions that show insight about the job and your passion for it. Review your résumé carefully and pick it apart because that is what interviewers will do. Prepare to talk about weak spots—turn them into positives. Finally, prepare 'stories' to use during the interview—scenarios to answer questions like 'tell me about a time when . . .' and stories that will illustrate your strengths."

Introduction

In Chapter 11, you learned how to compose effective cover letters and résumés. If the content and appearance of these documents present you as a person who meets the company's needs, you may receive an invitation to interview. A job interview is a mutual learning experience. The employer will learn more about you to determine if you are a good fit for the job, and you will learn more about the organization and the position to determine if the job is a good fit for you. Since you may get only one opportunity to persuade an employer that you are the right candidate, it is important to develop strong interview skills. The ACE process can help you develop those skills and improve your interview results in three ways.

First, ACE helps you analyze your communication goals and prepare effectively. Each step in the interview process has a different goal. For example, at a career fair your goal is to gather information about the company and make a good first impression so that you might later get an interview. At an on-campus interview, your goal is to impress the interviewer enough to be invited to visit the company. Analysis helps you focus on the goal and identify how best to achieve it. Analysis also helps you prepare to answer interview questions. You'll need to think about why an interviewer asks a specific question and then how to answer that question to portray your strengths. Finally, analysis helps you ask good questions during an interview. Analyze what you want to learn to help you compose questions that prompt interviewers to share this information.

ACE also helps you compose a professional image in your speaking, writing, and actions. Composing does not refer only to writing. Every time an interviewer asks you a question, you will need to compose your thoughts to identify a clear message and organize your answer to support that message. If you anticipate questions and prepare answers in advance, you will feel much less pressure during the interview. As you prepare for interviews, you also need to compose a professional image. How you look and how you act will affect an employer's perception of you just as strongly as what you say. Your professional image will help employers envision you as a member of their team.

Finally, ACE helps you evaluate your performance. In many ways, interviewing is a performance. When you finish an interview or when you hear from an employer, you will benefit from evaluating your performance. What did you do well? What are your concerns? What kind of responses did you get? This kind of evaluation and reflection helps you learn from the experience and perform better the next time.

This chapter will show you how to apply ACE throughout the interview process. In the chapter, you will learn how to:

- take advantage of different types of interview situations
- prepare for a job interview
- dress appropriately for the interview
- make the best impression during the interview
- follow up effectively

Study Question 12.1

How do I take advantage of different types of interviews?

■ Access this chapter's simulation entitled Interviewing, located at mybcommlab.com.

Although traditional one-on-one interviews are still common, you may participate in several different kinds of interviews. For example, your first contact with a company may be a mini-interview at a career fair. Later, the company may ask you to participate in a campus interview or telephone interview before inviting you to an in-person interview. Once at the company, you may be involved in panel or group interviews, action interviews, and testing situations before you meet with a hiring manager. Each of these interview formats has a different goal, and each format benefits from different preparation.

Capture interest in preliminary interviews

Preliminary interviews—including career fair interviews, on-campus interviews, and telephone interviews—give you the opportunity to learn about an employer and capture a recruiter's interest.

Career fairs

A **career fair** is a gathering of representatives or recruiters from many companies seeking to fill open positions. Your goals are to learn about the company and to impress these recruiters enough that they recommend you for an interview. Because you have only a limited amount of time, you need to be prepared to make an immediate impression. What's the first thing you're going to say? How will you market your skills to set yourself apart from the competition? To get the most benefit from a career fair, consider the following suggestions.

Arrive early. If possible, plan to arrive at a career fair when it opens rather than waiting until later in the day when recruiters have already seen many people. In addition to standing in shorter lines, you'll have more time to speak with recruiters.

Make a plan. Large career fairs can be overwhelming—both in the number of employers and the number of job seekers who attend. If you have the opportunity to go to a career fair a year or so before you are actually looking for a position, you will gain valuable knowledge that will help you prepare later on. Large career fairs often provide a layout of the room that shows where the booths for each company will be situated. Study the map to find out which employers will be at the fair, and, if possible, where their booths are situated. Plan a strategy for who you want to talk to first, second, and third.

Look the part. Dress like a businessperson rather than a college student. If you don't dress professionally, recruiters won't take you seriously. (More information about dressing professionally is presented in section 12.3.) In addition, adopt a confident and professional attitude and exhibit real interest in the company. The *A–Z Business Etiquette Guide* published by OfficeTeam, a division of Robert Half International, suggests, "passion for your work can translate into a compelling image—you'll be perceived as a confident, competent, talented professional."[1]

Be assertive. Approach recruiters and make the first move to start a conversation. Extend your hand and firmly shake the recruiter's hand (practice handshaking ahead of time). Begin the conversation with confidence: "Hi, I'm Sean Garrison, an accounting major from Southwest University. Here's my résumé. I want to be a _____ (state the name of a position you know they are looking to fill) and am interested in your company because _____."

Demonstrate your knowledge. Show that you are well prepared, organized, and interested in the company. Review the websites of the companies you want to meet with ahead of time so you are knowledgeable about their products or services, mission statements, and open positions. (More information about how to research companies is presented in section 12.2.) Identify the jobs you might be interested in and know something about the position. Consider printing the job descriptions so you can refer to them during the career fair to ask specific questions.

Ask good questions. Although you want to demonstrate that you already know something about the company, also prepare a list of questions to ask. Asking specific questions about the company's current projects or news items you have read indicates your interest in the company. In addition, you can then use the recruiter's answers when you interview at the company to further demonstrate your knowledge of the organization. Generic questions you can ask during career fairs include:

- What do you like most about working for your company?
- What advice do you have for job seekers interested in your company?
- Assuming I get in the door, what will the interview process be like?

Additional information about asking questions is presented in section 12.2.

Take notes. When you write down information a recruiter says, you send the message that you are interested in the company and value the information. Your notes may also help you prepare for onsite interviews.

Ask for a business card. Before moving on to the next company's booth, ask the recruiter for a business card. Make notes on the back of the card to help you remember the recruiter who gave it to you. Your notes might include the date and where you met, what you talked about, and something interesting about your conversation. For example, writing comments on the cards such as "funny jokes," "great career advice," or "stressed the importance of teamwork" will help you put names with faces and prepare personalized thank-you notes. Additional information on thank-you notes is presented in section 12.5.

Follow up. Having recruiters' business cards also helps you follow up after the career fair. A short email message thanking recruiters for their time and reiterating your interest in a particular position says a lot about your professionalism and attention to detail. You might also want to attach your résumé so they have an electronic version to

Career fair A gathering of representatives from companies seeking to fill open positions.

share with others at their company. Recall from Chapter 11 that you should try to send your résumé as a PDF rather than a Word document to ensure that the résumé will look the same to the recipient as it does on your computer.

On-campus interviews

Some employers send recruiters to campuses to conduct *first-round* interviews with a large pool of applicants. The recruiters who conduct on-campus interviews may be the same people who represent the company at career fairs, or they could be hiring managers from a specific unit or department of the company, such as IT or accounting. Many career services centers require students to register with the center in order to participate in on-campus interviews. In addition to ensuring you are eligible for on-campus interviews, registering with your school's career services office early in your college career allows you to take advantage of their resources.

On-campus interviews can range from 15 to 60 minutes and often use the traditional one-on-one format. Because the recruiter will typically interview a large number of applicants, it is important to set yourself apart from the competition. At this stage in the hiring process, the interviewer's goal is to narrow the candidate pool so that the *second-round* interviews—which are usually conducted by telephone or at the company's location—include a small set of highly qualified and competitive applicants. To ensure you make it to the next level, follow the same guidelines suggested for career fairs before participating in an on-campus interview.

Telephone interviews

Some companies use **telephone interviews** to filter candidates before scheduling onsite interviews, especially for candidates who need to travel a distance to participate in the interview. In some cases, you may be asked to call the company. In other situations, you will be answering their call. Either way, choose a quiet location where you feel comfortable and will not be disturbed. Telephone interviews may be challenging, but they also offer at least one advantage: during the interview, you can easily refer to resources such as printouts of the company website, notes for answering standard interview questions, and your own list of questions for the interviewer. Use the following guidelines to prepare for telephone interviews.

Know your audience. Before placing a telephone call, learn a little about the person you're calling. For example, assume that in response to your online job application, you received an email message from Pat Kuceyeski asking you to call to schedule an interview. Before you place the call, find out how to pronounce Pat's last name correctly. Also, find out if you are calling Mr. Kuceyeski or Ms. Kuceyeski. Calling the company's general number (receptionist) or human resources department should provide you with this information.

Begin the call professionally. When you place a telephone call, identify yourself before asking for the person you're calling, and indicate that you are returning a call or calling at the person's request: "Good afternoon. This is Michael Smith. Pat Kuceyeski asked me to call. Is she available?" When you receive a scheduled telephone call, do not answer immediately after the phone rings because you may appear too eager. Instead, answer after the second ring, take a deep breath, smile, and state your name: "Good morning. This is Michael Smith."

Know your medium. Use a landline rather than a cell phone to increase the chances of a good connection and minimize the possibility of a dropped or lost call. If a search committee is involved in the hiring process, several people will participate in the telephone interview. In these cases, they may be gathered in a conference room and use a single speakerphone to communicate with you. Write down the committee members' names as they introduce themselves. Ask for their job titles, if they don't provide them, so you can ask specific questions that relate to their positions. Communicating via speakerphone can be difficult because you have no visual cues to indicate when someone is waiting to speak. In addition, if many people speak at once, it is very difficult to identify to whom you should respond. During the conversation, feel free to ask people to repeat or reword a question if you did not hear them clearly or are not sure what they are asking you.

Avoid distracting noises. Take the phone call in a quiet room. Do not chew gum, drink beverages, or eat anything during a telephone interview. Avoid tapping your fingers or pencil, which communicates your nervousness. Press the mute key or cover the phone's mouthpiece if you need to clear your throat, cough, or sneeze. If using a landline, turn off your cell phone so you are not distracted by other calls or texts.

Project a professional voice. Speak clearly and at a normal pace (many people tend to speak too quickly when nervous). Be slightly more formal than you normally are. For example, say "yes" instead of "yeah." Avoid fillers, such as "like," "ah," and "um." Practicing can help you speak more fluently. Let the caller complete a question before jumping in to answer it (don't be too eager). Pause before speaking to gather your thoughts, then breathe deeply, articulate your words, and smile. Although no one can see you, smiling brightens the tone of your voice. Also consider dressing professionally if it will increase your motivation and confidence during the interview.

End the call professionally. Thank your interviewers for taking the time to speak with you. If you are talking to just one person, use his or her name. Here's an example: "Thank you, Mr. Paulson, for your time today. I appreciate the opportunity to discuss my qualifications for this position, and I look forward to hearing from you again. Do you know when you will make a decision?" Also, let the interviewer hang up first, both as a professional courtesy and as a practical matter. You want to be sure that the interviewer does not have any last-minute questions to ask before you hang up.

Sell your strengths during onsite company interviews

If you talked to a company's recruiter at a job fair or on-campus interview and participated in a telephone interview before scheduling a face-to-face interview, you will have gained valuable information about what the company is looking for in a job applicant. However, in many cases, your first contact with a company may be to schedule an interview in response to your cover letter and résumé. Interview experiences vary greatly from simple one-on-one interviews that may last only a half hour, to detailed agendas that span two days and involve many people in several interviews, presentations, and meals. FIGURE 12.1 outlines an intinerary for a student who interviewed for a management training program with a large multinational company. This interview experience included three meals with company representatives, a group interview, an action interview, a presentation, and a one-on-one interview with a senior-level manager. Preparation for this two-day event requires knowledge about the different interview formats.

One-on-one interviews

In a traditional one-on-one interview, you meet individually with an employer to discuss your qualifications for a position. In many cases, the person conducting the interview is the immediate supervisor for the position you want. In those cases, one goal of the interview is to establish that you have a natural fit with the organization and this person. The interview will determine—for both you and the supervisor—whether you would work well together on a day-to-day basis.[2] Therefore, when the supervisor asks if you have any questions, take the opportunity to gather information that will help you make a good decision about your potential working relationship. Ask questions about the supervisor's expectations, the challenges of the position, and daily activities.

Panel and group interviews

A **panel interview** involves several people, such as a search committee, who gather in a conference or seminar room with a job applicant to discuss the position. The interview process is similar to a traditional one-on-one interview, just with more people asking

Telephone interview An interview conducted by telephone, often used to narrow the candidate pool before scheduling an onsite visit.

Panel interview An interview format that involves several people, such as a search committee, who gather in a conference or seminar room with a job applicant to discuss the position.

FIGURE 12.1 Interview Itinerary

INTERVIEW SCHEDULE FOR BRIAN PEELE
MANAGEMENT TRAINING PROGRAM
April 12–13, 20XX

Wednesday, April 12

3:35 PM	American Airlines Flight #222 to Atlanta (ATL)
6:40 PM	Arrive Atlanta – Take Marriott Courtesy Shuttle to Hotel
7:30 PM	Meet Management Trainees David Whitaker and Mario Phillips in Marriott Lobby for Dinner
8:00 PM	Dinner at Ruth's Chris Steakhouse

Thursday, April 13

7:30 AM	Meet Alyson Prescott in Lobby for Breakfast (transfer to company headquarters)
9:00 AM	Group Interview with Search Committee
10:15 AM	Break
10:30 AM	Action Interview with Management Training Program Staff
12:00 PM	Lunch with Management Training Program Staff
1:30 PM	Presentation of Action Interview Results
2:00 PM	Interview with Division Head of Management Training Program
3:00 PM	Meet Mario Phillips to Drive to Airport (ATL)
6:05 PM	Return Flight – American Airlines Flight #559 (DFW)

questions. You may not know ahead of time whether your interview will be with just one or many people, so be prepared. Consider the following suggestions:

Shake hands with everyone. When you enter the room and see several people, take the initiative to approach each one and introduce yourself as you extend your arm to shake hands. Use a firm handshake, make eye contact, and smile. This is your chance to make a strong, professional first impression. When the interview concludes, repeat this process thanking each person for taking his or her time to meet with you.

Get everyone's name and position. As you shake hands, people may introduce themselves. If they offer a business card, take it. If they don't, after you've been seated, ask if you can take a moment to learn people's names and positions. However, don't ask for additional information at this point in the interview because that may take too much time away from the interview process. If you can, use people's names as you respond to their questions: "I appreciate your question, Mr. Lowry. I just finished a project on. . . ." Here's a helpful hint: when you write down names and titles, draw a box like the table you're sitting at and record their information on the paper in the order they're positioned around the room. This will give you an easy reference to use.

Balance your eye contact. Although one person may seem to be in a higher position than the rest of the panel, be sure to make eye contact with each person. Begin your responses by first looking at the person who asked the question, but ensure balanced eye contact with the rest of the panel during your response, and conclude your answer by returning your eyes to the questioner.

A **group interview** brings together several job candidates who are interviewed at the same time. This format provides employers the opportunity to evaluate applicants' collaborative skills as well as the knowledge and abilities they can offer. When participating in a group interview, listen intently, ask questions, and offer advice, but do not lead the group unless someone from the company's search committee asks you to do so. Group interviews can use the standard Q&A format, or they can be project-based action interviews as described next.

Action interviews

Action interviews require applicants to perform under work-based conditions. Action interviews are typically designed to assess your common sense, your time management skills, or your ability to think logically under pressure, your common sense. Some action interviews simulate project meetings or scenario discussions, while others offer opportunities to solve real problems, such as generating ideas for a marketing campaign or evaluating potential cost-savings strategies. Performing well in action interviews requires preparation and practice. If possible, ask your contact person two or three pertinent questions about the situation, for example:

- How many people will be involved in the action interview? What are their job titles?
- Will the action interview take the form of a discussion, or will you be asked to present an analysis or results at the conclusion of the exercise?
- What specific area will the action involve, such as marketing, management, or operations?
- Will it be simulated, such as case study, or a response to a real problem?
- Will you receive data ahead of time to research related information and possible options?

To get more comfortable answering action interview questions, search the web for "case interview" resources. You will find many examples of case scenarios and questions that you can use to help you practice.

Some action interviews are designed to assess your presentation skills, especially if you are applying for a position in an area such as sales, marketing, or management, where good presentation skills are needed right from the start. If you are asked to make a presentation at your interview and are not given a topic to address, ask your contact person if the company is currently dealing with a particular problem or obstacle, and take time to research it. Ask what kind of presentation equipment you will be able to use, the layout of the room you will be speaking in, how many people will be present, and whether handouts are expected. Refer to Chapter 10 for more specific presentation information.

Employment Tests

Employers often schedule an employability test before an in-person interview to give them time to measure and evaluate the test scores before discussing the results with the applicant. Tests vary widely and can measure personality style, leadership qualities, problem-solving abilities, analytical skills, judgment, and specific content knowledge related to the position.[3] Some of these tests are objective-based online assessments, such as the Myers-Briggs Type Indicator, which suggests personality types and tests of your computer skills. Other tests may use case-based writing-intensive formats or may combine multiple-choice questions and essay responses. The Praxis Pre-Professional Writing Skills Test uses a combined format to assess both grammar knowledge and writing ability.

Group interview An interview format in which an employer meets with several applicants at the same time to assess their approach to working collaboratively with others.

Action interview An interview format that requires applicants to make a presentation or perform under work-based conditions, which could be simulated or real.

Corporate culture refers to the personality of a company as reflected in its atmosphere, attitudes, values, and behaviors. You will see signs of a company's culture on its website: how does the company talk about itself and its values? When you visit for an interview, you will see signs in the office: how do people dress? Do they greet each other with first or last names? Are the offices formal and expensively decorated, or informal and individualized? How early do people come to work, and how late do they stay? Are relationships formal and hierarchical, or are they more informal and collegial?

During the interview process you have the opportunity to assess the company's culture. If you align well with that culture, you will most likely develop effective working relationships with your colleagues. If you do not perceive a good fit, you may not enjoy working for the company.

How can you determine a company's corporate culture, and—more importantly—whether you will be a good fit in that culture? The following suggestions will help you answer those questions.

Before the Job Interview

Read the company's mission or vision statement on its corporate website. Although these are often generalized statements about over-arching goals, some companies post more detailed content in their "About Us" pages. For example, Microsoft includes information about its corporate citizenship initiatives. Other information can be gathered by reading links to recent news items and corporate announcements. Download the company's annual report, and pay attention to the photos of the people they choose to display as well as the style and tone of the wording they use. Most importantly, talk to employees or people who know employees to get their sense of the company's culture. What is it like to work there?

During the Job Interview

While you are waiting in a reception area, assess the "atmosphere" of the workplace. What impression do you get of the people who work there? How do they interact with each other? During your interview, ask questions that will help you understand the company's corporate culture. However, avoid directly asking people how they would define it. Most employees won't know how to describe their company's culture, either because they don't think about it or because they are too immersed in it to objectively describe it.[4] Consider the following questions:[5]

- In your opinion, what does this company value the most from its employees?
- How does the company communicate its goals to employees?
- What performance criteria does this company use and how does it reward employees?

Pay attention to what happens during group or action interviews. Employers often use scenarios and role plays to assess how well a job candidate communicates and collaborates with others. If you feel comfortable with the company's way of working, that may signal you'd be a good fit.

After the Job Interview

Soon after your interview, think about the experience and visualize yourself in that workplace. How did you feel about the work environment and the people that you met? Make a decision about your fit with the company before you receive a job offer so you aren't distracted by the salary and benefits they provide. Your day-to-day happiness and long-term career success may be more closely tied to your corporate fit than to your bottom line.

mybcommlab

For a CULTURE exercise, go to Exercise 7 on page 467 or to this chapter's End-of-Chapter Exercises at mybcommlab.com.

How can I prepare for a job interview?

Whether you are participating in an on-campus interview or have progressed to an on-site interview, you will perform best if you are well prepared. Think of preparation as having three parts: learning as much as possible about the company, composing and practicing answers to potential interview questions, and composing questions that you can ask. By preparing well, you will be able to reduce performance anxiety and approach the interview as a conversation between colleagues in which you share information, ask good questions, and communicate the key points you want the company to know about you.

Analyze the company

The more you know about the company with which you are interviewing, the more prepared you will be to anticipate questions, tailor your responses, and ask good questions. University Career Services at Northwestern University recommends you research the following about an employer before interviewing:

- history, philosophy, and goals of the organization
- geographical location of headquarters, branches, and subsidiaries
- organizational size, number of offices/plants, and potential growth
- organizational culture and structure
- annual production and performance growth
- current and potential products and/or services
- training and promotional opportunities
- competitors
- descriptions of operating divisions
- organizational chart (include names of top executives)
- financial review of stock performance and shareholder reports
- contributions to the industry or field
- recent news/press releases

You can find much of this information by visiting the company's website and by reading its most recent annual report. For an outside point of view, look for articles in business publications and websites, including *Investor's Business Daily*, *Kiplinger's*, and *MarketWatch*. You can find articles in these and other publications by searching business journal databases such as Lexis-Nexis, ABI-Inform, EBSCO Business Source Premier, and Cengage Business & Industry. You can also use a web search engine such as Google or Bing to find articles and interviews with the company's top executives.

For publicly traded companies, financial information—including financial statements, significant competitors, industries and clients served, and SEC filings—is available through resources such as Yahoo! Finance, Dow Jones Interactive, Hoover's, Dun & Bradstreet, and Standard & Poor's. For private companies, financial information is more difficult to find. One possible source you may find at your library is *Hoover's Handbook of Private Companies*.

You also can more deeply research a specific company through LinkedIn and other social networking tools. People in your personal and professional networks may have friends or contacts who work there. Review profiles, make connections, and ask questions to learn more about the company. In fact, Dan Schawbel, an authority on personal branding, suggests doing a people search instead of a job search and using social media tools to connect with people who work at the company where you will be interviewing.[6] Another way to get an insider's perspective on a company is to take advantage of career resource websites like Vault.com and Glassdoor.com. On both sites, current employees provide their view of what it's like to work at a company. In addition, on Glassdoor, people who have interviewed with companies explain the interview process and the types of questions you are likely to receive.

new hires @ work

Jason Calcaño

Editorial Assistant
Pearson Education

Rutgers University, 2010

"Anytime you can mention an interesting fact about the company or demonstrate knowledge about what the company is doing or has done, you show that you have done your research and are serious about your interest."

Corporate culture The personality of a company as reflected in its atmosphere, attitudes, values, behaviors, and unstated assumptions.

Compose answers to typical questions

Interviewers often use standard questions to help them learn about a candidate and assess that person's suitability for a job. As part of your interview preparation, develop clear, concise answers to these questions, along with details that allow you to elaborate. Rather than bringing scripted responses with you, practice beforehand (and aloud) so your answers don't sound canned. FIGURE 12.2 lists some of the most common questions.

FIGURE 12.2 Common Employment Interview Questions

Questions about Yourself
1. Tell me about yourself.
2. How has your experience prepared you for this position?
3. What was the most useful criticism you received?
4. How do you motivate people?
5. How would you describe your leadership style?
6. How do you work under pressure?
7. Tell me about a time when you . . .
   • used your analytical skills
   • demonstrated planning skills
   • delegated responsibility
   • worked successfully under pressure
   • failed
   • used persuasion to change someone's point of view
   • made a difficult decision
8. What are your greatest strengths/weaknesses?
9. What are your career plans (short- and long-range)?
10. Are you planning to continue your education?
 	
Questions about Your Career and Past Jobs
11. What work experience has been the most valuable to you?
12. What contributions did you make at your last job?
	13. What did you like best or least about your last job?
	14. Why are you leaving your current position?
	
	Questions about Your Job Search
	15. Tell me about your job search. How will you make your decision?
	16. What challenges are you looking for in your next position?
	17. Describe your ideal job.
	18. What factors are most important to you in choosing an employer?
	19. What criteria are most important to you in choosing a position?
	
	Questions about the Job You Are Applying For
	20. What do you know about our company? What interests you the most?
	21. Why do you think you would like this job?
	22. How do you see yourself contributing to our organization?
	23. What are your salary expectations?
	24. How do you feel about traveling, working long hours, etc.?
	25. Why should we hire you?

The following advice will help you respond to several of these questions—ones that people often have trouble answering.

Tell me about yourself is not a request for your life story or complete biography. It is your opportunity to identify the skills that qualify you for the position. Prepare a 30- to 60-second summary of information that is relevant to the job. For example, why did you choose your major? What strengths or accomplishments uniquely qualify you for this position? What is your career goal (keeping in mind that employers will not be motivated to hire you if your career goal is to open your own business)? When relating prior work experiences, begin with the oldest relevant position and work your way up to the most current so that your story is coherent. Unless asked to go into more detail, just summarize related jobs, highlighting the experiences within those jobs that prepared you for this position.

What do you know about our company? What interests you the most? Answering these questions requires that you have done your research and know something about the company. You should also think about what you find interesting about the company and the possibility of working there. Do you like the industry or field? Do you admire the company's mission and vision? Do you respect their products, clients, or innovation? Do you believe you will fit into the culture of the company? Be prepared to talk intelligently about their business and how you can contribute.

Why should we hire you? Study yourself to determine how you fit the job and the company. Provide clear, specific evidence of your skills. You should have articulated the answer to this question in your cover letter. Bring a copy of your cover letter to the interview to refer to, if necessary.

Describe your ideal job. If you respond to this question by indicating the job you are applying for is your ideal job, you will sound insincere, especially if the job is an entry-level position. However, do not share information that would make you a less desirable candidate. For example, if in five years you want to start your own business but know you need experience first, don't share your entrepreneurial goals with a potential employer who is looking at you as a long-term human resource investment, not as a future competitor. When describing your ideal job, identify attributes that demonstrate your work ethic and interpersonal skills, for example "My ideal job is a position that does not feel like work. Every day I get to solve problems, help people, and contribute to the organization."

What's your greatest strength/weakness? Your greatest strength should be directly related to the job. Your weakness should be a real weakness rather than a backhanded compliment. You will sound insincere if you suggest that your greatest weakness is that you work too hard or that you're a perfectionist. According to Alison Green, hiring manager at AskAManager.com, "Candidates who can't or won't come up with a realistic assessment of areas where they could improve make me think they're lacking in insight and self-awareness—or, at a minimum, they're just making it impossible to have a real discussion of their potential fitness for the job."[7] Mention a real weakness that indicates you are aware of your shortcomings (we all have them) and are making an effort to enhance your skills. Identify constructive criticism you have received from previous employers or instructors, outline the steps you are taking to improve, note any progress, and predict your future success in this area. For example:

> *"Although I enjoy working collaboratively with others, in the past I have not been very good at delegating work. I tend to want to do it all myself. I realize this is not an effective method of getting work done, and I've made a point to improve that. For example, in my last project. . . ."*

or

> *"Although I've received positive feedback on my classroom presentations from my instructors, I do not feel that my speaking skills are as good as they can be. I've joined Toastmasters and plan to continue to improve my presentation skills."*

Why are you leaving your current position? If you are employed, do not speak negatively about your current job. According to a survey of 3,061 U.S. hiring managers conducted by Harris Interactive, a market research firm, this is one of the most common and most detrimental mistakes candidates make at interviews.[8] Focus on the job you are applying for as a way to advance your career—what you're moving toward more than what you're getting away from. Emphasize positive qualities, such as your desire for a greater challenge or more responsibility.

What are your career plans (short- and long-range)? In the short term, your goal should be to get the job you're applying for in the interview and prove to the company that you are a valuable member of their team. Long-range plans should suggest your continued growth and level of responsibility at the company. Use your research about the company to cite specific job titles or projects that you are interested in pursuing. Demonstrate that you are invested in a long-term relationship with the company.

What are your salary expectations? The best answer to this question is to suggest that you are flexible and willing to negotiate your salary based on industry averages and the current market conditions. Avoid stating a minimum amount, which might result in a lower salary than they had planned to offer you. Conversely, indicating a salary much higher than they budgeted could cause them to stop considering you a candidate. Karen Burns, author of *The Amazing Adventures of Working Girl,* suggests answering the question in one of these two ways: *"I'm pretty flexible about salary. However, I do believe that my compensation should be commensurate with my value to your company. What's your salary range, by the way?"* or, *"I've done a lot of research and learned that the going rate for this job ranges from X to Y thousand dollars. What's your salary range?"*[9]

Tell me about a time when you . . . ? Behavioral questions are designed to determine how you would make decisions, solve problems, or respond to stressful situations.[10]

Behavioral questions A type of interview question designed to determine how you would make decisions, solve problems, or respond to stressful situations.

Your answers to these questions should demonstrate your collaborative skills, innovative thinking, and leadership abilities.

One well-established method of responding to behavioral questions is to use the **STAR method**, which stands for situation, task, action, and result.[11] Using this framework, you develop a story that identifies a *situation* in which you completed a *task* (such as solving a problem or making a decision) by implementing a specific *action* that ended in a positive *result*. For example, consider the answer to a question about working well under pressure in FIGURE 12.3.

FIGURE 12.3
The STAR Method of Answering Behavioral Questions

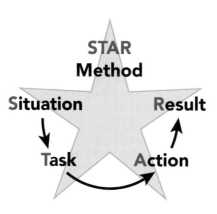

QUESTION
Tell me about a time when you worked successfully under pressure.

ANSWER
Situation: Last semester, I worked on a market research project for a small business near the university. Our team had difficulty collecting data. By the time we had collected it all, we had only one week to complete the project.

Task: In that one week, we needed to analyze all the data, develop a justified set of recommendations, and write a complete report for the client.

Action: Although I originally did not have a leadership role on the team, I took the lead and developed a work plan that delegated the work, set deadlines, and ensured that all the analysis was double checked by another member of the team. I also facilitated the team meeting when we developed recommendations.

Result: As a result of this approach, we not only completed our report on time, but our client agreed with our analysis and decided to implement three of our four recommendations.

As you plan answers, be sure to identify the three or four selling points that set you apart from other candidates—and develop STAR stories that give you the opportunity to highlight these attributes.

Preparing and practicing responses to interview questions will help you organize your answers and target the employer's needs. Practicing will also help you avoid saying too much. If you tend to talk a lot when you are nervous, or if you fall into a comfortable discussion with the interviewer, be careful about sharing too much information. If you inadvertently mention that you're always running your new baby to the doctor's office, or that a close relative was just diagnosed with cancer, the employer may worry that your family obligations will interfere with your job.[12]

In rare cases, employers may ask questions that are inappropriate or illegal. For example, employers are prohibited by federal law from asking personal questions about your family or health, though they may collect demographic information once you are employed. Application forms may request that you volunteer information about your nationality, ethnicity, or race to document equal employment opportunity the government requires, but you are not obligated to provide this data. Other inappropriate topics include your age, marital status, children (or whether you plan to have them), family history, religion, or affiliations. While employers may ask whether you have a disability or physical condition that would prevent you from fulfilling the requirements of the job, general questions about medical information are not allowed under federal law. As you prepare responses in advance, think about how you would handle inappropriate questions asking for information not related to the job. You can choose to answer, refuse to answer, or redirect the question to something that is more job-related. This last option is a useful skill to practice. For example, if an interviewer asks whether you have small children at home, you could say that you do not foresee any conflicts between family obligations and work.

Compose questions to ask

Interviewers commonly ask candidates *"What questions do you have?"* Not having good questions to ask is another common and detrimental interview mistake, according to the hiring managers surveyed by Harris Interactive.[13] You should ask three or four questions to demonstrate your interest in the job. However, Theresa Grothe, recruiter and staffing specialist for Boost Mobile, a division of Sprint Nextel, cautions not to ask questions that you could have easily researched on your own. For example, asking where the company's headquarters are located or how many employees they have tells the interviewer that you did not do your research.[14] Also avoid asking questions that are more relevant once you have been offered a position—for example, questions about benefits such as health insurance and retirement plans. If you have done your research, you should be able to ask several meaningful and appropriate questions about the company and the position. The questions that follow are general questions that may be relevant to ask no matter what company or position you are interviewing for.

Questions you can ask about the company:

1. The mission statement indicates that your goal is to. . . . How does the company fulfill this goal at an operational level on a day-to-day basis?
2. What are the company's plans for long-term growth?
3. Can you tell me about the typical career paths for people in the position for which I'm interviewing?
4. Does the company support professional development? What are typical opportunities in this area?
5. What advice do you wish you'd received when you were starting here?

Questions you can ask about the position:

1. What is a typical day like in this job?
2. What are the greatest challenges of this position?
3. How would I be evaluated in this position, and by whom?
4. Who last had this position, and is he/she available if I have questions once I start the job?
5. Who would I be working most closely with on a daily basis?
6. When do you expect to make a hiring decision?

Do not leave an interview without asking about the next steps.[15] You can ask when the company expects to make a decision or even if there's any reason why you might not be considered for the job. The answers to these questions will tell you how seriously you are being considered as a candidate.

Study Question 12.3

How should I dress for a job interview?

You may have heard the saying, "clothes don't make the man (or woman)," but what you wear certainly communicates a message about you. Employers cite dressing inappropriately as the biggest mistake job applicants make in interviews.[16,17] These unsuccessful applicants dress much too casually, wearing street clothes such as jeans, low-slung pants, short skirts, gym shoes, or sandals. Or they may wear tight clothing that is too revealing. When dressing for interviews, follow two key rules: wear business formal attire and look professional.

Wear business formal attire

Historically, business attire was very formal. Men wore three-piece suits and women wore dresses. Some businesses still adhere to a business formal dress code. For example,

STAR method A method of answering a behavioral interview question by explaining a **S**ituation, **T**ask, and **A**ction that led to a positive **R**esult.

in financial management and legal environments, attire is neutral and conservative. In many companies, however, the dress code is business casual, a professional but more relaxed way of dressing. In fact, according to a Gallup Poll, business casual is the most common form of dress in business today.[18] For men, business casual means a sweater, an ironed button-down or polo shirt, slacks or khakis with a belt, and dark socks and shoes. Women have more casual attire options—slacks, skirts, dresses,

TECHNOLOGY Managing Your Social Media Image

Social media can both enhance and detract from your professional image, depending on the content that's "out there" about you and who has access to it.

According to Ponemon Institute, an organization that conducts research on Internet privacy issues, human resource professionals frequently use Internet searches, blog entries, and social networking sites to screen job candidates. A Ponemon survey found that nearly one-third of those web searches led to the candidate being rejected.[19] Similarly, a 2010 survey commissioned by Microsoft found that 79% of U.S. hiring managers and job recruiters research job candidates online, and 70% of managers have rejected candidates based on what they found.[20] Consider, for example, the story of the college student applying for a management consulting internship who lost the job because he described himself on Facebook as being interested in drugs, sex, and violence—using very colorful language. Even though the recruiter knew the young man was not serious, the company did not want to risk hiring someone with such bad judgment.[21] By contrast, a strong online persona can help a job search. One director of a university career center tells the story of a company recruiting at the university who had difficulty deciding between two candidates until he researched them both on Google. He ultimately chose the one who had the stronger Google presence.[22]

To manage your online image, follow these guidelines:

Review your current online presence. Google your name to see what results an employer can find. If you believe any of the material may be harmful to you, then work to remove it from the web. Also, modify your Facebook and other social media privacy settings to allow only confirmed friends access to your page. If your friends and acquaintances have posted any negative pictures of you on Facebook, ask to have those pictures removed.

Use a unique and consistent name on all your web profiles. If you have an unusual name, people will easily be able to find you in a web search. However, if you have a common name, consider adding a middle name or middle initial to your web profiles and web entries so that you stand out among all the others who share your name.[23]

Join professional directories. To maximize the positive online information an employer may find about you, add yourself to professional directories such as LinkedIn and Plaxo. Professional networking sites like these enable you to post information about your education, work experience, and professional qualifications. You can also receive recommendations from colleagues and friends to substantiate your qualifications. You may find that you already have a profile on ZoomInfo. ZoomInfo, used heavily by recruiters, continuously updates information about businesses and employees and offers advanced tools to search the information. It combines community-contributed content with content acquired from ZoomInfo's proprietary web crawling to create more than 50 million profiles of business people. ZoomInfo encourages people to update their profiles and there is no cost to do so.

Source: Reprinted with permission from Zoominfo.

Consolidate your web presence by creating a central profile. For example, by creating a Google profile, you can control the information that will appear at the top of a Google search for your name. In this profile, you can create links to other sites on the web that you'd like a potential employer to see.

Search results for Mimi Bory, a New Hire at The Baltimore Zoo.
Source: Reprinted with permission from Mimi Bory.

For a TECHNOLOGY exercise, go to Exercise 12 on page 467 or to this chapter's End-of-Chapter Exercises at mybcommlab.com.

blouses, sweaters. FIGURE 12.4 provides examples of both business formal and business casual options.

Although business casual may be the dress code in the company where you are interviewing, unless you are explicitly told otherwise, your job interview clothing should be business formal. Wear a well-pressed professional business suit (jacket with matching slacks or skirt) in a conservative color. Your interview attire should conform to the one hanger rule—it should be a professional-looking outfit that looks like it was purchased on one hanger. In other words, the jacket and slacks (or skirt) are a set rather than mix-matched tops and bottoms that you piece together. Your goal at an interview is not to express your personality through clothing and accessories but to dress in a way that allows people to focus on what you say.

FIGURE 12.4 Business Attire

BUSINESS FORMAL

- Matching jackets and slacks or skirts
- Dark colors with light shirts
- Coordinating tie for men (no loud colors or patterns)
- Neutral or dark hose and dark shoes for women
- Dark socks and dark shoes for men
- Polished, unscuffed shoes
- Conservative jewelry

BUSINESS CASUAL

- Clothes that are pressed and clean
- Well-maintained shoes (no sneakers)
- Coordinating colors and accessories
- Good grooming

Look professional

Creating a professional look for an interview involves more than just selecting your clothing. In addition to the clothing suggestions outlined in the previous section, consider the following guidelines when preparing for an interview.

Tips for everyone

Dress for the position above the one you're applying for. Do some legwork by visiting the company, if possible, several days before your interview to observe what people are wearing as they enter the building. Practicing the commute ahead of time will also let you know how long it will take to get to the interview and, if you are driving, where you should park.[24] Alternatively, you can simply call the human resources department to ask about the company's dress code. However, even if business casual is the norm for employees, wearing more formal clothing is usually expected for interviews. If your contact person specifically suggests business casual for your interview, as many IT companies do, dress for the position above the one you want, to demonstrate your professionalism.

Ensure your clothing fits correctly. Buying a suit is not enough. To look professional, the suit may need to be altered to fit correctly. For both men and women, arm lengths for suits should extend just below the wristbone when the arm is at rest (not extended), and the shirtsleeve should extend a half-inch beyond the jacket. Slacks should be long enough to break in the front while the back of the pant hangs straight to the heel of the shoe. Generally speaking, your slacks are too short if you can see your socks when you walk and too long if they bunch or reach the floor. Practice wearing your professional business attire, including your portfolio and accessories, by walking down long hallways, going up stairs, and sitting in an office chair to ensure you are comfortable and feel relaxed, but look professional.

Wear a watch and turn off your cell phone. If you typically use the clock on your cell phone to know the time, buy a watch and turn off your cell phone. Leaving it on vibrate is not enough. Turning it off or silencing your phone demonstrates that you are fully focused on the job interview.

Use professional (conservative) grooming habits. It may seem obvious, but your professional attire is also complemented by your professional grooming habits. Because interview clothing and accessories are conservative, your grooming style should also be conservative. Short hair styles are most conservative, but women can wear longer hair if it is well-styled or tied back at the nape of the neck.[25] Women should avoid ornate hair clasps or barrettes. For men, facial hair is not recommended, but a neatly groomed mustache or goatee is acceptable. Nails, for both men and women, should be neat and trimmed short.

Avoid distracting odors. Do not wear cologne or perfume to an interview. People often perspire when they're nervous, which can increase the scent of a cologne or perfume. You want people to remember you because of your strengths and skills, not your smell. In addition, do not smoke or be near anyone who smokes before an interview. If you smell like a cigarette, a potential employer may infer that you are at a greater risk for health problems and consequently may be absent frequently or become a burden on the health-care plan as compared to a nonsmoking employee. Similarly, do not drink alcohol before or during an interview. To ensure your breath is fresh, use mints that dissolve quickly rather than chewing gum.

Hide or eliminate tattoos. Tattoos can hurt your chances of receiving a job offer. Cover all tattoos with clothing or makeup. If you plan a long-term business career, consider having visible tattoos removed.[26]

Leave your backpack at home. Look like a business professional rather than a student. Carry a dark-colored portfolio, briefcase, or messenger bag. Women should pack their essentials in one of these options, or also carry a small purse.

Tips for men

In addition to general business attire guidelines, men should ensure a professional image by considering the following guidelines.

Choose a contrasting but conservative shirt and tie. Solid-colored shirts are most versatile, but a simple stripe is also acceptable. White, cream, and gray shirt colors coordinate well with dark suits and a wide range of ties. Straight-collar shirts (with collar stays) are more formal than button-down shirts. Your tie should provide a contrast and/or a splash of color without a loud or distracting pattern (no cartoon characters!). For an added touch of style and class, purchase a coordinating pocket square for your external breast pocket.

Wear dark shoes. Wear dark-colored shined shoes (as dark or darker than your suit). If you purchase new shoes, break them in a few days before your interview and scuff the bottoms so they aren't slippery. For men, the color of your socks should match your suit or your shoes and be long enough so no skin shows when you sit and cross your legs.

Wear a belt or suspenders—not both. Dark-colored belts that match your shoes (cordovan, black, or brown) are more frequently worn than suspenders (also called braces by many upscale clothing stores). However, dark-colored suspenders, without flashy patterns are also acceptable and can set you apart from the competition. If you opt for suspenders, do not duplicate your efforts by wearing a belt, too. Choose one or the other.

Minimize jewelry. Men should not wear any jewelry other than a watch and a wedding ring or class ring. Cufflinks and tie tacks are acceptable if small and conventional. Earrings and other piercings do not reflect a convervative business image for men.

Tips for women

In addition to the general business attire guidelines, women can ensure a professional image by following these guidelines.

Wear a neutral-colored blouse under a conservative suit. Tailored pantsuits are as acceptable as suits with skirts. Avoid sleeveless tops or tops with distracting patterns. If you interview in a poorly ventilated room, you need to be able to remove your jacket, if necessary. Do not wear tight or revealing clothing. Necklines should cover cleavage and hemlines should come to the knee. Wear slips and camisoles as necessary to prevent see-through silhouettes.

Wear conservative shoes and hosiery. Close-toed and closed-heel shoes in a conservative color are the safest style. Ensure that your shoe color matches or is darker than your suit. If you're buying new shoes, break them in several days before your interview to ensure they do not pinch your feet, cause blisters, or slide on slick surfaces. Hose are required if you are wearing a skirt and are a good choice with slacks also. Avoid patterned hosiery, and choose a neutral color that is not darker than your suit.

Consider skirt lengths. If you wear a skirt, it should extend to the knee. Shorter skirts are not appropriate for interviews, and longer skirts may seem overly formal. Avoid skirts with front or side slits as they often show too much leg. Back slits should also be a conservative length. If you need to wear a slip, make sure it does not show.

Wear neutral, well-blended makeup. Avoid bright colors, even if they match your outfit. Soft hues that match your skin tone are best. Nails should be clean, well-manicured, and trimmed to a short length. If you wear nail polish, select beige, clear, or pale pink. Avoid nail art.

Minimize jewelry. Jewelry should be conservative and inconspicuous, complementing your outfit rather than making a bold statement. Wear no more than one ring per hand, no more than one earring per ear, and eliminate jewelry from all other piercings. Avoid bracelets and long earrings that jingle when you move.

Study Question 12.4

How should I act during the interview?

When you have confidence in your preparation and your appearance, you are ready to go to your interview. Your goal during the interview is to be your best self and make a strong, positive impression. To achieve this goal, you need to act like a professional from the moment you arrive until the end of the interview, including during meals.

Manage first impressions

You get just one shot at a first impression, and many employers will form their opinion of you within the first few seconds of meeting you. In fact, a survey of executives conducted by Robert Half Finance and Accounting, the world's largest financial recruiting firm, found that "Hiring managers often know whether they might hire someone soon after the opening handshake and small talk."[27] Therefore, be prepared to make a strong, positive first impression by considering these guidelines:

Arrive early. Know how long it will take you to get to the interview location, where you will be able to park, and if possible, how to get from the parking area to the interviewer's office or reception area. Alison Green of AskAManager.org advises that if you arrive more than 10 minutes early, wait in your car rather than in the reception area to avoid seeming too eager or making the interviewer feel obligated to meet with you ahead of schedule.[28] Plan to enter the reception area about 10 minutes before the interview time and, if time permits, use the restroom before the interview begins.

Look ready to work. Look like a professional who is ready to work by bringing the following in your portfolio or binder:

- a pad of paper and nice pen
- copies of your résumé printed on good paper
- your business cards with your name, email address, and phone number
- several copies of your list of references with complete contact information
- personal notes or website printouts about the company and the job
- a list of questions you plan to ask the interviewer
- personal items, such as mints and tissues

Make a good impression as you wait for your interview. One hiring manager explained some of the inappropriate waiting room behavior that he saw during job interviews: "One job applicant was leaning so far over a receptionist's desk that his feet were off the floor. I remember thinking, he's not even an employee yet, but he's already harassing the staff. In another situation, while several applicants were waiting together in a conference room for their individual interviews, two young men were arm wrestling."[29] In some cases, the waiting periods may be intentional to test your patience. How do you handle idle time? Look productive by reviewing your notes about the company and job, or ask someone for a recent copy of the company's annual report or product information.

Greet people professionally. Use people's names when you meet them ("Good afternoon, Mr. Williams. Thank you for taking time to meet with me today.") This practice personalizes the conversation, conveys politeness, and helps you remember the person's name after the fact. Use people's last names until they indicate their first names. Shake hands with everyone you meet, and practice your handshake ahead of time to ensure a firm, solid grip. Protocol experts Dale Web and Pauline Winick describe this as a web-to-web grasp. The "web" of your hand is the stretchy part between your thumb and index finger. The web of your hand should be firmly against the web of the other person's hand with a firm, but not overly aggressive, grip.[30]

Treat support staff with courtesy and respect. Be polite and respectful to everyone you meet during your interview experience, including the receptionist who asks you to wait in an outer office and the assistant who offers you a cup of coffee. One hiring manager noted, "We've canceled [second] interviews with candidates when we've heard negative things from our support people."[31]

Act professionally during the interview

Continue to support your positive first impression by using the following techniques to maintain a professional image throughout the interview experience:

Be aware of nonverbal gestures. When you follow an interviewer into an office or conference room, wait to be seated until you are invited. Practice good posture while seated. Be aware that you communicate with your whole body. Positive nonverbal gestures include smiling, maintaining eye contact, crossing your legs appropriately, using moderate hand movements, and leaning a bit forward to show your interest. Potential negative expressions are frowning, having no facial expression, staring, swinging a leg or tapping a foot, slouching or exhibiting poor posture, looking at your watch or phone, and leaning too far forward (which can be perceived as overly aggressive). When you are nervous, you may not be aware of your facial expressions or nervous habits. However, practicing interview skills with instructors or career service professionals will help you identify potential negatives.

Listen actively. Take notes during interviews. Ask questions if you don't understand something, such as industry terms or acronyms. Indicating you don't know a company-specific acronym is not a sign of weakness. In this case, asking what it means demonstrates your interest in the position as well as your willingness to ask questions. In fact, in some situations, an interviewer might purposefully use an acronym you wouldn't know to assess whether you are confident enough to ask questions.

Use appropriate eye contact. Make eye contact with people while they are speaking. While you are speaking, ensure eye contact with everyone in the room. If several people participate in your interview, begin your answer to a question by looking at the person who asked the question. Then, during natural pauses in your dialog, move your eye contact to someone else.

Avoid jokes or sarcasm. Don't try to be funny. Nervous energy can cause you to say things before you think about them. What might seem witty at the moment may in retrospect be in very poor taste. Don't joke about recent political scandals or news events. You never know on what side of the issue someone may be. Err on the side of caution by avoiding any jokes or sarcasm during interviews.

Avoid responding to negative comments. If during your interview you talk with someone who speaks negatively about the company or about other employees, do not agree with the comments or extend the discussion. Change the focus of the conversation by moving to a positive topic or asking a question. For example, "This office building is in a great location. Do you have a short commute?"

Be prepared for meals and social gatherings

Professional interviews often include meals, especially if you have to travel a great distance to participate in the interview. Although meals are intended to be social experiences rather than formal interviews, you are still being informally assessed during these gatherings. If the position you are interviewing for includes taking clients to business lunches or dinners, you will also be evaluated on your manners and table skills. Consider the following guidelines.

Plan for conversation. Be prepared for appropriate small talk while en route to and from meals and social gatherings as well as during them. Familiarize yourself with current events in the news and business world so that you can contribute to conversation about them or raise related topics. For example, you may ask about the company's budget outlook given recent market declines. However, avoid discussions about politics, religion, and other potentially personal or controversial topics. If your discussion of the stock market expands to personal financial holdings, change the subject back to neutral issues, such as market indicators or predictions about future growth. If you are interviewing in a different city, research their local news to be able to ask specific questions about the area's current events. Ask about local recreational activities, volunteer opportunities, and or professional networks.

Listen before talking, but talk to everyone. Whether during a meal function or large social gathering, pay attention to the topics people discuss and ask appropriate questions to stimulate the conversation. Listen more than you talk, but make a point to talk to as many people as you can. Use social gatherings as an opportunity to leave a positive, lasting impression.

Do not place your accessories on the table. Put your messenger bag, briefcase, portfolio, or purse on the floor or the back of your chair. This is true during office meetings, too. Accessories do not belong on tables. If the meal turns to business, you may retrieve your portfolio to make notes, but rest it on your lap or the edge of the table rather than using the table as a desk.

Do not be intimidated by formal table settings. Business lunches often occur at upscale restaurants where the table settings may include several kinds of glasses and utensils.

After you order, the waitperson will remove glassware or silverware that you will not need for the meal you ordered. When selecting utensils for a specific course, work from the outside in. In other words, as FIGURE 12.5 illustrates, forks for salad or a first course will be to the left of the dinner fork. If there is a fork and spoon at the top of the plate, those are intended for dessert. In large gatherings when the table is densely populated with drinking glasses and bread plates, it may not be immediately obvious which ones are yours. Here's a quick trick: remember BMW—bread, meal, water. Note how in the table setting in Figure 12.5, the bread plate is at the far left, the meal will be served in the middle, and the water glass (and other beverages) are on the right.

FIGURE 12.5
Formal Table Setting

Put your napkin on your lap. As soon as you are seated at the table, unfold your napkin and put it on your lap. It remains there throughout the entire meal. Your napkin stays in your lap until you leave the table. If you excuse yourself temporarily and plan to return to the table, place your napkin either to the right or left of your place setting. When not returning, place your napkin on the tablecloth to the left of your plate.

Order wisely. When ordering food, play "Simon Says" by following your host's lead. Do not order steak and lobster if everyone else is ordering soup and salads. If you are asked to order first, ask what's good there or defer to someone else indicating that you haven't quite decided yet. Choose menu options that are easy to eat, and avoid messy meals like spaghetti that can easily splatter on your suit. Never put more food in your mouth than you will be able to chew and swallow within a few seconds. Chances are good someone will ask you a question as you're putting food in your mouth, and it is never acceptable to remove the food to answer the question. Avoid alcoholic beverages.

Butter your plate before your bread. Use the butter knife (or dinner knife if there is no butter knife) to put a small serving of butter on your butter plate. Then tear your bread into bite-sized pieces and butter each piece as you eat it.

Put used silverware on your plate, not the table. When finished with your meal, place your silverware diagonally across your plate (at the 4 o'clock position).

Do not ask for a doggie bag. If you are nervous, you may not be hungry during the interview meal. However, it is not appropriate to ask for a doggie bag. It is not professional in formal situations to take your leftovers with you.

What can I do to follow up effectively?

Following an interview, you have many opportunities to evaluate your performance and keep the lines of communication open. You can continue to impress prospective employers by sending thank-you messages and checking on the status of your application in a professional manner. If you are offered a position, how you respond is particularly important. Whether you choose to accept, negotiate, or refuse the job offer, your response needs to reinforce the company's confidence that they made a good decision. Even if you are not offered a position, you have the option of responding to communicate your interest in future opportunities. You may also be able to gather some information about the results of any background checks that the company conducted.

Evaluate your performance

Each interview you have helps you refine your communication skills to prepare you for your next interview. Immediately after the interview, evaluate your performance by considering the following questions:

Did you make a good impression? This may be difficult to determine, but recalling the interviewers' subtle nonverbal messages can give you a clue. Did they take a quick glance at your clothing and nod approvingly or raise an eyebrow in surprise? Did they introduce you to other people or offer to take you on a quick tour of the office? They wouldn't show you around if they weren't impressed.

Did you stumble with any answers? If you found yourself searching for responses to certain questions, write them down and work on answers that you will remember next time. Create a list of bullet points you can recall to jog your memory. Chances are good you will face similar questions again.

What did you forget? Did you have everything you needed, such as pen and paper, and extra copies of your résumé? If you found yourself wishing you had brought extra change for the parking meter or the vending machine (after your interview), make a checklist of things to remember next time. Consider adding an extra pen as well as cough drops and a small bottle of hand sanitizer during cold and flu season.

What went well? In addition to the negatives, evaluate the positive aspects of your interview. When did you feel most comfortable? How can you duplicate that experience next time? Identify your strengths as well as your weaknesses to evaluate your performance and increase your interview success.

Compose thank-you messages

Within 24 hours after an interview, send a thank-you message to offer your sincere gratitude for the time people took out of their busy schedules to meet with you. If you collected business cards during your interview or made good notes, you will have all the contact information you need to thank each person who met with you.

Before writing each message, review the notes you took during the interview so that you can personalize the content. For example, you may have learned about a particular company project from one person and enjoyed a lunch conversation about a professional development opportunity with another person. Your thank-you messages should reflect your conversations with the person to whom you are writing and stress one or two key points: things you forgot to mention during the interview or points you want to highlight. Your thank-you note may take the form of an email, a letter, or a handwritten note. Email provides a quick method of delivering your gratitude but is a casual method of communication. Typed business letters may seem more "official," but handwritten thank-you notes demonstrate a personalized effort, especially if you have personalized stationery. From both professional and personal perspectives, people perceive a handwritten message as a sincere gesture that speaks volumes about your character and indicates a personal interest in the company or relationship.

As you compose the message, follow these guidelines:

- Keep the message short. One or two paragraphs are sufficient.
- Remind the audience of the position you interviewed for.
- Show your gratitude.
- Personalize the message and emphasize something you learned during the interview.
- Emphasize your strengths, your interest in the job, or your potential contribution to the company.
- Conclude the message with a positive, forward-looking statement that encourages a response, and include your contact information.

After you have written a draft, evaluate your message to review the content. Read it aloud to hear the style and tone of the words you used. Revise to ensure a professional impression, and ask a friend to help you proofread to guarantee you have not made any spelling or grammatical errors. FIGURE 12.6 provides an example.

FIGURE 12.6
Handwritten Thank-You Message

handwritten note

Dear Mr. Jacobson:

Thank you for the opportunity on March 15 to discuss my qualifications for the open training manager's position. I enjoyed our conversation, and after learning more about the organization, I am eager to become a part of the Higgins Consulting management team.

The company's current objective to expand training services to the IT market is an exciting, yet challenging, goal. I believe my minor in MIS combined with my marketing major can provide a perspective that will benefit the company in this effort.

I look forward to hearing from you by email (ematthews@gmail.com) or telephone (218.555.2552).

Sincerely,
Ellyn Matthews

Begins with a thank you followed immediately by the date of the interview and position.

Mentions information learned during the interview and integrates a strength that relates to an audience benefit.

Concludes with a positive, forward-looking statement that includes contact information for easy reference.

Compose follow-up messages

Following an interview, an employer may need several weeks to interview other applicants, contact references, and process background checks. Therefore, unless an employer indicated you would be contacted by a certain date, don't be concerned if it takes a while to receive a response. Analyze the situation to determine when you should follow up and with whom. Typically, after two weeks, you can inquire about the status of the position and communicate your continued interest. Consider the following guidelines.

Contact only one person. Follow-up with only your primary contact person with the company rather than emailing everyone you met during the interview.

Choose an appropriate medium. Use a communication medium that best suits the employer's preferences based on your initial communications. Email is the least invasive and most convenient to answer. By contrast, a telephone call indicates a more assertive attempt to contact the employer.

Be prepared to leave a message if calling. Your message should be concise yet complete. State your name, the position you are calling about, and the date of your interview. Indicate your continued interest in the position, and close with a request to return your call. Repeat your name and telephone number:

> "Good afternoon, Mr. Jacobson. This is Ellyn Matthews calling to follow up about the training manager's position I interviewed for on March 15. I am still very interested in this opportunity and curious about the status of the position. I look forward to hearing from you at your convenience. My number is 218.555.2552. Again, this is Ellyn Matthews at 218.555.2552. Thank you."

Resell your strengths if writing. FIGURE 12.7 provides an example of a follow-up email message. Use a format similar to a thank-you message, and include the following information:

- Begin by mentioning the interview, including the name of the position and when you interviewed.
- Identify any new strengths or skills you can use to sell yourself for the position.
- Reiterate your continued interest in the position.
- Conclude by requesting a response and providing your contact information.

Don't go overboard. Evaluate your message to ensure you don't seem overly anxious about the position. Also, do not use multiple methods of contacting an employer. Sending several emails and leaving multiple telephone messages could be interpreted as unprofessional and overzealous.

FIGURE 12.7 Follow-Up Email Message

email

Dear Mr. Jacobson:

Last month, I interviewed with you to discuss my qualifications for the training manager's position. I am still very interested in this opportunity and am writing to inquire about the status of the position.

Since we last spoke, I investigated some of the issues related to expanding your training services to the IT market. My research found that several competing consulting companies have been successful in this area by marketing their ability to provide industry-based certifications. I would enjoy the opportunity to discuss this research as well as my continued interest in becoming a Higgins Consulting employee.

Please contact me at your convenience by email (ematthews@gmail.com) or telephone (218.555.2552). I look forward to hearing from you.

Thank you,
Ellyn Matthews

Ellyn Matthews, Marketing Major
MIS Minor Concentration
McClellan University
ematthews@gmail.com
218.555.2552

Identifies when and for which position she interviewed.

Introduces new information and potential audience benefits.

Emphasizes continued interest in the position.

Concludes with a positive, forward-looking statement that includes contact information for easy reference.

Negotiate the details of a job offer, if necessary

When making a job offer, employers usually outline the salary and related benefits that come with the job. If you have researched the company, the job, and the industry in general, you will know if the offer is competitive. In some cases, you may choose to accept the offer as it is initially presented. In other cases, you may consider negotiating the terms of the offer. If you plan to negotiate your salary or benefits, request the job offer in writing to eliminate possible ambiguity about the terms of the offer. Before responding, do some additional research and analysis so that you can make well-informed decisions and reasonable requests.

Use your professional network for advice. Chapter 11 identified people to include in your professional network—faculty and staff members, advisors, career counselors, as well as friends and relatives in business positions. Share your offer with them and ask for their input about which elements of the offer are fair and which ones you might be able to negotiate.

Check library and career center resources. Salary surveys and related compensation packages are often published by industry-specific groups, such as American Accounting Association, or by general groups, such as the National Association of Colleges and Employers. The Bureau of Labor Statistics[32] publishes the *Occupational Outlook Handbook* that provides national averages for salaries and related information.

Consider the offer based on the cost of living for the specific geographic area. A job paying $50,000 will buy you more in some areas than it will in others. For example, renting an apartment in New York City costs much more than renting one in Columbus, Ohio, and a meal at a nice restaurant in Los Angeles will be more expensive than a comparable dining experience in Des Moines, Iowa. Several online cost-of-living calculators can help you determine equitable salary offers.

Ask about company policies. Most professional jobs provide a set salary and expect a 40-hour workweek. Ask about vacation time, sick leave, personal days, overtime, and flextime options. In many cases, these allowances can be negotiated, especially if the salary amount is not flexible. Other benefits to inquire about include health insurance, tuition reimbursement, professional development, and office equipment.

See FIGURE 12.8 for a sample negotiation letter. Evaluate your message to ensure it includes all the necessary content, sounds professional, and has no errors.

 ETHICS Asking for More Time to Consider a Job Offer

During your employment search, you may receive a job offer from one company before you have had a chance to interview with another company, perhaps even with a company for which you are more interested in working. Most employers request a response to a job offer within a few days.[33] What do you do?

Be honest. Indicate that you would like to be able to weigh all your options and have not yet completed all of your interviews. Show gratitude for the offer, but explain that you want to make an informed decision about your career options. However, be careful not to suggest that the current offer is not your first choice.

Show understanding for the employer's needs. The employer has a job to fill, has made you an offer, and may not have additional time to wait for a response. Other applicants next in line may be willing to make an immediate decision. Acknowledge that time is money and any delays negatively affect the employer's ability to fill the vacancy in a timely manner.

Do not burn your bridges. Do not accept an offer thinking that you can easily decline the offer in a few days. Doing so may "burn your bridges" with the company, making future employment opportunities less likely. Further, if you accepted an offer and signed a contract, you are legally bound to the requirements of the contract.

Go with your gut. Sometimes you simply have to make decisions without having all the information you would like to have. If you have interviews lined up or are waiting to hear from other employers about possible offers, make a decision about a current job offer based on the merits of the offer alone. Would you be happy in this job? Are you satisfied with the compensation package? Ask for advice from your professional network, but only you can answer these questions. ∎

mybcommlab

For ETHICS exercises, go to Exercise 21 on page 469 and Exercise 31 on page 470 or this chapter's End-of-Chapter Exercises at mybcommlab.com.

FIGURE 12.8 Job Negotiation Message

`letter`

Ellyn Matthews
1651 Randolph Avenue, Apt. 3G, McClellan, MI 49449
ematthews@gmail.com | 218.555.2552

April 23, 20XX

Mr. Stephen Jacobson
Higgins Consulting
8153 Higgins Road
Chicago, IL 60632

Dear Mr. Jacobson:

Thank you for your offer to join Higgins Consulting as your newest training manager. I am very interested in the position and pleased with the salary you quoted. However, before I feel comfortable accepting the job, I have two requests:

- Your offer included reimbursement for moving expenses up to $500. However, the three estimates I received all exceeded $1,000. Are you able to increase my reimbursement allocation?

- The benefits packet you sent mentions that Higgins Consulting reimburses MBA and other relevant graduate education after the employee's second year on the job. As you know, I have already begun my Master of Education degree in Global Training and Development in the online program at State University. I would like to keep my momentum going with this program. Will you be willing to start reimbursing these courses right away? What I learn from my coursework will be immediately useful on the job at Higgins, and I understand that Higgins will require repayment if I do not stay at the company for the required period of time.

I look forward to discussing these issues with you in more detail and appreciate the opportunity to begin my career as a Higgins employee. Please call (218.555.2552) or email (ematthews@gmail.com) at your convenience.

Sincerely,

Ellyn Matthews

Ellyn Matthews, Marketing Major
MIS Minor Concentration
McClellan University

Begins with gratitude for the offer and mentions positive aspects of the offer before indicating points of concern.

Issues for discussion are bulleted. They could also be numbered, making it easier to refer to the items in future communication.

Concludes positively and motivates action by including contact information.

PEARSON
mybcommlab

Apply Figure 12.8's key concepts by revising a new document. Go to Chapter 12 in mybcommlab.com and select Document Makeovers.

Compose acceptance messages for job offers you accept

When you decide to accept a job offer, analyze your medium options. Even if you plan to accept the position by telephone, following up in writing provides documentation for both you and the employer. Some companies request that applicants sign the bottom of the offer letter to indicate that they accept the offer. In these cases, you do not have to write a separate letter unless you want to negotiate the offer. Other companies will expect you to initiate a response. As you compose, organize the content directly, indicating at the beginning of your message that you are accepting the position. Finally, evaluate the message to ensure you are communicating professionally. See FIGURE 12.9 for an example of a job acceptance message sent by email.

FIGURE 12.9 Job Acceptance Message

email

Dear Mr. Jacobson:

I am following up on our telephone conversation earlier today to accept your offer for the training manager's position. I look forward to beginning my career at Higgins Consulting and will report to your office at 8:30 AM on Monday, June 24.

References telephone conversation to put the message in context.

Confirms beginning day and time.

As you requested, I called (and left a message for) Larry Ferguson in Human Resources to make an appointment to complete the paperwork for my relocation reimbursement. I hope to hear from him soon.

Documents the status of any requested action (in this case, contacting Human Resources).

Thank you again for this opportunity. I plan to be one of your greatest assets on the management team.

Concludes with gratitude and a forward-looking statement.

Sincerely,
Ellyn Matthews

Ellyn Matthews, Marketing Major
MIS Minor Concentration
McClellan University
ematthews@gmail.com
218.555.2552

Compose refusal messages for job offers you reject

If you receive a job offer for a position you are not interested in, you need to communicate to the company that you are not accepting the offer. As FIGURE 12.10 illustrates, the best medium for this communication depends on how you received the offer and whether the company asked you to respond in a particular way.

Regardless of the medium you use, maintain professionalism and courtesy in your message and buffer your "bad news" as shown in FIGURE 12.11. Evaluate the message by reviewing the content and revising, if necessary, to ensure a professional tone and style. Proofread carefully.

FIGURE 12.10 Selecting a Medium for Refusing a Job Offer

IF YOU RECEIVE A JOB OFFER BY . . .	RESPOND BY . . .	AND . . .
telephone conversation, and you know at that moment that you do not want the job,	declining the offer during the conversation,	there's no need to follow up in writing.
telephone message,	returning the call by telephone. Try to speak to the person, but if you can't, leave a voice-mail message to decline the job offer,	follow up with an email message or letter to confirm the information.
email message,	replying to the email, unless the employer requested you respond by calling,	if you leave a voice mail message, follow up with an email message.
formal letter,	mailing a formal letter in return,	as a professional courtesy, you may also choose to call the employer to indicate your refusal letter is in the mail.

FIGURE 12.11 Job Refusal Message

`letter`

Ellyn Matthews
1651 Randolph Avenue, Apt. 3G, McClellan, MI 49449
ematthews@gmail.com | 218.555.2552

April 30, 20XX

Mr. Stephen Jacobson
Higgins Consulting
8153 Higgins Road
Chicago, IL 60632

Dear Mr. Jacobson:

Thank you for the offer to join the Higgins Consulting team. I enjoyed meeting you and your staff and appreciated the opportunity to learn about your company.

Your collaborative work environment was energizing, and I could see myself fitting in well with your team. Although your offer is tempting, I have decided to accept a position in a city closer to my family. If in the future my circumstances change and I am more able to relocate, I would be very interested in working on your team.

Best wishes,

Ellyn Matthews

Ellyn Matthews, Marketing Major
MIS Minor Concentration
McClellan University

Begins with appreciation for the opportunity to interview for the position.

Buffers the bad news (the refusal) with gratitude, declines the offer, and identifies reasoning for the decision.

Concludes with a positive, friendly statement.

Respond to job rejections

When you are rejected for a job, you may feel hurt or angry. Rather than taking the rejection personally, use it as one last opportunity to make a good impression by writing a final letter to your interviewer, like the letter in FIGURE 12.12.

FIGURE 12.12 Response to Job Rejection

`letter`

Ellyn Matthews

1651 Randolph Avenue, Apt. 3G, McClellan, MI 49449
ematthews@gmail.com | 218.555.2552

April 23, 20XX

Mr. Stephen Jacobson
Higgins Consulting
8153 Higgins Road
Chicago, IL 60632

Dear Mr. Jacobson:

I just received your letter today, indicating that you have selected another candidate for the training manager position. Although I am disappointed, I appreciate your letting me know your decision in such a timely manner. I also appreciate the courtesy and professionalism you have shown during the entire interview process. ⟵ *Begins by graciously accepting the rejection and expressing gratitude.*

I want to reiterate my strong interest in working for Higgins Consulting. Please keep me in mind when you have another opening in the near future. ⟵ *Emphasizes continuing interest in the company.*

Again, thank you for the opportunity to interview, and best wishes to your company. ⟵ *Concludes positively.*

Sincerely,

Ellyn Matthews

Ellyn Matthews, Marketing Major
MIS Minor Concentration
McClellan University

If you suspect that you have not been hired based on negative results from a background check (for which the employer must receive your permission), you are entitled to receive a free copy of the background report from the employer or the company that prepared it. According to a poll by the Society for Human Resource Management, 96 percent of employers claim to perform background checks on potential employees and new hires.[34] Almost half of U.S. employers use credit checks to screen applicants.[35] Others verify claims made on your résumé and in the job interview as well as look at news reports and criminal records. Because many applicants are damaged by incorrect information in their background checks, you should request background check results to verify that the reports are correct and to prepare explanations that you can use in future interviews.

IN SUMMARY, the employment interview process is often a long one, incorporating many different kinds of interviews. Learning how to research and analyze a company in advance and how to present yourself as a professional helps prepare you for the interview. Learning how to answer and ask questions effectively helps you perform well in the interview. And learning how to respond to job offers and rejections helps ensure the best possible results at the end of the process. As you move through the process, you can expect to become more skilled at interviewing, especially if you evaluate your performance at each interview and make adjustments.

CHAPTER 12 Summary

12.1 How do I take advantage of different types of interviews? *(pages 434–440)*

- **Capture interest in preliminary interviews,** which often begin at career fairs. Since you will have only a few minutes with a recruiter, be assertive, demonstrate your knowledge, and ask good questions. Some companies also send recruiters to campus for preliminary, first-round interviews, which offer you a little more time to impress the recruiter with your knowledge and questions. If you live far from the company, you may also be interviewed by telephone, which requires you to use your best telephone skills.
- **Sell your strengths during onsite company interviews.** These interviews may combine several formats, including traditional one-on-one interviews, panel and group interviews, and action interviews. Before these interviews, you may be required to take tests, such as personality assessments, so results can be discussed during the interview.

12.2 How can I prepare for a job interview? *(pages 441–445)*

- **Analyze the company.** Conduct in-depth research into the company by reading the company's website and finding articles about the company on the web and in business publications. Learn more about the company's industry, competition, and financial performance. Find connections through social networking sites and use career resource websites like Vault.com.
- **Compose answers to typical questions.** Typical questions focus on you, your past employment, your job search, and your suitability for the job. For each question, plan a 30- to 60-second summary of your strengths, focusing on skills and qualities required for the job. Provide evidence that convinces the employer to hire you. Use the STAR method to respond to behavioral questions to demonstrate how you handled past challenges.
- **Compose questions to ask** about the company as well as the position to indicate your interest. Do not ask questions you could have easily found answered online.

12.3 How should I dress for a job interview? *(pages 445–449)*

- **Wear business formal attire** to an interview, even if the company culture is casual. Your goal is not to express your personality through your clothing but to allow people to focus on what you say.
- **Look professional** by ensuring your clothes fit properly, being conservative in your grooming and makeup, bringing a portfolio or business case, wearing a watch, and turning off your cell phone.

12.4 How should I act during the interview? *(pages 449–452)*

- **Manage first impressions** by arriving a few minutes early and looking ready to work. Greet people professionally, and treat support staff with courtesy and respect.
- **Act professionally during the interview** by avoiding negative nonverbal gestures, listening actively, and using appropriate eye contact, avoiding jokes or sarcasm, and not responding to negative comments.
- **Be prepared for meals and social gatherings.** Plan for conversation and small talk, be sure to talk to everyone at the table, and learn proper dining etiquette.

12.5 What can I do to follow up effectively? *(pages 453–461)*

- **Evaluate your performance** after each interview to assess how you can improve your skills.
- **Compose thank-you messages** that show gratitude, demonstrate what you learned, sell your strengths, and focus on audience benefits. Conclude with your contact information.
- **Compose follow-up messages** to inquire about the status of an open position if you have not heard anything after two weeks.
- **Negotiate the details of a job offer, if necessary,** when you receive an offer.
- **Compose acceptance messages for job offers you accept.** Start with the good news, confirm any important information, and conclude with gratitude.
- **Compose refusal messages for job offers you refuse.** Consider your medium options and use the indirect organizational plan. Conclude positively.
- **Respond to job rejections** by writing a professional letter expressing appreciation and continued interest. If you suspect that a negative background check played a part in your rejection, ask to see the report so that you can correct any errors in it and you can address the results in future interviews.

Are you an active learner? Go to mybcommlab.com to master Chapter 12 content. Chapter 12 interactive activities include:

- Customizable Study Plan and Chapter 12 practice quizzes
- Chapter 12 Simulation, Interviewing, that helps you think critically and prepare to make choices in the business world
- Flash Cards for mastering the definition of chapter terms
- Chapter 12 Video Exercise, Interviewing Skills, which shows you how textbook concepts are put into practice every day
- Interactive Lessons that visually review key chapter concepts
- Document Makeovers for hands-on, scored practice in revising documents

ACE Helps You
Analyze
Communication Goals and
Prepare Effectively for Interviews

- Analyze your professional image to determine how you want to present yourself.
- Analyze your social media content to ensure it supports your professional image.
- Before each interview, research company websites, articles, and industry news so that you can demonstrate your knowledge.
- Analyze your fit for the company and the job so that you can present yourself well.

ACE Helps You
Compose
a Professional Image in
Your Appearance,
Speaking, and Writing

Look Professional
- Arrive early for your interview.
- Dress like a businessperson rather than a college student.
- Use professional (conservative) grooming habits.
- Wear a watch and turn off your cell phone.
- Carry a well-stocked briefcase or portfolio.

Speak Well
- Prepare effective answers to standard interview questions.
- Compose answers to behavioral questions using the STAR method.
- Compose good questions to ask about the company and position.
- Be assertive when you shake hands and polite when you greet people. Use good eye contact.
- Communicate your interest and abilities and demonstrate professional enthusiasm.
- Restrain your nervous energy and project a professional voice.

Write Effectively
- Compose thank-you messages within 24 hours of the interview.
- Even if you respond to job offers and rejections on the telephone, follow up with formal letters that convey a positive impression.

ACE Helps You
Evaluate
Your Performance

- Evaluate positive aspects of your interview to replicate them in future interviews.
- Evaluate negative aspects of your interview and plan changes to improve future interviews.
- Evaluate your responses to interview questions and plan changes if necessary.

KEY TERMS QUICK ACCESS REVIEW

Action interview *p. 439*

Behavioral questions *p. 443*

Career fair *p. 434*

Corporate culture *p. 440*

Group interview *p. 439*

Panel interview *p. 437*

STAR method *p. 444*

Telephone interview *p. 436*

CASE STUDY Preparing for Interviews

Tabatha Martin and Jonathan Perkins met during their first year in college and became close friends. During their senior year, they begin their employment search—both are looking for entry-level positions in the financial sector. However, they have had very different experiences during college.

Tabatha double majored in finance and economics and minored in forensic accounting. She will graduate with a 3.85 grade point average. However, because she has been (and continues to be) a live-in caretaker for her elderly aunt for four years, Tabatha does not have any work experience other than the part-time job she held working as a research assistant for a professor in the economics department. She gained valuable research skills and was able to work from home, but is now concerned that her lack of "real-world" experience may hinder her ability to secure a good entry-level position. She was a member of the Finance Club but did not have the time to pursue leadership positions in the organization or participate in any other extracurricular activities.

Jonathan also majored in finance, but his grade point average is just 2.95. However, he had two summer internships, both for well-known financial corporations, and has exceptional letters of recommendation from his internship supervisors. Jonathan also worked 20 hours a week during his sophomore, junior, and senior years for a local bank where he was cross-trained in several positions. In addition to his work experiences, Jonathan held the positions of treasurer, vice president, and president of the Finance Club. He was also a member of the track team and volunteered at a homeless shelter.

Review Question 1: *Based on what you learned in Chapters 11 and 12, what challenges do you think Tabatha and Jonathan will encounter during their job search and interviews? What advice would you give them as they prepare to enter the job market?*

Preparing for Testing Situations— Personality Profiles

Tabatha and Jonathan review the job advertisements posted by the Career Center. One position stands out for both of them—a financial management position for BankTrust Corp. Although they hesitate to compete with each other, they decide to submit their résumés and see what happens. Two weeks later, they were surprised to learn that they both received invitations to interview next month. Their interviews are scheduled just two days apart. They know they have to prepare, but they aren't sure where to begin. They decide to collaborate to figure it out.

One concern they have is that the company asked them to provide their Myers-Briggs Type Indicator personality profiles as part of their application materials. BankTrust does not administer the personality test, but asks candidates to find online versions of the assessment if they do not know their personality profile. Candidates are told to prepare to describe their personality results during their interviews and, based on their personality results,

identify strengths and weaknesses that would be relevant for the financial management position. Although Tabatha and Jonathan have heard of the popular personality test, neither has taken the assessment.

Review Question 2: *Find a free online assessment for the Myers-Briggs personality test. Take the test to learn your own personality profile and read the style descriptions to understand all eight identifiers: extrovert (E) or introvert (I), sensing (S) or intuitive (N), thinking (T) or feeling (F), judging (J) or perceiving (P). Then consider the following questions:*

1. Does your profile sound like you? How does the description of your personality profile (such as INTJ) differ from your perceptions of yourself?

2. Ask close friends or relatives to read your profile description. Do they think the profile for your identification reflects your personality? In what ways do they agree with the profile? Disagree?

3. Consider how your personality profile would interact with other profiles. With which personalities would you work well? Which personalities would provide challenges?

4. How well-suited are you for your career choice based on your personality profile?

Purchasing Interview Outfits

In preparation for their interviews, Tabatha and Jonathan go shopping for professional business suits. Neither has a lot of money to spend on new clothes, but they know they need to invest in their careers by having appropriate business formal attire.

Review Question 3: *Assume Tabatha and Jonathan attend your school. Where would they find reasonably priced yet appropriate clothing for their interviews? Do some research, keeping in mind that they may need to have their clothing altered. Put together a complete outfit and accessories (including portfolio) for one of them (for Tabatha if you're female, and for Jonathan if you're male) making note of the items and prices. What's your total? Compare your findings with other students.*

Composing Answers to Standard Interview Questions

Tabatha and Jonathan meet for coffee a few days after they learn they both have interviews scheduled for the same position at BankTrust. They independently researched the BankTrust website to gather information about the company and the position. They share their perspectives of this information with each other to gain deeper insight into the company and how to best sell their respective strengths during their interviews. They review the standard interview questions and help each other brainstorm responses to the question: "Why should we hire you?"

Review Question 4: *Using the descriptions of Tabatha's and Jonathan's experiences during college, compose a list of bullet* *points they could use during their interview to highlight their qualifications and strengths. Compose five points for each candidate.*

Reacting to Difficult Interview Scenarios

Tabatha's Interview

Tabatha arrives to her interview on time, is well-prepared, and looks professional. Her initial nervousness is eased when she meets the interviewer, Jeannette Gus, who looks younger than Tabatha had expected and is very friendly. They chat amiably about the new office renovations as Jeannette gives Tabatha a brief tour en route to Jeannette's office. Once in her office, Jeannette gestures for Tabatha to sit in one of the guest chairs, while Jeannette sits next to her in the other guest chair. Tabatha is at first surprised not to be separated by the desk, but soon feels comfortable as they discuss her Myers-Briggs personality profile, her academic record, and her strengths for the position. However, near the end of their conversation Jeannette asks Tabatha a question that she is not sure how to answer.

"Your recommendations are exceptional, your academic record is strong, and I feel you have a good understanding of what would be expected of you here. However, I'm curious about your work history. Other than your research job on campus, I don't see any internships or industry experience. Why not?"

Tabatha is concerned that if she explains she is a caretaker for her elderly aunt, Jeannette might question Tabatha's ability to fulfill her full-time job requirements. Nonetheless, Tabatha does not want to lie about the reason for her lack of work experience. She feels her personal commitments should not have a bearing on her candidacy for the position, but does not know how to say that without sounding rude.

Review Question 5: *If you were Tabatha, how would you respond to Jeannette's question?*

Jonathan's Interview

Two days later, Jonathan meets with Jeannette to discuss his application for the same position. Jeannette is equally friendly with him, and as the interview draws to a close, Jonathan feels his interview is going very well. Jeannette praises his work experience and commends him on his ability to balance so many extracurricular activities with his schoolwork. Jeannette notes that Jonathan and Tabatha are from the same school and both listed the Finance Club on their résumé. When Jeannette asks Jonathan if he knows Tabatha, he acknowledges that he and Tabatha are friends and he is aware that she is also a candidate for the position. That's when the interview became tough.

Jeannette says, "I'll be honest with you, Jonathan. You interview well. Since you and Tabatha are friends, I feel comfortable telling you that the competition for the job is down to just the two of you. I don't want you to share any personal information, of course, but I am curious how you will answer this question: Why should I hire you instead of Tabatha?"

Jonathan is surprised by the question and does not know how to reply. He's usually good at thinking on his feet, but his mind races to try to find an answer that sells his strengths without disrespecting his friend. He also considers whether the question itself is Jeannette's way of assessing Jonathan's character. Will he find fault in Tabatha's weaknesses? Or will he reiterate his strengths without diminishing Tabatha's successes?

Review Question 6: *If you were Jonathan, how would you answer this question?*

Who Gets the Job?

Tabatha and Jonathan both receive offers at BankTrust. Jonathan is offered the financial management position that they had applied for, and Tabatha is given the opportunity to apply for a financial analyst position. The analyst position is lower ranking than the manager position, but Tabatha would be able to complete some of her work online from home, allowing her to continue to care for her elderly aunt. During her interview, Tabatha had decided to share her family situation. At the time, she assumed the information would keep her from getting the job. She had no idea it would open another, and more convenient, opportunity for her.

As they meet for lunch on the first day of their new jobs, Tabatha and Jonathan reflect on their employment search. They know their business communication skills helped them successfully navigate the job market and will continue to guide them throughout their professional careers. During their morning orientation training, they both signed up for BankTrust's professional development program so they could continue to enhance their financial management and business communication skills. Their managerial communication seminar begins next month.

CRITICAL THINKING

1. Although telephone interviews may cause less stress than face-to-face interaction, they do not provide you with visual cues that help you interpret people's feelings and attitudes. Identify the kinds of information that you might perceive from visual cues in an interview. What strategies could you use in a telephone interview to elicit this kind of information?

2. Personality assessments are subjective. How you answer the questions can be affected by recent experiences or your mood during the assessment. Additionally, in many cases your personality profile changes as you mature. Is it appropriate for an employer to evaluate a candidate based on a personality profile? What do you believe are valid uses for personality profiles in the interview process?

3. When applicants do not adequately prepare for standard interview questions, they often provide ineffective answers to inquiries about their weaknesses. Why is it a bad idea simply to admit a weakness like being late on deadlines, procrastinating, or disliking group work? Why does giving yourself a backhanded compliment (such as, I'm so focused on the details that I often don't see the big picture) come across as an insincere weakness? Why is it important always to include a description of how you are addressing the weakness?

4. Assume that during an interview, an employer states: "We work a lot of long hours here when we have large client proposals due. Sometimes we need people to stay very late or come in on a Sunday. Do you have any family obligations or religious restrictions that would limit your ability to do that?" How should an applicant respond to that question?

5. Jacob is very nervous as he waits alone in a conference room for his interview to begin. Based on the copies of his résumé at each

chair around the table, he knows several people will be asking him questions. He knows he is not good at remembering names, so he plans to make notes as people introduce themselves. However, when the group arrives all at once and quick introductions are made, Jacob is not able to make notes while he stands to shake hands with everyone. He asks for business cards, but no one has one to offer. How would you recommend that Jacob proceed? What are some ways that he can gather names and contact information during the interview?

6. Sam is preparing for a two-day interview at a large Fortune 500 company based in New York. Sam is from a small Midwest community and has never been to the east coast, much less a big city. Although he is very enthusiastic about the interview experience and is very interested in the company and the job, he is concerned about one of the meal events. On the first day of his interview, after a long afternoon of meetings, three people will be taking him to an Asian fusion restaurant. Sam found the restaurant online and read the menu but nothing looks good to him. He researched the words he didn't know, like miso, tandoori, and hoisin, but can't find a menu option other than egg drop soup that he would like. Sam prefers simple food like burgers and pizza. He thinks about asking his contact person for a change in venue or faking an allergy to soy products. What advice would you give Sam?

7. Employers' expectations about appropriate business attire may vary based on the industry. Why do you think people in financial management and legal professions often dress more formally than people who work in computer and service-based industries? If you are interviewing for a job in an industry that is more informal, what kind of clothing should you wear to the interview: business formal or business casual? Why would you make that choice?

8. Two weeks after her interview with a small company in town, Cara has not heard from the employer. She sends a follow-up email message, but a week later she still has not heard anything. She calls and leaves a message, and a week later has still not received a reply. She's very interested in the position, and the interviewer indicated it might take a couple of weeks to make a decision. However, after a month, Cara would at least like to know the status of her application. What advice would you give Cara? Explain why.

9. Assume you spent the last four months of your senior year looking for the perfect job. You interviewed with dozens of companies, but given the competitive job market, you haven't received any offers. Today, suddenly, you receive two very good offers from two very good companies. The salary and compensation packages are nearly identical, and the opportunities for advancement are similar. Both jobs are in the same town you currently live. How would you decide which job to take? Make a list of at least five criteria you would use to help you make a decision.

10. During March, Randy interviewed for five internships for the upcoming summer before his senior year. Of the five, he was most interested in Baylor Industries. By April 10, he had received offers from everyone except Baylor, who indicated they would make a decision by April 30 at the latest. Unfortunately, the other four companies needed his response before then. Randy figured that since he had received offers from the rest of the companies, his odds were fairly good to receive an offer from Baylor, too. But he wondered if he shouldn't take one of the four offers while he still had them rather than turn down a sure thing for a possibility. What if Baylor didn't make an offer? What would you do? Explain why.

DEVELOPING YOUR COMMUNICATION SKILLS

12.1 How do I take advantage of different types of job interviews? *(pages 434–440)*

EXERCISE 1 Capture interest in preliminary interviews: Career fairs

Attend a local career fair to observe the format and layout of the event. Note both the employers and the job seekers. Were there obvious differences in attire, professionalism, or image? Talk to students who spoke with recruiters. What kinds of questions did they ask? What was the experience like? What advice do the students recommend? Summarize your findings and highlight those that specifically relate to your career goals. Be prepared to present this information in class or in a message to your instructor.

EXERCISE 2 Capture interest in preliminary interviews: Telephone interviews

a. How often are telephone interviews conducted for both internship and entry-level positions in your discipline? Schedule an appointment with a career counselor, instructor, or academic advisor, and at least two business people (perhaps friends or relatives) to find out. Also, request their suggestions to help you prepare to project a professional image when participating in telephone interviews. Summarize your findings and be prepared to present the information in class or in a message to your instructor.

b. For each of the following scenarios, describe how you would respond:

1. You are in the middle of a telephone interview with three people who represent three different departments at the company where you applied for an internship. Someone asks you a question about what specific skills you possess that would support his department. However, you aren't sure which person asked the question.

2. During the same telephone interview, assume after you finish answering a question, there is nothing but silence. No one responds to your answer or asks another question. You are not sure whether the interviewers are confused or upset—or whether the connection has been lost.

3. Near the end of your telephone interview, your roommate and two friends enter the room, all three loudly talking about a party later tonight. They don't notice you're on the phone and continue their loud conversation despite your desperate waves for them to be quiet.

EXERCISE 3 Sell your strengths during onsite company interviews: Panel interviews

Describe a position in your intended field that you might apply for, and list the job titles or departments of potential panel members who might be involved in interviewing you. For example, if you are a management major, you might be interested in applying for an assistant sales manager position for a large retail firm. Panel members participating in the search committee for this position might include the sales manager, an associate sales manager, representatives from Sales and someone from Human Resources. Brainstorm two to three questions the team members might ask you that relate to their areas, and draft your answers.

EXERCISE 4 Sell your strengths during onsite company interviews: Group interviews

In some competitive interview situations, especially for internship opportunities, group interviews may include all (or many) of the applicants for the same position. Research tips for this kind of group interview experience. Summarize your findings in a one-page "tip sheet" that can be shared with the class as a resource.

EXERCISE 5 Sell your strengths during onsite company interviews: Action interviews

Assume that the itinerary for your two-day interview for your "ideal job" includes a 10-minute presentation to a panel of 10 people, each of whom has a say in your hiring decision and each of whom you would be working with (or for) if you were hired. Your contact person has told you that as one of the first events during your interview, your presentation should explain your academic and work background and outline your strengths, skills, and qualifications for the position. Each member of the panel will have already received a copy of your résumé, so your presentation should expand upon or explain your skills in greater detail. Create a slide presentation that outlines the content you would present.

EXERCISE 6 Sell your strengths during onsite company interviews: Pre-interview tests

Personality assessments are popular testing tools during applicant screening. You may be familiar with the Myers-Briggs or The Big 5 personality tests. Research free online tests, and take one you have not taken before. Write a memo to your instructor in which you identify the test you took and answer the following questions: What does the assessment indicate about your personality? Do you agree with the results? How do you think your personality type will affect your workplace interactions? How could you talk about your personality type in an interview?

EXERCISE 7 Exploring company culture
[Related to the Culture feature on page 440]

Imagine you are planning to interview with a large or well-known company and you want to learn more about that company's culture. Select a company that interests you and conduct an Internet search using the company's name and the term "corporate culture" or "company culture." Read at least five of the sources that your search identifies (or more if you like). Based on what you read, write a paragraph describing the company's culture. Include a reference list that identifies the sources you used.

12.2 How can I prepare for a job interview?

(pages 441–445)

EXERCISE 8 Analyze the company

Research a company you may be interested in working for, either as an intern or a full-time employee after graduation. Use the sources outlined in the chapter to gather in-depth information about the company and, if possible, identify a specific position

you would be interested in pursuing. Outline your findings for an in-class discussion, a short presentation, or a written summary to your instructor.

EXERCISE 9 Compose answers to typical questions

Outline your "ideal" job, including a description of the job title, basic duties and job requirements, company, and location. Which of the standard interview questions presented in Figure 12.2 (page 442) will be most challenging for you to answer when interviewing for this job? Explain why. Then draft responses for each question that relate to the duties and requirements you outlined.

EXERCISE 10 Compose answers to typical questions: the STAR method

The STAR Method is an effective format to use when responding to behavioral questions. Outline a scenario, task, action, and result you could use to respond to the following:

a. Describe a time when you worked well under pressure or organized a major project.

b. Describe something you have done that shows you have initiative and creativity.

c. Describe a time when you faced frustration. How did you deal with it?

Be prepared to share your responses in class or in a message to your instructor. Evaluate your response based on feedback you receive.

EXERCISE 11 Compose questions to ask

a. Imagine that you want to learn more about the corporate culture of a company that is interviewing you. In addition to observing people when you visit, what questions could you ask in an interview that will provide you insight?

b. Imagine that you want to communicate to your interviewer that you are interested in a long-term career with the company. What questions can you ask to communicate that impression?

c. Imagine that you want to find the specific tasks you would be doing if hired for a job. Compose two different questions that might help you get that information in an interview.

EXERCISE 12 Manage your social media image
[Related to the Technology feature on page 446]

Find three video résumés posted to YouTube or a similar online video site. Watch all three videos and assess their effectiveness. Do the individuals look and sound professional? Do they display any images other than themselves? Do they use sound or graphics effectively? Does the content they include sell their strengths? Do they (or their videos) portray any weaknesses? Would you hire these people? Summarize your answers to these questions and be prepared to discuss your findings in class or in a message to your instructor.

12.3 How should I dress for a job interview?

(pages 445–449)

EXERCISE 13 Wear business formal attire

Pat is a senior marketing major who spent college working two jobs: as a short-order cook at a local diner on weeknights and as a coach for a large K–12 indoor soccer league on the weekends. Pat is also on the school's soccer team and typically wears gym clothes to classes to be ready to go to soccer practice. Pat's wardrobe does not include any business-like clothing, not even business casual options. In preparation to begin interviewing for jobs, Pat knows investing in a business wardrobe is important. However, Pat does not have a lot of money to spend. Help Pat determine what to buy and where to buy it to stay within a reasonable budget (assume Pat's gender is the same as yours). Provide Pat with two interview options, complete with accessories and portfolio, as well as three business casual outfits that can be mixed and matched to extend the wardrobe. Research every detail: stores, labels, styles, shoes, etc. Be prepared to share your findings in class or summarize them in a message to your instructor.

EXERCISE 14 Look professional

Search "job interview" on YouTube, and find one or more videos of mock job interviews. Assess whether you believe the interviewee looks professional, based on the criteria in this chapter. Be prepared to share your findings in class or summarize them in a message to your instructor.

12.4 How should I act during the interview? *(pages 449–452)*

EXERCISE 15 Manage first impressions

a. You never know when you might have an opportunity to make an important first impression. Assume that you work part-time at a coffee shop on weekends. During a slow Sunday afternoon, you decide to review your human resources textbook to study for a test the next morning. As a customer walks to the counter, you close the book to greet her. After placing her order, the customer notices the book and asks if you're a student. You chat together for a few minutes about your major, the school, and the job market. She mentions she supervises the internship program at her company, which, coincidently, you've been trying to get into for nearly a year. This would be the perfect time to offer a 60-second summary of your qualifications and strengths—if you had ever developed one. Write a summary that you could memorize for occasions like these. Start with a general statement about who you are and what you want, and then use more specific information to describe your strengths and skills.

b. First impressions are made within the first few seconds. Therefore, it is important to ensure your confidence and enthusiasm from the very beginning of an interview. This chapter outlined several suggestions. Additional resources are available online. For example, some experts suggest using neuro-linguistic programming (NLP), which is the study of how people interact and respond to experiences. People trained in NLP learn how to assess a situation and modify their tone of speech, gestures, and facial expressions to put other people at ease and consequently make a positive first impression. Research information about neuro-linguistic programming and write a one-page paper summarizing what you learned that would help you improve your meeting-and-greeting skills. Be sure to cite your sources. Be prepared to share your summary in class or submit it to your instructor for evaluation.

EXERCISE 16 Act professionally during the interview

To maintain a professional image, you need to avoid responding negatively to questions or comments during an interview. Plan an effective response to the following questions:

a. What did you like least about your last job?

b. Tell me about a time when you worked with a difficult supervisor or colleague. How did you handle the situation?

EXERCISE 17 Be prepared for meals and social gatherings

Several business etiquette quizzes are available online. Check mybcommlab.com for links, or search online for the following titles or another interactive site.

- USA Today — Miss Business Manner's Etiquette Quiz
- GradView — Test Your Business Etiquette
- International Social and Business Savvy Quotient

Take the quiz and score your responses. What percentage did you answer correctly? Summarize the questions you answered incorrectly and be prepared to share what you learned in class or in writing to your instructor.

12.5 What can I do to follow up effectively?
(pages 453–461)

EXERCISE 18 Evaluate your performance

Register with your school's career services office, if you have not already done so, and schedule a mock interview with one of the career counselors. Ask for feedback from the counselor, and then evaluate your performance based on the criteria outlined in the chapter. Summarize your evaluation in a one-page memo or email to your instructor.

EXERCISE 19 Compose thank-you messages

Assume you responded to an advertisement for a summer internship with a local business, Metrix Marketing Consultants. After submitting your cover letter and résumé, the assistant to the human resources director (you forgot to record her name) called to invite you to participate in a panel interview. At the beginning of the interview, you wrote down the names and positions of the five panel members, none of whom were the person who called you nor the human resources director. Each panel member asked questions and responded to your questions. Philip Peterson, a marketing research analyst, appeared to be the most senior member of the panel, but he didn't lead the interview. In fact, none of the panel members *led* the interview. Phyllis McEwen started the interview with an overview of the process, and Kathy Hampton concluded the interview, asking if you had any questions and finally indicating that they would follow up in two weeks with a decision. At the end of the interview, you asked for business cards, but no one had one. Before you left, you thanked and shook hands with each person. It was a good interview. When you get home, you remember that you should write a thank-you note. Do you send a note to one person or to each of the five panel members? If you send five notes, do you say the same thing in each one or do you customize? Additionally, you're not sure if you have the correct spellings of their names: Phillip or Philip, Peterson or Petersen, McEwen or Macuen, Kathy or Cathy? Who do you contact and how? You don't have a phone number or email address for anyone and your résumé was submitted electronically on the company's website. Outline what you would do, who you would write to, and what you would say.

EXERCISE 20 Compose follow-up messages

Read Exercise 19 about the panel interview experience with Metrix Marketing Consultants. Assume three weeks have passed and you have not heard from anyone about the internship. How do you follow up in this situation? Whom do you contact? What medium should you use? What should you say? Justify your answers and be prepared to share them in class or submit them to your instructor.

EXERCISE 21 Answering difficult questions
[Related to the Ethics feature on page 456]

How would you answer these questions if they were asked at an interview?

a. *Tell me about a time when you had to delegate responsibility.* You can't remember a time when you delegated responsibility. How would you answer?

b. *Why did you leave your previous position?* You were fired from that job. How would you respond?

c. *This position includes a company car for regional sales calls, so if hired, your driving record will be checked for insurance purposes. That's not a problem, is it?* You have a DUI on your record. What could you say?

EXERCISE 22 Negotiate the details of a job offer

You are in the middle of your job search for a full-time position after graduation. You applied for several positions, interviewed for a few, and hope to hear from many more. Today you receive a letter from one of the companies that interviewed you offering you the position you wanted, but at the low end of the salary range they quoted you. You want to negotiate, but aren't sure how to ask for more money. Research salary negotiation strategies and suggestions, and summarize your findings in a one-page email message or memo to your instructor. Your instructor may ask you to present your summary in class.

EXERCISE 23 Compose acceptance messages for job offers you accept

Assume your friend, James, received an email offering him a summer internship. James is drafting his response and asked you for your input. Analyze his message (in the next column), and identify how you could improve it based on the criteria provided in the chapter.

EXERCISE 24 Compose refusal messages for job offers you reject

Refer to Exercise 23. Assume that James received a better summer job offer before he sent the acceptance message he drafted. Now he's work-

---

Thanks, Mr. Sills:

I really appreciate the job offer. I accept! I look forward to working with you and the rest of the staff at Media Designs, Inc., this summer.

In response to your question about when I can start, my last final exam is May 4, but I'd like to take a week or so to move out of my dorm and into the apartment I'm sharing with a friend for the summer. Would Monday, May 15, be okay? I'm also hoping to take a few days during the July 4 holiday for a family reunion.

When I interviewed for the position, you mentioned a salary range, but you didn't specify one in your email below. What's my salary?

Thanks again, I look forward to seeing you on the 15th.

Sincerely,

James

Accompanies Exercise 23

Dear Mr. Sills:

Thank you for your kind offer to intern with Media Designs, Inc., this summer. I regret to inform you that I have taken a better position.

Best wishes,

James

Accompanies Exercise 24

---

ing on a refusal message. Analyze his message above, and identify how he could improve it based on the criteria provided in the chapter.

EXERCISE 25 Respond to job rejections

Read Exercises 19 and 20. Assume you received an email message from Kathy Hamptom of Metrix Marketing Consultants. She thanked you for interviewing with the company and indicated they interviewed many well-qualified candidates. Although they were impressed with your application, they offered the position to someone who had more marketing experience. The message concluded by wishing you success in your continued job search.

Based on the advice in this chapter, you decide to write a follow-up message. Draft your response. Make up details as necessary.

WRITING

EXERCISE 26 Managing your social media image

Write a career summary that you could post on your blog, Facebook, Google Profile, or LinkedIn page. Research career summary content and then tailor yours to be unique to your skills and abilities as well as specific to your discipline. Keep your career summary to a single paragraph (roughly 100 words). Be prepared to share your summary in class or submit it to your instructor for evaluation.

EXERCISE 27 Writing your own recommendation letter

Find a job posting for an internship or job you would be interested in pursuing after graduation. Assume that you have applied for the position and scheduled an interview. The employer is requesting a letter of recommendation from your faculty advisor. When you ask your advisor for the letter, she indicates that she is really very busy and won't be able to provide a letter by the time you need it unless you draft it for her. She assures you that she'll edit it as necessary to make it sound like her, but needs you to put the content on the page and in an appropriate format. Research content for professional recommendation letters and then draft your own letter, being sure to integrate evidence that supports your qualifications for this specific job. Evaluate your letter and submit it and your job advertisement to your instructor for evaluation.

EXERCISE 28 Preparing responses to interview questions

Find a reputable resource that lists interview questions specific to your discipline. (Tip: you can search the web using the name of your field and the phrase "interview questions," for example "accounting interview questions.") Select five questions and draft your responses in a one-page report. Be prepared to share your questions and answers in class or submit your report to your instructor for evaluation.

EXERCISE 29 Composing targeted thank-you messages

Assume that earlier today you interviewed for a competitive summer internship with McMillen-Scott, Inc., a local company. Your contact person, Carla Ruiz, an assistant manager and director of the internship program, was in the reception area when you arrived. Carla greeted you and led you to a conference room where you met Ted Jacobs and Toby Smith, also assistant managers. During the next hour, you learned that the internship would give you a wide breadth of experience at the company by helping with several projects in three different departments while regular employees are out on vacation. Your interview concluded just before lunch, and although it wasn't planned as part of your interview experience, Ted and Toby invited you to have lunch with them. Carla had a lunch meeting with a client. During lunch, Ted and Toby shared their insights about the company and, in response to your request for career advice, talked at length about graduate school and professional development options. You thanked Toby when he paid for your lunch.

As you reflect on the interview and lunch, you realize the internship will require good time management and prioritization skills to balance the many projects and needs of different departments. Your skills in these areas are very strong, and you regret that you forgot to emphasize that during your interview. However, you decide you can work them into your thank-you messages to Carla, Ted, and Toby. Compose unique thank-you messages to each person, carefully evaluate your messages, and submit your documents to your instructor.

EXERCISE 30 Making follow-up decisions

Read the interview scenario outlined in Exercise 29. Carla indicated at the conclusion of your interview that they would be making a decision about the internship position within two weeks. Carla, Ted, and Toby responded to your thank-you messages within a day of receiving them to thank you for your interest in McMillen-Scott, Inc. Ted and Toby both stated that they enjoyed talking with you during lunch. Given the positive feedback, you were surprised two weeks later when you had not heard anything about the internship. When you call Carla to follow up, her assistant indicates that due to a death in the family, Carla would be out all week. The assistant did not have any information about the status of the internship position. Although Carla was your primary contact, you consider either calling or emailing Ted and Toby to find out about the internship. Explain your answers to the following questions:

a. Should you contact Ted and/or Toby, or should you wait until Carla returns?

b. If you decide to follow up before Carla returns, should you contact both Ted and Toby, or just one of them?

c. Should you call or email?

d. Should you offer your condolences to Carla? Or would that be considered too personal given that you don't know her that well?

Compose your follow-up message indicating which audience and medium options you would choose. Submit your responses to the questions and your follow-up message to your instructor.

EXERCISE 31 Requesting an extension on an offer response deadline [Related to the Ethics feature on page 456]

Read the interview scenario in Exercise 29 and the follow-up situation in Exercise 30. Assume you emailed one follow-up message to Ted and Toby and copied Carla on the cc line. Toby responded (copying both Ted and Carla) indicating that they were still very interested in your application, but that due to Carla's absence, the internship decision would be postponed until the end of the month. Toby apologized for the delay and encouraged you to "hang in there" awhile longer. You reply to all thanking Toby for the update and indicating your continued interest in the position.

The next day, you receive an offer from Joshua Barnett of DeLorean Consulting, another company you interviewed with for a summer internship. The pay is less than the amount Carla had indicated you could expect from McMillen-Scott, and the description of the DeLorean internship did not impress you during the interview. DeLorean is looking for someone to enter data, run reports, and occasionally fill in for absences in the mailroom. You decide that although the DeLorean internship would be better than nothing, you are really much more interested in the potential McMillen-Scott opportunity. However, Joshua's email offer indicated he needed your response by the 20th, and you know you won't hear from McMillen-Scott until the end of the month. Email Joshua Barnett to request an extension to the first of the next month. Carefully evaluate your message and submit it to your instructor.

EXERCISE 32 Accepting a job by voice mail and in writing

Read the interview scenario in Exercise 29, the follow-up situation in Exercise 30, and the extension request in Exercise 31. As you requested, Joshua Barnett of DeLorean Consulting graciously extended your deadline to respond to their interview offer. You were very pleased when you received Carla's official letter on the 29th to offer you the internship at McMillen-Scott. Her letter outlined your starting and ending dates, terms of employment, compensation, and job duties. The last paragraph of her letter requests that you respond by the 10th. However, she does not indicate whether you should call, email, or write a letter. All her previous messages had been by email, but you decide to call immediately to accept the offer. Unfortunately, Carla is in a meeting when you call, and you end up leaving a voice mail message. Decide whether you should email or write a letter to confirm your acceptance. Draft your voice mail message and written confirmation message, carefully evaluate them and submit them to your instructor.

EXERCISE 33 Writing an effective job refusal message

Read the interview scenario in Exercise 29, the follow-up situation in Exercise 30, the extension request in Exercise 31, and the job acceptance described in Exercise 32. Compose an email message to Joshua Barnett of DeLorean Consulting declining his internship offer. Carefully evaluate your message and submit it to your instructor.

COLLABORATING

EXERCISE 34 Role playing interview skills

In small groups of three or four, assign the roles of interviewer and interviewee to two students. The remaining student(s) will serve as an observer and recorder. The interviewee describes an entry-level job related to his/her career goal, and the interviewer selects three to five questions from the list of standard interview questions presented in Figure 12.2 (page 442). For five minutes, role-play an interview. The observer/recorder makes notes about the interviewee's responses, and at the conclusion of the interview, provides both positive and constructive feedback. Rotate roles and repeat the process ensuring that different interview questions are selected with each round. If time permits, ensure everyone in the group has had an opportunity to serve as the interviewee. Review the strengths and weaknesses of the group's collective interview responses. What similarities exist? What differences? Be prepared to present a summary of your findings in class or in a message to your instructor.

EXERCISE 35 Comparing personality types

As outlined in Exercise 6 (page 467), companies often use personality assessments to screen applicants. In small groups of two or three, find an online personality assessment, such as the Myers-Briggs or The Big 5, and determine your personality profile. Compare your profiles with each other. What are your similarities? What are your differences? If the two or three of you were assigned to work together on a project, what factors would you need to take into consideration to work effectively together? Summarize your findings and be prepared to present this information in class or in a message to your instructor.

SPEAKING

EXERCISE 36 Making informal/impromptu presentations

Select one of the interview questions listed in Figure 12.2 (page 442). In a one-minute informal presentation, respond to this question as you would during a job interview.

EXERCISE 37 Presenting research

Research one of the following topics and prepare a visual aid to support a three- to five-minute presentation:

a. Visit your school's career center, either in person or online. Research the career fair opportunities they provide or recommend in your area. Determine if they offer career-specific fairs, such as for business, health industry, or education occupations. Also, research the companies that recruit on campus outside of career fairs. Summarize your findings and highlight those that specifically relate to your career goals.

b. Select a company that you would be interested in working for after graduation. Research the company's website to become familiar with its history, mission and/or vision statement, financial health, and recent developments or projects. Brainstorm five questions specific to this company that you could ask during an interview. In your presentation, display the website highlighting the information upon which your questions are based. Then present your questions and explain how you would use the employer's answers to determine if the job is a good fit for you.

c. Interviews can be nerve-wracking experiences for even the most prepared applicants. Find at least two sources that provide stress-relieving suggestions you can use to reduce your anxiety before and during interviews. Explain the suggestions and, if possible, demonstrate them during your presentation.

d. Find online images or take photos of friends (or yourself) in "street clothes," business casual outfits, and business formal attire. Display the photos in a PowerPoint presentation that includes annotated descriptions of how or why the outfits fit into each category. Explain the outfits and their accessories during the presentation moving from most casual to most formal.

e. What are your salary expectations? Research salaries for jobs you are interested in pursuing after graduation. What is the range? What are the differences among various geographic regions? What differences in an applicant's qualifications would justify a salary at the upper end of the range? In addition to salary, what other benefits are included in typical compensation packages?

GRAMMAR

Spelling (See Appendix D—Section 4.0)

Rekey (or download from mybcommlab.com) the following paragraph, correcting the 10 incorrect homonyms or near homonyms, which a spell checker may not catch. Underline all your corrections.

Businesses rely on text messaging for many things besides advertising. Texting can compliment other forms of communication and surpass some for speed and affectiveness. To site one example, let's consider instant communication between a stockbroker and investor. The broker can council the investor about the movement of a stock price and get a "buy" or "sell" decision quickly. Vendors can confirm deliveries, customers can track shipments, and contractors can tell there on-sight crews to precede with construction. Another principle advantage of text messages is the ability to communicate silently. In situations where speaking may be awkward or impossible but immediate communication is important, texting makes more sense then a phone call. Instead of searching in vain for a place to take a call, a person can simply tap out a reply, waving the need for privacy.

Appendix A

Guide to Social Media in Business

Social media has changed the way that businesses communicate—with customers, employees, other businesses, and the general public.

Only a few years ago, if a business wanted to learn what issues were on customers' minds or what merchandise customers wanted, they would commission expensive marketing studies. Today, social media allows companies to ask questions quickly and directly, to read answers and analyze data, and to start a dialogue to gather more targeted information. For example, the Container Store asks its Facebook fans where they would like to see a new store located. Dell Computer asks customers to visit its Idea Storm page to suggest and vote on new product ideas. Comcast monitors Twitter feeds, listening for comments about the company and addressing them in a public forum. This social media interaction supports improved communication for businesses, and it creates a community of people who talk together about a business and its products.

The ways that businesses use social media to communicate are varied and dynamic—and are likely to evolve quickly over the course of your business career. This appendix, "Guide to Social Media in Business," offers a series of quick snapshots illustrating how businesses are using social media now to communicate, solidify their reputations, and build business. Its goal is to help you start thinking about how you can add value to your future employer's business by contributing to its social media efforts.

What Falls under the Social Media "Umbrella"?

When you hear the term *social media*, the first thing that comes to mind may be Facebook, the most prominent social networking site in the world with more than 500 million active users.[1] But the term *social media* goes beyond social networking. It refers to a broad group of Internet-based applications that encourage user interaction and the exchange of user-generated content. Figure A.1 outlines some of the types of social media that businesses use.

While all social media sites are Internet-based, a standard website is not considered social media. A standard website represents one-way communication from a company to its audience. By contrast, social media is *social*. It allows and encourages two-way communication as well as multiparty discussions. Social media is based on involvement, not just dissemination of information.

How Do Businesses Use Social Media to Communicate?

Social media can play a number of different roles in a company's business communication strategy. The following sections provide snapshots of how companies use social media tools as part of their business communication strategy.

Build a Customer Community

With a Facebook Fan Page and a Message Board

Beachbody, a fitness company that sells its exercise programs through the Internet and infomercials, sponsors both a message board and an official Facebook fan page for one of its most popular exercise programs, P90X, an intense set of 12 workouts. Both social media tools provide a community forum for customers and potential customers—a community that numbers more than 40,000 people on the message board and 200,000 people on

FIGURE A.1 Social Media in Business

CATEGORIES OF SOCIAL MEDIA	PURPOSE	EXAMPLES
Social networking sites	Member-only websites that allow individuals and organizations to connect with others who have shared interests	Facebook, MySpace, LinkedIn
Blogs	Interactive websites that allow content generators to provide comments and link with other content on the web and that allow visitors to leave comments in response	NutsaboutSouthwest.com Blogs.cisco.com/innovation
Online forums	Message and discussion boards where people who look for specific information on a topic can ask and answer questions	DigitalPoint
Social bookmarking sites	Collections of publicly accessible browser bookmarks on specific topics where users can submit links and vote to promote links they particularly like	Digg, Delicious
Media sharing	Sites where companies can upload and share videos, photos, and slides	YouTube, Flickr, Slideshare
User reviews and social searches	Sites where users rate and discuss products and services	Amazon, Yelp, TripAdvisor
Microblogs	Internet applications that allow users to broadcast brief posts to other subscribers of the service	Twitter
Crowdsourcing	Sites where people work collaboratively to develop content and knowledge	Wikipedia, Threadless, iStockPhoto

FIGURE A.2
Fans of P90X Use a Message Board to Communicate

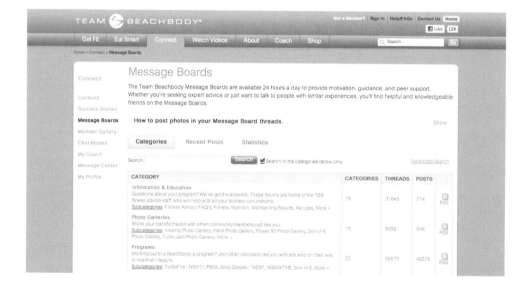

Facebook. As Figure A.2 illustrates, P90X fans use the message board and Facebook "wall" to communicate about the product with other "fans." They post pictures of their success, which provides inspiration to others, ask questions of other fans, and chat with the company's fitness advisors to get professional advice. Because Beachbody encourages interaction and commitment, they have achieved an important goal for social media: they have turned fans into friends.[2]

Interact with Customers and Gather Feedback

With Twitter

Many companies use Twitter to interact with customers in real time. For example, Best Buy has a dedicated Twitter account, called Twelpforce, where Best Buy "agents" can respond immediately to customer questions about products offered and address cus-

The Global Online Job Recruitment Company

Monster.com spent a long time listening to and learning from social media before developing their social media strategy. According to Kathy O'Reilly, Monster's Director of Social Media, "Most companies try to be everything to everyone. But we wanted to know where our audience was engaged, so we spent a lot of time determining where our customers were hanging out on social media."[3]

Monster's social media strategy involves engaging their audience on numerous platforms to achieve three business goals: assert brand leadership, drive traffic to their website, and create demand and preference for their products and services.

YouTube:
Engage with job seekers

Twitter:
Offer customer service

Blog:
Be a thought leader

tomer service issues. This Twitter account allows the "collective force of Best Buy's technology pros" to respond to customers one on one.[4] Whole Foods Market also monitors Twitter traffic to respond quickly to customer suggestions and complaints. Figure A.3 illustrates how a member of the Whole Foods Market integrated media team was able to defuse a customer's anger and elicit a compliment about the "excellent mushroom soup" in a brief conversation with only 140 characters per exchange.

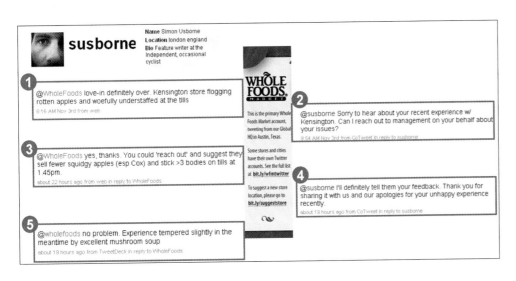

FIGURE A.3
Twitter Exchange Responding to Customer Complaint

Put a Personal Face on a Business

With Blogs and Twitter

People like to do business with companies and individuals they know—or feel that they know. Social media lets executives put a personal face on an organization, whether the organization is for-profit or not-for-profit. As a small business owner, Thomas Mahon uses his Englishcut.com blog, illustrated in Figure A.4, to talk directly to people who are interested in hand-tailored ("bespoke") suits, explaining to them the materials and process he uses. He posts pictures of himself and his staff at work—and of his suits in the process of being tailored. People who are interested in high-quality tailoring follow his blog to learn about the process, and when they are ready to buy a suit, they feel as though they already know Thomas. They are buying from a friend.

Similarly, Doug Ulman, the CEO of LIVESTRONG, frequently posts on the LIVE-STRONG blog (http://livestrongblog.org) and communicates through Twitter to strengthen the organization's connections with the LIVESTRONG community. He blogs and tweets about the LIVESTRONG movement, about cancer research, and about his own reading and travels. He says, "I think people want to know who you are, what you do, what makes you tick—not just hear your marketing agenda. They want to get to know you, and you can only engage them in that manner if you share some personal information and thoughts."[5] Ulman says that social media, especially Twitter, "has fundamentally changed the way we [LIVESTRONG] communicate with the LIVESTRONG movement. It has made us much more transparent. And it has allowed us to develop tons of deep relationships with people who we may not have otherwise met."[6]

Build a Reputation and Become a Thought Leader

With LinkedIn and Blogs

Social media offers businesspeople the opportunity to establish themselves as subject matter experts and thought leaders in a field. They can do this by writing their own subject matter blogs that engage audiences, demonstrate their expertise, and provide

FIGURE A.4
Small Business Blog

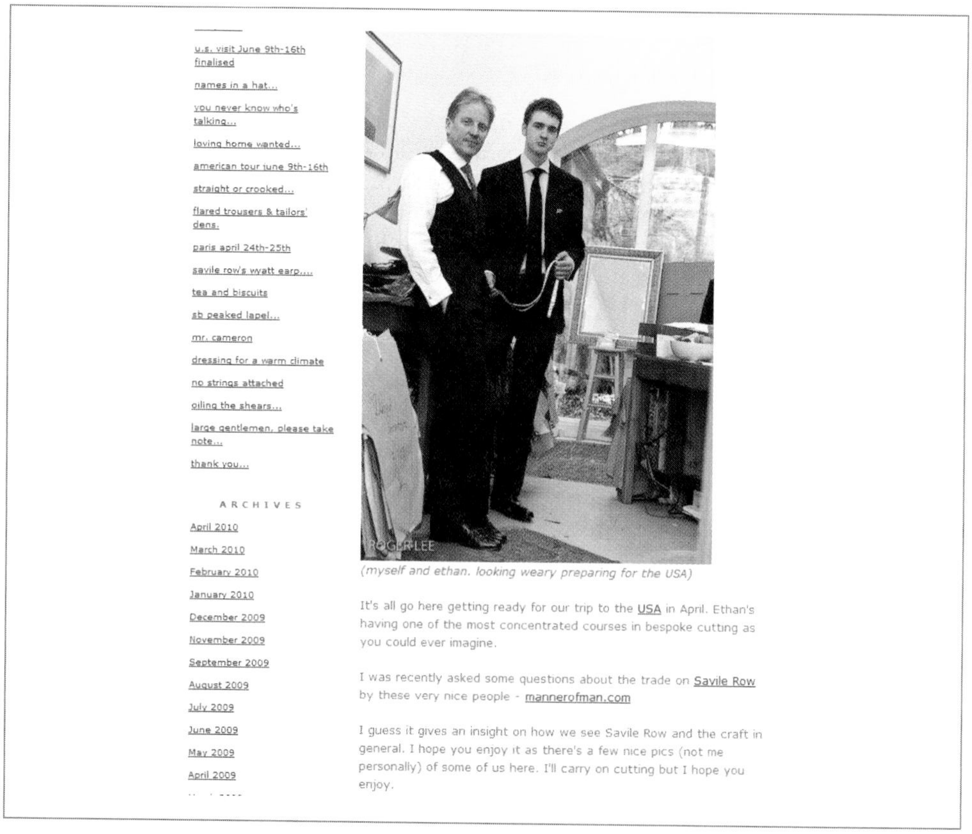

Associate Director of Commercial Analytics, Myrexis

Chris Pounds, with a 15-year career in the biotechnology industry, is currently the associate director of commercial analytics for a small biopharmaceutical company in Utah, focusing on market research and market strategy. He uses social media professionally to advance both his company's interests and his own career.

"Here are some ways I have tried to engage Web 2.0. Being active on **LinkedIn** helps me keep up with my former classmates and work colleagues. I am geographically isolated from nearly all of these folks, so seeing the changes in their status is a great prompt for me to check in with them, helping keep my less common connections fresh. As someone who works in competitive intelligence, I have also used LinkedIn to get a competitive assessment of the commercialization plans of potential partners or competitors. If I see certain positions posted or filled with new hires I will read that as a signal of their intentions and spending levels on a program.

With **Answers on LinkedIn,** I will watch to see what others are talking about and chime in when I can contribute something. This gives my small company a little more visibility and credibility by indicating that our staff has demonstrated expertise. I am also active on **vark.com,** answering questions there. Digging through notes or references to find a solution for someone else keeps my skills current.

I am a big fan of **Reader on Google** for RSS feeds, and follow 90 people who tag articles in various areas. Many of these fall into technical domains that are related to my work. For example we use **Google Apps** and often the new features in **Google Docs** get flagged with examples."[7]

links to relevant material on the Internet. For example, the Chicago restaurateur Rick Bayless has established himself as an expert on Mexican food and travel in Mexico not only by his books and television show, but also by his continual communication about Mexico and his willingness to share his knowledge. His blog includes pictures of Mexico and Mexican food, video links to stories about travel in Mexico, suggested recipes, and advice about where to buy ingredients.

Other people establish their expertise by monitoring questions asked in various discussion forums, including LinkedIn Answers. Chris Pounds, a director of a biopharmaceutical company in Salt Lake City, has established himself in LinkedIn as a biotech subject matter expert by answering questions posted on LinkedIn's biotechnology forum.

Educate

With YouTube

One way to engage audiences with social media is to provide them with value, such as education, information, insight, and connections to other sources. YouTube channels have become a valuable medium for companies to educate their customers and provide value. For example, salesforce.com, the enterprise cloud computing company, uses YouTube to host training videos and best practice webinars about their software. Potential customers also have access to the videos and comments from current customers. This education and validation builds consumer confidence.

Invite Participation

With Flickr

Flickr is an image and video hosting site. Most users are photographers—both amateur and professional—who share their images on the site. However, some corporations use Flickr as part of their social media strategy. For example, Coca-Cola has a Flickr group where individuals can upload photos related to Coca-Cola and its various beverage brands.

FIGURE A.6
Coca-Cola gathers and shares images
on Flickr

The Last Vegas

A Chicago-Based Hard Rock Band

Over the last 10 years, the Last Vegas has developed an international following. Adam Arling, the band's guitarist and business manager, credits this business success both to the quality of the band's music and the power of social media: Facebook, MySpace, Twitter, and YouTube.

"Social media is an invaluable tool for reaching people outside our local region. When we do a tour, we get Facebook fans from 20 different cities. All those people are connected to others who like similar music. There is a snowball effect, and we develop mini-markets all across the world. Facebook and Twitter get our name out, get more people to come to our shows, and help us market music and merchandise. YouTube helps also. We put some videos on YouTube, but more often fans who come to concerts take video and post it immediately, getting the word out about our concerts and giving people a taste of the show. We use MySpace for something completely different: it's a one-stop shop for booking agents and reviewers to download our pictures and other material. We've also begun to make our website more interactive because people want to come to a website and do things—see pictures of concerts, download songs, leave comments."[8]

What Guidelines Should You Follow for Using Social Media at Work?

In the early days of social media, employers were concerned that social media might interfere with employees' concentration at work. As a result, many companies blocked social media at work—and some still do. However, many businesses have come to realize that employees can be effective brand evangelists on social media—if the company provides guidelines for employees to follow and if employees are trained to communicate effectively within those guidelines. Organizations as diverse as The Coca-Cola Company[9] and the International Olympic Committee[10] have produced social media guidelines for their employees.

Unfortunately, not all companies have social media guidelines: in fact, a survey by Manpower found that fewer than 30 percent of companies have guidelines in place.[11] If the company you work for has no guidelines, the following suggestions provide a good starting point for professional behavior. They are adapted from the guidelines Monster.com has produced for its own employees.[12]

❶ **If it's personal, keep it personal.** For non–business-related topics, use your personal email and don't mention your employer.

❷ **If you are engaging in social media as part of your job, identify the company you work for.** Keep to topics related to your area of expertise, and let people know your views are yours, not the company's.

③ **Be honest and professional.** Act as you would in face-to-face conversations. Avoid discriminatory content. Avoid arguments. Identify who you are: "anonymous" is not professional.

④ **Respect and protect what's confidential.** Never reveal financial, legal, copyrighted, proprietary, or personal information about the company, customers, or employees.

⑤ **Recommend colleagues with care.** It's acceptable to provide personal recommendations about your experience but not an official recommendation on behalf of your company.

⑥ **Add value.** Share interesting, helpful information and ideas, and link to helpful content from your company's website. Your "brand" is the sum of what you share and how you share it.

⑦ **Know the risks.** Ignoring these rules could lead to termination.

Appendix B

Business Document Formatting Guide

This appendix provides standard formatting guidelines for basic business documents such as email messages, memos, and letters. In addition, it provides an annotated example of a report. For more complete report formatting directions, see Chapter 9. Your instructor (or employer) may request formats that vary from the samples provided. Whatever format you use, your goal should be to ensure a professional-looking message that effectively communicates your purpose.

Email Messages

Follow email formatting guidelines to ensure you include all the elements needed in business emails and to ensure that your content is easy to read on a computer or hand-held device.

Email Formatting Guidelines

A professional business email message includes the following elements:

- **Email addresses.** When composing an email message, place the recipient's email address on the "To" line. If you want to send the same message to several recipients, separate their email addresses with commas. If you want to send a courtesy copy ("cc") to a secondary audience, add their email addresses on the "cc" line. The "bcc" line is for "blind courtesy copy" and is used to send a copy of the message to people without the "To" and "cc" recipients' knowledge.

- **Subject line.** Always include a subject line that is short but meaningful. The best subject lines clearly communicate the purpose of your message. For example, sending an email message with "Sales Meeting" as the subject line is not meaningful. The recipients would have to open your message to know whether you are trying to schedule a sales meeting or following up after a meeting. If you are sending meeting minutes requiring no response, your subject line might be "Sales Meeting Minutes," which would indicate to recipients that the message could be read when the recipients have time. However, if you are trying to schedule a meeting and need their quick response, your subject line might be "Need Input for Meeting Date ASAP," which would prompt recipients to read the message right away.

- **Salutation.** The salutation or greeting addresses the message to the primary audience. How the message begins sets the tone for the rest of the document. Formal business emails frequently use "Dear" in the salutation, such as "Dear Mr. Smith." However, contemporary business writers are moving away from the traditional use of "Dear," especially in informal emails, often choosing instead to use a salutation such as "Hi, John" or "Hello, Mr. Smith." In some cases, you might simply use the person's name without any salutation, although some audiences may consider it rude to omit a salutation.

    Different salutations require different punctuation. In a formal email, a salutation like "Dear Mr. Smith" ends with a colon. There is no other punctuation. In the less formal salutation, "Hello, John," a comma separates the greeting from the name, and the salutation ends with a colon. In rare cases, you may see salutations formatted with *open punctuation,* which means neither the salutation nor the complimentary closing includes punctuation.

- **Name.** Whether you use a person's first or last name in the salutation depends on how you address the individual in face-to-face settings. If your boss has asked you to call him "John," address your email to him as "John" rather than "Mr. Smith." However, when emailing new clients or customers for the first time, do not assume they want you to use their first names. You practice better business etiquette by erring on the side of formality. Similarly, do not assume that a woman is a "Mrs." unless you know your recipient prefers "Mrs." It is better to use "Ms." or a professional title such as "Dr." or "Rev."

- **Paragraphs.** Short email messages may include just a few lines of text. Longer messages should use effective paragraphing techniques to organize the content logically:

  - Keep the first paragraph short (50 words or less) and get to the point of the message. Imagine that your audience is reading the message on a smart phone or other handheld device. Make sure the main idea shows on the first screen, without making your reader scroll. Do not begin with "This email is about. . . ." Your subject line tells the recipient the topic of the email.

  - The middle paragraph(s) should be relatively short. Average paragraphs are roughly 100 words in length. For longer messages that use several paragraphs, begin each paragraph with a topic sentence that identifies the main point of the paragraph.

  - End with a short paragraph requesting any action, indicating any deadlines, and maintaining goodwill with the audience.

- **Complimentary closing.** In formal situations, use a closing such as "Sincerely." In less formal messages, "Thanks" or "Regards" will suffice. The closing is followed by a comma and then your name on the next line. Using just your first name is fine for informal messages to people who will immediately recognize your email address. However, if you are writing to someone who does not know you, use your first name and last name. Do not use a personal title such as "Mr." or "Ms." with your name unless the recipient does not know you and cannot identify your gender from your first name (such as Pat, Chris, or Rathi). In these cases, use your personal title so the recipient knows to address you as either Mr. or Ms. in a response to your message.

- **Signature block.** Include an electronic signature block that displays all relevant contact information including your name, position title, department, company, email address, phone number, and fax number. You may wonder why you should include your email address in your signature block when the recipients will have your address in their inbox. If your message is forwarded, the email system may display your name rather than your email address, so the recipient will not know your email address. Further, if the recipient prints your email message, your email address may not be included in the printout.

Informal Email Format

FIGURE B.1 provides an example of an informal email message.

FIGURE B.1 Informal Email Message Format

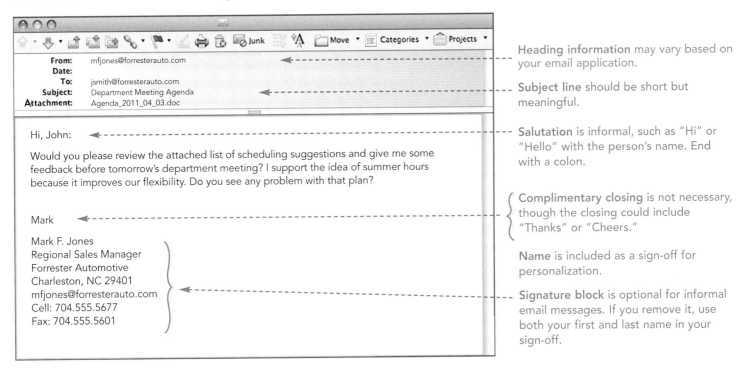

Heading information may vary based on your email application.

Subject line should be short but meaningful.

Salutation is informal, such as "Hi" or "Hello" with the person's name. End with a colon.

Complimentary closing is not necessary, though the closing could include "Thanks" or "Cheers."

Name is included as a sign-off for personalization.

Signature block is optional for informal email messages. If you remove it, use both your first and last name in your sign-off.

Formal Email Format

FIGURE B.2 provides an example of a formal email message.

FIGURE B.2 Formal Email Message Format

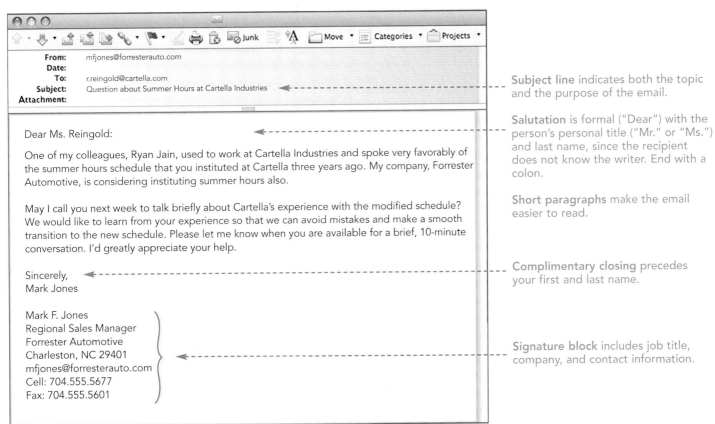

Subject line indicates both the topic and the purpose of the email.

Salutation is formal ("Dear") with the person's personal title ("Mr." or "Ms.") and last name, since the recipient does not know the writer. End with a colon.

Short paragraphs make the email easier to read.

Complimentary closing precedes your first and last name.

Signature block includes job title, company, and contact information.

Email Report Format

You can compose informal email reports to share information with people within your organization. Email reports may also be appropriate for external audiences if the context is informal and you know the audience prefers email over other medium options. FIGURE B.3 provides an example of an email report format. Notice that the salutation and complimentary closing are optional.

FIGURE B.3 Email Report Format

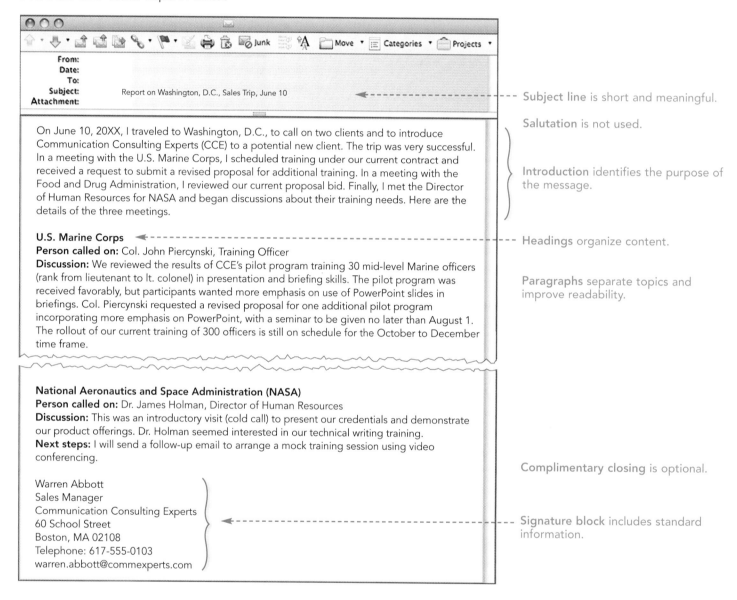

Subject line is short and meaningful.

Salutation is not used.

Introduction identifies the purpose of the message.

Headings organize content.

Paragraphs separate topics and improve readability.

Complimentary closing is optional.

Signature block includes standard information.

Memos

Memos are similar to email messages with the exception that they are either printed and distributed as hard copies or sent as email attachments. When printed, memos often accompany documents that cannot be sent electronically, such as forms requiring signatures or carbon documents completed in triplicate. When sent as email attachments, memos provide the formality of an official company document as compared to an informal email message. Memos are generally intended for internal audiences (people within an organization rather than customers or clients) and can be designed on letterhead or plain paper. Quite often, a company will determine a standard memo format that all employees should use to promote consistency in style throughout the organization.

Memo Formatting Guidelines

As with most business messages, organize the content by placing the main idea or reason for writing in the first line or paragraph of the memo. Short memos, such as the example in FIGURE B.4, may require only one paragraph. In longer memos, as shown in FIGURE B.5, organize the content by paragraph, using headings to separate topics as you would in a report. Use the following guidelines to ensure the document looks professional and projects a positive nonverbal image (keeping in mind that your instructor or company may provide specific design criteria):

- **Top margin.** Begin at the top margin setting, or a few lines below the company logo if using letterhead.
- **Memo headings.** The page title "Memorandum" (as shown in Figure B.4) is optional. However, four memo headings are required: TO:, FROM:, DATE:, and SUBJECT: (or RE:). Use colons to separate the heading labels from the text that follows the labels, and use the Tab key to move from the colon (:) to the text. Using spaces to move from the heading to the text does not exactly align the text.
- **TO/FROM content.** Be consistent with the use of personal titles (Mr., Ms., Dr.) and employment positions (such as Director of Sales). For example, if you are writing to "Mr. John Smith," include Mr. or Ms. with your name on the FROM line. However, if you are writing to "John Smith," do not include a personal title with your name. When including employment positions after a name, separate them from the name with a comma and use initial caps (such as "Mr. John Smith, Director of Sales"). In a printed memo, sign the hard copy by writing your initials next to your name.
- **Date.** Write out the date's month (for example, "January 10, 2012") on the date line.
- **Subject line.** Use a short (three- to five-word) subject line to indicate the topic of your message. Use one or two blank lines after the SUBJECT line to separate the memo headings from the message.
- **Salutation.** Memos do not use salutations since the recipient's name is prominently displayed on the TO line.
- **Body.** If the content of a memo is very short, such as the memo in Figure B.4, write the message in a single paragraph. If the content is lengthy, write multiple paragraphs. Make the first paragraph short (two to three lines) and get to the point (do not begin with "This memo is about . . ."). In a lengthy memo, keep the middle paragraphs short, roughly 100 words each. Be sure each paragraph has a purpose and begins with a topic sentence. Single space the paragraphs. Use one blank line between paragraphs. As noted earlier, use paragraph headings to separate major topics.
- **Second page heading.** For long memos that extend beyond one page, format second and subsequent page headings as shown in Figure B.5. Include the recipient's name, the page number, and date.

FIGURE B.4 Short Memo Format

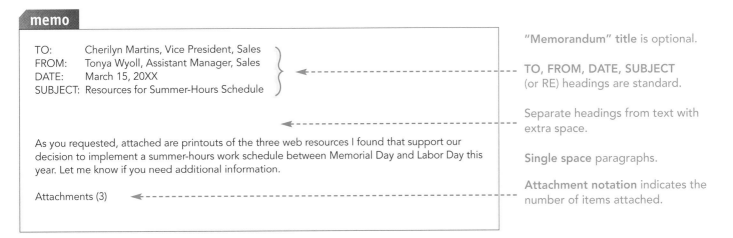

FIGURE B.5 Long Memo Format

memo

TO: Ms. Cherilyn Martins, Vice President, Sales
FROM: Ms. Tonya Wyoll, Assistant Manager, Sales
DATE: February 12, 20XX
SUBJECT: Proposal for Summer-Hours Work Schedule

Standard headings with aligned content, consistent use of titles, and a short but specific subject line.

No salutation is used.

At our last department meeting, we briefly discussed how a summer-hours work schedule might improve employee morale. I'd like to propose that we try a summer schedule this year. I believe this change will be very easy and will benefit our company. This memo summarizes the detailed content in my attached proposal.

First paragraph presents the main idea (direct organizational plan) and mentions the attached proposal.

How the Schedule Will Work
The summer schedule will begin on June 1 and end on August 31. During that period, employees can choose to work a normal 9 AM to 5 PM day or come in and leave an hour earlier (8 AM to 4 PM). This means all employees will be present during the core hours of 9 AM to 4 PM, when we are busiest. It also means we will not need to adjust lunch hours or breaks, since the proposed hours are very similar to our current working hours.

Specific headings let the audience know how the message is structured.

Ms. Cherilyn Martins, Page 2
February 12, 20XX

Second page heading includes recipient's name, page number, and date.

Next Steps
Please let me know if you need additional information, or if you would like me to draft a formal proposal to present at next week's upper management meeting. I look forward to your response.

No complimentary closing or signature block is used.

Attachments:
• Summer-Hours Work Schedule Report
• Web Resources

Attachment notation lists the documents attached.

- **Closing.** Do not use a complimentary closing or a signature block in a memo. Your name is displayed on the FROM line. However, if your message requests a reply, be sure to indicate your telephone number and/or email address in the last paragraph (for example, "Please call me at 555-1522 by Friday with your response.").
- **Attachment notation.** If you are attaching additional documents to your memo, describe them in the message (for example, "Attached is a list of resources you may find useful."). Then, remind the audience of the attachments by placing an "Attachment" notation at the end of your memo. Leave one blank line between the last paragraph and the attachment notation. You can include the number of attachments in parentheses (as shown in Figure B.4) or name the attachment(s) (as shown in Figure B.5).

Letters

Letters are generally intended for external audiences —people outside an organization such as customers or clients. They may also be used for formal correspondence within a company, such as letters of resignation or letters offering a promotion. Letters are printed on letterhead or sent as email attachments. Many companies use electronic letterhead templates so that letters attached to emails will look the same as printed letters.

Just as with memo formats, companies often promote consistency in style throughout an organization by identifying a standard letter format that all employees use. Two main letter-formatting styles exist:

- **Block style.** Place all parts of the letter at the left margin and do not indent paragraphs. See FIGURE B.6 for an example of a block style letter.

FIGURE B.6 Block Style Letter

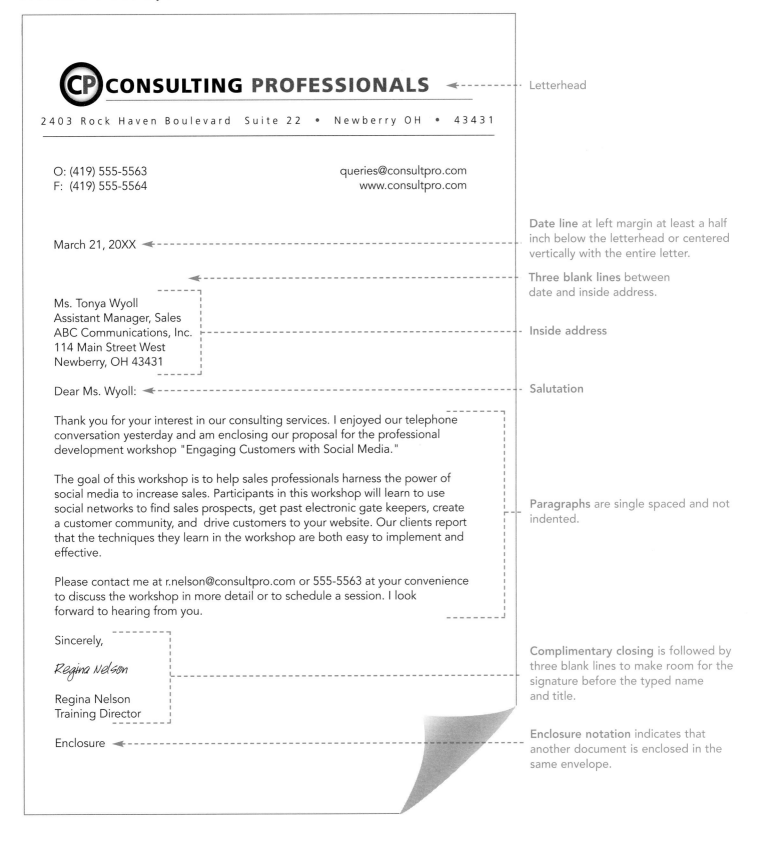

- **Modified block style.** This style begins the return address (if no letterhead is used), date, complimentary closing, and signature block at the center of the page. Paragraphs can be indented or not, depending on your preference. See FIGURE B.7 for an example of a modified block style letter.

FIGURE B.7 Modified Block Style Letter

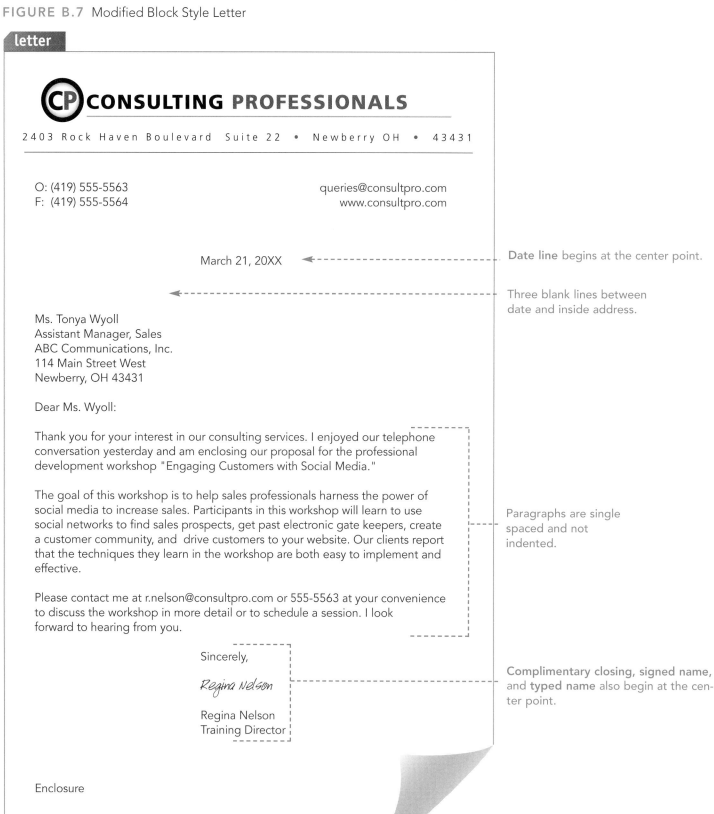

Date line begins at the center point.

Three blank lines between date and inside address.

Paragraphs are single spaced and not indented.

Complimentary closing, signed name, and typed name also begin at the center point.

Block style is the most efficient letter style because you do not have to indent or align any of the letter elements.

Letter Formatting Guidelines

When designing a letter, use the following guidelines to ensure that the letter looks professional and projects a positive nonverbal image.

- **Letterhead or return address.** Most companies create custom-designed letterhead with their logo and/or company name and address at the top (or sometimes at the bottom) of the page. When sending letters for personal business, you might create your own letterhead similar to the cover letter samples in Chapter 11. At a minimum, your personal letterhead should include your name and mailing address. You might also include your phone number and email address. If you are not using letterhead, provide your return address at the top of the page, starting either at the left margin (block style) or in the center of the page (modified block style). The return address includes your street address on the first line and your city, state, and zip code on the next line.

- **Date.** Write out the date as month, day, and year (for example, January 10, 2012). At a minimum, place the date a half inch (usually three lines depending the font size) below the letterhead. Typically, letters should be centered vertically on the page. If your letter is short, the date will be lower to balance the amount of blank space on the top and bottom of the page. If using a personal return address (with no letterhead), place the date on the line below your city, state, and zip code. Following the date, leave three blank lines (pressing the Enter key four times) between the date and inside address.

- **Special mailing notations and on-arrival notations.** If you are sending a letter by special delivery or certified mail, add these notations in ALL CAPS. If you are sending a letter to someone in a company but want to mark it as personal or confidential, add one of the following notations in ALL CAPS: personal, confidential, private and confidential, or strictly confidential. Place these notations two lines below the date and two lines above the inside address.

- **Inside address.** The inside address includes the name and address of the person to whom the letter will be sent. Follow these guidelines:
  - First line: Use "Mr." or "Ms." or some other courtesy title like "Dr." or "Professor" in front of the person's name. If you include an employment title like "Director of Marketing" after the name, capitalize it and separate it from the name with a comma.
  - Second line: Type the person's company name (if applicable).
  - Third line: Type the street address.
  - Fourth line: Type the city, state, and zip code. Use the two-letter state abbreviation (see the list of states, territories, and provinces on page A-19) and one space between all elements. Use a comma only between the city and state.
  - Leave one blank line between the inside address and the salutation.

- **Salutation.** The use of "Dear" in the salutation is traditional. However, it is not required in letters to people whom you know well. For formal letters, use the recipient's personal title (Mr. or Ms.) and last name. In informal situations and when you know the person well, use the recipient's first name. If you do not know the name of the person who should receive your letter, create an attention line to a position title (such as "Human Resources Director" or "Sales Department") in place of the salutation. Leave one blank line between the salutation and the first paragraph.

- **Open/closed punctuation.** Closed punctuation style uses a colon (:) after the salutation and a comma after the complimentary closing. Open punctuation style, which is used less frequently, uses no punctuation at the end of the salutation or after the complimentary closing.

- **Subject line.** Subject lines are optional in letters. If used, format the subject line as you would in a memo and place it below the salutation.

- **Body.** Begin with a short first paragraph (two to three lines) that gets to the point (do not begin with "This letter is about. . . ."). The middle paragraph(s) can be longer if necessary, up to eight or 10 lines of text in each paragraph. Be sure each paragraph has a purpose and begins with a topic sentence. Use headings, bulleted lists, or enumerations as needed. The last paragraph should be short (two to three lines). In the closing, let the audience know what they should do next, include contact information, and reinforce goodwill.

- **Second (and subsequent) page headings.** Use the same format for second page headings in letters as described for memos: include the recipient's name, page number, and date of the message.

- **Complimentary closing.** Start the signature block with a complimentary closing, such as "Sincerely" or "Best regards," followed by a comma (if using closed punctuation). Leave at least three blank lines between the closing and your typed name so you have enough room to sign your name.

- **Signed name.** On the printed copy, sign above your typed name. Your signature does not have to be legible, but it should fit neatly between the complimentary closing and your typed name. Celebrity-style signatures are not considered professional for business documents.

- **Typed name.** Your name (as the author of the letter) should be typed three lines below the complimentary closing. Do not use a personal title, such as "Mr." or "Ms.," with your name unless the recipient does not know you and cannot identify your gender from your first name (such as Pat, Chris, or Rathi). If you include your job title on the same line as your name, separate it with a comma. If your job title is long, place it on the line below your typed name.

- **Enclosure notation.** If you are including additional documentation with the letter, indicate that by typing "Enclosure" one line below your typed name.

- **Copy notation.** If you are sending a copy of the letter to someone else, indicate that by adding a "cc" notation below your typed name (or enclosure/attachment notation). The "cc" used to mean "carbon copy," but today it refers to "courtesy copy."

- **Postscript.** Commonly prefaced with "PS," postscripts are additional short content placed as an afterthought at the end of the message. They may be used in informal letters and sales letters (to retain the audience's attention), but should be avoided in most formal contexts. If the content is important, move it into the body of the message.

- **Vertical placement.** If the letter does not fill an entire page, center the content vertically (top to bottom) on the page. You can do this manually by positioning the cursor at the date, zooming out to a full page view, and then pressing the "Enter" key until approximately the same amount of space appears at the top (between the letterhead and the date line) and the bottom (between the last typed line and the bottom the of the page). Alternatively, you can use your word processor's page setup feature to change the page's vertical alignment to center. If you use this feature and plan to print your letter on company letterhead, first create a blank header and/or footer on your file that are the same size as any preprinted header and footer on the stationery. If you are writing your letter on "electronic" letterhead, be sure that the letterhead content is in the header portion of your page. Otherwise, the automatic centering feature will not work.

Envelope Format

Most word processing programs include a mailing feature that helps you format envelopes. Use a format similar to FIGURE B.8. Place the your return address on the front of the envelope in the upper left corner. If the company uses envelopes with a preprinted return address, you may add your name above the preprinted text. Begin the recipient's mailing address approximately in the center of the envelope. The U.S. Postal Service suggests typing the address in ALL CAPS with no punctuation, although some companies use initial caps for easier reading. The postal service also recommends using the recipient's ZIP+4 code.

FIGURE B.8 Envelope Style

Regina Nelson, Training Director
Consulting Professionals
2403 Rock Haven Boulevard, Suite 22
Newberry OH 43431-5589

Return address (writer's name, company, and mailing address) is typed in the top left corner (if not provided as envelope letterhead).

MS TONYA WYOLL
ASSISTANT MANAGER SALES
ABC COMMUNICATION INC
113 MAIN STREET WEST
NEWBERRY OH 43431-9271

Recipient's address is centered vertically between the return address and the bottom of the envelope and is indented so the text is aligned near the horizontal center.

Abbreviations of States, Territories, and Provinces

Refer to the following list of abbreviations when used in addresses in letters and envelopes. When addressing letters to international recipients, use the format shown in Figure B.8 and replace the state with the province or other principal subdivision. Add the country name in ALL CAPS in English on line by itself at the end of the address block.[1]

State	Abbr.	State	Abbr.	State	Abbr.	State	Abbr.
Alabama	AL	Indiana	IN	Nebraska	NE	Rhode Island	RI
Alaska	AK	Iowa	IA	Nevada	NV	South Carolina	SC
Arizona	AZ	Kansas	KS	New Hampshire	NH	South Dakota	SD
Arkansas	AR	Kentucky	KY	New Jersey	NJ	Tennessee	TN
California	CA	Louisiana	LA	New Mexico	NM	Texas	TX
Colorado	CO	Maine	ME	New York	NY	Utah	UT
Connecticut	CT	Maryland	MD	North Carolina	NC	Vermont	VT
Delaware	DE	Massachusetts	MA	North Dakota	ND	Virginia	VA
Florida	FL	Michigan	MI	Ohio	OH	Washington	WA
Georgia	GA	Minnesota	MN	Oklahoma	OK	West Virginia	WV
Hawaii	HI	Mississippi	MS	Oregon	OR	Wisconsin	WI
Idaho	ID	Missouri	MO	Pennsylvania	PA	Wyoming	WY
Illinois	IL	Montana	MT				

Abbreviations of Commonwealth/Territories

Name	Abbr.	Name	Abbr.	Name	Abbr.
American Samoa	AS	Guam	GU	Palau	PW
District of Columbia	DC	Marshall Islands	MH	Puerto Rico	PR
Federated States of Micronesia	FM	Northern Mariana Islands	MP	Virgin Islands	VI

Abbreviations of Military "States"

Name	Abbr.	Name	Abbr.	Name	Abbr.
Armed Forces Africa	AE	Armed Forces Canada	AE	Armed Forces Middle East	AE
Armed Forces Americas	AA	Armed Forces Europe	AE	Armed Forces Pacific	AP

Reports

A complete discussion of report formats is provided in Chapter 9. Refer to FIGURE B.9 for basic guidelines.

1. United States Postal Service. (2010). *Addressing international mail.* Retrieved from http://www.usps.com/international/addressingintlmail.htm

FIGURE B.9 Report Format

INTEGRATING BLOGGING INTO THE BUSINESS COMMUNICATION CURRICULUM AT WESTERN STATE UNIVERSITY

Prepared by
Courtney Patterson
School of Management Sciences
Western State University

August 1, 2010

Table of Contents

ii

Executive Summary

Purpose of This Report

Blogging is a growing medium of communication in business. However, the Western State University School of Management Sciences offers students no instruction in blogging. The purpose of this report is to analyze the current state of business blogging and to recommend ways that Western State University can prepare business students to be better communicators with new social media.

Research and Analysis

This report is based on extensive research, including a review of key documents and books about blogging, analysis of nearly 100 small business and corporate blogs, and analysis of blogging statistics using the data provided by Technorati (2008), an organization that analyzes blogs and trends in blogging and also periodically surveys bloggers and readers of blogs worldwide.

Key Findings

- Blogging has evolved from a purely personal form of online diary into a vehicle for widespread communication.

- Blogging has grown exponentially from just a few blogs in the early 1990s to more than 130 million today.

- As of 2006, an estimated 20,000 businesses regularly used blogs to communicate.

Conclusion

Blogging has become a key way businesses communicate with customers and other stakeholders. Use of blogs in business will likely continue to grow.

Recommendations

Since Western State University does not address blogging in any of its current management communication courses, and since blogging has evolved into a serious method for business communication, this report offers four recommendations:

1) **Address blogging and social media in BUAD 287: Business Communication—** at least one class session should focus on social media, including blogging.

2) **Add an elective course, History of Social Media,** which will focus on analyzing blogging and other forms of social media. This course will take a theoretical approach.

3) **Add an elective course, Social and Technological Business Communication,** which will be designed to give students practical instruction using social media as a form of business communication.

4) **Develop a school-wide Management Sciences blog** to provide students with hands-on experience in blogging.

iii

Introduction

The popular social medium of blogging is a powerful tool for business and corporate communication. Blogging gives corporations a personality and human voice, enhancing their ability to reach consumers. As the blogging world, or blogosphere, has grown, the corporate world has begun to adapt to the communication style that blogging makes possible. Moreover, individual experts in the important disciplines of economics, finance, investing, law, and marketing are writing extremely influential blogs on a range of important subjects affecting business, often creating mini-essays with detailed arguments on timely issues and trends.

Given the importance of blogging—especially in business—it is surprising that Western State University does not include instruction about blogging in its business communication curriculum. As a result, business students are graduating without a disciplined intellectual understanding about how to use blogging as a business communication tool.

This report addresses the question of whether and how Western State University should integrate blogging into its curriculum. This report is based on extensive research, including a review of key documents and books about blogging, analysis of nearly 100 small business and corporate blogs, and analysis of blogging statistics using the data provided by Technorati (2008), an organization that analyzes blogs and trends in blogging and also periodically surveys bloggers and readers of blogs worldwide.

This research supports the recommendation that WSU integrate blogging into the curriculum for three key reasons:

1) Business blogging has become a significant and credible form of communication.

2) Businesses are increasingly using blogs to communicate.

3) Effective blogging requires education.

To best prepare students to communicate effectively through workplace blogging, WSU should integrate blogging in the following ways:

- Add a module on blogging/social media to BUAD 287: Business Communication.

- Add two elective courses to the curriculum, focusing on social media in general, including blogging.

- Develop a school-wide Management Sciences blog to provide students with hands-on experience in blogging.

This report explores the reasons that blogging should be integrated into the curriculum, looks at current uses of blogging in the university, and then provides detailed discussion of where blogging can fit into the curriculum.

1

The **title page** typically includes the title of the report, the author's name, title, and company (or school) and date. Use balanced spacing between major elements. Do not paginate the title page.

Preliminary pages, such as the table of contents and executive summary, use lowercase Roman page numbers at the bottom of the page (left, center, or right aligned). Use a consistent location for all page numbers throughout the manuscript.

The **table of contents** lists the section titles and headings with their corresponding page numbers. Use dot leaders with a right-aligned margin tab to align numbers.

An **executive summary** is optional, depending on the formality and length of the report. If included, summarize the purpose, highlights, and main idea (or conclusion) of the report.

Headings can be boldfaced for emphasis. Use consistent styles for similar heading levels throughout the manuscript.

The **introduction** may be a separate section in formal reports, or it could be a paragraph or two at the beginning of the body of the report.

FIGURE B.9 Continued

Reasons to Incorporate Blogging into the Curriculum

Reason 1: Business Blogging Is a Significant and Credible Form of Communication

In the last 15 years, business blogging has evolved into a significant and credible platform for business communication. Large and small corporations are creating and managing blogs as an important way to reach customers and stakeholders.

The birth of blogging occurred in 1994 when a student at Swathmore College, Justin Hall, launched links.net (Rosenberg, 2009). In the early years, blogs were personal websites where site creators (bloggers) could keep an online, public diary of their lives. Blogs were usually written by individuals who would write from their subjective point of view on any topic, such as their particular events in their personal lives or their individual reactions to external events. As such, the first generation of blogs were highly individualized, with the specific life and experiences of the blogger as the main source of blog content.

As the number of blogs grew very quickly, bloggers who read and followed other individuals' blogs created what amounted to a viral social network from blogging, typically by linking to other blogs and other websites of interest. Blogs oriented to political discussion emerged on the scene in 2001, prompted by the controversial election of George W. Bush in 2000 as well as the events of September 11, 2001. By 2008, blogging became so critical to reaching audiences that 95 of the top 100 newspapers had reporter blogs (Technorati, 2008).

In its 2008 *State of the Blogosphere* report, Technorati stated that it had indexed 133 million blogs since 2002. Of this 133 million, 76,000 blogs have what is known as Technorati Authority (TA), a label denoting the number of blogs linking to a website in the last six months (the higher the number, the more TA the blog has). Thus, approximately 76,000 blogs are actively linking to other blogs and websites.

At the time of that report, close to one million posts were being created every day in up to 81 languages from 66 countries (Technorati, 2008). Blogging has expanded to include genre-specific blogs, such as political commentary blogs, media blogs that use music and video posts, and corporate blogs (Rettberg, 2008). Blogging has evolved from online personal diaries to commentary and discussion on social, political, legal and economic issues by academic scholars/expert professionals. Blogging has also become a vehicle for businesses to communicate with customers and stakeholders.

As blogging has evolved, so has its credibility as a communication medium. In its survey for the 2008 *State of the Blogosphere* report, Technorati asked a statistically valid representative sample of bloggers worldwide about the credibility of the blogging world. The results suggest blogging is becoming more credible as a source of information (see Figure 1).

Reason 2: Businesses Are Increasingly Using Blogs to Communicate

In the early days of blogging, prominent thinkers about blogging such as Rick Levine, Christopher Locke, Doc Searls, and David Weinberger (1999) prophesied the influence blogging could have on the corporate world. In *The Cluetrain Manifesto*, Levine et al. wrote: "A powerful global conversation has begun. Through the Internet, people are discovering and inventing new ways to share relevant knowledge with blinding speed. As a direct result, markets are getting smarter—and getting smarter faster than most companies" (1999, p. 10). They knew that, in order to survive, companies would have to learn from the technological changes occurring through blogging's conversational medium.

2

Figure 1 – Response to Survey About Credibility of Blogging

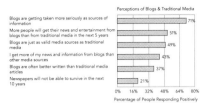

Perceptions of Blogs & Traditional Media

- Blogs are getting taken more seriously as sources of information — 71%
- More people will get their news and entertainment from blogs than traditional media in the next 5 years — 51%
- Blogs are just as valid media sources as traditional media — 49%
- I get more of my news and information from blogs than other media sources — 43%
- Blogs are often better written than traditional media articles — 37%
- Newspapers will not be able to survive in the next 10 years — 21%

Percentage of People Responding Positively (0%, 16%, 32%, 48%, 64%, 80%)

Adapted from Technorati (2008). *State of the Blogosphere*. http://technorati.com/blogging/stateof-the-blogosphere/

Corporations heeded this advice and now have a prominent place in the blogosphere. Technorati's 2004 estimate counted roughly 5,000 corporate blogs (Sifry, 2004), a number that some experts believe had quadrupled by 2006 (Cass, 2006). The official blog for Google (http://googleblog.blogspot.com/) is so widely read and linked that Technorati Authority rated it the 13th highest ranked blog among all categories of blogs.

Table 1 shows an alphabetized list of the top 75 business blogs in 2009 as measured by the *Financial Times ComMetrics Blog Index of Corporate Blogging Effectiveness* (2009). While many of the businesses listed are Internet related, a number of traditional technology, finance, industrial, and retail corporations are also on the list, for example, Alcoa, General Electric, Wells Fargo, and Wal-Mart. For WSU business communication students, such blogs would be worth studying as examples of effective blogging in a business setting. (The Appendix lists the URLs for the top 25 of these blogs.)

Blogging in Small Businesses. Businesses typically use blogs in one of two ways: to showcase the personnel/expertise of the corporation or to engage in product-related conversations with others in a public and widely read forum. For a smaller business, a blog can be an economical way of getting attention and attaining a global reach at little to no cost.

Small business blogs are particularly effective when they focus on the company's personality and expertise instead of on marketing its products. In effect, the credibility of a small business blog depends on showing passion rather than salesmanship (Herzlich, 2009; Scoble & Israel, 2006). A blog can act as a conduit for a small company to begin conversations that build consumer trust, rather than simply serve as another avenue for marketing products.

3

Table 1 – 75 Corporations Whose Blogs Appear in the *Financial Times ComMetrics Blog Index of Corporate Blogging Effectiveness*

ABB	Deutsche Bank	Johnson & Johnson	SAP
Accenture	Deutsche Telekom	Johnson Controls	Siemens
Adobe	E.ON	Kraft Foods	Sony
Alcoa	eBay	McDonald's	Swisscom
Amazon	EMC	Microsoft	Sygenta
American Express	Emerson Electric	Nestlé	Telenor Group
Arcelor Mittal	Ericsson	News Corporation	Telia Sonera
Aviva	Fedex	Nike	Telstra
Bank of America	Fiat	Nissan	Time Warner
Bayer	France Telecom	Nokia	Toyota
BBVA	General Electric	Novo Nordisk	Unilever
Berkshire Hathaway	GlaxoSmithKline	Oracle	UPS
BNP Paribas	GM	Petro Canada	Verizon Communications
Boeing	Google	Procter & Gamble	Viacom
Chevron	Henkel	Renault	Volvo
Cisco	Hewlett Packard	Reuters	Wal-Mart
Coca-Cola	IBM	Royal Bank of Canada	Wells Fargo
Daimler	InBev	Royal/Dutch Shell	Yahoo!
Dell	ING	Samsung	

Adapted from: Financial Times (2009). Powered by My.ComMetrics.com—updates available at http://FTindex.ComMetrics.com/

Thomas Mahon, for example, is a London tailor who started a blog called English Cut where he writes about the technical aspects of tailoring, such as the differences among suits and kinds of fabrics. As Figure 2 illustrates, Mahon does not primarily promote his own business. Instead, Mahon uses his blog to influence his customers' perceptions of him and his quality tailoring. His blog provides a public, yet informal place where consumers can view his life and his love for tailoring—and come to appreciate his work.

Blogs also offer small businesses the opportunity to become completely transparent with their consumer base (Halzack, 2008; Mahon, 2009; Rettberg, 2008; Scoble & Israel, 2006). For example, Honest Tea began its blog in 2005 expressly desiring openness with its consumers. Before Coca-Cola acquired a 40% share of Honest Tea, the company blogged about the decision and even responded to consumers' criticisms (Goldman, 2009). This transparency allows a company like Honest Tea to build consumer trust and credibility.

4

Figure 2 – Screen Shot of Thomas Mahon's Blog, EnglishCut.com

From: Englishcut.com

Blogging in Large Corporations. Larger companies also benefit from blogging's emphasis on personality and community. Whereas a smaller company may use a blog to inform readers of the company's qualifications and dedication to quality, an established, larger company can use blogging to rebrand itself as a more consumer-friendly, actively listening business.

Robert Scoble (2003), a Microsoft employee, used his blog to interview other Microsoft employees. By creating a personal face for a corporation nicknamed the "Evil Empire," Scoble did much to positively shift perceptions of Microsoft in less than six months. Multiple employees at Microsoft then began day-to-day blogs to provide information to customers.

Some corporations achieve this personal face by publishing blogs by their CEOs. Mark Cuban, owner of the Dallas Mavericks, writes the widely read blogmaverick.com, which has a Technorati Authority ranking of 837 (Technorati, 2008). Other corporations, like Wal-Mart, present the voice of the employee. In checkoutbloggers.com, Wal-Mart managers and associates spread the news about new gadgets, games, and Wal-Mart initiatives.

5

The **body** of the report can be single or double spaced. If double-spaced, indent paragraphs without adding extra space between paragraphs.

Page numbers for the body of the report use Arabic numerals that are positioned in the same location as the page numbers in the preliminary pages.

Place **figures** and **tables** after they are first introduced in the narrative. Use consistent styles for figure/table headings or captions.

(continued)

FIGURE B.9 Continued

[Page 6]

Established corporations also use blogs to enter into existing web-based conversations about the company's products or services. Corporate bloggers search online for mentions of their company, looking specifically for misinformation, rumors, or easily answered questions. By responding to these comments online, bloggers communicate that the company is interested in being an active participant of a community, not just in selling its products (Rettberg, 2008).

Finally, corporations also use "dark blogs," which are not available to the public, for internal communication. For example, one large European pharmaceutical company uses blogs as a form of internal knowledge sharing to pool competitive intelligence (Charman, 2005).

Reason 3: Effective Blogging Requires Education

Although blogs are a significant form of business communication, blogging requires a unique set of skills that need to be taught.

- **How to communicate professionally in informal language.** Blogs communicate information with a more personalized and individualized voice than most news, corporation, or media outlets do. Because of blogging's roots in personal journaling, blogs communicate with an informal language that typically represents the writer. Blogs are clearly authored by individuals, even if those individuals are doing so at the request of a corporation.

  This individualized voice leads to a number of advantages. Successful blogs allow corporations to connect to a wide range of consumers. The blogs also provide a forum for treating consumers as real humans through authentic conversation rather than through impersonal marketing and branding rhetoric, which is often criticized as insincere. Commentators have referred to this evolution of marketing communication as a corporate revolution (Rettberg, 2008; Scoble & Israel, 2006; Technorati, 2009).

- **How to generate consumer interest in a company without turning consumers off.** One of the easiest ways for a blog to be ineffective is if it is used as a product-advertising tool. To be effective, blogs should focus on communicating to consumers and investors information that is seen as objective as possible, without any sales pitches.

- **How to maintain transparency in writing.** Another pitfall for corporate bloggers is failing to take seriously the directive for transparency that personal communication demands. Scoble's (2003) Corporate Weblog Manifesto, posted on his blog, includes principles such as these: "Tell the truth, the whole truth, and nothing but the truth. If your competitor has a product that's better than yours, link to it" and "Post fast on both good news and bad … The trick to building trust is to show up." As *New York Times* columnist Marci Alboher (2007) points out, this "kind of transparency is a popular reason for blogging, particularly for companies that want to be identified as mission-oriented or socially responsible" (p. 3C). However, the failure to be transparent will make the company appear evasive.

- **How to use blogging as part of a larger communication strategy.** Bloggers have to deal with an audience that must be kept interested. One important and often overlooked challenge with blogging is its commitment: a blog must be a regularly updated forum. Without consistent updates, the blog will lose its readership (Alboher, 2007; "Blogging," 2009; Thompson, 2009; Scoble, 2003). Scoble (2003) stated this need for commitment in a clear axiom: "Demonstrate passion. Post frequently" (p. 18).

6

[Page 7]

Recommendations for Incorporating
Blogging into the WSU Curriculum

At first glance, it may look as if business blogging is only a function of corporate communication, and thus only marketing or journalism majors need to learn how to do it. However, as channels of business communication evolve, the curriculum for all business students must evolve with them. As this report has shown, blogging offers an intellectually rich and interesting business communication channel for the following reasons:

- Even in its short history, blogging has undergone dramatic changes.
- Thousands of corporations are blogging; a rich set of examples can easily be mined for detailed theoretical and practical studies.
- Blogging continues to evolve with the speed typical of most Internet phenomena.

WSU can prepare business students to communicate well in this channel by adopting the following additions and modifications to the management science curriculum:

Recommendation 1—Address Blogging/Social Media in BUAD 287: Business Communication

At least one week of classes in this mandatory course should be devoted to reviewing social media, including blogging. This basic introduction will alert all students to the importance of blogging in business.

Recommendation 2—Add 300-Level Elective: History and Theory of Social Media

Western State should add a course focusing on the *History and Theory of Social Media*. This course would survey the past and present developments of social media, including blogging as well as other new forms of social media (such as Twitter, Facebook, MySpace, Ning) and track how media has changed in the last two decades due to Internet technology. This course would take a theoretical and analytical approach to blogging and social media.

Recommendation 3—Add 300-Level Elective: Social and Technological Business Communication

Western State should add a course focusing on *Social and Technological Business Communication*. This course would provide practical knowledge on how businesses communicate through blogging and other social media, understand the challenges and opportunities for big and small businesses, and learn how to incorporate blogging and other social media into a firm's overall business communication strategy. The course would focus on giving students practical instruction in using blogging and social media. One model for such a course is Georgetown University's Social Media in Business, Development and Government (Georgetown University, 2009).

Recommendation 4—Create a School-Wide Blog for Students

Western State School of Management Science has the opportunity to model effective blogging for students by creating its own blog to communicate with stakeholders and by encouraging students to participate and to develop their own linked blogs.

7

*Use **bullets** and/or **enumerations** to help the reader understand the content.*

[Page 8]

References

Alboher, M. (2007, December 27). Blogging's low-cost, high-return marketing tool. *New York Times*, p. 3C.

BLOGGING: Natural selection. (2009, January 15). *New Media Age*. Retrieved from HighBeam Research: http://www.highbeam.com/doc/1G1-192295694.html

Cass, J. (2006, March 28). Fortune 500 take lead in corporate blogging: Only 0.73% of employers blog - while 4.6% of Fortune 500 blog. [Web log post]. Retrieved from http://blogsurvey.backbonemedia .com/archives/2006/03/fortune_500_tak_1.html

Charman, S. (2005). Dark blogs: The use of blogs in business. *Corante Research Report*. Retrieved from http://www.suw.org.uk/files/Dark_Blogs_01_ European_Pharma_Group.pdf

Cuban, C. (n.d.). *Blog maverick*. Retrieved from http://blogmaverick.com

Financial Times ComMetrics blog index 2009. (2009). Retrieved from http://ftindex.commetrics.com/

Georgetown University. (2009). *Social media in business development and government*. Retrieved from https://digitalcommons.georgetown.edu/blogs/msfs-556-spring2009/course-description/

Goldman, S. (2009, August 7). *For Honest Tea, Coke is it*. [Web log post]. Retrieved from http://www.honesttea.com/blog (category/from-seth-and-barry/

Halzack, S. (2008, August 25). Marketing moves to the blogosphere; Business model shifts to engage customers online. *Washington Post*, p. D1.

Levine, R., Locke, C., Searls, D., & Weinberg, D. (1999). *The cluetrain manifesto: The end of business as usual*. New York: Basic Books.

Mahon, T. (n.d.) *English cut*. Retrieved from http://englishcut.com

Rettberg, J. W. (2008). *Blogging*. Malden, MA: Polity Press.

Rosenberg, S. (2009). *Say everything: How blogging began, what it's becoming, and why it matters*. New York, NY: Crown Publishers.

Scoble, R. (2003, February 6). Corporate weblog manifesto. [Web log post]. Retrieved from http://scoble.weblogs.com/2003/02/26.html

Scoble R., & Israel, S. (2006). *Naked conversations*. Hoboken, NJ: John Wiley & Sons, Inc.

Sifry, D. (2004, October 17). *Oct 2004 state of the blogosphere: Corporate bloggers*. [Web log post]. Retrieved from http://www.sifry.com/alerts/archives/000390.html

Technorati (2008).*The state of the blogosphere 2008*. Retrieved from http://technorati.com/blogging/state-of-the-blogosphere/

Thompson, L. (2009). Blogs: If used properly, an investor-friendly tool. *Compliance Week*, 6(62), p. 60.

Wal-Mart (n.d.) *Check out blog*. Retrieved from http://checkoutblog.com

8

*Cite all sources in a **reference page**. List sources alphabetically and use a standard reference style, such as APA or MLA, to provide complete documentation.*

[Page 9]

Appendix
Ranking, Names, and URLs of the Top 25 Corporate Blogs

The 25 corporate blogs listed below received the highest rankings from The Financial Times (2009). The Financial Times ranks blogs by assessing how popular they are with Internet users or how many people are referring to them. In creating this index, The Financial Times uses the following metrics: Google PageRank, Technorati Ranking, Technorati Authority, Yahoo! InLinks, and Google Blog Search.

Rank	Company	URL
1	Google	http://googleblog.blogspot.com/
2	Viacom	http://splashpage.mtv.com/
3	Reuters	http://www.reuters.com/finance/deals
3	Yahoo!	http://www.ysearchblog.com/
3	Adobe	http://blogs.adobe.com/
6	Nokia	http://conversations.nokia.com/
7	Oracle	http://blogs.sun.com/jonathan/
8	Microsoft	http://blogs.msdn.com/ie/default.aspx
9	Dell	http://en.community.dell.com/blogs/direct2dell/
10	Amazon	http://affiliate-blog.amazon.com/
10	General Electric	http://www.gereports.com/
12	eBay	http://developer.ebay.com/community/blog/ and http://www.ebaypartnernetworkblog.com/en/
13	American Express	http://www.openforum.com/
14	Cisco	http://blogs.cisco.com/gov
14	Boeing	http://boeingblogs.com/randy/
14	Time Warner	http://searchblog.aol.com/
14	Coca-Cola	http://www.coca-colaconversations.com/
14	Toyota	http://pressroom.toyota.com/pr/tms/our-point-of-view.aspx
14	GM	http://gmreinvention.com/
14	Hewlett Packard	http://www.communities.hp.com/online/blogs/csremea/default.aspx
14	Wells Fargo	http://blog.wellsfargo.com/wachovia/
14	Accenture	http://www.accenture.com/Global/Accenture_Blogs/Accenture_High_Performance_Business_Blog/default.htm
14	E.ON	http://eon-uk.com/
14	Alcoa	http://www.alcoa.com/alcoa_recycling/en/home.asp
25	News Corporation	http://allthingsd.com/

9

*Place related information in **Appendices**. Continue pagination numbers and styles. If the report includes only one Appendix, label it Appendix. If the report includes multiple appendices, label them Appendix A, Appendix B, and so forth.*

Appendix C

Reference Styles

Any time you quote, paraphrase, or use material from a source, you need to acknowledge that contribution by providing citations within the body of the text and a complete, alphabetized reference (or works cited) list at the end of the document. This is true whether you are writing a report, presentation, web page, or blog.

Different fields of study use different reference styles, and your instructor, employer, or publisher will usually identify the style you are expected to use. Two styles are typical in business fields: APA style, found in the *Publication Manual of the American Psychological Association,* and the Chicago style (sometimes referred to as CMOS), found in the *The Chicago Manual of Style.* Your instructor may instead require you to use MLA style from the Modern Language Association.

Whichever reference style you use, you need to provide enough information so your readers can find the sources you reference. To do this, you first briefly identify the source being cited within the body of your document, using in-text citations, and then you provide complete information about the sources in an alphabetized reference list or works cited page at the end of the document.

This appendix provides a brief guide to APA and MLA reference styles, outlining the most common rules you will need to follow. For information about CMOS, go to mybcommlab.com. Each of these styles offers additional rules to cover special circumstances. If you need advice beyond the guidelines in this appendix, see the full manual for the style you are using.

APA In-text Citations

Within your text, indicate the source of a citation by inserting authors' last names, the year of publication, and in some cases the page on which the material can be found (or the paragraph in an online source). Where you place this information depends on whether you paraphrase the original source or quote the source word-for-word.

Paraphrased Content

Paraphrased content consists of information from a source presented in your own words. When paraphrasing, or referring to another work, the citation can be part of the narrative or placed at the end of the sentence (inside the ending punctuation). Citations for paraphrases must include author and date. In addition, APA guidelines encourage—but do not require—writers to include page or paragraph numbers to help readers find the paraphrased material in the original source.

For example, if the original source states: "transparency is a popular reason for blogging, particularly for companies that want to be identified as mission-oriented or socially responsible" (Alboher, 2007, p. 3C), paraphrased content could be worded in one of the following three ways:

Single-Author Paraphrased Source

In 2007, *New York Times* columnist Marci Alboher suggested that companies often use blogs to be transparent, especially those companies that want to be seen as fulfilling their stated mission or social responsibility initiatives. ◄------ The author's name and the publication date can be integrated into the text itself.

Or . . .

New York Times columnist Marci Alboher (2007) suggests that companies often use blogs to be transparent, especially those companies that want to be seen as fulfilling their stated mission or social responsibility initiatives.

Or . . .

Companies often use blogs to be transparent, especially those companies that want to be seen as fulfilling their stated mission or social responsibility initiatives (Alboher, 2007).

The following examples provide additional information about how to cite sources with multiple authors or cite multiple sources.

Multiple Authors of One Paraphrased Source

In the early days of blogging, prominent thinkers about blogging such as Rick Levine, Christopher Locke, Doc Searls, and David Weinberger (1999) prophesied the influence blogging could have on the corporate world.

Or . . .

In the early days of blogging, prominent thinkers about blogging prophesied the influence blogging could have on the corporate world (Levine, Locke, Searls, & Weinberger, 1999).

Multiple Sources Used to Support One Statement

Blogs also offer small businesses the opportunity to become completely transparent with their consumer base (Halzack, 2008; Mahon, n.d.; Rettberg, 2008; Scoble & Israel, 2006).

Multiple Sources by the Same Author to Support One Statement

Corporate blogging is predicted to increase substantially in the next decade (Haffner, M., 2006; Haffner, R., 2008).

Multiple Sources by the Same Author Published in the Same Year

The medium options for corporate blogging vary widely, from standard blog applications to social media outlets (Jones, 2009a; Jones, 2009b).

Two types of sources require only in-text citations and are not included in the reference list: classical or religious works (such as the Bible) that are divided into the same sections in all editions, and personal communications.

Personal Communication

Dr. Kenneth Darby, who studies corporate blogging, predicts social media will support new forms of industry blogging in the future (personal communication, November 2, 2012).

Quoted Content

Quoted—word for word—content from a source uses a citation style similar to that for paraphrases. However, the quoted text must also be surrounded by quotation marks or set off as a block of text if it is more than 40 words long. In addition, the page or paragraph number for quotations must always be included. Just as with paraphrased content, the exact placement of these elements varies. Note the following examples.

The author's name can be integrated into the text, with the date in parentheses immediately following the name. If the source has no date, use *n.d.* in the parentheses.

If the author's name is not integrated into the text, then the author's last name and the date—separated by a comma— appear in parentheses at the end of the sentence.

The first time you integrate authors' names into the text, use last names or full names. For more than five authors, use only the first author's name, followed by "et al." Order the names as they appear in the original. Use "and" to separate the last author's name from the previous name. For subsequent references, use the first author's name followed by "et al."

When the authors' names are not integrated into the text, use only their last names in the parentheses and use "&" to separate the last author's name from the previous name.

List sources alphabetically by authors' names. Use semicolons to separate sources.

When the names are the same, use first initials to determine the order of the sources.

Order the sources as they are ordered in the reference list, which assigns a letter after the date of sources written by the same author and published in the same year. Use that letter in the citation.

Identify personal communication with in-text citations only; APA style does not list personal communications on the reference page.

Single-Author Quoted Source

As New York Times columnist Marci Alboher (2007) points out, this "kind of transparency is a popular reason for blogging, particularly for companies that want to be identified as mission-oriented or socially responsible" (p. 3C).

Surround the quoted content with quotation marks. Put the date in parentheses after the author's name. Always place the page number after the quotation. Use a lowercase "p" followed by a period to abbreviate "page." If the quote spans more than one page, use "pp." Place the parentheses between the ending quotation mark and final period.

Or . . .

This "kind of transparency is a popular reason for blogging, particularly for companies that want to be identified as mission-oriented or socially responsible" (Alboher, 2007, p. 3C).

If all the citation elements appear in the parentheses, use commas to separate author, year, and page number.

Multiple-Author Quoted Source

In *The Cluetrain Manifesto*, Levine, Locke, Searls, and Weinberger (1999) wrote:

The first time a source is used, list all authors' names (up to five).

> A powerful global conversation has begun. Through the Internet, people are discovering and inventing new ways to share relevant knowledge with blinding speed. As a direct result, markets are getting smarter—and getting smarter faster than most companies. These markets are conversations. Their members communicate in language that is natural, open, honest, direct, funny and often shocking. Whether explaining or complaining, joking or serious, the human voice is unmistakably genuine. (p. 10)

When a quotation is longer than 40 words, do not enclose it in quotation marks. Instead, indent the content as a block quotation and place the page number after the final punctuation mark.

Or if cited previously in the document . . .

> In *The Cluetrain Manifesto*, Levine et al. (1999) wrote: "A powerful global conversation has begun. Through the Internet, people are discovering and inventing new ways to share relevant knowledge with blinding speed. As a direct result, markets are getting smarter—and getting smarter faster than most companies" (p. 10).

The second and all subsequent times you refer to a source with three or more authors, list only the first author with "et al." to represent "and others." (Note: Two-author sources should always list both authors, such as Scoble & Israel.)

Quotations with Words Omitted

> *The Cluetrain Manifesto* stated: "A powerful global conversation has begun. . . . Markets are getting smarter—and getting smarter faster than most companies" (Levine et al., 1999, p. 10).

Use ellipses (three spaced periods) to indicate you have omitted words from quoted text. If you have omitted words between two sentences, end the first sentence with a period and then provide the ellipsis (for a total of four spaced points).

APA Reference List

At the end of your paper, include a page titled "References," which presents an alphabetical list of all the sources you cited in your text. Reference list entries for most sources include four major elements in the following order: the author(s), year of publication, name of work, and publication information. The entire reference list is organized alphabetically according to the first word in the entry, usually the author's last name. If more than one source begins with the same word, then the order is determined by a different element—date of publication or name of the work—as described below.

Authors

- List authors' last names first, use initials only for authors' first and middle names, and use one space between initials.
- Separate authors' names with commas, even when only two authors are listed. Use an ampersand (&) before the name of the final author.
- If an author has a hyphenated first name, include the hyphen and a period after each initial.
- List all authors in the order they appear on the publication.
- If the source lists more than seven authors, list the first six followed by an ellipsis (. . .) to indicate a break in the list and then the final author's name. In this instance, use no ampersand (&) before the final name.
- If the author is an organization, use a period at the end of the name to separate the author content from the next element of the reference.

- If a work has no author, begin the entry with the title of the work.

Examples:

Goins, T., & Robbins, D. R.

Jones, A. P., Baker, M.-A., & Cawfrey, G. L.

Pental, F., Raley, M., Meyer, R., Peterson, B., Boyd, L., Tobbin, E., . . . Jones, L. E.

Year of Publication

- Place the year the source was published in parentheses immediately after the author information. If a work has no author, put the year after the name of the work.
- If no date is available, put n.d. in the parentheses.
- For newspaper and magazine articles, include the month and day of publication *after* the year.
- If a reference list contains multiple sources for the same author, order the sources from oldest to newest.
- If a reference list contains multiple sources written by the same author and published the same year, use the titles to determine alphabetic sequence and differentiate the sources with lowercase letters added to the dates.

Examples:

Newspaper/magazine article. - - - ➤ Halzack, S. (2008, August 25).

Two articles by the same author with
the same dates. - - - ➤ Albanese, A. R. (2006a). Google is not the net:

Albanese, A. R. (2006b). The social life of books: . . .

Two articles by the same authors but - - - ➤ Jones, A. P., Baker, M.-A., & Cawfrey, G. L. (2006).
with different dates.

Jones, A. P., Baker, M.-A., & Cawfrey, G. L. (2012).

Name of Work

The format you use depends on the type of work. Complete works, such as books and websites, have just one title. By contrast, journal, newspaper, and magazine articles have article titles as well as publication titles. If your audience will need additional information to identify what kind of work this is, place that descriptive information in brackets immediately after the title.

Articles and Blog Posts

- Use plain text. Do not italicize, underline, or use quotation marks around the title.
- Use sentence case, capitalizing only the first word of the title, and the first word of the subtitle, if it has one, and any proper nouns such as company names.
- Conclude with a period.

Books, Websites, Videos, Podcasts, etc.

- Italicize the title name. Do not underline.
- Use sentence case, capitalizing only the first word of the title, and the first word of the subtitle, if it has one, and any proper nouns such as company names.
- Conclude with a period.

Journals and Other Periodicals

- Italicize the title. Do not underline.
- Use title case, beginning the first word and each word of four letters or more with a capital letter. Also capitalize any major words that are shorter than four letters as well as the first word after a colon, dash, or period in a title.
- Conclude with a comma.

Examples:

Book - - - - - - - - - - - - - - - ➤ Levine, R., Locke, C., Searls, D., & Weinberg, D. (1999). *The cluetrain manifesto: The end of business as usual.* . . .

Newspaper article - - - - - - - - - - - ➤ Halzack, S. (2008, August 25). Marketing moves to the blogosphere; Business model shifts to engage customers online. *Washington Post,* . . .

Blog post - - - - - - - - - - - - - - ➤ Goldman, S. (2009, August 7). For Honest Tea, Coke is it [Web log message]. Retrieved from http://www.honesttea.com/blog/category/from-seth-and-barry/

Publication Information

How you list the publication information depends on the kind of source you reference. For example, journal articles usually require volume, issue, and page numbers. However, books list only the publishing company's location and name, and websites require only a "Retrieved from" web address.

Journal and Other Periodical Articles

Following the title of the periodical itself, provide the volume number in italics immediately followed by the issue number in plain text and in parentheses. No space separates the volume from the issue numbers. Follow the issue number with a comma and page numbers. Page numbers do not use a page abbreviation ("p"), as was used for in-text citations. Indicate the range of page numbers with an en dash. End with a period.

> Author, A. A., Author, B. B., & Author, C. C. (Year). Title of article. *Title of Periodical, volume*(issue), pages.

> Thompson, L. (2009). Blogs: If used properly, an investor-friendly tool. *Compliance Week, 6*(62), 60.

Books

List the city and name of publisher, separated by a colon. Include a period at the end.

> Author, A. A., & Author, B. B. (Year). *Title of publication.* City, ST: Publisher's Name.

> Levine, R., Locke, C., Searls, D., & Weinberg, D. (1999). *The cluetrain manifesto: The end of business as usual.* New York, NY: Basic Books.

Websites

Use "Retrieved from" followed by the URL. Remove the hyperlink (blue font color and underlines) format from web addresses and, when necessary, insert a space to allow long addresses to wrap effectively to the right margin. Do not use a period at the end of a web address.

> Author, A. A., & Author, B. B. (Year). *Title of website*. Retrieved from [URL]

> Mahon, T. (n.d.) *English cut.* Retrieved from http://englishcut.com

◄------ Check the fine print at the bottom of a website for copyright information. If no date is obvious, use "n.d." for "no date" in parentheses.

Other Types of Sources

Adapt the four-part citation elements to other types of reference sources. Here are some examples that may not fit the "normal" format. If it is not clear from the name what type of source it is, then provide descriptive information in brackets immediately after the title.

- **Annual report**

  Clanton Corporation. (2011). *2010 corporate annual report.* Retrieved from http://www.clantoncorp.com

- **Brochure**

  Montana State University Billings Career Services. (2009). *A polished interview* [Brochure]. Retrieved from http://www.msubillings.edu/careers/PDF/ Polished%20Interview%20Brochure%209.pdf

- **Government publication**

  U. S. Bureau of Labor Statistics, U.S. Department of Labor (2010). *Occupational outlook handbook,* (2010–11 ed.). Washington, DC: U.S. Government Printing Office. Retrieved from http://www.bls.gov/oco/

- **Online encyclopedia or dictionary**

  Johnson, C. (2010). Communication in organizations. In *Encyclopedia of business,* (2nd ed.). Retrieved from http://www.referenceforbusiness.com/encyclopedia/ Clo-Con/Communication-in-Organizations.html

- **Podcast**

  Wildhaber, J. (Writer) & Fogarty, M. (Producer). (2010, July 1). *Understanding voice and tone in writing* [Audio podcast]. Retrieved from http://grammar. quickanddirtytips.com/understanding-voice-and-tone-in-writing.aspx

- **Slide presentation** (found online)

  Baer, J. (2010). *11 must-dos for the serious blogger.* [Online presentation]. Retrieved from http://www.slideshare.net/jaybaer/11-must-dos-for-the-serious-blogger-2512783

- **Online Video** (YouTube)

  Krueger, B. (Producer). (2007). *Interview tips—Avoiding three common video resume errors* [Video file]. Retrieved from http://www.youtube.com/watch?v=R3t9ysT0A_U

Sample Reference Page

To indent second and subsequent lines of a reference citation, use your word processor's hanging indent paragraph format feature rather than manually tabbing or spacing the text.

References

Albanese, A. R. (2006a). Google is not the net: Social networks are surging and present the real service challenge—and opportunity—for libraries. *Library Journal, 131*(15), 32–34.

Albanese, A. R. (2006b). The social life of books: Write, read, blog, rip, share any good books lately? A conversation with Ben Vershbow. *Library Journal, 131*(9), 28–30.

Two journal articles with the same author and year: use "a" and "b" after the year to identify the source in in-text citations

BLOGGING: Natural selection. (2009, January 15). *New Media Age.* Retrieved from http://www.highbeam.com/doc/1G1-192295694.html

Online article – no author

Charman, S. (2005). Dark blogs: The use of blogs in business. *Corante Research Report.* Retrieved from http://www.suw.org.uk/files/ Dark_Blogs_01_European_Pharma_Group.pdf

Company report (Note that a space is added in the middle of the URL to allow it to wrap effectively.)

Financial Times (2009). FT ComMetrics blog index. Retrieved from http://ftindex.commetrics.com/

Webpage – corporate author

Goldman, S. (2008, August 25). For Honest Tea, Coke is it [Web log message]. Retrieved from http://www.honesttea.com/blog/category/from-seth-and-barry/

Blog post

Halzack, S. (2008, August 25). Marketing moves to the blogosphere; Business model shifts to engage customers online. *Washington Post*, p. D1.

Newspaper article

Levine, R., Locke, C., Searls, D., & Weinberg, D. (1999). The *cluetrain manifesto: The end of business as usual.* New York, NY: Basic Books.

Book — multiple authors

Mahon, T. (n.d.) *English cut.* Retrieved from http://englishcut.com

Website — no date

Rettberg, J. W. (2008). *Blogging.* Malden, MA: Polity Press.

Book — single author

Rosenberg, S. (2009). *Say Everything: How blogging began, what it's becoming, and why it matters.* New York: Crown Publishers.

Scoble, R., & Israel, S. (2006). *Naked conversations.* Hoboken, NJ: John Wiley & Sons, Inc.

Thompson, L. (2009). Blogs: If used properly, an investor-friendly tool. *Compliance Week, 6*(62), 60.

Journal article (Volume is italicized, issue is in parentheses, separated from the page number with a comma and space.)

Sample Documentation in Presentation Files

Whether you're creating a traditional presentation file or a report deck, cite your in-text sources on the slides, either immediately after the content or in the corner of the slide as shown. Add a reference page to the end of report deck files or presentation handouts so your audience can refer the original sources, if necessary.

THE MILLENNIAL APPROACH TO PROBLEM-SOLVING

"Rather than insisting on solving society's challenges using the inherited, but inevitably limited wisdom of experts, Millennials would prefer to share their ideas and let the group find the right answer through their combined experiences."

Source: Winograd & Hais (2009)

Source is added to the page where the original content appears. Use standard in-text citation formats.

REFERENCES

BLOGGING: Natural selection. (2009, January 15). *New Media Age.* Retrieved from Http://www.highbeam.com/doc/1G1-192295694.html

Charman, S. (2005), Dark blogs: The use of blogs in business. *Corante Research Report.* Retrieved from http://www.suw.org.uk/files/ Dark_Blogs_01_European_Pharma_Group.pdf

Rosenberg, S. (2009). *Say everything: How blogging began, what it's becoming, and why it matters.* New York: Crown Publishers.

Scoble, R., & Israel, S. (2006). *Naked conversations.* Hoboken, NJ: John Wiley & Sons, Inc.

Thompson, L. (2009). Blogs: If used properly, an investor-friendly tool. *Compliance Week,* 6(62), 60.

Winograd, M., & Hais, M. D. (2009, November 9). Who needs critical thinking skills when we've got facebook? [Web log post]. Retrieved from http://blog-jenniferlindsay.com/ 2009/11/09/who-needs-critical-thinking-skills-when-weve-got-facebook/

The complete reference citation is included in a reference page at the conclusion of the report deck (or presentation handout).

MLA In-text Citations

MLA uses a simple and consistent style for all references to a source, whether the content is paraphrased or quoted. Provide enough information in the citation to help your audience find the correct work on the reference list and find the cited material in the source itself. Typically, this means that citations include the author's last name and the page number for the cited material. If you are referring to an entire work and not a specific passage, no page number is needed. MLA documentation never includes publication dates in the parentheses.

The following examples correspond with the APA examples on pages A-23–A-29 but are formatted as MLA-style citations. Fewer examples are provided since MLA uses the same format for quoted content as it does for paraphrased content.

Paraphrased Content

When paraphrasing content—using original information in your own words—or even just referring to a source, cite the original work by including the author's name within the narrative or in an in-text citation at the end of the sentence (before the ending punctuation).

For example, if the original source states "transparency is a popular reason for blogging, particularly for companies that want to be identified as mission-oriented or socially responsible" (Alboher 3C), paraphrased content could be worded in either of the following ways:

Single-Author Source

If the author's name is used in the narrative, include only the page number in the parenthetical reference. Place the parentheses at the first natural pause, usually at the end of the relevant passage.

In 2007, *New York Times* columnist Marci Alboher suggested that companies often use blogs to be transparent, especially those companies that want to be seen as fulfilling their stated mission or social responsibility initiatives (3C).

Or . . .

If the author's name is not used in the narrative, both the author and page number(s) appear in parentheses (with no comma separating them).

Companies often use blogs to be transparent, especially those companies that want to be seen as fulfilling their stated mission or social responsibility initiatives (Alboher 3C).

Multiple Authors of One Source

If the authors' names are used in the narrative and you are referring to an entire work, rather than content from a specific page of the source, no parenthetical reference is necessary.

In the *Cluetrain Manifesto*, Rick Levine, Christopher Locke, Doc Searls, and David Weinberger prophesied the influence blogging could have on the corporate world.

Or . . .

When including multiple authors' names in the parenthetical reference, separate the last name with "and".

In the early days of blogging, prominent thinkers about blogging prophesied the influence blogging could have on the corporate world (Levine, Locke, Searls, and Weinberger).

Or . . .

Whether in the narrative or in parentheses, texts with more than three authors can be cited with the name of the first author, followed by *et al.*

In the early days of blogging, prominent thinkers about blogging prophesied the influence blogging could have on the corporate world (Levine, et al.).

Multiple Sources Used to Support One Statement

When citing multiple sources in one reference citation, list sources alphabetically and separate with semicolons. When citing websites without page numbers or books in their entirety, no page numbers are needed.

Blogs also offer small businesses the opportunity to become completely transparent with their consumer base (Halzack D1; Mahon; Rettberg; Scoble and Israel).

Multiple Sources by the Same Author to Support One Statement

To differentiate between two works by the same author, include the first word or an abbreviated form of the title after the author's name (with comma) and before the corresponding page number (no comma).

Corporate blogging is predicted to increase substantially in the next decade (Haffner, *Blogs* 26; Haffner, *Corporate* 2).

Personal Communication

In contrast to APA style, in MLA, personal communications like interviews, letters, and emails are listed in the reference list, so the in-text citation does not need to indicate that the source is a personal communication.

This personal communication needs no citation because the source is identified in the Works Cited list.

Dr. Kenneth Darby, who studies corporate blogging, predicts social media will support new forms of industry blogging in the future.

Quoted Content

Quoted—word for word—content from a source uses a citation style similar to that for paraphrases. However, the quoted text must also be surrounded by quotation marks or set off as a block of text if it is more than four lines long. In addition, the page or paragraph number for quotations must always be included. Note the following examples.

Single-Author Quoted Source

As *New York Times* columnist Marci Alboher points out, this "kind of transparency is a popular reason for blogging, particularly for companies that want to be identified as mission-oriented or socially responsible" (3C).

Or . . .

This "kind of transparency is a popular reason for blogging, particularly for companies that want to be identified as mission-oriented or socially responsible" (Alboher 3C).

> Surround the quoted content with quotation marks. Always place the page number after the quotation. The number is not preceded by the word "page" or abbreviation "p." Place the parentheses between the ending quotation mark and final period.

> If the author's name is not used in the narrative, both the author and page number(s) appear in parentheses (with no comma separating them).

Multiple-Author Quoted Source

When a source has two or three authors, list all their names in the citation. When a source has more than three authors, you may either list all their names or the name of the first author, followed by "et al." ("and others") in plain text, not italics.

In *The Cluetrain Manifesto*, Levine, Locke, Searls, and Weinberger wrote:

A powerful global conversation has begun. Through the Internet, people are discovering and inventing new ways to share relevant knowledge with blinding speed. As a direct result, markets are getting smarter—and getting smarter faster than most companies. These markets are conversations. Their members communicate in language that is natural, open, honest, direct, funny and often shocking. Whether explaining or complaining, joking or serious, the human voice is unmistakably genuine. (10)

Or. . .

In *The Cluetrain Manifesto*, Levine et al. wrote: "A powerful global conversation has begun. Through the Internet, people are discovering and inventing new ways to share relevant knowledge with blinding speed. As a direct result, markets are getting smarter—and getting smarter faster than most companies" (10).

> When a quotation is longer than four lines, do not enclose it in quotation marks. Instead, indent the content as a *block quotation* and place the page number after the final punctuation mark.

Quotations with Words Omitted

The Cluetrain Manifesto stated: "A powerful global conversation has begun. . . . Markets are getting smarter—and getting smarter faster than most companies" (Levine, Locke, Searls, and Weinberger 10).

> Use ellipses (three spaced periods) to indicate you have omitted words from quoted text. If you have omitted words between two sentences, end the first sentence with a period and then provide the ellipsis (for a total of four spaced points).

MLA Works Cited List

At the end of your paper, include a "Works Cited" list: a double-spaced alphabetical list of all the sources you cited in your text.

Works Cited list entries for most sources include four major elements in the following order: the author(s), name of work, publication information, and medium of publication (print or web). In addition, some sources require supplemental information to help a reader find the material. These major elements are separated by periods. The entire reference list is organized alphabetically according to the first word in the entry, usually the author's last name. If more than one source begins with the same word, then the order is determined by a different element—author's first name or name of the work—as described in the following sections.

Authors

- List the first author's last name first, followed by his/her full first name (and middle initial or name if available).
- For an entry with one author, follow the first name with a period.
- For entries with two or three authors, list all the authors in the order they appear on the publication. Use a comma to separate names (even when only two authors are listed) and list the remaining authors with their first names before their last names. Use "and" before the last author's name.
- For entries with more than three authors, you may either list all the authors as described above or give the first author's name only, followed by "et al." ("and others") in plain text, not italics.
- If the author is an organization, use a period at the end of the name to separate the author name from the next element of the reference.
- If a work has no author, begin the entry with the title of the work.
- If you have cited more than one work by a specific author, order the entries alphabetically by title. For every entry after the first, use three hyphens in place of the author's name.

Examples:

Smith, John.

Smith, John, and Mary Jones.

Smith, John, Mary Jones, and Tom Baker.

Smith, John, Mary Jones, Tom Baker, and Lenore Kaplan.

Or Smith, John, et al.

Clanton Corporation.

Name of Work

In MLA style, all titles use title case: the first letter of every word is capitalized, except for *a, an, the,* and short prepositions. Put quotation marks around titles of short works, like articles in periodicals, book chapters, and specific pages on a website. Follow the title with a period, inside the closing quotation mark, unless the title itself concludes with different punctuation, such as a question mark. Use italics for titles of long works, like books, plays, encyclopedias, and entire websites. Follow the title with a period or other end punctuation if the title itself includes it.

Examples:

Book --------------------->
Levine, Rick, Christopher Locke, Doc Searls, and David Weinberg. *The Cluetrain Manifesto: The End of Business as Usual.* . . .

Newspaper article --------------->
Halzack, Sarah. "Marketing Moves to the Blogosphere: Business Model Shifts to Engage Customers Online." . . .

Blog post --------------------->
Goldman, Seth. "For Honest Tea, Coke Is It." . . .

Publication Information and Medium of Publication

After the title of the work, include additional publication information to identify the source. The format will depend on the kind of source you cite.

Journal or Other Periodical Articles

For journal articles, include the following publication information, in this order:

- **Journal title:** Put the journal name in italics. Do not use punctuation at the end of the journal name.

- **The volume and issue numbers:** Cite them as a single number sequence separated by a period. For example, "2.3" indicates the article can be found in the third issue of the second volume. In cases where issues are combined, such as the third and fourth, use a hyphen to separate the numbers (for example, "2.3-4"). Use no punctuation after the issue number. Leave one space before the date.
- **Date of the publication:** For a scholarly journal, put the year of publication in parentheses followed by a colon. For other periodicals, include the day, month, and year if they are available, followed by a colon. Leave one space before the page numbers.
- **Inclusive page numbers:** List the page numbers from the beginning of the article to the end using hyphens to separate page spreads and commas to indicate page breaks (such as 12-16, 20). Do not repeat hundreds or thousands. Use a concise form such as, 167-89 or 1125-30.
- **Medium of publication:** Indicate the medium of the publication you are referencing, such as Print or Web.

   Example:

   Scholarly Journal:

   Last name, First name and First name Last name. "Title of Article." *Title of Periodical* Volume.Issue (Year): pages. Medium of publication.

   Goins, Tamara, and David R. Robbins. "An Analysis of Corporate Blogging." *The Delta Pi Epsilon Journal* 53.3 (2012): 38-48. Print.

   Newspaper:

   Halzack, Sarah. "Marketing Moves to the Blogoshpere; Business Model Shifts to Engage Customers Online." *Washington Post* 25 August 2008, sec. D: 1. Print.

Books

For books, include the following publication information, in this order:

- **Editions or series numbers:** When applicable, provide series numbers, versions, or editions of the publication after the book's title.
- **City of publication:** List the city where the book, which can generally be found on the book's title page or copyright page. If the book lists several locations, include only the first. Use a colon between the city of publication and the publisher.
- **Publisher:** You may abbreviate the name of the publisher, if it is long. For example, Cambridge University Press can be written as Cambridge UP. Use a comma between the publisher's name and year of publication.
- **Year of publication:** Use the latest date listed on the copyright page. This should be the date of the edition that you indicate right after the book's name. Follow the date with a period.
- **Medium of publication:** Indicate the medium of the book's publication you are referencing, either Print or Web.

   Example:

   Last name, First name, First name Last name, and First name Last name. *Title of Book*. City: Publisher, Year. Medium.

   Levine, Rick, Christopher Locke, Doc Searls, and David Weinberg. *The Cluetrain Manifesto: The End of Business as Usual*. New York: Basic Books, 1999. Print.

Web-Based Sources

For web-based sources, include the following publication information, in the following order. All items are followed by a period except for publisher, which is followed by a comma.

- **Website title:** If a website has a title that is distinct from the article or page you are citing, include the website's title, italicized.
- **Publisher's name:** Include the company, sponsor, or publisher name if one is listed. If none exists, use N.p. to document "No publisher." Use a comma to separate the publisher's name from the date that follows.

- **Date of publication:** If a date of publication (or last updated) is present, cite it, placing the day before the month and then the year (for example, 4 Sept. 2009). Do not use commas, but use periods for the month abbreviation. Do not abbreviate May, June, or July. If no date is available, use "n.d."
- **Medium of publication.** Include the word "Web" to indicate this is an online source.
- **Date of access.** Identify the date you accessed the website using the same date format (day before abbreviated month followed by year).
- **Web address.** The URL is optional. The MLA 7th edition suggests that readers can more easily access websites by searching for author and/or title names, rather than keying in the complete URL. However, if you do include a URL, enclose it in angle brackets (< . . .>) followed by a period.

> **Example:**
>
> Last name, First name, First name Last name, and First name Last name. *Title of Website.* Name of Publisher, Date of Publication. Medium. Date of Access.
>
> Mahon, Thomas. *English Cut.* N.p., n.d. Web. 15 July 2009.
>
> "Financial Times ComMetrics Blog Index." *ComMetrics: Tools for Benchmarking Social Media.* ComMetrics, 2009. Web. 15 July 2009.

Supplemental Information

This content can include additional information that will help the audience identify the source. Such content may include parts in a series (such as, "Pt 2 of a series") followed by the name of the series or the name of a musical score. This information usually comes at the end of the entry. However, if you are providing supplemental information about the form that a source takes, MLA recommends putting that information directly after the title of the source.

Other Types of Sources

Apply the four-part citation elements to other types of reference sources. Here are some examples that may not fit the "normal" format. If it is not clear from the name what type of source it is, then provide descriptive information immediately after the title.

- **Annual report**

  Clanton Corporation. *2010 Corporate Annual Report.* n.d. Web. 1 July 2010.
- **Brochure**

  Montana State University Billings Career Services. *A Polished Interview.* Montana State University, 2009. Web. 1 Aug. 2009.
- **Government publication**

  U. S. Bureau of Labor Statistics, U.S. Department of Labor. *Occupational Outlook Handbook,* 2010-11 ed. Washington: U.S. Government Printing Office, 2010. Web. 15 July 2010.
- **Online encyclopedia or dictionary**

  Johnson, Clint. "Communication in Organizations." *Encyclopedia of Business,* 2nd ed. Reference for Business, 2010. Web. 15 July 2010.
- **Podcast**

  Wildhaber, Julie. "Understanding Voice and Tone in Writing." Podcast. *Grammar Girl.* Quick and Dirty Tips, 1 July 2010. Web. 15 July 2010.
- **Slide presentation** (found online)

  Baer, Jay. "11 Must-Dos for the Serious Blogger." Slide Presentation. *SlideShare.* Slideshare, Inc., n.d. Web. 15 July 2010.
- **Online Video** (YouTube)

  Krueger, Brian. "Interview Tips – Avoiding Three Common Video Resume Errors." Video. *YouTube.* YouTube, 10 April 2007. Web. 15 July 2010.

- **Interview**

  Hodge, Elizabeth. Personal interview. 22 July 2009.

  Hodge, Elizabeth. Telephone interview. 31 August 2009.

- **Email**

  Hodge, Elizabeth. "Re: Additional Blogging Information." Message to the author. 24 July 2009. E-mail.

Sample Works Cited Page

Double space throughout the works cited page. To indent lines following the first line, use your word processor's hanging indent paragraph format feature rather than manually tabbing or spacing the text.

Works Cited

Albanese, Andrew Richard. "Google is Not the Net: Social Networks Are Surging and Present the Real Service Challenge—and Opportunity—for Libraries." *Library Journal* 131.15 (2006): 32–34. Print.

--- "The Social Life of Books: Write, Read, Blog, Rip, Share Any Good Books Lately? A Conversation with Ben Vershbow." *Library Journal* 131.9 (2006): 28–30. Print.

> Two sources by the same author: use—rather than repeating the name the second (and subsequent) time(s).

"BLOGGING: Natural Selection." *New Media Age* 15 January 2009. *HighBeam Research*. Web. 10 July 2009.

> Article from online database—no author

Charman, Suw. "Dark Blogs: The Use of Blogs in Business." *Corante Research Report*. Traction Software, 13 June 2005. Web. 15 July 2009.

> Company report

"Financial Times ComMetrics Blog Index." *ComMetrics: Tools for Benchmarking Social Media.* ComMetrics, 2009. Web. 15 July 2009.

> Webpage—no author

Goldman, Seth. "For Honest Tea, Coke Is It." *Honesttea.com*. Honest Tea, Inc., 25 Aug. 2008. Web. 10 Aug. 2009.

> Blog post

Halzack, Sarah. "Marketing Moves to the Blogosphere; Business Model Shifts to Engage Customers Online." *Washington Post* 25 August 2008, sec. D:1. Print.

> Newspaper article

Levine, Rick, Christopher Locke, Doc Searls, and David Weinberg. *The Cluetrain Manifesto: The End of Business as Usual*. New York: Basic Books, 1999. Print.

> Book—multiple authors

Mahon, Thomas. *English cut*. N.p. n.d. Web. 15 July 2009.

> Webpage—no date

Rettberg, Jill Walker. *Blogging*. Malden: Polity Press, 2008. Print.

> Book—single author

Rosenberg, Scott. *Say Everything: How Blogging Began, What It's Becoming, and Why It Matters*. New York: Crown Publishers, 2009. Print.

Scoble, Robert, and Shel Israel. *Naked Conversations*. Hoboken: John Wiley & Sons, Inc., 2006. Print.

> Book—two authors

Thompson, Louis. "Blogs: If Used Properly, An Investor-friendly Tool." *Compliance Week* 6.62 (2009): 60. Print.

> Journal article

Sample Documentation in Presentation Files

When citing sources in presentation files or report decks, use an in-text citation on the slide where the content is presented and add a "Works Cited" page at the conclusion of the file.

THE MILLENNIAL APPROACH TO PROBLEM-SOLVING

"Rather than insisting on solving society's challenges using the inherited, but inevitably limited wisdom of experts, Millennials would prefer to share their ideas and let the group find the right answer through their combined experiences."

Source: Winograd and Hais

Source is added to the page where the original content appears. Use standard in-text citation formats.

WORKS CITED

"BLOGGING: Natural selection." *New Media Age* 15 January 2009. HighBeam Research. Web. 10 July 2009.

Charman, Suw. "Dark blogs: The Use of Blogs in Business." *Corante Research Report*. Traction Software, 13 June 2005. Web. 15 July 2009.

Rosenberg, Scott. *Say Everything: How Blogging Began, What It's Becoming, and Why It Matters*. New York: Crown Publishers. 2009. Print.

Scoble, Robert and Shel Israel. *Naked conversations*. Hoboken, NJ: John Wiley & Sons, Inc. 2006. Print.

Thompson, L.ouis. "Blogs: If Used Properly, An Investor-friendly Tool. *Compliance Week*, 6.62 (2009): 60. Print.

Winograd, Morley and Michael D. Hais. "Who Needs Critical Thinking Skills When We've Got Facebook?" *Jennifer Lindsay Digital*. Jennifer Lindsay Digital, 9 Nov. 2009. Web. 10 Jan. 2010.

The complete reference citation is included in a Works Cited list at the conclusion of the report deck (or presentation handout).

Appendix D

Grammar, Punctuation, Mechanics, and Conventions

This appendix begins with a diagnostic test to help you identify strengths and weaknesses in your sentence-level writing skills. Identify the areas that you need to improve, and then use this appendix to refresh your understanding of the rules, check your writing, and correct any mistakes.

The numbered sections cover the basics of grammar, punctuation, mechanics, and conventions in written business communication. Headings such as **GRAMMAR ALERT!** and **PUNCTUATION ALERT!** draw attention to especially common writing errors.

Sentence-Level Skills Diagnostic Test

The following test covers common sentence-level errors. After you have completed the test, ask your instructor for the answer sheet to score your answers. Use the **Skills Assessment** table following the test to record your scores in each category. The assessment will identify the skill areas you need to strengthen and where to find their associated rules in this appendix.

Use and Formation of Nouns and Pronouns

Each of the following sentences is either correct or contains an error. If the sentence is correct, write "C" in the blank. If the sentence contains an error, underline the error and write the correct form in the blank.

1. _____ Our supervisor wanted George and I come in early on Tuesday.

2. _____ If your sure that everyone has left, turn out the lights.

3. _____ I will speak with whoever is in the office this morning.

4. _____ For three months in a row this Dealership had the highest sales.

5. _____ There are fewer jobs and less employments during a recession.

Use and Formation of Adjectives and Adverbs

Each of the following sentences is either correct or contains an error. If the sentence is correct, write "C" in the blank. If the sentence contains an error, underline the error and write the correct form in the blank.

6. _____ Most consumers prefer the least costly of the two service plans.

7. _____ He sees badly in the dark because of his cataracts.

8. _____ Remember to drive slow in a school zone.

9. _____ Wasn't it snowing real hard last evening?

10. _____ The timing of the winter sale was absolutely perfect.

Sentence Fragments, Run-On (Fused) Sentences, and Comma Splices

Each of the following sentences is either correct or incorrect. If the sentence is correct, write "C" in the blank. If it is incorrect, insert the punctuation and/or wording that would make the sentence correct. Adjust capitalization as necessary.

11. _____ When people enjoy their jobs. They usually perform better.

12. _____ Many younger employees rate job satisfaction over high salary, they want meaningful work.

13. _____ Baby boomers, on the other hand, have spent their lives working to get ahead their goal has been to reach the top.

14. _____ Finding the right balance between work, family, and leisure that fits a person's personal and professional goals.

15. _____ Women usually have a more difficult time than men, however, achieving this balance.

Subject-Verb Agreement and Pronoun-Antecedent Agreement

Each of the following sentences is either correct or contains an error. If the sentence is correct, write "C" in the blank. If the sentence contains an error, write the correction in the blank.

16. _____ Each generation defines their relationship to work.

17. _____ There is sometimes considerable differences in attitudes.

18. _____ Members of one generation believes in "living to work."

19. _____ Conversely, the goals and philosophy of the next generation is "working to live."

20. _____ To be satisfied, everybody has to find what works best for them.

Commas

Each of the following sentences is either correct or incorrect in its use of commas. If the sentence is correct, write "C" next to it. If it is incorrect, insert or delete punctuation to make it correct.

21. _____ Many cultures value recreation, and family time highly and business practices reflect these norms.

22. _____ In Europe for example workers get at least a month of vacation in the summer.

23. _____ Although some businesses stay open many are closed for most of August.

24. _____ Posting an "On Vacation" sign in the window collecting the family and gassing up the car business owners across the continent head for the beach or the mountains.

25. _____ This practice of closing up shop and going on vacation for a month which annoys Americans traveling abroad in August is considered "therapeutic and necessary for good physical and mental health" says Doris Pernegger an Austrian travel agent.

Commas and Semicolons

Each of the following sentences is either correct or incorrect in its use of commas and semicolons. If the sentence is correct, write "C" next to it. If it is incorrect, insert or delete punctuation to make it correct.

26. _____ In France the workweek is 35 hours; but most Americans still work a 40-hour week.

27. _____ The number of hours one can work is set by national law in many countries, however U.S. labor laws allow for variations among employee categories.

28. _____ Many U.S. companies classify workers as "exempt" employees, who may work extra hours without extra pay, "non-exempt" employees, who must be paid a minimum wage and receive higher overtime pay for extra hours, and part-time employees, who may be covered by minimum-wage laws but who are not necessarily being paid a higher wage for overtime.

29. _____ The average worker in Germany spends about 1,500 hours on the job per year; the average worker in India annually spends about twice that number on the job.

30. _____ The most leisure time contrary to popular belief was enjoyed by prehistoric hunter-gatherers, not modern humans.

Other Punctuation Marks

In each of the following sentences, insert or delete colons, end punctuation, apostrophes, parentheses, quotation marks, dashes, and hyphens as needed. If a sentence is correct, write "C" next to it.

31. _____ Some of the benefits of a four day workweek may be: improved levels of education (extra time for classes), improved health less stress, and money saved on transportation.

32. _____ If we dont have to drive to work as often, we reduce carbon related automobile emissions.

33. _____ Some economists argue that unemployment will decrease if the workweek is shortened a big if.

34. _____ This is the theory: People working fewer hours will create a demand for additional workers in order to produce the same amount of goods and services.

35. _____ The old expression work smarter, not harder describes my philosophy.

Capitalization

In each of the following sentences insert or delete capital letters as needed. If a sentence is correct, write "C" next to it.

36. _____ In the Western world the workweek for many employees is Monday through friday.

37. _____ Of course, doctors and nurses, people with md or rn after their name, as well as public safety and hospitality employees often work weekend shifts.

38. _____ the workweek in a number of muslim countries is Sunday through Thursday or Saturday through Wednesday, because Friday is a Holy Day.

39. _____ My Mother says Washington's and lincoln's birthdays used to be celebrated separately, but they have been lumped together to create presidents' day, giving many employees a three-day weekend in mid-february.

40. _____ We say "tgif," meaning "Thank Goodness It's Friday," to salute the end of the workweek.

Numbers

Each of the following sentences is either correct or incorrect in the way numbers are expressed. If the sentence is correct, write "C" next to it. If it is incorrect, insert the necessary changes.

41. _____ South Koreans average thirty-four percent more work hours per year than U.S. workers.

42. _____ Most South Koreans start work at eight a.m., take a break for dinner, and don't leave work until after 10 o'clock at night.

43. _____ 2004 marked the end of the 6-day workweek in South Korea; before then, everyone worked Saturdays.

44. _____ A South Korean accountant averaged about twenty-seven hundred dollars a month in 2005; the average annual income was 22,928 dollars, or 18,544,199 Korean wons.

45. _____ Since Korean employees are expected to stay at their desks until their superiors leave, we really shouldn't complain about our measly 5 8-hour days.

Spelling

In each of the following sentences, correct spelling as needed. If a sentence is correct, write "C" next to it.

46. _____ Before making a judgement about excepting a job offer, you might want to explore what "work" means in that companies' culture.

47. _____ Some people find it inconcievable that they are expected to wear a suit and tie to work; its tee shirts and flip-flops for them.

48. _____ Does the employer have a flextime policy, leting you come and go as you please as long as you meet your deadlines and attend meetings?

49. _____ What seems like a miner inconvience when your first hired may be a major hurdle after you have been on the job awhile.

50. _____ Ask yourself weather you can accommodate the company policies and expectations or if you would be happyer and more productive in a different inviroment.

Sentence-Level Skills Assessment

In TABLE D.1, record the number of questions you answered **incorrectly** in each category. If you got more than two answers wrong in any category, it is likely that you are making similar errors in your writing. Review the relevant sections of the appendix. If you are still having trouble with sentence-level errors in any category, you may want to seek additional help at your school's writing center or writing lab.

TABLE D.1 Skills Assessment Table

QUESTIONS	SKILL AREA	NUMBER OF INCORRECT ANSWERS	SECTION(S)
1–5	Nouns and Pronouns		1.1.1., 3.1.2.
6–10	Adjectives and Adverbs		1.1.3.
11–15	Fragments, Run-On (Fused) Sentences, Comma Splices		1.2.2., 1.3.1., 1.3.2.
16–20	Subject-Verb Agreement, Pronoun-Antecedent Agreement		1.1.2., 1.3.3., 1.3.4.
21–25	Commas		2.2.–2.2.4.
26–30	Commas and Semicolons		2.3.
31–35	Other Punctuation Marks		2.4.–2.7.
36–40	Capitalization		3.1.–3.1.2.
41–45	Numbers		3.2.–3.2.11.
46–50	Spelling		4.0

TABLE D.2 Functions of Parts of Speech

FUNCTION	PART OF SPEECH	EXAMPLES
naming	nouns pronouns	computer, IBM, email you, itself, hers, everyone
showing action or being	verbs	email, was, will hire, has run
modifying	adjectives adverbs	expensive, clear, legal quickly, really, well
connecting	prepositions conjunctions	in, under, after, of, to, on and, but, although, since
exclaiming	interjections	oh, well, hey, indeed Ouch! Help! Stop! Wow!

■ 1. Sentences

A sentence is often described as a group of words that expresses a complete thought. However, a sentence does more than that. Sentences convey information and establish relationships between ideas. Your ability to communicate well—effectively manage sentences and their parts—will contribute to to your success in the workplace.

1.1. Parts of Speech

Words in sentences belong to categories that describe their function within the sentence. Just as particular departments within a business have particular functions—accounting, sales, shipping and receiving—words are categorized according to the functions they serve in sentences. These categories are commonly called the **parts of speech**. Knowing the names and functions of the parts of speech enables people to talk about how sentences work—or don't work when there are errors.

As you can see from the examples in TABLE D.2, the same word (e.g., *email*) may serve different functions, depending on its use in a sentence.

1.1.1. Naming Words: Nouns and Pronouns

a. **Nouns** name persons, places, things, and concepts. They can be classified as indicated in TABLE D.3.

Many nouns form the plural **regularly** by adding *-s* or *-es* at the end: *report, reports; expense, expenses*. Some nouns have an **irregular** plural form, often formed by a change in vowel: *man, men; mouse, mice; goose, geese*.

b. **Pronouns** replace or refer to nouns. The word that a pronoun replaces or refers to is called its **antecedent** (meaning "to go before"): *Shanice* said *she* received the memo. *She* is the pronoun; *Shanice* is the antecedent. Like nouns, pronouns can be classified, as described in TABLE D.4.

c. **Pronoun case.** As TABLE D.5 illustrates, pronouns show their function in a sentence by means of **case: subjective, objective**, or **possessive**.

TABLE D.3   Types of Nouns

TYPE OF NOUN	FUNCTION	EXAMPLES
Common nouns	Refer to general groups, people, places, things, and ideas. They are not capitalized.	intern, street, company, soda, capitalism
Proper nouns	Refer to particular people, places, things, and ideas. They are capitalized.	Monica, Wall Street, Progressive Insurance Company, Coca-Cola, Marxism
Count nouns	Refer to people, places, and things that can be counted individually. Count nouns have singular and plural forms	two interns, 15 insurance companies, one customer, $3 million, raindrops, job
Mass nouns (noncount nouns)	Refer to things that cannot be counted individually but that exist in a mass or aggregate. Mass nouns do not usually have plural forms, and they take singular verbs.	rain, milk, steel, money, overstock, The *milk is* cold.
Collective nouns	Refer to groups that are singular in form but, depending on context, may be singular or plural in meaning.	committee, team, sales force, board of directors, faculty, staff, herd, flock The *staff* [collectively] *is* meeting this afternoon. The *staff* [individually] *are* registering for the conference.
Abstract nouns	Refer to intangible conditions, qualities, or ideas	wealth, illness, technology, sound, capitalism
Concrete nouns	Refer to things perceived by the five senses	euros, diabetes, sonogram, applause, stockholder

TABLE D.4   Types of Pronouns

TYPE OF PRONOUN	FUNCTION	EXAMPLES
Personal pronouns	Refer to specific persons, places, things	I, me you, she, her, he, him, it, they, their, them
Indefinite pronouns	Do not refer to specific persons, places, things; do not require antecedents. Pronouns indicating individuals are singular: any, each, every, -body, -one, -thing, no. Pronouns indicating several are plural: all, many, most, some.	all, any, anyone, anybody, both, each everyone, everybody, everything, many, most, none, no one, nobody, nothing, some, somebody, something *Everybody hopes* for a raise. *Some are* counting on it.
Relative pronouns	Introduce subordinate clauses that refer to a noun or pronoun the clause modifies	that, who, whom, whose, which The vice president *who gave the presentation* used to be my boss.
Interrogative pronouns	Introduce questions	what, who, whom, whose, which *What* happened next?
Demonstrative pronouns	Identify particular people or things	this, that, these, those *Those* are the most recent sales figures available.
Intensive pronouns	Emphasize the antecedent	Same form for both types: myself, yourself, himself, herself, itself, ourselves, yourselves, themselves
Reflexive pronouns	Refer to the receiver of an action who is the same as the performer of the action	a. The *President himself* will attend the conference. b. *We* congratulated *ourselves* on a job well done.
Reciprocal pronouns	Refer to separate parts of a plural antecedent	each other, one another The new *employees* introduced themselves to *each other*.

TABLE D.5 Pronoun Cases

PERSONAL PRONOUNS: SINGULAR	FUNCTIONING AS A SUBJECT SUBJECTIVE CASE	FUNCTIONING AS AN OBJECT OBJECTIVE CASE	FUNCTIONING TO SHOW POSSESSION POSSESSIVE CASE
First person (denotes person speaking)	I *I* sent an email.	me Rob sent an email to *me*.	my, mine *My* mailbox was full.
Second person (denotes person or thing spoken to)	you Were *you* the recipient?	you Mae saw *you* in the lobby.	your, yours Did you find *your* ticket?
Third person (denotes person or thing spoken of)	he, she, it *It* came in the mail.	him, her, it I found *it* on the desk.	his, her, hers, its The storm ruined *his* travel plans.
PERSONAL PRONOUNS: PLURAL	**SUBJECTIVE CASE**	**OBJECTIVE CASE**	**POSSESSIVE CASE**
First person (persons speaking)	we When *we* arrived, the meeting had already started.	us Let *us* know the date.	our, ours *Our* flight was canceled.
Second person (persons or things spoken to)	you As new employees, *you* have temporary security clearances.	you I wish *you* the best of luck.	your, yours *Your* supervisors will distribute the new software.
Third person (persons or things spoken of)	they It was *they* who completed the project.	them The department head recommended *them* for a raise.	their, theirs They earned *their* reward.
RELATIVE OR INTERROGATIVE PRONOUNS	**SUBJECTIVE CASE**	**OBJECTIVE CASE**	**POSSESSIVE CASE**
Singular and plural forms are the same	who Lee was the person *who* phoned.	whom To *whom* am I speaking?	whose Please tell me *whose* turn is next.

GRAMMAR ALERT! MISUSE OF PRONOUN CASE

If a pronoun is in the wrong **case,** the sentence will be grammatically incorrect.

Use the objective case for the object of a transitive verb (a verb that passes the action to a recipient—or object—of that action).

Incorrect   The division manager asked him and *I* to report our findings.
(Incorrect use of subjective case: *I* is not the subject of the sentence.)

Correct   The division manager asked him and *me* to report our findings.
(Correct use of objective case: The pronoun *me* is the object of the verb *asked*.)

Use the subjective case with intransitive verbs such as linking or being verbs.

Incorrect   The principal researchers on the project were *him* and *me*.
(Incorrect use of objective case: The subject antecedent, *researchers*, and pronouns referring to it are linked by a "be" verb—*were*—so both are subjective case.)

Correct   The principal researchers on the project were *he* and *I*.

Use the subjective case when answering a caller's question, "Is [your name] there?"

Incorrect   This is *me*. (Incorrect use of objective case; *me* renames the subject *this, which refers to the antecedent subject [your name] in the question,* so use subjective case.)

Correct   This is *she*.

Sometimes you can hear the correct case if you modify the wording of the sentence and start with the pronoun(s) in the subject spot: *He and I* were the principal researchers on the project. Another test is to switch to the plural: The division manager asked *us* to report our findings. *Us* sounds (and is) correct, so the corresponding singular objective form, *him and me*, will be correct.

SPELLING ALERT! MISUSE OF APOSTROPHE

Do not confuse their/they're, your/you're, or its/it's. Possessive pronouns are never formed with an apostrophe, but contractions ending in -s always are.

They're the lawyers who handle corporate mergers in *their* law firm. (contraction of *they are*; possessive pronoun)

Your application is due if *you're* interested in being considered for the job. (possessive pronoun; contraction of *you are*)

You can't tell a book by *its* cover, although *it's* tempting to try. (possessive pronoun; contraction of *it is*)

1.1.2. Action and Being Words: Verbs

Verbs express action, occurrence, or state of being.

Action	Stock prices *rose* in late December.
Occurrence	That often *happens* at the end of the year.
State of Being	The phenomenon *is known* as the "year-end bump."

a. **Verb forms.** Verbs change form to show **time (tense), person, number, voice, and mood,** as illustrated in TABLE D.6.

b. **Expletives** are introductory words such as *there* or *it* followed by a linking verb (*is, are, was, were*).

   It is probable that Jean won't attend.

   There were six people on the conference call.

   Expletives function more as signal expressions used for emphasis than as true conveyers of content. For example, *There were six people on the conference call* could as easily be expressed as *Six people were on the conference call.* Examine your writing to eliminate expletives, when possible. Although they can be used effectively to manage the pace and emphasis in a sentence, expletives can also add words that may not be necessary.

GRAMMAR ALERT! SUBJECT-VERB AGREEMENT ERROR

Verbs must agree with their subjects in person and number. The subject cannot be in a prepositional phrase. Find the true subject and make the verb agree.

Incorrect	The members of the Federal Reserve Board *sets* interest rates. (Verb *sets* is incorrect because subject *members* is plural.)
Correct	The *members* of the Federal Reserve Board *set* interest rates.

Contractions should be separated and matched with the correct person.

Incorrect	He *don't* want to be late, and I don't either. (Verb form *don't* or *do not* disagrees with third-person singular subject *he*.)
Correct	He *doesn't* want to be late, and I don't either. OR He *does not* want to be late, and I *do not* either.

Also see "Subject-Verb Agreement" in *Common Sentence Errors*.

Wordy	It is probable that Jean won't attend.
Revised	Jean probably won't attend.

GRAMMAR ALERT! AGREEMENT ERROR WITH *THERE*

When a sentence begins with the expletive *there*, the verb is singular or plural depending on the number of the noun or pronoun that follows it. In other words, the verb must agree with the true grammatical subject of the sentence; *there* and *here* are adverbial modifiers and cannot be grammatical subjects.

Incorrect	There was two possible solutions.
Correct	There *were* two possible *solutions*.

To check for correct agreement between subject and verb, try putting the sentence in subject-verb word order: Two possible *solutions were* there.

TABLE D.6   Features of Verbs

FEATURE	VARIATIONS	EXAMPLE
Time	Present, Past, Future (Tense)	The stock market *rose* 58 points. Prices **will increase**.
Person	first, second, third	*You and I think* it is a bull market. *He thinks* it is a bear market.
Number	singular, plural	A rising *tide raises* all boats, but ill financial *winds raise* many fears.
Voice: Active voice Passive voice	Subject performs action of verb. Subject receives action of verb.	Corporate losses *caused* a market decline. The market decline *was caused* by corporate losses.
Mood: Indicative Imperative Subjunctive	Indicates whether action expresses a fact or question (indicative), gives a command (imperative), or expresses a condition contrary to fact (subjunctive).	Indicative: She *saves* part of every paycheck. *Does* she *save* part of every paycheck? Imperative: *Save* part of every paycheck. Subjunctive: If she *were saving* part of every paycheck, she would be financially secure. [But the fact is she is not saving, so she is not secure.]

TABLE D.7 Types of Conjunctions

TYPE	FUNCTION	EXAMPLES
Coordinating conjunctions	Join words, phrases, or clauses of equal grammatical rank	and, but, or, nor, for, so, yet
Correlative conjunctions	Work in pairs to join words, phrases, or clauses of equal grammatical rank	both/and, either/or, neither/nor, not/but, not only/but also
Subordinating conjunctions	Join clauses that are not of equal rank. The clause beginning with the subordinating conjunction cannot stand by itself as a sentence.	after, although, as, because, before, if, since, rather than, that, unless, when, where, whether, while
Conjunctive adverbs	Join independent clauses only, clauses that can stand by themselves as sentences. These are adverbs, not true conjunctions, so they need to be preceded by a semicolon.	however, therefore, nevertheless, furthermore, instead, besides, consequently, then, meanwhile, thus

1.1.3. Modifying Words: Adjectives and Adverbs

a. **Adjectives** modify nouns and pronouns: Put the expense report in the *tall, gray filing* cabinet. Adjectives answer the questions *which one? what kind of?* or *how many?*

"Modify" means to identify, describe, limit, or qualify in some way. For example, the *tall, gray filing* cabinet describes the height, color, and type of cabinet, differentiating it from the low, white equipment cabinet next to it.

b. **Adverbs** modify verbs, adjectives, other adverbs, and occasionally prepositions, conjunctions, or even whole sentences: I *quickly* located the cabinet but *unfortunately* could *not* pull *open* the *very firmly stuck* drawer. Adverbs answer the questions *how? when? where? why? to what extent?* or *to what degree?*

c. **Degree of comparison.** Many adjectives and adverbs change form to indicate three degrees of **comparison:**

- **positive** (nothing being compared)
- **comparative** (higher or lower degree when comparing two)
- **superlative** (highest or lowest degree when comparing three or more)

The changes in form are indicated three ways.

1. By adding *-er* or *-est* to the positive form of a one-syllable adjective or adverb or an adjective that ends in *-ly*: *tall, taller, tallest; few, fewer, fewest; fast, faster, fastest; friendly, friendlier, friendliest*

2. By adding the prefix words *more* and *most* or *less* and *least* to the positive form of adjectives with three or more syllables or adverbs with two or more syllables: *expensive, less expensive, least expensive; simply, more simply, most simply*

3. By using an irregular form: *good, better, best; bad, worse, worst*

Some adjectives are considered **absolute,** not comparable. Absolute adjectives include *perfect, unique, square, straight, endless,* and *dead*. Something cannot be *more dead* than something else; it can, however, be *almost* or *nearly dead*.

GRAMMAR ALERT! MISUSE OF *BAD* AND *GOOD*

Use adjectives, not adverbs, with linking verbs (*be, become, is, are, was, were*) and verbs of the senses (*feel, smell, taste, look, appear, seem*). One of the most common adjective/adverb errors is confusion of *good* and *well, bad* and *badly*.

Incorrect	He *looks well* in that suit. (An adjective should be used instead of the adverb *well,* because it describes the subject, *he.*)
Correct	He *looks good* in that suit.
Incorrect	She *felt badly* about missing the appointment. (The "sensing" verb *felt* requires an adjective, not an adverb, because it describes the subject, *she.*)
Correct	She *felt bad* about missing the appointment.
But	Because her fingers were numb with cold, she *felt badly* and couldn't tell her car key from her house key. (The adverb form *badly* is correct because it describes the verb, her ability to feel or touch.)

1.1.4. Connecting Words: Prepositions and Conjunctions

a. **Prepositions** connect a noun or pronoun (called the "object" of the preposition) to some other word in a sentence. These prepositional "phrases" usually function as modifiers, describing the words to which they are connected: The office *on the left* belongs to the corporate lawyer. Common prepositions include *in, out, up, down, before, behind, over, under, to, from, above, below, on, off, by, through, around*. Although we sometimes end sentences with prepositions in conversation ("Where are you from?"), try to avoid these "danglers" in writing. Follow the preposition with a noun or a pronoun as the object, unless doing so makes the sentence unusually awkward.

b. **Conjunctions** connect words, phrases, or clauses to show relationships between them: **coordination, correlation,** or **subordination.** The difference between them is described in TABLE D.7.

Note that some conjunctions also function as other parts of speech. For example, *after* can be a preposition or a conjunction, depending on whether it is followed by a noun or pronoun as an object or begins a phrase or clause containing a verb form.

> **GRAMMAR ALERT!** AGREEMENT ERROR WITH PREPOSITIONAL OBJECT
>
> The object of a preposition cannot be the subject of a sentence. Consequently, the verb should not be made to agree with it but rather with the true subject of the sentence.
>
> | Incorrect | The box of name badges are on your desk. (The subject is not *badges*; *badges* is the object of the preposition *of*.) |
> | --- | --- |
> | Correct | The *box* of name badges *is* on your desk. (The subject is *box*; the verb *is* agrees with the subject.) |

Prepositional Phrase	Jason returned to the office *after* lunch. (*Lunch* is a noun.)
Conjunction Joining Independent Clauses	Jason returned to the office *after* he finished lunch. (*He finished lunch* is a clause.)

1.1.5. Exclaiming Words: Interjections

Interjections are considered a part of speech, but their only function is to express strong feeling. While a few interjections can be interpreted as single-word commands with understood subjects or objects (*Help! Stop!*), most are grammatically unconnected to the rest of the sentence. An interjection may be accompanied by an explanation mark if the emotion is to be interpreted as particularly strong: "*Ouch!* I just got a paper cut from that file folder."

Interjections are common in speech, so they may be appropriate (if used with discretion) in written business messages that are more informal and conversational. Conversely, they are seldom appropriate in formal business writing, unless used for instructions that must grab the reader's attention.

Spoken Conversation	*Hey,* Lynn, do you have a minute?
Informal Email	*Wow!* I was impressed by her accomplishments.
Written Instructions	*Attention!* Set the brake before starting the engine.

Be aware that interjections that might be appropriate for texting friends will create an unprofessional, immature tone in business correspondence.

1.2. Sentence Parts and Patterns

As the old song says, "The knee bone is connected to the thigh bone," not to the heel bone or the toe bone. Understanding the components that make up a sentence and how they work together can help writers and speakers eliminate errors and use language more effectively.

1.2.1. Subjects and Predicates

The largest structural parts of sentences are their subjects and predicates. The **subject** explains who or what the sentence is about, who is performing or receiving the action described in the sentence. The **predicate** states the action or state of existence.

a. **Simple subject and predicate.** A sentence can be as short as two words—one word for the subject, and one word for the predicate: *Prices rose.* If the sentence is a command with an understood subject, it can even be just one word: *Run!* Usually sentences are longer, with their subjects and predicates composed of more words, conveying more information: *The prices for new homes rose in the third quarter.* However, every sentence can be pared down to its essential elements, the **simple subject** (noun, pronoun, or noun equivalent) and **simple predicate** (verb): *Prices rose.*

b. **Complete subject and predicate.** The simple subject along with all its modifiers is called the **complete subject.**

   The **prices** for new homes rose in the third quarter.

   Similarly, the simple predicate along with all its modifiers, objects, and complements is the **complete predicate.**

   The prices for new homes **rose in the third quarter.**

   In the sentence above, the complete predicate includes only the verb and its modifiers: **rose in the third quarter.** That is because the verb *rose* is an intransitive verb: a verb that does not take an object.

   If the verb is a transitive verb—one that takes an object—the complete predicate will include a **direct object** that receives the action of the verb: We *bought* **a house.** It may also include an **indirect object,** telling to or for whom or what the action occurred: The real estate agent *sent* **us** the contract.

   If the predicate has a linking verb, it may include a **complement**—a noun, pronoun, or adjective that "completes" the verb, renaming or describing the subject: The house *is* **a two-story colonial.** The price *was* **reasonable.**

c. **Inverted word order** can sometimes make locating the subject and predicate difficult. For example, questions have inverted word order, in which the verb (or part of a verb phrase) precedes the subject. In the following questions, the simple predicates are *did rise* and *are*. The simple subjects are *prices* and *they*: **Did** home prices **rise** last month? **Are** they still reasonable?

1.2.2. Phrases and Clauses

a. **Phrases** are word groups that may contain a subject or a predicate, but not both. They function as a single part of speech, as described in TABLE D.8.

b. **Clauses** are word groups that have both a subject and a predicate. The subject and predicate may contain no modifiers or many; they may contain no phrases or many.

   Prices rose. (no modifiers)

   Prices *for new homes* rose *in the third quarter.* (two modifying phrases)

   An **independent clause** (main clause) can stand by itself as a complete sentence, but a **dependent clause** cannot stand alone.

   Dependent clauses (also called subordinate clauses) add information to the main idea, but they are incomplete without the main clause to which they are attached. You can identify an adverbial dependent clause by the subordinating conjunction that connect it to the main clause (see "Connecting Words"). You can identify an adjectival subordinate clause (also called a relative clause) by the relative pronoun (*who, whom, whose, that,* or *which*] or the relative adverb (*when, where,* or *why*) that connects it to the main clause. TABLE D.9 illustrates the differences between independent and dependent clauses.

TABLE D.8   Functions of Phrases

FUNCTION OF PHRASE	EXAMPLE	EXPLANATION
Functions as noun	*Remembering all my computer passwords* is difficult.	Noun phrase takes subject position in sentence.
Functions as verb	I *have been writing* them on sticky notes.	Verb phrase takes verb position in sentence.
Functions as adjective	Dozens *of these notes* are stuck to my computer. *Looking at all these notes stuck on my computer*, I wish I did not need this memory aid	Adjectival prepositional phrase modifies noun *dozens*, telling what kind. Present participial phrase *looking at all these notes* modifies the pronoun *I*. Past participial phrase *stuck on my computer* modifies the noun *notes*, telling which ones.
Functions as adverb	*However,* I can't seem to remember my passwords from one day to the next.	Adverbial prepositional phrase modifies verb *seem to remember*, telling when.

TABLE D.9   Independent versus Dependent Clauses

Independent	*I can't remember my passwords* because I have too many of them. (Italicized words can stand alone.)
Dependent	I can't remember my passwords *because I have too many of them.* (Italicized words cannot stand alone.)
Independent	*I can't even remember the password* that I selected yesterday. (Italicized words can stand alone.)
Dependent	I can't even remember the password *that I selected yesterday.* (Italicized words cannot stand alone.)
Independent	*Now I just need to find the sticky notes* where I wrote down my passwords. (Italicized words can stand alone.)
Dependent	Now I just need to find the sticky notes *where I wrote down my passwords.* (Italicized words cannot stand alone.)

PUNCTUATION ALERT! SENTENCE FRAGMENT

Do not punctuate a **dependent clause** as if it were a sentence. Doing so creates a sentence fragment (see "Common Sentence Errors: Sentence Fragments").

Incorrect	My computer doesn't work. Although the technician checked it. (*Although the technician checked it* is a dependent clause—a sentence fragment, not a complete sentence.)
Correct	My computer doesn't work although the technician checked it.

1.2.3. Sentence Types: Simple, Compound, Complex, Compound-Complex

Sentences can be classified according to the number and types of clauses they contain. Good communicators take advantage of these sentence types to express their ideas most effectively. From simple to complex, sentence structure can help create and reinforce meaning. TABLE D.10 illustrates the four sentence types.

Subjects and predicates may have compound elements, but those compound elements do not necessarily make the sentence itself compound. For example, a simple sentence with a compound verb is still a simple sentence: People **live** longer *but* **save** less.

TABLE D.10   Sentence Types

SENTENCE TYPE	STRUCTURE	EXAMPLES
Simple	One **independent** clause; no *dependent* clauses	**People want to save for retirement.**
Compound	Two or more **independent** clauses; no *dependent* clauses	**People want to save for retirement**, but **they seldom do it.**
Complex	One **independent** clause; one or more *dependent* clauses	*Although people want to save for retirement*, **they seldom do it voluntarily.**
Compound-Complex	Two or more **independent** clauses; one or more *dependent* clauses	**People say** *that they want to save for retirement*, but **they seldom do it** *while they are young.*

PUNCTUATION ALERT! MISUSE OF COMMA

Do not punctuate a simple sentence with a compound subject or compound predicate as if it were a compound sentence. Before putting a comma in front of *and* or *but*, check to make sure the conjunction connects two independent clauses.

Incorrect	I turned off my computer, and then went to get the mail. (This is a single independent clause with a compound predicate.)
Correct	I turned off my computer and then went to get the mail.
Correct	I turned off my computer, and then I went to get the mail. Each clause is independent, so the comma is required.)

1.3. Common Sentence Errors

The most frequent sentence errors are **fragments, run-ons** or **fused sentences, comma splices,** and **agreement errors.** The first three errors occur because the writer has incorrectly indicated where one sentence stops and another begins. These errors can prevent readers from understanding the meaning the writer intended. Although our daily speech is full of these "not sentence" constructions, listeners have many more cues to help determine meaning—including the opportunity to ask questions. Business writers need to get it right the first time, or they may cause serious miscommunication.

1.3.1. Sentence Fragments

A sentence contains at least one independent clause, having a subject and a verb, and can stand alone as a complete thought. When a word group (phrase or dependent clause) lacking these characteristics is punctuated as if it were a sentence, a **fragment** results. A fragment can be corrected by rewriting it as a complete sentence. Join the fragment to the sentence before or after it, or supply the missing subject or verb to make the fragment an independent clause.

Incorrect	People would rather have rewards now. Than wait patiently for rewards in the future. (phrases punctuated as a sentence)
Correct	People would rather have rewards now than wait patiently for rewards in the future.
Incorrect	Behavioral economists say people choose immediate rewards. Because they overly discount the future. (dependent clause punctuated as a sentence)
Correct	Behavioral economists say people choose immediate rewards because they overly discount the future.
Incorrect	People buying things on credit that they can't afford. (phrases and dependent clause punctuated as a sentence)
Correct	People buy things on credit that they can't afford.

Compound predicates (joined by *and, but, or, yet*, and so on) are sometimes punctuated as complete sentences, especially when the sentence is long. However, if the clause beginning with "but" is short, combine it with the first sentence.

Incorrect	Sometimes people have to run up their credit card bills. But they shouldn't make a habit of it.
Correct	Sometimes people have to run up their credit card bills, but they shouldn't make a habit of it.

A polite request or command may appear to be missing a subject, and therefore be a sentence fragment; however, the sentence is complete because the subject is the understood pronoun *you*.

Correct	Please send your response as soon as possible. (The understood subject is *you*.)

1.3.2. Run-On (Fused) Sentences and Comma Splices

Run-on or **fused sentences** are independent clauses joined together without a connecting conjunction.

Classical economists believe humans rationally weigh costs and benefits **conversely, behavioral economists point out humans' irrational decision making.**

Comma splices are independent clauses joined together by a comma.

Rational humans are marvelous in theory, **in reality they do not exist.**

Run-ons and comma splices are both incorrect, and both can be fixed in one of five ways:

1 **Connect the independent clauses with a comma and a co-ordinating conjunction.**

   Classical economists believe humans rationally weigh costs and benefits, *but* behavioral economists point out humans' irrational decision making.

2 **Connect the independent clauses with a semicolon.**

   Rational humans are marvelous in theory; in reality they do not exist.

3 **Make a separate sentence of each independent clause.**

   Classical economists believe humans rationally weigh costs and benefits. Conversely, behavioral economists point out humans' irrational decision making.

4 **Change one independent clause to a dependent clause.**

   Although rational humans are marvelous in theory, in reality they do not exist.

5 **Change one independent clause to a phrase.**

   Marvelous in theory, rational humans do not exist in reality.

1.3.3. Subject-Verb Agreement

Subjects and verbs need to agree in number and person. If the subject of a clause is singular, the verb must be singular as well; if plural, it must be plural. If the subject is in third person, the verb must reflect that. (Also see 1.1.2 "Action and Being Words: Verbs.") Agreement errors are most common in the following instances.

- **Words and phrases between subject and verb.** Locate the subject and verb and make them agree, ignoring everything in between.

   The *aroma* of baking cupcakes *convinces* me to start my diet tomorrow. (The verb *convinces* should agree in number with the subject *aroma*, not with *cupcakes*, the object of the preposition *of*.)

   Even though words such as *with*, *together with*, and *as well as* suggest plural meaning, they are not part of the subject. When they follow singular subjects, use singular verbs.

   Temptation, as well as immediate sweet rewards, *undermines* my willpower.

- **Indefinite pronouns as subjects.** Use singular verbs with indefinite pronouns indicating one: *another, each, either, much, neither, one*, and all pronouns ending in *-one, -body*, and *-thing*.

   Everybody believes in doing what is best for the future; nevertheless, *each* of us occasionally *gives* in to immediate gratification.

   Use plural verbs with indefinite pronouns indicating more than one: *both, few many, others*, and *several*.

   Many behave irrationally, but *few view* their choices as irrational.

   The indefinite pronouns *all, any, most, more, none*, and *some* take either a singular or a plural verb, depending on whether the noun to which they refer is singular or plural.

   Some people are good at delaying gratification, but *none find* it very easy. (*None* refers to *people* and so requires the plural verb *find*.)

   Most of the cake is gone, but some is still on the plate. (*Most* and *some* refer to one item—most of it and some of it.)

- **Collective nouns as subjects.** Collective nouns are singular in form but name a group of persons or things: *committee, crowd, jury, team, task force*. Use a singular verb when the group is considered as a unit acting collectively as one. Use a plural verb when the members of the group are acting separately as individuals.

   The *task force has* reported its findings to the director. (Task force is considered a unit acting collectively.)

   The *task force have* agreed to conduct follow-up studies in their own departments. (Individuals on the task force are acting separately.)

   OR

   The task force *members have* agreed to conduct follow-up studies in their own departments.

- **Plural forms that have singular meanings.** Some nouns are plural in form but singular in meaning: *economics, mathematics, news, measles*. Use a singular verb with these.

   Behavioral *economics explains* why consumers can't resist a sale.

However, some nouns in plural form, such as *athletics, politics, statistics*, and *acoustics*, may be singular or plural, depending on whether they refer to a singular or plural idea.

   The Republican Party's *politics is* generally conservative, although members' *politics reflect* a wide spectrum of views.

> **GRAMMAR ALERT!** DATA
>
> A singular verb is often used with the word *data*: *The data appears in the appendix*. However, people in technical and scientific fields typically think of data as plural, as compilations of separate pieces of numerical information. Therefore, they usually prefer plural verbs: *The data appear in the appendix*. Follow the practice of the business, industry, or field for which you are writing. If the word *data* is considered plural in meaning, use a plural verb: *The data are reliable. Her data show* that more testing should be done. The singular form is *datum*, or you can write about an individual *data point*.

- **Subjects joined by coordinating conjunctions *and, or*, or *nor*.** Use a plural verb when two or more subjects are joined by *and*, unless the parts of the compound subject refer to the same thing.

   Our *wants and* our *needs are* often not the same thing.

   Robert's *son and executor* of his estate *has signed* the documents.

   When *each* or *every* precedes a compound singular subject joined by *and*, the subject is considered singular and takes a singular verb.

   Every employee and his or her guest *has been issued* an identification badge.

   When subjects are joined by *or, nor*, or *not only/but also*, the verb should agree in number with the subject that is nearer.

   Neither the employee *nor* her *guests have been issued* badges, so either the receptionist *or* the *department head has to call* Security for clearance.

   Neither the guests *nor* the *employee has been issued* badges.

- **Relative pronouns *who, which*, and *that* as subjects.** When the relative pronoun *who, which*, or *that* is the subject of a dependent clause, make the verb agree with the pronoun's antecedent.

   Please give me a list of the *guests who need* badges. (*Who* refers to the antecedent *guests*, so the verb must be plural.)

- **Inverted word order.** Be sure to check agreement when the verb comes before the subject. Test for correctness by putting the subject first. (Also see 1.1.2.b. "Expletives.")

   After a vacation *comes* the *reality* of an overflowing in-box. (The *reality* of an overflowing in-box *comes* after a vacation.)

   There *appears* to be no *excuse* for his behavior. (No *excuse* for his behavior *appears* to be there.)

- **Quantities.** Total amounts are usually considered a single unit and take singular verbs.

Two weeks is not enough vacation, according to Europeans.

I think *$100 is* outrageous for weekly parking.

If the individual parts of a unit are being emphasized, choose a plural verb.

Twenty-four grams of fat *have* to be spread over three meals, not eaten in a single sitting.

If a percentage refers to things that are plural and countable, the verb should be plural.

Thirty percent of the engine parts *do* not pass quality standards.

If a percentage refers to something that is singular, the verb is singular.

Ten percent of his income *goes* to charity.

The number takes a singular verb, but *a number* takes a plural verb.

A number of faulty parts *were found,* although *the number* of returns *was* low.

- **Business names, products, titles, and words used as words.** Even if the form of a business name or product or the title of a work is plural, it takes a singular verb because it is a single thing. The same is true for words discussed as words.

  I think *Twinings makes* the best cup of Earl Grey tea.

  Hot, Flat, and Crowded by Thomas Friedman *has* sold millions of copies.

  Geese is the plural of *goose.*

1.3.4. Pronoun-Antecedent Agreement

Pronouns must agree in number with their antecedents, the words to which they refer. Most agreement situations are obvious: The *interns* received *their* orientation yesterday. However, the following situations can be tricky.

- **Indefinite pronouns.** As the word "indefinite" suggests, these pronouns do not refer to specific persons, places, or things: for example, *some, all, many,* and *anyone* are indefinite pronouns. Although people tend to use plural pronouns when speaking, in writing use singular pronouns to refer to indefinite pronoun antecedents such as *person, one, any, each, either,* and *neither* and indefinite pronouns ending in *-one, -body,* and *-thing,* such as *anybody, someone,* or *everything.*

  Incorrect *Everybody* knows *they* should dress appropriately for a job interview.

  Correct *Everybody* knows *he or she* should dress appropriately for a job interview.

- **Collective nouns.** Use a singular pronoun if the antecedent is a group being considered as a unit. Use a plural pronoun if the members of the group are being considered individually.

  The review *panel* started *its* tour of the laboratory at 9:30 AM. (The panel toured as a group.)

  The review *panel* asked many questions when *they* met with the research director. (Individual members of the group asked questions.)

- **Compound antecedents.** Antecedents connected by *and* take plural pronouns. Pronouns referring to compound antecedents connected by *or* or *nor* should agree with the antecedent closer to it. If that choice is awkward or ambiguous, do not use a pronoun.

  Incorrect If you ask either Jenny or Paul, they will help you.

  Incorrect If you ask either the supervisors or Jenny, they will help you.

  Correct If you ask *Jenny and Paul, they* will help you.

  Correct If you ask either *Jenny or Paul, one of them* will help you.

  Correct If you ask either Jenny *or the supervisors, they* will help you.

  Correct If you ask either the supervisor*s or Jenny, someone* will help you. (Avoid using the grammatically correct pronoun, *she,* because the resulting sentence implies that the supervisors will not help: If you ask either the supervisors *or Jenny, she* will help you.)

When a compound antecedent is introduced by *each* or *every,* or when it refers to a single person or thing, use a singular pronoun.

Each hospital and clinic has *its* own evacuation plan.

The president and CEO delivered *his* annual state-of-the-company speech.

1.3.5. Vague Pronoun Reference

The antecedent to which a pronoun refers should be clear. Pronouns should refer to

- only one antecedent. It may be plural or compound, but it should be only one.
- an antecedent that is nearby. Readers generally assume the antecedent is the closest previous noun or noun substitute.
- a specific antecedent, not an implied person or thing or the general idea of a preceding clause or sentence. A pronoun should refer to a noun or noun substitute that exists in a previous phrase or clause. Revise if *this, that,* or *which* refers to the general idea of a preceding clause or sentence.

  Vague We need to survey more customers. *This* will give us better data, so we can develop better products. *They* will benefit in the long run. (*This* vaguely refers to the whole idea in the previous sentence. *They* could refer to customers, data, or products; the closest noun, *products,* doesn't make sense.)

  Clear We need to survey more customers. A bigger sampling will give us better data, so we can develop better products. Customers will benefit in the long run.

■ 2. Punctuation

Punctuation marks fall into four basic categories: (1) end punctuation that marks the endings of sentences and indicates how the sentence is to be read; (2) internal punctuation that shows the relationship of individual words or sentence parts to the rest of a sentence; (3) direct-quotation punctuation that indicates speakers and changes of speaker as well as where words have been added or omitted from the original text; and (4) word punctuation that indicates words or letters having a special use. These functions are illustrated in the sections that follow.

2.1. End Punctuation

The punctuation at the ends of sentences signals where ideas stop and marks the end of complete grammatical units that can stand alone. End punctuation also indicates whether the sentence is to be understood as a question (**question mark**), statement, command, indirect question, or polite request (**period**), or strong expression of emotion (**exclamation point**).

Examples:

I will now ask your name.

Tell me your name.

Will you please state your name.

What is your name?

What a wonderful name!

2.1.1. Question Marks

Direct questions are punctuated with a question mark: *What time is the meeting? She asked me, "What time is the meeting?"*

2.1.2. Periods

Periods mark the ends of statements and commands as well as indirect questions and polite requests. An **indirect question** implies a question but does not actually ask one: *She asked me what time the meeting is.* One clue that the previous sentence is not a direct question is the word order: The subject and verb are not inverted in indirect questions, as they are in a direct question (what time *is the meeting?*). A **polite request** may be phrased like a question, but it is really a command stated nicely. Therefore, it is often punctuated with a period rather than a question mark *When you have scheduled the meeting, would you please let me know.* Deciding whether a sentence is a polite request or a question may also have to do with who is making the request. A polite request that is a command from a supervisor would require a period: *"Will you please attend the meeting for me."* A polite request for a favor from a coworker would require a question mark: *"Will you please attend the meeting for me?"*

Periods also are normally used with initials and with abbreviations ending with lowercase letters.

Dr. Janice Brown Sen. Ben Cardin St. Jerome Mr. Kim

Academic degrees and professional certifications in some fields omit the period from abbreviations; for example, PhD, RN, or MD may appear without periods. Consult the style manual of the profession if in doubt. Your company may also have a style manual that specifies how abbreviations are to be handled in company correspondence and publications.

2.1.3. Exclamation Points

Interjections and sentences that require strong emphasis or express extreme emotion are often punctuated with exclamation points: *Attention! Fire on the third floor! Evacuate the building using the stairs!*

Unfortunately, many people have adopted the habit of sprinkling their writing liberally with exclamations, particularly in text messages and emails: *OMG!! Guess who showed up at the company party?!* More formal business communication should contain few if any exclamation points. Overusing exclamations either diminishes their effect or makes the writing sound hysterical and immature. In some fields, such as court reporting, exclamation points are never used.

2.2. Commas

Commas separate parts of a sentence, guiding readers through complex constructions, indicating modifiers, separating series, and generally ordering things into understandable units of meaning. Think of commas as markers that signal changes in the road. Although there are many rules for using commas, most business writing relies on a fairly limited number.

2.2.1. Between Clauses

- **Independent clauses joined by coordinating conjunctions** *and, but, or, nor, for, so, yet.* The comma before the coordinating conjunction linking the clauses signals that one complete thought is finished and another is about to begin.

  I prepared the slides, *and* Mavis printed the handouts.

  The comma can be omitted between very short clauses if there is no possibility of confusion: You drive *and* I'll navigate.

  Do not use a comma with a coordinating conjunction linking compound predicates (verbs plus objects or complements plus modifiers). Check to be sure the conjunction links independent clauses.

Incorrect	I prepared the slides for the meeting, and then printed the handouts.
Correct	I prepared the slides for the meeting, and then I printed the handouts.
Or	I prepared the slides for the meeting and then printed the handouts.

  Also see 1.2.3. "Sentence Types: Simple, Compound, Complex, Compound-Complex."

- **Dependent clauses and phrases preceding the independent clause.** The comma following an introductory dependent clause or phrase signals that the main clause containing the main idea is about to begin. It helps the reader differentiate modifying information from the meat of the sentence, announcing "OK, now pay attention. Here comes the most important stuff."

  When the presentation was finished, the speaker answered questions.

  Having missed the first 15 minutes, I was a bit confused.

  If it will not cause misreading, the comma can be omitted after very short introductory clauses or phrases.

Clear	After lunch we returned to the office.
Confusing	Before long smears appeared on the glass.
Clear	Before long, smears appeared on the glass.
Confusing	After she ate lunch was served to the rest of us.
Clear	After she ate, lunch was served to the rest of us.

2.2.2. Between Adjectives

- **Coordinate and cumulative adjectives.** If each adjective in a series modifies the noun separately, they are **coordinate** and need commas between them.

  The *personable, youthful, but knowledgeable* guide led the way.

  If any adjective in a series forms a total concept along with the noun, they are cumulative and do not need commas.

  International currency exchange rates are posted on the Internet. (Currency exchange rates is a total concept.)

  To test for coordinate adjectives, see if the adjectives can be rearranged and if *and* can be inserted between them without altering the basic meaning: *knowledgeable and youthful and personable* guide. If the result is nonsense, the adjectives are cumulative, interdependent, and should not be separated from each other by commas: *international currency exchange rates* must appear in that order, or the statement makes no sense.

2.2.3. Between Items in a Series

Three or more words, phrases, or clauses in a series are said to be **serial** or **coordinate.** Their equal importance is indicated by their equal grammatical rank and parallel grammatical form.

- **Serial words, phrases, or clauses.** Serial items are differentiated from one another by the commas between them.

  Many U.S. companies have found that outsourcing call-center jobs *cuts costs, increases productivity, and allows 24-hour global service.*

  Although writing in newspapers, magazines, and websites often omits the comma before the conjunction, use it in business writing to prevent misreading—which could be not only confusing but also costly.

Confusing	Charge the plane tickets for the vice president, board chairwoman and president and CEO to the corporate account. (Three tickets or four?)
Clear	Charge the plane tickets for the vice president, board chairwoman, and president and CEO to the corporate account. (Three tickets, because the president and the CEO are the same person.)

2.2.4. Around Clauses, Phrases, or Words

a. **Nonrestrictive clauses and phrases.** If the information in a modifying clause or phrase can be omitted without changing the basic meaning of a sentence, it is **nonrestrictive** and is set off by commas. If readers would be unable to understand the sentence's core meaning without the modifying

information, it is **restrictive** and is not set off by commas. Restrictive modifiers limit meaning to a particular set within a category and are crucial to the sentence.

Nonrestrictive	The sales award went to McKenzie, *who landed six new accounts.* (The clause provides additional information about McKenzie, but without it we would still know who got the award.)
Restrictive	Everyone *who has been with the company for three years* is eligible for profit sharing. (The clause restricts who qualifies; otherwise, the company would have to include all employees in profit sharing.)

GRAMMAR ALERT! *THAT* AND *WHICH*

That and *which* are not interchangeable. Use *that* to introduce restrictive clauses and *which* to introduce nonrestrictive clauses:

The retirement plan *that I chose* is split between annuities and stock funds. The stock funds, *which are invested in Fortune 500 companies,* showed a good return last year.

Remember that nonrestrictive clauses, *which are set off by commas,* can be removed without destroying the basic meaning of the sentence. Most of the time, if you use *that,* you will be making the correct choice.

Use *who,* not *which* or *that,* when referring to people; use *which* or *that* when referring to things or ideas:

Incorrect	Dr. Phillips is the only veterinarian *that* keeps Sunday hours.
Correct	Dr. Phillips is the only veterinarian *who* keeps Sunday hours.

---

b. **Appositives.** An appositive is a noun, with or without modifiers, that identifies the noun immediately preceding it. Appositives can be nonrestrictive or restrictive, accordingly written with or without commas.

  Mnemonics, *memory aids,* can help you learn things. (nonrestrictive)

  The mnemonic *"every good boy does fine"* refers to the musical notes E, G, B, D, and F. (restrictive)

  I learned that mnemonic from Mr. Glonner, *my third-grade music teacher.* (restrictive)

c. **Direct address and other parenthetical elements.** If you insert the name of the person to whom you are speaking or writing into a sentence, you are using **direct address.** Set these names off with commas: Thank you, *Leela,* for closing the door. *Committee members,* are we ready to vote?

  Parenthetical elements such as interjections, transition words, words expressing contrast, and other interrupting words that are unrelated to the grammatical structure of a sentence should also be set off with commas.

  Yes, everyone is present and ready to vote. We shall, *therefore,* proceed. *Oh,* before we do, someone needs to second the motion. Parliamentary procedure, *unlike the consensus method,* requires a second.

d. **Dates and places.** Dates and places in sentences are treated similarly to parenthetical elements. In general, place a comma after each element. Exceptions: Do not put a comma between the state and zip code. If there is no day-date, do not put a comma between the month and year. If the date is written day-month-year, use no commas.

> *October 29, 1929,* is known as Black Tuesday, the day the New York stock market crashed.

> No American will forget *11 September 2001.*

> Isn't NBC's headquarters at *30 Rockefeller Plaza, New York, NY 10112,* in mid-town Manhattan?

> The annual convention will be held in *Boise, Idaho,* next year and *Toronto, Canada,* the year after that.

e. **Direct quotations.** Direct quotations are set off with commas. Any comma at the end of a quotation **always** goes inside the quotation marks. Also see 2.5, "Quotation Marks."

> The manager told the sales associates, "We need better customer service."

> "I'm hearing too many complaints," she explained, "and we're losing business."

Use a question mark at the end of the quotation if it is a question.

> "Does anyone have a suggestion?" she asked.

f. **Salutations.** In formal business correspondence, punctuate the salutation or greeting with a colon, not with a comma. Commas should be reserved for personal, social correspondence written on personal stationery. Follow this convention even if you know the recipient and use his or her first name in the salutation.

> **Not** Dear Dr. Spaulding, or Dear Jerry,
>
> **But** Dear Dr. Spaulding: or Dear Jerry:

The colon announces that the subject of the correspondence is business—but conventions are somewhat more flexible for business email. See Appendix B for formatting examples.

2.3. Semicolons

In a sentence, semicolons have two distinctly different uses.

2.3.1. Joining Independent Clauses

Use a semicolon between grammatically independent clauses that are closely related in thought. In these instances, the semicolon is the equivalent of a period. It signals the end of one complete thought and the beginning of another. Reserve semicolons for sentences in which the thoughts in the independent clauses are closely related. If the thoughts are not closely related, use a period. When the second clause is introduced by a conjunctive adverb (*however, moreover, therefore, consequently*), place a comma after the conjunctive adverb. Do not use a semicolon between independent clauses joined by coordinating conjunctions (*and, but, so, for*), unless the clauses are quite long or internally punctuated.

> **Incorrect** Pollution threatens air quality; and everything that breathes is at risk.
>
> **Correct** Pollution threatens air quality; everything that breathes is at risk.
>
> **Correct** Pollution threatens air quality; consequently, everything that breathes is at risk.

2.3.2. Between Items in a Series

Use semicolons between serial items if any parts of the series have internal commas. The semicolons help readers sort things into the appropriate subsets and prevent misreading.

> Over the last 20 years, international negotiators have tried to reach agreement about global emission standards several times, including the Montreal Protocol of 1989; the Kyoto Protocol adopted on December 11, 1997; and the largely unsuccessful Copenhagen Climate Conference held December 7–18, 2009.

2.4. Colons

A colon signals that what follows will explain, clarify, or illustrate preceding information.

2.4.1. Preceding a List

Use a colon after phrases such as *the following* or *as follows* to signal the beginning of a list or series.

> Businesses can be "greener" and also save money by taking *the following steps:* insulate the building well, switch to fluorescent lighting, and recycle disposable items.

2.4.2. Preceding an Explanation or Illustration

Use a colon between explanatory material and the independent clause that introduces it.

> Polluting industries that balk at stricter standards usually offer one reason: the expense of compliance.

2.4.3. Preceding a Rule, Formal Quotation, or Subtitle

> Carpenters follow this advice: cut once, measure twice. (rule)

> The Declaration of Independence assumes inherent human rights: "We hold these truths to be self evident." (formal quotation)

> *The World is Flat: A Brief History of the Twenty-First Century* (subtitle)

PUNCTUATION ALERT! MISUSE OF COLONS

Be sure that a complete sentence, not a partial statement, precedes the colon—even if the clause ends with *including* or *such as.* Do not put a colon between a verb and its object or complement or between a preposition and its object.

Incorrect	Our office has adopted "green" initiatives including: recycling soda cans and installing energy-efficient light bulbs.
Correct	Our office has adopted "green" initiatives, including recycling soda cans and installing energy-efficient light bulbs.
Correct	Our office has initiated two successful green initiatives: recycling soda cans and installing energy-efficient light bulbs.

(continued)

PUNCTUATION ALERT! MISUSE OF COLONS continued	
Incorrect	I try to cut down carbon emissions by: biking to work, combining errands, and driving a hybrid car.
Correct	I try to cut down on carbon emissions by biking to work, combining errands, and driving a hybrid car.
Correct	I try to cut down on carbon emissions in the following ways: biking to work, combining errands, and driving a hybrid car.

However, if the items following a verb or preposition are presented as a vertical list, use a colon.

Correct	Signs that the planet is warming include:
	• melting glaciers
	• invasive tropical species in temperate zones
	• more frequent violent weather systems

2.5. Quotation Marks and Italics

Quotation marks and italics indicate that words are being used in a distinct way, most commonly to identify direct address, titles, and special meaning or emphasis.

2.5.1. Quotation Marks

Use quotation marks to signal direct quotations, titles of shorter works, and words that are being used in a special sense.

a. **Direct quotation.** Use double quotation marks for language that has been reproduced exactly as someone spoke or wrote it. Use single quotation marks to indicate a quotation within a quotation.

> According to this morning's news, "The President reminded his audience that economic recessions can be partly psychological. President Roosevelt said, 'We have nothing to fear but fear itself.' You know, he was right."

According to American punctuation usage, periods and commas always go inside single and double quotation marks. Colons and semi-colons always go outside quotation marks. Question marks and exclamation points, go either inside or outside the quotation marks, depending on whether the punctuation is part of the quotation or part of the sentence in which the quotation appears.

> "Shouldn't we recycle these computer printouts?" Marge asked.

> Did Marge say, "We should recycle these computer printouts"?

> I am sick of hearing the expression "waste not, want not"!

> Did Marge ask, "Shouldn't we recycle these computer printouts?" (This sentence requires only one question mark—inside the quotation marks—to signal that both the main sentence and the quoted sentence are questions.)

b. **Titles that are part of longer works.** Use quotation marks around titles of short stories, poems, chapters, articles, sections, songs, or episodes that are part of whole works. The title of the complete work in which a shorter work appears is italicized. Also see 2.5.2, "Italics."

> The article "Putting Green Technology into Bricks" in *The Wall Street Journal* makes the point that venture capital investment in the "green" building sector has nearly doubled in the past year.

c. **Words used as words or in a special sense.** Quotation marks signal that a word is being used in a special way. In the previous example, the quotation marks around "green" in *"green" building sector* alert the reader that "green" doesn't mean buildings painted green but green in the sense of "ecologically friendly."

2.5.2. Italics

Italics are used to distinguish titles of whole works from parts of works, to indicate some special uses of words, and to provide emphasis.

a. **Titles.** Place titles of works in italics; place title of parts of works in quotation marks:

> One of my favorite features in *The New York Times Magazine* is William Safire's "On Language" column

> If the word *The* is part of the title, be sure to capitalize and italicize it.

Some well-known titles of works are not italicized: religious works such as the Bible (and books of the Bible), the Koran, and the Talmud, and founding governmental documents such as the Declaration of Independence, the Bill of Rights, the Magna Carta, and the U.S. Constitution.

b. **Letters, numbers, words used as words, foreign words, names of ships and aircraft.** Italics are used to signal that a letter, number, or word is being identified as such.

> To an American, a *7* written by a German looks more like the number *1*.

Italics are also used to identify foreign words that have not been accepted into English.

> One of my favorite William Safire columns is a discussion of the Yiddish word *schlep.*

Words that have become part of the English language need not be italicized: bourgeois, milieu, zeitgeist, fiesta. Names of ships and aircraft are italicized but not the abbreviations that precede them: U.S.S. *Saratoga*, H.M.S. *Bounty*, the space shuttle *Atlantis.*

c. **Emphasis.** Italics can also be used for special emphasis.

> This is absolutely the *last* time we can accept a late shipment.

However, as with exclamation points, in business writing emphasizing too many words soon becomes tiresome to readers. It is like crying wolf; soon no one is paying attention, even when the wolf really is at the door. Use italicized emphasis sparingly.

2.6. Apostrophes

Apostrophes have two main functions in business writing: to show possession and to indicate the omission of a letter.

2.6.1. Possessive Case

a. **Singular nouns, plural nouns that do not end in -s, and indefinite pronouns.** Also see 1.1.1.b. "Pronoun Case." TABLE D.11 provides examples of how to form the possessive.

TABLE D.11 Examples of forming the possessive with 's

ADD 's TO SHOW POSSESSION	SINGULAR NOUNS	PLURAL NOUNS NOT ENDING IN -s	INDEFINITE PRONOUNS
Examples	my child's education, the boss's office, an individual's rights, a person's income, Dow Jones's sales, James's paycheck	his children's education, the mass media's influence, the people's choice, the mice's mutations	another's misfortune, someone's benefit, nobody's fault

In compounds, make only the last word possessive.

> his brother-in-law's mortgage (singular possessive)
> mothers-in-law's Christmas gifts (plural possessive)
> somebody else's parking space
> the writer-in-residence's latest one-act play

b. **Plural nouns ending in -s.** Add the apostrophe after the -s.

> the presidents' terms in office
> the stocks' dramatic rebound after the sell-off
> the pharmaceutical companies' profits
> the auto workers' union

c. **Joint possession.** Make the last noun possessive. In cases of individual possession, make both nouns possessive.

> Beth and Earl's project is due tomorrow. (joint possession)
> Beth's and Earl's offices are on different floors. (individual possession)

d. **Personal pronouns.** Do not use an apostrophe to form the possessive of personal pronouns. The pronouns *his, hers, its, ours, yours, theirs,* and *whose* are possessive as they stand.

> Ours is the second house on the right.
> Its expiration date is past.
> Be especially careful not to confuse *its* (possessive form of *it*) and *it's* (the contraction for *it is*) or *whose* (possessive form of *who*) and *who's* (contraction for *who is*).

2.6.2. Contractions

Apostrophes in contractions show where letters or numbers have been omitted.

> can't = cannot   they're = they are   o'clock = of the clock
> it's = it is   won't = will not
> the crash of '29 = the crash of 1929

2.7. Other Punctuation Marks

In business writing, following internal punctuation marks are used less frequently than commas, semicolons, and colons. However, when they are called for, it is important to use them correctly.

2.7.1. Parentheses, Dashes, Brackets, and Ellipses

Parentheses, dashes, brackets, and ellipses signal that words are being inserted or being left out.

a. **Parentheses.** Use parentheses to set off incidental or nonessential information.

> Mortgages that are "underwater" (meaning the property is worth less than the amount owed on it) have resulted in numerous foreclosures.
> The findings of the study (pp. 12–14) are quite surprising.

b. **Dashes.** If you want more emphasis for inserted incidental information, surround it with a pair of **dashes** instead of parentheses. You may also use dashes to emphasize important information. If the emphasized word or phrase comes at the end or beginning of the sentence, separate it from the rest of the sentence with only one dash.

> Wilkins missed the start of the meeting—again—and so didn't hear about the new deadline.
> The two problems we discussed at the meeting—absenteeism and tardiness—cost us thousands of dollars each month.
> Absenteeism and tardiness—these problems cost us thousands of dollars each month.
> Wilkens will never get promoted—unless he changes his behavior.

Be careful not to overuse dashes in formal business documents, especially for incidental information. They can give writing a breezy, chatty tone that is better reserved for email and notes to close associates.

c. **Brackets.** If you insert information, explanation, or comment into quoted material, use **brackets** to indicate that the words are not those of the quoted speaker or writer. To make a quotation grammatical when you insert it into your writing, you may sometimes have to add or change a word. These additions or changes should also be bracketed.

> "Innovation is not necessarily discovering new things, but discovering how to use old things [in a new way]," he said.

d. **Ellipses.** When quoting an author or speaker, you may choose to use only part of the material. You need to be honest with your readers and let them know that you have omitted some words or sentences. Use **ellipses,** spaced periods, to show the omission. If you are leaving out words within a sentence, use three ellipsis marks. If the omission comes at the end of a sentence, use three ellipses followed by whatever is the punctuation mark at the end of the quoted sentence.

> "While the rest of the industry has retreated, . . . green construction has actually grown," says Paul Holland, a

partner at venture firm Foundation Capital. He continues, "Why wouldn't smart contractors promote green construction for schools, shopping centers, [and] office buildings . . . ?"

If the omission comes between two sentences, end the first quoted sentence with the appropriate punctuation mark. Then indicate the omission with the ellipses.

> Holland is not surprised by the trend toward green construction: "While the rest of the industry has retreated, it makes sense that green construction has actually grown. . . . Why wouldn't smart contractors promote green construction for schools, shopping centers, office buildings and other major construction projects?"

If you find that the quotation is lengthy and you are removing words at more than one or two spots, it is better to summarize or paraphrase the ideas rather than butchering the original passage. Remember that you need to cite the source of paraphrases and summaries, just as you do for quotations.

2.7.2. Hyphens

Hyphens are used to form compound words, to write some numbers expressed as words, and to attach some prefixes and suffixes. A hyphen may also be used when it is necessary to divide a word at the end of a line. In this case, divide the word between syllables as shown in a dictionary. Most word processing programs take care of this issue by "wrapping" the word to the next line.

a. **Compound words.** Hyphens are used to join words into a single concept: *second-string* quarterback. Most hyphenated compounds are adjectives: *well-known* company, *back-ordered* items. Omit the hyphen when the first word is an adverb ending in *-ly*: *slowly rising* temperature, *previously paid* bill.

PUNCTUATION ALERT! MISUSE OF HYPHENS

When a compound modifier follows the word it modifies, the hyphen is omitted:

> The company is *well known* for its progressive policies.
> Your items have been *back ordered*.

Compound nouns used as adjectives before another noun are not hyphenated either: *data processing* software; *high school* reunion; *income tax* return; *life insurance* policy.

---

b. **Numbers as words.** Use a hyphen to form fractions and compound numbers twenty-one through ninety-nine when they are spelled out as words: *two-fifths, one-third, twenty-six.*

c. **Prefixes and suffixes.** Use a hyphen with the prefixes *all-, self-, ex-,* and the suffix *-elect: all-important, self-evident, ex-mayor, president-elect.* Do not capitalize *ex-* or *-elect,* even when it is part of a title that precedes a name: *ex-President* George Bush, *Councilwoman-elect* Betsy M. Clark. Do not use hyphens with prefixes such as *anti, extra, inter, non, pre, pro, re,* and *un: interoffice* memorandum, *pretrial* motion. The exception is if the prefix occurs before a proper noun or the first letter of the root word is the same as the last

letter of the prefix: *anti-American* demonstration, *non-negotiable* demands.

Some words have changed over time from a hyphenated form to a single word. For example, *co-worker* has lost its hyphen and is now commonly written as *coworker.* When in doubt about whether a prefix is hyphenated, consult an up-to-date dictionary.

■ 3. Mechanics and Business Conventions

Written English has many conventions, standard ways of doing things that developed over time: "It's just the way things are." Business writing has some of its own conventions that differ from standard written English and from writing in the sciences or the humanities. Where these differences are important, they will be noted in the following sections.

3.1. Capitalization

Text messaging and social media have spawned writing that features little or no capitalization. In these cases, the technology drives the behavior: it is difficult to capitalize on a small keypad where each key functions for several letters. However, the correct use of capital letters is still important for clarity in emails, business letters, memos, reports, and presentation decks. Capital letters signal beginnings as well as differentiate between the particular and the general.

3.1.1. First Words

Capitalize the first word of a sentence, a direct quotation, a complete sentence enclosed within parentheses or brackets, and a complete sentence following a colon.

> *Job* interviews can be nerve wracking. (sentence)
>
> He said, "*Please* have a seat." (direct quotation)
>
> Sales for the last three quarters have been flat. (*See* Table 2 for specific figures.) (sentence in parentheses)
>
> There two alternatives: *We* can raise prices, or we can cut costs. (complete sentence following colon)

3.1.2. Proper Nouns vs. Common Nouns

Proper nouns name particular persons, places, and things: Steve Jobs, Grand Hyatt, Honda Accord. Common nouns name general categories of persons, places, and things: investor, hotel, automobile.

a. **Proper nouns and adjectives formed from them.** The names of particular persons, places, and things are capitalized, as are nicknames, adjectives, and abbreviations formed from them. Foreign countries and languages are always capitalized. The words Internet and Web are always capitalized (as in "search the Internet" and "surf the Web"), but do not capitalize intranet or website.

William Jefferson Clinton prefers to be called *Bill.*

> How many people know that *IBM* is the abbreviation for the *International Business Machine Corporation*?
>
> The *National Cathedral* stands on the highest point in *Washington, D.C.*
>
> Claire took a job with a *French* pharmaceutical company.

I did most of the research on the *Internet*.

Post your résumé on your website.

b. **Places and directions.** Follow the conventions of standard American English. Capitalize place names following the examples in TABLE D.12.

- Official place names are capitalized.
- Common nouns that are part of official place names are also capitalized.
- Place names that simply refer to a general category are not capitalized.

Directions are capitalized if they serve as recognized names of regions or are part of an official name: the *South* of France, *Northwest* Airlines. They are not capitalized when they refer to points of the compass: the *east* side of town, a *westerly* breeze. Some directional nouns and adjectives may appear either way: the southern hemisphere, the Southern Hemisphere. When in doubt, check a dictionary.

c. **Brand and product names, organizations and institutions.** The brand names of products and the names of organizations and institutions are proper nouns and, therefore, are capitalized: Jell-O, Citibank, General Electric Company, Chicago Cubs, Google, the National Science Foundation, the Mayo Clinic, the United States Senate.

Take care to capitalize and spell brand names correctly. Most of them are registered trademarks, even though they may be widely used as generic terms. A generic term following a brand name is not capitalized.

Incorrect	post-it notes, jello, realtor, xerox, kleenex, ipod
Correct	Post-it notes, Jell-O, Realtor, Xerox, Kleenex tissues, iPod
Correct	sticky notes, gelatin, real estate agent, photocopy, tissues, portable media player

d. **Titles, offices, positions, and abbreviations.** Capitalize titles, offices, and positions when they precede a proper name. Capitalize abbreviations of professional certificates and degrees when they follow a proper name.

Secretary of State Clinton   Dr. Snow   Professor Okpala

Bridget Brennan, CPA   Ty Ray, RN   Chairman Bill Gates

Do not capitalize a title, office, or position that follows a name unless the office is one of high distinction. Do not capitalize a title, office, or position that follows a name if the title is preceded by "the."

Incorrect	Bill Gates, Chairman of Microsoft Corporation.
Correct	Bill Gates, chairman of Microsoft Corporation
Incorrect	John Roberts, the Chief Justice of the United States
Correct	John Roberts, Chief Justice of the United States or
	John Roberts, the chief justice of the United States

e. **Organizations and parts of organizations.** Names of specific organizations are capitalized, as are the official names of parts of organizations: *Clark Equipment Company, Off-Road Vehicles Division, Department of Internal Affairs.* When the organization or a part is being referred to in a general way, do not capitalize: the *dealership*, the *internal affairs department.*

Department names deserve special mention because the conventions governing their capitalization can be confusing. Should it be Accounting Department or accounting department? If it is the actual name of the department in your organization or you know it is the actual name of the department in another organization, then it is capitalized. Otherwise, don't capitalize department names: Send your résumé to our Human Resources Department. He sent his résumé to their personnel department.

When writing about your own company or organization, observe its capitalization conventions. Many organizations capitalize words that would not be capitalized in standard usage. Consider, for example, this sentence from a Ford Motor Company annual report: "We believe we are on track for the total Company and North American Automotive pre-tax results. . . ." Although contrary to standard convention, Ford's documents always capitalize *Company,* even when the word stands alone. The words *North American Automotive* refer to the official title of a Ford business unit and therefore conform to standard capitalization conventions.

f. **Courses, academic subjects, majors, and degrees.** Capitalize specific course titles but not majors or general areas of study. Capitalize the abbreviation of a degree, but not a generic degree name.

Patrick needs business law, *Intermediate Chinese,* and *Economics 315* to complete his bachelor's degree. He hopes his B.S. in international business will help him land a job with a global company.

g. **Days of the week; months; holidays; holy days and names; historical events, periods, and documents; and seasons.**

TABLE D.12 Capitalizing Place Names

OFFICIAL PLACE NAME: CAPITALIZE	GENERAL CATEGORY: DON'T CAPITALIZE
West Virginia	the western Virginia plateau
Woodrow Wilson High School graduate	high school graduate
Miami International Airport	the Miami airport
Seattle is in the Pacific Northwest.	Is Seattle northwest of Tacoma?
The Office of the Vice President is on the third floor of the Arnold Administration Building.	The vice president's office is on the third floor of the administration building.

Tuesday	Easter	Labor Day	The Great Depression
November	Ramadan	Yom Kippur	the Fourth of July
Black Friday	Allah	Treaty of Versailles	the Middle Ages

Do not capitalize seasons: *summer* vacation, last *spring*, *midwinter* doldrums, *fall* foliage.

h. **Titles of works.** Capitalize the first word of a title and all other words except articles (*a, an, the*) and prepositions (for example, *for, to, in, from*). Some styles recommend capitalizing prepositions longer than five or more letters, such as *before, after*, and *inside*. The first word following the colon in a subtitle is always capitalized, even if it is a preposition or article.

The Wealth of Nations   *The Wall Street Journal*

BusinessWeek   "Why China Is No Match for the Internet"

Predictably Irrational: The Hidden Forces That Shape Our Decisions

From Here to Eternity

3.2. Numbers

The conventions for expressing numbers vary from field to field. Historians spell out numbers from one to 100; psychologists spell out only those less than 10. Lawyers may follow a number expressed as a word with the figure (numerals) in parentheses; business people do not. Chemists use decimals instead of fractions to indicate parts of a whole. As a general rule, the more numbers are used in a field, the more likely they are to be expressed as figures rather than words. Business is such a field.

3.2.1. Words vs. Figures

Amounts expressed as figures in a sentence are usually easier to read than amounts expressed as words. Consequently, business writers generally express only numbers from one through nine as words and use figures for 10 and greater: *four* customers, *24* orders.

Use commas in numbers of four figures or more: *2,400*; *76,000,000*. Numbers of one million or more can be expressed in a combination of figures and words: *12 billion* light years, *6.2 million* people.

> **NUMBER ALERT!** FIGURES IN PARENTHESES
>
> Do not follow a number expressed as a word with a parenthetical figure for the same number.
>
>   **Incorrect**   We are shipping three (3) printers by UPS.
>
>   **Revised**   We are shipping three printers by UPS.
>
> Although technical and legal writing sometimes follow this practice, business writing does not. The repetition is unnecessary.

3.2.2. Consecutive Numbers

Unrelated numbers that appear next to each other should be separated by a comma to avoid confusion. If the sentence remains potentially confusing, reorder the words.

Of the three, two shipments were damaged.

The report stated that in 2010, 468 orders were delayed.

The report stated that 468 orders were delayed in 2010.

3.2.3. Related Numbers

Related numbers appearing in the same sentence or same paragraph should be expressed in the same way. Opinions differ regarding whether to use figures or words. However, readers appreciate simplicity: if any of the numbers is greater than 10, use figures.

Members of Congress against the law outnumber those in favor by 10 to 1.

While most auto enthusiasts own 3 or 4 cars, John owns more than 20.

3.2.4. Indefinite or Approximate Numbers

Spell out numbers that express approximate quantities: *hundreds* of tickets, *tens* of *thousands* of gallons, *millions* of dollars.

3.2.5. Numbers at the Beginning of Sentences

Always spell out a number that begins a sentence, even if it would ordinarily be written as a figure.

Fifty thousand students from India are studying in the United States today.

If spelling out the number makes the sentence awkward, rewrite it so that another word comes first.

   Awkward   Two-thousand seven was the beginning of a severe economic recession.

   Revised   In 2007, a severe economic recession began.

3.2.6. Fractions and Ordinals

Express fractions as words, unless the fraction is a mixed number (a whole number and a fraction).

Only one-third of the members were present, so we did not have a quorum.

The administrative staff is 1 1/2 times larger than it was 10 years ago.

Express ordinals (*first, second, tenth*, and so on) as words, unless they are longer than one word.

The board always meets on the fourth Tuesday, which is the 25th of this month.

3.2.7. Decimals and Percentages

Express decimals as figures. To avoid misreading, place a zero before the decimal if there is no whole number.

We drove 388.4 miles on one tank of gas, but ran out of fuel 0.6 miles from home.

More than 2.8 million bachelor's degrees in science and engineering were awarded worldwide in 2003; Asian students earned 1.2 million of them.

Express percentages as figures, followed by the word *percent*. Use the % symbol only in tables, charts, and graphs.

> Science and engineering jobs are increasing 5 percent per year.

3.2.8. Money

Express precise amounts of money in figures, but do not use decimals and zeros with whole amounts: *$14.25*; a *$50* check (not a $50.00 check); *$5* worth of quarters (not $5.00 worth); a condominium priced at *$389,000*.

Express indefinite or approximate amounts of money in words: *almost thirty* pesos; a *few hundred* euros; *over a trillion* dollars.

Express amounts of money of one million or more by combining figures and words: *$2.5 million*; *€ 30 billion*.

3.2.9. Dates and Times

In U.S. business documents, dates are usually written month, day, year. Place a comma between the day and the year. When the date occurs in a sentence, place a comma after the year also. Incomplete dates have no commas. Many other countries use international style: day, month, and year, with no commas. In either case, express dates in figures, spelling out the month.

> June 14, 2010   June 2010   June 14   14 June 2010
>
> The contract was signed on June 14, 2010, after all parties had agreed to terms.

Express hours and minutes as figures when using AM and PM in small caps (also spelled a.m. and p.m.). Use words with fractional times and with *o'clock*. Times on the hour do not require zeros unless the sentence contains another time in hours and minutes.

> 10:45 AM   eleven o'clock   half past eight
> from 4:00 PM to 5:30 PM   from 4 PM to 5 PM

3.2.10. Measurements and Compound-Number Adjectives

Express precise units of measurement in figures, even if the number is less than 10. Within a sentence, spell out the unit name, rather than abbreviating it: the room measured *9 feet* by *12 feet*. In the case of compound-number adjectives, when quantities and units are next to each other, write one number as a word and the other as a figure to avoid confusion. Spell out the first of the two or the shorter of the two.

> six 10-foot poles   24 two-liter bottles   8 two-ton trucks

3.2.11. Addresses and Telephone Numbers

If you have direct information about how to write a specific address—for example, from letterhead stationery, the return address on an envelope, the signature block with address from an email, or an example from a website—use the same format. Lacking direct information, use the following guidelines.

Express street numbers from one through nine in words; use figures for those 10 and higher. Express building numbers

as figures, except for the number one. Ordinarily in formal business correspondence, words that are part of the address, such as *street, avenue, boulevard, place, way, terrace,* and compass points (*north, west,* and so on), are not abbreviated.

> 305 Fourth Avenue   One West 16th Street
> 1437 Wooten Parkway

Use figures for highway numbers: I-80, U.S. 17, A-5.

Telephone numbers are always expressed as figures. Although the U.S. style is to place a hyphen between the parts of a telephone number, with the globalization of business the trend is to adopt international style, which places one space between the international code, country code, city code, and number.

> **U.S. Style**   1-505-555-4523
> **International Style** 001 505 555 4523

3.3. Abbreviations, Acronyms, and Initialisms

Abbreviations, acronyms, and initialisms are a kind of shorthand, allowing writers to avoid awkward, laborious repetition of lengthy names and terminology. They work fine when everyone knows what they mean, when they do not create confusion, and when writers follow generally accepted guidelines.

3.3.1. Definitions, Forms, and Functions

a. **Abbreviations.** An **abbreviation** is a shortened version of a word or series of words, usually formed by cropping or contracting the word or by combining the first letter of each word: *Dr.* (doctor), *Mr.* (mister), *Pres.*, (president), *etc.* (et cetera).

b. **Acronyms.** An **acronym** is an abbreviation formed from the first letters of a series of words, with the combination pronounced as a word: scuba (self-contained underwater breathing apparatus), OSHA (Occupational Safety and Health Administration), UNICEF (United Nations Children's Emergency Fund).

c. **Initialisms.** An **initialism** is an abbreviation formed from the first letters of a series of words, but the letters are pronounced separately: CIA (Central Intelligence Agency), MIT (Massachusetts Institute of Technology), PM (post meridian), UPS (United Parcel Service), CEO (chief executive officer), ROI (return on investment), mph (miles per hour).

3.3.2. When to Use Abbreviations—or Not

Within the text of business documents, generally do not use abbreviations unless they are well known to your readers. Remember that abbreviations common to a particular business or subject may be unfamiliar to readers outside that field. In general, save abbreviations for tables, charts, graphs, and other places where space is limited.

When you feel an abbreviation is appropriate (to avoid repetition of a lengthy name or term, for instance), always spell out the term in its first use and write the abbreviation in parentheses unless it is commonly understood, and cannot be confused with some other term. For example, AMA can stand for either the American Management Association or the American

Medical Association, so it needs to be spelled out at the first use: *He is a member of the American Management Association (AMA). He became president of the AMA last year.* In some cases, an abbreviation may be more widely recognized than the name for which it stands and therefore not require being spelled out at the first use: for example, FBI (Federal Bureau of Investigation). Assess your audience, and act accordingly. When in doubt, provide the parenthetical information.

The following guidelines will help you decide how and when to abbreviate.

a. **Titles before names.** Except for *Mr., Mrs., Ms.,* and *Dr.,* courtesy and professional titles are generally spelled out in formal business writing.

   Ms. Eames   Dr. Sanchez   Senator Lewkowski

   President Lee   Lieutenant Wells   Professor Jones

b. **Titles appearing independently or following names.** Academic, religious, military, and civilian titles that follow a proper name or stand alone should not be abbreviated: John Wells, the *lieutenant* who handled the arrest, appeared as a witness for the prosecution.

c. **Academic degrees and professional certifications.** Degrees and certifications are abbreviated when they follow a proper name. These abbreviations can also stand by themselves. However, do not use both a professional title before a name and the equivalent degree after it.

   | Incorrect | Dr. Lenora Sanchez, MD, also holds a PhD from Stanford. |
   | Correct | Lenora Sanchez, MD, also holds a PhD from Stanford. |

d. **Company names.** Use abbreviations for only those words that the company itself abbreviates: Eli Lilly and *Company,* but Barnes *&* Noble, *Inc., IBM, AT&T.*

e. **Names of people; countries, states, and place names; days, months, and holidays; organizational units; and academic subjects.** Ordinarily, spell out first names. Use initials if that is what the individual uses professionally or prefers: *I. F.* Stone, Dr. *H. C.* Brown. Countries and states may be abbreviated when part of mailing addresses, but should be spelled out in the text of documents. Days and months are often abbreviated in informal notes and emails but should be spelled out in more formal documents. Similarly, organizational units (such as departments and divisions) as well as academic subjects should be spelled out.

   | Incorrect | Chas. was transferred to our biochem div. in the UK during Mar. but he emailed his report last Tues. in time for the BOT meeting. |
   | Correct | Charles was transferred to our biochemistry division in the United Kingdom during March, but he emailed his report last Tuesday in time for the board of trustees meeting. |

f. **Units of measurement, times, and dates.** Use abbreviations for units of measurement when they are expressed as figures—13 *oz*, 28 *mpg*, 6 *ft* 2 *in.*—unless they are in full sentences. Then spell them out (see 3.2.10). Use abbreviations for exact times and dates: 9:30 *AM*, 4:00 *PM*, 800 *BC*, *AD* 1603

3.3.3. Spacing and Punctuation of Abbreviations

For most **lowercase abbreviations** that stand for multiple words, put a period after each letter of the abbreviation with no spaces between them: *i.e., e.g., c.o.d.*

Exceptions are lowercase abbreviations for precise units of measurement following figures. These are abbreviated without periods with one space between the figure and the abbreviation: for example, *23 mpg, 65 mph, 90 wpm, 10 ft, 7 in, 3 yd, 5 gal, 40 km, 3 1/2 tsp, 2 mg.* Note that the singular and plural forms are the same when used with figures: *3 yd,* not *3 yds.*

Most **capitalized abbreviations** do not use periods or internal spaces: *MD, RN, CPA, ACLU, IRS, SEC.* Opinions differ on whether abbreviations for academic degrees such as Ph.D., M.S., and B.A. should contain periods; however, the trend is toward omitting them: *PhD, MS, BA.*

■ 4. Spelling

Use your computer's spell checker to help you edit your work. However, it is important to proofread documents carefully and more than once. Spell checkers will not catch homonyms (words that are similar in sound but different in meaning: *council, counsel; to, two*), misspelled proper names, dropped endings, and other errors. The following "rules of thumb" can help you deal with some of the spelling questions that occur most often.

4.1. Four Rules of Thumb for Adding Endings

a. **Suffix added to one-syllable word.** Double the final consonant before the suffix if a vowel precedes the consonant and the suffix begins with a vowel. Do not double the final consonant if the suffix begins with a consonant. TABLE D.13 illustrates this rule.

TABLE D.13 Adding a Suffix to a One-Syllable Word

VOWEL PRECEDES CONSONANT	SUFFIX BEGINS WITH VOWEL: DOUBLE FINAL CONSONANT	VOWEL PRECEDES CONSONANT	SUFFIX BEGINS WITH CONSONANT: DO NOT DOUBLE FINAL CONSONANT
stop	sto**pp**ing	live	live**ly**
drop	dro**pp**ed	fit	fit**ness**
put	pu**tt**ing	Ship	ship**ment**

TABLE D.14 Adding a Suffix to a Word Ending with -*e*

ROOT FORM	SUFFIX BEGINS WITH VOWEL: DROP FINAL -*e*	ROOT FORM	SUFFIX BEGINS WITH CONSONANT: RETAIN FINAL -*e*
locate	loca*tion*	manage	manag*ement*
use	us*able*	use	us*eful*
come	com*ing*	sure	sur*ely*

TABLE D.15 Adding a Suffix to a Word Ending with -*y*

ROOT FORM	SUFFIX BEGINS WITH LETTER OTHER THAN *i*: CHANGE -*y* TO *i*	ROOT FORM	SUFFIX BEGINS WITH *i*: RETAIN FINAL -*y*
mercy	merci*ful*	comply	compl*ying*
ninety	ninet*ieth*	rectify	rectif*ying*
company	compan*ies*	thirty	thirty*ish*
deny	den*ial*	deny	den*ying*

b. **Stress on final syllable.** Double the final consonant before a suffix if the last syllable is accented: *submit, submitted; occur, occurrence; regret, regretted; propel, propeller.* Note that for suffixes added to *program,* the -*m* may or may not be doubled. Both are considered correct: *programmed, programed; programming, programing.* Just make the spelling consistent throughout the document.

c. **Final -*e* dropped.** For words ending in -*e*, drop the -*e* before the suffix if the suffix begins with a vowel but not if the suffix begins with a consonant. TABLE D.14 illustrates this rule.

The -*e* is retained after a soft *c* or *g* before *a* or *o*: *noticeable, changeable.* It is dropped in some words taking the suffix -*ful*, -*ly*, or -*ment*: *awe, awful; due, duly; true, truly; judge, judgment; acknowledge, acknowledgment.*

d. **Final -*y* changed to *i*.** For words ending in -*y*, change the *y* to *i* unless the suffix begins with *i*. TABLE D.15 illustrates this rule.

4.2. Memory Aids for *ie* and *ei*

The rhyming jingle heading in TABLE D.16 will help you remember whether to choose *ie* or *ei*. Common exceptions to this rule include *either, neither, leisure, foreigners, height, seize, being* and *weird.*

TABLE D.16 Choosing *ie* or *ei*

WRITE *i* BEFORE *e*	EXCEPT AFTER *c*	OR WHEN SOUNDED LIKE *a* AS IN *NEIGHBOR* AND *WEIGH*
relief	conceive	eight
believe	ceiling	freight
yield	deceive	reign
wield	receive	vein

4.3. Commonly Misspelled Words

Spelling a word correctly from memory is still faster than using a spell checker. All of us have personal spelling challenges that we simply have to keep working on throughout our careers. The following list contains words that are frequently misspelled in business writing. Renew your efforts to master the ones that are problems for you.

absence	alignment	assistant	campaign
accessible	all right	attendance	canceled
accommodate	amateur	bankruptcy	catalog
achieve	among	believable	ceiling
acknowledgment	analyze	benefited	changeable
advisable	annually	bulletin	collateral
advantageous	apparent	bureau	column
aggressive	argument	calendar	committee

competitor	existence	maintenance	questionnaire
concede	extraordinary	manageable	receipt
conceive	familiar	mileage	receive
congratulations	fascinate	misspell	recommend
consensus	feasible	mortgage	remittance
convenient	flexible	necessary	repetition
courteous	foreign	negligence	restaurant
criticism	forty	negotiable	rhythm
debt	fourth	ninety	ridiculous
deceive	freight	noticeable	secretary
definitely	government	occasional	seize
description	grateful	occurrence	separate
desirable	guarantee	omission	sergeant
develop	harass	omitted	sincerely
dilemma	hors d' oeuvre	opportunity	succeed
disappoint	illegible	paid	suddenness
disbursement	immediate	parallel	surprise
discrepancy	incidentally	pastime	tenant
dissatisfied	independent	perceive	thorough
efficient	indispensable	permanent	truly
eighth	irresistible	personnel	unanimous
eligible	itinerary	persuade	until
embarrassment	jewelry	precede	usable
emphasis	judgment	prerogative	usage
entrepreneur	knowledgeable	privilege	vacuum
environment	labeling	procedure	volume
emphasize	legitimate	proceed	weird
especially	leisure	profited	yield
exaggerate	license	pursue	

4.4. Commonly Confused Words

The following words are homonyms, or near homonyms—words that sound the same but have different spellings and meanings. Spell checkers won't catch these confusions. Check your writing to be sure you have chosen the correct word and spelling for the meaning you intend.

accede	to agree to		assure	to inform confidently
exceed	to go beyond		ensure	to make certain
accept	to receive		insure	to protect from financial loss
except	to exclude		biannual	occurring twice a year
access	to gain admittance		biennial	occurring every two years
excess	too much, more than enough		capital	money or wealth; seat of government
advice	(noun) a suggestion		capitol	building housing state or national governing body
advise	(verb) to suggest			
affect	to influence		choose	(present-tense verb) to select
effect	(verb) to bring about; (noun) result		chose	past tense of *choose*
aid	(verb) to help		cite	to quote or refer to
aide	(noun) an assistant		sight	to see, the ability to see
allowed	permitted		site	location
aloud	audible, out loud		coarse	rough in texture, not delicate
all ready	prepared		course	route taken, movement in a direction, duration
already	previously, by now			
ascent	act of rising		complement	to add to or complete
assent	agreement		compliment	to flatter

conscience	sense of right and wrong	moral	virtuous, good character; lesson of a story or tale
conscious	aware, alert	morale	state of mind, sense of well-being
council	governing body or advisory group	overdo	to act in excess
counsel	(verb) to advise; (noun) advice, a lawyer	overdue	past the due date, unpaid
defer	to put off until later	passed	(verb) to move, go around, hand out
differ	to be different from; to disagree	past	(noun, adjective) time before the present
desert	to abandon; arid wasteland	patience	willingness to wait, perseverance
dessert	last course of a meal, usually sweet	patients	recipients of medical treatment
device	a mechanism or instrument	peace	absence of conflict
devise	to plan, create, arrange	piece	a portion, fragment
disburse	to pay out	pedal	a foot lever
disperse	to scatter	peddle	to sell
discreet	careful, circumspect	persecute	to torment
discrete	separate, individual	prosecute	to bring legal action
do	to perform, fulfill, complete	personal	individual, private
due	payable, debt owed	personnel	employees
elicit	to draw out	populace	the population, the people
illicit	illegal, unlawful	populous	densely populated
eligible	qualified, worthy	precede	(verb) to come before
illegible	not legible, impossible to read	proceed	(verb) to move ahead, advance
envelop	to surround	principal	chief or main; leader or head; sum of money
envelope	container for a letter	principle	basic law or general rule
everyday	ordinary	right	correct
every day	each day	rite	ceremony
farther	a greater distance	write	to form words on a surface
further	additional	role	a part that one plays
forth	forward	roll	(noun) a list; (verb) to tumble
fourth	ordinal form of the number four	stationary	fixed, not moving
holey	full of holes	stationery	writing paper
holy	sacred	than	as compared with
wholly	entirely, completely	then	at that time
hear	(verb) to perceive by ear	their	(pronoun) possessive form of *they*, belonging to them
here	at or in this place	there	(adverb) in that place
human	characteristic of humans	they're	contraction for *they are*
humane	kind	to	(preposition) suggesting "toward"
incidence	frequency	too	(adverb) also, an excessive degree
incidents	events, occurrences	two	the number
imply	to express indirectly, to suggest	vain	futile, useless; excessive pride in appearance or achievements
infer	to conclude from evidence, deduce	vein	tubular, branching vessel; bed of minerals; line of thought or action
instance	example, case	waist	area between rib cage and pelvis
instants	brief moments, seconds	waste	(verb) to use carelessly (noun) undesirable by-product
interstate	between states	waive, waiver	to set aside; intentional relinquishment of right or claim
intrastate	within a state	wave	a swell of water; a sweeping gesture
its	possessive form of *it*	weather	atmospheric conditions
it's	contraction for *it is*	whether	if
later	afterward	who's	contraction for *who is*
latter	the second or last of two	whose	possessive form of *who*
lay	to place, put down	your	possessive form of *you*
lie	to recline	you're	contraction for *you are*
lead	chemical element, metal; (verb) to guide		
led	(verb) past tense of lead, guided		
lean	to rest at an angle		
lien	a claim against property for debt		
loose	not tight; (verb) to free		
lose	to misplace, to be deprived of		
miner	a person who works in a mine		
minor	a person who is not of legal age; something comparatively less		

Appendix E

Answer Key to Grammar Exercises

Chapter 1   Nouns and Pronouns
(See Appendix D, Section 1.1.1.)

Rekey (or download from mybcommlab.com) the following paragraph, correcting the errors in use or formation of nouns and pronouns. Underline all your corrections.

> Whomever answers the phone may be the only contact a caller has with a business. Everyone has their own personal preferences. However, find out how your employer wants the telephone answered, what your expected to say. When you pick up the phone, its important to speak politely and provide identifying information. Clearly state the company's name and you're name. Should you identify the Department, too?
>
> These are the kinds of question's to settle before the phone rings. If the caller asks for you by name, say, "This is me." Don't leave the caller wondering who he or she has reached. Remember that when on the telephone at work, you are the Company.

Answer:

The 10 correct answers are highlighted in color and listed in the order they appear in the paragraph.

1. Whoever answers
2. Everyone has his or her own
3. what you're expected
4. the phone, it's important
5. and your name.
6. identify the department
7. kinds of questions to settle
8. "This is I."
9. wondering whom he
10. you are the company.

Chapter 2   Verbs
(See Appendix D, Section 1.1.2.)

Rekey (or download from mybcommlab.com) the following paragraph, correcting the errors in use or formation of verbs. Underline all your corrections.

> If my first boss had ran his businesses the way he answered the phone, he would have went broke long ago. Usually he grabbed the receiver and growls, "Barker." The person at the other end probably thought, "That don't that sound

like a human, more like a rottweiler." If George Barker was a dog, he would probably be more courteous on the phone. No doubt there was lots of offended customers. The other day he asked my co-worker, Jess, and me to stop by his office. He still answer the phone the same way. George's phone offenses amounts to quite a long list. Instead of "barking," there is several other things he could say. "Hello, Barker Contracting" or "This is George Barker" make a better impression.

Answer:

The 10 correct answers are highlighted in color and listed in the order they appear in the paragraph.

1. If my first boss had run
2. have gone broke
3. he grabs the receiver
4. "That doesn't sound
5. Barker were a dog,
6. there were lots
7. still answers the phone
8. offenses amount to
9. there are several
10. George Barker" makes a better impression.

Chapter 3   Adjectives and Adverbs
(See Appendix D, Section 1.1.3.)

Rekey (or download from mybcommlab.com) the following paragraph, correcting the errors in use or formation of adjectives and adverbs. Underline all your corrections.

> Does your telephone etiquette speak good of you? Because most people answer their own phones at work, poor phone manners make both you and your company look badly. Which greeting will make the best impression: "How may I help you?" or "What do you want?" It is important to sound cheerfully on the phone.
>
> Even if you don't feel well, try to respond positively. A more simple way to sound positive is to smile when speaking. Smiling actually does make a person seem more friendlier over the phone. Some people like to have the most unique telephone greeting in the office: "Yo, super service representative Skip speaking!" A greeting like that just makes "Skip" seem real unprofessional. Instead of being named "Best Employee of the Month," he is likely to be awarded "Worse Phone Manners of the Year."

Answer:

The 10 correct answers are highlighted in color and listed in the order they appear in the paragraph.

❶ speak well
❷ look bad.
❸ make the better impression
❹ sound cheerful
❺ feel good,
❻ A simpler way
❼ more friendly
❽ have a unique telephone greeting [eliminate "in the office"]
❾ seem really unprofessional.
❿ "Worst Phone Manners

Chapter 4   Prepositions and Conjunctions
(See Appendix D, Section 1.1.4.)

In the following paragraph, identify the prepositions (P), coordinating conjunctions (CC), correlative conjunctions (CorC), subordinating conjunctions (SC), and conjunctive adverbs (CA). There are a total of 10 prepositions and conjunctions. Count correlative conjunction pairs as one.

> The way you begin a business call is very important; however, the conclusion is equally important. Have you ever been caught in an awkward spot, wondering who should end the call? If you initiated the call, the convention is for you to conclude it. After you have obtained the information you need, thank the person you called and then say good-bye. The person at the other end either can just say good-bye or can end with a pleasantry: for example, "I'm glad I could help."

Answer:

The 10 prepositions and conjunctions are highlighted in color and listed in the order they appear in the paragraph. Correlative conjunction pairs are counted as one.

❶ important; however (CA),
❷ caught in (P) an awkward spot
❸ If (SC) you
❹ is for (P) you
❺ After (SC) you
❻ called and (CC) then
❼ person at (P) the other
❽ either (CorC) can . . . or (CorC) can
❾ with (P) a pleasantry
❿ for (P) example

Chapter 5   Phrases and Clauses
(See Appendix D, Section 1.2.2.)

In the following paragraph, circle or highlight each phrase. Underline each dependent clause once and each independent clause twice. There are a total of 10 dependent and independent clauses and a total of 15 phrases.

> In the list of tech-etiquette offenders, the "misguided multitasker" may be the worst, although the "broadcaster" is a close second. Holding their BlackBerries under the table, multitaskers send email or text messages during meetings. The nonverbal message that they are sending to everyone else is that the meeting is not important to them. Broadcasters use their cell phones anytime, anywhere, and they apparently don't mind being overheard by others. On a crowded elevator, they will discuss the intimate details of a medical procedure or talk loudly about confidential business matters.

Answer:

The phrases are highlighted in color, with the type of phrase indicated in parentheses: noun (N), verb (V), prepostion (Pr), or participial (Pa). The dependent clauses are underlined once, and independent clauses are underlined twice. There are a total of 10 clauses and a total of 15 phrases.

> In the list (P) of tech-etiquette offenders (P), the "misguided multitasker" may be (V) the worst, although the "broadcaster" is a close second. Holding their BlackBerries (Pa) under the table (P), multitaskers send email or text messages during meetings (P). The nonverbal message that they are sending (V) to everyone else (P) is that the meeting is not important to them (P). Broadcasters use their cell phones anytime, anywhere, and they apparently don't mind being overheard (N) by others (P). On a crowded elevator (P), they will discuss (V) the intimate details of a medical procedure (P) or they will talk loudly about confidential business matters (P).

Chapter 6   Common Sentence Errors: Run-Ons and Comma Splices
(See Appendix D, Section 1.3.)

Rekey (or download from mybcommlab.com) the following paragraph, correcting the 10 run-on or fused sentences and comma splices. Underline all your corrections.

> One business etiquette consultant believes that good telephone manners begin in childhood, children should be taught how to answer the phone courteously and take messages. Diane Eaves says, "I work with a lot of people who are technically ready for work however, they apparently missed a lot of the teaching of manners." For instance, asking who is calling can be taught in childhood then it will be a habit. Parents know how annoying it is to have a child report that "somebody called and wants you to call back" Sonny doesn't remember who it was and didn't write down the number. Thank goodness for caller ID it can be a big help, nevertheless, children should be taught to ask for and write down names and numbers. It's surprising how many people don't identify themselves when they make business calls, they expect listeners to recognize their voice. That may be OK if you speak frequently with the caller on the other hand it's mystifying when a voice you don't recognize launches right into a subject. It is the caller's responsibility to identify

himself or herself, if he or she doesn't you can politely say, "Excuse me, I didn't catch your name."

Answer:

The 10 run-on (RO) sentences and commas splices (CS) are identified in the first paragraph. They are corrected in the second paragraph.

Run-Ons (RO) and Comma Splices (CS) Identified

One business etiquette consultant believes that good telephone manners begin in childhood, (CS) children should be taught how to answer the phone courteously and take messages. Diane Eaves says, "I work with a lot of people who are technically ready for work (RO) however, they apparently missed a lot of the teaching of manners." For instance, asking who is calling can be taught in childhood (RO) then it will be a habit. Parents know how annoying it is to have a child report that "somebody called and wants you to call back" (RO) Sonny doesn't remember who it was and didn't write down the number. Thank goodness for caller ID (RO) it can be a big help, (CS) nevertheless, children should be taught to ask for and write down names and numbers. It's surprising how many people don't identify themselves when they make business calls, (CS) they expect listeners to recognize their voice. That may be OK if you speak frequently with the caller (RO) on the other hand it's mystifying when a voice you don't recognize launches right into a subject. It is the caller's responsibility to identify himself or herself, (CS) if he or she doesn't you can politely say, "Excuse me, (CS) I didn't catch your name."

Run-Ons and Comma Splices Corrected
(answers will vary)

One business etiquette consultant believes that good telephone manners begin in childhood. Children should be taught how to answer the phone courteously and take messages. Diane Eaves says, "I work with a lot of people who are technically ready for work; however, they apparently missed a lot of the teaching of manners." For instance, asking who is calling can be taught in childhood; then it will be a habit. Parents know how annoying it is to have a child report that "somebody called and wants you to call back." Sonny doesn't remember who it was and didn't write down the number. Thank goodness for caller ID. It can be a big help. Nevertheless, children should be taught to ask for and write down names and numbers. It's surprising how many people don't identify themselves when they make business calls. They expect listeners to recognize their voice. That may be OK if you speak frequently with the caller. On the other hand it's mystifying when a voice you don't recognize launches right into a subject. It is the caller's responsibility to identify himself or herself. If he or she doesn't, you can politely say, "Excuse me. I didn't catch your name."

Chapter 7   Common Sentence Errors: Subject-Verb Agreement
(See Appendix D—Section 1.3.)

Rekey the following paragraph (or download a copy from mybcommlab.com and edit), correcting the 10 errors in subject-verb agreement. Underline all your corrections.

When making a business call, being put on hold for countless minutes fray even patient people's nerves. Having to wait, as well as not knowing for how long, are upsetting. Each of us have our own way of coping with this irritant. *The Sounds of Silence* apply not only to the Simon and Garfunkle song but also to endless minutes on hold. Three minutes feel like forever to the person waiting. If you must put someone on hold, there is several things you should do. First, ask, "May I put you on hold?" and then give the caller an estimate of the probable waiting time. The person on the other end might be one of those callers who really need to know how long the wait might be. The unknown number of minutes are what drive people crazy. Data collected by Hold On America, Inc., shows that callers become frustrated after 20 seconds. After 90 seconds, 50 percent of callers hangs up.

Answer:

The 10 subject-verb agreement errors are highlighted in color in the first paragraph. They are corrected in the second paragraph.

Agreement Errors Identified

When making a business call, being put on hold for countless minutes fray even patient people's nerves. Having to wait, as well as not knowing for how long, are upsetting. Each of us have our own way of coping with this irritant. *The Sounds of Silence* apply not only to the Simon and Garfunkle song but also to endless minutes on hold. Three minutes feel like forever to the person waiting. If you must put someone on hold, there is several things you should do. First, ask, "May I put you on hold?" and then give the caller an estimate of the probable waiting time. The person on the other end might be one of those callers who really need to know how long the wait might be. The unknown number of minutes are what drive people crazy. Data collected by Hold On America, Inc., shows that callers become frustrated after 20 seconds. After 90 seconds, 50 percent of callers hangs up.

Verbs Corrected

When making a business call, being put on hold for countless minutes frays even patient people's nerves. Having to wait, as well as not knowing for how long, is upsetting. Each of us has our own way of coping with this irritant. *The Sounds of Silence* applies not only to the Simon and Garfunkle song but also to endless minutes on hold. Three minutes feels like forever to the person waiting. If you must put someone on hold, there are several things you should do. First, ask, "May I put you on hold?" and then give the caller an estimate of the probable waiting time. The person on the other end might be one of those callers who really needs to know how long the wait might be. The unknown number of minutes is what drives people crazy. Data collected by Hold On America, Inc., show that callers become frustrated after 20 seconds. After 90 seconds, 50 percent of callers hang up.

Common Sentence Errors: Pronoun-Antecedent Agreement
(See Appendix D—Section 1.3.)

Rekey (or download from mybcommlab.com) the following paragraph, correcting the 10 errors in pronoun-antecedent agreement. Underline all your corrections.

Everybody has preferences about their communication tools. A person may prefer email rather than telephone, so they might respond to a voicemail message by sending an email instead of returning the call. If you ask either of my managers, Jenny or Kurt, they will tell you that I would rather email them. Business professionals will often choose the one with which he or she is most at ease. Considering its total number of calls versus emails per month, the sales team obviously would rather talk than write. Each of these communication media has their advantages and disadvantages. Text messages and email may be best because it will be delivered whether the recipient is there or not. On the other hand, someone who leaves a voicemail message probably assumes you will call them back, not send a text. Otherwise, they would have texted you instead of calling.

Answer:

The 10 pronoun-antecedent agreement errors are highlighted in color in the first paragraph (The antecedent is in blue and the pronoun is in red). They are corrected in the second paragraph. (The corrections are in red and alternative options are in parentheses in blue).

Agreement Errors Identified

Everybody has preferences about their communication tools. A person may prefer email rather than telephone, so they might respond to a voicemail message by sending an email instead of returning the call. If you ask either of my managers, Jenny or Kurt, they will tell you that I would rather email them. Business professionals will often choose the one with which he or she is most at ease. Considering its total number of calls versus emails per month, the sales team obviously would rather talk than write. Each of these communication media has their advantages and disadvantages. Text messages and email may be best because it will be delivered whether the recipient is there or not. On the other hand, someone who leaves a voicemail message probably assumes you will call them back, not send a text. Otherwise, they would have texted you instead of calling.

Agreement Errors Corrected

Everybody has preferences about his or her communication tools. A person (people) may prefer email rather than telephone, so he or she (they) might respond to a voicemail message by sending an email instead of returning the call. If you ask either of my managers, Jenny or Kurt, she or he will tell you that I would rather email her or him. Business professionals will often choose the one with which they are most at ease. Considering their total number of calls versus emails per month, the sales team obviously would rather talk than write. Each of these communication media has its advantages and disadvantages. Text messages and email may be best because they will be delivered whether the recipient is there or not. On the other hand, someone (people) who leaves (leave) a voicemail message probably assumes you will call him or her (them) back, not send a text. Otherwise, he or she (they) would have texted you instead of calling.

Chapter 8 Commas: Clauses and Phrases
(See Appendix D—Section 2.2.)

Rekey (or download from mybcommlab.com) the following paragraph, correcting the 10 errors in the use of commas with independent clauses, dependent clauses, and phrases. Underline all your corrections.

Although most final job interviews are face to face telephone interviews have become common for screening interviews. Employers find that phone interviews are not only economical but they are also an effective way to determine which candidates merit a closer look. While you are on the job market a potential employer or networking contact might call, and ask, "Do you have a few minutes to talk?" Being interviewed over the phone isn't easy so you need to be prepared. What initially seems like an informal conversation about a job might actually be the first round of screening, or the first test of your communication skills. After the initial introductions and pleasantries let the caller take the lead, and guide the conversation. When you answer questions keep your responses short and to the point. The caller will ask follow-up questions if necessary, and will bring the interview to a close.

Answer:

The 10 correct uses of commas are highlighted in color and listed in the order they appear in the paragraph. The reason for each is given in parentheses.

1. Although . . . face to face, telephone (introductory dependent clause)
2. economical, but they are (independent clauses joined by coordinating conjunction)
3. While . . . job market, a potential employer (introductory dependent clause)
4. might call and (compound predicate requires no comma)
5. isn't easy, so you (independent clauses joined by coordinating conjunction)
6. screening or the first test (compound predicate requires no comma)
7. pleasantries, let the caller (long introductory phrase)
8. take the lead and guide (compound predicate requires no comma)
9. When you answer questions, keep (introductory dependent clause)
10. if necessary and will bring (compound predicate requires no comma; "if necessary" requires no special emphasis)

Commas: Coordinates, Cumulatives, and Series
(See Appendix D—Section 2.2.)

Rekey (or download from mybcommlab.com) the following paragraph, correcting the 10 errors in the use of commas with coordinate and cumulative adjectives and with serial words, phrases, and clauses, Each missing or unnecessary comma counts as one error. Underline all your corrections.

After you have sent out résumés and applied for jobs, be ready willing and able to handle a telephone interview. Keep your résumé a pad and pen and a bottle of water near the phone. You will need your résumé for reference the pad and pen to take notes and the water in case your throat gets dry. Is your cell phone, service, provider reliable, or do you have to worry about dropped calls? If so, consider using a landline. Send roommates, friends, spouses, children and pets from the room when a potential employer calls. You want to be completely calmly focused and undistracted during a telephone interview.

Answers:

The 10 correct uses of commas are highlighted in color and listed in the order they appear in the paragraph. The reason for each is given in parentheses.

❶.❷   ready, willing, and able (coordinate adjectives)

❸.❹.❺   your résumé , a pad and pen, and a bottle (serial elements)

❻.❼   your résumé for reference, the pad and pen to take notes, and the water (serial elements)

❽   cell phone service provider (cumulative adjectives: no commas)

❾   spouses, children, and pets (serial nouns)

❿   completely, calmly focused (coordinate adverbs)

Commas: Restrictive and Nonrestrictive Elements
(See Appendix D—Section 2.2.)

Rekey (or download from mybcommlab.com) the following paragraph, correcting the 13 errors in the use of commas with restrictive, nonrestrictive, or parenthetical words, phrases, or clauses. Each missing or unnecessary comma counts as one error. There are also two mistakes in the use of that, which, or who. Underline all your corrections.

Anyone, who has been through an employment interview, knows it is nerve-wracking. A telephone interview which provides none of the nonverbal cues available in a face-to-face situation can be even trickier. The interviewer's word choice, tone of voice, and level of enthusiasm may therefore be important indicators. The interviewee the person that is being interviewed must listen carefully. The advice, "sit up and pay attention," certainly applies in this situation. Companies, who use telephone interviews for employment screening, have heard it all everything from bad grammar to burping.

Answer:

The 13 errors in the use of commas with restrictive, nonrestrictive, or parenthetical words, phrases, or clauses and the two mistakes in the use of *that, which*, or *who* are highlighted in color. The reason for each is given in parentheses. Each missing or unnecessary comma counts as one error.

❶.❷   Anyone who has . . . interview (restrictive clause identifies who and requires no commas)

❸.❹   interview, which provides . . . situation, can (nonrestrictive clauses requires commas)

❺.❻   may, therefore, be (parenthetical element)

❼.❽   interviewee, the person who is being interviewed, must (nonrestrictive appositive requires commas; *who* is the correct pronoun for referring to a person, *interviewee*)

❾.❿   advice "sit up and pay attention" (restrictive appositive requires no commas)

⓫.⓬   Companies that use telephone interviews for employment screening (restrictive clause requires no commas; *that* is the correct pronoun for referring to a thing, *companies*)

⓭   have heard it all, everything (nonrestrictive appositive explaining *all* requires comma)

Chapter 9   Semicolons and Colons
(See Appendix D—Sections 2.3. and 2.4.)

Rekey (or download from mybcommlab.com) the following paragraph, correcting the 10 errors or omissions in the use of semicolons and colons. Underline all your corrections.

In the online article "How to Give a Professional Voicemail Greeting The Business Etiquette of Voicemail Greetings," author James Bucki asks, "What would I want to know from the voicemail greeting?" The greeting may be perfectly clear to you however, the caller may be mystified. His advice create the greeting as if you were the listener at the other end. As a general rule, the length of a voicemail greeting should be: no longer than 20–25 seconds. Some of the most annoying greetings are: long introductions, greetings that are too casual or personal, and background music of any kind (especially music that drowns out the message). Avoid endings that are not business related (such as "have a blessed day"); because they may strike customers and clients as presumptuous. Here is an example of a bad voicemail greeting; "Hi. This is Accounting. Leave me a message." Callers have no idea whether they have reached the right person; nor do they know if they even have the right company. Too little information is bad, conversely, so is too much information. Business callers don't want personal details, including: the fun spot where you are vacationing; or that you are out sick with the flu.

Answer:

The 10 correct uses of semicolons and colons are highlighted in color and listed in the order they appear in the paragraph. The reason for each is given in parentheses.

❶   "How to . . . Voicemail Greeting: The Business . . . Greetings" (preceding subtitle)

❷   clear to you; however, (independent clause introduced by conjunctive adverb)

❸   His advice: create the greeting (preceding an explanation or rule)

❹   greeting should be (delete colon) no longer (no colon between verb and complement)

❺   greetings are (delete colon) long introductions (no colon between verb and complement)

6 blessed day") (delete semicolon) because they ("because" clause is dependent)

7 voicemail greeting: (colon preceding an illustration)

8 is bad; conversely, so (independent clause introduced by conjunctive adverb)

9 details, including (delete colon) (not preceded by a complete statement)

10 vacationing (delete semicolon) or (not followed by an independent clause)

Quotation Marks and Italics
(See Appendix D—Section 2.5)

Rekey (or download from mybcommlab.com) the following paragraph, correcting the 10 errors or omissions in the use of quotation marks and italics. Count pairs of quotation marks as one. Underline all your corrections.

It's a *good* idea to review the voicemail greeting on your personal phone, especially if potential employers might call. As part of his greeting, my friend Joe recorded John Cleese speaking lines from the *Dead Parrot Sketch* from the British television comedy "Monty Python's Flying Circus." His friends all thought it was really funny, using the words hilarious and clever to describe the greeting. One afternoon he retrieved a phone message that said, You really should use a more professional greeting. The voice continued, I called to offer you a job interview, but I've changed my mind. Joe thought, 'I wouldn't want to work for someone who didn't understand the humor in the "Dead Parrot Sketch", anyway. Sounds like this guy just doesn't get it.' Maybe not, but Joe's chances with that company are kaput.

Answer:

The 10 correct uses of quotation marks and italics are highlighted in color and listed in the order they appear in the paragraph. The reason for each is given in parentheses. Pairs of quotation marks count as one error

1 It's a good idea (the word needs no special emphasis)

2 "Dead Parrot Sketch" (title of a segment, part of a longer work)

3 *Monty Python's Flying Circus* (title of television program, complete work)

4 using the words "hilarious" (direct quotation)

5 and "clever" (direct quotation)

6 "You really . . . greeting." (direct quotation)

7 "I called . . . my mind." (direct quotation)

8,**9** "I wouldn't . . . in the 'Dead Parrot Sketch,' anyway . . . doesn't get it." (quotation and quotation within a quotation)

10 are *kaput*. (2.5.2. foreign word)

Chapter 10   Apostrophes
(See Appendix D—Section 2.6.)

Rekey (or download from mybcommlab.com) the following paragraph, correcting the 10 errors or omissions in the use of apostrophes. Underline all your corrections.

Practicing for a telephone interview will give you confidence that you wont blow the real thing. Ask one of your parents' or a friend to conduct a mock interview with you. Have him or her phone you and ask an interviewers questions. Its also helpful to get a spouses' or father's-in-laws critique of your answers. Ask one of them to listen in, or, whats even more useful, tape record the mock interview for later analysis. Pay attention not only to the content of your answers, but also to the vocal quality; is your's clear, without too many "uhm's," "you knows," and "likes"? The practice sessions payoff is your improved interviewing skills.

Answer:

The 10 correct uses of apostrophes are highlighted in color and listed in the order they appear in the paragraph. The reason for each is given in parentheses.

1 you won't (contraction of *will not*)

2 parents (plural but not possessive)

3 an interviewer's (singular possessive)

4 It's also (contraction of *it is*)

5 spouse's (singular possessive)

6 father-in-law's (singular possessive)

7 what's (contraction of *what is*)

8 Is yours (possessive form of *you*)

9 uhms (not possessive)

10 practice session's (singular possessive)

Parentheses, Dashes, Brackets, and Ellipses
(See Appendix D—Section 2.7.)

Rekey (or download from mybcommlab.com) the following paragraph, inserting parentheses, dashes, brackets, and ellipses where required. There are 10 omissions. Consider pairs of parentheses or brackets as a single omission. Underline all your corrections. In cases where there is more than one possibility, be ready to explain your choice.

The time to research a potential employer is before not after the job interview. Interviewers expect job applicants to know something about a company's products goods or services its markets local, national, international and its operating locations. Job applicants can begin their research on an Internet search engine Google or Bing. Career advisor Martin Reis writes on his blog, "A company's URL Uniform Resource Locator is the gateway to a wealth of information new products, financial statements, press releases, the corporate mission statement. . ." There is something else a company's web site may reveal its corporate culture. Web page photos can provide clues about dress standards casual or traditional, employee diversity ethnicity, gender, age, and community involvement.

Answer:

The 10 correct insertions of parentheses, dashes, brackets, and ellipses are highlighted in color and listed in the order they appear in the paragraph. The reason for each is given in parentheses.

Pairs of dashes, parentheses and brackets are considered a single insertion. Answers may vary.

① before—not after—the job interview. (emphasis)

② a company's products (goods or services), (incidental information)

③ its markets (local, national, international), (incidental information)

④ search engine—Google or Bing. (emphasis on inserted information)

⑤ company's URL [Uniform Resource Locator] (editorial information inserted into direct quotation)

⑥ information—new products (emphasis on inserted information)

⑦ mission statement . . . . "(words omitted from end of direct quotation; requires ellipses and period)

⑧ may reveal—its corporate culture. (emphasis)

⑨ dress standards (casual or traditional), (incidental information)

⑩ employee diversity (ethnicity, gender, age), (incidental information)

Chapter 11   Capitalization
(See Appendix D—Section 3.1.)

Rekey (or download from mybcommlab.com) the following paragraph, correcting the 30 errors or omissions in the use of capital letters. Underline all your corrections.

Robin thompson, owner of etiquette network and Robin Thompson charm school, says, "personal phone calls are fine, so long as you limit them and choose the appropriate time." She also believes cell phones should be turned off at work; If you are at work, that means you have a desk phone and can be reached at that number most of the time. Cell phones and pagers don't belong in business meetings, either, she says. Would you interrupt your Vice President to answer your cell phone? (you wouldn't if you want to keep working for the Company.) Of course, when you are flying to Corporate Headquarters on the West Coast from the Regional Office in north Dakota, a cell phone can be a life saver. Because you had to take your daughter to her spanish lesson, you've missed your plane. The head of the division of specialty products wants that report by 5 PM, president McMillan is expecting you for lunch, and your son forgot to order his date's corsage for the High School prom tonight. Note to self: text son about picking up tuxedo. Instead of a Master's Degree in business, you're thinking maybe you should have majored in Emergency Management. Thank heavens you have a blackberry.

Answer:

The 30 correct uses of capital letters are highlighted in color and listed in the order they appear in the paragraph. The reason for each is given in parentheses.

① Robin Thompson,

② owner of Etiquette

③ Network and

④ Robin Thompson Charm

⑤ School (proper nouns: name of person; name of companies)

⑥ "Personal (first word of sentence)

⑦ work; if you (sentence following a semi-colon requires no capital)

⑧ your vice

⑨ president (common noun)

⑩ (You wouldn't (first word of complete sentence in parentheses)

⑪ the company.) (common noun)

⑫ corporate (common noun)

⑬ headquarters (common noun)

⑭ regional

⑮ office

⑯ North Dakota (proper noun: state)

⑰ Spanish lesson (adjective formed from proper noun: language)

⑱ Division of

⑲ Specialty

⑳ Products (proper noun: official name of part of organization)

㉑ President McMillan (proper noun: official title or position)

㉒ high

㉓ school (common noun)

㉔ Note to self: Text son (first word of complete sentence following a colon)

㉕ master's

㉖ degree (common nouns: generic degree name)

㉗ emergency

㉘ management (common noun: academic major)

㉙ Black

㉚ Berry (proper noun: brand/product name. This product name illustrates "camel case" or "medial capitals": compound words in which the first letters of the parts are capitalized. Names using camel case should always be capitalized as branded or trademarked—for example, PowerPoint.)

Numbers
(See Appendix D—Section 3.2.)

Rekey (or download from mybcommlab.com) the following paragraph, correcting the 15 errors in the use of numbers. Underline all your corrections.

20 years ago mobile phones were novel and expensive. In the nineteen-eighties cellular telephones, luxury items used only by top executives, cost almost $4,000 and weighed more than 2 pounds. Today, of course, even ten-year-olds have them, and the lightest ones weigh two.65 ounces. Some people have more than one mobile phone; imagine carrying 2 2-pound phones in your purse. The International Telecommunications Union estimates that there are approximately 4,6000,000,000 mobile telephones

in use worldwide. That amounts to about sixty percent of the world's population. China ranks number 1 with a little over 57 percent of Chinese using cellular telephones. India ranks 2nd, adding more than six (6) million subscribers a month. According to The Washington Post, nearly ½ of the Indian population has wireless service – 3 times the number of landlines in the country. The United States ranks third, with 91% of us using cell phones.

Answer:

The 15 correct uses of numbers are highlighted in color and listed in the order they appear in the paragraph. The reason for each is given in parentheses.

❶ Twenty years (word, not figure, at beginning of sentence)

❷ In the 1980s (year date)

❸ almost four thousand dollars (approximate amounts of money)

❹ weighed more than two pounds. (approximate measurement)

❺ 10-year-olds (number 10 or greater)

❻ 2.65 ounces. (precise measurement, decimal)

❼ two 2-pound phones (measurements, compound-number adjectives)

❽ approximately 4.6 million (decimals)

❾ about 60 percent (percentage)

❿ number one (number less than 10)

⓫ ranks second (one-word ordinal number)

⓬ more than six million (approximate number; do not use parenthetical figure)

⓭ one-half of (fraction that is not a mixed number)

⓮ three times (number less than 10)

⓯ with 91 percent (*percent* as word when part of paragraph, not table or graph)

Chapter 12 Spelling
(See Appendix D—Section 4.0.)

Rekey (or download fron mybcommlab.com) the following paragraph, correcting the 10 incorrect homonyms or near homonyms, which a spell checker may not catch. Underline all your corrections.

Businesses rely on text messaging for many things besides advertising. Texting can compliment other forms of communication and surpass some for speed and affectiveness. To site one example, let's consider instant communication between a stockbroker and investor. The broker can council the investor about the movement of a stock price and get a "buy" or "sell" decision quickly. Vendors can confirm deliveries, customers can track shipments, and contractors can tell there on-sight crews to precede with construction. Another principle advantage of text messages is the ability to communicate silently. In situations where speaking may be awkward or impossible but immediate communication is important, texting makes more sense then a phone call. Instead of searching in vain for a place to take a call, a person can simply tap out a reply, waving the need for privacy.

Answer:

The 11 correct homonyms are highlighted in color and listed in the order they appear in the paragraph. See Handbook Section 4.4. for an extended list of commonly confused words and their meanings.

❶ can complement

❷ and effectiveness

❸ To cite

❹ can counsel

❺ tell their

❻ on-site

❼ to proceed

❽ Another principal

❾ sense than

❿ reply, waiving

Appendix F

Proofreader's Marks and Corrections Symbols

Symbol	Meaning	Symbol Used in Context	Corrected Copy
═	Align horizontally	effective ᵐᵉˢsage	effective message
‖	Align vertically	1. Laptop computer 2. Monitor	1. Laptop computer 2. Monitor
(bf)	Boldface	Recommendations (bf)	**Recommendations**
≡	Capitalize	Mcdonald's Corporation	McDonald's Corporation
⨆⨅	Center	⨆Awards Ceremony⨅	Awards Ceremony
⌣	Close up space	summer- hours program	summer-hours program
ℓ	Delete	harrassment and abuse	harassment
(ds)	Double-space	text in first line text in second line (ds)	text in first line text in second line
∧	Insert	back shirts (and white)	black and white shirts
∨	Insert apostrophe	our teams goals	our team's goals
∧	Insert comma	a, b and c	a, b, and c
⸗	Insert hyphen	first quarter sales	first-quarter sales
⊙	Insert period	Baca et al	Baca et al.
∨ ∨	Insert quotation marks	This team isn't cooperating.	This "team" isn't cooperating.
#	Insert space	real estate testcase	real estate test case
(ital)	Italics	Quarterly Report (ital)	*Quarterly Report*
/	Lowercase	BRADFORD, South of here	Bradford, south of here
⌎⌏	Move down	Sincerely,	Sincerely,
⌐	Move left	Attention: ⌐Sales Representatives	Attention: Sales Representatives
⌐	Move right	February 2, 2011 ⌐	February 2, 2011
⌐	Move up	FIRST-QUARTER SALES	FIRST-QUARTER SALES
(STET)	Restore	staff talked openly and frankly (STET)	staff talked openly
⌇	Run lines together	Manager, Marketing	Manager, Marketing
(ss)	Single space	photo on first page photo on second page	photo on first page photo on second page
⬭	Spell out	(COD)	cash on delivery
(sp)	Spell out	(sp) ABC	Association for Business Communication
⌐	Start new line	Maria Cardoni, Manager, Customer Service	Maria Cardoni, Manager, Customer Service
¶	Start new paragraph	¶ The business world evolves continually, requiring you to adapt both as an employee and a communicator.	The business world evolves continually, requiring you to adapt both as an employee and a communicator.
∿	Transpose	images, words and actions	words, images, and actions

Glossary

A

Abstract One or two paragraphs, included at the beginning of a formal, informational report, that either (a) describe the content of the report so that a reader can decide whether to read the report or (b) briefly summarize the report, including the main points, conclusions, and recommendations. *p. 291*

Abstract wording Language that refers to broad concepts that an audience can interpret in multiple ways. *p. 90*

Action interview An interview format that requires applicants to make a presentation or perform under work-based conditions, which could be simulated or real. *p. 439*

Active listening A learned skill that requires you to focus on the speaker, make sense of the information that is presented, and when possible, provide feedback about the information to ensure understanding. *pp. 10 and 32*

Active voice A sentence structure in which the subject performs the action of the verb. *p. 93*

Affective conflict A conflict that results from differences in personalities and relationships. If affective conflicts remain unstated and unaddressed, they can lead to tension, stress, and dysfunctional work processes. *p. 41*

Agenda A detailed plan or outline of the items to be discussed at a meeting. *p. 54*

AIDA An acronym used in marketing to suggest the organization of sales communication: Attention, Interest, Desire, Action. *pp. 164 and 412*

Analytical report A report that analyzes information to solve a problem or support a business decision. *p. 288*

Analyzing The process of looking critically at four elements of your message: purpose, audience, content, and medium. *p. 72*

Animations Software effects that control when and how elements appear on your slide when you present. *p. 358*

Announcement A communication that publicly notifies an audience of information they need or want to know. *p. 121*

Appendix A section (or multiple sections called appendices) included at the end of a formal report or proposal that provides supplementary information. *p. 291*

Argumentation A persuasive appeal that supports a position with reasons and evidence. *p. 149*

Attachment A document that is included with a letter or memo report to provide supplementary information. *p. 291*

Audience Anyone who receives a message and for whom a message is intended; the audience can be one person or many, depending on the number of recipients. *pp. 10 and 72*

Audience benefits Advantages the recipient gains from agreeing with or acting on your message; The positive outcomes your audience will experience by responding favorably to your request. *pp. 74 and 114*

B

Barrier An obstacle that gets in the way of effective communication. *p. 7*

Behavioral questions A type of interview question designed to determine how you would make decisions, solve problems, or respond to stressful situations. *p. 443*

Buffer An introductory sentence or paragraph that leads up to and softens the bad news. *p. 190*

Bullet point list A vertically formatted list, with each item preceded by a dot or other simple shape. *p. 84*

Business case A justification for a proposal showing that the recommended course of action is good for an organization and makes business sense. *p. 260*

C

Career fair A gathering of representatives from companies seeking to fill open positions. *p. 434*

Chronological résumé A traditional résumé style that lists content sequentially, starting with the most recent experience. *p. 400*

Clarity The quality of being unambiguous and easy to understand. Clear communication uses relatively simple words in well-constructed sentences and well-organized paragraphs. *pp. 15 and 90*

Clichés Commonplace and often overused phrases that have lost their force and meaning. *p. 94*

Cognitive conflict A conflict that results from differences in understanding content or tasks. Working through a cognitive conflict often leads to better decisions and work products. *p. 41*

Collaboration The process of working together to achieve a common goal. *p. 21*

Collectivist culture A culture that puts the good of the group or organization before people's individual interests. *p. 49*

Combined résumé A résumé style that takes advantage of both the chronological and functional methods of organizing content by highlighting work experience by date and skill sets by category. *p. 400*

Communication The process of planning, creating, delivering, and interpreting messages both verbally (through writing and speaking) and nonverbally (through gestures and symbols). *p. 5*

Communication strategy A plan for what and how you are going to communicate to ensure your message achieves your purpose. *p. 9*

Competitive proposal A proposal that will compete with other proposals for the same sale, funding, or opportunity. *p. 256*

Composing The multi-step process of producing content, organizing it so that it is understandable from the audience's perspective, putting it into coherent sentences and logical paragraphs, and then designing a format or delivery approach that is professional and makes the communication easy to follow. *p. 72*

Comprehension How well you understand what you hear or read. *p. 33*

Concession An admission that the opposing point of view has merit but does not invalidate your argument. *p. 144*

Conciseness Using no more words than necessary for a message to accomplish its purpose; Expressing an idea clearly in the fewest possible words. *pp. 15 and 91*

Concrete wording Language that is specific, making it likely that everyone will interpret it the same way. *p. 91*

Confirmation An acknowledgment that you have received information or understood a message correctly. *p. 120*

Congratulatory message Communication sent to recognize someone's achievements or important events. *p. 127*

Content The substance of your message. *p. 72*

Context A set of circumstances that influences the purpose of communication, the best medium to use to communicate the message, and even how receivers interpret a message; A term that describes how people in a culture deliver, receive, and interpret messages. Low-context cultures rely on explicit language to communicate. High-context cultures derive meaning not just from words but from everything surrounding the words. *pp. 8 and 47*

Convenience sample A survey population selected because you have easy access to that group. *p. 231*

Corporate culture The personality of a company as reflected in its atmosphere, attitudes, values, behaviors, and unstated assumptions. *p. 440*

Cover letter A persuasive letter or email sent to a prospective employer along with a résumé that "sells" your résumé to the employer. *p. 411*

Cover message A letter, memo, or email accompanying a formal report or proposal, designed to explain the document and persuade the audience to read it. *p. 270*

Credibility An audience's belief that you have expertise and are trustworthy based on your character, reputation, and behavior. *p. 147*

Culture The learned and shared patterns in a society. People demonstrate their culture through values, ideas, and attitudes. *pp. 19 and 46*

Customer claim A request that a store or a vendor accept a return, refund money, exchange an item, or perform a repair. *p. 161*

D

Data graphics Visual representations of data, in tables and graphs, that allow you to see relationships and trends much more clearly than text alone. *p. 318*

Decode To interpret the words and actions of a message and attach meaning to them. *p. 7*

Deliverables The items or services you agree to deliver to your audience. *p. 260*

Direct organizational plan Stating the purpose and main idea of the message before the supporting details. *p. 81*

Drafting A creative process that involves getting information on the paper or computer screen before revising and editing it. *p. 82*

E

Encode To translate the meaning of the message into words, images, and actions. *p. 6*

Ethics A set of principles that guide decision making and lead someone to do the right thing. *p. 16*

Ethnocentrism An inappropriate belief that your own culture is superior to all others. *p. 47*

Evaluating The practice of critically reviewing and judging communication; The process of reviewing your communication to ensure it is complete, clear, concise, easy to understand, and error-free. *pp. 36 and 72*

Executive summary A condensed description of a document that summarizes key ideas; A separate, standalone mini-report—included at the beginning of a formal analytical report—that completely summarizes the main ideas and recommendations of the report and may be read instead of the main report. *pp. 257 and 291*

External audiences People with whom you communicate outside your organization. *p. 86*

External benefits Advantages that someone else—a third party—gains when your audience complies with a request. *p. 115*

F

Fallacy A violation of logical reasoning that leads to a flawed argument. *p. 152*

Feasibility report A report that analyzes whether a plan can be implemented as proposed. It may also consider how to change the plan to make it feasible. *p. 296*

Feedback Any form of verbal or nonverbal response. *p. 7*

For-your-information message A message written as an act of kindness to pass along information you think someone may appreciate knowing. *p. 128*

Forming A stage of team development in which members get to know each other. *p. 52*

Functional résumé A contemporary résumé style that emphasizes categories of skills rather than job experience. *p. 400*

G

Goodwill The positive relationship between you (or your company) and your audience. *pp. 73 and 184*

Goodwill message Any message that gives you the opportunity to establish and maintain a positive relationship with your audience. *p. 112*

Grant proposal A proposal requesting funding, typically from governmental agencies or charitable foundations. *p. 267*

Graphs A visual representation of data that illustrates the relationship among variables, usually in relationship to *x*- and *y*-axes. *p. 319*

Group interview An interview format in which an employer meets with several applicants at the same time to assess their approach to working collaboratively with others. *p. 439*

Groupthink A process by which a group reaches a decision by eliminating all critical thinking that threatens consensus. *p. 45*

I

Idiom An expression that means something other than the literal meaning of its words. *p. 50*

Impromptu speaking Speaking without advance knowledge of the topic or question. *p. 373*

Indirect organizational plan Stating the purpose and main idea of the message after the supporting details. *p. 81*

Individualistic culture A culture that values an individual's achievements, satisfaction, and independent thinking. *p. 48*

Informational report A report that provides readers with facts that they can easily understand and refer to when necessary. Meeting minutes, trip reports, and progress reports are types of informational reports. *p. 288*

Internal audiences People with whom you communicate inside your organization. *p. 85*

Internal benefits Advantages that the audience will directly receive from complying with your request. These may include a reduced workload, increased professional recognition, or financial gains. *p. 114*

Interpretation Analyzing the meaning of what you hear, read, or see to determine its intention. *p. 33*

Interview A research method involving a structured discussion between two or more people, usually in a question-and-answer format. *p. 235*

J

Jargon The specialized language of a specific field. *p. 50*

L

Letters Formal correspondence, generally intended for external audiences. *p. 86*

Limitations The characteristics of the research that prevent you from generalizing your findings more broadly. *p. 221*

M

Mean The average derived by adding all responses and dividing the sum by the number of responses. *p. 234*

Median The number that represents the middle number in a distribution or the most central number. *p. 234*

Medium A channel used to transmit a message. Senders can choose a medium from many options, including face-to-face conversation, videoconference, telephone, letter, memo, email, brochure, website, and group meeting. *pp. 7 and 72*

Meeting minutes Notes that describe what was discussed at a meeting, what was decided, and what actions will follow. *p. 54*

Memos Hardcopy documents, following a set format, typically sent to internal audiences. *p. 85*

Message headlines Slide headlines that summarize the key message of each slide. *p. 348*

Minutes A written report of a meeting that identifies who was present, summarizes the discussion, and records specific decisions and action items. *p. 296*

Mode The number that most frequently appears in a distribution. *p. 235*

Monochronic culture A culture that values punctuality and efficiency. *p. 49*

N

Network The people you know who are aware of your career goals and can help you learn about career opportunities. *p. 395*

Noncompetitive proposal A proposal that has no competition because your audience will not be considering any offers other than yours. *p. 256*

Nonverbal communication Messages conveyed through means other than words, for example tone of voice, facial expressions, gestures, and body language. *p. 33*

Norming A stage of team development in which team members learn how to manage conflict and work with each other effectively. *p. 53*

O

Observational research A research method that involves watching people perform relevant activities and recording details about what you observe. *p. 237*

Outcome What you want your audience to know or do as a result of the communication. *p. 73*

P

Panel interview An interview format that involves several people, such as a search committee, who gather in a conference or seminar room with a job applicant to discuss the position. *p. 437*

Parallel phrasing Using the same grammatical form for each item in a list. *p. 123*

Paraphrase Restating someone's point in different words; A version of what someone else says, but in your own words and with your own emphasis. *pp. 35 and 328*

Passive listening Hearing what someone says without actively paying attention to ensure understanding. *p. 32*

Passive voice A sentence structure in which the subject is passive and receives the action expressed by the verb. *p. 93*

Performing A stage of team development in which team members work collaboratively and achieve a high level of productivity. *p. 53*

Persuasion The process of influencing your audience to agree with your point of view, recommendation, or request. *pp. 11, 74, 142*

Persuasive request A request that persuades the audience to do you a favor by making the audience feel good about doing the favor and, if possible, stressing audience benefits. *p. 160*

Plagiarism Intentionally or unintentionally failing to acknowledge others' ideas in your work. *p. 327*

Polychronic culture A culture that has a relaxed attitude toward time and punctuality. *p. 49*

Power distance A characteristic of cultures that describes how the culture perceives inequality and authority. *p. 48*

Primary audience The person or people to whom your message is addressed; The direct recipients of your message. *pp. 74 and 143*

Primary research Collecting your own original data. *p. 76*

Primary sources Sources from which you collect your own raw data. *p. 221*

Professionalism The qualities that make you appear businesslike in the workplace. *p. 13*

Proofreading A systematic process of reviewing writing for errors. *p. 94*

Proposal A communication designed to persuade a business decision maker to adopt a plan, approve a project, choose a product or service, or supply funding. *p. 254*

Purpose The intended outcome of a communication that defines what you want the audience to know, do, or feel about the subject of your message; The reason why you are communicating and the outcome you want to achieve. *pp. 10 and 72*

Q

Qualitative research Research that provides insight into the attitudes, values, and concerns of research subjects through interviews and observation. *p. 221*

Quantitative research Research that relies on numerical data, such as that gathered from structured survey responses to which you can assign numbers. *p. 221*

Quotations Any phrases, sentences, paragraphs—even single, distinctive words—that you take from any of your sources. *p. 328*

R

Random sample A population selected broadly from all available members of the population you want to study. *p. 231*

Range The span between the highest and lowest values. *p. 234*

Recommendation A business message that suggests a solution to a business problem. *p. 155*

Redundancy Unnecessary repetition of an idea. *p. 92*

Reference list A list of secondary research sources used in a research report. *p. 291*

Refutation A response intended to prove an objection is wrong. *p. 144*

Report deck A report document written in PowerPoint or other presentation software. *p. 289*

Request for proposal (RFP) An invitation for suppliers to competitively submit proposals to provide a product or service. *p. 255*

Revising A logical process that involves evaluating the effectiveness of your message in relation to your audience and purpose and then making changes in content, organization, or wording, as necessary. *p. 83*

Routine business message A nonsensitive, straightforward communication that asks questions, answers questions, provides information, or confirms agreements. *p. 112*

S

Sample A representative portion of your population. *p. 231*

Scope The range of your research: a broad scope includes a wide range of content, while a narrow scope focuses on specific aspects of the topic. *p. 221*

Secondary audience People other than the primary audience who may read or hear your message. These include people to whom you have sent a copy of your message as well as people to whom your audience has forwarded a copy. *pp. 74 and 143*

Secondary research Searching published reports, articles, and books for information other people have collected. *p. 76*

Secondary sources The results of other people's research that you consult as part of your research. *p. 221*

Slang Nonstandard, informal language that may communicate well within a certain group but often excludes people from different countries, cultures, and social groups. *p. 94*

Slide deck A set of slides used for a presentation. *p. 348*

Slide master A tool within presentation software that allows you to select design features that will apply to all slides. *p. 353*

Social media Web-based applications such as Facebook and Twitter, designed to promote social interaction. *p. 5*

Solicited proposal A proposal that your audience has requested. *p. 255*

Solicited sales communication A response to a request for sales information. *p. 165*

Stand-alone presentation A slide deck that makes sense without the benefit of a presenter. *p. 348*

STAR method A method of answering a behavioral interview question by explaining a **S**ituation, **T**ask, and **A**ction that led to a positive **R**esult. *p. 444*

Stereotypes Oversimplified images or generalizations of a group. *p. 47*

Storming A stage of team development in which teams experience conflict and begin to confront differences. *p. 53*

Storyboard A slide-by-slide sketch of the presentation that is used as a tool for organizing the flow of the presentation. *p. 353*

Style How you express yourself. *p. 92*

Subject line The line at the top of an email that communicates what the message is about and influences whether the audience will open the message. *p. 82*

Summary Very brief version of text, using your own words. *p. 328*

Survey population The audience from whom you want to collect survey responses. *p. 231*

Survey A predetermined list of questions used to collect a structured set of information from a selected audience. *p. 231*

Sympathy message (also called condolences) A message that expresses compassion and understanding when someone experiences a loss. *p. 128*

T

Tables A graphic that arranges data in columns and rows, allowing you to read down or across to see different relationships. *p. 319*

Targeted sample A sample that consists of only specific people from the group you are studying. *p. 231*

Team Two or more people who recognize and share a commitment to a specific, common goal and who collaborate in their efforts to achieve that goal. *p. 51*

Telephone interview An interview conducted by telephone, often used to narrow the candidate pool before scheduling an onsite visit. *p. 436*

Tertiary sources Books and articles that synthesize material from secondary sources. *p. 221*

Thank-you message An expression of appreciation when someone has done something for you. *p. 124*

Title page The first page of a formal report, which includes identifying information, such as the report's title; the name of the person or organization for whom the report was written; the author's name, position, and organization; and the date of submission. *p. 301*

Tone The image of yourself that your language projects based on how the message sounds to the recipient. *p. 92*

Topic sentence Sentence that identifies the main point or overall idea of the paragraph. Most frequently, it is the first sentence in a paragraph. *p. 84*

Topic-specific headings Section or paragraph titles that are short but include key ideas. They are often in the form of a short sentence and include a verb. *p. 84*

U

Uncertainty avoidance A measure of how comfortable a culture is with ambiguity, risk, and change. *p. 49*

Unsolicited proposal A proposal that your audience is not expecting. *p. 255*

Unsolicited sales communication Sales messages you send to audiences who did not request the information, also called "cold-call sales messages." *p. 165*

V

Visual aid presentation A presentation in which the speaker's words carry the main story of the presentation, and the slides provide illustration and backup. *p. 348*

W

Writer's block An inability to begin or continue writing. *p. 83*

Y

"You" perspective An approach to communication that presents the information from the audience's point of view. The "you" perspective focuses on what the audience needs and how the audience benefits from your message. *p. 114*

References

CHAPTER 1

1. U.S. Department of Labor, The Secretary's Commission on Achieving Necessary Skills. (1991). *What work requires of schools. A SCANS report for America 2000.* Retrieved from http://wdr.doleta.gov/SCANS/whatwork/whatwork.pdf
2. North, A., Hargrave, B., & Worth, W. E. (2007, October). *Workplace competencies and skills: Advertised online June 2007.* Presented at Association of Business Communication Convention. Washington, DC.
3. National Commission on Writing. (2004). *Writing: A ticket to work or a ticket out – A survey of business leaders.* Retrieved from http://www.host-collegeboard.com/advocacy/writing/publications.html
4. The Conference Board (2008). *New graduates' workforce readiness: The mid-market perspective.* Retrieved from http://www.conference-board.org/publications/publication detail.cfm?publicationid=1422
5. Graduate Management Admissions Council (2006). *Corporate recruiters survey report.* Retrieved from http://www.gmac .com/NR/rdonlyres/6838813E-4238-4B78-9C3D-F4AC11592 BA6/0/CorpRecSurvey06SurveyReport.pdf
6. Washington sees results from plain talk initiative. (2006, December 10). *USA Today.* Retrieved from http://www.usatoday .com/news/nation/2006-12-10-washington-plain-talk_x.htm
7. Towers Watson (2009). *Capitalizing on effective communication: How courage, innovation, and discipline drive business results in challenging times. 2009/2010 Communication ROI Study*™. Summary retrieved from http://www.towerswatson .com/assets/pdf/670/NA-2009-14890.pdf
8. Marketing Profs Research. (2009). *The state of social media marketing.* Los Angeles, CA: Marketing Profs LLC. Cited in Harte, B. (2009, December 10). Introducing 'The State of Social Media Marketing' report. [Web log message]. Retrieved from http://www.mpdailyfix.com/introducing-the-state-of-social-media-marketing-report/
9. Mitchelmore, S., & Rowley, J. (2010). Entrepreneurial competencies: A literature review and development agenda. *International Journal of Entrepreneurial Behavior & Research, 16*(2), 92.
10. See, for example Roebuck, D. B., Sightler, K. W., & Brush, C. C. (1995). Organizational size, company type, and position effects on the perceived importance of oral and written communication skills. *Journal of Managerial Issues, 7,* 99–115. Also see Wilhelm, W. (1999). A Delphi study of desired entry-level workplace skills, competencies, and proof-of-achievement products. *Delta Pi Epsilon Journal (41)*2, 105–22.
11. Byant, A. (2010, March 12). Three good hires? He'll pay more for one who's great. *New York Times.* Retrieved from http:// www.nytimes.com/2010/03/14/business/14corners.html? scp=1&sq=tindell&st=cse
12. Fisher, A. (1998, December 7). The high cost of living and not writing well. *Fortune, 138*(11), 244.
13. Barnlund, D. (1970). A transactional model of communication. (p. 83). In K. K. Sereno & C. D. Mortensen (Eds.), *Foundations of Communication Theory* (pp. 83–102). New York, NY: Harper & Row.
14. Grognet, A., & Van Duzer, C. (2003). *Listening skills in the workplace.* Retrieved from Spring Institute for International Studies website: http://www.springinstitute.org/Files/listeningwkplc.pdf
15. Bezos, J. (2009). An apology from Amazon. [Discussion board message]. Retrieved from Kindle Community Discussion Board: http://www.amazon.com/tag/kindle/forum/?_encoding= UTF8&cdForum=Fx1D7SY3BVSESG&cdMsgNo=1&cdPage= 1&cdSort=oldest&cdThread=Tx1FXQPSF67X1IU&display- Type=tagsDetail&cdMsgID=Mx2G7WLMRCU49NO#Mx2G7 WLMRCU49NO&tag=kwab-20
16. Gerstner, L. (2002). *Who says elephants can't dance? Leading a great enterprise through dramatic change.* New York, NY: HarperCollins Publishers, Inc.
17. Richman, J. (2010, February). The seven uses of social media in business—The 7 "C"s. [Web log message]. Retrieved from http://www.doseofdigital.com/2010/02/the-seven-uses-social-media-business/
18. Gartner, Inc. (2009, March 26). Gartner highlights four ways in which enterprises are using *Twitter.* Retrieved from http:// www.gartner.com/it/page.jsp?id=920813
19. Selling Power (Producer). (2010, April 4). *How Kodak leverages social media.* [Video file]. Retrieved from http://www .youtube.com/watch?v=GlE8_mKjPnQ
20. Donnelly, S. (2008, February 1). What pharma can learn from Novartis' YouTube campaign. *PharmaExec.com.* Retrieved from http://pharmexec.findpharma.com/pharmexec/article/ articleDetail.jsp?id=490707&sk=&date=&pageID=2
21. Spencer-Oatley, H. (2007). Rapport in an international business meeting: A case study. [Online forum comment]. Retrieved from http://dialogin.com/index.php?id=58&tx_ mmforum_pi1[action]=list_post&tx_mmforum_pi1[tid]= 54&tx_mmforum_pi1[page]=1&tx_mmforum_pi1[sword]= international%20business%20meetings#pid275
22. For insight into China's younger workforce, see Lynton, N., & Thøgersen, K. H. (2010, January 25). Reckoning with Chinese Gen Y. *Bloomberg Businessweek.* Retrieved from http://www .businessweek.com/print/globalbiz/content/jan2010/ gb20100125_065225.htm. Also see Lynton, N., & Thøgersen, K.H. (2010, February 16). Working with China's Generation Y. *Bloomberg Businessweek.* Retrieved from http://www .businessweek.com/print/globalbiz/content/feb2010/ gb20100216_566561.htm
23. Power, W. (1996, January 15). Neither rain nor snow shall keep workers from calculating NAVs. *The Wall Street Journal*, p. B1.
24. Jobs, S. (2007, September 6). Steve Jobs' letter to iPhone customers. *The Wall Street Journal.* Retrieved from http://online .wsj.com/article/SB118910674094519630.html

CHAPTER 2

1. Emanuel, R., Adams, J., Baker, K., Daufin, E., Ellington, C., Fitts, E., & Okeowo, D. (2008). How college students spend their time communicating. *International Journal of Listening, 22*(1), 13–28.
2. Maes, J., Weldy, T., & Icenogle, M. (1997). A managerial perspective: Oral communication is most important for business students in the workplace. *Journal of Business Communication, 34*(1), 67–80.
3. Nichols, R. (1957). Listening is a 10-part skill. Retrieved from The International Listening Association: http://www.listen .org/images/pdf/listening10partskill2.pdf
4. Wolvin, A., & Coakley, C. G. (1996). *Listening.* (5th ed.) Madison, WI: Brown and Benchmark.

5. Tannen, D. (1991). *You just don't understand: Women and men in conversation.* London: Virago.

6. Toivane, J., Väyrynen, E., & Seppäne, T. (2005). Gender differences in the ability to discriminate emotional content from speech. *Proceedings, FONETIK 2005* (pp. 119–122). Göteborg, Sweden: Department of Linguistics, Göteborg University.

7. Azar, B. (2000, January). What's in a face? *Monitor on Psychology, 31*(1). Retrieved from http://www.apa.org/monitor/jan00/sc1.aspx

8. Jack, R. E., Blais, C., Scheepers, C., Schyns, P., & Caldera, R. (2009). Cultural confusions show that facial expressions are not universal. *Current Biology, 19*, 1543–1548.

9. Faust, D. G. (2009, October 31). Leadership without a secret code. Interview conducted by Adam Bryant. *New York Times.* Retrieved from http://www.nytimes.com/2009/11/01/business/01corner.html

10. Giles, H., & Le Poire, B. (2006). The ubiquity and social meaningfulness of nonverbal communication. In V. Manusov & M. L. Patterson (Eds.), *The Sage Handbook of Nonverbal Communication* (pp. xv–xxiii). Thousand Oaks, CA: Sage Publications.

11. Pentland, A. (2008). *Honest signals.* Cambridge, MA: MIT Press.

12. Pentland, A. (2008). *Honest signals.* Cambridge, MA: MIT Press.

13. Knapp, M., & Hall, J. (2009). *Nonverbal communication in human interaction.* (7th ed.) Belmont, CA: Wadsworth Publishing.

14. Bippus, A., & Young, S. (2005). Owning your emotions: Reactions to expressions of self- versus other-attributed positive and negative emotions. *Journal of Applied Communication Research, 33*(1), 26–45.

15. Novak, D. (2009, July 11). At Yum Brands, rewards for good work. Interview conducted by Adam Bryant. *New York Times.* Retrieved from http://www.nytimes.com/2009/07/12/business/12corner.html

16. Tannen, D. (1991). *You just don't understand: Women and men in conversation.* London: Virago.

17. Zimmermann, D. H., & West, C. (1975). Sex roles, interruptions and silences in conversation. In B. Thorne & N. Henley (Eds.), *Language and sex: Difference and dominance* (pp. 105–129). Rowley, MA: Newbury House.

18. Lakoff, R. (1975). *Language and woman's place.* New York: Harper & Row.

19. Hosman, L. A. (1999). The evaluative consequences of hedges, hesitations, and intensifiers: Powerful and powerless speech styles. *Human Communication Research, 15*, 383–406.

20. Blankenship, K., & Holtgraves, B. (2005). The role of different markers of linguistic powerlessness in persuasion. *Journal of Language and Social Psychology, 24*(1), 3–24.

21. Centre for Effective Dispute Resolution (2006). Conflict is costing business £33 billion every year. Retrieved from http://www.cedr.com/index.php?location=/news/archive/20060526_232.htm

22. Bobinski, D. (2006). *The hidden costs of conflict.* Retrieved from http://www.management-issues.com/2006/8/8/opinion/the-hidden-costs-of-conflict.asp

23. Duxbury, L., & Higgins, C. (2003). *Worklife conflict in Canada in the new millennium: A status report.* Retrieved from the Public Health Agency of Canada website: http://www.phac-aspc.gc.ca/publicat/work-travail/pdf/rprt_2_e.pdf

24. De Dreu, C., & Van De Vliert, E. (1997). *Using conflict in organizations.* Thousand Oaks, CA: Sage Publications.

25. Zupeck, R. (2008, January 2). Six tips to managing workplace conflict. *CNN.com/living.* Retrieved from http://www.cnn.com/2008/LIVING/worklife/01/02/cb.work.conflict/index.html

26. Wilmot, W., & Hocker, J. (2007). *Interpersonal conflict* (7th ed.). New York: McGraw-Hill, 138–165.

27. Rabe, C. B. (2006). *The innovation killers: How what we know limits what we can imagine—and what smart companies are doing about it.* New York: AMACOM.

28. Hall, E. T. (1977). *Beyond culture.* New York: Anchor Books.

29. Hofstede, G. (1997). *Cultures and organizations: Software of the mind.* New York: McGraw Hill.

30. Formula for success. (1992, December). *Financial World, 161*(24), 40.

31. ITIM International. (2009). *Geert Hofstede cultural dimensions.* Retrieved from http://www.geert-hofstede.com/hofstede_united_states.shtml

32. Morrison, T. (2000, January 11). The problem of proxemics. *Industry Week.* Retrieved from http://www.industryweek.com/articles/global_business_basics_1907.aspx

33. United States Department of Labor (n.d.). *Indonesia.* Retrieved from http://www.dol.gov/ILAB/media/reports/iclp/sweat/indonesia.htm

34. Chandrasekaran, R. (2001, February 23). Indonesian workers in Nike plants list abuses. *Washington Post.* (F.ed.), p. E1.

35. Cushman, J. H. (1998, May 13). Nike pledges to end child labor and apply U.S. rules abroad. *New York Times.* Retrieved from http://www.nytimes.com

36. Oxfam. (2006). *Offside! Labour rights and sportswear production in Asia.* Retrieved from http://www.oxfamamerica.org/newsandpublications/publications/research_reports/research_paper.2006-05-23.7997564894. See also, Keady, J. (2010, July 27). How did student activists beat Nike? [Web log message]. Retrieved from http://www.educatingforjustice.org

37. O'Brien, M. (1995). *Who's got the ball? (And other nagging questions about team life).* San Francisco: Jossey-Bass.

38. Larson, C., & LaFasto, F. (1989). *Teamwork: What must go right/what can go wrong.* Newbury Park, CA: Sage.

39. Tuckman, B. W. (1965). Developmental sequence in small groups. *Psychological Bulletin, 63*, 384–399.

40. Katzenbach, J., & Smith, D. (1993). *The wisdom of teams: Creating the high performance organization.* Boston: Harvard Business School Press.

41. Lewin, K., Llippit, R. & White, R. K. (1939). Patterns of aggressive behavior in experimentally created social climates. *Journal of Social Psychology, 10*, 271–301.

CHAPTER 3

1. Gurchiek, K. (2008). Workplace flexibility has bottom-line implications. *Society for Human Resource Management.* Retrieved from http://www.shrm.org/hrnews_published/ARCHIVES/CMS_025558.asp

2. Kawasaki, G. (2010, March 19). Just give him 5 sentences, not 'War and Peace.' Interview by Adam Bryant. *New York Times.* Retrieved from http://www.nytimes.com/2010/03/21/business/21corner.html

3. Benefit. (n.d.). In The Princeton Language Institute (Ed.), *Roget's 21st century thesaurus* (3rd ed.). Retrieved from http://thesaurus.reference.com/search?r=20&q=benefit

CHAPTER 4

1. Gibson, S. (2005, October 15). Finance gets the message. *E-Week.* Retrieved from http://www.eweek.com/c/a/Messaging-and-Collaboration/Finance-Gets-the-Message/

2. Radicati Group. (2009). *Instant Messaging Market: 2009–2013.* Retrieved from http://www.radicati.com/wp/wp-content/uploads/2009/12/Instant-Messaging-2009-Brochure.pdf. See also Gartner, Inc. (2007, June 21). Gartner predicts instant messaging will be de facto tool for voice, video and text chat by the end of 2011. Retrieved from http://www.gartner.com/it/page.jsp?id=507731

3. Garrett, R. K., & Danziger, J. N. (2007). IM=Interruption management? Instant messaging and disruption in the workplace. *Journal of Computer-Mediated Communication, 13*(1). Retrieved from http://jcmc.indiana.edu/vol13/issue1/garrett.html

4. Osterman Research. (2005). *A short & simple guide to managing instant messaging in the workplace.* Retrieved from http://www.imbrellasoftware.com/osterman.pdf

5. Kotler, P. (2001). *Marketing management: Millennium edition.* Englewood Cliffs, NJ: Prentice Hall.

6. Bittner, M. J. (1990). Evaluating service encounters: The effects of physical surroundings and employee responses. *Journal of Marketing, 54*(2), 69–82.

7. Hill, D., & Baer, R. (1993). Excuse making: A prevalent company response to complaints? *Journal of Consumer Satisfaction, Dissatisfaction and Complaining Behavior, 6*, 143–151.

8. Strauss, J., & Hill, D. (2001). Consumer complaints by email: An exploratory investigation of corporate responses and customer reactions. *Journal of Interactive Marketing, 15*(1), 63–73.

9. Hudson, L. (2009, September 19). Fitting in, and rising to the top. An Interview with **A**dam Bryant. *New York Times.* Retrieved from http://www.nytimes.com/2009/09/20/business/20corner.html

CHAPTER 5

1. Aristotle. (1924). Rhetoric. In W. R. Roberts (Ed., & Trans.). Retrieved from http://www.molloy.edu/sophia/aristotle/rhetoric/rhetoric1a_txt.htm. (Original work written ca. 350 B.C.E.) Aristotle called these three elements *ethos, logos,* and *pathos.*

2. As examples, see Conger, J. (1998, May–June). The necessary art of persuasion. *Harvard Business Review*, 84–95; and Cialdini, R. (2001, October). Harnessing the science of persuasion. *Harvard Business Review*, 72–79.

3. Stiff, J. B., & Mongeau, P. A. (2002). *Persuasive communication* (2nd ed.). New York: The Guilford Press, 107.

4. Wallace, E. (2009, May–June). *Business relationships that last.* Austin, TX: Greenleaf Book Group Press. Also, Conger, J. (1998, May–June). The necessary art of persuasion. *Harvard Business Review*, 84–95.

5. Cialdini, R. (2009). *Influence: Science and practice* (5th ed.). Boston, MA: Pearson/Allyn & Bacon, 142–152.

6. Eisenstein, P. A. (2010, February 17). Toyota official says credibility is damaged. *MSNBC.* Retrieved from http://www.msnbc.msn.com/id/35369379/ns/business-autos/

7. Stiff, J. B., & Mongeau, P. A. (2002). *Persuasive communication* (2nd ed.). New York: The Guilford Press, 213–236.

8. Chaffin, B. (2009, October 15). IDC puts U.S. Apple's Mac market share at 9.4% for September quarter. *The Mac Observer.* Retrieved from http://www.macobserver.com/tmo/article/idc_puts_u.s._apples_mac_market_share_at_9.4_for_september_quarter/

9. Lin, E., & Hildebrandt, J. (2004). Good business to give credit where it's due. *Singapore Business Times,* Retrieved from http://www.bain.com/bainweb/publications/publications_detail.asp?id=17378&menu_url=publications_results.asp

10. Farrington, J. (2008). Customer complaints: The income multiplier effect. *CRM-Daily.com.* Retrieved from http://www.crm-daily.com/story.xhtml?story_id=122002AUBP0I&full_skip=1

11. Conger, J. (1998, May–June). The necessary art of persuasion. *Harvard Business Review*, 84–95.

12. Maslow, A. (1998). *Toward a psychology of being* (3rd ed.). Hoboken, NJ: Wiley. (Original work published in 1962.)

13. Cialdini, R. (2001, October). Harnessing the science of persuasion. *Harvard Business Review*, 72–79.

14. Gordon, J. (2006, May–June). *Presentations that change minds.* New York: McGraw-Hill, 69–98. Also, Conger, J. (1998, May–June). The necessary art of persuasion. *Harvard Business Review*, 93.

15. *Brazil's weeping President Luiz Inacio Lula da Silva revels in 2016 Olympics vote* (2009, October 3). Telegraph.co.uk. Retrieved from http://www.telegraph.co.uk/sport/othersports/olympics/news/6257463/Brazils-weeping-President-Luiz-Inacio-Lula-da-Silva-revels-in-2016-Olympics-vote.html

16. Grohmann, K. (2009, October 2). *Olympics-FIFA's Blatter moved by Lula's Rio 2016 bid speech.* Reuters. Retrieved from http://www.reuters.com/article/olympicsNews/idUSL257623920091002

17. Conger, J. (May–June 1998).The necessary art of persuasion. *Harvard Business Review*, 92–93.

18. Diana, Princess of Wales. (1997, June 12). *Responding to landmines: A modern tragedy and its consequences.* Keynote speech delivered at a seminar co-hosted by the Mines Advisory Group and the Landmine Survivors Network. London, England. Retrieved from http://gos.sbc.edu/d/diana.html

19. O'Brien, M. (1995). *Who's got the ball? (And other nagging questions about team life).* San Francisco, CA: Jossey-Bass.

20. Making room for emotions at work. (2005). Retrieved from http://www.managingpeopleatwork.com/Article.php?art_num=3902

21. Cialdini, R. (2009) *Influence: Science and practice.* Boston, MA: Pearson/Allyn & Bacon, 49.

22. Communicaid Group, Ltd. (2009). Doing business in Mexico: Mexican social business and culture. Retrieved from http://www.communicaid.com/access/pdf/library/culture/doing-business-in/Doing%20Business%20in%20Mexico.pdf

23. UK Trade and Investment. (2010, February 29). Doing business in the Netherlands. Retrieved from www.invest.uktradeinvest.gov.uk/download/107212_100410/Doing%20Business%20in%20Netherlands.html

24. Aune, K., & Basil, M. (1994). A relational obligations approach to the foot-in-the-mouth effect. *Journal of Applied Social Psychology, 24*, 546–556.

CHAPTER 6

1. Jansen, F., & Janssen, D. (2010). Effects of positive politeness strategies in business letters. *Journal of Pragmatics, 42* (9), 2531–2548.

2. Droste, T. (2003). Using e-mail efficiently for clear communication. *Monster Forums.* Retrieved from http://forums.monster.com/forum.asp?forum=2716

3. Cho, H. (2006, September 11). You've got mail. You're fired. *Baltimore Sun.* Retrieved from http://www.baltimoresun.com/business/bal-cho0911,0,6366979.column

4. Gardner, M. (2006, September 18). You've got mail: "We're letting you go." *Christian Science Monitor.* Retrieved from http://www.csmonitor.com/2006/0918/p13s02-wmgn.html

5. Sussman, S., & Sproull, L. (1999). Straight talk: Delivering bad news through electronic communication. *Information Systems Research, 10*(2), 150–166.

6. Kraemer, B. (2009, January 22). *Ballmer's e-mail to Microsoft employees: Job cuts "crucial."* Retrieved from http://www.crn.com/software/212901935

7. United Airlines. (2006). *Announcing new benefits and changes to your Mileage Plus program.* Retrieved from http://www.united.com/page/article/0,6722,51635,00.html?jumpLink=%2Fawardchanges

8. Storti, C. (2007). *Speaking of India: Bridging the communication gap when working with Indians.* Boston, MA: Intercultural Press.

9. Hart, C. W. L., Heskett, J. L., & Sasser, W. E., Jr. (1990, July–August). The profitable art of service recovery. *Harvard Business Review*, 148–156.

10. TARP (Technical Assistance Research Programs). (1986). *Consumer complaint handling in America: An updated study.* Washington, DC: The Office of the Special Advisor to the Pres-

ident for Consumer Affairs, Technical Assistance Research Programs.

11. Patel, A., & Reinsch, L. (2003). Companies can apologize: Corporate apologies and legal liability. *Business Communication Quarterly, 11*(1), 9–25.

12. Neelman, D. (2007). *David Neelman's flight log.* Retrieved from http://www.jetblue.com/about/ourcompany/flightlog/archive_february2007.html

CHAPTER 7

1. Booth, W., Colomb, G., & Williams, J. (2008). *The craft of research* (3rd ed.). Chicago, IL: University of Chicago Press, 41–43.

2. O'Leary, M. (2008). New portals enrich STM menu. *Information Today* (April). Retrieved from http://www.deepwebtech.com/talks/InfoTodayReprint.pdf

3. U.S. Department of State. (2009). *Independent states in the world.* Retrieved from http://www.state.gov/s/inr/rls/4250.htm

4. Gordon, R. (Ed.) (2005). *Ethnologue: Languages of the world* (15th ed.). Dallas, TX: SIL International. Retrieved from http://www.ethnologue.com/

5. Patton, M. Q. (2002). *Qualitative evaluation and research methods.* Thousand Oaks, CA: Sage Publications.

6. SLS Consulting. (2006). *The potential for greater fiber recovery from magazines, catalogs, and direct mail.* Retrieved from http://www.dmaresponsibility.org/Recycle/ThePotentialForGreaterFiberRecovery.pdf

7. U.S. Copyright Office. (2009, May). *Fair use.* Retrieved from http://www.copyright.gov/fls/fl102.html

8. American Wind Energy Association. (2008). *AWEA small wind turbine global market study 2008.* Retrieved from http://www.awea.org/smallwind/pdf/2008_AWEA_Small_Wind_Turbine_Global_Market_Study.pdf

9. United Nations Development Programme. (2007). *Fighting climate change: Human solidarity in a divided world.* Retrieved from http://hdr.undp.org/en/media/HDR_20072008_EN_Complete.pdf

10. Element K. (2003). *Learning management systems in the work environment: Practical considerations for the selection and implementation of an e-Learning platform.* Retrieved from http://www.elementk.com/c/document_library/get_file?uuid=c9ce5712-0896-49d2-8ff2-4225a95a2cc4&groupId=2814201

CHAPTER 8

1. Lagerwerf, L., & Bossers, E. (2002). Assessing business proposals: Genre conventions and audience response in document design. *Journal of Business Communication, 39,* 437–460.

2. Gambles, I. (2009). *Making the business case: Proposals that succeed for projects that work.* Farnham, Surrey, England: Gower Publishing, Ltd.

3. LaDuc, L. (2003). A hermeneutic rubric for teaching ethical communication via "real world" proposal writing. *Proceedings of the 2003 Association for Business Communication Annual Convention.* Retrieved from at http://www.businesscommunication.org/conventions/2003proceedings.html

4. Gambles, I. (2009). *Making the business case: Proposals that succeed for projects that work.* Farnham, Surrey, England: Gower Publishing, Ltd.

5. Business Meeting Etiquette (2008). Chinatrade.com. Retrieved from http://www.chinatrade.com/blog/business-meeting-etiquette

6. Beamer, L. (1998). Bridging business cultures. *China Business Review, 25*(3), 54–58.

7. Schuster, C. (2005, January 1). How to manage a contract in China. *Business Credit.* Retrieved from http://www.allbusiness.com/accounting/3487269-1.html

8. Hugget, K. (2003, June). Brazil-USA: Learning to bridge cultures. *Brazzil.com.* Retrieved from http://www.brazzil.com/2003/html/news/articles/jun03/p114jun03.htm

9. Hupert, A. (2009, April 30). Chinese negotiation—Doing the business vs. doing the deal. *Chinese Negotiation.* Retrieved from http://www.chinesenegotiation.com/2009/04/chinese-negotiation-%E2%80%93-doing-the-business-vs-doing-the-deal/

10. Katz, L. (2008, March). Negotiating international business: Italy. In *Negotiating international business: The negotiator's reference guide to 50 countries around the world.* Retrieved from http://www.globalnegotiationresources.com/cou/Italy.pdf

11. The Wal-Mart Foundation. Our mission. (n.d.). Retrieved from http://walmartstores.com/CommunityGiving/203.aspx

12. Hofstede, G. (2009). Geert Hofstede's cultural dimensions. Retrieved from http://www.geert-hofstede.com/hofstede_japan.shtml

CHAPTER 9

1. Couture, B., & Rymer, J. (1993). Situational exigence: Composing processes on the job by writer's role and task value. In R. Spilka [ed.] *Writing in the workplace: New research perspectives* (pp. 4–20). Carbondale, IL: Southern Illinois University Press.

2. Weiss, E. H. (2005). *The elements of international English style: A guide to writing correspondence, reports, technical documents, Internet pages for a global audience.* New York, NY: Sharpe.

3. Mydans, S. (2007, April 7). Across cultures, English is the word. *New York Times.* Retrieved from http://www.nytimes.com/2007/04/09/world/asia/09iht-englede.1.5198685.html?_r=1&scp=1&sq=Across%20Cultures%20English%20is%20the%20Word&st=cse

4. Wynne, A. (2009, June 8). The language of empire. *Foreign Policy.* Retrieved from http://experts.foreignpolicy.com/posts/2009/06/08/domination_by_language

5. Mulvihill, T. (2002). International publishing. *Planet Publish.* Retrieved from http://www.planetpublish.com/mainpage.asp?webpageid=140

6. Fenstermacher, H. (2003). No pain, no gain. Content fitness for everyone. *Architext.* Retrieved from http://www.architext-usa.com/downloads/Content%20Fitness_CSN.pdf

7. Yeh, A. (2005, April 13). New dawn in a shared language. *Financial Times.* Retrieved from http://www.ft.com/cms/s/0/95e7a436-abb7-11d9-893c-00000e2511c8.html

8. For example, see McKinsey & Co. (2010, January). *Electrical vehicles in cities: Shanghai charges up.* Retrieved from http://online.wsj.com/public/resources/documents/mckinsey_electric_vehicle_0113.pdf and Bain & Co. (2005, March 23). *City of Atlanta building permitting project: Permitting improvement action plan.* Retrieved from http://www.atlantaga.gov/client_resources/government/planning/buildings/coa_building_permitting_project.pdf

9. Sedlack, R., Shwom, B., & Keller, K. (2009). *Graphics and visual communication for managers.* 2nd ed. (p. 69). Mason, OH: South-Western Cengage Learning.

10. Harris, R. (2000). *Information graphics: A comprehensive illustrated reference: Visual tools for analyzing, visualizing, and communicating.* New York, NY: Oxford University Press.

11. Tufte, E. (1983). *The visual display of quantitative information.* Cheshire, CT: Graphics Press.

12. INSEE (2009). *National Institute of Statistics and Economic Studies.* Retrieved from http://www.insee.fr/en/default.asp

13. Environmental Paper Network. (2007). *The state of the paper industry: Monitoring the indicators of environmental*

performance. Retrieved from http://www.environmental-paper.com/documents/StateOfPaperIndSm.pdf

14. Vertis Communications. (2007). *Online response to direct mail has increased since 2003.* Retrieved from http://www.vertisinc.com/files/PressReleases/071112PR_VCF_DM_TechSavvy_Consumers.pdf

CHAPTER 10

1. The Conference Board. (2008). *New graduates' workforce readiness: The mid-market perspective.* Retrieved from http://www.conference-board.org/Publications/describe.cfm?id=1422

2. The Conference Board. (2008). *New graduates' workforce readiness: The mid-market perspective.* Retrieved from http://www.conference-board.org/Publications/describe.cfm?id=1422

3. Munter, M. (2003). *Guide to managerial communication* (6th ed.). (p. 112). Upper Saddle River, NJ: Prentice Hall.

4. United States Copyright Office. (2009, May). *Copyright: Fair use.* Retrieved from http://www.copyright.gov/fls/fl102.html

5. Kagawa, H. (1997). T*he inscrutable Japanese.* Tokyo: Kodansha Bilingual Press.

6. Donahue, R. (1998). *Japanese culture and communication: Critical cultural analysis.* Lanham, MD: University Press of America.

7. Krakovsky, M. (2009). National poker face. *Psychology Today, 42*(1), 20.

8. Vertis Communications. (2007). *Online response to direct mail has increased since 2003.* Retrieved from http://www.vertisinc.com/files/PressReleases/071112PR_VCF_DM_TechSavvy_Consumers.pdf

CHAPTER 11

1. National Association of Colleges and Employers. (2010). *2010 internship and coop survey.* Retrieved from http://www.naceweb.org/products/1020internship_co-op_survey/

2. Marte, J. (2009, September 29). An internship from your couch. *Wall Street Journal.* Retrieved from http://online.wsj.com/article/SB10001424052748704471504574441132945681314.html

3. Cited in Gutner, T. (2009, March 31). Career journal: Graduating with a major in go-getting. *Wall Street Journal* (Eastern edition, New York), p. D6.

4. Bruzzese, A. (2010, March 25). Online résumés can trigger identity theft. *USA Today.* Retrieved from http://www.usatoday.com/money/jobcenter/workplace/bruzzese/2010-03-25-online-resume-hazards_N.htm. Also see Identitytheft.com (2010). Online résumé could result in ID theft. Retrieved from http://www.identitytheft.com/article/posting_your_resume_online

5. Prentice, K. (n.d.). Making employers click (online) for you. Retrieved from http://www.jobweb.com/studentarticles.aspx?id=2249

6. Gutner, T. (2009, March 31). Career journal: Graduating with a major in go-getting. *Wall Street Journal* (Eastern edition, New York), p. D6.

7. Langfitt, F. (2006, November 27). Social networking technology boosts job recruiting. *National Public Radio.* [Radio broadcast]. Transcript retrieved from http://www.npr.org/templates/story/story.php?storyId=6522523

8. Jaffe, M. (2010, May 4). Should you include your photo on LinkedIn? [Web log message]. Retrieved from http://blogs.bnet.com/career-advice/?p=779

9. Haefner, R. (2009). More employers screening candidates through social networking sites. *Careerbuilder.* Retrieved from http://www.careerbuilder.com/Article/CB-1337-Getting-Hired-More-Employers-Screening-Candidates-via-Social-Networking-Sites/

10. Frazier, E. (2010, May 17). Facebook post costs waitress her job. *Charlotte Observer.com.* Retrieved from http://www.charlotteobserver.com/2010/05/17/1440447/facebook-post-costs-waitress-her.html

11. Balachandran, M., & Blair, R. B. (2007). Résumé preferences of U.S. businesses. *Business Education Digest, XVI,* 60–69.

12. Dumas, M. (2007). 5 résumé writing myths. *Résumé Writing & Career Marketing Insider.* [Web log message]. Retrieved from http://blog.distinctiveweb.com/distinctive_documents_car/2007/07/5-resume-writin.html

13. Lee, K. S. (2009). Top 10 résumé mistakes IT pros should avoid. Retrieved from http://www.globalknowledge.com/training/generic.asp?pageid=1560&country=United+States

14. Win at work. (2009, May 1). *U.S. News & World Report. 146*(4), 32.

15. Balachandran, M., & Blair, R. B. (2007). Résumé preferences of U.S. businesses. *Business Education Digest (XVI),* 60–69.

16. Schullery, N. M., Ickes, L., & Schullery, S. E. (2009). Employer preferences for résumés and cover letters. *Business Communication Quarterly, 72*(2), 163–176.

17. Balachandran, M., & Blair, R. B. (2007). Résumé preferences of U.S. businesses. *Business Education Digest, XVI,* 60–69.

18. Balachandran, M., & Blair, R. B. (2007). Résumé preferences of U.S. businesses. *Business Education Digest, XVI,* 60–69.

19. MacMillan, D. (2007, May 7). The art of the online résumé: How to get yours past electronic filters that cull the herd of applicants. *BusinessWeek.* Retrieved from http://www.businessweek.com/print/magazine/content/07_19/b4033099.htm

20. Tomassi, K. D. (2006, May 23). Most common resume lies. *Forbes.com.* Retrieved from http://www.forbes.com/2006/05/20/resume-lies-work_cx_kdt_06work_0523lies.html

21. Feltham, C. (2007). InterContinental executive walks out after lying on CV. *The Independent.* Retrieved from http://www.independent.co.uk/news/business/news/intercontinental-executive-walks-out-after-lying-on-cv-453236.html

22. Martin, D. (2004). The myth of the one-page résumé. *Sales & Marketing Management, 156*(10), 50.

23. Hachey, J-M. (2006, July/August). International resumes. *Transitions Abroad Magazine.* Retrieved from www.transitions-abroad.com/publications/magazine/0609/international_resumes.shtml

24. Langfitt, F. (2006). Job hunters seek winning edge in video résumés. *National Public Radio.* [Radio broadcast]. Transcript retrieved from http://www.npr.org/templates/story/story.php?storyId=6631326

25. Cote, T. (2009, February 25). 10 video résumé do's & don'ts. *Austin News KXAN.com.* Retrieved from http://www.kxan.com/dpp/home/Video_Resume_Tips

26. Balachandran, M., & Blair, R. B. (2007). Résumé preferences of U.S. businesses. *Business Education Digest, XVI,* 60–69.

27. Schullery, N. M., Ickes, L., & Schullery, S. E. (2009). Employer preferences for résumés and cover letters. *Business Communication Quarterly, 72*(2), 163–176.

28. Korkki, P. (2009, February 15). A cover letter is not expendable. *New York Times (Late Edition),* Section BU, p. 10.

CHAPTER 12

1. Office Team. (2005). *A–Z business etiquette guide, 6.* Retrieved from http://www.docstoc.com/docs/1146794/Robert-Half-Business-Etiquette-Guide

2. Martin, C. (2010). The one-on-one interview. *Monster.ca.* Retrieved from http://interview.monster.ca/7120_en-CA_p1.asp

3. Stevenson, J. C. (2007). Questions and answers: The evolving art of the job interview. *BusinessWest, 24*(2), 53.

4. Edmonds, C., & Glaser, B. (2010, January). Culture by default or by design? *Talent Management Magazine, 6*(1), 36–39.

5. Hansen, R. S. (2010). Uncovering a company's corporate culture is a critical task for job-seekers. *Quintessential Careers*. Retrieved from http://www.quintcareers.com/employer_corporate_culture.html

6. Shawbel, D. (2009). *Me 2.0: Build a powerful brand to achieve career success*. New York: Kaplan Publishing.

7. Win at work. (2009). *U.S. News & World Report, 146*(4), 32.

8. Answer the phone? Sniff armpits? Top 10 interview gaffes (2008, May 13). *Reuters*. Retrieved from http://www.reuters.com/article/idUSSP687020080313

9. Win at work. (2009, May 1). *U.S. News & World Report. 146*(4), 32.

10. Stevenson, J. C. (2007, May 28). Questions and answers: The evolving art of the job interview. *BusinessWest, 24*(2), 53.

11. Byham, W. C., & Pickett, D. (1997). *Landing the job you want: How to have the best job interview of your life*. New York: Three Rivers Press.

12. Melone, L. (2007, August 2). Why you didn't get the job. OC Metro, 54.

13. Answer the phone? Sniff armpits? Top 10 interview gaffes. (2008, May 13). *Reuters*. Retrieved from http://www.reuters.com/article/idUSSP687020080313

14. Melone, L. (2007, August 2). Why you didn't get the job. *OC Metro,* 54.

15. Melone, L. (2007, August 2). Why you didn't get the job. *OC Metro,* 54.

16. Melone, L. (2007, August 2). Why you didn't get the job. *OC Metro,* 54.

17. Answer the phone? Sniff armpits? Top 10 interview gaffes. (2008, May 13). *Reuters.* Retrieved from http://www.reuters.com/article/idUSSP687020080313

18. Lynch, C. G. (2009, April 28). Build a better online persona: Four steps. *CIO.com.* Retrieved from http://www.cio.com/article/490992/Build_a_Better_Online_Persona_Four_Steps

19. Du, W. (2007, August 14). Job candidates get tripped up by Facebook. *MSNBC.com.* Retrieved from http://www.msnbc.msn.com/id/20202935/print/1/displaymode/1098/

20. Crosstab. (2010, January). *Online reputation in a connected world.* Retrieved from http://www.microsoft.com/privacy/dpd/research.aspx

21. Finder, A. (2006, June 11). For some, online persona undermines a résumé. *New York Times.* Retrieved from http://www.nytimes.com/2006/06/11/us/11recruit.html

22. Covello, L. (2008, May 16). How to keep your online persona in check. *FoxBusiness.com.* Retrieved from http://www.foxbusiness.com/story/personal-finance/online-persona-check-999698680/

23. Carroll, J. (2007, October 4). "Business casual" most common work attire: Women more likely than men to wear formal business clothing on the job. *Gallup.* Retrieved from http://www.gallup.com/poll/101707/Business-Casual-Most-Common-Work-Attire.aspx

24. Win at work. (2009, May 1). *U.S. News & World Report. 146*(4), 32.

25. Melone, L. (2007, August 2). Why you didn't get the job. *OC Metro,* 54.

26. Kilgannon, C. (2009, April 1). When tattoos hurt job prospects. *New York Times* [Weblog entry]. Retrieved from http://cityroom.blogs.nytimes.com/2009/04/01/when-tattoos-hurt-job-prospects/

27. Act fast: Survey finds employers form opinions of job interviewees within 10 minutes. (2007, April 12). *PRNewswire.* Retrieved from http://www.accessmylibrary.com/coms2/summary_0286-30293924_ITM

28. Green, A. (2008, December 12). 5 small things that annoy interviewers. *U.S. News and World Report.* Retrieved from http://money.usnews.com/money/blogs/outside-voices-careers/2008/12/29/5-small-things-that-annoy-interviewers.html

29. Snyder, M. J. (2009, July 22). Personal communication.

30. Lorenz, K. (2009, September 29). Six tips for a perfect handshake. *CareerBuilder.com.* Retrieved from http://www.careerbuilder.com/Article/CB-431-Getting-Hired-Six-Tips-for-a-Perfect-Handshake/

31. Melone, L. (2007, August 2). Why you didn't get the job. *OC Metro*, 58.

32. Bureau of Labor Statistics. (2010, January). *Occupational outlook handbook, 2010–2011 Edition.* Retrieved from http://www.bls.gov/oco

33. Bureau of Labor Statistics. (2010, January). Evaluating a job offer. *Occupational outlook handbook, 2010–2011 Edition.* Retrieved from http://www.bls.gov/oco/oco20046.htm

34. Benedict, A. (2006). *Weapons in the workplace survey report.* Alexandria, VA: Society for Human Resource Management. Retrieved from http://www.shrm.org/Research/SurveyFindings/Documents/2006%20Weapons%20In%20The%20Workplace%20Survey%20Report.pdf

35. Hsu, T. (2009, June 7). Trapped. It's hard to get a job if your credit is bad. *Los Angeles Times.* Retrieved from http://articles.latimes.com/2009/jun/07/business/fi-cover-badcredit7

APPENDIX A

1. Facebook. (2010). *Pressroom.* Retrieved from http://www.facebook.com/press/info.php?statistics

2. Charney, M. (n.d.). Facebook for employers: Make friends, not fans. [Web log message]. *Monster.* Retrieved from http://hiring.monster.com/hr/hr-best-practices/recruiting-hiring-advice/attracting-job-candidates/facebook-for-employers.aspx

3. O'Reilly, K. (2010, October 5). Personal interview.

4. Twelpforce Best Buy. (2010). Retrieved from http://twitter.com/#!/TWELPFORCE

5. Van Grove, J. (2010, May 11). Top 5 social media tips for C-suite execs. *Mashable.* Retrieved from http://mashable.com/2010/05/11/social-media-tips-execs

6. Ulman, D. (2010, May 20). Doug visits Twitter HQ. [Web log message]. *Livestrong.* Retrieved from http://livestrongblog.org/author/doug-ulman/

7. Pounds, C. (2010, September 29). Personal interview.

8. Arling, A. (2010, September 3). Personal interview.

9. The Coca-Cola Company. (2009, December). Online social media principles. Retrieved from http://www.thecoca-colacompany.com/socialmedia/

10. International Olympic Committee. (2009). *IOC blogging guidelines for persons accredited at the XXI Olympic Winter Games, Vancouver 2010.* Retrieved from http://www.olympic.org/Documents/Reports/EN/en_report_1433.pdf

11. Manpower. (2010, January). Social networks vs. management? *Harness the power of social media.* Retrieved from http://www.manpower.com/research/research.cfm

12. O'Reilly, K. (2010, October 5). Social media: Are you doing it effectively? [PowerPoint webinar presentation].

Credits

Index

Page numbers in *italic* indicate figures. Key terms and the page number on which they are defined appear in **boldface**.